ON THE SKIRTS OF CANAAN
IN THE IRON AGE

Bifacial feminine head, 7th century B.C.
(Amman, Archaeological Museum, J. 11689).

ORIENTALIA LOVANIENSIA
ANALECTA
153

ON THE SKIRTS OF CANAAN IN THE IRON AGE

Historical and Topographical Researches

BY

EDWARD LIPIŃSKI

UITGEVERIJ PEETERS en DEPARTEMENT OOSTERSE STUDIES
LEUVEN – PARIS – DUDLEY, MA
2006

Library of Congress Cataloging-in-Publication Data

Lipiński, Edward.
On the skirts of Canaan in the Iron Age: historical and topographical researches / by Edward Lipiński.
p. cm -- (Orientalia Lovaniensia analecta ; 153)
Includes bibliographical references and index.
ISBN-13: 978-90-429-1798-9 (alk. paper)
ISBN-10: 90-429-1798-9 (alk. paper)
1. Middle East--History--To 622. I. Title II. Series.

DS62.2.L57 2006
933--dc22 2006046035

D. 2006/0602/87
ISBN-10 90-429-1798-9
ISBN-13 9789042917989

CONTENTS

FOREWORD

The history of Canaan in the Iron Age was generally written from the perspective of the Deuteronomistic History, roughly corresponding to the biblical books of the Former Prophets. Even recent studies, using extra-biblical written sources, and archaeological research in the "Bible Lands" are often viewing the history of the region in centripetal relation to the core of the biblical account. The scope of this book is to inverse this relation and to focus on "the skirts of Canaan", while regarding the Kingdom of Israel, the Kingdom of Judah, the "United Monarchy", the "Divided Monarchy", as external and sometimes marginal players of the regional history. This approach nevertheless casts one's eyes on the biblical history, but viewed from a different angle.

The resulting chapters are no full-fledged presentations of the Philistine, Ammonite, Moabite, Edomite history, which could not be written in any case. They treat of selected topics, which are somehow echoed in the Bible, but are being inserted here in a historical framework provided mainly by extra-biblical information. There will be no discussion about High and Low Chronology, because external synchronisms and data will be used, as much as possible. Absolute chronology must in fact be based here on epigraphic finds, carbon C-14 analyses of short-lived material, foreign imports, Mycenaean, Greek, Cypriot, Phoenician, and Edomite pottery types, artefacts with pharaonic cartouches. Dating of Philistine, Israelite, and Judaean pottery, even of architectural remains in the concerned area, not seldom rests at the end on unsubstantiated assumptions, like the "axiomatic" linkage of certain pottery assemblages to Sennacherib's campaign in 701 B.C., on misinterpretations of some sources, like the passage of Papyrus Harris I alluding to "Sea Peoples" settled in Egyptian fortresses, or on a naïve reading of the Scripture, especially of the Deuteronomistic History. Published results of the sole study of the pottery in question can safely be used only for establishing a relative chronology of comparable sites and archaeological levels.

The work is based on writer's courses and lectures, spread over several years and places. The presentation of the topics is here updated and integrated in the framework of ten chapters. A particular attention is paid to phonological, lexicographic, and palaeographic aspects of the encountered problems. The first chapter examines the passage from the Late

Bronze to the Iron Age in Canaan and Syria, especially in the light of epigraphic and archaeological data from Ugarit, Emar, and Egypt. This preliminary reassessment is followed by an examination of the Philistine origins, of the "Sea Peoples'" settlement in Canaan, and of the traces of surviving Philistine identity in Iron Age II.

By *ca.* 950 B.C., the Levantine crisis of the "Dark age" was surmounted, the transition to a new ethno-political spectrum was achieved and new structures were established. Along the Syro-Phoenician coast, the Phoenician city-states managed nevertheless to preserve the system current in the area during the Late Bronze Age. The southern coastal area, dominated by the Philistine pentapolis, changed rapidly into a group of individual city-states with institutions most likely similar to the Phoenician ones. Inland, Aramaean territorial states came into existence in northern and southern Syria, while central Syria was ruled by a Neo-Hittite dynasty with Hamath as capital. In Canaan, the short-lived United Monarchy of David was based on Israelite tribal traditions in the north, which became the kingdom of Israel after Solomon's death, while clans of various origins formed the land of Judah, ruled from Jerusalem by the dynasty founded by David. In Transjordan, the tribal forces, already active in the area during the 10th-9th centuries B.C., developed into the kingdoms of Ammon, Moab, and Edom, but their sedentarization proceeded somewhat slower than in Cisjordan. Around 900 B.C., all these entities were independent from each other and also from the "great powers", which tried from the mid-10th century on to recover a dominant position in Syria-Palestine. The Egyptian attempts by Siamun and Shoshenq I were short-lived, but Assyria pursued its imperial policy through more than two hundred fifty years, with various intensity, with reversals and interruptions. It had also positive aspects, especially during the period of the *pax Assyriaca*.

Chapter III of the book is thus devoted to the role of Egypt in Canaan during Iron Age II. Special attention is paid to the topographical list of Shoshenq I and to the Egyptian interventions during the Assyrian period. The following chapter deals with the Phoenicians, in particular with the Tyrian king-list, the chronology and foreign policy of Tyre, also in relation to the Kingdom of Israel. Chapter V on the Aramaeans is meant as a synthesis and a complement to the previous writer's work on *The Aramaeans*. There follow five chapters on Bashan, Gilead, Ammon, Moab, and Edom. Several topographical and historical questions are dealt with, like the location of Abel-Bēth-Maaka, Abel-mayim, Dan, Maḥanaim, Penuel, the distribution of Mesha's fortresses in Greater Moab, and the Edomite expansion in the Negeb during Iron Age II.

References to earlier literature are selective. As a rule, opinions showing either an insufficient awareness of textual and literary criticism, or an inadequate knowledge of linguistic changes or phenomena, are not discussed at length, because the basic principles of the art cannot be explained once and again. At any rate, the footnotes make no attempt at full documentation. The policy has been to cite books and articles in full at the first occurrence in each chapter, even if the work in question has already been cited in an earlier chapter. The devices *op. cit.* and *art. cit.* will always refer to a publication cited previously in the same chapter. The exceptions are limited to abridged titles, listed among the abbreviations of journals and series, in alphabetical order. The names of persons and places, when currently used, are given here in their usual form, but names of archaeological sites and of persons mentioned in inscriptions are transcribed or transliterated in a precise way, eventually with their alternative pronunciations or appellations. However, the traditional spelling is often followed for Arabic toponyms occurring regularly in publications, for instance Tell al-Kheleifeh. In any case, the same spelling is kept for each place name throughout the whole work.

The writer wishes to thank Dr. Fawwaz Al-Khraysheh, Director-General of the Department of Antiquities of the Hashemite Kingdom of Jordan, for authorizing the photographical reproduction of several art objects from the Archaeological Museum of Amman. He also wishes to express his gratitude to Peeters publishers and the Orientaliste typography for the work finalized with their well-known precision and skill.

ABBREVIATIONS

AA(A)S	: *Annales Archéologiques (Arabes) Syriennes.*
AASOR	: *Annual of the American Schools of Oriental Research.*
ABEL, *Géographie*	: F.M. ABEL, *Géographie de la Palestine* I-II, Paris 1933-38.
ADAJ	: *Annual of the Department of Antiquities of Jordan.*
AfO	: *Archiv für Orientforschung.*
AfO, Beih.	: Archiv für Orientforschung, Beiheft.
AHw	: W. VON SODEN, *Akkadisches Handwörterbuch* I-III, Wiesbaden 1965-81.
AION	: *Annali dell'Istituto Orientale di Napoli.*
AIPHOS	: *Annuaire de l'Institut de Philologie et d'Histoire Orientales et Slaves.*
AJA	: *American Journal of Archaeology.*
ANEP	: J.B. PRITCHARD, *The Ancient Near Eastern Pictures relating to the Old Testament,* 2nd ed., Princeton 1969.
ANET	: J.B. PRITCHARD (ed.), *The Ancient Near Eastern Texts relating to the Old Testament*, 3rd ed., Princeton 1969.
AnOr	: Analecta Orientalia.
ANRW	: H. TEMPORINI - W. HAASE (eds.), *Aufstieg und Niedergang der römischen Welt,* Berlin-New York.
AnSt	: *Anatolian Studies.*
AOAT	: Alter Orient und Altes Testament.
AOS	: American Oriental Series.
ARM(T)	: *Archives royales de Mari* (transcrites et traduites).
AS	: Assyriological Studies.
ASAÉ	: *Annales du Service des Antiquités de l'Égypte.*
ASOR	: American Schools of Oriental Research.
AUSS	: *Andrews University Seminary Studies.*
BA	: *(The) Biblical Archaeologist.*
BAH	: Bibliothèque archéologique et historique de l'Institut Français d'Archéologie de Beyrouth.
BAR	: British Archaeological Reports International, Oxford.
BASOR	: *Bulletin of the American Schools of Oriental Research.*
BENZ	: F.L. BENZ, *Personal Names in the Phoenician and Punic Inscriptions* (Studia Pohl 8), Rome 1972.
BIFAO	: *Bulletin de l'Institut Français d'Archéologie Orientale*, Le Caire.
BiOr	: *Bibliotheca Orientalis.*
BKAT	: Biblischer Kommentar. Altes Testament.
BM	: Inventory numbers of the British Museum.
BMB	: *Bulletin du Musée de Beyrouth.*
BN	: *Biblische Notizen.*

BTAVO : Beihefte zum Tübinger Atlas des Vorderen Orients.
BTS : Beiruter Texte und Studien.
BZAW : Beihefte zur Zeitschrift für die alttestamentliche Wissenschaft.

CAD : *The Assyrian Dictionary of the Oriental Institute of the University of Chicago*, Chicago-Glückstadt 1956 ff.
CAH : *The Cambridge Ancient History*, Cambridge.
CCCM : Corpus Christianorum. Continuatio Mediaevalis, Turnhout.
CCSL : Corpus Christianorum. Series Latina, Turnhout.
CGC : Catalogue général du Musée du Caire / Cairo Museum General Catalogue.
CIS I : *Corpus Inscriptionum Semiticarum. Pars I inscriptiones Phoenicias continens*, Paris 1881 ff.
CIS II : *Corpus Inscriptionum Semiticarum. Pars II inscriptiones Aramaicas continens*, Paris 1889 ff.
CIS IV : *Corpus Inscriptionum Semiticarum. Pars IV inscriptiones Himyariticas et Sabaeas continens*, Paris 1889 ff.
CRAI : *Comptes rendus de l'Académie des Inscriptions et Belles Lettres.*
CSCO : Corpus Scriptorum Christianorum Orientalium.
CSEL : Corpus Scriptorum Ecclesiasticorum Latinorum, Wien 1866 ff.
CSHB : Corpus Scriptorum Historiae Byzantinae.
CTN : Cuneiform Texts from Nimrud, London.
DBS : *Dictionnaire de la Bible. Supplément,* Paris 1928 ff.
DCPP : E. LIPIŃSKI (ed.), *Dictionnaire de la civilisation phénicienne et punique*, Turnhout 1992.
DDD : K. VAN DER TOORN - B. BECKING - P.W. VAN DER HORST (eds.), *Dictionary of Deities and Demons in the Bible*, 2nd ed., Leiden-Grand Rapids 1999.
DEB : *Dictionnaire encyclopédique de la Bible*, Turnhout 1987.
DJD : Discoveries in the Judaean Desert.
DMOA : Documenta et Monumenta Orientis Antiqui, Leiden.
DNWSI : J. HOFTIJZER - K. JONGELING, *Dictionary of the North-West Semitic Inscriptions*, Leiden 1995.
DUSSAUD, *Topographie* : R. DUSSAUD, *Topographie historique de la Syrie antique et médiévale* (BAH 4), Paris 1927.

EA : The El-Amarna tablets numbered according to J.A. KNUDTZON, *Die El-Amarna - Tafeln* (VAB 2), Leipzig 1915; A.F. RAINEY, *El Amarna Tablets 359-379* (AOAT 8), 2nd ed., Kevelaer - Neukirchen - Vluyn 1978; W.L. MORAN, *Les lettres d'El Amarna* (LAPO 13), Paris 1987; ID., *The Amarna Letters*, Baltimore 1992.
ErIs : Eretz-Israel.
ESI : *Excavations and Surveys in Israel.*

FGH	: F. JACOBY (ed.), *Fragmente der griechischen Historiker*, Berlin-Leiden 1923-58.
FHG	: C. MÜLLER (ed.), *Fragmenta Historicorum Graecorum*, Paris 1841-70.
GCS	: Die griechischen christlichen Schriftsteller.
GM	: *Göttinger Miszellen.*
HARDING, *Arabian Names*	: G. LANKESTER HARDING, *An Index and Concordance of Pre-Islamic Arabian Names and Inscriptions* (Near and Middle East Series 8), Toronto 1971.
HAT	: Handbuch zum Alten Testament.
HSM	: Harvard Semitic Monographs.
HSS	: Harvard Semitic Series.
HTR	: *The Harvard Theological Review.*
HUCA	: *Hebrew Union College Annual.*
IAA Reports	: Reports of the Israel Antiquities Authority.
ICC	: The International Critical Commentary.
IDAM	: Israel Department of Antiquities and Museums.
IEJ	: *Israel Exploration Journal.*
JANES	: *The Journal of the Ancient Near Eastern Society of the Columbia University.*
JAOS	: *Journal of the American Oriental Society.*
JARCE	: *Journal of the American Research Center in Egypt.*
JASTROW	: M. JASTROW, *A Dictionary of the Targumim, the Talmud Babli and Yerushalmi, and the Midrashic Literature* I-II, New York 1886-1903.
JBL	: *Journal of Biblical Literature.*
JCS	: *Journal of Cuneiform Studies.*
JEA	: *Journal of Egyptian Archaeology.*
JEOL	: *Jaarbericht van het Vooraziatisch-Egyptisch Genootschap "Ex Oriente Lux".*
JESHO	: *Journal of the Economic and Social History of the Orient.*
JHS	: *Journal of Hellenic Studies.*
JNES	: *Journal of Near Eastern Studies.*
JNSL	: *Journal of the Northwest Semitic Languages.*
JPOS	: *Journal of the Palestine Oriental Society.*
JSS	: *Journal of Semitic Studies.*
K.	: Inventory numbers of the Kuyundjik collection in the British Museum.
KAI	: H. DONNER - W. RÖLLIG, *Kanaanäische und aramäische Inschriften*, Wiesbaden 1962-64 (3rd ed., 1971-76).
KAT	: Kommentar zum Alten Testament.

KTU	: M. DIETRICH - O. LORETZ - J. SANMARTÍN, *The Cuneiform Alphabetic Texts from Ugarit, Ras Ibn Hani and Other Places (KTU: second, enlarged edition)*, Münster 1995.
LÄg	: W. HELCK - E. OTTO - W. WESTENDORF (eds.), *Lexikon der Ägyptologie* I-VI, Wiesbaden 1972-86.
LAPO	: Littératures anciennes du Proche-Orient.
LIPIŃSKI, *Aramaeans*	: E. LIPIŃSKI, *The Aramaeans: Their Ancient History, Culture, Religion* (OLA 100), Leuven 2000.
LIPIŃSKI, *Dieux et déesses*	: E. LIPIŃSKI, *Dieux et déesses de l'univers phénicien et punique* (Studia Phoenicia XIV; OLA 64), Leuven 1995.
LIPIŃSKI, *Itineraria Phoenicia*	: E. LIPIŃSKI, *Itineraria Phoenicia* (Studia Phoenicia XVIII; OLA 127), Leuven 2004.
LIPIŃSKI, *Semitic*	: E. LIPIŃSKI, *Semitic Languages: Outline of a Comparative Grammar* (OLA 80), 2nd ed., Leuven 2001.
MARI	: *Mari. Annales de recherches interdisciplinaires.*
MDAIR	: *Mitteilungen des Deutschen archäologischen Instituts. Römische Abteilung.*
MDOG	: *Mitteilungen der Deutschen Orient-Gesellschaft zu Berlin.*
MGWJ	: *Monatschrift für Geschichte und Wissenschaft des Judentums*, Breslau.
MIFAO	: Mémoires de l'Institut Français d'Archéologie Orientale, Le Caire.
MUSJ	: *Mélanges de l'Université Saint-Joseph*, Beyrouth.
MVÄG	: Mitteilungen der Vorderasiatisch - Ägyptischen Gesellschaft.
ND	: Inventory numbers of the Nimrud excavations.
NEAEHL	: E. STERN (ed.), *The New Encyclopedia of Archaeological Excavations in the Holy Land*, Jerusalem 1993.
NESE	: *Neue Ephemeris für semitische Epigraphik.*
OBO	: Oriens Biblicus et Orientalis.
OEANE	: E.M. MEYERS (ed.), *The Oxford Encyclopedia of Archaeology in the Near East* I-V, New York-Oxford 1997.
OIP	: Oriental Institute Publications.
OLA	: Orientalia Lovaniensia. Analecta.
OLP	: *Orientalia Lovaniensia. Periodica.*
OLZ	: *Orientalistische Literaturzeitung.*
Orientalia	: *Orientalia.* Nova series.
PAT	: D.R. HILLERS - E. CUSSINI, *Palmyrene Aramaic Texts*, Baltimore 1996.
PECS	: R. STILLWELL - W.L. MACDONALD - M.H. MACALLISTER (eds.), *The Princeton Encyclopedia of Classical Sites*, Princeton 1976.
PEFQ	: *Palestine Exploration Fund. Quarterly Statement.*

PEQ	: *Palestine Exploration Quarterly.*
PL	: J.P. MIGNE (ed.), *Patrologia Latina*, Paris 1844-55.
PNA	: K. RADNER - H.D. BAKER (eds.), *The Prosopography of the Neo-Assyrian Empire* I-III, Helsinki 1998 ff.
PRU	: J. NOUGAYROL / Ch. VIROLLEAUD, *Le Palais royal d'Ugarit* II-VI, Paris 1955-70.
PSBA	: *Proceedings of the Society of Biblical Archaeology.*
PW	: A. PAULY - G. WISSOWA *et al.* (eds.), *Real-Encyclopädie der classischen Altertumswissenschaft.*
RA	: *Revue d'assyriologie et d'archéologie orientale.*
RAO	: Ch. CLERMONT-GANNEAU, *Recueil d'archéologie orientale* I-VIII, Paris 1885-1921.
RB	: *Revue biblique.*
RÉG	: *Revue des Études Grecques.*
RÉS	: *Répertoire d'épigraphie sémitique,* Paris 1905 ff.
RGTC	: Répertoire géographique des textes cunéiformes, Wiesbaden 1974 ff.
RHA	: *Revue hittite et asianique.*
RHR	: *Revue de l'histoire des religions.*
RIH	: Inventory numbers of the Rās Ibn Hani excavations.
RIMA I	: A.K. GRAYSON, *Assyrian Rulers of the Third and Second Millennia BC (to 1115 BC)* (Royal Inscriptions of Mesopotamia. Assyrian Periods 1), Toronto 1987.
RIMA II	: A.K. GRAYSON, *Assyrian Rulers of the Early First Millennium BC* I: *1114-859 BC* (Royal Inscriptions of Mesopotamia. Assyrian Periods 2), Toronto 1991.
RIMA III	: A.K. GRAYSON, *Assyrian Rulers of the Early First Millennium BC* II: *858-745 BC* (Royal Inscriptions of Mesopotamia. Assyrian Periods 3), Toronto 1996.
RIMB II	: G. FRAME, *Rulers of Babylonia from the Second Dynasty of Isin to the End of Assyrian Domination: 1157-612 BC* (Royal Inscriptions of Mesopotamia. Babylonian Periods 2), Toronto 1995.
RLA	: *Reallexikon der Assyriologie und vorderasiatischen Archäologie.*
RS	: Inventory numbers of the Ras Shamra - Ugarit excavations.
RSF	: *Rivista di Studi Fenici.*
RSO	: *Rivista degli Studi Orientali.*
SAA I	: S. PARPOLA, *The Correspondence of Sargon II, Part I* (State Archives of Assyria I), Helsinki 1987.
SAA II	: S. PARPOLA - K. WATANABE, *Neo-Assyrian Treaties and Loyalty Oaths* (State Archives of Assyria II), Helsinki 1988.
SAA VII	: F.M. FALES - J.N. POSTGATE, *Imperial Administrative Records, Part I* (State Archives of Assyria VII), Helsinki 1992.
SAA X	: S. PARPOLA, *Letters from Assyrian and Babylonian Scholars* (State Archives of Assyria X), Helsinki 1993.

SAA XI	: F.M. FALES - J.N. POSTGATE, *Imperial Administrative Records, Part II* (State Archives of Assyria XI), Helsinki 1995.
SAA XVI	: M. LUUKKO - G. VAN BUYLAERE, *The Political Correspondence of Esarhaddon* (State Archives of Assyria XVI), Helsinki 2002.
SAAB	: *State Archives of Assyria Bulletin.*
Sabaic Dictionary	: A.F.L. BEESTON - M.A. GHUL - W.W. MÜLLER - J. RYCKMANS, *Sabaic Dictionary / Dictionnaire sabéen*, Louvain-la-Neuve - Beyrouth 1982.
SAIO I	: E. LIPIŃSKI, *Studies in Aramaic Inscriptions and Onomastics* I (OLA 1), Leuven 1975.
SAIO II	: E. LIPIŃSKI, *Studies in Aramaic Inscriptions and Onomastics* II (OLA 57), Leuven 1994.
SAK	: *Studien zur altägyptischen Kultur.*
SAOC	: Studies in Ancient Oriental Civilization.
SC	: Sources chrétiennes, Paris.
SIMA	: Studies in Mediterranean Archaeology.
SMEA	: *Studi Micenei ed Egeo-Anatolici.*
TAD I-III	: B. PORTEN - A. YARDENI, *Textbook of Aramaic Documents from Ancient Egypt* I. *Letters*, Jerusalem 1986; II. *Contracts*, Jerusalem 1989; III. *Literature, Accounts, Lists*, Jerusalem 1993.
TCL	: Textes cunéiformes du Louvre.
TCS	: Texts from Cuneiform Sources.
ThWAT I-VIII	: J. BOTTERWECK - H. RINGGREN - H.-J. FABRY (eds.), *Theologisches Wörterbuch zum Alten Testament*, Stuttgart 1970-95.
Tigl. III	: H. TADMOR, *The Inscriptions of Tiglath-pileser III, King of Assyria. Critical Edition with Introduction, Translation, and Commentary*, Jerusalem 1994.
TPOA	: J. BRIEND - M.-J. SEUX, *Textes du Proche-Orient ancien et histoire d'Israël*, Paris 1977.
TSSI I-III	: J.C.L. GIBSON, *Textbook of Syrian Semitic Inscriptions* I. *Hebrew and Moabite Inscriptions*, 2nd ed., Oxford 1973; II. *Aramaic Inscriptions*, Oxford 1975; III. *Phoenician Inscriptions*, Oxford 1982.
UF	: *Ugarit-Forschungen.*
VTS	: Supplements to Vetus Testamentum.
WA	: Western Asiatic Antiquities, British Museum, London.
WO	: *Die Welt des Orients.*
WVDOG	: Wissenschaftliche Veröffentlichungen der Deutschen Orient-Gesellschaft.

WZKM	: *Wiener Zeitschrift für die Kunde des Morgenlandes.*
YNER	: Yale Near Eastern Researches.
YOS	: Yale Oriental Series.
ZA	: *Zeitschrift für Assyriologie und vorderasiatische Archäologie.*
ZAH	: *Zeitschrift für Althebraistik.*
ZÄS	: *Zeitschrift für ägyptische Sprache und Altertumskunde.*
ZAW	: *Zeitschrift für die alttestamentliche Wissenschaft.*
ZDMG	: *Zeitschrift der Deutschen Morgenländischen Gesellschaft.*
ZDPV	: *Zeitschrift des Deutschen Palästina-Vereins.*

CHAPTER I

THE END OF THE BRONZE AGE

The Levant underwent significant changes and transformations between 1200 and 950 B.C., a period which corresponds to the final decades of the Late Bronze Age and to Iron Age I. The Bronze Age Canaanite and North-Syrian city-state system was then replaced by an ethno-political structure in which the various regions of the Levant were inhabited by different peoples. This change was accompanied by the collapse of the Hittite empire, by a considerable shrinking of the Assyrian power basis, and by the evanescence of the Egyptian control in Syro-Phoenicia and in Canaan, with concomitant and widespread destructions of the urban centres. The consequence was the abrupt end of historical records provided by the cuneiform archives of Ḫattuša, Emar, and Ugarit, which were not replaced by a sufficient amount of reliable indigenous sources. Only a few inscriptions, especially from Byblos, and some passages hypothetically distinguishable in the biblical accounts can be considered as historical sources related to this period. This lack of indigenous documents is by no means filled by the rare external references in Egypt and in Assyria, although one cannot neglect the "Israel Stela" of Merneptah, the Medinet Habu inscriptions and reliefs, which describe the wars of Ramesses III against the "Sea Peoples" in his 8th year, the statements in Papyrus Harris I and Papyrus Louvre N 3136, that Ramesses III settled his defeated foes in strongholds to fight the Libyans, the Tale of Wenamon and the *Onomasticon* of Amenemope, two literary works from the 11th century B.C., as well as the annals of Tiglath-pileser I (1114-1076 B.C.). The approximate date of the end of the Ugarit and Emar archives has also its importance, while the archaeological evidence can be crucial in establishing the chronology of this period and in setting the broad limits of the areas occupied by the different peoples.

The immediate cause of the momentous changes in the Levant seem to have been the large-scale migrations that occurred at the end of the Bronze Age and were probably brought about by a severe and protracted famine in Anatolia. The Hittite king thus urges the king of Ugarit to send a ship and a crew to transport grain from Mukish to the Hittite harbour town of Ura in Cilicia, as a "matter of life and death", since there is starvation in the land[1]. In 1211, to alleviate the famine Merneptah has even shipped a huge gift of corn to Hatti[2]. Syria and Palestine were affected directly by the migrations of the "Sea Peoples" along the Mediterranean coasts and by the expansion of the Aramaeans who spread inland all over the Fertile Crescent. Their movements coincided with the settlement of various Transjordanian and Cisjordanian nomadic tribes, taking advantage of the collapse of the Egyptian power in Canaan.

Ugarit between Egypt and the Hittites

The end of Ugarit, in north-western Syria, is usually placed about 1180 B.C. because of the assumed chronological link between the destruction of the city and Ramesses III's battles with the "Sea Peoples" in his 8th year (1175 B.C.). However, nothing substantiates this assumption and Papyrus Harris I states that, after defeating and capturing his foes, Ramesses III settled them in his strongholds in Egypt, probably to the south-west of the Delta, facing the Libyans. The slightly higher date of 1185 B.C. was proposed on basis of the letter RS 86.2230, which Beya, "Chief of the troops of the Great King, the King of Egypt", had sent to Ammurapi[3]. The man must be identical with the "Great Chancellor of the entire land" Bay, active until the end of the Nineteenth Dynasty, during the reigns of Siptah, who was a minor (*ca.* 1193-1187 B.C.), and of Siptah's mother Tewosret (*ca.* 1193-1186)[4]. On this basis, however, 1185 B.C. can only be regarded as a *terminus post quem* for the fall of Ugarit. Although we have no direct evidence to establish the interval between the arrival of Beya's letter and the destruction of Ugarit and of the nearby site of Rās Ibn Hani, these events can hardly be dated to *ca.* 1185 or 1180 B.C.

[1] RS 20.212 and RS 26.158, published by J. NOUGAYROL, in *Ugaritica* V, Paris 1968, No. 33, p. 105-107, and No. 171, p. 323-324.

[2] Line 24 of the great Karnak inscription: K.A. KITCHEN, *Ramesside Inscriptions* IV, Oxford 1982, p. 5; ID., *Ramesside Inscriptions. Translated & Annotated. Translations* IV, Malden 2003, p. 4; C. MANASSA, *The Great Karnak Inscription: Grand Strategy in the 13th Century BC* (Yale Egyptological Studies 5), New Haven 2003, p. 158. Cf. H. KLENGEL, *Geschichte des hethitischen Reiches*, Leiden 1999, p. 310, n. 4.

[3] J. FREU, *La tablette RS 86.2230 et la phase finale du royaume d'Ugarit*, in *Syria* 65 (1988), p. 395-398; ID., *La fin d'Ugarit et de l'Empire hittite. Données nouvelles et chronologie,* in *Semitica* 48 (1999), p. 17-39. An even higher date is defended by I. SINGER, *New Evidence on the End of the Hittite Empire*, in E.D. OREN (ed.), *The Sea Peoples and Their World: A Reassessment*, Philadelphia 2000, p. 21-33, probably because he still dates the reign of Siptah to 1197-1192 B.C. (see p. 28, n. 2).

[4] H. ALTENMÜLLER, *Die Verspätete Beisetzung des Siptah,* in *GM* 145 (1995), p. 29-36.

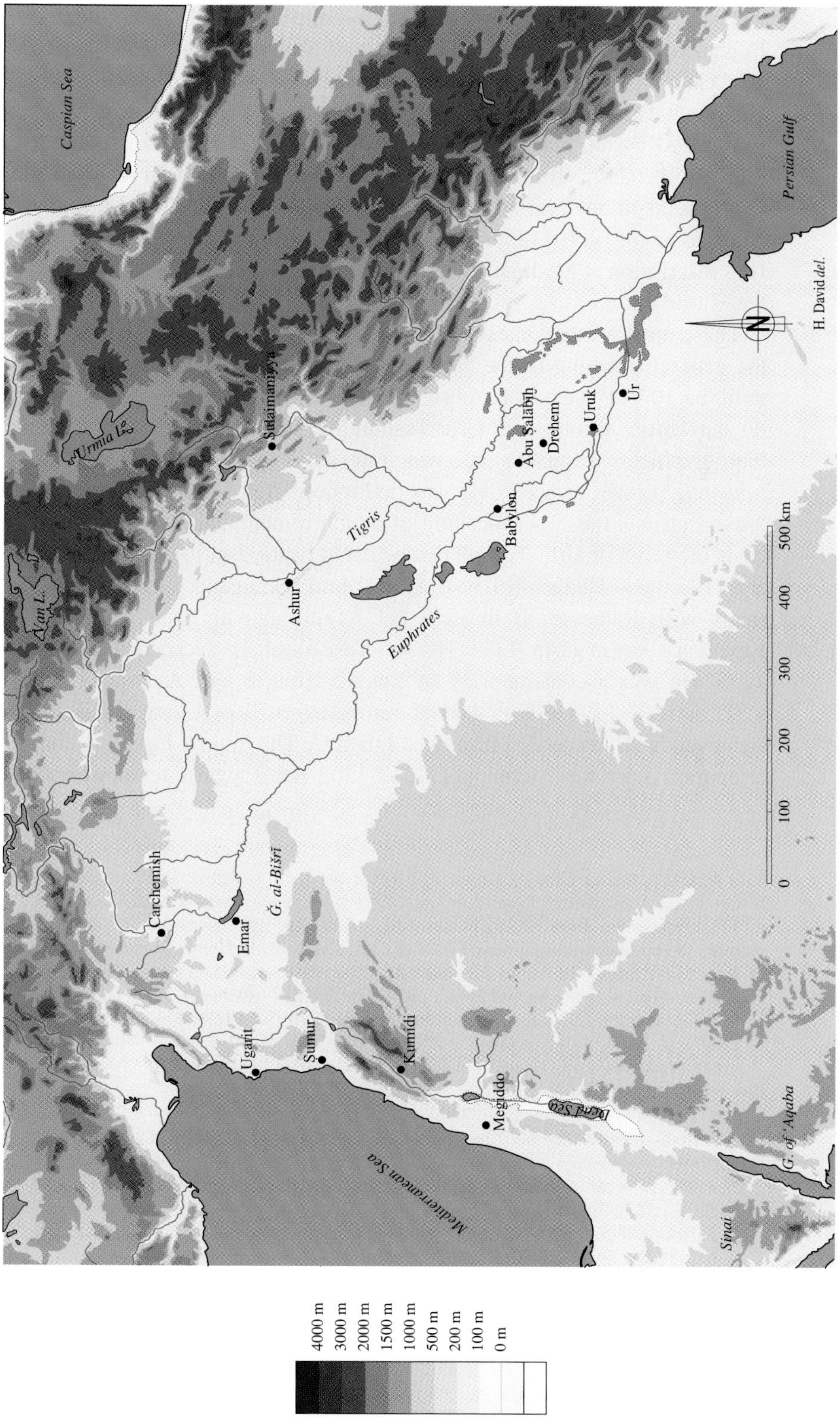
Caspian Sea
Persian Gulf
Mediterranean Sea
Dead Sea
G. of 'Aqaba
Sinai
Urmia L.
Van L.
Tigris
Euphrates
Ğ. al-Bišrī
Carchemish
Emar
Ugarit
Sumur
Kumidi
Megiddo
Ashur
Sulaimaniyya
Babylon
Abu Salabih
Drehem
Uruk
Ur
N
0 100 200 300 400 500 km
H. David del.
4000 m
3000 m
2000 m
1500 m
1000 m
500 m
200 m
100 m
0 m

Middle East.

The unexpected discovery of the so-called *Südburg* inscription at Boghazköy-Ḫattuša, in 1988, showed that Shuppiluliuma II led extensive campaigns in western Anatolia, annexing lands and cities to his kingdom. This information will probably take a long time to be fully recognized by all, and publications on the end of the Bronze Age still refer "to the short, ill-fated reign of ... Shuppiluliuma II"[5]. In reality, his reign seems to have lasted longer than previously assumed and it might be dated to *ca.* 1200-1180 B.C., ending just a few years before Ramesses III's inscription at Medinet Habu mentions, in 1175 B.C., the collapse of the Hittite empire.

These approximate dates of Shuppiluliuma II's reign result also from the general lowering of the chronology. Muwatalli II probably reigned until the 10th/11th year of Ramesses II[6], i.e. 1269 B.C. His legitimate heir on the Hittite throne was Urḫi-Teshub/Murshili III, as shown by the hieroglyphic seal impressions, which attribute to Urḫi-Teshub the title *tuḫkanti*, "crown prince"[7]. He was dethroned after a peaceful period of "seven years", the exact meaning of which remains uncertain[8]. On this basis the reign of Urḫi-Teshub can be dated cautiously to *ca.* 1268-1261 B.C. His uncle Hattushili III assumed then the kingship, signed a peace treaty with Ramesses II in 1258 B.C.[9], and sent his daughter to the Egyptian court in 1245 B.C.[10] His son Tudhaliash IV succeeded him *ca.* 1235. He was a contemporary of Tukulti-Ninurta I of Assyria (1240-1205 or 1233-1197 B.C.)[11] and of Ammištamru II of Ugarit[12]. His son Arnuwanda III succeeded him *ca.* 1210 B.C. The latter's Egyptian contemporary ruler was Merneptah (1212-1202 B.C.), whose relations with

[5] A. Caubet, *The Case of Ugarit and Carchemish: A Contrast*, in W.G. Dever - S. Gitin (eds.), *Symbiosis, Symbolism, and the Power of the Past*, Winona Lake 2003, p. 17-21, quotation from p. 19. In her bibliography (p. 20), the author nevertheless includes the pertinent publications of D. Hawkins, *The New Inscription from the Südburg of Boğazköy-Ḫattuša,* in *Archäologischer Anzeiger* 1990, p. 305-314; Id., *The Hieroglyphic Inscription of the Sacred Pool Complex at Hattusa (Südburg)*, Wiesbaden 1995.

[6] A. Hagenbuchner, *War der* ^{LÚ}tuḫkanti Neriqqaili *ein Sohn Ḫattušilis III.?*, in *SMEA* 29 (1992), p. 111-126 (see p. 116).

[7] J.D. Hawkins, *Urhi-Tešub*, tuhkanti, in G. Wilhelm (ed.), *Akten des IV. Internationalen Kongresses für Hethitologie*, Wiesbaden 2001, p. 167-179.

[8] H. Klengel, *op. cit.* (n. 2), p. 228.

[9] E. Edel, *Der Vertrag zwischen Ramses II. von Ägypten und Hattusili III. von Hatti*, Berlin 1997.

[10] In the 34th year of Ramesses II: H. Klengel, *op. cit.* (n. 2), p. 242-243.

[11] *Ibid.*, p. 279-281, 390.

[12] J. Nougayrol, *Le Palais royal d'Ugarit* IV, Paris 1956, p. 8; J. Munn-Rankin, in *CAH* II/2, 3rd ed., Cambridge 1975, p. 291.

the court of Ugarit[13], probably with Ibiranu, seem to explain, why Ibiranu had to be reminded by the Hittite king that he was supposed to appear before his suzerain or at least send an ambassador[14]. Apparently, he was in no great hurry either to fulfil the military obligations of a vassal[15]. Arnuwanda died without offspring[16] and his younger brother Shuppiluliuma II took over *ca.* 1200, imposing a new treaty on Niqmaddu of Ugarit[17], who had just ascended the throne of his father Ibiranu. Niqmaddu's reign cannot have been very long and Ammurapi, still a minor[18], was made king of Ugarit *ca.* 1190 B.C.

It does not appear that Ugarit fell about the same time as Ḫattuša. No link can be established between the two events: Ḫattuša was already abandoned by a part of its population and was no longer the capital of the Empire, when it was partially destroyed by the Kaška tribes[19], while Ugarit was deserted because of an overwhelming invasion of the "Sea Peoples". Besides, Ugarit is not mentioned in Ramesses III's account on the advance of the "Sea Peoples", although good relations between Ugarit and Egypt seem to have thrived until the last days of Ugarit. Moreover, if Shuppiluliuma II still concluded treaties with Talmi-Teshub of Carchemish[20] and Niqmaddu of Ugarit[21] in the first decade of the 12th century, the divorce adjudicated by Talmi-Teshub, king of Carchemish, to Ammurapi and Eḫli-Nikkal, the daughter of the Hittite king,

[13] RS 88.2158, published by S. LACKENBACHER, *Une correspondance entre l'administration du pharaon Merneptah et le roi d'Ugarit*, in M. YON *et al.* (eds.), *Le pays d'Ougarit autour de 1200 av. J.-C.*, Paris 1995, p. 77-83.

[14] RS 17.247: J. NOUGAYROL, *op. cit.* (n. 12), p. 191. Cf. RS 34.136: F. MALBRAN-LABAT, in P. BORDREUIL (ed.), *Ras Shamra-Ougarit* VII. *Une bibliothèque au sud de la ville*, Paris 1991, p. 29-31, No. 7.

[15] RS 17.289: J. NOUGAYROL, *op. cit.* (n. 12), p. 192. Cf. RS 34.143: F. MALBRAN-LABAT, in *op. cit.* (n. 14), p. 27-29, No. 6.

[16] A. GOETZE, *Keilschrifturkunden aus Boghazköi* XXVI. *Historish-politische Texte*, Berlin 1933, No. 33, col. II, 6 ff. Cf. H. KLENGEL, *op. cit.* (n. 2), p. 297, 298.

[17] A.-S. DALIX, *Šuppiluliuma (II?) dans un texte alphabétique d'Ugarit et la date d'apparition de l'alphabet cunéiforme,* in *Semitica* 48 (1999), p. 5-15. A new edition of the tablet is provided by D. PARDEE, *Le traité d'alliance RS 11.772+,* in *Semitica* 51 (2003), p. 5-31. The tablet (*KTU* 3.1) should be added to the list of documents from the reign of Shuppiluliuma II in H. KLENGEL, *op. cit.* (n. 2), p. 300-308.

[18] RS 34.129, published by F. MALBRAN-LABAT, in P. BORDREUIL (ed.), *Ras Shamra-Ougarit* VII. *Une bibliothèque au sud de la ville*, Paris 1991, No. 12, line 6: LUGAL EN-*ka ṣe-ḫe-er*.

[19] J. SEEHER, *Die Zerstörung der Stadt Hattuša*, in G. WILHELM (ed.), *Akten des IV. Internationalen Kongresses für Hethitologie*, Wiesbaden 2001, p. 623-634.

[20] H. KLENGEL, *op. cit.* (n. 2), p. 301; I. SINGER, *The Treaties between Karkamish and Hatti*, in G. WILHELM (ed.), *Akten des IV. Internationalen Kongresses für Hethitologie*, Wiesbaden 2001, p. 635-641.

[21] Se here above, n. 17.

without the latter's intervention, seems to indicate that all links with Ḫattuša were already disrupted by that time, the more so that the financial solution of the divorce was rather favourable to the king of Ugarit[22]: Eḫli-Nikkal was allowed to keep her dowry, but she had to give up a royal residence, which she occupied and was reluctant to leave. The documents related to this affair might thus be dated to *ca.* 1180 B.C.

A few years later, all links between Ugarit and Carchemish seem to have been broken as well, because of the Aramaean invasions of the area to the west of the great bend of the Euphrates, culminating in the fall of Emar *ca.* 1175 B.C.

The end of Emar

For the date of Emar's fall authors are generally relying on the fortunate discovery of a dated tablet in the destruction level of a private house[23]. The tablet is a legal document from the second year of Meli-Shipak, king of Babylon, whose reign is now dated to 1181-1167 B.C.[24] The second year of his reign corresponds then to 1180/79. This date only provides a *terminus post quem* for the fall of Emar, since we have no evidence whatsoever to establish the interval between the writing of the tablet and the destruction of the city. The approximate date of 1175 is suggested by a cuneiform tablet and a bulla, both most likely from Emar, which mention Kuzi-Teshub, the son of Talmi-Teshub, king of Carchemish, but do not yet attribute the royal title to Kuzi-Teshub himself, as do somewhat later impressions of his royal seal[25]. The date *ca.* 1175 B.C. is also supported by the chronology of the rulers of Emar, which

[22] RS 17.226 and RS 17.355: J. NOUGAYROL, *op. cit.* (n. 12), p. 206-210. RS 20.216 (J. NOUGAYROL, in *Ugaritica* V, Paris 1968, No. 35, p. 108-110) might be related to the same case. Cf. M. LIVERANI, *Storia di Ugarit* (Studi semitici 6), Roma 1962, p. 132. The earlier opinion regarding the documents as related to a divorce of Ammurapi's son should be abandoned. Exaggerated doubts about the nature of the affair are expressed by S. LACKENBACHER, *Textes akkadiens d'Ugarit* (LAPO 20), Paris 2002, p. 126-130.

[23] D. ARNAUD, *Les textes d'Emar et la chronologie de la fin du Bronze Recent,* in *Syria* 52 (1975), p. 87-92; ID., *Recherches au pays d'Aštata. Emar VI,* Paris 1985-87, No. 26.

[24] J. BOESE, *Burnaburiaš II., Melišipak und die Mittelbabylonische Chronologie,* in *UF* 14 (1982), p. 15-26. These dates are now followed also by H. GASCHE - J.A. ARMSTRONG - S.W. COLE - V.G. GURZADYAN, *Dating the Fall of Babylon. A Reappraisal of Second-Millennium Chronology*, Ghent-Chicago 1998. J.A. BRINKMAN, *Meli-Šipak,* in *RLA* VIII, Berlin 1993-97, p. 52, dated the reign of Meli-Shipak to 1186-1172 B.C.

[25] Cf. J.D. HAWKINS, *Kuzi-Tešub and the "Great Kings" of Karkamiš,* in *AnSt* 38 (1988), p. 99-108 (see p. 99, n. 1).

allows dating the archives to the period 1260-1175 B.C.[26], corresponding to four generations with an average reign-span of 25 years, the first and the fourth reigns being shorter[27]. Another chronology, assuming the existence of an earlier dynasty with four rulers and attributing the most recent documents (*ca.* 1210-1185) to a period without known kings of Emar[28], lacks any solid foundation. No member of the assumed earlier dynasty bears the royal title, while the persons in question seem to belong to the later period of the archives[29].

Yaṣi-Dagan (*ca.* 1260-1245 B.C.)
|
Baal-kabar I (*ca.* 1245-1220 B.C.)
|
Zu-Ashtarti (*ca.* 1220-1210 B.C.) — Pilsu-Dagan (*ca.* 1210-1190 B.C.)
|
Elli/Illi (*ca.* 1190-1175 B.C.)
|
Baal-kabar II (crown prince)

The ruling dynasty of Emar in the 13th-12th centuries B.C.

The first siege of Emar by "the king of the Mountain people", LUGAL ERIM.MEŠ ^{kur}*Ḫar-ri*[30], occurred during the reign of Pilsu-Dagan, *ca.* 1200 B.C. The existence of the Hurrian state of Hanigalbat had come to an end *ca.* 1258[31] and its former territory, though pervaded by Aramaean

[26] Somewhat higher dates 1310-1187 B.C. were proposed by D. ARNAUD, *art. cit.* (n. 23), on basis of the texts found by the French archaeological mission and of a slightly higher general chronology.

[27] The sequence of the Emar dynasty was established by F.M. FALES, *Notes on the Royal Family of Emar*, in D. CHARPIN - F. JOANNÈS (eds.), *Marchands, diplomates et empereurs. Études sur la civilisation mésopotamienne offertes à Paul Garelli*, Paris 1991, p. 81-90.

[28] A. SKAIST, *The Chronology of the Legal Texts from Emar,* in *ZA* 88 (1998), p. 45-71.

[29] E. LIPIŃSKI, *The Hosts of the Mountain*, forthcoming.

[30] D. ARNAUD, *op. cit.* (n. 23), No. 42, 9-10; cf. D. ARNAUD, *Textes syriens de l'âge du Bronze Récent* (Aula Orientalis. Suppl. 1), Sabadell-Barcelona 1991, No. 9, 21-22; A. TSUKIMOTO, *Akkadian Tablets in the Hirayama Collection* (I), in *Acta Sumerologica* 12 (1990), p. 177-259 (see p. 190, No. 7, 29-30); G. BECKMAN, *Texts from the Vicinity of Emar in the Collection of Jonathan Rosen*, Padova 1996, No. 77, 34-35.

[31] A. HARRAK, *Assyria and Ḫanigalbat* (Texte und Studien zur Orientalistik 4), Hildesheim 1987, p. 188.

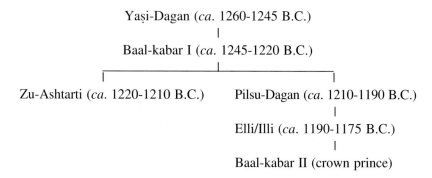

tribesmen, belonged then firmly to the Assyrian empire of Tukulti-Ninurta I, and "a king of the Mountain people" could hardly come from this region. The [kur]*Ḫar-ri,* called also *Ṭár-wu* /*Ṭawru*/[32], should rather be Mount Bishri, called "Mountains of the Aḫlamū", *šá-da-an Aḫ-la-mi-i*, by Tukulti-Ninurta I[33], and known as a main Aramaean centre in the 12th century B.C., at the time of Tiglath-pileser I (1113-1077 B.C.)[34]. This first attack did not disrupt the relations of Emar with Carchemish and Ugarit, but the fall of Emar about twenty-five years later, towards the end of Talmi-Teshub's reign[35], and the Aramaean push westward into Syria and along the valleys of the Euphtates and its tributaries certainly caused a break-up of international relations and of the exchange of correspondence not only between Carchemish and Ugarit, but also between Carchemish and the Egyptian centre of Kumidi, in the Beqa' Valley. This probably explains the mention of Carchemish among the countries being ruined in 1175 B.C. or somewhat later, when the Medinet Habu inscriptions were redacted. The fact that the dates of Ramesses III's battles against the "Sea Peoples" and the fall of Emar are more or less coinciding does not prove that the "Sea Peoples" were also responsible for the destruction of Emar and of other inland cities[36]. Aramaean tribes are much better candidates of the disruption of Late Bronze Age conditions in the area of the Middle Euphrates[37].

32 D. ARNAUD, *op. cit.* (n. 30), Nos. 25, 2-3 and 44, 2-3. The equivalence of the two appellations has been first noticed by M. ASTOUR, *Who was the King of the Hurrian Troops at the Siege of Emar?,* in M.W. CHAVALAS (ed.), *Emar*, Bethesda 1996, p. 25-56 (see. p. 32, n. 28). For their interpretation see here below, Chapter V, p. 206.

33 *RIMA* I, text A.0.78.23, p. 273, line 70. Cf. J.-R. KUPPER, *Les nomades en Mésopotamie au temps des rois de Mari*, Paris 1957, p. 110 and 136.

34 *RIMA* II, text A.0.87.1, p. 23, lines 43-63; text A.0.87.2, p. 34, lines 28-29; text A.0.87.3, p. 37, lines 29-30; text A.0.87.4, p. 43, line 34; text A.0.87.12, p. 59-60, lines 4'-8'.

35 M.L. ADAMTHWAITE, *Late Hittite Emar. The Chronology, Synchronisms, and Socio-Political Aspects of a Late Bronze Age Fortress Town* (Ancient Near Eastern Studies. Suppl. 8), Louvain 2001, follows an inconsistent chronology, since he dates Talmi-Teshub to 1235-1210 and Ammurapi of Ugarit to 1200-1182 B.C., although Talmi-Teshub has ruled over the financial consequences of Ammurapi's divorce.

36 *Pace* J. BOESE, *art. cit.* (n. 24), p. 18; M. YON, *The End of the Kingdom of Ugarit*, in W.A. WARD - M.S. JOUKOWSKY (eds.), *The Crisis Years: The 12th Century B.C. - From Beyond the Danube to the Tigris*, Dubuque 1992, p. 111-122 (see p. 117); A. CAUBET, *Reoccupation of the Syrian Coast after the Destruction of the "Crisis Years", ibid.*, p. 123-131 (see p. 129); J.-Cl. MARGUERON, *Emar, Capital of Aštata in the Fourteenth Century BCE,* in *BA* 58 (1995), p. 126-138 (see p. 127).

37 H. KLENGEL, *op. cit.* (n. 2), p. 318, n. 35; LIPIŃSKI, *The Aramaeans*, p. 44; I. SINGER, *art. cit.* (n. 3), p. 25; M.R. ADAMTHWAITE, *op. cit.* (n. 35), p. 278-280.

Bronze plaque representing a Canaannite dignitary
of the Late Bronze period, found at Hazor
(Photo: Courtesy of the IDAM).

The last days of Ugarit

Ugarit was not destroyed by the Aramaeans and its fall should be dated later than the capture of Emar by these tribesmen. It had to defend itself against the "Sea Peoples", and the navy of Ugarit, like the fleets of the Phoenician cities, was able to protect the town against them for a few decades. However, Ugarit did certainly feel insecure and this is the reason, why its ruler resorted to seek protection from the king of Egypt by becoming his vassal. This situation is clearly implied by the Ugaritic drafts of two letters sent by Ammurapi to the pharaoh, most likely to Ramesses III (1182-1151 B.C.). They can date from the period following Ramesses III's victories in 1175 B.C., in the battles on land and sea, fought probably at the border of Amurru and off its coast. In fact, Ramesses III's inscriptions seem to indicate that the raiders were stopped at the frontier of the Egyptian sphere of influence in Syro-Phoenicia[38].

Both letters contain very elaborate courtesy addresses to the pharaoh and record that the king of Ugarit is his vassal: *ht.'ank.'bdk*, "See, I am your servant"[39], ['*an*]*k.'bdk.l.p'n* [*b'ly.ql*]*t*, "I am your servant, I fell at the feet of my lord"[40]. The better preserved text from Rās Ibn Hani contains wishes also at the address of the cavalry and the chariots of the pharaoh, alluding to the importance of this Egyptian power basis in the concrete situation of Ugarit: *yšlm* [...] *l.'inšk.l.ḥwtk* [*l.śśw*]*k.lmrkbtk*, "May there be welfare ... to your people, to your land, to your horses, to your chariots"[41].

The letter RS 34.356 most likely belonged to the archive of Urtenu, a very important figure of the last decades of Ugarit, possibly the prefect to whom the Hittite king had addressed the letter RS 34.129, in which the king of Ugarit, most likely Ammurapi, is qualified as "young"[42]. Ammurapi was apparently set on the throne while yet a boy. This must have happened *ca.* 1190 B.C. Urtenu probably had a long career, but the provenance of a document from his archive does not prove that it dates

[38] See here below, p. 43-44.

[39] RS 34.356, recto 5 = *KTU* 2.76. The text was published by P. BORDREUIL, *Quatre documents en cunéiformes alphabétiques mal connus ou inédits*, in *Semitica* 32 (1982), p. 7-14 and Pls. I-II (see p. 10-12 and Pl. II).

[40] RIH 78/3+30, recto 5-6 = *KTU* 2.81.The text was published by P. BORDREUIL - A. CAQUOT, *Les textes en cunéiformes alphabétiques découverts en 1978 à Ibn Hani*, in *Syria* 56 (1980), p. 343-373 (see p. 356-357).

[41] RIH 78/3+30, recto 6-8 = *KTU* 2.81.

[42] See here above, p. 27, n. 18.

from his tenure of office. In fact, the Akkadian letter RS 92.2009 from this archive, concerning communication between Urḫi-Teshub (*ca.* 1268-1260 B.C.) and elders of Ugarit[43], shows that the presence of such a document in Urtenu's house only provides a general date in the 13th-12th centuries B.C. Of course, one should keep in mind that several hundred tablets from this house are not yet published. New information shall undoubtedly provide new insights. In the meantime, however, one can cautiously regard Ibiranu, not Ammurapi, as the author of the letter RS 88.2158 sent by the king of Ugarit to Egypt during the reign of Merneptah (1212-1202 B.C.). He probably tried to obtain an Egyptian backing in a period of somewhat strain relations with the Hittites.

The Hittite king and even the king of Carchemish, probably Kuzi-Teshub, have instead disappeared from the Ugaritian horizon when Ammurapi's letters were sent to the pharaoh. They could be dated *ca.* 1170 B.C. We do not know how long lasted Urtenu's tenure of office and whether his house contains documents from the last years of Ugarit, which had to be finally abandoned by its inhabitants. They had apparently had enough warning to escape, for no skeletons were found in streets or houses other than those buried in the tombs, and for some precious artefacts were hidden in walls or beneath the floors in the vain hope that they might one day be recovered[44]. People left probably for inland regions not yet occupied by Aramaeans, like the Anṣariyah range, which has always been a refuge place. Scattered peasants and herdsmen remained around Ugarit and Rās Ibn Hani, where the Late Bronze Age palaces had been abandoned and then destroyed, more or less at the same time as Ugarit.

There is obviously no written evidence dating these events, but Rās Ibn Hani was soon resettled by people who produced Mycenaean IIIC:1b pottery of the same type that appears on Cyprus in the Late Cypriot IIIA period (*ca.* 1175-1125 B.C.) and along the Levantine coast from Cilicia to Philistia. The settlement of the "Sea Peoples" is rightly connected with the appearance of this ware[45]. Now, the affinities between Aegean pottery and the pottery of the Philistines can be "from

[43] For Urḫi-Teshub, see H. KLENGEL, *op. cit.* (n. 2), p. 218-235.

[44] Cl. F-A. SCHAEFFER, *Neue Endeckungen in Ugarit*, in *AfO* 20 (1963), p. 206-215 (see p. 206); ID., *Neue Endeckungen und Funde in Ugarit (1962-1964)*, in *AfO* 21 (1966), p. 131-137 (see p. 131-132).

[45] A.E. KILLEBREW, *Aegean-Style Early Philistine Pottery in Canaan during the Iron I Age: A Stylistic Analysis of Mycenaean IIIC:1b Pottery and Its Associated Wares*, in E.D. OREN (ed.), *The Sea Peoples and Their World: A Reassessment*, Philadelphia 2000, p. 233-253, in particular the summary on p. 243 and the conclusions on p. 244.

no earlier than the middle of the 12th century"[46]. Also the decorative patterns of Philistine ware, very similar to those of the pottery group from Late Helladic IIIC Middle on the Island Cos[47], can serve as a reliable chronological indicator and date the Mycenaean IIIC:1b pottery of Philistia and of the "Sea Peoples" to the later part of the 12th century B.C. Therefore, the destruction of Ugarit and of Rās Ibn Hani can probably be dated to *ca.* 1160, closer to the end of the Egyptian occupation of Kāmid el-Lōz, *ca.* 1150 B.C. or somewhat later[48]. Ammurapi was then about forty years old.

The introduction of Mycenaean IIIC:1b ware at Rās Ibn Hani[49] points to a settlement of newcomers from the Aegean in the mid-12th century B.C. It is worth noting that some types of pottery continue local traditions[50], indicating that the new settlers intermingled with small autochthonous groups, like in Philistia. There is likewise gradual evolution from "monochrome" to "bichrome" pottery[51], again like in the Philistine settlements. The precise origin of the newcomers is unknown, but they certainly belong to the large movement of peoples in Anatolia and the Aegean, who abandoned their lands completely. This implies serious climatic changes and a widespread disruption of agriculture. Some pieces of evidence support this assumption precisely in the 12th century B.C. Thus, abnormal fluctuations were observed in the Yassihöyük / Gordion (Anatolia) tree-ring sequence in the decades of the mid-

[46] Ph.P. Betancourt, *The Aegean and the Origin of the Sea Peoples*, in E.D. Oren (ed.), *The Sea Peoples and Their World: A Reassessment*, Philadelphia 2000, p. 297-303, quotation from p. 300.

[47] T. Dothan - A. Zukerman, *A Preliminary Study of the Mycenaean IIIC:1 Pottery Assemblages from Tel Miqne-Ekron and Ashdod,* in *BASOR* 333 (2004), p. 1-54, in particular p. 35-41 and 44.

[48] R. Hachmann, *Kamid el-Lōz* 16. *'Schatzhaus'-Studien* (Saarbrücker Beiträge zur Altertumskunde 59), Bonn 1996, p. 19-20.

[49] A. Bounni - J. & E. Lagarce - N. Saliby - L. Badre, *Rapport préliminaire sur la troisième campagne de fouilles (1977) à Ibn Hani (Syrie),* in *Syria* 56 (1979), p. 217-294 and Pls. V-VIII, especially p. 245-257 and Fig. 25; L. Badre, *Les Peuples de la Mer à Ibn Hani?,* in *Atti del I Congresso Internazionale di Studi Fenici e Punici*, Roma 1983, Vol. I, p. 203-209; J. & E. Lagarce, *The Intrusion of the Sea Peoples and Their Acculturation: A Parallel between Palestinian and Ras Ibn Hani Data*, in S. Soath (ed.), *Studies in the History and Archaeology of Palestine* III, Aleppo 1988, p. 137-169. A few fragments of Mycenaean IIIC:1b ware have been identified at Ugarit according to J.-Y. Montchambert, *Du Mycénien IIIC à Ougarit,* in *Orient-Express* 2 (1996), p. 45-46. For expressed doubts, cf. A. Caubet, *Ras Shamra-Ugarit before the Sea Peoples*, in E.D. Oren (ed.), *The Sea Peoples and Their World: A Reassessment*, Philadelphia 2000, p. 35-51 (see p. 49).

[50] J. & E. Lagarce, *art. cit.* (n. 49), p. 154-155; A. Caubet, *art. cit.* (n. 36), p. 127.

[51] J. & E. Lagarce, *art. cit.* (n. 49), p. 153.

12th century B.C.[52] Comparable phenomena occurred in Western Europe about the same time. Thus, Irish oaks show up poor growing seasons in that period[53].

The dating of the fall of Ugarit to *ca.* 1160 B.C. is not contradicted by the fact that the final level of Ugarit has provided imported pottery from the extreme end of Late Helladic or Mycenaean IIIB[54], which might be even later than 1150 B.C. On the other hand, the locally made Mycenaean IIIC:1b pottery, found in the post-destruction level at Rās Ibn Hani[55], close to Ugarit, is convincingly dated in Palestinian sites between *ca.* 1140-1130 and 1100 B.C.[56], while its Cypriot and Aegean prototypes should be dated to *ca.* 1175-1125 B.C.[57] Since there was no important gap between the destruction of the Ugaritian settlement at Rās Ibn Hani and the reoccupation of the site[58], the end of Ugarit can indeed

[52] P.I. Kuniholm, *Archaeological Evidence and Non-Evidence for Climatic Change*, in *Philosophical Transactions of the Royal Society of London* A 330 (1990), p. 645-655 (see p. 653).

[53] M.G.L. Baillie, *Irish Oaks Record Volcanic Dust Veils Drama!*, in *Archaeology Ireland* 2/2 (1988), p. 71-74; Id., *Marker Dates - Turning Prehistory into History*, in *Archaeology Ireland* 2/4 (1988), p. 154-155.

[54] J.-Cl. & L. Courtois, in *Ugaritica* VII, Paris 1978, for instance, p. 310-311, No. 12; p. 344-345, No. 6. For an earlier characterization of this pottery type, see F.H. Stubbings, *Mycenaean Pottery from the Levant*, Cambridge 1951, p. 71 ff. See now A. Leonard, *An Index to the Late Bronze Age Pottery from Syria-Palestine* (SIMA 114), Jansered 1994.

[55] See above, n. 49.

[56] I. Finkelstein, *The Date of the Settlement of the Philistines in Canaan*, in *Tel Aviv* 22 (1995), p. 213-239, especially p. 224; Id., *The Stratigraphy and Chronology of Megiddo and Beth-shan in the 12th-11th Centuries B.C.E.*, in *Tel Aviv* 23 (1996), p. 170-184, in particular p. 178. See also P. Warren - V. Hankey, *Aegean Bronze Age Chronology*, Bristol 1989, p. 165, 168; D. Ussishkin, *Megiddo at the End of the Late Bronze Age*, in *Tel Aviv* 22 (1995), p. 240-267, especially p. 264, and here above, note 45. This pottery type was first isolated from the whole complex of the so-called "Philistine pottery" (cf. T. Dothan, *The Philistines and their Material Culture*, Jerusalem 1982, p. 94-218) by B. Hrouda, *Die Einwanderung der Philister in Palästina. Eine Studie zur Seevölkerbewegung des 12. Jahrhunderts*, in *Vorderasiatische Archäologie, Studien und Aufsätze A. Moortgat ... gewidmet*, Berlin 1964, p. 126-135, especially p. 130-131.

[57] After the study of A. Furumark, *The Mycenaean IIIC Pottery and its Relation to Cypriote Fabrics*, in *Opuscula Archaeologica* 3 (1944), p. 194-265, large quantities of Mycenaean IIIC:1b were found in various Cypriot sites, at Enkomi, Kouklia, Kition, Palaeokastro-Maa, Athienou. This pottery can be compared to the similar Mycenaean ware from Tarsus (cf. E. French, *A Reassessment of the Mycenaean Pottery at Tarsus*, in *AnSt* 25 [1975], p. 53-75), but it is convenient to relate it first of all to the Late Helladic IIIB pottery from mainland Greece, where this particular ware is characteristic of pre-destruction Mycenae, the end of which can be dated *ca.* 1130 B.C.; cf. V.R. D'A. Desborough, in *CAH* II/2, 3rd ed., Cambridge 1975, p. 668-669. There is some discrepancy in the terminology used by some authors.

[58] A. Bounni - N. Saliby - J. & E. Lagarce, *Ras Ibn Hani*, in *Syrian-European Archaeology Exhibition / Exposition Syro-Européenne d'Archéologie*, Damas 1996, p. 107-112, especially p. 110.

be dated near 1160 B.C., with the following tentative chronology of its last kings, where the figures are just a calculated guess: Ibiranu, *ca.* 1210-1200; Niqmaddu, *ca.* 1200-1190; Ammurapi, *ca.* 1190-1160 B.C.

Merneptah and the "Sea Peoples"

The presence of a large quantity of the Late Mycenaean IIIC:1b pottery in the post-destruction level of Rās Ibn Hani and at Philistine sites links the end of Ugarit with the migration of the "Sea Peoples". The term "Sea Peoples" was coined in the modern research as a common appellation of several sea-borne peoples who, according to Egyptian sources, came first from the west via Libya, then by sea and by land from the east, in an attempt to invade Egypt[59]. Their first mention dates from the reign of the pharaoh Merneptah who boasts in his records at Karnak and Athribis that he won a great victory at Per-Ir in his 5th year (1208 B.C.) on an army of Libyans and Meshwesh, who were supported by "foreigners from the sea"[60]. The battle must have taken place to the south-west of the Delta. The "Sea Peoples" participating in it were mercenaries serving in the Libyan forces and no migrants coming to settle in Egypt. Strictly speaking, therefore, this was no invasion of the "Sea Peoples". Nevertheless, it is interesting to recall the names given to them in Merneptah's inscriptions. The great Karnak inscription enumerates them in lines 1, 14, 52-53, 56: *'I-q-w-š* (Ahhiyawa, Achaeans), *Tw-r-š* (Tro-

[59] A survey with literature is given by I. SINGER, *The Origin of the Sea Peoples and Their Settlement on the Coast of Canaan*, in M. HELTZER - E. LIPIŃSKI (eds.), *Society and Economy in the Eastern Mediterranean (c. 1500-1000 B.C.)* (OLA 23), Leuven 1988, p. 239-250. One should add, in particular: C. VANDERSLEYEN, *Le dossier égyptien des Philistins*, in E. LIPIŃSKI (ed.), *The Land of Israel: Cross-Roads of Civilizations* (OLA 19), Leuven 1985, p. 39-54; T. & M. DOTHAN, *People of the Sea. The Search for the Philistines*, New York 1992; E. NOORT, *Die Seevölker in Palästina* (Palaestina antiqua 9), Kampen 1994; E.D. OREN (ed.), *The Sea Peoples and Their World: A Reassessment*, Philadelphia 2000; A. KILLEBREW - G. LEHMANN - M. ARTZY (eds.), *The Philistines and Other Sea Peoples*, forthcoming.

[60] A detailed and accurate study of Merneptah's great inscription at Karnak is provided by C. MANASSA, *op. cit.* (n. 2), p. 162, line 52. See also K.A. KITCHEN, *op. cit.* (n. 2), p. 2-12, especially p. 8, line 52 (Karnak); p. 19-22, especially p. 22, line 13 (Athribis), and ID., *op. cit.* (n. 2), *Translations* IV, p. 2-10, in particular p. 2 and 7 (Karnak), 19 (Athribis). The Egyptian phrase "foreigners from the sea" corresponds to the etymological meaning of the name Ahhiyawa or Achaeans, "water people", i.e. Aegeans, as shown by O. CARRUBA, *Ahhija e Ahhijawa, la Grecia e l'Egeo,* in Th. P. J. VAN HOUT - J. DE ROOS (eds.), *Studio historiae ardens. Ancient Near Eastern Studies Presented to Ph. H.J. Houwink ten Cate*, Leiden 1995, p. 7-21; ID., *La Grecia e l'Egitto nel II millennio*, in *Istituto Lombardo. Accademia di Scienze e Lettere. Rendiconti. Classe di Lettere e Scienze Morali e Storiche* 129 (1995), p. 141-160.

jans), *R-kw* (Lycians), *Š-r-d-n* (Sherdana), and *Š-k-r-š* (Shagalasha), "Northerners coming from all lands" (line 1).

Ahhiyawa lay west of the Anatolian mainland, across the sea, and could be reached by boat via the islands[61]. It was a powerful state, although Achaea was restricted in the first millennium B.C. to south-east Thessaly and the north coast of the Peloponnesus. The *'I-q3-(ỉ-)w3-š3* mentioned among the "Sea Peoples" in Merneptah's inscriptions are Achaean Greeks[62]. Allied to the Libyans and fought by Merneptah in 1208 B.C., they may have come from the Peloponnesus, but they may also have been Achaeans from Anatolia[63] or Cyprus[64]. The large amounts of Mycenaean pottery discovered at Tarsus, Kazanlı, and Mersin suggest that these Cilician places were either Mycenaean emporia or had capacious Mycenaean warehouses about the 14th-13th centuries B.C.[65] Besides, coastal sites of West Anatolia are now providing solid evidence of Mycenaean settlement and influence in the form of pottery, imported and locally made, and of typical Mycenaean tombs, mainly in the central area between Bodrum and İzmir, considerably increasing the evidence of Mycenaean settlement in this region[66]. We can thus assume an Achaean presence on this coast. The Achaeans are no longer mentioned in 1175 B.C. among the enemies of Ramesses III, and cannot be connected directly with the Philistines.

As for the *Tw-r-š* of Merneptah's and Ramesses III's inscriptions, they must be people from the region of Troy rather than Tarsus[67]. In fact,

[61] Summary presentation by J.D. HAWKINS in the important article by D.F. EASTON - J.D. HAWKINS - A.G. & E.S. SHERRATT, *Troy in Recent Perspective,* in *AnSt* 52 (2002), p. 75-109 (see p. 100).

[62] As shown by O. CARRUBA, *art. cit.* (n. 60).

[63] Cf. O. CARRUBA, *art. cit.*, in *Istituto Lombardo...* (n. 60), p. 151-152. These can only be Achaeans emigrated or ousted from Greece, since Ahhiyawa was not located on the Anatolian mainland; cf. lately J.D. HAWKINS, in *art. cit.* (n. 61), p. 100.

[64] They could be identified with the immigrants of the latest phase of Late Cypriote II B, prior to the appearance of the Mycenaean IIIC:1b pottery. The opposite opinion was rightly criticized by A. MAZAR, *The Emergence of the Philistine Material Culture*, in *IEJ* 35 (1985), p. 95-107 (see p. 104-106).

[65] C. MEE, *Aegean Trade and Settlement in Anatolia in the Second Millennium B.C.*, in *AnSt* 28 (1978), p. 121-156; I. SINGER, *art. cit.* (n. 59), p. 244; M. MARAZZI, *Mykener in Vorderasien,* in *RLA* VIII, Berlin 1993-97, p. 528-534, in particular the map on p. 530; M. POPKO, *Religions of Asia Minor*, Warsaw 1995, p. 157. See also C. ÖZGÜNEL, *Mykenische Keramik in Anatolien* (Asia Minor Studien 23), Bonn 1996, especially p. 6-7 with references.

[66] References can be found in D.F. EASTON *et al.*, *art. cit.* (n. 61), p. 96. For instance, Mycenaean *tholos* tombs have been found at Panaztepe, in Western Anatolia: M.J. MELLINK, *Archaeology in Anatolia*, in *AJA* 92 (1988), p. 101-131, especially p. 114-115.

[67] Tarsus is called *Tarša* in Hittite texts: A. GOETZE, *Kizzuwatna and the Problems of*

Tw-r-š should be identified with the city *Taruiša* in Hittite sources[68], since the Neo-Egyptian spelling ***Tw**-r-š* usually indicates the syllable *ta*[69]. Now, *Taruiša* is most likely Troy[70]. *R-kw* is certainly "greater Lycia", as shown by the Yalburt inscription, which records a campaign of Tudhaliash IV to several localities in the Lukka lands, identified with toponyms in Lycia[71]. Lycians appear already as pirates in a piece of Amarna correspondence (*EA* 38), in which the king of Alashiya complains of "men of Lukki" raiding his country (*EA* 38, 6-12). The king also protests to the pharaoh that people of Alashiya are not among the Lycian raiders, as the king of Egypt had previously thought (*EA* 38, 13-22).

The *Š-r-d-n*, known also from texts of Ugarit[72], appear in Egyptian documents as early as the reign of Amenhotep III (1392-1354 B.C.), when pharaoh's army encountered Sherdana warriors at Byblos[73]. By the

Hittite Geography, New Haven 1940, p. 54-56; D.F. EASTON *et al.*, *art. cit.* (n. 61), p. 97. The West Semitic spelling was *Trz.*

[68] G.F. DEL MONTE - J. TISCHLER, *Die Orts- und Gewässernamen der hethitischen Texte* (RGTC 6), Wiesbaden 1978, p. 408.

[69] R. HANNIG, *Die Sprache der Pharaonen. Grosses Handwörterbuch Ägyptisch-Deutsch (2800-950 v. Chr.)*, 2nd ed., Mainz a/R 1997, p. LIV.

[70] J.D. HAWKINS, in *art. cit.* (n. 61), p. 98-100. See also F. STARKE, *Troia im Kontext des historisch-politischen und sprachlichen Umfeldes Kleinasiens im 2. Jahrtausend,* in *Studia Troica* 7 (1997), p. 447-487. The usual speculative reference to the Etruscans is not illuminating in the present state of our knowledge, even if we link them with HERODOTUS, *History* I, 94, to the Tyrsenoi of Lydia. Neither should *Tw-r-š* be related to the Lycian place name *Trusñ*, in Greek Τρύσα; cf. E. KALINKA, *Tituli Asiae Minoris* I. *Tituli Lyciae lingua Lycia conscripti,* Wien 1901, No. 44b, 15.

[71] M. POETTO, *L'iscrizione luvio-geroglifica di Yalburt* (Studia Mediterranea 9), Pavia 1993. For earlier research on the location of Lukka, cf. W. RÖLLIG, *Lukka, Lukki*, in *RLA* VII, Berlin 1987-90, p. 161-163. See also T.R. BRYCE, *The Lukka Problem - and a Possible Solution*, in *JNES* 33 (1974), p. 395-404; ID., *Lukka Revisited*, in *JNES* 51 (1992), p. 121-130, especially p. 128-130. Bryce assumes that Lycaonia was the original home of these people. Its name is a Grecized form of Anatolian **Lukka-wani*, "inhabitant of Lukka", as shown convincingly by E. LAROCHE, *Lyciens et Termiles*, in *Revue archéologique* 1976, p. 15-19 (see p. 17-18). Instead, there are no solid arguments in favour of a location of Lukka in northern Anatolia, as proposed by H. OTTEN, *Das Land Lukka in der hethitischen Topographie*, in J. BORCHHARDT - G. DOBESCH (eds.), *Akten des II. Internationalen Lykien-Symposions*, Wien 1993, p. 117-121 (see p. 119 and 121). Cf. also J.M. MELLINK, *Homer, Lycia and Lukka*, in J. CARTER - S.P. MORRIS (eds.), *The Ages of Homer: A Tribute to Emily Townsend Vermeule*, Austin 1995, p. 33-43; R. LEBRUN, *Réflexions sur le Lukka et environs au 13ème s. av. J.-C.*, in K. VAN LERBERGHE - A. SCHOORS (eds.), *Immigration and Emigration within the Ancient Near East. Festschrift E. Lipiński* (OLA 65), Leuven 1995, p. 139-152; W. JENNIGES, *Les Lyciens dans l'Iliade: sur les traces de Pandaros*, in L. ISEBAERT - R. LEBRUN (eds.), *Quaestiones Homericae*, Louvain-Namur 1998, p. 119-147, especially p. 123-125 and 141.

[72] They are called there *Ṯrtnm* with several variants; cf. LIPIŃSKI, *Itineraria Phoenicia*, p. 242-243.

[73] W. HELCK, *Die Beziehungen Ägyptens und Vorderasiens zur Ägäis bis ins 7.*

Ramesses III on bas-relief at Medinet Habu
(Photo: Dirk Huyge).

reign of Ramesses II (1279-1212 B.C.) the Sherdana appear as Egyptian mercenaries[74], and in the 13th century B.C. they were likewise incorporated at Ugarit in the royal service system[75]. The *Š-k-r-š* were connected already by Gaston Maspero[76] with Sagalassos (Ağlasun), in Pisidia.

Jahrhundert v. Chr. (Erträge der Forschung 120), Darmstadt 1979, p. 133. Cf. K. SETHE - W. HELCK, *Urkunden der 18. Dynastie*, Leipzig-Berlin 1906-58 (reprint, 1984), p. 1821: 13 ff.

74 *ANET*, p. 255b; K.A. KITCHEN, *Pharaoh Triumphant. The Life and Times of Ramesses II, King of Egypt*, Warminster 1982, p. 40-41. For references to battle reliefs with Sherdana fighting alongside Egyptian troops, see C. MANASSA, *op. cit.* (n. 2), p. 78-79.

75 M. HELTZER, *Some Questions Concerning the Sherdana in Ugarit*, in *IOS* 9 (1983), p. 9-16.

76 G. MASPERO, *Histoire ancienne des peuples de l'Orient*, Paris 1875, p. 195-196; ID., *Études de mythologie et d'archéologie égyptiennes*, Paris 1893-1916, Vol. III, p. 104-105. For the Hellenistic and later attestations of the city and its location, see L. ZGUSTA, *Kleinasiatische Ortsnamen* (Beiträge zur Namenforschung. Beihefte, N.F. 21), Heidelberg 1984, p. 522-523, §1141.This location does not imply, of course, that the *Š-k-r-š* of the Late Bronze Age were occupying the very same area as the Hellenistic city of Sagalassos, although the favourable conditions of its surroundings could have attracted part of the coastal *Š-k-r-š* population. For the natural environment of Sagalassos, see N. WAELKENS - J. POBLOME (eds.), *Sagalassos* IV (Acta Archaeologica Lovaniensia. Monographiae 9), Leuven 1997, p. 225-252.

Ramesses III and the "Sea Peoples"

The Libyans defeated at Per-Ir by Merneptah waited until the 5th year of Ramesses III, i.e. 1178 B.C., to invade Egypt again, this time without the assistance of the "Sea Peoples". Information is provided by the inscriptions and scenes sculptured on the walls of Ramesses III's funerary temple at Medinet Habu and by the narrative of Papyrus Harris I, which to some extent supplements the temple record and describes the Libyan penetration in Egypt from Merneptah's reign until year 5 of Ramesses III[77]. The progression of events is obliterated by the triumphal and stereotyped wording of the Egyptian texts to the extent that the Libyan invasion of year 5 was viewed sometimes as a prelude to the attack by the "Sea Peoples" in year 8[78], although no "Northerners" appear this time among the enemies. The account of this invasion was even regarded as a literary echo of the Libyan war in year 5 of Merneptah[79]. Fortunately, the monumental record allows distinguishing these conflicts, in particular those of year 5 (1178 B.C.) and of year 8 (1175 B.C.)[80], in which the attackers were the "Sea Peoples" and the battle field lay on the Syro-Phoenician coast, not on the western bank of the Nile.

Where the Egyptians encountered the Libyans in 1178 is not known, but the latter were utterly defeated by Ramesses III[81]. Egypt enjoyed peace for two years, but in 1175 it had to face the "Sea Peoples". This was their first real attempt to migrate to Canaan by sea and by land. The invasion was repulsed by Ramesses III in 1175 B.C. The Medinet Habu reliefs depict a land battle and a naval battle. The bas-relief picturing the

[77] Papyrus Harris I (BM 10053), 76, 11-77, 2. Cf. P. GRANDET, *Le Papyrus Harris I* (Bibliothèque d'étude 109-110), Le Caire 1994, Vol. I, p. 337; C. MANASSA, *op. cit.* (n. 2), p. 131.

[78] R.D. BARNETT, *The Sea Peoples*, in *CAH* II/2, 3rd ed., Cambridge 1975, p. 359-378 (see p. 371); W.F. ALBRIGHT, *Syria, the Philistines, and Phoenicia, ibid.*, p. 507-536 (see p. 507).

[79] L. LESKO, *The Wars of Ramses III,* in *Serapis* 6 (1980), p. 83-86. Cf. C. MANASSA, *op. cit.* (n. 2), p. 131, n. 37.

[80] The inscription of year 5 is reproduced in *Medinet Habu* I (OIP 8), Chicago 1930, Pls. 27-28. The inscription and the reliefs referring to year 8 can be found *ibid.*, Pls. 29-46. All the texts are given also by K.A. KITCHEN, *Ramesside Inscriptions* V, Oxford 1983, p. 20-43, where the Philistines are mentioned on p. 25, 28, 36, 37, 40. See also p. 73 and 102. One should refer besides to a stele from Deir el-Medina: *ibid.*, p. 91-92. The main inscriptions are transcribed and translated by A.J. PEDEN, *Egyptian Historical Inscriptions of the Twentieth Dynasty* (Documenta Mundi. Aegyptiaca 3), Jansered 1994, p. 7-22 (Year 5) and 23-36 (Year 8). Selected passages are translated in *ANET*, p. 262-263.

[81] Papyrus Harris I, 77, 3-77, 6: P. GRANDET, *op. cit.* (n. 77), Vol. I, p. 337.

One of the five ox-carts carrying the "Sea Peoples"
with women and children on bas-relief at Medinet Habu
(*Medinet Habu* I, Chicago 1930, Pl. 34).

land battle is very significant because it represents not only the "Sea Peoples" in battle chariots, but also the families of the warriors drawn in four ox-carts with solid wheels. Thus the invaders appear as migrants and not merely as a military force. The main Medinet Habu inscription mentions five peoples: the Philistines (*P-r-s-t*), well known from the Bible, the Sicals (*Ṯ-k-r*), already referred to in a letter from the king of Hatti to the prefect of Ugarit[82] and mentioned later in the Tale of Wenamon from the 11th century B.C.[83], the Shagalasha (*Š-k-r-š*), probably

[82] RS 34.129, the photographs of which are published in *Ugaritica* VII, Paris 1978, Pl. XI (p. 417). Their decipherment was provided by M. DIETRICH - O. LORETZ, *Das 'seefahrende Volk' von* šikila *(RS 34.129),* in *UF* 10 (1978), p. 53-56, and the identification with *Ṯ-k-r* was proposed by G.A. LEHMANN, *Die* šikalaju - *Ein neues Zeugnis zu den "Seevölker" Heerfahrten im späten 13. Jh. v. Chr. (RS 34.129),* in *UF* 11 (1979), p. 481-494. See also I. SINGER, *art. cit.* (n. 59), p. 245-246. The outdated identification with Teucrians still occurs in several publications, e.g. in D.E. GERSHENSON, *A Greek Myth in Jeremiah*, in *ZAW* 108 (1996), p. 192-200 (see p. 198-199).

[83] Photographic edition by M.A. KOROSTOVTSEV, *The Journey of Wen-Amon to Byblos* (in Russian), Moscow 1960; hieroglyphic transcription by A.H. GARDINER, *Late-Egyptian Stories* (Bibliotheca Aegyptiaca 1), Bruxelles 1932, p. 61-76. The Tale of Wenamon is a literary work and no official report; see the discussion in G. BUNNENS, *L'expansion phénicienne en Méditerranée*, Bruxelles-Rome 1979, p. 45-51, with earlier literature. Add now B.U. SCHIPPER, *Die Erzählung des Wenamun* (OBO 209), Freiburg/Schweiz-Göttingen 2005. For the Sicals, the personal names and the place names of the Tale of Wenamon, cf. A. SCHEEPERS, *Anthroponymes et toponymes du récit d'Ounamon*, in E. LIPIŃSKI (ed.), *Phoenicia and the Bible* (Studia Phoenicia XI; OLA 44), Leuven 1991, p. 17-83.

linked with Sagalassos in Pisidia[84], the Danunians (*D-n-w-n, D-n-w*), known later as *Dnnyn* in Phoenician[85] and Δαναοί in Greek, from Cilicia (Adana), and the Weshesh (*W-š-š*), who have been related among others to Iasos, a Carian city[86], but whose name is closer to Ουασσος, a Carian locality near Halicarnassus[87]. The Sherdana are not mentioned in the Medinet Habu inscriptions related to the 1175 war, but Papyrus Harris I, 76, 7, lists the "Sherdana of the Sea" among the other "Sea Peoples" vanquished by Ramesses III:

> "I extended all the frontiers of Egypt and overthrew those who had attacked them from their lands. I slew the Danunians in their islands, while the Sicals and the Philistines were made ashes. The Sherdana and Weshesh of the Sea were made non-existent, taken captive all together and brought in captivity to Egypt like the sands of the shore. I settled them in strongholds bound in my name. The military classes were as numerous as hundred-thousands. I assigned portions for them all with clothing and provisions from the treasuries and granaries every year" (Papyrus Harris I, 76, 6-9).

The obvious Aegeo-Anatolian origin of these peoples explains why their invasion first struck the land of the Hittites, Tarḫuntassa in Cilicia (*Q-d-ỉ*[88]), Carchemish, West Anatolia (Arzawa)[89], and Cyprus (Alashiya). Although the Medinet Habu inscription says in a poetical style that these lands "have been cut off all at once", one cannot consider as granted on this basis that Ḫattuša, the Hittite capital, was meant or that its end had been caused by the "Sea Peoples". The destructions recorded

[84] Cf. here above, note 76. Beside the main texts, the *Š-k-r-š* are also mentioned in the inscription of a column fragment; cf. K.A. KITCHEN, *op. cit.* (n. 2), *Translations* IV, p. 19.

[85] *KAI* 24, 7; 26A, I, 2.3.4.5-6.17-18.21; II, 8.16-17 = *TSSI* III, 13, 7; 15, I, 2.3.4.5-6.17-18.21; II, 8.16-17.

[86] G.A. WAINWRIGHT, *Some Sea-Peoples*, in *JEA* 47 (1961), p. 71-90, especially p. 71, n. 3; R.D. BARNETT, in *CAH* II/2, 3rd ed., Cambridge 1975, p. 377. The Aegean character of Iasos results from excavations: Cl. LAVIOSA, *Les fouilles de Iasos*, in *Proceedings of the Xth International Congress of Classical Archaeology*, Ankara 1978, p. 1093-1099, with previous literature. For its location, cf. L. ZGUSTA, *op. cit.* (n. 76), p. 191, §358.

[87] L. ZGUSTA, *op. cit.* (n. 76), p. 456, §996.

[88] The place name *Q-d-ỉ,* attested from the time of Tuthmosis III, might be a variant of *Ḫ-t-3*, based not on Hittite or Luwian pronunciation, but on a language of South Anatolia, one could call Proto-Lycian. Hittite *ḫ* can in fact correspond in the first millennium B.C. to Lycian *q*, like in *Tarḫu-*, attested in Lycian A as *Trqqs* and in Lycian B as *Trqqiz*. Cf. G. NEUMANN, *Lykisch,* in *Altkleinasiatische Sprachen*, Leiden 1969, p. 358-396 (see p. 378); M. POPKO, *Ludy i języki starożytnej Anatolii*, Warszawa 1999, p. 124. On the other hand, Egyptian *d* often marks a phoneme /ṭ/, which was articulated either as a glottalized or pharyngealized *t*, or possibly as a geminated *t*.

[89] Apasa / Ephesus was the capital city of Arzawa to which the Cayster Valley belonged. The interpretation "Arwad", proposed in *Syria* 71 (1994), p. 374, is untenable.

by the Egyptians might refer generally to Hittite-controlled territories, especially to coastal areas like Amurru, mentioned explicitly in the Medinet Habu inscription. In fact, the pottery of the main destruction level at Tell al-Kāzil, the ancient Ṣumur in Amurru, seems to belong to a period anterior to the last pre-Philistine levels in South-Canaanite cities and to date back to *ca.* 1200-1175 B.C., since even Late Mycenaean IIIA and Late Ugaritian 2 wares have been found in that level[90], while the post-destruction layers contain wares also from the 11th century[91]. At the site of Carchemish, instead, no ample archaeological evidence of a destruction in the 12th century B.C. was found and the city was flourishing once again in Iron Age I.

The first scenes of the Medinet Habu bas-reliefs depicting these events show Ramesses III mobilizing his troops and setting out for Djahi against the "Sea Peoples"[92]. Djahi is a general term referring to Syro-Canaanite coastal regions, but the inscriptions refer more precisely to Amurru, while no expected Palestinian toponyms are mentioned. We know besides that Kumidi, the residence of pharaoh's representative in the Beqa' Valley, was in Egyptian hands at least until 1150 B.C.[93] All this means that Ramesses III's defensive frontier was not in Palestine but in Syria, at the border with Amurru[94], which was in the 13th century B.C. a kind of buffer state between the Hittite empire and the Egyptian sphere of influence in Syro-Phoenicia. The land battle against the "Sea Peoples" was thus probably fought in the coastal plain of northern Lebanon or Syria, whereas the following sea battle was won by Ramesses III off the coast, as suggested by the phrase "river-mouths". It is normally used for the mouths of the Nile in the Delta, but the context suggests to localize the battle near the mouth of the Nahr al-Kebir[95], the ancient Eleutherus. "It is a considerable stream even in the summer, and in the rainy season

[90] L. BADRE *et al.*, *Tell Kazel (Syrie). Rapport préliminaire sur les 4e-8e campagnes de fouilles (1988-1992)*, in *Syria* 71 (1994) p. 259-359, see p. 310-346, especially p. 345-346. See also E. CAPET - E. GUBEL, *Tell Kazel: Six Centuries of Iron Age Occupation (c. 1200-612 B.C.)*, in G. BUNNENS (ed.), *Essays on Syria in the Iron Age* (Ancient Near Eastern Studies. Suppl. 7), Louvain 2000, p. 425-457.

[91] L. BADRE *et al.*, *art. cit.* (n. 90), p. 297-309.

[92] *Medinet Habu* I, Pls. 29 ff.

[93] R. HACHMANN, *op. cit.* (n. 48), p. 19-20.

[94] A. ALT, *Kleine Schriften zur Geschichte des Volkes Israel* I, 2nd ed., München 1959, p. 228-229. The opposite opinion was held by R. STADELMANN, *Die Abwehr der Seevölker unter Ramses III.*, in *Saeculum* 19 (1968), p. 156-171, followed by M. BIETAK, *The Sea Peoples and the End of the Egyptian Administration in Canaan*, in *Biblical Archaeology Today, 1990*, Jerusalem 1993, p. 292-306.

[95] Already Cl. F.-A. SCHAEFFER, *Enkomi-Alasia* I, Paris 1952, p. 60, believed that the sea battle occurred near Arwad, off the Amurru coast.

Prisoners captured by Ramesses III from among the "Sea Peoples"
on bas-relief at Medinet Habu
(*Medinet Habu* I, Pl. 44).

is a barrier to intercourse, caravans sometimes remaining encamped on its banks for several weeks, unable to cross"[96]. The river reaches the sea a little north of Arqa and formed marches. If this localization is correct, the Egyptians took their final decisive action against the "Sea Peoples" off the coast of Amurru. The scene depicting the victory celebration on the relief logically follows the sea battle, which has ended this campaign and strengthened the Egyptian control on Canaan in general and on the seacoast in particular. From the account in the Papyrus Harris I it is clear that the captive "Sea Peoples" were settled in strongholds in Egypt[97], not in Canaan, as often assumed[98].

[96] J. KENRICK, *History and Antiquities of Phoenicia*, London 1855, p. 8, who quotes J.L. BURCKHARDT, *Travels in Syria and the Holy Land*, London 1822, p. 161, and F.R. CHESNEY, *Narrative of the Euphrates Expedition* I, London 1854, p. 450. See also F. WALPOLE, *The Ansayrii and the Assassins* III, London 1851, p. 49.

[97] Papyrus Harris I (BM 10053), 76, 6-9. Cf. W. ERICHSEN, *Papyrus Harris I. Hieroglyphische Transkription* (Bibliotheca Aegyptiaca 5), Bruxelles 1933, p. 92. Translation in *ANET*, p. 262a; P. GRANDET, *op. cit.* (n. 77), Vol. I, p. 336-337.

[98] For example, R.D. BARNETT, in *op. cit.* (n. 78), p. 377-378.

Ramesses III specifically claims that he settled Sherdana warriors in fortresses after the 1175 war against the "Sea Peoples"[99], and Papyrus Louvre N 3136, a literary composition based on historical records from the time of Merneptah and Ramesses[100], clearly indicates that Philistines and Sherdana fought against the Libyans alongside Egyptian troops in the year 11 war (1172 B.C.)[101]. These Sherdana are called *Šrdn n n3 nḫt.w*[102], "Sherdana of the strongholds", in contrast to the *Šrdn n p3 ym*[103], "Sherdana of the sea", a qualification assigned to the congeners among the "Sea Peoples" attacking Egypt. The reference to the Philistines, first mentioned in 1175, shows that these were captured in year 8 at the border of Amurru and that they were settled in fortresses along the western border of Egypt, facing the Libyans. This means that the Philistine settlement in Canaan cannot be regarded as a consequence of the 1175 war. It is linked to much later events, posterior to the reign of Ramesses III and related to the complete collapse of the Egyptian empire in Canaan around 1130 B.C.

Canaan under the Twentieth Dynasty

According to Papyrus Harris I, 9, 1-3[104], Ramesses III has built a temple for Amon in Pa-Canaan, i.e. Gaza, but the number of archaeological findings dated to his reign is even more indicative of direct Ramesses III's rule in Canaan than the information gleaned in this papyrus. Not only the main stronghold of Bēth-shan provided a statue of this pharaoh[105], as well as reliefs and inscriptions with his cartouches[106], but also other centres yielded dated material, such as bronze door fittings

[99] Papyrus Harris I, 76, 8-9: P. GRANDET, *op. cit.* (n. 77), Vol. I, p. 336-337.

[100] A. SPALINGER, *The Transformation of an Ancient Egyptian Narrative: P. Sallier III and the Battle of Kadesh*, Wiesbaden 2002, p. 359-365, Pls. I-III; C. MANASSA, *op. cit.* (n. 2), p. 125-133.

[101] Papyrus Louvre N 3136, II, 8-9.

[102] Papyrus Louvre N 3136, II, 9.

[103] Papyrus Harris I, 76, 7: P. GRANDET, *op. cit.* (n. 77), Vol. I, p. 336; Epigraphic Survey, *Medinet Habu* VIII (OIP 94), Chicago 1970, Pl. 600B, fourth figure; *ANEP*, No. 9.

[104] Papyrus Harris I, 9, 1-3. Translation in *ANET*, p. 260b-261a; P. GRANDET, *op. cit.* (n. 77), Vol. I, p. 232. See also H.J. KATZENSTEIN, *Gaza in the Egyptian Texts of the New Kingdom*, in *JAOS* 102 (1982), p. 111-113.

[105] F.W. JAMES, *The Iron Age at Beth Shan. Study of Levels VI-IV*, Philadelphia 1966, p. 34-38.

[106] *Ibid.*, p. 161-179, Fig. 88-99.

from Lachish[107], an ivory pen case from Megiddo[108], a faience vessel from Gezer[109], all bearing the name of Ramesses III. The relatively high percentage of scarabs with the name of Ramesses III from Tell al-Far'ah South, Tell Ğemmeh, Lachish, Bēth-Shemesh, Ashdod, Megiddo, and Bēth-shan[110] are rightly seen as further indications of Egyptian rule during his reign. In particular, the scarab from Bēth-Shemesh and two scarabs from Tell al-Far'ah South could be identified as official seals of temple estates in this region during the reign of Ramesses III[111]. An Egyptian hieratic ostracon from Tell aš-Šerī'a (Tel Sera'), dating to the 12th century B.C., is of particular interest since it bears the date "Year 22", certainly referring to a regnal year of Ramesses III (1161 B.C.), the only monarch to fit this date[112], which is largely posterior to the incursion of the "Sea Peoples" in 1175 B.C. Also two hieratic fragments from Tell al-Far'ah South have been ascribed to the time of Ramesses III[113]. The latest Egyptian temple at Kumidi seems even to have been built during the reign of Ramesses III and to have been destroyed only in the second half of the 12th century B.C.[114]

In any case, Egyptian presence in Canaan is attested also under the reign of Ramesses IV (1151-1145 B.C.), whose name appears on a stone block found at Tell Dalhamiyah[115], south of the Sea of Galilee, and on scarabs from Lachish[116], Tell al-Far'ah South[117], Bēth-

[107] D. USSISHKIN, *Levels VII and VI at Tel Lachish and the End of the Late Bronze Age in Canaan*, in J.N. TUBB (ed.), *Palestine in the Bronze and Iron Age. Papers in Honour of Olga Tufnell*, London 1985, p. 213-228, especially p. 218, Pl. IV.

[108] G. LOUD, *The Megiddo Ivories* (OIP 52), Chicago 1939, p. 11-12, Pl. 62:377.

[109] R.A.S. MACALISTER, *The Excavations of Gezer 1902-1905 and 1907-1909*, London 1912, Vol. II, p. 235-236, Fig. 388-390.

[110] The bibliography is collected by E. OREN, *'Governor's Residencies' in Canaan under the New Kingdom: A Case Study in Egyptian Administration*, in *Journal of the Society for the Study of Egyptian Antiquities* 14 (1984), p. 37-56, especially p. 46-56.

[111] C. UEHLINGER, *Der Amun-Tempel Ramses' III. in* p3-kn'n, *seine südpalästinensischen Tempelgüter und der Übergang von der Ägypter- zur Philisterherrschaft. Ein Hinweis auf einige wenig beachtete Skarabäen,* in *ZDPV* 104 (1988), p. 6-25, especially p. 9-15.

[112] O. GOLDWASSER, *Hieratic Inscriptions from Tel Sera' in Southern Canaan*, in *Tel Aviv* 11 (1984), p. 77-93, especially p. 87.

[113] O. GOLDWASSER - S. WIMMER, *Hieratic Fragments from Tell el-Far'ah (South),* in *BASOR* 313 (1999), p. 39-42.

[114] R. HACHMANN, *op. cit.* (n. 48), p. 19-20.

[115] J. LECLANT, *Fouilles et travaux en Égypte et au Soudan, 1980-1981*, in *Orientalia* 51 (1982), p. 411-492 (see p. 485).

[116] R. KRAUSS, *Ein wahrscheinlicher Terminus* post quem *für das Ende von Lachisch VI*, in *MDOG* 126 (1994), p. 123-130; N. LALKIN, *A Ramesses IV Scarab from Lachish,* in *Tel Aviv* 31 (2004), p. 17-21.

[117] J.L. STARKEY - L. HARDING, *Beth-Pelet* II, London 1932, p. 24-26, Pls. LII, 129 and LV, 297.

Shemesh[118], Gezer[119], Rās al-'Ain (Tel Aphek)[120], Bēth-shan[121], probably Tell aṣ-Ṣāfī (Gath)[122], Tell ar-Reqeish[123], and Tell Zakariyah (Azekah)[124]. The Timna copper mine was in operation at least until the time of Ramesses V (1145-1141 B.C.)[125] and the copper base of a statue of Ramesses VI (1141-1134 B.C.) found at Megiddo[126] evidences the Egyptian control of northern Canaan in the second half of the 12th century B.C. In the south, it lasted until the end of the century, since the cartouche of Ramesses VIII (1133-1126 B.C.) appears on an ivory knob from Ekron[127], while the throne name of Ramesses IX (1126-1108 B.C.) can be read on a faience fragment of a tile at Gezer[128], and scarabs with the name of Ramesses X (1108-1098 B.C.) have been found at Tell al-Far'ah South[129] and at Ḫirbet al-Mšāš (Tel Masos)[130].

With the exception of the camp set up by the "Sea Peoples" in Amurru before 1175 B.C. and mentioned in the Medinet Habu inscription, the settlement of the "Sea Peoples" in the Levant seems to have

[118] E. GRANT, *Ain Shems Excavations* II, Haverford 1932, Pl. 51:40.

[119] R.A.S. MACALISTER, *op. cit.* (n. 109), Vol. II, p. 296, Fig. 157:18.

[120] O. KEEL - M. SHUVAL - C. UEHLINGER, *Studien zu den Stempelsiegeln aus Palästina/Israel* III (OBO 100), Fribourg-Göttingen 1990, p. 26, confirming the original dating by R. GIVEON, *Scarabs from Recent Excavations in Israel* (OBO 83), Fribourg-Göttingen 1988, No. 40.

[121] J.M. WEINSTEIN, *The Scarabs, Plaques, Seals, and Rings*, in F.W. JAMES - P.W. MCGOVERN (eds.), *The Late Bronze Age Egyptian Garrison at Beth Shan: A Study of Levels VII and VIII*, Philadelphia 1993, p. 221-225 (see p. 221).

[122] B. PORTER - R.L. MOSS, *Topographical Bibliography of Ancient Egyptian Hieroglyphic Texts, Reliefs, and Paintings* VII. *Nubia, the Deserts, and Outside Egypt*, Oxford 1951, p. 372.

[123] W. CULICAN, *The Graves at Tell er-Reqeish*, in *The Australian Journal of Biblical Archaeology* 2/2 (1973), p. 66-105, especially p. 93, Fig. 14:1.

[124] B. PORTER - R.L. MOSS, *op. cit.* (n. 122), p. 372.

[125] B. ROTHENBERG, *The Egyptian Mining Temple at Timna*, London 1988, p. 277.

[126] J.H. BREASTED, in *Megiddo* II (OIP 62), Chicago 1948, p. 135-138. Cf. I. SINGER, *The Political Status of Megiddo VIIA*, in *Tel Aviv* 15-16 (1988-89), p. 101-112, especially p. 106-107; D. USSISHKIN, *art. cit.* (n. 56), p. 259-260; J.M. WEINSTEIN, *The Collapse of the Egyptian Empire in the Southern Levant*, in W.A. WARD - M.S. JOUKOWSKY (eds.), *The Crisis Years: The 12th Century B.C. - From Beyond the Danube to the Tigris*, Dubuque 1992, p. 142-150 (see p. 147).

[127] S. GITIN, *Philistia in Transition: The Tenth Century BCE and Beyond*, in S. GITIN - A. MAZAR - E. STERN (eds.), *Mediterranean Peoples in Transition: Thirteenth to Early Tenth Centuries BCE, in Honor of Trude Dothan*, Jerusalem 1998, p. 162-183 (see p. 174).

[128] R.A.S. MACALISTER, *op. cit.* (n. 109), Vol. II, p. 250; Vol. III, Pl. CXCV:74.

[129] W.M.F. PETRIE, *Beth Pelet* I, London 1930, p. 7, Pl. XXII, 202.

[130] B. BRANDL, *The Tel Masos Scarab: A Suggestion for a New Method for the Interpretation of Royal Scarabs*, in *Scripta Hierosolymitana* 28 (1982), p. 371-405.

started only in the mid-12th century B.C., first in the north, for example at Rās Ibn Hani, near their Anatolian and Cypriot bases, later in the south, probably not before *ca.* 1130 B.C.

CHAPTER II

PHILISTINES

Settlement

The migration and the settlement of the Philistines in the southern coastal plain of Canaan followed the same paradigm as the invasion of other "Sea Peoples". In other words, their settlement was no mercantile phenomenon[1]. Nor did they serve at first as mercenaries in the strongholds of the Egyptian administration in Canaan and settled along the Canaanite coast with the consent of the pharaoh. They just took advantage of the weakening and final collapse of the Egyptian domination in the country, and occupied the coastal region. The clearest chronological criterion to date this invasion and its immediate aftermaths is the end of maritime trade links with the Aegean and Cyprus, disrupted by the "Sea Peoples", and the consequent disappearance of imported Mycenaean IIIB and Cypriot pottery. These wares were succeeded, after a destruction of the city, by the first appearance of Philistine pottery.

The date of these events can be established on archaeological grounds. Imported Late Helladic or Mycenaean IIIB and Cypriot wares were found at Megiddo in Stratum VIIB and in Stratum VIIA[2], which is dated by the bronze base of a statue of Ramesses VI (1141-1134 B.C.). This means that the disruption of the trade links with the Aegean and Cyprus happened only about 1140-1130 B.C. The destruction levels of the main Philistine cities, so far excavated, such as Ashdod, Ashkelon, Ekron, and Gath, must be dated therefore to *ca.* 1130 B.C., and be followed by partly new settlements with a distinct new culture. This is indeed the situation attested at these four sites, especially thanks to major amounts of locally produced Mycenaean IIIC:1b pottery, also called "Monochrome" by opposition to the somewhat later Philistine

[1] This is stressed correctly by T.J. BARAJO, *The Philistine Settlements as Mercantile Phenomenon?,* in *AJA* 103 (1999), p. 513-530.

[2] I. FINKELSTEIN, *The Stratigraphy and Chronology of Megiddo and Beth-Shan in the 12th-11th Centuries B.C.E.,* in *Tel Aviv* 23 (1996) p. 170-180, especially p. 171; A. LEONARD - E.H. CLINE, *The Aegean Pottery at Megiddo: An Appraisal and Reanalysis,* in *BASOR* 309 (1998), p. 5-39.

black and red "Bichrome" ware, fashionable in the 11th and the early 10th century B.C. Of much importance is the fact that this Mycenaean IIIC:1b pottery, which constituted a luxury table ware, is accompanied by a larger quantity of locally made kitchen vessels in Aegean style[3], such as plain ware "kalathoi" (baskets) and one-handle cooking pots and jugs. This domestic pottery is a significant ethnic indicator which reveals the presence of a new population, native from the Aegean realm. However, locally produced Philistine ware is always found together with a larger assemblage of local pottery made in Canaanite tradition. We may therefore assume that the Philistines became overlords in an area which remained to a large extent populated by Canaanites[4], while the newcomers were few thousands at the most[5]. This is confirmed by the acculturation of the Philistines, who with the time started using Canaanite dialects and bearing Semitic names[6].

The Philistines' cultural assimilation, however, did not bring their ethnic identity to an end. Throughout the Iron Age, they retained a distinct

[3] T. DOTHAN - S. GITIN, *Tel Miqne - Ekron: The Rise and Fall of a Philistine City*, in *Qadmoniot* 27 (1994), p. 2-28 (in Hebrew), especially p. 10. The importance of this fact is stressed by S. BUNIMOVITZ - A. YASUR-LANDAU, *Philistine and Israelite Pottery: A Comparative Approach to the Question of Pots and People*, in *Tel Aviv* 23 (1996), p. 88-101, especially p. 92-93. See also A. MAEIR, *Philister-Keramik*, in *RLA* X, Berlin 2003-05, p. 528-536.

[4] A. MAZAR, *The Emergence of the Philistine Material Culture*, in *IEJ* 35 (1985), p. 95-107, especially p. 106-107.

[5] I. FINKELSTEIN, *The Philistine Countryside*, in *IEJ* 46 (1996), p. 225-242, especially p. 235-236; ID., *The Philistine Settlements: When, Where and How Many?*, in E.D. OREN (ed.), *The Sea Peoples and Their World: A Reassessment*, Philadelphia 2000, p. 159-180 (see p. 172-173). L.E. STAGER, *The Impact of the Sea Peoples in Canaan (1185-1080 BCE)*, in T.E. LEVY (ed.), *The Archaeology of Society in the Holy Land*, New York 1995, p. 332-348, estimates the number of newcomers at *ca.* 25,000.

[6] B.J. STONE, *The Philistines and Acculturation: Culture Change and Ethnic Continuity in the Iron Age*, in *BASOR* 298 (1995), p. 7-32. However, non-Semitic names occur as well: J. NAVEH, *Writing and Scripts in Seventh Century B.C.E. Philistia: The New Evidence from Tell Jemmeh*, in *IEJ* 35 (1985), p. 8-21 and Pls. 2-4; A. KEMPINSKI, *Some Philistine Names from the Kingdom of Gaza*, in *IEJ* 37 (1987), p. 20-24. See below, p. 65-70. Instead, the names of the Egypto-Aramaic papyrus fragment from Göttingen, dating probably from the 7th century B.C. and published by R. DEGEN, *Ein Fragment des bisher ältesten aramäischen Papyrus*, in *NESE* 2 (1974), p. 65-70 = *TAD* III, C3.2, are not related to Anatolian anthroponomy. The alleged ending *š* is an abbreviation for *šeqel* (cf. E. LIPIŃSKI, rev. in *BiOr* 37 [1980], p. 6). If we follow the reading of *TAD, S'dt* (line 4) may be compared to *S'DT* in HARDING, *Arabian Names*, p. 318, and *M'dt* may be Old Persian *Māhī-dāta* (W. HINZ, *Neue Wege im Altpersischen*, Wiesbaden 1973, p. 47), spelled elsewhere in Aramaic *Mhdt* (R.A. BOWMAN, *Aramaic Ritual Texts from Persepolis* [OIP 91], Chicago 1970, No. 5, line 3), *Mḥdd* (cf. J. NAVEH - Sh. SHAKED, *Amulets and Magic Bowls. Aramaic Incantations of Late Antiquity*, Jerusalem 1985, p. 156-157) or *Mhdṭ* (I. JERUZALMI, *Les coupes magiques araméennes de Mésopotamie*, Paris 1964, p. 114-126, line 6). The other names are apparently Semitic.

Locally made Mycenaean IIIC:1b pottery from Ekron Stratum VII,
ca. 1130-1100 B.C.
(Photo: *Tel Miqne-Ekron Excavation* by T. Dothan and S. Gitin).

material culture and the independence of their city-states, although their combined population in the 8th century B.C. is estimated at only *ca.* 50,000 people[7], half the population of Judah in the same period, and even less in Iron Age I: *ca.* 30,000 people[8].

The migration of the Philistines has often been identified with the movements of the Achaean Greeks[9]. Instead, the biblical tradition brings the Philistines from the island of Caphtor, i.e. Crete[10]. Also the Kerethite and Pelethite guards of David and of Solomon seem to be "Cretans and Philistines"[11], while Cretan traditions have been emphasized in the decoration of Philistine pottery[12]. Although the name *'kyš / Ikausu* borne by a king of Ekron in the 7th century B.C. seems to be 'Αχαιός[13], this was

[7] M. Broshi - I. Finkelstein, *The Population of Palestine in Iron Age II*, in *BASOR* 287 (1992), p. 47-60, especially p. 53-54.

[8] I. Finkelstein, *art. cit.*, in *The Sea Peoples* (n. 5), p. 172-174.

[9] Cf. here above, p. 37.

[10] M. Weippert, *Kreta. A. Philologisch*, in *RLA* VI, Berlin 1980-83, p. 225-230. See also J. Prignaud, *Caftorim et Kerétim*, in *RB* 71 (1964), p. 215-229; M. Delcor, *Les Kerethim et les Crétois*, in *Vetus Testamentum* 28 (1978), p. 409-422 = Id., *Études bibliques et orientales de religions comparées*, Leiden 1979, p. 314-327.

[11] II Sam. 8, 18; 15, 18; 20, 7.23; I Kings 1, 38.44; I Chron. 18, 17.

[12] F. Schachermeyr, *Die Levante im Zeitalter der Wanderungen vom 13. bis 11. Jahrhundert v. Chr.* (Die ägäische Frühzeit V), Wien 1982, p. 244-249.

[13] S. Gitin - T. Dothan - J. Naveh, *A Royal Dedicatory Inscription from Ekron*, in *IEJ* 47 (1997), p. 1-16, especially p. 11.

a widespread personal name in the Aegean[14] and may just testify to a Greek influence. Other borrowings point at first sight in the same direction: the Philistine word *sərān(īm)*, "princes", has been compared with τύραννος[15], and Hebrew *pilegeš*, "concubine", is very likely borrowed from a Philistine noun related to παλλακίς[16]. Considering the names of the other "Sea Peoples", however, Anatolian connections are very likely, also because Anatolian sites have started to show "Mycenaean" pottery similar to the Philistine[17].

It seems that the Anatolian provenance of the Philistines can be proved directly. One of the Hittites' allies at the battle of Qadesh in 1275 B.C. was called *P-d-s* according to the Egyptian scribes[18]. Now, *P-d-s* is rightly taken as an equivalent of Hittite *Pitašša*[19], which was generally located in the area of the Salt Lake (Tuz Gölü) and of the plain of Konya, but has also been equated with Pisidia[20]. If there were several regions bearing this name, that may reappear later in Carian Πήδασα[21], at least the Bronze Age *Pitašša* has to be located in West Anatolia, close to Arzawa, probably north-west of Konya, in the area of Yalburt and of the present-day town of Ilgın.

[14] P.M. FRASER - E. MATTHEWS, *A Lexicon of Greek Personal Names* I, Oxford 1987, p. 97.

[15] It has been compared also with hieroglyphic Luwian *tarwanis*; cf. F. PINTORE, *Seren, Tarwanis, Tyrannos*, in O. CARRUBA - M. LIVERANI - C. ZACCAGNINI (eds.), *Studi orientalistici in ricordo di Franco Pintore* (Studia Mediterranea 4), Pavia 1983, p. 285-322; W. HELCK, *Ein sprachliches Indiz für die Herkunft der Philister,* in *BN* 21 (1983), p. 31. However, this has been contested: G.A. LEHMANN, *Die "Seevölker"*, in H. MÜLLER-KARPE (ed.), *Herrschaften an der Levantküste* (Jahresbericht des Instituts für Vorgeschichte der Univ. Frankfurt a/M 1976), München 1977, p. 78-111 (see p. 104, n. 33); E. EDEL, *Bemerkungen zu Helcks Philisterartikel in BN 21,* in *BN* 22 (1983), p. 7-8.

[16] J.P. BROWN, *Israel and Hellas* I (BZAW 231), Berlin 1995, p. 65-70.

[17] See here above, p. 37.

[18] The texts of the Qadesh battle are now collected in K.A. KITCHEN, *Ramesside Inscriptions* II, Oxford 1969-79, p. 2-147; for *P-d-s*, see p. 3, line 3 (of the edition by Ch. KUENTZ, *La bataille de Qadech* [MIFAO 55], Le Caire 1928-34); p. 17, line 45; p. 32, line 86; p. 111, line 44. The texts are translated by K.A. KITCHEN, *Ramesside Inscriptions, Translated & Annotated. Translations* II, Oxford 1996, p. 2-26, see p. 2, line 3; p. 4, line 45; p. 5, line 86; p. 16, line 44.

[19] G.F. DEL MONTE - J. TISCHLER, *Die Orts- und Gewässernamen der hethitischen Texte* (RGTC 6), Wiesbaden 1978, p. 318-319; G.F. DEL MONTE, *Supplement* (RGTC 6/2), Wiesbaden 1992, p. 127. The spelling with geminated *šš* should have been preserved, like in St. DE MARTINO, *Pitašša,* in *RLA* X, Berlin 2003-05, p. 579.

[20] F. CORNELIUS, *Geographie des Hethiterreiches*, in *Orientalia* 27 (1958), p. 225-251, 373-398 (see p. 393 and 396).

[21] L. ZGUSTA, *Kleinasiatische Ortsnamen* (Beiträge zur Namenforschung. Beihefte, N.F. 21), Heidelberg 1984, p. 489, §1084-1 (Πήδασα, Πίδασα), and p. 490, Map 393.

Given that the constant spelling of the toponym is *Pitašša*, with geminated *š*, it may stand for **Pitasθa*, since /θa/ is usually expressed in cuneiform writing by *ša*. Considering the well-known spelling variation *t/d - l* in Anatolian languages[22], **Pitasθa* may very well correspond to Hebrew *Pəlišti* and Assyrian *Palastu*, *Pilište/i* or *Piliste/i*[23]. We shall see in fact that this variation *t/d - l* is attested in the notation of the Philistine language as well[24]. As for the Egyptian spelling *P-d-s*, it presents no particular problem, since the foreign interdental /θ/ can be expressed in Egyptian by *s*, like in *'-s-t-r-t* for *'Aṯtartu*. Thus, **Pitasθa* could normally be written *P-d-s*. If this explanation is correct, a solution is offered to the problem of the strange absence of the Philistines from Hittite texts. At the same time, their homeland appears to be close to the southwest Anatolian regions from which other "Sea Peoples" are native.

By the late 11th century B.C. the main Philistine centres of Canaan had expanded to urban proportions, covering in the period of their major development an area of about 60 ha at Ashkelon[25], 8 ha at Ashdod[26], 30 ha at Ekron[27], and 40-50 ha at Gath[28]. A substantial Philistine settlement

[22] H. KRONASSER, *Vergleichende Laut- und Formenlehre des Hethitischen*, Heidelberg 1956, § 72a; E. LAROCHE, *Comparaison du louvite et du lycien* II, in *Bulletin de la Société de Linguistique* 55 (1960), p. 155-185, especially p. 181; L. ZGUSTA, *Kleinasiatische Personennamen*, Prag 1964, p. 143, § 252 and n. 57b; H. KRONASSER, *Etymologie der hethitischen Sprache* I, Wiesbaden 1966, p. 61-64, § 50; G. NEUMANN, *Lykisch*, in *Altkleinasiatische Sprachen*, Leiden 1969, p. 358-396, especially p. 376-377; A. HEUBECK, *Lydisch*, *ibid.*, p. 397-427, especially p. 405. As examples, one can mention Lametru = Demeter, Lygdamis = Tugdamme, Labarna = Tabarna, κανδαύλης = *χñtawata*, "king". See also F. STARKE, *Labarna*, in *RLA* VI, Berlin 1980-83, p. 404-408.

[23] At any rate, the change σθ > στ is attested also in ancient Greek: M. LEJEUNE, *Phonétique historique du mycénien et du grec ancien*, Paris 1972, p. 60, § 47. A less satisfactory approach would regard the final *-t* as a suffix, paralleled by the ending *-ti* of proper names.

[24] See here below, p. 89.

[25] L.E. STAGER, *art. cit.* (n. 5), p. 335. Cf. ID., *Ashkelon*, in *NEAEHL*, Jerusalem 1993, Vol. I, p. 103-112.

[26] L.E. STAGER, *art. cit.* (n. 5), p. 336. Cf. M. DOTHAN, *Ashdod*, in *NEAEHL*, Jerusalem 1993, Vol. I, p. 93-101.

[27] S. GITIN, *Philistia in Transition: The Tenth Century and Beyond*, in S. GITIN - A. MAZAR - E. STERN (eds.), *Mediterranean Peoples in Transition - Thirteenth to Early Tenth Centuries BCE*, Jerusalem 1998, p. 162-183 (see p. 167). Cf. T. DOTHAN - S. GITIN, *Miqne, Tel (Ekron)*, in *NEAEHL*, Jerusalem 1993, Vol. III, p. 1051-1059; EAD.-ID., *Miqne, Tel*, in *OEANE*, New York 1997, Vol. IV, p. 30-35; U. POPLUTZ, *Tel Miqne / Ekron. Geschichte und Kultur einer philistäischen Stadt*, in *BN* 87 (1997), p. 69-99.

[28] A.M. MAEIR, *Tell eṣ-Ṣafi / Gath, 1996-2002*, in *IEJ* 53 (2003), p. 237-246 (see p. 239, 244); ID., *The Historical Background and Dating of Amos vi 2: An Archaeological Perspective from Tell eṣ-Ṣāfi / Gath*, in *Vetus Testamentum* 54 (2004), p. 319-334; J. UZIEL - A.M. MAEIR, *Scratching the Surface at Gath: Implications of Tell eṣ-Ṣafi / Gath Surface Survey*, in *Tel Aviv* 32 (2005), p. 50-75 (see p. 61-62, 65).

existed also at Tell Qasile and at Azor (Arabic *Yāzūr*), 7 km east of Jaffa, where an important cemetery was exposed[29]. The *Onomasticon* of Amenemope, which dates from the 11th century B.C., mentions Azor (*'I-s-r*)[30] after Ashkelon (*'I-s-q-nr-n*), Ashdod (*'I-s-d-d*), and Gaza (*G-ḏ-t*), and before the somewhat damaged name of the Shephelah (*S3-b-p3-ỉ-r-ỉw*)[31], where Ekron and Gath were situated. After a gap, in which one place name is lost, possibly Ekron or Gath, the *Onomasticon* mentions *Š-r-d-n*, *Ṯ-k-r*, and *P-r-s-t*, thus implying that also the Sherdana were then settled in Palestine. The sequence of the names in this section of the list does not seem to follow a geographic order and it is difficult therefore to assign a particular territory to the Sherdana. It was assumed that they occupied the area of Akko[32], or settled at al-Aḥwat in the northern part of central Canaan[33], or else in the territory between the Soreq brook (Wādī aṣ-Ṣarar) and the Yarkon River (Nahr al-'Auğa), regarded as the original settlement of Dan. In this hypothesis, Sherdana would have

[29] A. BEN-TOR - M. DOTHAN, *Azor*, in *NEAEHL*, Jerusalem 1993,Vol. I, p. 125-129.

[30] *Onomasticon* of Amenope, No. 265, published by A.H. GARDINER, *Ancient Egyptian Onomastica* I, Oxford 1947, p. 24 ff. Cf. A. ALT, *Syrien und Palästina im Onomastikon des Amenope*, in *Schweizerische Theologische Umschau* 20 (1950), p. 58-71, especially p. 65-66 = A. ALT, *Kleine Schriften zur Geschichte des Volkes Israel* I, 2nd ed., München 1959, p. 238-240.

[31] No. 266. The transcription is regular, but the final *-ỉw* indicates that the *nisbe*-form was used with loss of the feminine ending *-t,* like in Hebrew *Timnī* from *Timnā*. Instead, *-t* is preserved in *š-b-p3-r-ṯ n G-b-r-y* and *š-b-p3-r-ṯ w-r-k-y-t* in Shoshenq's List, Nos. 73-74 and 75-76, to be used according to the readings of its definitive publication in *Reliefs and Inscriptions at Karnak* III. *The Bubastite Portal* (OIP 74), Chicago 1954, Pls. 2-9. Probably this is an area of the Beersheba Valley (cf. here below, p. 116). K.A. KITCHEN, *The Third Intermediate Period in Egypt (1100-650 B.C.)*, 3rd ed., Warminster 1995, p. 439, is certainly right in refusing the identification of *š-b-p3-r-ṯ n G-b-r-y* with Ezion-Geber.

[32] M. DOTHAN, *'Akko, 1980,* in *IEJ* 31 (1981), p. 110-112 (see p. 111); ID., *The Significance of Some Artisans' Workshops along the Canaanite Coast,* in M. HELTZER - E. LIPIŃSKI (eds.), *Society and Economy in the Eastern Mediterranean (c. 1500-1000 B.C.)* (OLA 23), Leuven 1988, p. 295-303 (see p. 298-299, 301-302); ID., in *NEAEHL*, Jerusalem 1993, Vol. I, p. 21.

[33] Grid ref. 1590/2100: A. ZERTAL (ed.), *El-Aḥwat: A Fortified Sea People Site near Naḥal 'Iron*, Haifa 1996 (in Hebrew); A. ZERTAL - A. ROMAN, *El-Aḥwat - 1993-1996,* in *ESI* 110 (1999), p. 32-34; A. ZERTAL - N. MIRKAM, *The Manasseh Hill Country Survey* III. *From Naḥal 'Iron to Naḥal Shechem,* Tel Aviv 2000 (in Hebrew), p. 133-138; A. ZERTAL, *The 'Corridor-Builders' of Central Israel: Evidence for the Settlement of the 'Northern Sea Peoples'?*, in V. KARAGEORGHIS - C.E. MARRIS (eds.), *Defensive Settlement of the Aegean and the Eastern Mediterranean after c. 1200 B.C.*, Nicosia 2001, p. 215-232; ID., *Philistine Kin Found in Early Israel,* in *Biblical Archaeology Review* 28/3 (2002), p. 18-31, 60-61. According to I. FINKELSTEIN, *El-Aḥwat: A Fortified Sea People City?,* in *IEJ* 52 (2002), p. 187-199, this is an ordinary Iron Age I village, inhabited by local people.

been understood later as *šūr Dān*, "enclosure of Dan", or *šār*[34] *Dān*, "arable land of Dan"[35]. However, no evidence supports either of these opinions. Beside, the *Onomasticon* may refer to Sherdana troops once employed in the Egyptian army, settled in Canaan peacefully and remained in the country after the collapse of the Egyptian empire.

Dan's presence in the area of the Aijalon and Soreq vales, described in Josh. 19, 40-47a, does not match the information provided by other sources. The alleged boundaries of Dan's domain probably correspond to a district of the Persian province of Ashdod in the 5th-4th centuries B.C.[36] The mention of Ekron (Josh. 19, 40) does not create any difficulty, although the excavations of Ḫirbet al-Muqanna' (Tel Miqne) did not uncover any occupational traces between the first quarter of the 6th century B.C. and the Roman period. In fact, the town was known under its old name in Hellenistic times (I Macc. 10, 89). This implies a continuous occupation of the broader area of Ekron, with 'Ακκαρών being possibly located at 'Aqir (Kiryat Ekron), 10 km north-west of Ḫirbet al-Muqanna'. Shifting of a settlement with its own name occurred quite often for various historical or geographic reasons. Eusebius' indications seem to confirm the location of 'Ακκαρών near Reḥovot, "between Ashdod and Iamnia" as shown also on the Madaba map, and at the same time they preserve the souvenir of the ancient site near the village of Gallaia (Ǧiliya)[37].

[34] This word is attested only in Jer. 5, 10 and in Job 24, 11 by a feminine plural *šrwt(yh)* or *šwrt(m)*, but it must be related to Sabaic *s¹r*, "cultivated land besides a flood-bed" or "communal agricultural land", "irrigated land"; cf. *Sabaic Dictionary*, p. 128, s.v. *S¹RR*, and p. 130, s.v. *S¹YR*. See also K. Conti Rossini, *Chrestomathia Arabica Meridionalis Epigraphica*, Roma 1931, p. 195 and 200; W.W. Müller, *Epigraphische Nachlese aus Ḥāz*, in *NESE* 1 (1972), p. 75-85 (see p. 80, with partly problematic etymologies); M.A. Ghūl, *Early Southern Arabian Languages and Classical Arabic Sources*, Irbid 1993, p. 158, translating *CIS* IV, 37, 5 and *RÉS* 4775, 2.

[35] E. Lipiński, *Sea Peoples and Canaan in Transition, c. 1200-950 B.C.*, in *OLP* 30 (1999), p. 1-35 (see p. 14). For J.N. Tubb's hypotheses, see here below, p. 64.

[36] The historicity of this unsuccessful settlement is nevertheless accepted by H.M. Niemann, *Die Daniten*, Göttingen 1985. According to N. Na'aman, *Two Notes on the History of Ashkelon and Ekron in the Late Eighth-Seventh Centuries B.C.E.*, in *Tel Aviv* 25 (1998), p. 219-227 (see p. 223-225), Dan's artificial domain roughly overlapped the Philistine territory of the kingdom of Ekron in the late 8th-7th centuries B.C. See also A. Demsky, *The Boundary of the Tribe of Dan (Joshua 19:41-46)*, in Ch. Cohen - A. Hurvitz - Sh.M. Paul (eds.), *Sefer Moshe. The Moshe Weinfeld Jubilee Volume*, New York 2004, p. 261-284. Cf. further Judg. 1, 34 and here below, p. 251-254.

[37] M. Du Buit, *Kh. Muqenna'-Éqrôn*, in *RB* 65 (1958), p. 410-411, summarizing the Hebrew original of J. Naveh, *Khirbet al-Muqanna'-Ekron: An Archaeological Survey*, in *IEJ* 8 (1958), p. 87-100, 165-170. Cf. Eusebius of Caesarea, *Onomasticon*, in E. Klostermann (ed.), *Eusebius: Das Onomastikon der biblischen Ortsnamen*, Leipzig 1904, p. 22:6-10 and p. 72:5-7.

In the centre of this area lies Timnah (Tell al-Baṭaši), the Philistine city associated with Samson in Judg. 14-15. The excavation of the site, conducted in 1977-1989[38], in particular the recovered pottery, reveals a continuation of the Late Bronze tradition under assumed Philistine suzerainty. Archaeological findings do not show that the city was protected by a wall, which at any rate does not appear as an early element of the Philistine material culture. A gap in the occupation of the site seems to occur in the 10th century, unless all 11th-century pottery should be lowered to the 10th century. An inferior lifestyle is manifest in Stratum IV, that must belong to the 9th century B.C. The town came probably to an end towards the end of this century, possibly as a result of Hazael's campaign in the south, *ca.* 810 B.C. (II Kings 12, 18-19). Timnah was thereafter abandoned until the late 8th century B.C., when it was resettled and fortified by a king of Judah. The city was besieged and captured in 701 B.C. by Sennacherib, who does not say that he razed and burned it[39]. In fact, the conquest of Timnah by the Assyrians does not seem to have affected its city wall, which continued to be used throughout the 7th century B.C.

The material culture of Bēth-Shemesh, some 7 km further east, shows a comparable mixture of Late Bronze traditions and Philistine features in Iron Age I [40]. The legend of the Ark of Yahwe in I Sam. 6, hardly anterior to the late 10th century B.C., should not hinder defining the ethnicity of the population of Bēth-Shemesh in Iron Age I on the basis of its material culture[41]. Gezer, with its 5 percent of Philistine pottery, appears

[38] Grid ref. 1416/1325: A. MAZAR, *Batash, Tel (Timnah),* in *NEAEHL*, Jerusalem 1993, Vol. I, p. 152-157; G.L. KELM - A. MAZAR, *Timnah: A Biblical City in the Sorek Valley*, Winona Lake 1995; A. MAZAR, *Timnah (Tel Batash)* I (Qedem 37), Jerusalem 1997; A. MAZAR - N. PANITZ-COHEN, *Timnah (Tel Batash)* II. *The Finds from the First Millennium BCE* (Qedem 42), Jerusalem 2001. Both authors date Stratum IV from the 10th century B.C., although its pottery parallels the wares of Stratum VII at Tell Rās Abu Ḥumeid (Tel Ḥamid), dated by carbon C-14 to the 9th century. They further date Stratum III from the 8th century, but the bulk of its pottery belongs to the very end of this century.

[39] D.D. LUCKENBILL, *The Annals of Sennacherib* (OIP 2), Chicago 1924, p. 32, lines 6-7; E. FRAHM, *Einleitung in die Sanherib-Inschriften* (AfO, Beih. 26), Wien 1997, p. 54, line 46.

[40] S. BUNIMOVITZ - Z. LEDERMAN, *Beth-Shemesh*, in *NEAEHL*, Jerusalem 1993, Vol. I, p. 249-253. Stratum III, the single Iron I level, is characterized by Philistine pottery. The destruction at the end of this period, in the mid-10th century B.C., possibly occurred during the assumed Siamun's campaign (see below, p. 95-98). The Judaean city of Stratum IIa, rebuilt fairly soon after its destruction, shows a marked decline from the finest days of the Philistine rule.

[41] The legend in its original form may date from the late 10th century B.C. Its aim was probably to integrate the area of Bēth-Shemesh into the kingdom of Judah; cf. H.J. STOEBE, *Das erste Buch Samuelis* (KAT VIII/1), Gütersloh 1973, p. 112.

instead as a Canaanite town with some Philistine population or suzerainty[42]. Timnah, Bēth-Shemesh, and Gezer thus demonstrate a moderate Philistine penetration in the foothills east of the coastal plain. A series of sites were settled by the Philistines also along the Yarkon River, especially the harbour town of Tell Qasile[43], founded on virgin soil. In the southern Shephelah, exceptional tombs reveal Philistine occupation at Tell 'Eitun[44], 11 km south-east of Lachish. In the area to the south-east and south of Gaza, the importance of which cannot be determined as yet[45], Philistine settlement is attested at Tell aš-Šerī'a (Tel Sera')[46], Tell Ǧemmeh[47], and Tell al-Far'ah South[48].

No Philistine texts are extant, except some stone stamp seals with cryptic signs recalling the still undeciphered Cypro-Minoan script[49]. We also know very little about the Philistine internal organization. In the earlier phase of their settlement, the city-states were governed by the *sərānīm*, but their rulers bore later the Semitic title of *śar*, used in the royal inscription from Ekron. An inscription incised by an attendant on a storage jar from Ekron also uses the title *b'l*, "lord", to designate king Padi: *lb'l wlpdy*[50], "belonging to the lord, viz. to Padi"[51].

42 S. BUNIMOVITZ, *Problems in the Ethnic Identification of the Philistine Material Culture,* in *Tel Aviv* 17 (1990), p. 210-222 (see p. 212). Cf. W.G. DEVER (ed.), *Gezer* IV, Jerusalem 1986, p. 60-116.

43 Grid ref. 1309/1678: A. MAZAR, *Excavations at Tell Qasile* I-II (Qedem 12, 20), Jerusalem 1980-85; T. DOTHAN - I. DUNAYEVSKY - A. MAZAR, *Qasile, Tell*, in *NEAEHL*, Jerusalem 1993, Vol. IV, p. 1204-1212.

44 See A. MAZAR, *Archaeology of the Land of the Bible: 10,000-586 B.C.E.*, New York 1990, p. 312, 314-315, 324, 326, 502.

45 We still lack sufficient archaeological data. Minimal information was provided by the excavations of W.J. PHYTHIAN-ADAMS, *Reports on Soundings at Gaza*, in *PEQ* 55 (1923), p. 11-36, and recent French excavations have so far reached a small sector from the end of the 7th century B.C.: J.-B. HUMBERT, *Gaza*, in *Nouvelles de Jérusalem*, Jérusalem 1997, p. 73. See, at present: A. CLARKE *et al.*, *Gaza Research Project: 1998 Survey of the Old City of Gaza*, in *Levant* 36 (2004), p. 31-36.

46 Grid ref. 119/088: E.D. OREN, *Sera', Tel*, in *NEAEHL*, Jerusalem 1993, Vol. IV, p. 1329-1335.

47 Grid ref. 097/088. Stratum VII from the 11th century B.C.: G.W. VAN BEEK, *Jemmeh, Tell*, in *NEAEHL*, Jerusalem 1993, Vol. II, p. 667-674, especially p. 669-670.

48 Grid ref. 100/076: J. WALDBAUM, *Philistine Tombs at Tell Fara and their Aegean Prototypes*, in *AJA* 70 (1966), p. 331-340; T. DOTHAN, *The Philistines and Their Material Culture,* Jerusalem 1982, p. 29-30, 260-268; A. MAZAR, *art. cit.* (n. 4), p. 97-98; Y. YISRAELI, *Far'ah, Tell el- (South),* in *NEAEHL*, Jerusalem 1993, Vol. II, p. 441-444.

49 A. MAZAR, *op. cit.* (n. 44), p. 326.

50 S. GITIN - M. COGAN, *A New Type of Dedicatory Inscription from Ekron,* in *IEJ* 49 (1999), p. 193-202; S. GITIN, *Israelite and Philistine Cult and the Archaeological Record in Iron Age II: The "Smoking Gun" Phenomenon*, in W.G. DEVER - S. GITIN (eds.), *Symbiosis, Symbolism, and the Power of the Past*, Winona Lake 2003, p. 279-295 (see p. 288).

51 For this use of "pleonastic" *w*-, see M. POPE, *"Pleonastic" Wāw before Nouns in Ugaritic and Hebrew,* in *JAOS* 73 (1953), p. 95-98; P. WEINBERG-MØLLER, *"Pleonastic"*

The first term, attested only in the plural, is cognate with Greek τύραννος and Hieroglyphic Hittite / Luwian *tarwanis*. F. Pintore has provided an accurate study of the meanings of the words in question and of their historical interrelationship[52]. In particular, he linked their use to shifts in leadership types in Greece and Anatolia from the 12th through the 7th century B.C. Their Aegeo-Anatolian origin is certain and confirms the assumed provenance of the Philistines. The term *śar* is instead Semitic and corresponds to Hebrew *śar* and Akkadian *šarru*, while *b'l* is the term used by the subjects to designate their king[53].

The Sical ruler of Dor is called *b3-dì-r* in the story of Wenamon[54]. This does not seem to be a proper name[55], but a title the spelling of which points at Semitic *badal* or *badīl*, already attested at Ebla as *badalum*, in Ugaritic as *bidalu*, and in Phoenician as *bdl*[56], although one may prefer the reading *b'l* in one of the instances[57]. A connection with the term ^{LÚ}*piduri* found in Hittite texts[58] is less likely, although the cuneiform sign *pi* might also be read *bi*. The Egyptian spelling suggests the vocalization *badīl*, which is precisely the Arabic noun meaning "substitute", "deputy". It does not seem therefore that *b3-dì-r* renders the title of a chieftain in the language of the "Sea Peoples".

Waw in Classical Hebrew, in *JSS* 3 (1958), p. 321-326; M. DAHOOD, *Ugaritic Studies and the Bible*, in *Gregorianum* 43 (1962), p. 55-79 (see p. 66-67); ID., *Hebrew-Ugaritic Lexicography II*, in *Biblica* 45 (1964), p. 393-412 (see p. 404-405); L. PRIJS, *Ein "Waw der Bekräftigung"?*, in *Biblische Zeitschrift*, n.s., 8 (1964), p. 105-109; C.H. GORDON, *Ugaritic Textbook*, Roma 1965, p. 129, §13.103; E. LIPIŃSKI, *La Royauté de Yahwé dans la poésie et le culte de l'ancien Israël*, 2nd ed., Brussel 1968, p. 211, n. 6; J. TROPPER, *Ugaritische Grammatik* (AOAT 273), Münster 2000, p. 783-785, §83.112; LIPIŃSKI, *Semitic*, §49.3.

52 See here above, p. 52, n. 15.

53 For instance, RS 34.148, lines 5 and 12: P. BORDREUIL (ed.), *Ras Shamra-Ougarit* VII. *Une bibliothèque au sud de la ville*, Paris 1991, p. 163, No. 91. Cf. also Ch.R. KRAHMALKOV, *Phoenician-Punic Dictionary* (Studia Phoenicia XV; OLA 90), Leuven 2000, p. 110, who reads *hny b'lk*, "I, your king, am here", in *KAI* 2, 2 = *TSSI* III, 5, 2.

54 A. SCHEEPERS, *Anthroponymes et toponymes du récit d'Ounamon*, in E. LIPIŃSKI (ed.), *Phoenicia and the Bible* (Studia Phoenicia XI; OLA 44), Leuven 1991, p. 17-83 (see p. 38-41).

55 See *ibid.*, p. 39-40.

56 E. LIPIŃSKI, Š u - b a l a - a k a *and* badalum, in H. WAETZOLDT - H. HAUPTMANN (eds.), *Wirtschaft und Gesellschaft von Ebla* (Heidelberger Studien zum Alten Orient 2), Heidelberg 1988, p. 257-260; ID., *Wares Ordered from Ben-Ḥarash at Akko*, forthcoming.

57 Ch.R. KRAHMALKOV, *loc. cit.* (n. 53). The triangular shape of the letter suggests reading *bdl* with a *daleth*, but one might assume that the circle of an *'ayin* was intended.

58 J. FRIEDRICH, *Hethitisches Wörterbuch, 3. Ergänzungsheft*, Heidelberg 1966, p. 45, 51; cf. F. SCHACHERMEYR, *op. cit.* (n. 12), p. 114, n. 1; I. SINGER, *The Origin of the Sea Peoples and Their Settlement on the Coast of Canaan*, in M. HELTZER - E. LIPIŃSKI (eds.), *Society and Economy in the Eastern Mediterranean (c. 1500-1000 B.C.)* (OLA 23), Leuven 1988, p. 239-250 (see p. 247-248).

It is not possible to distinguish chieftains of the "Sea Peoples" on the triumphal relief carvings, which adorn the mortuary temple of Ramesses III at Medinet Habu[59]. These show battle scenes involving warriors who can be identified as Philistines, Sicals, Shagalasha, Denyen, and Weshesh. They all wear headdresses consisting either of a horned helmet or of a band with feathers sticking up from it. However, a limestone relief of a pavilion at Medinet Habu shows a row of six bound prisoners in kneeling posture[60]. Four of them are chieftains of the "Sea Peoples", all bearded and labelled with names[61]. The chieftain of the Sicals wears a band with hair or helmet projecting from it. The Sherdana chief wears a helmet with side points and horns between which is a ball-tipped projection. The latter seems to distinguish him from the warriors with horned helmet, represented on the battle scenes. The chieftain of the Shagalasha is characterized by long hair held by a band and extending backwards, while the Trojan (*Tw-r-š*) chief seems to wear a tightly fitting cap. The figure of the chieftain of the Philistines is missing.

An Egyptian statuette bears an inscription datable to the Twenty-second Dynasty (*ca.* 9th century B.C.) and mentioning a certain "Patesi, son of Ephay, ambassador from the Canaan of the Philistines" (*wpw.tỉ n p3-Kn'n n Prst*)[62]. The presence of such a representative in Egypt is not surprising, but his title, taken at face value, would signify that he acted on behalf of the whole Philistine pentapolis. However, *P3-Kn'n* usually designates Gaza, and the man must have been an "emissary from Gaza in Philistia".

[59] *Medinet Habu* I (OIP 8), Chicago 1930, Pls. 32-43, especially Pls. 37 and 39. See also Sh. WACHSMANN, *To the Sea of the Philistines*, in E.D. OREN (ed.), *The Sea Peoples and Their World: A Reassessment*, Philadelphia 2000, p. 103-143, in particular the figures on p. 106-107 and 110-114.

[60] Epigraphic Survey, *Medinet Habu* VIII (OIP 94), Chicago 1970, Pl. 600B; *ANEP*, No. 9, with earlier literature and a reproduction from W. WRESZINSKI, *Atlas zur altägyptischen Kulturgeschichte*, Leipzig 1923-36, Vol. II, Pl. 160b (upper).

[61] J. SIMONS, *Handbook for the Study of Egyptian Topographical Lists Relating to Western Asia*, Leiden 1937, p. 176; cf. p. 6 and 85-86.

[62] G. STEINDORFF, *The Statuette of an Egyptian Commissioner in Syria,* in *JEA* 25 (1939), p. 30-33, Pl. VII; A. ALT, *Ein Gesandter aus Philistäa in Aegypten,* in *BiOr* 9 (1952), p. 163-164; G. VITTMANN, *Ägypten und die Fremden im ersten vorchristlichen Jahrtausend*, Mainz a/R. 2003, p. 37, 57, 59, Fig. 21. Palaeography and orthography do not favour the much later dating, *ca.* 600 B.C., proposed by A.J. SPALINGER, *Egypt and Babylonia: A Survey (c. 650 B.C.-550 B.C.),* in *SAK* 5 (1977), p. 221-244 (see p. 229); B. PORTEN, *The Identity of King Adon,* in *BA* 44 (1981), p. 36-52 (see p. 44); D.B. REDFORD, *Egypt, Canaan, and Israel in Ancient Times*, Princeton 1993, p. 442.

Struggle for central Canaan

The Philistine expansion, consisting mainly in plundering expeditions, led in the 11th century to conflicts with the Israelites, who in Iron Age I had begun to settle in the central hill country of Canaan, in Upper Galilee, and in northern Transjordan. Already in the 5th year of Merneptah (1208 B.C.) according to the "Israel Stele"[63], they had confronted the Egyptian chariots, possibly in the coastal plain or in the Jezreel Valley[64], where they were trying to penetrate. Since "Israel" is the only name in the stele context which is written with the determinative of people rather than land, it is likely that the Israelites were still semi-nomadic pastoralists at that time[65]. As long as their peaceful movements followed the immemorial pattern of transhumance between the desert fringe and the sparsely populated central highlands of Palestine, they did not constitute any threat to the Egyptian control of the coastal area, but an infiltration

[63] CGC 34025; the text of the stele and of its duplicate is available in K.A. KITCHEN, *Ramesside Inscriptions* IV, Oxford 1982, p. 12-19. English translation by J.A. WILSON, in *ANET*, p. 376-378; K.A. KITCHEN, *Ramesside Inscriptions. Translated & Annotated. Translations* IV, Malden 2003, p. 10-15 (see p. 15). Photograph in *ANEP*, Nos. 342-343. A detailed analysis is provided by M.G. HASEL, *Domination and Resistance: Egyptian Military Activity in the Southern Levant, ca. 1300-1185 B.C.*, Leiden 1998, p. 194-217, 257-271; ID., *The Structure of the Final Hymnic-Poetic Unit on the Merenptah Stela*, in *ZAW* 116 (2004), p. 75-81.

[64] If they are not represented as Shasu prisoners on a Merneptah's relief at Karnak, as suggested by A.F. RAINEY, *Israel in Merneptah's Inscription and Reliefs*, in *IEJ* 51 (2001), p. 57-75, in particular p. 68-75, they might be figured in a battle scene: L.E. STAGER, *Merneptah, Israel, and Sea Peoples: New Light on an Old Relief*, in *Naḥman Avigad Volume* (ErIs 18), Jerusalem 1985, p. 56*-64* and Pl. IV, 2; F. YURCO, *Merneptah's Canaanite Campaign*, in *JARCE* 23 (1986), p. 189-215; M.G. HASEL, *op. cit.* (n. 63), p. 199-201. The opposite view held by D.B. REDFORD, *The Ashkelon Relief at Karnak and the Israel Stela*, in *IEJ* 36 (1986), p. 188-200; ID., *Egypt and Western Asia in the Late New Kingdom: An Overview*, in E.D. OREN (ed.), *The Sea Peoples and Their World: A Reassessment*, Philadelphia 2000, p. 1-20 (see p. 4), fails explaining the battle scene above Ashkelon, which depicts Israel according to Yurco, and Merneptah's cartouches on the wall, which appear as the original ones.

[65] The opinion that Israel designates, in the context of the stele, a settled agricultural population is defended by M.G. HASEL, *Israel in the Merneptah Stela*, in *BASOR* 296 (1994), p. 45-61; ID., *op. cit.* (n. 63), p. 201-203, cf. p. 77-80, and by A. NICCACCI, *La Stèle d'Israël. Grammaire et stratégie de communication*, in M. SIGRIST (ed.), *Études égyptologiques et bibliques à la mémoire du Père B. Couroyer* (Cahiers de la Revue Biblique 36), Paris 1997, p. 43-107. However, it is unlikely that *prt* in the inscription refers to "grain" and not to the "offspring" of Israel; cf. A.F. RAINEY, *art. cit.* (n. 64), p. 57-68. At any rate, the "classical" opposition of nomadic shepherds and settled farmers does not seem to suit the area concerned, as shown by U. ZWINGENBERGER, *Dorfkultur der frühen Eisenzeit in Mittelpalästina* (OBO 180), Freiburg/Schweiz-Göttingen 2001, p. 513-552, in particular p. 550.

of pastoral clans into the Sharon plain or the Jezreel Valley had to meet Egyptian reaction, especially if these pastoralists were to appear as allies of some rebellious Canaanite cities, such as Ashkelon, Gezer, and Yeno'am, all mentioned in the same context.

The mention of Israel after Yeno'am and the assumption that Merneptah's victory hymn lists the enemies following a south-north itinerary led Y. Aharoni to the conclusion that Israel was living at that time in Galilee[66]. Unfortunately, the exact location of Yeno'am is still debatable and the use of the south-north itinerary in this poetical composition is unproven.

Yeno'am is mentioned in several Egyptian documents, but only two of them provide information about its location: the topographical list of Amenhotep III from Qōm al-Ḥēṭān (Thebes)[67] and Amarna letter 197[68]. The list mentions Yeno'am with Taḥshi, Damascus, Edrei, Boṣrah, and Qanawāt, while *EA* 197 locates it in the same region with Ashtarot, Boṣrah, and Ḫaluni. The city should thus lay in Bashan, most likely at 'Ēn-Nu'ēme, also called Nu'ēmet Der'ā, 7 km north-east of Edrei[69]. The village, rebuilt in 1857, occupies a mound (alt. 637 m), where G. Schumacher could still recognize "a few antiquities"[70]. No local king is ever mentioned at Yeno'am and Merneptah probably went there in the first years of his reign to subdue unruly populations. There is so far no evidence that in the late 13th century Israel was living in that area or even further north. The Egyptians could have encountered its clans on their march through Canaan or on their way back. This Merneptah's campaign was possibly conducted two or three years earlier than the date indicated on the "Israel Stele", which is focussed on pharaoh's victory over the Libyans in year 5. Therefore, the "Wells of Merneptah", mentioned in a border official's journal from Merneptah's year 3 and preserved in Papyrus Anastasi III, rev. 6, 4[71], can be regarded as a record of the campaign in Canaan. This could be a reference to the "Waters of

[66] Y. AHARONI, *The Settlement of the Israelite Tribes in Upper Galilee*, Jerusalem 1957 (in Hebrew).

[67] E. EDEL, *Die Ortsnamenlisten aus dem Totentempel Amenophis III.* (Bonner Biblische Beiträge 25), Bonn 1966, BN, right 2.

[68] S. AḤITUV, *Canaanite Toponyms in Ancient Egyptian Documents,* Jerusalem 1984, p. 198-200.

[69] K. BAEDEKER, *Palestine et Syrie*, 4th ed., Leipzig 1912, map before p. 153.

[70] G. SCHUMACHER, *Das Südliche Basan,* in *ZDPV* 20 (1897), p. 65-227 and Pl. I (map), in particular p. 130, cf. p. 204, 211. See also J.G. WETZSTEIN, *Reisebericht über Hauran und die Trachonen*, Berlin 1860, p. 85.

[71] *ANET*, p. 258b.

(Mer)neptah" (Josh. 15, 9; 18, 5), located at Liftā, 4.5 km north-west of the Old City of Jerusalem[72].

We do not know whether the name "Israel" refers in Merneptah's hymn to a single tribe, that became the core of later Israel (cf. Gen. 32, 29), or already designates a tribal league or "amphictyony"[73], as the one alluded to in the Song of Deborah, which is a composite work, but remains one of the oldest known pieces of Hebrew poetry (Judg. 5). It mentions the six tribes of Israel which fought against Sisera (Ephraim, Benjamin, Makīr, Zebulun, Issachar, and Naphtali), as well as those that did not participate in the fight (Reuben, Gilead, Dan, Asher, and Meroz). The most southern tribe was Benjamin, as its name indicates, i.e. "Meridionals". Judah, Simeon, Gad, and Levi are not referred to, simply because they were no members of the league. The enemy mentioned in Judg. 5, 26.28 was Sisera, whose name is Anatolian. It is not encountered so far in epigraphic texts, but its elements Σεισα- / Σισα- / *Ziza-* and *-ara* occur in Anatolian anthroponomy. It is likely therefore that Sisera was a Philistine war-lord. Also the reference of Judg. 5, 6 to Shamgar Ben-Anat connects the war against Sisera with the fight against the Philistines and the period of the "judges" (cf. Judg. 3, 31). The complementary details of the account in Judg. 4 belong to a later elaboration by a storyteller, who did not understand the historical situation of the 11th century, when the Philistines were trying to penetrate further inland.

If the so-called "minor judges" of Israel were chief magistrates of the league and if their list is authentic[74], as often assumed, the framework of its fragments[75] would cover a period of about a century and thus correspond to the span of time from the beginning of the 11th century to Saul's election as war-lord and "judge", *ca.* 1000 B.C. In fact, the real length of David's and Solomon's reigns is unknown, for the "forty

[72] ABEL, *Géographie* II, p. 398; Y. AHARONI, *The Land of the Bible*, London 1967, p. 172-173.

[73] The concept of "amphictyony" was introduced in biblical scholarship by M. NOTH, *Das System der zwölf Stämme Israels* (Beiträge zur Wissenschaft vom Alten und Neuen Testament, 4th ser., 1), Stuttgart 1930. Despite the criticism expressed in some quarters, e.g. by C.H.J. DE GEUS, *The Tribes of Israel. An Investigation into Some of the Presuppositions of Martin Noth's Amphictyony Hypothesis* (Studia Semitica Neerlandica 18), Assen 1976, the basic thesis of M. Noth remains valid and cannot be questioned seriously.

[74] The basic study is that by M. NOTH, *Das Amt des "Richters Israels"*, in *Festschrift A. Bertholet*, Tübingen 1950, p. 404-417. See also E. LIPIŃSKI, *Juge*, in *DEB*, Turnhout 1987, p. 703-704, with literature, and H. NIEHR, *šāpaṭ*, in *ThWAT* VIII, Stuttgart 1985, col. 408-428, especially col. 423-424, with literature.

[75] Judg. 4, 4-5; 10, 1-5; 12, 7-15; I Sam. 7, 15-17a.

years" of their rule[76] are just a symbolic and approximate figure which reveals that no royal annals were available for these kings. We may guess that their reign in Israel lasted for less than fifty years and that Saul's shorter reign started at the beginning of the 10th century B.C. Saul's kingship united the two charges of "judge" and of war-lord in one person (I Sam. 8, 20), and it was supposed to be permanent, contrary to the function of former charismatic war-lords, the "great judges" (Othniel, Ehud, Barak, Gideon, Jephthah)[77], appointed for the duration of the danger, often just in one tribe as initially Jephthah in Gilead and Saul in Benjamin. Even Saul's kingship seems to have been actually limited to Benjamin, Ephraim, and Gilead. His main task consisted in fighting the Philistines after the Israelite defeat at Aphek, at the edge of the coastal plain (I Sam. 4), and opposing the Philistine penetration in the heartland of Israelite settlement in the central hill country.

It seems in fact that the Philistines undertook large-scale movements to the north and the north-east, but it is difficult to decide in concrete cases, whether destruction was caused by Philistines, Phoenicians, Israelites or Egyptians. Dor was destroyed in the 10th century B.C.[78], as well as several sites in the Jezreel Valley, where Philistine pottery was found[79], and also in the hill country. The flourishing settlements of Megiddo (Stratum VIA)[80] and of Jokneam (Stratum XVII)[81], which were still continuing the Canaanite tradition of the Late Bronze Age and show interrelations with Phoenicia, came then to an end in a violent destruction and fierce conflagration. The same happened then to Shiloh in the hill country[82], where the latest central sanctuary of the Israelite league

[76] II Sam. 5, 4; I Kings 11, 42.

[77] See above, n. 74.

[78] E. STERN, *Dor - Ruler of the Seas,* Jerusalem 1994, p. 92, 98-99. See here below, p. 95-98.

[79] A. RABAN, *The Philistines in the Western Jezreel Valley,* in *BASOR* 284 (1991), p. 17-27.

[80] A. ZARZEKI-PELEG, *Hazor, Jokneam and Megiddo in the Tenth Century B.C.E.,* in *Tel Aviv* 24 (1997), p. 258-288, especially p. 258-260. See also R.M. ENGBERG, *Historical Analysis or Archaeological Evidence: Megiddo and the Song of Deborah,* in *BASOR* 78 (1940), p. 4-7; D.L. ESSE, *The Collared Pithos at Megiddo: Ceramic Distribution and Ethnicity,* in *JNES* 51 (1992), p. 81-103, especially p. 101-103. For the continued Canaanite tradition, cf. the overview by A. MAZAR, *op. cit.* (n. 44), p. 356.

[81] A. BEN-TOR, *Jokneam,* in *NEAEHL,* Jerusalem 1993, Vol. III, p. 805-811, in particular p. 808-809.

[82] I. FINKELSTEIN, *The Archaeology of the Israelite Settlement,* Jerusalem 1988, p. 225-226. According to U. ZWINGENBERGER, *op. cit.* (n. 65), p. 451, archaeological data do not provide any clue indicating that Ḫirbet Selūn (Shiloh) was an important religious centre rather than a simple village.

was located and the destruction of which is still recorded in Jer. 7, 12 and 26, 6. A layer of ash, burnt debris, and broken pottery vessels on the floors evidence an earlier destruction of Bēth-shan (Stratum Lower VI = S-3), probably at the end of the 12th century B.C.[83] There is no doubt that the city of Stratum Lower VI was an important Egyptian stronghold in the days of the Twentieth Dynasty. Therefore, its end can presumably be related to the collapse of the Egyptian rule in Canaan and linked to the Philistine presence in the country after 1130 B.C. No "Sea People" settled at Bēth-shan and its destruction was followed by a long gap corresponding to the period in which the Philistines hung the bodies of Saul and his sons on the city-walls, after the battle of Gilboa (*ca.* 975 B.C.). The city seems to have been uninhabited at that time, since people came from Jabesh of Gilead to recover the bodies from the wall (I Sam. 31, 10b-13). These circumstances correspond in a remarkable way to the archaeological findings. The city of Stratum Upper VI = S-2, similar to the contemporary Stratum VIA at Megiddo, was rebuilt only later in the 10th century[84], but destroyed again after a few decades, probably in the same chain of events that affected the cities in the Jezreel Valley.

There are no solid indications that Philistines or other "Sea Peoples", like the Sherdana, have ever pushed further to the south-east, settled in the central Jordan Valley[85], and practiced there metal industry. The "double-jar" burials at Tell as-Sa'īdīyeh, which record Anatolian usages, may possibly indicate the presence of Hittite refugees, who would have reached Transjordan by means of an overland route following the collapse of the Hittite empire[86]. Alternatively, they could belong to a Sherdana unit, gar-

[83] A. MAZAR, *Beth Shean in the Iron Age: Preliminary Report and Conclusions of the 1990-1991 Excavations,* in *IEJ* 43 (1993), p. 201-229, especially p. 204-217; ID., *Beth-Shean: Tel Beth-Shean and the Northern Cemetery,* in *NEAEHL*, Jerusalem 1993, Vol. I, p. 214-223, especially p. 217-218. For the dating of Stratum Lower and Upper VI, see I. FINKELSTEIN, *art. cit.* (n. 2), p. 173-180

[84] A. MAZAR, *The Excavations at Tel Beth-Shean in 1989-1990,* in *Biblical Archaeology Today, 1990,* Jerusalem 1993, p. 606-619, especially p. 617; ID., *art. cit.* (n. 83), p. 223, 228-229; ID., *art. cit.* (n. 83), in *NEAEHL*, Vol. I, p. 217-218.

[85] J.N. TUBB, *The Role of the Sea Peoples in the Bronze Industry of Palestine / Transjordan*, in J.E. CURTIS (ed.), *Bronze Working Centres of Western Asia*, London 1988, p. 251-270. This hypothesis was convincingly refuted by O. NEGBI, *Were there Sea Peoples in the Central Jordan Valley at the Transition from the Bronze Age to the Iron Age?*, in *Tel Aviv* 18 (1991), p. 205-243; EAD., *"Were there Sea Peoples in the Central Jordan Valley at the Transition from the Bronze Age to the Iron Age?" Once Again*, in *Tel Aviv* 25 (1998), p. 184-207. See also E.J. VAN DER STEEN, *Tribes and Territories in Transition. The Central East Jordan Valley in the Late Bronze Age and Early Iron Ages: A Study of the Sources* (OLA 130), Leuven 2004, p. 66-68.

[86] R. GONEN, *Burial Patterns and Cultural Diversity in Late Bronze Age Canaan* (ASOR. Dissert. Ser. 6), Winona Lake 1992, p. 30.

risoned there in the frame of the Egyptian occupation forces[87]. As for the tablets from Deir ʻAlla, first labelled as "Aegean", they might be related to Proto-Canaanite[88], but they are still undeciphered.

Phoenician expansion southward could not endanger the cities of the Philistine pentapolis, but there was an impending threat of Egyptian invasion, that materialized in the 10th century B.C.[89] As for the biblical texts recording the relations of the Philistines with David, their detailed analysis seems superfluous, since they have been examined so many times, also in recent years[91], and are of doubtful historical value. According to I Kings 5, 1, the Philistine cities were Solomon's vassals: "Solomon was the suzerain of all the kingdoms from the river (of) Philistia to the frontier of Egypt; they paid tribute and were subject to him all his life". The phrase *'ereṣ Pəlištīm* apposed to *hannahar* indicates that "the river" in question was the Yarkon River (Nahr al-ʻAuğa), considered as the northern border of Philistia[90]. The Hebrew phrase of I Kings 5, 1 was misunderstood by a later editor, responsible for verse 4, where Solomon becomes the king of the whole Persian satrapy of Abar-Nahara, from the "crossing" of the Euphrates to Gaza, and this misinterpretation is followed in II Chron. 9, 26. However, even the text of I Kings, 5, 1 is not based on an authentic old source, as shown by the plethoric phrases "all the kingdoms" and "all his life"[92]. It just expresses a later belief that Solomon was a powerful king and thus reflects the "Myth of Solomon".

Iron Age II: Philistine names

The heartland of Philistia lies south of the Yarkon River, but it was largely Canaanized in Iron Age II. It is even difficult to assess to what

87 J.N. TUBB, *An Aegean Presence in Egypto-Canaan*, in W.V. DAVIES - L. SCHOFIELD (eds.), *Egypt, the Aegean and the Levant: Interconnections in the Second Millennium BC*, London 1995, p. 136-145; ID., *Sea Peoples in the Jordan Valley*, in E.D. OREN (ed.), *The Sea Peoples and Their World: A Reassessment*, Philadelphia 2000, p. 181-196.

88 H.J. FRANKEN, *Excavations at Tell Deir 'Alla: The Late Bronze Age Sanctuary*, Leuven 1992, p. 176.

89 See here below, respectively p. 174, 176, and 95-130.

90 The Philistines did apparently not gain military control over the Yarkon basin. They rather interacted there with the highland settlers: A. GADOT, *Aphek in the Sharon and the Philistine Northern Frontier*, in *BASOR* 341 (2006), p. 21-36.

91 C.S. EHRLICH, *The Philistines in Transition: A History from ca. 1000-730 B.C.E.*, Leiden 1996; P. MACHINIST, *Biblical Traditions: The Philistines and Israelite History*, in E.D. OREN (ed.), *The Sea Peoples and Their World: A Reassessment*, Philadelphia 2000, p. 53-83.

92 M. NOTH, *Könige* I (BKAT IX/1), Neukirchen-Vluyn 1968, p. 75-76.

extent the inhabitants of Philistia in the 8th and 7th centuries B.C. were the direct descendants of the Philistines who settled there in the late 12th century B.C. They were certainly influenced by Canaanite culture, as shown by the West Semitic names of most of their kings, like Hanun, Ṣidqa, Mitinti, Aḥimilki, Padi, Adon. Only Akayos, a king of Ekron[93] and a king of Gath[94], as well as *M'k*, the latter's father[95], bear non-Semitic names. The patronymic *M'k* may in fact be compared with Μύαξ, a name attested at Rhodes[96], off the Anatolian coast. The same name seems to occur in a Neo-Assyrian text from the 7th century B.C., where it is spelled in the genitive *Mì-ia-ki*[97]. However, the inscriptions from Philistia, collected and published by J. Naveh[98], contain several names of commoners that are related to the anthroponomy of south-western Anatolia.

A seal from the 8th or 7th century B.C., bearing the letters *Drymš / 'lyqm*, was published by W.F.M. Petrie in 1928, in the archaeological report of his excavations at Tell Ǧemmeh[99]. A. Alt has immediately suspected that *Drymš* was a Philistine name[100] and his opinion is confirmed by the Lycian name Δερειμις from Trysa[101]. The final *-š* indicates the desinence, like in other Semitic quotations of Anatolian names[102]. Since the patronymic *'lyqm* is Semitic, we do not deal here with a newcomer native from Lycia, but with a Philistine family preserving an Anatolian tradition through the ages.

93 *'kyš* in line 1 of the inscription published by S. GITIN - T. DOTHAN - J. NAVEH, *art. cit.* (n. 13); J. NAVEH, *Achish-Ikausu in the Light of the Ekron Dedication*, in *BASOR* 310 (1998), p. 35-37. This is probably the same name as *'kys*, attested on a Carthaginian stele (*CIS* I, 5984, 2) and classified as Greek by BENZ, p. 193. The name of the same king is spelt *I-ka-ú-su* in Esarhaddon's inscriptions: E. FRAHM, *Ikausu*, in *PNA* II/1, Helsinki 2000, p. 508-509. This spelling corresponds to a name *Ika(y)os*, with the initial *a* vowel assimilated to the *y*-glide, which is not marked as such in cuneiform script.

94 *'kyš* in I Sam. 21, 11-13.15; 27, 2-12; 28, 1-2; 29, 2-9; I Kings 2, 39-40.

95 The name is Semiticized in *Mā'ōk*, "crushed", in I Sam 27, 2, and in *Ma'ᵃkāh* in I Kings 2, 39 (cf. here below, p. 238-239).

96 P.M. FRASER - E. MATTHEWS, *op. cit.* (n. 14), p. 321b.

97 H.D. BAKER, *Meiaku*, in *PNA* II/2, Helsinki 2001, p. 747.

98 J. NAVEH, *art. cit.* (n. 6). Opinions concerning proper names in these inscriptions are collected and discussed by F. ISRAEL, *Note di onomastica semitica 8: L'onomastica della regione filistea ed alcune sue possibili sopravvivenze nell'onomastica fenicio-punica*, in P. FILIGHEDDU (ed.), *Circolazioni culturali nel Mediterraneo antico*, Cagliari 1994, p. 127-188, in particular p. 151-165.

99 W.F.M. PETRIE, *Gerar*, London 1928, p. 19, Pl. XLIII, 1.

100 A. ALT, *Zwei neue Philisternamen?*, in *ZAW* 47 (1929), p. 250-251.

101 L. ZGUSTA, *Kleinasiatische Personennamen*, Prag 1964, p. 146, §274-2.

102 LIPIŃSKI, *Itineraria Phoenicia*, p. 130.

A second inscribed object from the 8th or 7th century B.C., found at Tell Ǧemmeh and published by W.F.M. Petrie[103], is a potsherd with five incised letters to be read *lrḥlk*[104], with a shaft added to the head of *r* and badly sloped to the left. Despite the partly questionable reading *lrylk* by Petrie, J. Hempel assumed that the name was Philistine[105]. Its Phoenician interpretation by B. Delavault and A. Lemaire was based on the erroneous decipherment *lbmlk*[106], while J. Naveh suggested the reading *l'ḥlk*, with a doubtful *aleph*[107]. The name *rḥlk* ought to be read with an initial vowel *a*-, not indicated after the preposition *l*-. It should be identified with the Greek name 'Αρχέλοχος or 'Αρχίλοχος, attested in the Aegean as early as the 8th or 7th century B.C.[108] The different notation of χ in Semitic script can be explained by the contiguous trill consonant *r*[109]. The name may reveal a Greek presence in Philistia, but it rather witnesses an ancient onomastic tradition brought from the Aegean and preserved by the Philistines.

The inscription of a jar fragment found at Ashdod was read *ldggrt* by J. Naveh[110]. The shape of the letters, mainly of the assumed *gg*, is so far unique and it is certainly not reminiscent of any Phoenician script[111]. The letters *gg* are similar, but the longer headline and the slightly curved shaft of the second *g* suggest reading it as *p*. This would provide a personal name *Dgprt*, the components of which would be *doga*- and *parta*-. The first one is attested in Pisidia by Δογα-μοας[112], while the second

[103] W.F.M. Petrie, *op. cit.* (n. 99), p. 19, Pl. XLIII, 2. Photograph in *IEJ* 35 (1985), Pl. 2B.

[104] The *ḥ* was correctly recognized by J. Naveh, *art. cit.* (n. 6), p. 16.

[105] J. Hempel, *Chronique,* in *ZAW* 47 (1929), p. 62-75 (see p. 65).

[106] B. Delavault - A. Lemaire, *Les inscriptions phéniciennes de Palestine,* in *RSF* 7 (1979), p. 1-39 and Pls. I-14 (see p. 26-27, Pl. XIII, 50).

[107] J. Naveh, *art. cit.* (n. 6), p. 16.

[108] P.M. Fraser - E. Matthews, *op. cit.* (n. 14), p. 58b and 88a. The aphaeresis of initial *a* is a less likely solution, as this is a rare phenomenon in Greek onomastics, as shown already by F. Bechtel, *Aphärese in griechische Personennamen?*, reprinted in *Kleine onomastische Beiträge*, Königsstein 1981, p. 49-57. There are however examples of aphaeresis in the Pamphylian dialect (southern Anatolia), and some isolated cases in Boeotian; cf. R. Kotansky - J. Curbera, *Unpublished Lead Tablets in the Getty Museum*, in *Mediterraneo Antico* 7 (2004), p. 684-691, with photos I-IV (see p. 689 with n. 9).

[109] Lipiński, *Semitic*, §27.8.

[110] J. Naveh, *art. cit.* (n. 6), p. 11, 16-17, Pl. 2D.

[111] This was suggested by M. Dothan, *Ashdod - Seven Seasons of Excavations,* in *Qadmoniot* 17 (1972), p. 2-13 (in Hebrew), especially p. 11, and assumed as granted by B. Delavault - A. Lemaire, *art. cit.* (n. 106), p. 28, No. 49.

[112] L. Zgusta, *op. cit.* (n. 101), p. 150, §292.

one occurs in Epichoric Lycian *Ddawã-parta*[113] and in other names[114]. The meaning of both elements is unknown.

An ostracon from Tell Ğemmeh, dated stratigraphically by G.W. Van Beek to the late 8th century or the early 7th century B.C.[115], mentions eight persons with their name and patronymic[116]. Only the first name is introduced by the preposition *l* and followed by the word *bn*, "son of", preceding the patronymic: *lhrš.bnkš*, with an additional lost word. The name *Hrš* may be related to Greek Ορας and Epichoric Lycian *Hura*[117], while *Kš* apparently corresponds to the Lycian proper name Κεισος[118].

Line 2 mentions *Wnnt.'dnš*. *Wnnt* seems to be an Anatolian name, possibly to be identified with Οενουναου?θ?, attested in Pisidia[119]. This reading corresponds better than Οενουναο[ς][120] to M.M. Hardie's description of the final signs[121]. As Adon (*'dn*) was the name of the last king of Ekron[122], it is quite possible that *'dnš* is the same name, adapted to the pattern of Philistine anthroponomy, like Ἄδωνις in Greek[123]. This would show again that the persons in question belonged to a family settled in Philistia since several generations.

In line 3, the Semitic name *Šlm* is followed by the Anatolian patronymic *'nš,* which may correspond to Ενας, Εννης, Εννις[124]. The same situation occurs in line 4, where Semitic *B'lšm'* (< *B'lšm'*), "Baal heard"[125], is followed by the patronymic *Šgš*, apparently Anatolian Σιγγις[126] or the like, attested in Lydia. Also in Lydia (İzmir) occurs the probable name 'Ρύκω[127], that could correspond to *Rkh* of line 5:

113 *Ibid.*, p. 144, §261-2.

114 *Ibid.*, p. 418-419, §1209-1210.

115 G.W. Van Beek, *Tel Gamma,* in *IEJ* 24 (1974), p. 274-275 (see p. 274).

116 IDAM 84.208, published by J. Naveh, *art. cit.* (n. 6), p. 11-15, Pl. 3A.

117 L. Zgusta, *op. cit.* (n. 101), p. 379, §1100-1 and 2; Ph.H.J. Houwink ten Cate, *The Luwian Population Groups of Lycia and Cilicia Aspera during the Hellenistic Period,* Leiden 1961, p. 164-165.

118 L. Zgusta, *op. cit.* (n. 101), p. 221, §571.

119 M.M. Hardie, *The Shrine of Men Askaenos at Pisidian Antioch,* in *JHS* 32 (1912), p. 111-150, especially p. 141, No. 63. No photograph and no copy of the inscription are provided.

120 This reading is proposed by L. Zgusta, *op. cit.* (n. 101), p. 396, §1154-4.

121 M.M. Hardie indicates that a somewhat elongated letter is engraved between *O* and the final letter which appears as ∊, possibly the left side of a *Θ*.

122 *TAD* I, A1.1, line 1; cf. B. Porten, *Appeal of Adon, King of Ekron, to Pharaoh,* in W.W. Hallo (ed.), *The Context of Scripture* III, Leiden 2002, p. 132-133.

123 P.M. Fraser - E. Matthews, *op. cit.* (n. 14), p. 14c.

124 L. Zgusta, *op. cit.* (n. 101), p. 163, §334-4 to 6.

125 J. Naveh, *art. cit.* (n. 6), p. 13.

126 L. Zgusta, *op. cit.* (n. 101), p. 465, §1429.

127 A.E. Contoléon, *Inscriptions inédites,* in *RÉG* 13 (1900), p. 493-503 (see p. 497, No. 7). For a different reading and proposed emendations, see L. Zgusta, *op. cit.* (n. 101), p. 139, n. 44.

rkh.šm'š. The patronymic *Šm'š* may be related to various Anatolian names, but it might be Semitic as well: for instance, one may surmise a name reduced to the theophorous element *Šamaš* with an *aleph* indicating the vowel *a*, like in some Phoenician inscriptions from Cilicia[128]. One may also consider that this is the name *Šm'* written *Šm'* with the Anatolian termination *-š*.

In line 6, the man called *b'l'.ḥmš* or *yymš* certainly bears a Semitic name reduced to the theophorous element *B'l* with a hypocoristic ending. His patronymic is more likely *Ḥmš*, both on palaeographic and onomastic grounds. Since *ḥ* often corresponds to κ in Hellenistic and Graeco-Roman times[129], this name may be identified with Κουμας or Κωμασις[130], attested in Pisidia. *Ntn.ppš* in line 7 bears a Semitic name, probably shortened from *Ntnb'l*. His patronymic is instead Anatolian and can be related to Παππας, Παππος, often attested in Lycaonia and Lycia, also in other parts of south-western Anatolia[131]. In line 8, one should read *ṭb.šl*[..] rather than *ṭy.šl*[..]. The first name is apparently Semitic and this might also be the case for the patronymic, if one restores *Šl*[*m*], which occurs in line 3.

Another ostracon from Tell Ğemmeh, dated "stratigraphically to the early or mid-7th century B.C."[132], fully preserves three names or patronymics[133]. *Klyṭbš* in line 2 appears to be the Greek proper name Κλεότιμος, attested on Cyprus already in the 6th century B.C.[134] Its spelling with internal *y* marking the glide ε-ο is not surprising, as also Κλέων is transcribed *'klyn* in Punic[135]. As for the *b* of *Klyṭbš* instead of the expected *m*, it seems to witness the Lycian alternation *b:m*, attested by the Greek transcriptions Πυρίματις / Πυριβάτης of the Lycian name *Purihimeti* and by the Lycian spelling *Telebehi* of the toponym Τελμησσός (Fethiye)[136], which is likely to reproduce the older form of the name, anterior to the change *s* > *h*. The other two names of the ostracon are apparently Lycian. *Qsryh* in line 3 can be compared with Epi-

[128] LIPIŃSKI, *Itineraria Phoenicia*, p. 132.
[129] For instance, see *ibid.*, p. 113.
[130] L. ZGUSTA, *op. cit.* (n. 101), p. 254, §729-1, and p. 263, §780.
[131] L. ZGUSTA, *op. cit.* (n. 101), p. 414-415, §1199-20 and 21.
[132] G.W. VAN BEEK, *Tel Gamma*, in *IEJ* 22 (1972), p. 245-246 (see p. 246); ID., *Tell Ğemmeh*, in *RB* 79 (1972), p. 596-599 (see p. 597-598).
[133] IDAM 84.207, published by J. NAVEH, *art. cit.* (n. 6), p. 11-15, Pl. 3B.
[134] P.M. FRASER - E. MATTHEWS, *op. cit.* (n. 14), p. 263a-b.
[135] *CIS* I, 143, 1= *KAI* 66, 1; cf. BENZ, p. 194.
[136] G. NEUMANN, *Beiträge zum Lykischen II*, in *Die Sprache* 8 (1962), p. 203-212 (see p. 203-204); W. JENNIGES, *Mystagogus Lycius*, Bruxelles 1996, p. 27.

choric Lycian *Xisterija*[137], attested at Pinara, at least if we assume a dissimilation *ss* > *st* or an assimilation *st* > *ss*. The final *h* may be either a vowel letter marking the final *-a* or the Lycian genitive ending *-h*, what is more likely since *Qsryh* is a patronymic. The same explanation can be applied to *Brṣyh* in line 4, if this is a Lycian equivalent of the Carian name Βρύαξις / Βρύασσις, attested also in Lydia and on the island Cos[138]. There is also an older attestation of Βρύησις on a gem from the 6th or 5th century B.C.[139]

These names may have been borne by native Philistines, like those of the preceding ostracon. Both ostraca may even be contemporary from a palaeographic point of view[140], but one cannot rule out the possibility that the men of the second ostracon were foreigners or mercenaries, as the names preserved contain no trace of Canaanite influence.

An Anatolian name is borne also by Goliath. Since the familiar biblical story need not here be rehearsed, we may pass at once to the problem which his name presents, for its usual connection with the Anatolian element *watta-* does not match the spelling *Glyt*. Considering the alternation *k/g* in the nominal element *kula / gula*[141], the name of Goliath, if properly transmitted, can be related instead to *Kuliet*, a proper name attested in Hittite[142]. Its meaning is so far unknown.

9th-8th centuries B.C.

Philistine history in Iron Age II is the history of the individual city-states, rather than that of an organized Pentapolis acting in concert. Even the concept of Pentapolis, based on biblical tradition and referring to Gaza, Ashkelon, Ashdod, Ekron, and Gath, is not entirely correct, since "Gibbethon, which belongs to the Philistines" (I Kings 15, 27; 16, 15-17), seems to play an important role, not only as a town close to the boundaries of Israel and Philistia, and therefore coveted by the kings of Israel in the outgoing 10th and early 9th centuries[143], but also on its own

[137] L. Zgusta, *op. cit.* (n. 101), p. 234, §620.

[138] L. Zgusta, *op. cit.* (n. 101), p. 129, §196-1 and 2 with n. 88-91.

[139] J. Boardman, *Greek Gems and Finger Rings*, London 1970, p. 186.

[140] J. Naveh, *art. cit.* (n. 6), p. 15.

[141] Ph.H.J. Houwink ten Cate, *op. cit.* (n. 117), p. 151. The element *kula / gula* occurs, for instance, in the name of the Śam'alian king *Kula-muwa*, whose name was conventionally read "Kilamuwa" (*ca.* 840-810 B.C.)

[142] E. Laroche, *Les noms des Hittites*, Paris 1966, p. 97, No. 613. The suffix *-iyat*, *-iet* occurs frequently in older Hittite names at Kaniš (Kültepe); cf. *ibid.*, p. 309.

[143] C.S. Ehrlich, *op. cit.* (n. 91), p. 66-69.

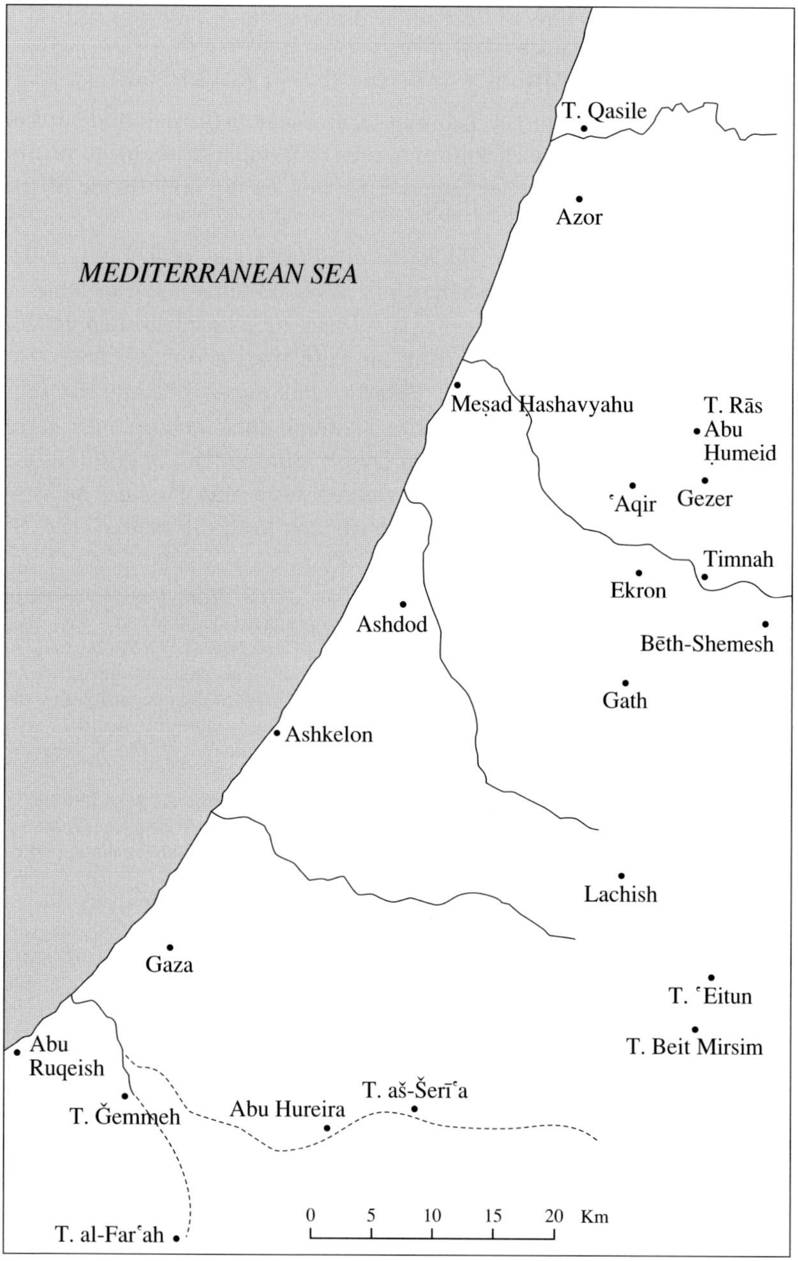
T. Qasile
Azor
MEDITERRANEAN SEA
Meṣad Ḥashavyahu
T. Rās Abu Ḥumeid
ʿAqir
Gezer
Timnah
Ekron
Ashdod
Bēth-Shemesh
Gath
Ashkelon
Lachish
Gaza
T. ʿEitun
T. Beit Mirsim
Abu Ruqeish
T. Ğemmeh
Abu Hureira
T. aš-Šerīʿa
T. al-Farʿah
0 5 10 15 20 Km

Philistia.

merits, since its capture by Sargon II deserved to be represented on a relief in the palace of Khorsabad (Dur-Sharrukin)[144]. This fortified city was tentatively located at Tell al-Melāt, west of Gezer[145], but the large site of some 10 hectares at Tell Rās Abu Ḥumeid (Tel Ḥamid), 6 km north-west of Gezer and 2.5 km south-east of Ramleh[146], seems to justify the repeated sieges by Israel better[147], as well as the importance of the town in Sargon II's eyes.

The relative might of the Philistine city-states was probably a sufficient deterrent to protect their territory from possible Judaean attacks, since the late hints in II Chron. 17, 10-11 and 26, 6 that Jehoshaphat (*ca.* 875-851 B.C.) received tribute from the Philistines and that Uzziah (*ca.* 786-735 B.C.) conquered Gaza, Yabneh, and Ashdod[148], are not substantiated by more reliable reports, although their source may have referred to historical events. Section D4 of "Stratum IX" at Ashdod, the partial destruction of which was attributed to Uzziah[149], must be connected with Stratum X and certainly goes back to the 9th century B.C.[150]

[144] M. EL-AMIN, *Die Reliefs mit Beischriften von Sargon II. in Dur-Sharrukin,* in *Sumer* 9 (1953), p. 35-59, 214-228 (see p. 36-37); N. FRANKLIN, *The Room V Reliefs at Dur-Sharrukin and Sargon II's Western Campaigns,* in *Tel Aviv* 21 (1994), p. 255-275 (see p. 260, 265, 267, Fig. 5). See here below, p. 139. The study of the relief by G. SCHMITT, *Gabbutunu,* in *ZDPV* 105 (1989), p. 56-69, reaches the conclusion that the city represented was located in the area of Deir al-Balaḥ and cannot be identified with biblical Gibbethon. See instead A. FUCHS, *Die Inschriften Sargons II. aus Khorsabad,* Göttingen 1994, p. 277, 433.

[145] G. VON RAD, *Das Reich Israel und die Philister,* in *Palästinajahrbuch* 29 (1933), p. 30-42 (see p. 38-39). The site has been very partially excavated: A. SHAVIT, *Tel Malot,* in *ESI* 12 (1993), p. 49-50, who believes that the results of this partial excavation agree with von Rad's proposal to identify the site with Gibbethon.

[146] This mound with pottery from the Neolithic, Chalcolithic, Intermediate Bronze, and Late Bronze Age through the Arab period was described by B. MAZAR, *Gath and Gittaim,* in *IEJ* 4 (1954), p. 227-235, who identified it with biblical Gath. The salvage excavation of the "lower terrace" (*ca.* 4 ha) did not provide any significant results for the Iron Age: Y. DAGAN, *Southern Route,* in *ESI* 15 (1996), p. 122; O. TAL, *Tel Hamid (The Lower Terrace), 1995, 1996,* in *IEJ* 47 (1997), p. 273-275; O. TAL - N. BLOCKMAN, *A Salvage Excavation at Tel Hamid (The Lower Terrace),* in *Tel Aviv* 25 (1998), p. 142-173. Instead, the excavation of the "western terrace" (grid ref. 1397/1456) revealed an Iron Age city: S. WOLFF - A. SHAVIT, *Tel Ḥamid,* in *ESI* 109 (1999), p. 68*-70*; S. WOLFF, *Tel Ḥamid,* in *ESI* 110 (1999), p. 55*-56*; S. WOLFF - A. SHAVIT, *Tel Ḥamid: An Iron Age Site in the Inner Coastal Plain* (IAA Reports), Jerusalem, forthcoming.

[147] N. NA'AMAN, *Borders and Districts in Biblical Historiography* (Jerusalem Biblical Studies 4), Jerusalem 1986, p. 107-108, n. 49.

[148] C.S. EHRLICH, *op. cit.* (n. 91), p. 69-70, 74-77, 144-146, 153-155. See also here below, p. 78.

[149] M. DOTHAN *et al.*, *Ashdod II/III* ('Atiqot. English Series 9-10), Jerusalem 1971, p. 21; M. DOTHAN - Y. PORATH, *Ashdod IV* ('Atiqot. English Series 15), Jerusalem 1982, p. 55-56; M. DOTHAN, *art. cit.* (n. 26), p. 99.

[150] There seems to be no independent "Stratum IX": I. FINKELSTEIN - L. SINGER-AVITZ, *Ashdod Revisited,* in *Tel Aviv* 28 (2001), p. 231-259 (see p. 242-244); ID., *"Ashdod Revis-*

The destructions noticed in the lower city should then be attributed to Hazael's thrust to the south in the latter part of his reign (*ca.* 810 B.C.), when he seized Gath and marched on Jerusalem (II Kings 12, 18-19)[151]. The destruction of the Philistine city of Ekron, dated by the excavators to the 10th century B.C., is attributed to the pharaoh Siamun or to a conflict with Ekron's Israelite neighbours[152]. The chronology, the circumstances, and the aftermaths of the disaster are so far not clear. In particular, there is no solid evidence for the existence of the city in the 9th century, and one may assume that the complete absence of Ekron in the stories of Samson, in Judg. 14-15, is due to its destruction. In fact, this omission requires an explanation, as Ashdod, Ashkelon, and Gaza are mentioned, while Ekron is not, although it was a town very close to Timnah, the centre of the Samson stories. They may have been written down in the 9th century B.C., when Ekron was possibly a ghost town.

The first definitive reference to Philistia in Assyrian sources dates from the reign of Adad-nirari III (810-783 B.C.), who boasts of having collected tribute from Philistia[153]. Seventy years later, in 734 B.C., Tiglath-pileser III invaded the country, sacked Gaza, and forced vassalage on Hanun, its king[154], and then upon Mitinti, king of Ashkelon[155], soon replaced by Rukibtu[156]. This campaign had little to do, as it seems, with the Syro-Ephraimite war waged by Damascus and Israel against Judah. As suggested by Tiglath-pileser III's thrust down to the border of Egypt, it rather resulted from the Assyrian desire of controlling the road

ited" - Maintained, in *Tel Aviv* 31 (2004), p. 122-135 (see p. 125-127), in response to D. BEN-SHLOMO, *The Iron Age Sequence of Tel Ashdod,* in *Tel Aviv* 30 (2003), p. 83-107 (see p. 91-95). The pottery of "Stratum IX", briefly presented by M. DOTHAN - Y. PORATH, *op. cit.* (n. 149), p. 25-26, goes back to the 9th century B.C.

151 LIPIŃSKI, *Aramaeans*, p. 387.

152 S. GITIN, *The Philistines: Neighbors of the Canaanites, Phoenicians and Israelites,* in D.R. CLARK - V.H. MATTHEWS (eds.), *100 Years of American Archaeology in the Middle East,* Boston 2004, p. 57-85 (see p. 60).

153 C.S. EHRLICH, *op. cit.* (n. 91), p. 79-85.

154 *Tigl. III*, p. 138 and 140, Summ. 4, lines 8'-17'; p. 170, Summ. 7, rev., lines 12'-13'; p. 176 and 178, Summ. 8, lines 14'-19'; p. 188, Summ. 9, rev., lines 13-16. The submission of Hanun is represented on Tiglath-pileser III's orthostats: C. UEHLINGER, *Hanun von Gaza und seine Gottheiten auf Orthostatenreliefs Tiglatpilesers III.*, in U. HÜBNER - E.A. KNAUF (eds.), *Kein Land für sich allein. Studien zum Kulturkontakt in Kanaan, Israel / Palästina und Ebirnâri für M. Weippert* (OBO 186), Freiburg/Schweiz-Göttingen 2002, p. 92-125. For a survey of the well-known data concerning Gaza at this period, see: N. NA'AMAN, *The Boundary System and Political Status of Gaza under the Assyrian Empire,* in *ZDPV* 120 (2004), p. 55-72.

155 *Tigl. III*, p. 82, Ann. 18 and 24, lines 8' and 12'-13'a; cf. p. 170, Summ. 7, rev., line 11'.

156 *Tigl. III*, p. 82, Ann. 18 and 24, lines 10' and 16'.

to the Nile delta and to the terminal of the lucrative desert trade from Arabia to the Mediterranean harbours of Philistia[157].

The erection of the large emporium at Abu Ruqeish / Tell ar-Reqeish, precisely in the second half of the 8th century B.C.[158], is probably a result of Tiglath-pileser III's policy. If the creation of this huge trade centre, 15 km south-west of Gaza, at the terminal of the caravan routes from South Arabia, was not a somewhat earlier initiative of a Tyrian king, acting "by great cleverness in trading" (Ez. 28, 5), Tiglath-pileser III certainly had the power of charging a Phoenician ruler with the establishment of such an emporium and commanding Hanun of Gaza to supply manpower. Large scale excavation of this site, which comprises an area between 8 and 10 ha, could provide more information.

Tribute from Philistine cities is recorded in Assyrian documents of this period[159], showing that Assyria did not want to alter their semi-independent status, since Philistines were acting as useful brokers in the delicate trade relations with Egypt. However, the Assyrian dynastic crisis in 722 B.C. provided the opportunity for a general western revolt led by the king of Hamath, acting apparently in concert with Hanun, king of Gaza[160], and with Egypt. Sargon II was able to confront the anti-Assyrian coalition in 720 B.C. He won a decisive victory at Qarqar over the Syrian members of the alliance, conquered Hamath[161], and swiftly marched southwards to Philistia. He took Hanun captive after seizing the Egyptian-held city of Raphia, and made Gaza once again a vassal city. Tell Rafāḥ on the coast is the site of a landing place at a small bay, now sanded up, while the main city, represented on a relief in Sargon II's palace at Khorsabad[162], lay inland, near Bīr Rafāḥ, where the mound raised up to some 50 m.

[157] C.S. EHRLICH, *op. cit.* (n. 91), p. 86-104.

[158] W. CULICAN, *The Graves at Tell er-Reqeish,* in *The Australian Journal of Biblical Archaeology* 2/2 (1973), p. 66-105 = W. CULICAN, *Opera Selecta,* Göteborg 1986, p. 85-124; R. HESTRIN - M. DAYAGI-MENDELS, *Another Pottery Group from Abu Ruqeish,* in *The Israel Museum Journal* 2 (1982), p. 49-57; E. OREN - N. FLEMING - S. KORNBERG - R. FEINSTEIN - P. NAḤSHONI, *A. Phoenician Emporium on the Border of Egypt,* in *Qadmoniot* 19 (1986), p. 83-91 (in Hebrew); E.D. OREN, *Ruqeish,* in *NEAEHL,* Jerusalem 1993, Vol. IV, p. 1293-1294; Y. HUSTER, *Tell er-Ruqeish,* in *ESI* 111 (2000), p. 87*-88*.

[159] *SAA* I, 110, rev. 4-13; *SAA* VII, 58, I, 3'; *SAA* XI, 34, 14; 50.

[160] For Hanun, see A. FUCHS, *Ḫanūnu,* in *PNA* II/1, Helsinki 2000, p. 457b.

[161] LIPIŃSKI, *Aramaeans*, p. 316-317.

[162] The Room V reliefs, related to Sargon II's campaign in 720 B.C., were lost when the ship carrying them sunk in the Shatt al-Arab waterway in 1855. Their only record is preserved in the drawings made at the site by M.E. Flandin and in the notes compiled by P.E. Botta: P.E. BOTTA - M.E. FLANDIN, *Monument de Ninive*, Paris 1849, in particular Vol. II, Pls. 86-93. Raphia (grid ref. 077/078) was recognized on Lower Relief 2 (Pl. 86)

Other wall reliefs from Room V at Khorsabad portray the capture of Gibbethon, of Ekron, and of a large unnamed city with an acropolis, which must be Gaza[163]. The relief depicts Gibbethon (*Gabbutunu*) in a conventional manner, located on higher ground and protected by a city-wall with towers. However, its defenders are represented as ambidextrous Cushites[164]. This could imply the presence of some troops sent by Shabako (721/0-707/6), but it is more likely that the artist simply followed the anachronistic representation of the Egyptian defenders of Raphia on Lower Reliefs 2-4, pictured as if they were Cushites.

Ekron is represented with two city-walls, a detail which seems to reveal an attempt at expressing the importance of the town. The first wall was apparently conceived by the artist as surrounding the whole settlement, while the second wall, higher and reinforced by towers, was probably supposed to protect the upper city[165]. The accuracy of the Assyrian palace bas-reliefs should not be underestimated. On the relief picturing the capture of Lachish by Sennacherib's army, for instance, the artist shows simultaneously the battle and its outcome. He depicts men and women emerging from the city and carrying their belongings, but he neither represents flocks and herds taken away as booty, as some other Neo-Assyrian bas-reliefs do, nor indicates that the city is burnt and its walls demolished. He thus draws quite a realistic scene, knowing that livestock has been kept in the city to supply the Assyrian troops scheduled to quarter at Lachish.

The third town on the Khorsabad reliefs is very likely Gaza, depicted as a much larger city. Gaza was the main target of the campaign and its importance had to be expressed visually. Its siege is represented on Lower Reliefs 5b-7, while Lower Reliefs 8-9 show the deportation of the elders of Gaza, accompanied by their wives and children. Probably headed by Hanun, known to have been captured and deported to Assyria, they proceed towards Sargon II represented on Relief 2 in Door O.

by M. EL-AMIN, *art. cit.* (n. 144), p. 35-41. Cf. N. FRANKLIN, *art. cit.* (n. 144), p. 259-260, 264-267. See here below, p. 139, 141, 143.

163 The city was identified as Gaza by M. EL-AMIN, *art. cit.* (n. 144), p. 40, followed by E. UNGER, *Gaza in assyrischer Darstellung*, in *RLA* III, Berlin 1957-71, p. 153. The uncertain results of the Ashdod excavations (see below, n. 171) do not favour the identification of the unnamed city with Ashdod, as proposed by N. FRANKLIN, *art. cit.* (n. 144), p. 260-261, 269-270. See here below, p. 141.

164 This Lower Relief 5a of Khorsabad Room V should be connected with Lower Reliefs 5b-13; cf. E. UNGER, *Gabbutunu*, in *RLA*, Berlin 1957-71, p. 129-130.

165 Comp. D. USSISHKIN, *The Fortifications of Philistine Ekron*, in *IEJ* 55 (2005), p. 35-65, in particular p. 61-63. See here below, p. 145.

In fact, two reliefs of the series show Sargon II standing on his chariot as captives are brought before him[166]. This is an artistic convention, which does not imply *per se* that the three towns Gibbethon, Ekron, and Gaza were captured in 720 B.C., and not in 712 B.C., for instance, when the king did not participate in the campaign. The double representation of Sargon nevertheless favours the dating of the scenes to 720 B.C.[167], although it cannot be regarded as an absolute criterion, lest one should neglect the ideological meaning of the sculptures displayed in the palace and of the inscriptions, in which Sargon II always speaks in the first person and is supposed to have accomplished everything personally.

In 713 B.C., Azuri of Ashdod was deported for treachery and replaced by his brother Ahi-Meti, bearing the Egyptianized name "Brother of Maat". However, an uprising forced him to fly from the city and the Ashdodites made a certain Yamani their king. Yamani, "Ionian", named also ^{m}*Ia-ad-na*, "Cypriot", was probably a ship-owner and businessman trading with Greece and Cyprus, as his surnames suggest. He tried to form a large anti-Assyrian coalition, but a swift Assyrian campaign[168], referred to in Is. 20, 1-6, crushed the rebellion in 712 B.C. Yamani fled to Egypt, but Shebitko, the Cushitic ruler of the country, extradited him to Sargon II in 707/6 B.C.[169]

Fragments of a basalt victory stele of Sargon II were uncovered in the excavations of Ashdod[170], which have also shown that the city-walls were destroyed at that time, corresponding to the end of Strata VIII-VII[171]. People of Ashdod, Gath, and Ashdod-Yam were then deported

[166] Room V of the Khorsabad palace, Reliefs 2 in Door O and 13.

[167] J.E. READE, *Sargon's Campaigns of 720, 716 and 715 B.C.: Evidence from the Sculptures,* in *JNES* 35 (1976), p. 95-104 (see p. 100-101).

[168] H. WINCKLER, *Die Keilschrifttexte Sargons*, Leipzig 1889, p. 186-189; A. FUCHS, *op. cit.* (n. 144), p. 132-135 and 326, Ann. 241-254; p. 219-221 and 348, Displ. 90-109. Cf. *ANET*, p. 285a, 286a-287a; *TPOA*, p. 113-115; K. RADNER, *Iamāni*, in *PNA* II/1, Helsinki 2000, p. 491.

[169] Lines 19-21 of the inscription published by G. FRAME, *The Inscription of Sargon II at Tang-i Var,* in *Orientalia* 68 (1999), p. 31-57 and pl. I-XVIII. Cf. D.B. REDFORD, *A Note on the Chronology of Dynasty 25 and the Inscription of Sargon II at Tang-i Var,* in *Orientalia* 68 (1999), p. 58-60, and here below, p. 143 with n. 266.

[170] H. TADMOR, *Fragments of an Assyrian Stele of Sargon II*, in *Ashdod II/III* ('Atiqot. English Series 9-10), Jerusalem 1971, p. 192-197, Pls. XCVI-XCVII; Z.J. KAPERA, *The Ashdod Stele of Sargon II,* in *Folia Orientalia* 17 (1976), p. 87-99.

[171] Contrary to M. DOTHAN *et al.*, *op. cit.* (n. 149), p. 21, 115; M. DOTHAN, *art. cit.* (n. 26), p. 100, who link the destruction of Stratum VII with the twenty-nine years long siege of Ashdod by Psammetichus I, recorded by HERODOTUS, *History* II, 157 (see below, p. 156, n. 346). The distinction of Stratum VIII and Stratum VII is highly problematic: I. FINKELSTEIN - L. SINGER-AVITZ, *art. cit.* (n. 150), in *Tel Aviv* 28 (2001), p. 244-246, 250-252; 31 (2004), p. 127-128. In their interpretation, which seems to be correct, the for-

with their belongings. The mention of Gath between Ashdod and Ashdod-Yam suggests that the town depended then from Ashdod and indicates that it was conquered by the Assyrians in the same circumstances. Gath, called *Gimtu* in Sargon II's inscriptions[172], is rightly identified with Tell aṣ-Ṣāfī (Tel Ṣafit)[173], almost 20 km southeast of Ashdod. The fragments of an Assyrian stele found there in the British excavations of 1899[174] and the recent excavations of the site confirm its identification with Gath[175]. In any case, the erection of a stele and the mention of Gath in Sargon II's inscriptions show that the city of the Philistine pentapolis had not lost all its importance in the 8th century. Ashdod-Yam, the harbour of Ashdod, was situated at Mīnet Esdūd or Mīnet al-Qal'a, 5 km north-west of Tel Ashdod[176]. Tell Ḫeiḍar (Tel Mor) instead, on the right bank of Nahr as-Sukreir (Naḥal Lachish), 8 km north of Ashdod[177], was then no more than an unfortified village (0.6 ha).

Documents from the time of Sargon II refer to military bases and international trade centres established by the Assyrians in the broader Gaza area[178]. Beside the Assyrian citadel of Tell aš-Šerī'a[179] and the large Assyrian-type building at Tell Ǧemmeh[180], one should mention Tell Abu Salima[181], east of al-'Arīš, and the large fortified site of Tell ar-Reqeish (Abu Ruqeish) on the coast, 15 km south-west of Gaza[182].

tified city of Stratum VIII-VII was destroyed by Sargon II. The destruction was attributed to a king of Judah in the later source of II Chron 26, 6.

172 A. FUCHS, *op. cit.* (n. 144), p. 134, Ann. 250-251; p. 220, Displ. 104-105. Cf. *ANET*, p. 286a; *TPOA*, p. 114.

173 W.M. SCHNIEDEWIND, *The Geopolitical History of Philistine Gath,* in *BASOR* 309 (1998), p. 69-77.

174 P.J. BLISS - R.A.S. MACALISTER, *Excavations in Palestine 1898-1900*, London 1902, p. 28-43, in particular p. 41. This stele must have been erected by Sargon II, since no other Assyrian king mentions Gath (*Gimtu*). Cf. H. TADMOR, *art. cit.* (n. 170), p. 192-194.

175 A.M. MAEIR - C.S. EHRLICH, *Excavating Philistine Gath: Have we found Goliath's Hometown?,* in *Biblical Archaeology Review* 27/6 (2001), p. 22-31; C.S. EHRLICH, *Die Suche nach Gat und die neuen Ausgrabungen auf Tell eṣ-Ṣāfī*, in U. HÜBNER - E.A. KNAUF (eds.), *Kein Land für sich allein. Studien zum Kulturkontakt in Kanaan, Israel/Palästina und Ebirnâri für M. Weippert*, Freiburg/Schweiz-Göttingen 2002, p. 56-69, and the publications quoted here above, p. 53, n. 28.

176 J. KAPLAN, *Ashdod-Yam*, in *NEAEHL*, Jerusalem 1993, Vol. I, p. 102-103.

177 Grid ref. 1175/1370.

178 C.J. GADD, *Inscribed Prisms of Sargon II from Nimrud,* in *Iraq* 16 (1954), p. 173-201, Pls. XLIII-LI (see p. 179, col. IV, 46-48); A. FUCHS, *op. cit.* (n. 144), p. 88 and 314, Ann. 17-18. See also here p. 127, 140-141, 376.

179 E.D. OREN, *Sera', Tel,* in *NEAEHL*, Jerusalem 1993, Vol. IV, p. 1329-1335.

180 G.W. VAN BEEK, *Jemmeh, Tell,* in *NEAEHL*, Jerusalem 1993, Vol. II, p. 667-674.

181 R. REICH, *The Identification of the 'Sealed* kāru *of Egypt',* in *IEJ* 34 (1984), p. 32-38.

182 See here above, p. 74, n. 158.

During the rebellions that broke out after Sargon II's death on the battlefield in Anatolia, in 705 B.C., Ṣidqa replaced the loyal ruler at Ashkelon and Padi, the vassal king of Ekron, was deposed and handed over to Hezekiah, king of Judah[183]. The latter never ruled the city-state, as erroneously claimed in some publications[184]. The three Judaean jar handles with the *lmlk* stamp and the single four-winged stamp with the inscription *lmlk ḥbrn* ("for the king, [from] Hebron"), found during the excavation, are easily explained by the vicinity of Jerusalem and trade relations in the 7th century B.C. They have the same meaning as the Phoenician-type vessels unearthed at Tell al-Muqanna'. Instead, Hezekiah may have occupied Gath, the population of which was partly deported by the Assyrians in 712 B.C. The so-called "Azekah fragment" of the incomplete Sennacherib's "Letter to the God"[185], written apparently during the campaign of 701 B.C., mentions the capture of Azekah and of another city, described as "a royal [city] of the Philistines, which H[ezek]iah had captured and strengthened for himself". This reference to an earlier event very likely concerns the capture of Gath by Hezekiah in 705 B.C., when the news of Sargon II's death in Anatolia had reached Judah. II Kings 18, 8 alludes to Hezekiah's campaign against the Philistines "as far as Gaza and its vicinity", thus in the direction of Tell aṣ-Ṣāfī, and the brief account in II Chron. 26, 6 may be based on a historical source[186], which concerned Hezekiah's campaign against the Philistines, not Uzziah's, as stated in the text.

The phrase "royal city" does not hamper the identification of the unnamed city with Gath, since *āl šarrūti* had quite a large meaning in Neo-Assyrian inscriptions[187], while Gath was a very large site at that

[183] D.D. LUCKENBILL, *op. cit.* (n. 39), p. 29-34 (third campaign); E. FRAHM, *op. cit.* (n. 39), p. 53-55, lines 39-58; *ANET*, p. 287-288; *TPOA*, p. 119-121.

[184] In particular: *Tel Miqne-Ekron: Summary of Fourteen Seasons of Excavation 1981-1996*, Jerusalem 2005, p. 7, referring to Judaean seal impressions on jar handles: "One four-winged example bears the inscription *lmlk hbrn* ('belonging to the King of Hebron'), dating to the brief period when Ekron was ruled by Hezekiah, King of Judah".

[185] K. 6205+82-3-3-23, 131, lines 11'-20'; cf. the discussion of the opinions by E. FRAHM, *op. cit.* (n. 39), p. 229-232. The present writer maintains the identification of the city with Azekah, as done originally by N. NA'AMAN, *Sennacherib's 'Letter to God' on His Campaign to Judah,* in *BASOR* 214 (1974), p. 25-39 (see p. 34-35). See here below.

[186] W. RUDOLPH, *Chronikbücher* (HAT I/21), Tübingen 1955, p. 284-285; C.S. EHRLICH, *op. cit.* (n. 91), p. 75-77, 153-155. A literary commonplace, like the breaching of the wall, which parallels II Chron. 25, 23, does not constitute an argument against the historicity of the capture of Gath.

[187] Y. IKEDA, *Royal Cities and Fortified Cities,* in *Iraq* 41 (1979), p. 75-87. The identification of the "royal city" with Ekron, proposed by S. MITTMANN, *Hiskia und die Philister,* in *JNSL* 16 (1990), p. 91-106, who is followed by G. GALIL, *Conflicts between Assyrian Vassals,* in *SAAB* 6 (1992), p. 55-63 (see p. 61-62), and N. NA'AMAN, *Hezekiah*

Philistine cult stand from Ashdod
(Photo: Courtesy of the IDAM).

time, with a superficies estimated at 50 hectares[188]. In the light of Sennacherib's texts, the jar handles with royal Judaean stamps from Tell aṣ-Ṣāfī[189] might confirm the short occupation of the site by Judaean forces in 705-701 B.C. However, excavators connect the stamp impressions with Temporary Stratum 3[190], which represents the occupation of the site in the 7th century B.C. Stamped *lmlk* jars are found even in late 7th-century B.C. contexts and this must also be the case of the specimens found at Tell aṣ-Ṣāfī, since the same stratum yielded two handles stamped with the so-called "rosette", which may have been a royal symbol in the days of the last kings of Judah. At any rate, the general use of the two-winged *lmlk* stamp continued throughout the 7th century until the last decades of the Judaean monarchy, when the "rosette" symbol came into use. Therefore, the traditional seventh-century date for the bulk of two-winged and even four-winged stamps remains the most probable hypothesis. This was true thirty-five years ago[191] and is even more evident today, since the fifty or more *lmlk* seal impressions found at Bēth-Shemesh come from the latest Iron Age level at the site, Stratum IIc[192]. The many stamped *lmlk* jars from Stratum III at Lachish only confirm this view, despite the well-known opinion of D. Ussishkin[193]. Some date certainly from the second half of the 7th century B.C., for names like *'ḥzyh, Šbnyh, 'zryh* with the spelling *-yh* of the theophorous element occur on official seal impressions from the same Stratum III[194]. Now, such spellings do not appear before the mid-7th century B.C.[195]

and the Kings of Assyria, in *Tel Aviv* 21 (1994), p. 235-254 (see p. 245-246), can safely be discarded; cf. here below.

188 See here above, p. 53, n. 28.

189 J. Uziel - A.M. Maeir, *art. cit.* (n. 28), p. 62, with further references.

190 A.M. Maeir, *art. cit.* (n. 28), in *IEJ* 53 (2003), p. 244b.

191 H.D. Lance, *The Royal Stamps and the Kingdom of Judah,* in *HTR* 64 (1971), p. 315-332. Add the information provided by the evidence from Jerusalem: A.D. Tushingham, *New Evidence Bearing on the Two-Winged* lmlk *Stamp*, in *BASOR* 287 (1992), p. 61-66.

192 S. Bunimovitz and S. Lederman, quoted by J. Finkelstein - N. Na'aman, *The Judahite Shephelah in the Late 8th and Early 7th Centuries BCE,* in *Tel Aviv* 31 (2004), p. 60-79 (see p. 68).

193 D. Ussishkin, *The Destruction of Lachish by Sennacherib and the Dating of the Royal Judean Storage Jars,* in *Tel Aviv* 4 (1977), p. 28-60.

194 G. Barkay - A.G. Vaughn, Lmlk *and Official Seal Impressions from Tel Lachish,* in *Tel Aviv* 23 (1996), p. 61-74 (see p. 66 and 71, No. 57); Id., *New Readings of Hezekian Official Seal Impressions,* in *BASOR* 304 (1996), p. 29-54 (see p. 44-45); Id., *The Royal and Official Seal Impressions from Lachish,* in D. Ussishkin (ed.), *The Renewed Archaeological Excavations at Lachish (1973-1994),* Tel Aviv 2004, Vol. IV, p. 2148-2173 (see p. 2162, No. 1, and p. 2164, No. 57), cf. *ibid.*, p. 2137, No. 78.

195 R. Zadok, *The Pre-Hellenistic Israelite Anthroponomy and Prosopography* (OLA 28), Leuven 1988, p. 185.

The identification of the unnamed city of the "Azekah fragment" with Gath is strongly supported by geographic and archaeological data, while its identification with Ekron[196] raises serious difficulties:

a) Ekron's location on flat land (Tell al-Muqanna') does not correspond to the topography of the site described in the "Azekah fragment" as "exceedingly difficult [to ascend]", a reference to the steep ascent to Tell aṣ-Ṣāfī from the Wādī ad-Daḥr (Elah Valley).

b) The "palace like a mountain" corresponds to the summit of the tell with the Crusader castle, described by William, archbishop of Tyre[197]: *Mons sublimis poterat appellari, et loco nomen arabice Telle Saphi, quod apud nos interpretatur "Mons" sive "Collis Clarus"... Nomenque ei vulgari indicunt appellatione Blanche Guarda, quod latine dicitur "Alba Specula".*

c) "The moat dug around" the town is a unique feature, which has been discovered in the excavation of Tell aṣ-Ṣāfī in 1996-2002, but was misinterpreted as a siege trench[198]. The moat, which is over 2 km long, from 3 m to 5 m deep, and 4 m wide at the bottom, surrounds the site from the east, south, and west. It was dug manually in Iron Age II and contains material parallel to Temporary Stratum 4, which dates obviously from the 8th century B.C.

d) Sennacherib's inscriptions do not mention any siege or capture of Ekron, and no evidence of a destruction in the late 8th century was found in the course of the excavations at Tell al-Muqanna'.

e) Capture of Azekah is mentioned before the capture of the "Philistine royal city", which should therefore lay to the south of Azekah, which is not the case of Ekron.

f) The pottery of Temporary Stratum 4 at Tell aṣ-Ṣāfī parallels vessels of the 8th century B.C. from Stratum IV at Lachish[199], contains the newly defined "pre-*lmlk*" jars of the late 8th century B.C.[200], and may thus date from the period immediately preceding Sennacherib's attack in 701 B.C.

[196] See here above, p. 78 and 80, n. 187.

[197] WILLIAM OF TYRE, *Chronicon* XV, 25, 13-27, in R.B.C. HUYGENS (ed.), *Guillaume de Tyr: Chronique* (CCCM 63-63A), Turnhout 1986, p. 708.

[198] A.M. MAEIR, *art. cit.* (n. 28), in *IEJ* 53 (2003), p. 244-246.

[199] I. SHAI and A.M. MAEIR, quoted by L. SINGER-AVITZ, *Arad: The Iron Age Pottery Assemblages*, in *Tel Aviv* 29 (2002), p. 110-214 (see p. 163). Cf. O. ZIMHONI, *The Pottery of Levels V and IV and Its Archaeological and Chronological Implications*, in D. USSISHKIN (ed.), *The Renewed Archaeological Excavations at Lachish (1973-1994)*, Tel Aviv 2004, Vol. IV, p. 1643-1778.

[200] A.M. MAEIR, *art. cit.* (n. 28), in *IEJ* 53 (2003), p. 243.

In 701 B.C., Sennacherib invaded Philistia and captured the cities of Bēth-Dagan, Jaffa, Banay-Barqa, and Azor, all belonging to the city-state of Ashkelon, the ruler of which, Ṣidqa, was deported to Assyria and replaced by Sharru-lu-dari, son of Rukibtu. The anti-Assyrian elite of Ekron requested assistance from the Cushite king of Egypt, but the battle of Eltekeh, fought north of Yabneh by the Egyptian army, did not stop Sennacherib's progression. Without fight, as it seems, Ekron submitted then to Sennacherib, who did not need to besiege and conquer the city by forcible means. He simply "drew near", *aqrib*[201]. Ekron's anti-Assyrian nobles were executed and Padi restored to the throne after his release by Hezekiah. To show his gratitude and loyalty, he sent one talent of silver to Sennacherib in 699 B.C.[202]

Judah had not only to pay a heavy tribute, but a large strip of Judaean territory, briefly described in II Chron. 28, 18, was attributed by Sennacherib to Mitinti, king of Ashdod, loyal to Assyria[203], to Padi, king of Ekron, and to Ṣilli-bēl, king of Gaza[204]. According to the Bull Inscription from the palace at Nineveh, even the newly appointed king of Ashkelon received some Judaean settlements[205]. In the actual context of II Chron. 28, 18, the cause of these events is ascribed to the reign of the "bad" king Ahaz, but this just reflects Chronicler's theological views. Sennacherib's annals do not mention any destruction and burning of Hezekiah's towns, as they do in other circumstances[206], but simply record the carrying off of spoils. There seems to have been no systematic scorched earth policy. The redistribution of Judaean territories among the Philistine neighbours of Judah appears thus as an act planned at least to some extent before the attack and capture of these settlements. Lachish, saved from destruction, became the headquarters of Sen-

201 D.D. LUCKENBILL, *op. cit.* (n. 39), p. 32, line 8; E. FRAHM, *op. cit.* (n. 39), p. 54, line 46.

202 *SAA* XI, 50.

203 D.D. LUCKENBILL, *op. cit.* (n. 39), p. 30, line 54; E. FRAHM, *op. cit.* (n. 39), p. 53, line 37.

204 D.D. LUCKENBILL, *op. cit.* (n. 39), p. 33, lines 31-34: E. FRAHM, *op. cit.* (n. 39), p. 54, line 53.

205 D.D. LUCKENBILL, *op. cit.* (n. 39), p. 70, lines 29-30.

206 For instance, D.D. LUCKENBILL, *op. cit.* (n. 39), p. 28, lines 18-19: "I besieged, I captured, I destroyed, I devastated, I burnt with fire"; p. 36-37, lines 11-12: "I captured and carried off their spoil, I destroyed, I devastated, I burnt with fire"; p. 38, lines 30-31: "I carried away from them as spoil, I destroyed, I devastated, and I burnt with fire"; p. 38, line 45: "I destroyed, I devastated, I burnt with fire"; p. 40, lines 78-80: "I besieged, I conquered, I despoiled, I destroyed, I devastated, I burnt with fire, with the smoke of their conflagration I covered the wide heavens like a hurricane"; etc.

nacherib and of his troops[207]. Assyrian policy in dealing with vassal states usually called for the stationing of a garrison at some distance from the capital[208]. The situation of Lachish was particularly fit for this purpose, since it allowed an easy control not only of the Judaean territory, but also of the Philistine cities of Ashdod, Ashkelon, and Gaza.

7th century B.C.

During the rest of Sennacherib's reign[209] and during the reigns of Esarhaddon and of Ashurbanipal, the kings of Gaza, Ashdod, Ashkelon, and Ekron are listed among the loyal vassals of Assyria. Philistia provided corvée workers and, as a buffer zone between Assyria and Egypt, it also supplied troops to the Assyrian army campaining in Egypt[210]. Moreover, in the treaty between Esarhaddon and Baal of Tyre, the Philistine coast is treated as Assyrian territory[211] and, in the Eponym Canon, the year 669 is called after an Assyrian governor of Ashdod[212], through there was a local king of Ashdod at that time.

Assyrian economic policy was probably the driving force of Ekron's olive oil industry in the late 8th and 7th centuries B.C. In fact, the industrial zone of the lower city, precisely in the area where the olive complex was discovered (Field III), yielded pottery types dated by the excavators to the late 8th century B.C.[213] Also Field IV in the centre of the lower

[207] II Kings 18, 14; 19, 8; Is. 36, 2; 37, 8; II Chron. 32, 9. In the "Azekah fragment", line 5', Sennacherib most likely calls Lachish his army unit's place, when he describes Azekah as a city located "between my [ar]my unit ([*ki-i*]*ṣ-ri-a*) and the land of Judah"; cf. E. FRAHM, *op. cit.* (n. 39), p. 230. Azekah, identified as Tell Zakariya, lies in fact about half-way between Tell ad-Duweir (Lachish) and Jerusalem. This means that Sennacherib's "Letter to the God" was written from the perspective of his stay at Lachish.

[208] I. EPH'AL, *Assyrian Domination in Palestine*, in *The World History of the Jewish People* IV/1, Jerusalem 1979, p. 276-289 (see p. 287).

[209] There was no second Sennacherib's campaign in Palestine between 688 and 686 B.C.; cf. K.A. KITCHEN, *op. cit.* (n. 31), p. 550. Taharqo's inscription found on the quay of Karnak in 1990 does not overturn the available evidence, despite the attempt of W.H. SHEA, *The New Tirhaqah Text and Sennacherib's Second Campaign,* in *AUSS* 35 (1997), p. 181-187.

[210] *ANET*, p. 291, 294.

[211] *SAA* II, 5, III, 15'-22'.

[212] A.R. MILLARD, *The Eponyms of the Assyrian Empire: 910-612 BC* (SAA Studies 2), Helsinki 1994, p. 52, sub 669, where one should read [*šá*]-*kìn As-du*-[*di*], as proposed by A UNGNAD, *Eponymen,* in *RLA* II, Berlin-Leipzig 1938, p. 412-457 (see p. 429 and 455a). Cf. A. ALT, *Kleine Schriften zur Geschichte des Volkes Israel* II, 2nd ed., München 1959, p. 234-241 and 246-247.

[213] This is recognized by T. DOTHAN - S. GITIN, *art. cit.* (n. 27), in *NEAEHL*, p. 1057, although S. Gitin constantly dates the olive oil industry of Ekron to the 7th century B.C.:

town provided number of store jars and asymmetric bowls or "scoops" attributed to the same period[214]. Specific vessel-types cannot provide a precise date in "the late eighth century BCE": they could belong to the 7th century as well. Instead, the Assyrian relief representing the siege of Ekron in 720 B.C. seems to indicate that the lower city was walled and thus occupied at that time. Its fortification could thus be dated from the last quarter of the 8th century B.C.[215], supporting the assumption that economic and industrial activity was in full swing at Ekron before the 7th century B.C. This development must have generated the city's repopulation with craftsmen brought also from Judah and the former kingdom of Israel. Ekron grew then to eight times the size of the earlier settlement. The four-horned altars, seventeen of which were found at Ekron, reveal the provenance of a part of the new population, migrated to Ekron from Israelite territories, where such stone altars had been cut for centuries. Instead, one can hardly believe that the technology of the olive oil production, no evidence of which has been found so far at the site in earlier periods, had the same Israelite origin.

Ekron's exceptionally large centre of olive oil industry is paralleled in the nearby towns of Timnah[216] and Bēth-Shemesh[217], which were given

S. GITIN, *Tel Miqne-Ekron in the 7th C. BC City Plan Development and the Oil Industry*, in M. HELTZER - D. EITAM (eds.), *Olive Oil in Antiquity*, Haifa 1987, p. 81-97, Figs. 1-13; ID., *Tel Mikne Ekron: The Type-Site for the Inner Coastal Plain in the Iron Age II Period*, in *AASOR* 49 (1989), p. 23-58 (see p. 28-36); ID., *Philistia in Transition: The Tenth Century BCE and Beyond*, in S. GITIN - A. MAZAR - E. STERN (eds.), *Mediterranean Peoples in Transition: Thirteenth to Early Tenth Centuries BCE*, Jerusalem 1998, p. 162-183 (see p. 167-173); ID., *The Philistines: Neighbors of the Canaanites, Phoenicians and Israelites*, in D.R. CLARK - V.H. MATTHEWS (eds.), *100 Years of American Archaeology in the Middle East*, Boston 2004, p. 57-85, with former literature.

214 T. DOTHAN - S. GITIN, *art. cit.* (n. 27), in *NEAEHL*, p. 1056-1057. Cf. S. GITIN, *Scoops: Corpus, Function and Typology*, in M. HELTZER - A. SEGAL - D. KAUFMAN (eds.), *Studies in the Archaeology and History of Ancient Israel in Honour of M. Dothan*, Haifa 1993, p. 99*-126* (see p. 106* with n. 25).

215 See here above, p. 75, and below, p. 145. Nothing proves so far that the lower city was walled already in the mid-8th century.

216 A. MAZAR, *The Northern Shephelah in the Iron Age: Some Issues in Biblical History and Archaeology*, in M.D. COOGAN - J.C. EXUM - L.E. STAGER (eds.), *Scripture and Other Artifacts*, Louisville 1994, p. 247-267 (see p. 260-263); ID., *Timnah (Tel Batash)* I. *Text* (Qedem 37), Jerusalem 1997, p. 155-161, 211-218, 262-263; A. MAZAR - N. PANITZ-COHEN, *Timnah (Tel Batash)* II. *The Finds from the First Millennium BCE* (Qedem 42), Jerusalem 2001, p. 281-282.

217 D. MACKENZIE, *Excavations at Ain Shems (Beth-Shemesh)* (Palestine Exploration Fund Annual 2), London 1912-13, p. 99-100; E. GRANT - G.E. WRIGHT, *Ain Shems Excavations (Palestine)* IV, Haverford 1939, Pls. 19:5; 20:3; 21:1; Vol. V, Haverford 1939, p. 74-76, Fig. 5.

by Sennacherib to the king of Ekron in 701 B.C.[218] The twelve olive oil installations found at Bēth-Shemesh must date in fact from the 7th rather than the 8th century B.C. In fact, they belong to Stratum IIc[219], characterized by pottery of Lachish Stratum III, including some fifty jar handles with the *lmlk* stamp[220], and they must be related to the re-activation of the water reservoir, certainly after Sennacherib's destruction[221] of Stratum IIb, which seems to begin in the early 8th century B.C.[222] However, the presence of jars with the *lmlk* stamp indicates that Bēth-Shemesh was given back to the king of Judah, certainly Manasseh (698-642 B.C.). In the same period, Lachish must have been abandoned by the Assyrian troops. They left taking their belongings and only three objects can be associated directly with their presence at Lachish: fragments of two bowls and a glazed vase[223]. One might perhaps add the anomalous vessel assemblage from Locus 4421[224], possibly dating from the time of the Assyrian headquarters.

New Judaean inhabitants seem to appear at Lachish only in the mid-7th century B.C., as shown by the drastic change in the ceramic culture in Level III[225]. A new Judaean population was then settled also at Bēth-Shemesh, where the olive-oil industry should probably be linked to this re-settlement and not to an enlargement of Ekron's facilities. In fact, a large state-organized oil production is attested in the same period at the Judaean site of Tell Beit Mirsim, a comparatively small mound in the

[218] II Chron. 28, 18 regards the occupation of these towns as a punishment of the sins of king Ahaz, but the historical event behind these facts must be the campaign of Sennacherib in 701 B.C.; cf. D.D. LUCKENBILL, *op. cit.* (n. 39), p. 33, lines 31-34; E. FRAHM, *op. cit.* (n. 39), p. 54, line 53.

[219] D. MACKENZIE, *loc. cit.* (n. 217); S. BUNIMOVITZ - Z. LEDERMAN, *Tel Beth Shemesh*, in *IEJ* 50 (2000), p. 254-258 (see p. 256); *ESI* 20 (2000), p. 105*-108* (see p. 106*); *ESI* 113 (2001), p. 98*-100* (see p. 99*); I. FINKELSTEIN - N. NA'AMAN, *art. cit.* (n. 192), p. 74. A firmer judgment will possibly be easier after the publication of the final report of the excavations by S. Bunimovitz and Z. Lederman.

[220] A.G. VAUGHN, *Theology, History, and Archaeology in the Chronicler's Account of Hezekiah*, Atlanta 1999, p. 190. Cf. I. FINKELSTEIN - N. NA'AMAN, *art. cit.* (n. 192), p. 68.

[221] A. FANTALKIN, *The Final Destruction of Beth Shemesh and the* Pax Assyriaca *in the Judahite Shephelah: An Alternative View,* in *Tel Aviv* 31 (2004), p. 245-261, in particular p. 246-253.

[222] I. FINKELSTEIN, *Chronology Rejoinders,* in *PEQ* 134 (2002), p. 118-129 (see p. 121-123).

[223] D. USSISHKIN, *Excavations and Restoration Work at Tel Lachish 1985-1994: Third Preliminary Report,* in *Tel Aviv* 23 (1996), p. 3-60 (see p. 18-20); ID., *The Renewed Archaeological Excavations at Lachish (1973-1994)*, Tel Aviv 2004, Vol. IV, p. 1904-1905.

[224] O. ZIMHONI, *op. cit.* (n. 199), p. 1694, 1707.

[225] O. ZIMHONI, *op. cit.* (n. 199), p. 1706.

low hill country south-west of Hebron. In Stratum A, W.F. Albright found six or seven "dye-plants"[226], which were proved to be olive-oil presses[227]. He estimated that the 3-ha town could have contained some thirty similar installations[228]. Albright dated Stratum A from the 7th century B.C., a date supported by two impressions of the seal "belonging to Eliakim, steward[229] of Yaukin[230]", *l'lyqm n'r Ywkn*[231]. The discovery of the same seal impressions at Tell Beit Mirsim, Bēth-Shemesh, and Ramath Raḥel undoubtedly points at a high official or household manager of a king or rather crown prince of Judah, obviously Jehoiachin, son of Jehoiakim (609-598 B.C.). Their presence in destruction levels probably indicates that these three sites have been destroyed by the Babylonians in 597 B.C., a date which some archaeologists prefer to ignore[232]. This Nebuchadnezzar II's intervention ends the series of his personal campaigns in Canaan, in 604-597 B.C., crowned by the re-conquest of Gaza. From the point of view of regional history, the events of 587 B.C. have instead a local importance, which is inflated because a religious significance is attached to the destruction of the temple in Jerusalem.

After the breakdown of the Assyrian power, *ca.* 620 B.C., Philistia came into the Egyptian sphere of influence. Egyptian armies commanded by Necho II traversed the region in 610/609 B.C.[233], but were

[226] W.F. ALBRIGHT, *The Excavations at Tell Beit Mirsim* III. *The Iron Age* (AASOR 21-22), New Haven 1943, p. 55-60.

[227] G. DALMAN, *Arbeit und Sitte in Palästina* V, Gütersloh 1937, p. 77-78, contesting the interpretation of W.F. ALBRIGHT, *The Archaeology of Palestine and the Bible*, New York 1932, p. 119 ff., and followed by D. EITAM, *Olive Presses in the Israelite Period,* in *Tel Aviv* 6 (1979), p. 146-155; R. FRANKEL, *Ancient Oil Mills and Presses in the Land of Israel*, in E. AYALON (ed.), *History and Technology of Olive Oil in the Holy Land*, Arlington 1994, p. 19-89 (see p. 36-40).

[228] W.F. ALBRIGHT, *op. cit.* (n. 227), p. 56.

[229] For the meaning of *n'r*, cf. H.F. FUHS, *na'ar*, in *ThWAT* V, Stuttgart 1986, col. 507-518; *DNWSI*, p. 741-742. The epigraphic attestations of the title *n'r* are collected by R. DEUTSCH - M. HELTZER, *Forty New Ancient West Semitic Inscriptions*, Tel Aviv-Jaffa 1994, p. 52-53. The title seems to have been used in the last quarter of the 7th century and the early 6th century B.C.

[230] *Ywkn* is probably an abbreviation of the name Joiachin or Jehoiachin: D. DIRINGER, in D.W. THOMAS (ed.), *Documents from Old Testament Times*, London 1958, p. 224.

[231] N. AVIGAD - B. SASS, *Corpus of West-Semitic Stamp Seals*, Jerusalem 1997, p. 243-244, No. 663. Palaeography suggests the second half of the 7th century B.C. Dating should be based on the innovative features of the script, like the head of the *mēm*, not on the conservative ones.

[232] The idiosyncratic comments of I. FINKELSTEIN - N. NA'AMAN, *art. cit.* (n. 192), p. 62-63, can best be understood as a special pleading and an attempt at preserving the conventional dating of the pottery related to the Lachish III horizon, attributed by them to the second half of the 8th century B.C.

[233] II Kings 23, 29; II Chron. 35, 20.

defeated in 605 B.C. by Nebuchadnezzar II, still crown prince at that time[234]. Despite the assistance requested from Egypt by king Adon of Ekron[235], Philistia was soon overrun by the Babylonians[236], Ashkelon was laid waste in 604 B.C.[237], and her king Aga' exiled[238]. Ekron met the same fate[239], probably in 602 B.C.[240], the city-walls of Ashdod were dismantled[241], and the city ruler brought captive to Babylon, just like the last king of Gaza[242]. However, the Babylonian army was defeated in the winter 601/600 B.C. by the Egyptians, who managed to reconquer Gaza[243] and to keep it until its recapture by the Babylonians, probably in 598/7 B.C.[244]

While an Assyrian document from Nineveh is still dated in 619 B.C. by the name of a governor of Ṣumur[245], in coastal Syria, fifteen years later the Babylonians were bringing a radical change in the Levantine

[234] A.K. Grayson, *Assyrian and Babylonian Chronicles* (TCS 5), Locust Valley 1975, p. 99, Babylonian Chronicle 5, lines 1-8; cf. Jer. 46, 2-12.

[235] *TAD* I, A1.1. Cf. B. Porten, *art. cit.* (n. 62).

[236] Jer. 25, 20; 47, 4-5; Am. 1, 8; Zeph. 2, 4-7.

[237] A.K. Grayson, *op. cit.* (n. 234), p. 100, Babylonian Chronicle 5, lines 15-20. Cf. E. Lobel - D. Page, *Poetarum Lesbiorum Fragmenta*, Oxford 1955, B 16, 10-11; Jer. 47, 6-7. Traces of a massive destruction have been uncovered in the excavations; cf. L.E. Stager, *Ashkelon and the Archaeology of Destruction: Kislev 604 BCE*, in *J. Aviram Volume* (ErIs 25), Jerusalem 1996, p. 61*-74* (see p. 62*-67*).

[238] E.F. Weidner, *Jojachin, König von Judah, in babylonischen Keilschrifttexten,* in *Mélanges syriens ... R. Dussaud*, Paris 1939, Vol. II, p. 923-935, Pls. I-V (see p. 928).

[239] S. Gitin, *Last Days of the Philistines,* in *Archaeology* May/June 1992, p. 26-31 (see p. 30).

[240] See also here below, p. 159-160. Year 604 B.C., proposed by S. Gitin, *art. cit.* (n. 213), in *100 Years*, p. 75-76, can be safely excluded, since the Babylonian Chronicle for Nebuchadnezzar II's year 1 is preserved and only mentions Ashkelon. Ekron was too important to be simply omitted. As nothing proves that Nebuchadnezzar interrupted his Palestinian campaigns in 603 B.C. to cope with a rebellion in Babylonia, year 603 B.C. offers another possibility; cf. B. Porten, *art. cit.* (n. 62), p. 49; S. Gitin, *art. cit.* (n. 213), in *AASOR* 49 (1989), p. 46. In any case, it is unlikely that this occurred after 595 B.C., as suggested by N. Na'aman, *Nebuchadnezzar's Campaign in Year 603 B.C.E.,* in *BN* 62 (1992), p. 41-44.

[241] M. Dothan - Y. Porath, *op. cit.* (n. 149), p. 41, 57; M. Dothan, *art. cit.* (n. 26).

[242] *ANET*, p. 308a.

[243] E. Lipiński, *The Egypto-Babylonian War of the Winter 601-600 B.C.,* in *AION* 32 (1972), p. 235-241. See also J. Quaegebeur, *À propos de l'identification de la 'Kadytis' d'Hérodote avec la ville de Gaza,* in K. Van Lerberghe - A. Schoors (eds.), *Immigration and Emigration within the Ancient Near East. Festschrift E. Lipiński* (OLA 65), Leuven 1995, p. 245-270.

[244] The general note of II Kings 24, 7, placed between the sections dealing with Jehoiakim and Jehoiachin, should refer to year 598 B.C. and thus indicate that this date marks the end of Egyptian presence north of the Wādī al-'Arīš.

[245] K. Radner (ed.), *PNA* I/1, Helsinki 1998, p. XIX.

world in which Philistia had prospered. The destructions caused by the Babylonian army in the Philistine city-states and the deportation of the productive core of their population brought about a terrible blow from which the Philistine culture never recovered.

Culture and religion

If Philistia was initially a kind of "amphictyony"[246], this was no more the case in Iron Age II, when strong assimilation with the native Canaanite population had already taken place and the institution of *sərānīm* replaced by dynastic monarchies, like in the Phoenician city-states. This is shown clearly by the Ekron dedicatory inscription with names of five rulers: Akayos, son of Padi, son of Yasod, son of Ada, son of Ya'ar[247]. Thanks to the Assyrian inscriptions, a similar genealogy can be reconstructed at Ashkelon: Sharru-lu-dari, son of Rukibtu, son of Mitinti. Despite the Semitic names of almost all the rulers of the Philistine city-states and the use of a Canaanite dialect with a variant of the Phoenician script, a distinct Philistine material culture survived until the 6th century B.C., even with local variations in the pottery and art objects. The urban development of the cities is remarkable, with formidable fortifications, appearing in the 9th-8th centuries, and an orthogonal town planning attested at Tell Qasile as early as the 10th or early 9th century and found later at Timnah and possibly at Ekron, in the 7th century B.C.

A housing quarter was unearthed at Tell Qasile with houses, workshops, and storehouses. The houses were square and built to a standard plan with an area of about 100 m^2 per dwelling. The latter comprised two rectangular rooms with a central courtyard, divided in two by a row of wooden pillars. One part was roofed, the other open. This plan, known as the "four-room house", appears in Iron Age II in the northern kingdom of Israel, sometimes in Judah, and apparently also in Edom, at Tell al-Kheleifeh.

The economic wealth and vitality of Philistia, that brought about the urban renaissance, lasted almost to the end of the 7th century B.C. They

[246] B.D. Rathjen, *Philistine and Hebrew Amphictyonies*, in *JNES* 23 (1964), p. 100-104.

[247] S. Gitin - T. Dothan - J. Naveh, *art. cit.* (n. 13). The "Homeric" interpretation of these names by A. Demsky, *On the Inscription of Ekron*, in Qadmoniot 31 (1998), p. 64-65 (in Hebrew), is unconvincing: *'kyš* = Anchises, *Pdy* = Pandion, *Ysd* = Hesiod, *'d'* = Idaios.

are demonstrated in the excavated industrial quarters at Ashdod, Ekron, Timnah, while Bēth-Shemesh was most likely depending then from Judah. The produce of the specialized olive oil industry, developed during the 7th century B.C. at the three last-mentioned sites[248], had to be exported, possibly through Ekron's coastal outpost at Meṣad Ḥashavyahu[249]. The Greek and Eastern Greek pottery found there in a well-planned fortress[250] parallels the same kind of fine wares imported to Ekron[251] and Timnah[252], while Hebrew ostraca from that site indicate that Judaean corvée workers, possibly native from territories given by Sennacherib to the Philistine king, were put at work there by the royal administration[253].

If the political and civic institutions of the Philistines are hardly known, we are somewhat better informed about their religion, although *Ptgyh* is the only non-Semitic deity of the Philistines so far attested[254]. She is very likely Πελαγία, the well known epithet of Aphrodite "Marine"[255]. The spelling *Ptgyh* of the Ekron inscription again reflects the Anatolian alternation of *t/d* and *l*[256] in the notation of the speech sounds inherited by the Philistines in their home country. The worship of this goddess among Philistines is so far documented in the 7th century B.C. by the large temple complex 650, which has been uncovered at

248 See above, p. 83-85.

249 A. MAZAR, *op. cit.* (n. 216), *Timnah (Tel Batash)* I, p. 9. Imported pottery recovered in the destruction level of Meṣad Ḥashavyahu indicates that this was an active settlement in the second half of the 7th century B.C.; cf. A. FANTALKIN, *Meẓad Ḥashavyahu: Its Material Culture and Historical Background*, in *Tel Aviv* 28 (2001), p. 3-165, in particular the conclusions on p. 128-136, but without entering in the speculations on the precise date of the destruction.

250 J. NAVEH, *The Excavations at Meṣad Hashavyahu. Preliminary Report,* in *IEJ* 12 (1962), p. 89-113, Pls. 9-12. Further literature in J. NAVEH, *Hashavyahu, Mezad,* in *NEAEHL*, Jerusalem 1993, Vol. II, p. 585-586.

251 S. GITIN, *art. cit.* (n. 213), in *AASOR* 49 (1989), p. 40 and 44-45, No. 8.

252 A. MAZAR, *op. cit.* (n. 44), p. 534.

253 N. NA'AMAN, *The Kingdom of Judah under Josiah,* in *Tel Aviv* 18 (1991), p. 3-71 (see p. 47). However, there is no evidence that this administration was appointed by the king of Judah, when Judah was subject to Egypt. No remains have been found at Meṣad Ḥashavyahu which could point to an Egyptian control of the fortress. Cf. J. NAVEH, *art. cit.* (n. 250), p. 99, n. 16, and here below, p. 156.

254 See the royal inscription from Ekron; cf. here above, n. 13. A different reading of the name (*Ptnyh*) and an interpretation *Potnia*, "Mistress", were proposed by A. DEMSKY, *The Name of the Goddess of Ekron A New Reading*, in *JANES* 25 (1997), p. 1-5; ID., *On the Inscription of Ekron*, in *Qadmoniot* 31 (1998), p. 64-65 (in Hebrew). The new reading is untenable palaeographically and the interpretation "Potnia" lacks, therefore, any support.

255 J. SCHMIDT, *Pelagia* 1., in *PW* XIX/1, Stuttgart 1937, col. 228.

256 See here above, p. 53, n. 22.

Ekron[257]. The date of its foundation is somewhat in doubt, because the inscription of Akayos, king of Ekron in the second quarter of the 7th century B.C., cannot provide an absolute date for the building of the sanctuary. The verb *bn*, used in line 1, can mean "he built", but also "he rebuilt", "he restored"[258]. The inscription was found among the destruction debris of Stratum IB[259] and no reason is given why it should be dated from the beginning of Stratum IC[260]. According to the excavators, there was continuous occupation from Stratum II to Stratum IC, at least on the upper part of the mound. Neither the passage from Stratum II to Stratum IC nor the distinction of Stratum IC and Stratum IB in the temple area are sufficiently clear. The same must be said about the date of the foundation of the temple of Pelagia, the more so because N. Na'aman suggests to date Stratum IC from the mid-8th century B.C.[261] Besides, the question whether this temple was preceded at the site by an earlier shrine remains unanswered. Yet, the side-rooms of the sanctuary contained a treasure of precious items, some quite old as an ivory knob with the cartouche of Ramesses VIII, while a cartouche of Merneptah was found at the entrance of the temple.

The other deities worshipped by the Philistines according to literary sources bear Semitic names and cannot be identified in the present state of our knowledge with any deity of the "Sea Peoples". Beside *Ptgyh*, we can only rely on archaeological sources[262].

Three terms designate the sanctuary in short epigraphs on jar fragments found next to the temple complex in Stratum IB, dating to the late 7th century B.C.[263] Two are Semitic, viz. *mqm* and *'šrt*, the third one

[257] S. GITIN - T. DOTHAN - J. NAVEH, *art. cit.* (n. 13), p. 3-8.

[258] This goes against the opinion of P. JAMES, *The Date of the Ekron Temple Inscription. A Note,* in *IEJ* 55 (2005), p. 90-93.

[259] S. GITIN - T. DOTHAN - J. NAVEH, *art. cit.* (n. 13), p. 7.

[260] S. GITIN - T. DOTHAN - J. NAVEH, *art. cit.* (n. 13), p. 16.

[261] N. NA'AMAN, *Ekron under Assyrian and Egyptian Empires,* in *BASOR* 332 (2003), p. 81-93.

[262] A good survey of the earliest period is provided by A. MAZAR, *The Temples and Cult of the Philistines*, in E.D. OREN (ed.), *The Sea Peoples and Their World: A Reassessment*, Philadelphia 2000, p. 213-232.

[263] S. GITIN, *Seventh Century B.C.E. Cultic Elements at Ekron,* in *Biblical Archaeology Today, 1990*, Jerusalem (1993), p. 248-258 (see p. 250-252); ID., *Tel Miqne-Ekron in the 7th century B.C.E. The Impact of Economic Innovation and Foreign Cultural Influences on a Neo-Assyrian Vassal City-State*, in S. GITIN (ed.), *Recent Excavations in Israel: A View to the West,* Dubuque, Iowa, 1995, p. 57-79 (see p. 72-73); ID., *The Neo-Assyrian Empire and Its Western Periphery: The Levant, with a Focus on Philistine Ekron*, in S. PARPOLA - R.M. WHITING (eds.), *Assyria 1995*, Helsinki 1997, p. 77-103 (see p. 98 and 102, Fig. 22); ID., *art. cit.* (n. 213), in *Mediterranean Peoples in Transition*, p. 175 and 179, Fig. 16.

must be Philistine, probably *⸢ṣ⸣q⸢n⸣dš*. They are always introduced by the preposition *l*: "belonging to / for the sanctuary".

The phrase *lmqm* echoes the Hebrew use of *māqōm* in the sense of "holy place", "sanctuary". This connotation is commonly acknowledged in phrases like "*māqōm* of Shechem" (Gen. 12, 6), "*māqōm* of Yahwe" (Jer. 7, 12; Ps. 132, 5), "*māqōm* of the Name of Yahwe" (Is. 18, 7), also "the *māqōm*"[264]. Besides, *māqōm* occurs frequently in the Deuteronomistic formulas "the *māqōm* which Yahwe has chosen" or *hammāqōm hazzeh*, "this *māqōm*"[265].

The ending *-t* of the second term *'šrt* suggests a Phoenician origin, while the Hebrew word would have been *'*^{a}*šērāh*. This common noun, attested in Akkadian (*aširtu, ešertu, išertu*), Phoenician (*'šrt*), Aramaic (*'trt*), and Hebrew with the meaning "sanctuary", is confounded by several authors with the theonym *'Āṯ(i)ratu*[266]. Such confusions seem to witness an inadequate knowledge of Semitic grammar and vocabulary, of literary sources, and of religious history. This question does not need to be discussed in the present context.

The third term, probably *⸢ṣ⸣q⸢n⸣dš*, is most likely Philistine. It ends in *-š* like Philistine personal names[267] and the common noun *pilegeš*, close to Greek παλλακίς and Latin *paelex*, "concubine". The first letter is partly preserved and the visible shaft suggests a *ṣade* rather than a *ḥeth*, as there is no trace of the cross-lines. The element *ṣq-* is apparently related to Greek σηκ-, Indo-European **tuaq*, "(sacred) enclosure", while *-nd-* seems to be the Anatolian suffix *-ant-*, which has several functions[268]. One of them consists in forming collective nouns, like *parnant-*, "farm", from *parna-*, "house"[269]. The element *-ant-* appears as -ανδ- or *-nd-* in Greek and Aramaic notations of the first millennium B.C., as shown by *Santa*, written Σανδα, or *Ḫant-*, indicated as Κανδ-/Κενδ-

264 Gen. 22, 8-9; 28, 11.19; II Kings 5, 11; Ezra 8, 17; cf. A.H.J. GUNNEWEG, *Esra* (KAT XIX/1), Gütersloh 1985, p. 150.

265 J. GAMBERONI, *māqôm*, in *ThWAT* IV, Stuttgart 1984, col. 1113-1124 (see col. 1121-1123).

266 E. LIPIŃSKI, *Athirat*, in *Encyclopaedia of Religion*, 2nd ed., Vol. I, New York 2005.

267 See here above, p. 66 ff.

268 J. FRIEDRICH, *Hethitisches Elementarbuch*, 2nd ed., Vol. I, Heidelberg 1960, §48; E. LAROCHE, *Études de toponymie anatolienne*, in *RHA* 16/69 (1961), p. 57-98 (see p. 73 ff.); ID., *Un 'ergatif' en indo-européen de l'Asie Mineure*, in *Bulletin de la Société de Linguistique* 57 (1962), p. 23-43 (see p. 23 ff.); M. POPKO, *Ludy i języki starożytnej Anatolii*, Warszawa 1999, p. 69.

269 M. POPKO, *loc. cit.* (n. 268). The distinction between *-ant-* and *-and-* is somewhat problematic, and many Anatolian place names in *-and-* seem to express a collective notion: Arnuw-anda, Aryk-anda, Cary-anda, Kur-anda, Law-anda, Marass-anda, Milawanda, Oino-anda, Saluw-anta, Zippal-anda.

and *Ḥnd-/Knd-*. In fact, "by the regular voicing of stops after nasals in at least Lycian and Lydian and probably throughout first-millennium Anatolia, an original **-nt-* would result in [*-nd-*]"[270]. The noun *ṣqndš* thus seems to designate a "sacred precinct", a "holy place", like Greek σήκωμα.

The full inscription reads *qdš l*⸢*ṣ*⸣*q*⸢*n*⸣*dš*, a phrase paralleled by *qdš l'štrt*, "holy thing belonging to / for the sanctuary". Similar phrases occur in Hebrew, thus *qdš* ... *lkhn(ym)*, "holy thing belonging to / for the priest(s)" (Numb. 6, 20; Ez. 45, 4). Instead, the inscription *qdš khnm lby*[*t Yhw*]*h*, " holy thing of the priests belonging to / for the House of Yahwe", is a modern forgery, engraved on a ceremonial pomegranate in ivory, dating back to the Late Bronze Age[271]. Even the syntax of the inscription is awkward and seems to reveal a second thought of the engraver, eager to mention the priests as well as the temple of Yahwe. This probably reflects a modern and lucrative approach.

The excavations at Tell Qasile have revealed another Philistine cultic centre with three successive temples[272]. To date, it is the only one that can be dated to the first centuries of the Philistine settlement in Canaan, since no definite proof of the cultic character of Building 350 at Ekron has been provided so far. The earliest sanctuary at Tell Qasile consisted of a small brick chapel with a raised platform, on which the statue of the deity probably stood, and with benches for offerings along the walls. East of the structure[273], a broad courtyard with layers of ash and animal bones evidenced the sacrificial activity. In a second phase, a minor shrine was built near the main temple. The resulting plan exactly parallels the disposition of the later temple complex at Ekron, where a large courtyard occupies the space east of the main sanctuary, while a chapel stands in its south-western corner, next to the main structure. The major architectural features at Ekron record the Phoenician temples of Citium on Cyprus. The courtyard enclosed by a portico closely parallels the Cit-

[270] H.C. MELCHERT, *The God Sanda in Lycia?*, in P. TARACHA (ed.), *Silva Anatolica. Anatolian Studies Presented to Maciej Popko*, Warsaw 2002, p. 241-251, quotation from p. 243-244, n. 17; cf. H.C. MELCHERT, *Anatolian Historical Phonology*, Amsterdam-Atlanta, 1994, p. 300 and 356.

[271] Y. GOREN *et al.*, *A Re-examination of the Inscribed Pomegranate from the Israel Museum*, in *IEJ* 55 (2005), p. 3-20. Cf. A. LEMAIRE, *Une inscription paléo-hébraïque sur grenade en ivoire*, in *RB* 88 (1981), p. 236-329 and Pls. V-VI; N. AVIGAD, *The Inscribed Pomegranate from the "House of the Lord"*, in *The Israel Museum Journal* 8 (1989), p. 7-16.

[272] A. MAZAR, *art. cit.* (n. 262), p. 215-223.

[273] See the plan in S. GITIN, *art. cit.* (n. 27), in *Mediterranean Peoples in Transition*, p. 177, Fig. 11.

First Philistine sanctuary at Tell Qasile
(Archive photo of the excavation by A. Mazar).

ian temenos of temple 1 with porticos whose roof was supported on rows of pillars[274], and Ekron's pillared sanctuary appears as a facsimile of the Citian main shrine, especially in Floor 2a, the beginnings of which are dated to *ca.* 800 B.C.[275]

Among the cult objects found at Tell Qasile, two types of clay figurines decidedly continue a Mycenaean tradition. One type of figurines, called "Ashdoda" due to the discovery of a complete example at Ashdod, schematically represents a goddess seated on a chair[276]. The second type shows mourning women with hands on their head[277]. The abundant ritual vessels either continue Canaanite artistic traditions or indicate connections with the Aegean and Cyprus.

Several Philistine cemeteries have been uncovered and a variety of burial practices have been observed: single graves dug into the ground,

[274] V. KARAGEORGHIS, *Kition: Mycenaean and Phoenician Discoveries in Cyprus*, London 1976, p. 98-99.

[275] *Ibid.*, 138-139, Fig. 19, cf. p. 173.

[276] T. DOTHAN, *op. cit.* (n. 48), p. 234-237; A. MAZAR, *Some Aspects of the "Sea Peoples'" Settlement*, in M. HELTZER - E. LIPIŃSKI (eds.), *Society and Economy in the Eastern Mediterranean (c. 1500-1000 B.C.)* (OLA 23), Leuven 1988, p. 251-260, especially p. 259-260; A. MAZAR, *art. cit.* (n. 44), p. 223-224.

[277] T. DOTHAN, *op. cit.* (n. 48), p. 237-239; A. MAZAR, *op. cit.* (n. 44), p. 324, fig. 8.16.

rectangular cists, "coffins" made by joining two large jars, a praxis well attested in Late Bronze Age Anatolia[278]. Some evidence for cremation was found at Azor, but the extent of this burial custom among the "Sea Peoples" requires further research, that should take south-western Anatolian usages into account. The grotesque anthropoid coffins, used in Canaan in the 13th and early 12th centuries B.C., are not Philistine. They are local artefacts, inspired by Egyptian burial practices[279].

[278] H.H. von der Osten, *The Alishar Hüyük Seasons of 1930-32* II (OIP 24), Chicago 1937, p. 84-108; K. Emre, *Yanarlar: A Hittite Cemetery near Afyon*, Ankara 1978, in particular p. 123-137.

[279] A. Mazar, *op. cit.* (n. 44), p. 283-285. See also M.G. Hasel, *op. cit.* (n. 63), p. 110-111.

CHAPTER III

EGYPT AND CANAAN IN IRON AGE II

The collapse of the Egyptian empire in Canaan during Iron Age I does not mean that pharaohs have renounced to re-impose their control over that region. The traditional road to Canaan was partly blocked by the well equipped and warlike manhood of the Philistine pentapolis, but an impending threat of Egyptian invasion is often assumed on the basis of a fragmentary relief found by P. Montet at Tanis and of the topographical list of Shoshenq I.

Siamun

The Tanis relief represents a youthful king Siamun smiting an enemy kneeling before him[1]. This is a traditional iconographic pattern, but this particular scene shows the enemy holding the double axe with flaring crescentic blades[2]. Now, such an axe is of Aegean origin and can imply a link with the "Sea Peoples", in general, and with the Philistines, in particular, either as a symbol or as an actual weapon. As the warrior holds it not by its handle, possibly broken, but by its socket, the scene seems to signify that the foe is powerless against the king[3]. This scene does not prove that Siamun ran a victorious campaign against the Philistines, but the destruction of Dor *ca.* 980/970 B.C. according to the carbon-14 chronology[4] can be linked with the reign of this pharaoh (979/8-960/59 B.C.). The massive destruction deposits of Tel Dor, found in Stratum

[1] P. MONTET, *Le drame d'Avaris: Essai sur la pénétration des Sémites en Égypte*, Paris 1940, p. 196, Fig. 58; ID., *Tanis*, Paris 1942, p. 102-103, Fig. 26, and photograph in *Tanis. L'or des pharaons*, Paris 1987, p. 78. The fragment belonged to a building erected under Psusennes I (*ca.* 1039-991 B.C.) and completed by Siamun.

[2] The photograph shows that this is no 8-shaped Hittite shield, as sometimes assumed: B.U. SCHIPPER, *Israel und Ägypten in der Königszeit* (OBO 170), Freiburg-Göttingen 1999, p. 27; E. LIPIŃSKI, *"Sea Peoples" and Canaan in Transition c. 1200-950 B.C.*, in *OLP* 30 (1999), p. 1-35 (see p. 22). See here p. 97.

[3] K.A. KITCHEN, rev. in *BiOr* 58 (2001), col. 379. More comments on this fragmentary relief are provided by K.A. KITCHEN, *Egyptian Interventions in the Levant in Iron Age II*, in W.G. DEVER - S. GITIN (eds.), *Symbiosis, Symbolism, and the Power of the Past*, Winona Lake 2003, p. 113-132 (see p. 118-121).

[4] Cf. lately A. GILBOA - I. SHARON - J. ZORN, *Dor and Iron Age Chronology: Scarabs, Ceramic Sequence and ^{14}C,* in *Tel Aviv* 31 (2004), p. 32-59, in particular p. 53.

XII of Area B1[1] and in Stratum IX of Area G[5], can indeed be dated from the time of Siamun and they could witness an Egyptian invasion. However, Iron Age I pottery uncovered at Dor does not reveal the presence of a settled "Sea People". The Sicals seen by Wenamon at Dor were either seamen or mercenaries, while the local governor, the *b3-dỉ-r*, was apparently the "deputy" of the king of Tyre. The Sicals of Southern Phoenicia probably intermingled later with the Canaanite population, as suggested by the cremation burials of Achzib.

A Siamun's scarab has nevertheless been recovered at Dor, but it belonged to a necklace found in Stratum VII of Area G, thus lost about 900 B.C.[6], with no direct relation to the assumed Siamun's campaign *ca.* 975 B.C. In the same period, the relatively small (*ca.* 8 ha), unfortified Philistine city of Ashdod was destroyed (Stratum XI)[7], as well as the Philistine settlement of Tell Qasile (Stratum XI)[8]. The same events have possibly marked the end of the equally unwalled town of Stratum V at Ekron (Tel Miqne)[9]. While Ashdod seems to have been abandoned for a short period, perhaps Ekron as well, Tell Qasile and Dor were rebuilt. The floors sealing this destruction stratum at Dor and denoted by pottery from the mid-10th century B.C. very likely represent the new city, which is characterized by an assemblage of cultic vessels[10].

Another destruction followed after a few decennia. Above Strata XI-X of Dor Area B[1], archaeologists encountered a thick layer of ash,

[5] E. STERN - J. BERG - I. SHARON, *Tel Dor, 1988-1989: Preliminary Report*, in *IEJ* 41 (1991), p. 46-61, especially p. 58-60; E. STERN - I. SHARON, *Tel Dor, 1992: Preliminary Report*, in *IEJ* 43 (1993), p. 126-150, especially p. 149-150; E. STERN - J. BERG - A. GILBOA - I. SHARON - J. ZORN, *Tel Dor, 1994-1995: Preliminary Stratigraphic Report*, in *IEJ* 47 (1997), p. 29-56, especially p. 42, n. 25, and p. 52-55.

[6] S. MÜNGER, *Egyptian Stamp-Seal Amulets and Their Implications for the Chronology of the Early Iron Age*, in *Tel Aviv* 30 (2003), p. 66-82; A. GILBOA *et al.*, *art. cit.* (n. 4), p. 34-55.

[7] I. FINKELSTEIN - L. SINGER-AVITZ, *Ashdod Revisited*, in *Tel Aviv* 28 (2001), p. 231-259 (see p. 238-239); ID., "*Ashdod Revisited*" - *Maintained*, in *Tel Aviv* 31 (2004), p. 122-135 (see p. 125-127), in response to D. BEN-SHLOMO, *The Iron Age Sequence of Tel Ashdod*, in *Tel Aviv* 30 (2003), p. 83-107 (see p. 91-95).

[8] Comp. A. MAZAR, *Qasile, Tell*, in *NEAEHL*, Jerusalem 1993, Vol. IV, p. 1204-1212 (see p. 1211).

[9] S. GITIN, *The Philistines: Neighbors of the Canaanites, Phoenicians and Israelites*, in D.R. CLARK - W.H. MATTHEWS (eds.), *100 Years of American Archaeology in the Middle East*, Boston 2004, p. 57-85 (see p. 60). For the lack of fortification in the early Iron Age Strata VII-IV of Ekron, see D. USSISHKIN, *The Fortifications of Philistine Ekron*, in *IEJ* 55 (2005), p. 35-65.

[10] E. STERN, *Dor - Ruler of the Seas*, Jerusalem 1994, p. 92; E. STERN - I. SHARON, *Tel Dor, 1993: Preliminary Report*, in *IEJ* 45 (1995), p. 26-36, especially p. 28.

Siamun's fragment from Tanis
(Photo: P. Montet's excavations).

resulting from the strong fire that burned to red the bricks of the town. The accumulation of some 2 m of burnt debris was sealed by the floors above, in which Cypriot and Phoenician vases of the later 10th and early 9th century B.C. were found. The transitional Stratum IX yielded a potsherd with a rim fragment of a Euboean cup, characterized by a scribbled zigzag on the lip and datable to the second half of the 10th century

B.C.[11] This second destruction could thus be linked with Shoshenq I's invasion of Canaan, although a Phoenician attack, possibly by Hiram I, king of Tyre (*ca.* 950-917 B.C.), cannot be excluded. At any rate, Dor is not mentioned in the preserved sections of Shoshenq I's list of toponyms. In the same period, Tell Qasile was destroyed in another mighty conflagration[12], which could be related to a Shoshenq I's campaign. The site lies only at a distance of 28 km from Gezer, which was burnt in the same years[13], not at the time of Siamun, whose name is often associated to the biblical passage of I Kings 9, 16, where an unnamed pharaoh is said to have captured the town of Gezer, burnt it down, and given it with his daughter's hand in marriage to Solomon[14].

Gezer, in fact, appears to have been destroyed in the 10th century B.C., so much easier that it was then unfortified, like Tell Qasile and other Philistine cities. However, the unburnished red slip pottery of the concerned Strata X-IX suggests a date closer to the end of the 10th century and the pharaoh who burnt Gezer should thus be identified with Shoshenq I[15]. The attempt at relating the destruction of Gezer to the hypothetical political relationship between Siamun and Solomon cannot be justified factually, since Siamun's death most likely precedes Solomon's accession. The first need is to have the chronology right.

Authors slavishly following the Deuteronomistic scheme of forty regnal years ascribed in the Bible to David and Solomon seem not to understand that "forty years" are just a symbolic indication of a life-long reign, and to forget that the middle life expectancy in Antiquity is esti-

[11] N. COLDSTREAM, *Some Aegean Reactions to the Chronological Debate in the Southern Levant,* in *Tel Aviv* 30 (2003), p. 247-258 (see p. 253-255). Cf. E. STERN, *New Finds from Dor concerning the Establishment of the First Phoenician City-State at the Site* (in Hebrew), in *F.M. Cross Volume* (ErIs 26), Jerusalem 1999, p. 176-185 (see p. 183, Fig. 16).

[12] Tell Qasile Stratum X was destroyed in the early Xth century B.C. according to A. MAZAR, *Excavations at Tell Qasile* I-II (Qedem 12, 20), Jerusalem 1980-85; T. DOTHAN - I. DUNAYEVSKY - A. MAZAR, *Qasile, Tell,* in *NEAEHL*, Jerusalem 1993, Vol. IV, p. 1204-1212 (see p. 1211). The dating is probably too high; it is certainly much too high in A. BEN-TOR - D. BEN-AMI, *Hazor and the Archaeology of the Tenth Century B.C.E.*, in *IEJ* 48 (1998), p. 1-37 (see p. 33).

[13] There is no circumstantial evidence of a conquest of this area by David, as assumed, for instance, by A. MAZAR, *Archaeology of the Land of the Bible: 10,000-580 B.C.E.*, New York 1990, p. 311, 374.

[14] J. ČERNÝ, *Egypt: From the Death of Ramesses III to the End of the Twenty-First Dynasty,* in *CAH* II/2, 3rd ed., Cambridge 1975, p. 606-657 (see p. 656-657), followed by E. LIPIŃSKI, *art. cit.* (n. 2), p. 22.

[15] I. FINKELSTEIN, *Gezer Revisited and Revised,* in *Tel Aviv* 29 (2002), p. 262-296 (see p. 282-283). The reply of W.G. DEVER, *Visiting the Real Gezer: A Reply to Israel Finkelstein*, in *Tel Aviv* 30 (2003), p. 259-282, does not deal with Strata X-IX.

mated at about twenty-five or thirty years. There were no annals extant from the time of Solomon and the length of his reign was thus unknown to the Deuteronomistic historiographers. Since a regnal period within one generation is generally estimated at 22 to 27 years, a modern historian can only assume with some likelihood that the reigns of David and Solomon lasted together about fifty years[16] and that Solomon's reign represented a span of time hardly longer than twenty-five years, perhaps only twenty years. In the period concerned, the Twenty-second Libyan Dynasty provides an eloquent illustration of the average span of a reign, since its ten kings reigned about 230 years. With 926/5 B.C. probably corresponding to Rehoboam's fifth year (I Kings 14, 29), 931/0 was the likeliest year of Solomon's death and *ca.* 956/5 or 951/0 his likely accession year[17]. Instead, the 19-year reign of Siamun falls close to 979/8-960/59 B.C. and an independent reign of 14/15 years seems required for Psusennes II, *ca.* 960/59-945 B.C.[18] The accession of Shoshenq I falls then to 945 B.C., which means that his reign coincided closely with fifteen Solomon's regnal years. Thus, chronologically, Shoshenq I is the best candidate for having been the pharaoh that took Gezer and married off a daughter to Solomon.

Campaigns of Shoshenq I in Canaan

The military campaigns carried out by Shoshenq I in Canaan are recorded at Karnak by a scene carved on the outer wall of the so-called Bubastite Portal. "The king is shown in the conventional manner, towering over a group of kneeling enemy chieftains, grasping them by the hair with his left hand and raising his mace to slay them with his right hand. Beyond the captives are figures of Amun and, on a smaller scale, the goddess Wast, the former presenting the scimitar of victory to the king. Both deities hold five cords which are attached to the necks of Asiatic

[16] Even "sixty years", once proposed by the writer (rev. in *Chronique d'Égypte* 76 [2001], p. 160), seems to be a too long period. In fact, David spent several years in the service of king Saul and of the Philistines, while Solomon became king when his father was already quite old (I Kings 1, 1-4). For a recent attempt at justifying a Solomon's reign of approximately forty years, see L.K. HANDY, *On the Dating and Dates of Solomon's Reign,* in L.K. HANDY (ed.), *The Age of Solomon*, Leiden 1997, p. 96-105.

[17] This would be confirmed by the Tyrian king-list, as presented by JOSEPHUS FLAVIUS, *Against Apion* I, 18, §121-126. Cf. E. LIPIŃSKI, *Ba'li-Ma'zer II and the Chronlogy of Tyre,* in *RSO* 45 (1970), p. 59-65 (see p. 62-65), but see here below, p. 166-174.

[18] K.A. KITCHEN, *The Third Intermediate Period in Egypt (1100-650 B.C.)*, 3rd ed., Warminster 1995, p. 465, and in M. BIETAK (ed.), *The Synchronization of Civilizations in*

captives. The bodies of the captives, arranged in ten rows, are in the form of oval enclosures, nine of which bear the names of Egypt's traditional enemies and the reminder names of places of Palestine conquered by the king"[19].

Authors dealing with this important document, dating from the end of Shoshenq I's life, regard it as the record of a single campaign, mentioned in I Kings 14, 25-26 and II Chron. 12, 2-4.9. Instead, the fact that the inscription of the Bubastite Portal does not date the scene by the corresponding year in the reign of Shoshenq I (*ca.* 945-924 B.C.) and that the topographical list opens with the names of the "Nine Bows" indicate that the scene is supposed to give a global vision of the victorious campaigns led by the pharaoh during the twenty-one years of his reign. It is clear from the layout and content of the inscription that several expeditions are meant, in various parts of Palestine and most likely in different years. This interpretation is confirmed by the allusion to Shoshenq I's Asiatic wars on the fragmentary El-Hiba relief[20], which can hardly refer to a single campaign of the pharaoh at the very end of his reign.

The title "copy of A[siatics]" (No. 10) on the Bubastite Portal refers to the represented captives. It is followed by a first group of towns (Nos. 11-13 and 24-26), which opens apparently with Gezer (*g*[*ḏr*]), formerly read Gaza (*g*[*ḏt*]), and further mentions five towns in the vicinity of Gezer[21]. This group may refer to the first Palestinian campaign of Shoshenq I, alluded to in I Kings 9, 16. Uncertain is the reason why such expedition was undertaken. If it was aimed at weakening the Philistine cities, it was largely unsuccessful, since none of them is recorded among the towns captured by the pharaoh. The unwalled town of Gezer was an easy target, but keeping an Egyptian enclave at Gezer was a hazardous enterprise and this was the probable reason why Shoshenq I gave it with his daughter's hand in marriage to Solomon, possibly *ca.* 935 B.C.

the Eastern Mediterranean during the Second Millennium B.C., Wien 2000, p. 29-42.

[19] I.E.S. EDWARDS, *Egypt: From the Twenty-Second to the Twenty-Fourth Dynasty,* in *CAH* III/1, 2nd ed., Cambridge 1982, p. 534-581, quotation from p. 545.

[20] E. FEUCHT, *Relief Scheschonqs I. beim Erschlagen der Feinde aus El-Hibe,* in *SAK* 9 (1981), p. 105-117 and Pl. II.

[21] N. NA'AMAN, *Israel, Edom and Egypt in the 10th Century B.C.E.*, in *Tel Aviv* 19 (1992), p. 71-93 (see p. 79-80 with n. 8). The readings are based on the copies made during the epigraphic survey conducted at Karnak by the Oriental Institute of Chicago: *Reliefs and Inscriptions at Karnak.* Vol. 3. *The Bubastite Portal* (OIP 74), Chicago 1954. Some evident place names, like Megiddo, exclude the hypothesis of F. CLANCY, *Shishak/Shoshenq's Travels*, in *Journal for the Study of the Old Testament* 86 (1999), p. 3-23, who limits Shoshenq's campaign to the Judaean Shephelah.

Detail from the Bubastite Portal of Shoshenq I (Karnak).

This diplomatic marriage creates no problem in the 10th century B.C. Its dismissal on anachronistic grounds[22] is rightly criticized by K.A. Kitchen[23]. Not only Psusennes II (960/59-945 B.C.) gave the hand of his daughter Makare to a foreign noble, Osorkon, the son of the Libyan chief of the Meshwesh, before the latter took the Egyptian throne as Shoshenq I, but Shoshenq I and his successors repeatedly gave their daughters in marriage to prominent commoners[24], all the more so to foreign kings. As for Solomon's building activity at Gezer, alluded to in I Kings 9, 17 after the mention of his marriage with a pharaoh's daughter, it seems to be confirmed, at least to a certain extent. A dating was attempted on the basis of the red-slipped, irregularly burnished pottery, which appears in Stratum VIII (*ca.* 935-835 B.C.) on the floors of the six-chambered gate and of "Palace 10,000", west of the gate[25]. However, this analysis does not provide precise absolute dates and assumes that the Solomonic building activity at Gezer preceded the destruction of the

[22] B.U. SCHIPPER, *op. cit.* (n. 2), p. 84-107.
[23] K.A. KITCHEN, rev. in *BiOr* 58 (2001), col. 380-381.
[24] K.A. KITCHEN, *op. cit.* (n. 18), p. 479, Table 12, and p. 594.
[25] Cf. the meticulous analysis of this pottery by J.S. HOLLADAY, *Red Slip, Burnish, and the Solomonic Gateway at Gezer*, in *BASOR* 277-278 (1990), p. 23-70.

city by Shoshenq I. In fact, the defence system of Stratum VIII suggests three successive building phases. The earliest one, which could date from the last years of Solomon's reign, should be represented by the six-chambered gate, constructed of large field stones, and by a casemate wall, flanking the gate but probably not surrounding the entire settlement[26]. The enclosure was thus not completed, probably because of the death of Solomon and of the splitting of the Monarchy. In a second phase, an "ashlar palace" was built somewhere on the tell, as well as an outer gate constructed of fine ashlar masonry and related to an "outer wall" with ashlar towers and ashlar-built sections[27]. Ashlars have also replaced some field stones in the facade of the six-chambered gate. These constructions may date from the early Omride period. In the third phase, reused ashlars, probably brought from the disused "ashlar palace", served to build a massive wall on the acropolis[28]. The works may have been interrupted here in the mid-9th century by an enemy assault that left destruction traces, mainly near the city gate.

Shoshenq I's campaign mentioned in I Kings 14, 25-26 and II Chron. 12, 2-4.9 is most likely the one that brought the pharaoh to Megiddo (No. 27), where he erected a monumental stele[29]. E.A. Knauf even suggests reading Nos. 28-31 on the Bubastite Portal as an epithet of Megiddo, written in a hieroglyphic transcription of a Canaanite or Hebrew sentence: "Megiddo (No. 27): Valiant is the hand of the King (Nos. 28-29). His Ma[jesty] showed favour upon them (Nos. 30-31)"[30]. It is clear from the toponyms of the Bubastite Portal that the objective of the expedition was the kingdom of Israel, not Judah and Jerusalem. The obvious explanation is that Shoshenq I was acting as an ally of Rehoboam, Solomon's son, in order to overthrow Jeroboam, despite the asylum that was granted to him in Egypt until Solomon's death (I Kings 11, 40; 12, 2-3). Of course, Shoshenq I's intervention was paid largely

[26] I. FINKELSTEIN, *art. cit.* (n. 15), p. 284. No new elements are provided by W.G. DEVER, *art. cit.* (n. 15), p. 268-269.

[27] The line of the "outer wall" is adapted to the position of the pre-existing six-chambered gate: A. KEMPINSKI, rev. in *IEJ* 22 (1972), p. 185; D. USSISHKIN, *Notes on Megiddo, Gezer, Ashdod, and Tel Batash in the Tenth to Ninth Centuries B.C.*, in *BASOR* 277-278 (1990), p. 71-91 (see p. 75); cf. I. FINKELSTEIN, *Penelope's Shroud Unravelled: Iron II Date of Gezer's Outer Wall Established*, in *Tel Aviv* 21 (1994), p. 276-282.

[28] I. FINKELSTEIN, *art. cit.* (n. 15), p. 284-285.

[29] D. USSISHKIN, *art. cit.* (n. 27), p. 71-74. Contrary to the opinion of F. CLANCY, *art. cit.* (n. 21), and others, it is certain that the stele was erected by Shoshenq I: K.A. KITCHEN, *The Shoshenqs of Egypt and Palestine*, in *Journal for the Study of the Old Testament* 93 (2001), p. 3-12.

[30] E.A. KNAUF, *Shoshenq at Megiddo,* in *BN* 107-108 (2001), p. 31.

by Rehoboam (I Kings 14, 26; II Chron 12, 9). Deuteronomistic historiographers apparently found this information in the annals of Rehoboam (I Kings 14, 29), but they incorrectly deduced from this notice that Shoshenq I's campaign had been directed against Jerusalem[31], which is not even mentioned on the Bubastite Portal. As for the account of II Chron 12, 2-12, it is an elaboration by the Chronicler, based on the Book of Kings[32]. The addition of the Sukkites and Cushites (II Chron. 12, 3) reflects his usual misconception of real history and confirms his tendency to add the Cushites, where they do not belong to[33]. As for the Sukkites, probably mentioned in the 5th century B.C. on an ostracon from Elephantine (*Sky*')[34], one should stress that they simply cannot be identified with the Egyptian *Ṯktn*[35]. The provenance of the ostracon from a Persian garrison and the reference to the Persian official Rauka leave little doubt that the Sukkites in question are the Sakā of the Achaemenid inscriptions, sometimes named with the Cushites, like in II Chron. 12, 3, especially in the phrase: "from the Sakā, which are beyond Sogdiana, to Cush"[36]. The Chronicler obviously used information from the 5th-4th centuries B.C. to illustrate an event from the 10th century B.C.

Authors generally assume that Shoshenq I's army had crossed the Jordan south of the Jabboq, at Adam (No. 56), came to Succoth (No. 55) and continued eastward to Penuel (No; 53). This line of march - or the inverse one - is usually explained in the light of Jeroboam's fortification of Penuel (I Kings 12, 25), and confirms Shoshenq I's goal, which was to overpower Jeroboam.

The erection of the monumental stele at Megiddo, in an inhabited town, seems to indicate that Shoshenq I intended to hold the city and to revive the Ramesside control over the important trade route through the Jezreel Valley, establishing a centre of Egyptian power at Megiddo, but the reign of Shoshenq I came to an abrupt end and Egyptian sources shed no light on Osorkon I's (924-889 B.C.) relations with his eastern

31 N. NA'AMAN, *art. cit.* (n. 21), p. 85. The evidence provided by the toponymic list of Shoshenq I shows how erroneous is the whole approach of K.A. WILSON, *The Campaign of Pharaoh Shoshenq I into Palestine*, Tübingen 2005, who thinks that the campaign was aimed at supporting Jeroboam I in his bid to rule Israel as a separate state and that it was directed solely against the kingdom of Judah.

32 N. NA'AMAN, *art. cit.* (n. 21), p. 85-86.

33 II Chron. 12, 3; 14, 8.11-12; 16, 8; 21, 16.

34 *TAD* IV, D7.24, 3.

35 This obsolete and dull identification is stated again by K.A. KITCHEN, *op. cit.* (n. 18), p. 295, n. 289-292; ID., rev. in *BiOr* 58 (2001), col. 382. It was rightly ignored by U.B. SCHIPPER, *op. cit.* (n. 2).

36 E. LIPIŃSKI, *Sukkiens*, in *DEB*, Turnhout 1987, p. 1221-1222, with further literature.

neighbours. Like his father, he gave a bust of himself to the king of Byblos, Elibaal, who followed the example of Abibaal by dedicating the figure to the Lady of Byblos[37]. The gifts show that the kings were on friendly terms and most likely indicate that trade connections were maintained between Egypt and Phoenicia which, among others, exported timber from the Lebanon woods. One can expect therefore that kings of the Twenty-second Dynasty also tried to keep open the land route through the Jezreel Valley, but earlier evidence is so far missing. Instead, archaeological data show that a number of major structures at Megiddo were burnt or wilfully destroyed, while the superimposed Stratum IVA radically differs from the previous city of Stratum VA-IVB. At least some of the destructions may be ascribed to the recapture of Megiddo by one of the kings of Israel, *ca.* 900 B.C.

Nos. 66-150 of Shoshenq I's topographical list mention settlements situated to the south and southwest of Judah, beyond the borders of the kingdom. It is quite clear that military operations in this area could not be conducted by the king in the same season as the campaign in central Palestine and in the Jabboq Valley. It probably antedates the attack on Israel in the fifth year of Rehoboam. Its background may be revealed by a very fragmentary stele discovered at Karnak, which mentions a border incident that led to a severe retaliation by Shoshenq I[38]. The fragment did unfortunately not preserve the date of the reprisal, but it locates it on the shores of Kem-wer, one of the Bitter Lakes on the isthmus of Suez. It is likely therefore that the unnamed enemy was a tribe of the Negeb highlands which had penetrated in the eastern Delta. The retaliation - to be effective - had to go beyond the scene of the incident and strike the attackers in their own realm, in the Negeb.

This expedition could even have a second background, if the fragmented speech of Shoshenq I on the stele from Karnak alludes to a request by an official or ruler to come to restore order[39]. Since the campaign in the Negeb avoided crossing the southern borders of Judah, the request may have been sent to Shoshenq I also by Solomon in the last years of his rule. But this is so far a sheer hypothesis. At any rate, the expedition aimed also at displaying pharaoh's might in the Negeb, as shown by the many place names of this part of the list.

[37] See here below, p. 165-166.

[38] G. LEGRAIN, *Rapport sur les travaux exécutés à Karnak du 31 octobre 1902 au 15 mai 1903*, in *ASAÉ* 5 (1904), p. 1-43 (see p. 38-39); D.B. REDFORD, *Studies in Relations between Palestine and Egypt during the First Millennium B.C.* II: *The Twenty-Second Dynasty,* in *JAOS* 93 (1973), p. 3-17 (see p. 10); I.E.S. EDWARDS, in *op. cit.* (n. 19), p. 546; K.A. KITCHEN, *op. cit.* (n. 18), p. 294.

[39] D.B. REDFORD, *art. cit.* (n. 38), p. 10-11; K.A. KITCHEN, *op. cit.* (n. 18), p. 294.

Campaign of Shoshenq I in the Negeb

This largest segment of Shoshenq I's topographical list includes 85 name ovals, but 11 are completely destroyed[40] and there are at least 18 compound names requiring two or three ovals each. We are thus left with some 55 toponyms, 19 of which are more or less damaged[41]. The linguistic accuracy of the list is remarkable and its preparation is obviously the work of experienced scribes, probably having a knowledge of the "Negebite" language. Some variations in the spelling can be explained by the fact that the list is ultimately based on spoken language, not on written records, and that different scribes have probably registered the data from which the list was compiled. The list is of special importance also because it provides the only detailed enumeration of ancient settlements in the Negeb and contains information of linguistic, ethnic, and religious nature. Unfortunately, several places have not been identified so far, but some can be located with a fair degree of probability and others provide some valuable insights. The transcription of Egyptian spellings, given below, will be in general reasonably complete and accurate in an attempt at avoiding eventual misinterpretations. However, not all distinctively transcribed hieroglyphs have preserved their particular phonemic value in the first millennium B.C. For instance, *z* and *ś* then had an approximate sound-value *s*, and *ṯ* was pronounced like *t*, except in traditional orthography, which hardly plays a role in Shoshenq's text. The list uses several generic terms: these will be examined first, before analyzing the particular place names.

The word *ḥ-q-r*[42] or *ḥ-g-r*[43] appears eight times in the list and obviously corresponds to Hebrew *ḥāṣēr*, Old Arabian and Arabic *ḥẓr*, Aramaic *ḥṭr*, Ugaritic *ḥṭ̱r*, "enclosure", "sheepfold", hardly "farm", and never "fort", "fortress". It has been erroneously equated with the West Semitic noun *ḥgr*, which literally designates what is reserved, prohibited, inaccessible, walled off. Hence *ḥ-q-r* / *ḥ-g-r* was often mistranslated "fortress"[44]. As well known, however, Egyptian *q* (*ḳ*) and *g* are

[40] Nos. 113-115, 138, 141-144, 147-149.

[41] Nos. 79, 81-83, 116, 118-120, 125, 129-138. The article by I. FINKELSTEIN, *The Campaign of Shoshenq I to Palestine. A Guide to the 10th century BCE Polity,* in *ZDPV* 118 (2002), p. 109-135, hardly contains any new constructive elements concerning the Negeb campaign (p. 113-117).

[42] Nos. 68, 71, 77, 87, 107.

[43] Nos. 94, 96, 101.

[44] B. MAZAR, *Cities and Districts in Eretz-Israel*, Jerusalem 1976, p. 132-138 (in Hebrew). Cf. J.E. HOCH, *The Supposed* Ḥgr *"Fort" in Negeb Place Names of the Shishak Toponym List*, in A. HARRAK (ed.), *Contacts between Cultures* I, Lewiston-Queenston 1992, p. 262-266.

used regularly to mark Semitic /γ/, for instance in *Q-ḏ-t* and *G-ḏ-t*, "Gaza". Now, etymological *ṯ* in certain phonetic contexts tends to be pronounced as /γ/ in Ugaritic[45] and probably in other Semitic languages of the Late Bronze and Early Iron Ages. Since pharyngealization characterized the emphatic phonemes in ancient Semitic, like in present-day Arabic, this accessory feature of the phoneme could under certain conditions supplant the basic character of the interdental fricative *ṯ*. This was apparently the case in the "Negebite" language spoken at the time of Shoshenq I, just as it happened in Ugaritic.

The noun *ḥ-q-r* / *ḥ-g-r* is preceded seven times in Shoshenq's list by the sign *p3* and it is then followed by the proper name of the enclosure, like Hebrew *Ḥăṣar Gaddāh*, *Ḥăṣar 'Ēnān*, *Ḥăṣar Šū'āl*, etc. It is used once without *p3*, but with the ending *-m*, interpreted as the desinence of the absolute masculine plural by M. Noth[46]. B. Mazar suggested then that *ḥ-q-r-m* should introduce the two following toponyms[47], but N. Na'aman argued that *Ḥ-q-r-m* was an independent place-name with the suffix *-aim*[48]. However, the diphthong *-aim* would have been indicated in Egyptian, while the "recumbent lion"-sign currently has the phonetic value *rw*. It rather suggests the reading *ru* or *rū*, although this is no firm rule. *Ḥ-q-r-m* seems thus to be a singular with mimation, like Sabaic *Ḥẓrm*[49] or *'I-d-m-m* further in the topographical list (Nos. 98, 128). In fact, mimation was extensively used in Old Arabian proper names and we may assume that this was the case also in "Negebite", which exhibits some Old Arabian features. At any rate, each name ending in *m* must be judged on its merits without having recourse to "shorthands".

Four places are said to be *ỉ-d-r-ỉ*, which is obviously *'iddar(u)*, "threshing floor"[50], a synonym of *g-r-n-ỉ* (No. 127). These names pro-

[45] C.H. GORDON, *Ugaritic Textbook*, Roma 1965, p. 27-28, §5.8-10; LIPIŃSKI, *Semitic*, §10.9. The uvular articulation of *ṯ* was probably occasioned by the phonetic structure of roots containing sonorants, such as /m/ and /r/ in the case of *ḥṯr*; cf. E. GREENSTEIN, *On a New Grammar of Ugaritic*, in *IOS* 18 (1998), p. 397-420 (see p. 404); H. GZELLA, rev. in *BiOr* 62 (2005), col. 311. For correct readings of Ugaritic *ṭ*, when etymological *ṯ* is not expressed by *ġ*, see D. FREILICH - D. PARDEE, *{ẓ} and {ṭ} in Ugaritic: A Re-examination of the Sign-Forms,* in *Syria* 61 (1984), p. 25-36.

[46] M. NOTH, *Die Wege der Pharaonenheere in Palästina und Syrien IV. Die Schoschenk-Liste,* in *ZDPV* 61 (1938), p. 277-304 (see p. 296) = M. NOTH, *Aufsätze zur biblischen Landes- und Altertumskunde* II, Neukirchen-Vluyn 1971, p. 73-93 (see p. 87).

[47] B. MAZAR, *The Campaign of Pharaoh Shishak in Palestine*, in P.A.H. DE BOER (ed.), *Congress Volume. Oxford 1959* (VTS 7), Leiden 1960, p. 57-66 (see p. 64-65).

[48] N. NA'AMAN, *Arad in the Topographical List of Shishak,* in *Tel Aviv* 12 (1985), p. 91-92.

[49] HARDING, *Arabian Names*, p. 193.

[50] Nos. 100, 116, 117, 146.

vide an important indication of agriculture practiced at least by some of the semi-nomadic clans of the Negeb. Such threshing places were located in an enclosure, as shown by the toponym *Ḥṣr-'dr* in Numb. 34, 4 and possibly by the compound name of Nos. 100-102 in Shoshenq's list.

The generic term *ḥ3-y-d-b3* appears twice in the list (Nos. 103, 105). Since *ḥ* and *ḫ* have merged in "Negebite", as shown by the theonym *Y-w-r-ḥ-m*[51], while Egyptian *d* may correspond to West Semitic *ṭ*, the word in question seems to be a *fay'al / fay'āl* derivative of *ḫṭb*, "precinct wall" in Old Arabian[52]. The same nominal pattern is used for Old Arabian toponyms like Bayḥān, Daydān, Ġaymān, Ḫaybar, Mayfa'at, Raydān, Šayhad, Taymān, etc., and for the Moabite city name Ḏaybān (*Dybn*).

Two places are characterized as *'-rw-d-ỉ* (Nos. 108, 110), too quickly identified with Tell 'Arad despite the two attestations of the name, followed by a qualification. The noun *'rd* is probably related to Neo-Assyrian *ḫarādu*, "to watch", and to the Palmyrene plural *'rdyn*[53]. This word appears in a military context and could mean "watch post"[54], like Greek φυλακή or φυλακτήριον. It is not attested in Hebrew and Shoshenq's list must here use the "Negebite" term of the semi-nomadic population living in the area concerned during the early Iron Age. The "recumbent lion" hieroglyph (*rw*) of the list does not require *per se* the vowel *u*, but we shall see that Josephus Flavius mentions a town Ἄρυδδα. For the sake of simplicity, we shall nevertheless follow the usual transcription *'-r-d-ỉ*.

The Arad of the Madaba map can be a third "Watch post" of the region[55]. The mosaic gives this name to a *castrum* situated half-way between Beersheba and Asemona. It would seem therefore that this is the *castrum* with the St. George hospital mentioned *ca.* 570 A.D. by the

[51] See here below, p. 123.

[52] M.A. GHŪL, *Early Southern Arabian Languages and Classical Arabic Sources*, Irbid 1993, p. 121-126.

[53] H. SEYRIG, *Antiquités syriennes 8. - Trois bas-reliefs religieux de type palmyrénien*, in *Syria* 13 (1932), p. 258-266 and Pls. LV-LVII (see p. 259-260 and Pl. LVI); J. CANTINEAU, *Tadmorea* I, in *Syria* 14 (1933), p. 169-202 (see p. 178-180 with a facsimile of the inscription). The reading was corrected by J.T. MILIK, *Inscription araméenne en caractères grecs de Doura-Europos et une dédicace grecque de Cordoue*, in *Syria* 44 (1967), p. 289-306 (see p. 295, n. 1). The corrected reading is not taken into account by D.R. HILLERS - E. CUSSINI, *Palmyrene Aramaic Texts*, Baltimore 1996, PAT 2757, line 2.

[54] The translation "catapult", proposed in *DNWSI*, p. 887, following J.T. MIILK, *loc. cit.* (n. 53), is based on Arabic *'arrādat*.

[55] Greek Αραδ may also transcribe *ḥarad*, "narrow pass"; cf. LIPIŃSKI, *Itineraria Phoenicia*, p. 317.

Antonini Placentini Itinerarium, which locates it 20 Roman miles south of Elusa (al-Ḫalaṣa)[56], but without giving its full name. This should bring us to Subeita, which was a Nabataean and Byzantine town[57]. However, it is surprising that the city does not appear on the map under its own name and that the picture indicates a *castrum*, while the site shows no evidence of fortifications. Josephus Flavius refers to a place in the Negeb, called Ἄρυδδα and followed by Ἄλουσα and Ὤρυβδα[58]. Ἄλουσα is no doubt Ḫalaṣa, *ΕΛΟΥϹΑ* on the Madaba map, Ὤρυβδα is *'Ōrḥ-'Ubda*, "Way(-station) of Oboda", thus 'Abda[59], and Ἄρυδδα must be a fort near the Naqb al-'Arūd, possibly Ḥorvat Qaṣra, situated on the summit of a hill and used in Nabataean and Roman times as a watchtower and way-station along the ancient road leading from Petra to Gaza[60]. These features are precisely matching the etymological meaning of *'rd*. The spelling *ΑΡΑΔ* of the Madaba map may be based on the Septuagint, where Αραδ is mentioned next to Ασεμωνα in Numb 34, 4[61].

A further Arad possibly appears in an Edomite ink inscription on a large jar from the mid-7th century B.C., found at Umm al-Biyāra, near Petra. The inscription was deciphered by J.T. Milik[62], but the third letter of line 2 seems to have a rather long down-stroke and to be *r* instead of *d*, which is legless or short-legged in Edomite script[63]. One can thus read:

šmn.r[ḥṣ/qḥ.••]	"Pure/Fragrant oil, [a jar?],
m'rd?.m['n?]	from the 'Arad of M[a'ān?],
bd. •••.bn?•[••]	through N, son of N".

[56] *Antonini Placentini Itinerarium* 35, in *Itineraria et alia geographica* (CCSL 175), Turnhout 1965, p. 146-147.

[57] Grid ref. 114/032: A. NEGEV, *Sobata*, in *NEAEHL*, Jerusalem 1993, Vol. IV, p. 1404-1410.

[58] JOSEPHUS FLAVIUS, *Jewish Antiquities* XIV, 1, 4, §18. These toponyms close a list of places conquered by Alexander Yannai (103-76 B.C.) on the Nabataeans. Although A. SCHALIT, *Alexander Yannai's Conquests in Moab*, in *M. Schwabe Volume* (ErIs 1), Jerusalem 1951, p. 104-121 (in Hebrew), locates them all in Moab, the last three names should be identified as sites west of the Arabah, as done by ABEL, *Géographie* II, p. 148.

[59] The identification is confirmed by the discovery of coins of Alexander Yannai at the site: A. NEGEV, *The Architecture of Oboda. Final Report* (Qedem 36), Jerusalem 1997, p. 1.

[60] Grid ref. 1585/9966: R. COHEN, *Negev Emergency Survey,* in *IEJ* 32 (1982), p. 163-165 (see p. 163-164).

[61] The masoretic text reads *'Addar*, possibly alluding at 'Ain al-Qudeirat: ABEL, *Géographie* I, p. 340. In fact, the Targum Yerushalmi identifies *'Aṣəmōn* with *Qysm*, the 'Ain al-Quṣeima: ABEL, *Géographie* I, p. 306; II, p. 47, 254-255.

[62] J.T. MILIK, in C.-M. BENNETT, *Fouilles d'Umm el-Biyara,* in *RB* 73 (1966), p. 372-403, Pls. XIV-XXV (see p. 398-399, Pl. XXIIa).

[63] L.G. HERR, *The Formal Scripts of Iron Age Transjordan,* in *BASOR* 238 (1980), p. 21-34 (see p. 30). Edomite inscriptions now provide more examples of the letter.

The jar was sent from a place called *'rd.m*[••], which must have laid on a caravan route. The element "Arad" was apparently qualified by a name beginning with *M*, possibly Ma'ān, the large oasis on the pilgrims' route to Mecca, 33 km south-east of Umm al-Biyāra.

Several 'Arrad or 'Arrada, with long *r*, are known in Syria. There is a village 'Arrad south of Damascus[64] and there is an 'Arrada west of the city[65]. In northern Syria, Tell 'Arrada[66] is probably the site of uru*A-ri-di* (genitive), mentioned in Neo-Assyrian texts[67]. The long *r* creates no problem for the identification of the Syrian toponyms with the biblical one, since long or geminated *r* does not appear in Hebrew.

Three names of Shoshenq's list are introduced by the determinative *p3 n-g-b*[68], which parallels the Hebrew appellations "the *negeb* of Judah", "the *negeb* of Caleb", "the *negeb* of the Jeraḥme'elites", "the *negeb* of the Kenites", "the *negeb* of the Kerethites" (I Sam. 27, 10; 30, 14), "the *negeb* of Arad" (Judg. 1, 16), probably "the *negeb* of Ziqlag" (I Sam. 30, 1)[69]. Most of these places were supposed to have been raided and plundered by David's men or by the "enclosure-men", the *'ămālēqī*[70]. Such a context indicates that the word is etymologically related to the Amorite and Ugaritic verb and noun *ngb*[71]. We read in a Mari letter: *ṣa-bu-šu ṣí-di-tam na-gi-ib*[72], "his army is supplied with victuals". The Hittite-Akkadian bilingual of Hattushili I (*ca.* 1550-1520 B.C.) from Boghazköy mentions the *ṣabē* (ZAB.MEŠ) *nagbāti*, "the troops (which have been) supplied"[73]. At Ugarit, we find: *'dn ngb*[74], "a wealth of supplies", and *ṣb'i / ṣb'a ngb*[75], "the army (which has been) sup-

[64] DUSSAUD, *Topographie*, p. 322, n. 5.

[65] DUSSAUD, *Topographie*, p. 395, n. 8.

[66] DUSSAUD, *Topographie*, p. 497 and Map XV, A, 1.

[67] LIPIŃSKI, *Aramaeans*, p. 126. One should keep here in mind that Hurro-Urartian *arde* means "city".

[68] Nos. 84, 90, 92.

[69] The absence of the article before *ngb* indicates that the word was used initially in the construct state and that *w'l* has been added before *Ṣqlg*, when the meaning of *ngb* was no longer understood. On the various pre-Judaean populations of the region, one can see D. JERICKE, *Die Landname im Negev. Protoisraelitische Gruppen im Süden Palästinas. Eine archäologische und exegetische Studie*, Wiesbaden 1997.

[70] See here below, p. 368, 370.

[71] The North-West Semitic lexeme *ngb* is closely related to Akkadian *nagbu*, meaning "entire amount" of something, not "totality" in the absolute sense. This is well explained by J. SILVA CASTILLO, *Nagbu: Totality or Abyss in the First Verse of Gilgamesh*, in *Iraq* 60 (1998), p. 219-221.

[72] Ch.-F. JEAN, *ARM* II, 69, rev., line 6'.

[73] H.H. FIGULLA, *Keilschrifturkunden aus Boghazköi* I, Berlin 1921, No. 16, III, 61-62. Cf. Th.H. GASTER, *The Canaanite Epic of Keret*, in *Jewish Quarterly Review* 38 (1947), p. 285-293 (see p. 290).

[74] *KTU* 1.14, II, 32; IV, 13.

[75] *KTU* 1.14, II, 33; IV, 14.

plied". The *ngb* of Shoshenq's list and of the above mentioned biblical passages must thus be a "store", probably a compound or facility with supplies belonging to a semi-nomadic clan or tribe.

The earliest attestations of the word in Egyptian texts occur at the time of Tuthmosis III (*ca.* 1479-1425 B.C.). *Ngb* was perhaps regarded as a place name, but its meaning appears clearly in the autobiography of Amen-em-heb, an official in pharaoh's army[76]. In lines 3-5 of his inscription he boasts of "having plundered a storage (*n-g-b3*) area and taken three Asiatic men as living prisoners". The text does not specify the location of the region in question. The word *ngb* occurs also in the great topographical list of Tuthmosis III, where the toponym has been carved in two ovals: *n-g-b ỉ-š Š-ḫ-n*[77], "Store of the men of Šiḫān". The place is called *CEANA* on the Madaba map and can be identified with Ḫirbet Siḥān, 10 km south-east of Gaza[78]. Its name appears also in the Babylonian Talmud where it is spelled *Š'wn'* (*Šə'ōnā*)[79].

The original meaning of the word *ngb* is lost in later Hebrew texts, but the feminine participle *ngbh*, "supplying", is still attested in the Aramaic text of I Enoch 76, 8, where it is commonly mistranslated. The text can be restored confidently on the basis of the Ge'ez version: "[And through the next gate, the one in the middle, comes forth a wind], which they call **supplier** of dew, [rain, well-being, and life]". The concerned phrase is preserved in Aramaic: *dy qryn lh ngbh ṭl*[80], with the ancient West Semitic meaning of *ngb*. The feminine *ngbh* is used because the participle, followed by direct objects, qualifies *rwḥ*, "wind", which is a feminine noun.

Later Hebrew language uses *ngb* in the sense of "arid land". This word has no etymological link with the older *ngb* and is borrowed, probably through Aramaic, from Akkadian *nagbu*, "groundwater" reachable by digging wells in arid and semi-arid land, hence the meaning "dry soil" in Middle Aramaic and Late Biblical Hebrew, with derivatives. The Akkadian word *nagbu* is formed with the *ma-* > *na*-prefix[81] either

[76] The bibliography is given in *ANET*, p. 240b. Older literature is collected by R. De Langhe, *Les textes de Ras Shamra-Ugarit et leurs rapports avec le milieu biblique de l'Ancien Testament* II, Gembloux-Paris 1945, p. 122.

[77] List I, 57-58 in J. Simons, *Handbook for the Study of Egyptian Topographical Lists Relating to Western Asia*, Leiden 1937. The name suggests the presence of hot springs; cf. M. Bonechi, *Remarks on the III Millennium Geographical Names of the Syrian Upper Mesopotamia,* in *Subartu* IV/1 Turnhout 1998, p. 219-241 (see p. 221-222).

[78] Abel, *Géographie* II, p. 451.

[79] Babylonian Talmud, *Niddah* 65a.

[80] J.T. Milik, *The Books of Enoch*, Oxford 1976, p. 285.

[81] Lipiński, *Semitic*, §29.26.

from *kuppu*, "perennial source", paralleled by *gubbu*, when it means "groundwater", or from *gabbu*, "totality", when it is used in the sense of "entire amount". The first root is Afro-Asiatic, as shown by Egyptian *qbb-wt*, "groundwater".

The loanword *ngb*-II does not mean "desert" in Aramaic and Hebrew, but designates land with water beneath its surface, that can be reached by digging wells, thus "water-producing land". Water was drawn from the wells by hand, rope, and bucket or by various ingenious devices. The amount of water that could be obtained by such a method, even where the water was near the surface, was small by modern standards. Hebrew writers or redactors, certainly posterior to the early Persian period, used *h-Ngb* with a definitive article to designate such an "arid land", i.e. the southern region of Judah. The word is even attested with the plain sense "south", most likely from the end of the 4th century B.C. on[82].

Two names of Shoshenq's list are introduced by the word *š-b-p3-r-ṯ* (Nos. 73, 75). Its spelling suggests connecting it with Akkadian *šappalu*, "very low", *šuppulu*, "very deep", etc., Arabic *sufālat^{un}*, "lowest part", Sabaic *s^{1}fl*, "lowland", *s^{1}flt*, "low-lying fields", Hebrew *šəpēlāh*, "lowland". Geminated plosives happen to be dissimilated in the spoken language[83] and the Egyptian spelling might reflect such a dissimilation. However, an indubitable *b/p* equivalence is provided by the hieroglyphic spellings *K-b-n* and *K-p-n* of the name of Byblos, while scribal practice does not imply *per se* that *b-p3* corresponds to a geminated consonant. The final *-t* of the feminine noun was not dropped in "Negebite", which preserved it at least until the 10th century B.C., like Moabite did it down to the 9th century. Of course, the identification of the lowland in question

[82] In Ex. 27, 9; 36, 23; 38, 9, *negeb* duplicates the older designation *tēmānāh* of the southern side or direction. It seems that the Septuagint translation was made from a text established before the addition of *negeb*, "south". This meaning occurs quite often in Josh. 13-19, a composition of the late Persian period, by no means a compilation from late preexilic times, as stated by N. LISSOVSKY - N. NA'AMAN, *A New Outlook at the Boundary System of the Twelve Tribes*, in *UF* 35 (2003 [2004]), p. 291-332. The early monarchic period is proposed by A. DEMSKY, *The Boundary of the Tribe of Dan (Joshua 19, 41-46)*, in C. COHEN - A. HURVITZ - S.M. PAUL (eds.), *Sefer Moshe. The Moshe Weinfeld Jubilee Volume*, New York 2004, p. 261-284. Such approaches mean a step backward when compared with M. NOTH, *Überlieferungsgeschichtliche Studien*, 2nd ed., Tübingen 1957, p. 183-189; ID., *Das Buch Josua* (HAT I/7), 2nd ed., Tübingen 1953, p. 10-11. Cf. E. LIPIŃSKI, *The Territory of Tyre and the Tribe of Asher*, in ID. (ed.), *Phoenicia in the Bible* (Studia Phoenicia XI; OLA 44), Leuven 1991, p. 153-166. Of course, earlier sources have been used in Josh. 13-19, but they can hardly be identified, for such lists do not lend themselves easily to literary criticism and traditio-historical analysis.

[83] E. LIPIŃSKI, *Dissimilation of Gemination*, forthcoming.

cannot be based on the current Hebrew use of the toponym Shephelah, although the latter is already used in the *Onomasticon* of Amenemope (11th century B.C.).

The generic element of some place names has possibly been omitted by the scribes, but this can hardly be proved in particular cases. On the other hand, generic names can be used without further qualification. The best example is *'Ābēl*, in hieroglyphic script *ỉ-b-r*, "meadow", but *'ṭm* seem to be another, well-attested case. A few terms, apparently used also as generics, will be examined below.

The first toponym of the section, viz. *'ỉ-ḏ3-m-ỉ* (No. 66), has been equated with *'ṣm* in Josh. 15, 29; 19, 3; I Chron. 4, 29. It is obvious that this place name, as well as the *'ṣmwn* of Numb. 34, 4-5 and Josh. 15,4, cannot be related to Hebrew *'ṣm* (*'ṯm* > *'ẓm*), "bone"[84]. These toponyms derive from *'ṣm*, which gives in Arabic the verb *'aṣama*, "to safeguard", and in Sabaic the noun *'ṣm*, "safekeeping" obtained by offerings brought to a deity or a temple[85].

The root forms also place names, like *'ṣm-m*[86], identified as 'Uṣām (Yemen), 'Aṣim in the Hauran[87], and 'Aṣūm east of Tripoli (Lebanon), nowadays pronounced 'Aṣūn[88]. Biblical *'ṣm* has been localized at Ḫirbet al-A'ẓam, 25 km south-east of Beersheba and 10 km south of Bīr 'Ar'ara (Aroer)[89], in an area allotted to the tribe of Simeon. However, the Arabic place name just means "bigger ruin", it does not correspond phonetically to the hieroglyphic spelling, and other doubts about this identification have been expressed as well[90].

The second place *'I-n-m-r-ỉ* (No. 67) looks either like the Sabaic "broken" plural *'nmr*, which designates parts of a dam structure[91], or like the

84 M. NOTH, *op. cit.* (n. 82), p. 149: "Knochen", "Knochen(-Ort)".

85 Cf. K. CONTI-ROSSINI, *Chrestomathia Arabica Meridionalis Epigraphica*, Roma 1931, p. 211.

86 *CIS* IV, 307, 1-2.

87 DUSSAUD, *Topographie*, p. 372.

88 E. WARDINI, *Lebanese Place-Names* (OLA 120), Leuven 2002, p. 147, 302, 646. - JOSEPHUS FLAVIUS, *Jewish Antiquities* IX, 1, 4, §17, apparently read *b'ṣm gbr* instead of *b'ṣywn gbr* in I Kings 22, 49, since he translates "because of (their) huge mass". The same reading led possibly to the translation of Ezion-Geber by *Kərak Tarnəgōlā'*, "Fort of the Cock", in Targum Pseudo-Jonathan to Deut. 2, 8 and in the Targum to II Chron. 8, 17; 20, 36 (A. SPERBER, *The Bible in Aramaic* IVA, Leiden 1968, p. 40, 50), *'ṣm* being then understood as "safe place". *Geber* can mean "cocq", e.g. in the Mishnah, *Yōmā* I, 8, and in the Talmud (JASTROW, p. 208b).

89 ABEL, *Géographie* II, p. 51, 254.

90 S. AḤITUV, *Canaanite Toponyms in Ancient Egyptian Documents*, Jerusalem 1984, p. 93.

91 *CIS* IV, 329, 2; 337, 4.

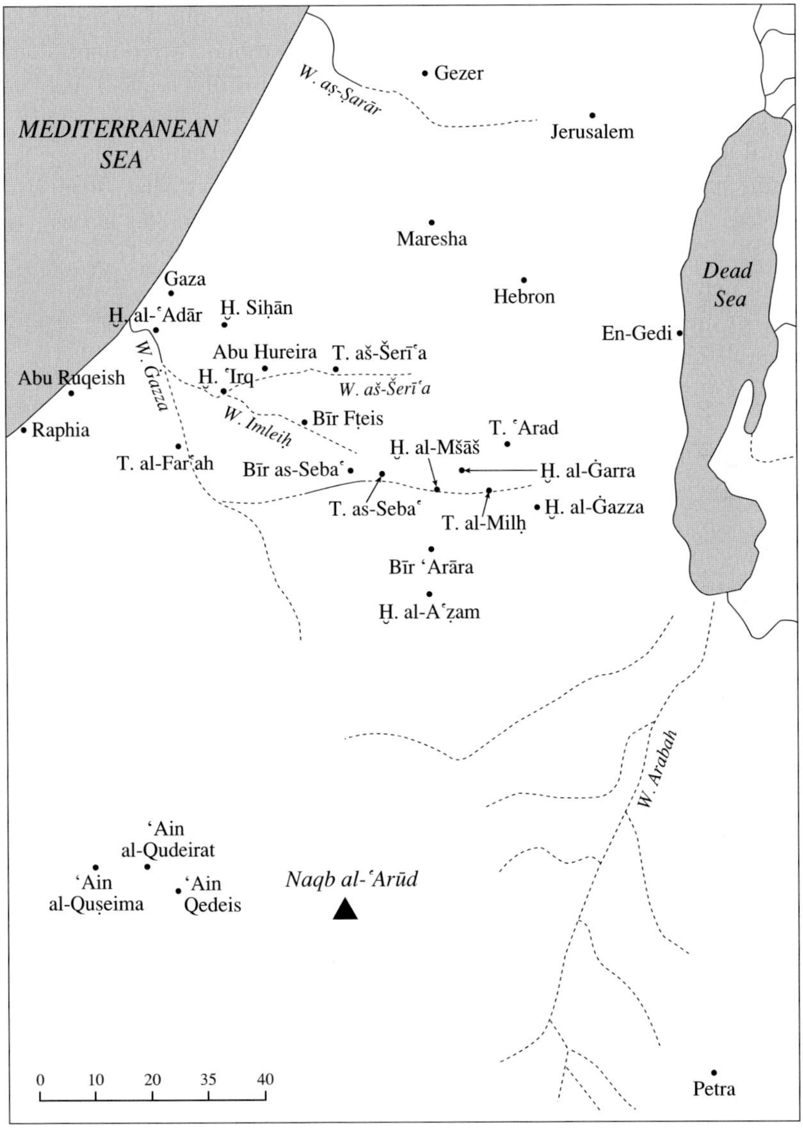
MEDITERRANEAN SEA
W. aṣ-Ṣarār
Gezer
Jerusalem
Maresha
Hebron
Dead Sea
En-Gedi
Gaza
Ḫ. al-ʿAdār
Ḫ. Siḥān
Abu Hureira
T. aš-Šerīʿa
W. aš-Šerīʿa
Abu Ruqeish
Ḫ. ʿIrq
W. Ġazza
Raphia
W. Imleiḥ
Bīr Fṭeis
T. ʿArad
T. al-Farʿah
Ḫ. al-Mšāš
Bīr as-Sebaʿ
Ḫ. al-Ġarra
T. as-Sebaʿ
T. al-Milḥ
Ḫ. al-Ġazza
Bīr ʿArāra
Ḫ. al-Aʿẓam
W. Arabah
ʿAin al-Qudeirat
ʿAin al-Quṣeima
ʿAin Qedeis
Naqb al-ʿArūd
0 10 20 35 40
Petra

Negeb.

Old Arabian tribal name *'nmr*, apparently a "broken" plural or an elative of *nmr*[92]. If it is a structure, the name may designate a series of stone walls or dams built across the shallow watercourse of a wadi[93]. Alternatively, channels or reservoirs might be intended. The Negebite site has not been identified, but the next place, Bīr Fṭeis, suggests localizing *'ṣm* and *'nmr* along the Wādī aš-Šerī'a or the Wādī Imleiḥ, where also underground water is abundant and good[94]. It is possible, in fact, to localize *P3 ḥ-q-r F-t-y-š-ỉ* (Nos. 68-69) with a fair degree of accuracy. This must be Bīr Fṭeis, the Φωτις of the Madaba mosaic, on the well-known track leading from Gaza to the Beersheba Valley. The nearby Tell al-'Uṣīfer provides evidence for Iron Age occupation[95].

The next name *'I-r-h-r-r* (No. 70) has been related to *Yəhallēl-'Ēl* in I Chron. 4, 16[96]. The doubts expressed by S. Aḥituv[97] are not entirely justified, because one should reckon with migratory movements of semi-nomadic clans, especially between the lowlands and the highlands. However, the two names are not identical and do not have the same meaning. Shoshenq's list probably refers to *'Āl-Hilāl*, the "Clan of the New Moon", which was still worshipped in the 6th century A.D. on the Sinai Peninsula[98]. Instead, the Calebite clan of I Chron. 4, 16 is called *Yəhallēl-'Ēl*, "Let (the clan) praise God", a name which may result from a deliberate change of *'Āl-Hilāl*. This tribal name is paralleled in the 7th century B.C. by ^{lú}*A'-lu ša* ^{d}*A-tar-sa-ma-a-a-in* [99]. The territory of the Negebite clan can be situated between Bīr Fṭeis and Tell as-Seba', mentioned in the following ovals.

Shoshenq's list provides the earliest attestations of the word *'āl*, "clan", in the first millennium B.C. (Nos. 70, 97, 126, 132), but there are many examples of this West Semitic term in the Mari archives from the

[92] HARDING, *Arabian Names*, p. 80 and 599-600, often with mimation.

[93] For such dams of desert farmers, cf. L.E. STAGER, *Farming in the Judean Desert during the Iron Age*, in *BASOR* 220-221 (1975-76), p. 145-158 (see p. 151-157).

[94] ABEL, *Géographie* I, p. 151.

[95] Y. AHARONI, *The Land of the Bible. A Historical Geography*, London 1967, p. 288; S. AḤITUV, *op. cit.* (n. 90), p. 111. Cf. ABEL, *Géographie* I, p. 151, 406; II, p. 89, 273, 409.

[96] Y. AHARONI, *op. cit.* (n. 95), p. 289. Such a comparison implies that a divine name *'Il* appears as the first element in toponyms. This unlikely opinion is expressed by N. NA'AMAN, *Israel, Edom and Egypt in the 10th Century B.C.E.*, in *Tel Aviv* 19 (1992), p. 71-93 (see p. 81).

[97] S. AḤITUV, *op. cit.* (n. 90), p. 92, n. 172.

[98] *Antonini Placentini Itinerarium* 38, in *op. cit.* (n. 56), p. 148-149.

[99] LIPIŃSKI, *Aramaeans*, p. 609-610 with references. Cf. I. EPH'AL, *The Ancient Arabs*, Jerusalem 1982, p. 162, 163, 166, 168.

17th century B.C. They are not distinguished orthographically from the Akkadian word *ālu*, "city", but already in 1957 J.-R. Kupper expressed his surprise at the frequent mentions of "cities" of nomadic or semi-nomadic tribes[100]. In such texts, *ālu* means "clan", eventually "camp". The use of the plural or of the suffix in "our *ālu*" or "your *ālu*" rather supports the first meaning. For instance, Baḫdi-Lim writes to the king: "The Ḫanaeans came back from the transhumance and dwell in the midst of the **clans** (*ālāni*)"[101]. Kibri-Dagan, governor of Terqa, complains about the Benjaminites: "I wrote to the **clans** (*ālāni*) of the Benjaminites and the sheikh of Dumtān answered me: 'Let the enemy come and take us away from our **clan**' (*ālīni*)"[102]. He even menaces them: "Whoever you are, should a man from your **clan** (*ālīka*) go to the Highland and you don't seize him and bring him to me, you will indeed not live!"[103]. There is a difference in the life conditions of the Negebites and of the semi-nomads of the Middle Euphrates, since the latter are closely monitored by a higher central authority. The word *'l* (*'āl*) appears often in Thamudic, Nabataean, and Ṣafaitic inscriptions, where it usually precedes the proper name of the tribe or clan.

We find further *P3 ḥ-q-r Í-b-r-m* (Nos. 71-72), where a word like "life stock" or "well" might be understood after *ḥ-q-r*, before the name *'Abrām*[104]. Contrary to *í-b-r* in No. 122, the *Í-b-r-m* cannot be explained as a "broken" plural with added mimation. As a rule, names of the *'f'l* pattern lack mimation in Old Arabian. One can assume that the same grammatical principle is applicable in "Negebite". Abram's tradition was of old linked to this area and a confirmation dated to the 10th century B.C. does not come as a surprise. The place in question was very likely Tell as-Seba' with the deep well hewn into the bedrock on the south-eastern slope of the mound[105]. "The Enclosure (of the flock/well) of Abram" would then correspond to the settlement of Strata IX-VIII rather than Stratum VII, which consisted of an oval line of attached dwellings of the four-room type.

[100] J.-R. Kupper, *Les nomades en Mésopotamie au temps des rois de Mari*, Paris 1957, p. 13-14, 56-57.

[101] *ARM* II, 48, 8-9.

[102] *ARM* III, 38, 15-22.

[103] *ARM* II, 92, 14-19.

[104] Cf. Gen. 13, 7; 21, 33. For this interpretation, see: W. Spiegelberg, *Ägyptologische Randglossen zum Alten Testament*, Strassburg 1904, p. 14; Abel, *Géographie* II, p. 89; S. Aḥituv, *op. cit.* (n. 90), p. 109.

[105] Z. Herzog, *Water Supply at Tel Beersheba,* in *Qadmoniot* 35 (2002), p. 87-101 (in Hebrew).

The next two place names are introduced each by *Š-b-p3-r-ṯ: Š-b-p3-r-ṯ n G-b-r-ỉ* (Nos. 73-74) and *Š-b-p3-r-ṯ w-r-k-y-t* (Nos. 75-76). Both places should be located in the valley east of Beersheba. The first one is qualified by a noun, *gbr* or *gbl*, the second one by an adjective meaning "outer", perhaps "upper", or the like. If *G-b-r-ỉ* stands for **gabbār*, "strong man", "ruler", the "Lowland of the Ruler" should correspond to Stratum III of Ḫirbet al-Mšāš, which in the 10th century B.C. was the main centre of the entire region[106] and covered an area of *ca.* 6 ha. The "Outer lowland" then designates the region situated farther from this centre, probably eastward, in the area of Tell al-Milḥ.

The next place is again an enclosure: *P3 ḥ-q-r n '-ḏ-y-tỉ* (Nos. 77-78). It cannot be located, but its name is identical to that of the Sabaean tribe of the Banū 'Uṯkulān 'Uṣayyat (*bnw 'ṯkln 'ṣyt*)[107]. The reading of No. 79 is uncertain, but one can read *Ḏ-p-q-ỉ* in No. 80. This place is commonly identified with Σαπεκ in the Septuagint addendum to I Sam. 30, 28a, but its location is unknown[108]. Nos. 81-83 are damaged and the doubtful reading *T-⌜p⌝-*[...] in No. 82 does not justify the identification of this place with Bēth-Tappuach near Hebron[109].

We are on more solid ground with a clan name introduced by *ngb: P3 n-g-b '-ḏ-ḥ-ṯ* or *P3 n-g-b '-ḏ-n-ṯ* (Nos. 84-85), pending on the reading of the horizontal hieroglyph over *ṯ* as a "tooth"-sign or a "tongue"-sign *ns* with a value *n*. In the second case, the 'Eznite clan of II Sam. 23, 8 could be referred to[110], but the *n*(*s*) reading is unlikely and the clan must therefore be considered unknown[111]. The toponym written *T-tỉw-šd-d-n-w* (No. 86) cannot be identified, but it offers an excellent sense, which reveals an aspect of the pastoral livelihood of the Negebite population and confirms the relation of their dialects to the languages spoken in Transjordan. The place name should be read *Taiš-dan*(*nu*), "Strong billy goat". It alludes to the leader of the flock, qualified by *dan*(*nu*). The adjective *dan*, "strong", does not occur in Hebrew, but it appears in Ammonite and Moabite proper names. We encounter *Kmš-dn*, "Chemosh is strong", in Moabite[112], and *'ly-dn*, "My god is strong", in Ammonite[113].

106 Z. HERZOG, *The Fortress Mound at Tel Arad: An Interim Report,* in *Tel Aviv* 29 (2002), p. 3-109 (see p. 87-88).

107 HARDING, *Arabian Names*, p. 407 and 424.

108 K.A. KITCHEN, *op. cit.* (n. 18), p. 440-441 with bibliography in n. 88.

109 I Chron. 2, 43; cf. S. AḤITUV, *op. cit.* (n. 90), p. 188.

110 Y. AHARONI, *op. cit.* (n. 95), p. 289.

111 S. AḤITUV, *op. cit.* (n. 90), p. 149.

112 N. AVIGAD - B. SASS, *Corpus of West Semitic Stamp Seals,* Jerusalem 1997, p. 380, No. 1030.

113 *Ibid.*, p. 335-336, No. 898, and p. 336-337, No. 902.

P3 ḥ-q-r Š-n-y-ỉ (Nos. 87-88) is attested as *Šūniy*, name of a "son" and clan of Gad, respectively in Gen. 46, 16 and Numb. 26, 15. The reading is clear and does not require any correction. It could point at a connection of the Negebite clan with Transjordan. *H-q-q* (No. 89) is unidentified and so far unexplained, but the name could exhibit a reduplicated root morpheme *haiq* > *hāq* with the assimilation **hāqhāq* > *haqqāq*. One should not forget that Shoshenq's list is based on records of a spoken language. Now, *haiq* is a designation of "ostrich" in Arabic.

P3 n-g-b w-h-ṯ-w-r-k (Nos. 90-91) bears a name interesting from the linguistic point of view, because it shows that "Negebite" has preserved the initial semi-vowel *w*, like Arabic, without changing it in *y*. This feature is still attested by the Negebite place name *'ltwld* in Josh. 15, 30; 19, 4[114], where *wld* appears, probably the "broken" plural *awlād*. The specific name in the list resembles the Arabic phrase *wahata wa-lakka*, "he pressed and crushed". Both roots *wht* and *lk* are attested in Old Arabian[115]. Nos. 90-91 of Shoshenq's list seem thus to designate a factory specialized in olive oil or wine production and storage. Wine seems logical, for grapes were commonly cultivated in the Negeb. Since neither afformatives nor preformatives are appended to *wht* and *lk*, these appear to be absolute infinitives suggesting a translation: "Store of pressing and crushing (olives/grapes)".

P3 n-g-b 'I-š3-ḥ3-t-ỉ (Nos. 92-93) occurs in I Chron 4, 11, where one should read *'ḥ Yšwḥh*. Like in other instances, Shoshenq's list preserves the final *t* of the feminine. *P3 ḥ-g-r Ḥ-n-n-ỉ* (Nos. 94-95) bears a widespread personal name. It can be related to Ben-Hanan in I Chron. 4, 20. The next compound toponym is *p3 ḥ-g-r 'I-r-q-d* (Nos. 96-97), where the proper name of the enclosure is probably *'Āl-Gad*, "Clan of Gad" (good fortune). This name is abridged in Josh 15, 27 to Ḥăṣar Gaddāh. Eusebius identified it erroneously with En-Gedi[116], while an equation with the Βεταγιδεα of the Madaba map was proposed by S. Aḥituv[117]. The latter place is Ḫirbet al-Ğindi, about 15 km east of Gaza[118], a location which is perhaps too westerly to fit Shoshenq's list at this point. At any rate, there is no phonetic connection with Ḫirbet al-Ġazza (Ḥorvat 'Uza), south-west of Rās Zuweira[119]. Instead, a relation to the Transjor-

[114] Cf. also I Chron. 4, 29 (*twld*) and see here below, p. 123 and 410.

[115] *CIS* IV, 604, 2.3.5 (*mwht*); *RÉS* 3610, 2 (*lkk*).

[116] EUSEBIUS OF CAESAREA, *Onomasticon*, in E. KLOSTERMANN (ed.), *Eusebius: Das Onomastikon der biblischen Ortsnamen*, Leipzig 1904, p. 68:18.

[117] S. AḤITUV, *op. cit.* (n. 90), p. 110.

[118] ABEL, *Géographie* II, p. 265.

[119] ABEL, *Géographie* II, p. 344.

danian tribe of Gad cannot be excluded, the more so because *P3 ḥ-q-r Š-n-y-ỉ* (Nos. 87-88) points in the same direction.

The next name is *'I-d-m-m* (No. 98). It occurs again as No. 128 and is spelled *'I-t-m-m* in the great topographical list of Tuthmosis III[120]. "Edomites" as toponym or tribal name in the 10th century B.C. is certainly no plausible guess. *'I-d-m-m* seems to be a generic designating a particular kind of structure and, as a rule, it should then be determined by a qualification. In this hypothesis, the second *m* can hardly be explained as the desinence of the plural or be regarded as a mimation. It could instead be the enclitic particle *-ma*, used with Amorite and Ugaritic nouns in the construct state[121], especially when these nouns are monosyllabic. Since hieroglyphic *d* and *t* can stand for Semitic *ṭ*, while *'ṭm* occurs in place names, one should take the word **'aṭmu* into consideration, when analyzing *'I-d-m-m / 'I-t-m-m*. The geography of al-Ya'qubi (9th century A.D.) mentions a place called al-Aṭmim in central Syria[122]. It is said to be an ancient city and corresponds to the present-day Tell Laṭmin[123]. In northern Syria, there is a village called Aṭma, also with ancient remains[124], and a toponym *'ṭmt* occurs in Sabaic inscriptions[125]. In Mishnaic Hebrew and in Aramaic, the root *'ṭm* designates something solid: *'ōṭem* is a substruction filled with earth[126], *'iṭmā* seems to be a dam[127], and *'aṭmātā də-šūrā* are apparently buttresses or piers of a wall[128]. These architectural connotations of the root suit a dam checking the flow of water in a wadi or a fortified place: an earth rampart with an eventual superstructure or piers buttressing a defence wall. Since No.

[120] List I, 36 in J. SIMONS, *op. cit.* (n. 77).

[121] LIPIŃSKI, *Semitic*, §33.16. For the enclitic *mēm* in Hebrew, see : C. COHEN, *The Enclitic-*mem *in Biblical Hebrew*, in C. COHEN - A. HURVITZ - S.M. PAUL (eds.), *Sefer Moshe. The Moshe Weinfeld Jubilee Volume*, New York 2004, p. 231-260.

[122] Y. AL-YA'QUBI, *Kitāb al-buldān*, in M.J. DE GOEJE (ed.), *Bibliotheca geographorum arabicorum* VII, Leiden 1892, p. 112; cf. G. LE STRANGE, *Palestine under the Moslems*, London 1890, p. 404.

[123] DUSSAUD, *Topographie*, p. 207-208 and Map VIII, B, 1.

[124] E. LITTMANN, *Zur Topographie der Antiochene und Apamene*, in *Zeitschrift für Semitistik* 1 (1922), p. 163-195 (see p. 174); DUSSAUD, *Topographie*, p. 224 and Map XII, B, 3.

[125] *RÉS* 4176, 3.

[126] Mishnah, *Middoth* IV, 6; *Parah* III, 6; cf. JASTROW, p. 24a and 43 .

[127] Babylonian Talmud, *Qiddushin* 70b.

[128] Babylonian Talmud, *Erubin* 57b. M. SOKOLOFF, *A Dictionary of Jewish Babylonian Aramaic of the Talmudic and Geonic Periods*, Ramat-Gan 2002, p. 107, translates *'aṭmā* by "foundation wall" and derives it from Aramaic *'ṭm'* (< *'ẓm*) "bone". This is unlikely, considering the frequent use of *'ṭm* in toponymy. The noun is a derivative of the same root as the verb *'ṭm*, "to stop up", "to keep back".

99 is a plain proper name *Ḥ-n-n-y* that can hardly stand on its own, *'I-d-m-m* can be regarded as a construct state with the enclitic *-ma*, unless *Ḥananiy* is used in apposition to a plural, admittedly an awkward construction. In both cases, one obtains a good place name, which unfortunately cannot be identified. The second *'I-d-m-m* (No. 128) could be explained in a similar way, as well as *'I-t-m-m* in Tuthmosis III's list, where *'I-t-m-m* is followed by *Q-ś-w-n* (No. 37), usually identified with *Qšywn* in the territory of Issachar[129]. However, a place name *'ṭmm* without any qualification cannot be excluded, as shown by al-Aṭmim and Aṭma, and this explanation is preferable at least in No. 128. One can also add here that the Septuagint transcription Οθομ of Hebrew *'tm* in Ex. 13, 20 could be inspired by *'ōṭem*, and we may even assume that *'yṭm* in I Chron. 4, 32 can stand for an original *'ṭm*. This place name of the territory allotted to Simeon would then witness the disappearance of the phonetic opposition between ' and ' in Late Biblical Hebrew[130].

Ḥ-n-n-y is followed by a "threshing floor", *'I-d-r-ỉ* (No. 100). One wonders whether this name should not be linked to the next place name *P3 ḥ-g-r Ṯ-rw-w3-n* (Nos. 101-102), thus: "threshing floor: Enclosure of Tolon" or "Tilon", but best "Tilwān", a settlement mentioned in I Chron. 4, 20. However K.A. Kitchen suggests identifying *'I-d-r-ỉ* (No. 100) with Ḥăṣar 'Addār (Numb. 34, 4)[131], located by Y. Aharoni at 'Ain Qadeis[132], 10 km south-east of 'Ain al-Qudeirat. This proposal is based on the passage of Numb. 34, 3-12, which is an addition to the "Sacerdotal Document" (P) of the Pentateuch[133]. Considering its use of *ngb* in the sense of "south" (Numb. 34, 3-4), it cannot be dated before the 4th century B.C. This dating logically concerns at least the whole section of Numb 33, 50-34, 29. Following Numb. 34, 3-4, one should identify Qadesh-Barnea with 'Ain Qadeis, Ḥăṣar 'Addār with 'Ain al-Qudeirat, and 'Aṣəmōn with al-Quṣeima, as confirmed by Talmud Yerushalmi[134]. In consequence, there is no reason why *'I-d-r-ỉ* (No. 100) should be identified with 'Ain Qadeis. Instead, it might refer to 'Ain al-Qudeirat, unless the next names refer to the area around this oasis.

[129] Josh. 19, 20; 21, 28.

[130] This is a more likely explanation than the pharyngealization '> ', which happens rarely. Cf. E.Y. Kutscher, *Studies in Galilean Aramaic*, Ramat-Gan 1976, p. 81-82.

[131] K.A. Kitchen, *op. cit.* (n. 18), p. 440, n. 96.

[132] Y. Aharoni, *op. cit.* (n. 95), p. 65.

[133] M. Noth, *Überlieferungsgeschichtliche Studien*, 2nd ed., Tübingen 1957, p. 192-195.

[134] See here above, p. 108 with n. 61.

We thus find side by side *Ḥ3-y-d-b-ỉ3 Š-r-n-r-ỉ-m* (Nos. 103-104) and [*Ḥ3*]*-y-d-b-ỉ3 Dỉ-w3-ṯ* (Nos. 105-106), two "precincts" (**ḥyṭb*). The first one seems to be called **Šarān Ri'm* or *Ar'ām*, a "broken" plural. *Š-r-n* has probably the same meaning as Hebrew and Moabite *Šrn*[135]. In the Negeb, the *r'm* is hardly a "wild ox" or "buffalo". It must be an "antelope", the addax or the Arabian oryx, a large size antelope with long horns and long tufted tail, probably referred to in Ps. 92, 11 and called *r'm*. The presence of such desert animals nevertheless implies the vicinity of perennial water courses or sources providing a water supply. This could be the case in the fertile valley watered by the 'Ain al-Qudeirat, where an enclosed settlement, erroneously called "early fortress", can be dated from the second half of the 10th century B.C.[136] This enclosure can then be the "Precinct of the Plain of Antelopes". The second specific *Dỉ-w3-ṯ* should be compared with the Sabaic tribal name *Dw't*[137]. If the Negebite tribe was living in the neighbourhood of 'Ain al-Qudeirat, one might point either at 'Ain Qadeis or at the so-called "Aharoni fortress" near 'Ain al-Quṣeima. An oval enclosed settlement of 42 m by 32 m existed at 'Ain Qadeis, possibly in the 10th century B.C.[138], and the enclosed settlement near 'Ain al-Quṣeima seems to go back to the same period[139]. The name **ḥyṭb* used for these two enclosures instead of **ḥṣ̱r* may witness a different dialect, spoken further to the south. One might object that the suggested locations are too southerly to fit Shoshenq's list at this point, but a small task-force could be dispatched to 'Ain al-Qudeirat, 'Ain Qadeis, and 'Ain al-Quṣeima to manifest the Egyptian presence there.

The next place names must belong to the Beersheba Valley and its surroundings. The independent toponym *Ḥ-q-r-m*, "Enclosure" (No. 107) without qualification, is followed by two place names designated as "Watch posts": *'-rw-d-ỉ Rw-b3-t* (Nos. 108-109) and *'-rw-d-ỉ n b-p3-ỉt-ṯ Y-w-r-ḥw-m* (Nos. 110-112). The usual simplified transcriptions are *'-r-*

[135] Mesha inscription, line 13.

[136] Grid ref. 0955/0062: R. Cohen, *Kadesh-Barnea. A Fortress of the Time of the Judaean Kingdom*, Jerusalem 1983, p. IX-XI.

[137] *CIS* IV, 407, 19; cf. Harding, *Arabian Names*, p. 245. The name might be related to Akkadian *dūtu*, "manliness", but this is only a guess.

[138] Grid ref. 1034/0002: R. Cohen, *'Ein Qedeis,* in *IEJ* 27 (1977), p. 171; Id., *Ain Qedeis - 1976,* in *RB* 85 (1978), p. 429. Y. Aharoni, *Forerunners of the* Limes*: Iron Age Fortresses in the Negev,* in *IEJ* 17 (1967), p. 1-17 (see p. 8), identified this site with *Ḥăṣar 'Addār* (Numb. 34, 4).

[139] Grid ref. 087/012: Z. Meshel, *The "Aharoni Fortress" near Quseima and the "Israelite Fortresses" in the Negev,* in *BASOR* 294 (1994), p. 39-67.

d-ỉ R-b-t and *'-r-d-ỉ n b-ỉ-t Y-w-r-ḥ-m*, as the use of the "tusk of elephant" (*ḥw*) does not involve any determined vowel. Most authors identify *'-r-d-ỉ* with Tell 'Arad, assuming that the place kept the name it was given in the Iron Age. This implies a continuous occupation of the surrounding area, at least by semi-nomadic populations. In fact, a village called Arad was still known to Eusebius of Caesarea[140], 20 miles from Hebron and 4 miles from Malḥata. This location fits Tell 'Arad inasmuch as it is about 30 km south of Hebron, but it is situated 13 km north-east of Tell al-Milḥ, i.e. 8 miles[141].

Regarding Shoshenq's list, no serious concern seems to have appeared in view of two distinct places called *'-r-d-ỉ*. The opinion regarding them as sites in the same neighbourhood is nevertheless unfounded, because the Egyptian scribes may have grouped compound names with the same generic element. Moreover, the commonly accepted translation of *'-r-d-ỉ r-b-t* by "Great(er) Arad" does not make much sense, if this was the name of the small village of Arad Stratum XII, the superficies of which is estimated at 0.5 ha. Besides, the common noun *'-r-d-ỉ*, "watch post", is most likely masculine and there is no reason why *r-b-t* should be a feminine adjective. As a rule, admittedly, place names are of the feminine gender, but a "greater watch post" does not seem to belong to this nominal category. In the best case, it can be compared with place names whose generic is *bēt*, "house", and those are masculine.

Some authors were upset by the absence of Arad in the biblical lists of settlements in southern Judah (Josh. 15, 21-32) and Simeon (Josh. 19, 1-9; I Chron. 4, 28-33), and thus changed the *'Eder* of Josh. 15, 21 into 'Arad[142]. However, the *Codex Alexandrinus* of the Septuagint identifies it with Εδραιν, shown on the Madaba map, that clearly supports its location at Ḫirbet al-'Adār, 7 km south of Gaza, on the right bank of the Wādī Ġazza[143]. The absence of Arad means probably that the redactors of the biblical lists incorporated material from a period when the generic meaning of *'rd*, "watch post", was still understood and in consequence the specific name was used[144].

140 E. KLOSTERMANN (ed.), *op. cit.* (n. 116), p. 14:2-3.

141 See here below, p. 399-400.

142 ABEL, *Géographie* II, p. 88, 248, 309; Y. AHARONI, *op. cit.* (n. 95), p. 298.

143 Cf. ABEL, *Géographie* II, p. 248, 309.

144 *B-ngb* in Josh. 15, 21, which indicates a date in the Late Persian period, must be a gloss added to "border of Edom". The opposite suggestion was made by M. NOTH, *Das Buch Josua* (HAT I/7), 2nd ed., Tübingen 1953, p. 88. For Josh. 13-19, see also here above, p. 111, n. 82.

In passages based on aetiological accounts, Arad is associated to Ḥormah, thus in Numb. 21, 1-3 and Josh. 12, 14. Now, Ḥormah is preceded in the biblical lists by *Bt*(*w*)'*l*[145], attested under various spellings, as Bethul (Josh. 19, 4), Bethuel (I Chron. 4, 30), and Bethel (I Sam. 30, 27). Although Ḥormah is a reference to ruins, rather than an existing town, it seems nevertheless reasonable to assume that *Bt*(*w*)'*l* is the specific name of an Arad, abridged from *'-r-d-ỉ n* ***b-ỉ-t*** *Y-w-r-ḥ-m*(***-ỉ-r***), Shoshenq's *Y-w-r-ḥ-m* being probably shortened from *Yrḥm'l*, as attested later in Hebrew and in Moabite[146]. Tell 'Arad would thus be the second *'-r-d-ỉ* of Shoshenq's list. The identification of this place with the enclosed settlement of Stratum XII is unlikely. The great similarity between the pottery assemblages of Strata XII and XI[147] indicates that they are not separated by a large gap and do not cover a very long time-span. Since Stratum XI goes back to the same period as Lachish Level IV and dates therefore from the 8th century B.C., the beginning of Stratum XII cannot be placed in the mid-10th century B.C. It should be dated, at the earliest, in the first half of the 9th century B.C.

The location of the first *'-r-d-ỉ* can be inferred hypothetically from two data, at first from the meaning of the generic "watch post", which distinguishes both sites from places qualified as *š-b-p3-r-ṯ,* "lowland". It should thus refer to settlements or structures on high ground. Coming from the west, the first conspicuous site of the kind in the Beersheba Valley is Ḫirbet al-Ġarra (Tel 'Ira), which raises about 100 m above the valley and is characterized by steep ridges on each side[148]. Further to the east, the site of Tell 'Arad fits the characteristics of *'-r-d-ỉ* with the

[145] Josh. 15, 30; I Chron. 29, 30; cf. Josh. 19, 4. The toponym is corrupted to *Ksyl* in Josh. 15, 30, but *yl* preserves the phonetic spelling of the divine name *'Il*. Besides, a place name *Bethula* is attested at the time of the Crusaders in the same area: G. BEYER, *Civitas Ficuum*, in *ZDPV* 69 (1953), p. 75-87. It is identified with *Bt*(*w*)'*l* by A. ALT, *Anhang*, *ibid*., p. 85-87, who proposes locating the place at Ḫirbet al-Qaryatein (alt. 912 m), *ca*. 8 km north of Tell 'Arad. He assumes that *Civitas Ficuum* was intended to be a translation of *Qaryat-tīn,* "Village of Figs", while *Bethula* was supposed to be the older name of the place. In the present writer's opinion, the latter could possibly be taken from a nearby site, somehow related to Tell 'Arad, which was still settled in the early Arab period.

[146] The legend *l-Yrḥm'l bn hmlk* occurs on a bulla and a scaraboid from the 7th century B.C.: N. AVIGAD, *Hebrew Bullae from the Time of Jeremiah: Remnants of a Burnt Archive*, Jerusalem 1986, p. 27-28, No. 8 = N. AVIGAD - B. SASS, *op. cit.* (n. 112), p. 175, No. 414; R. DEUTSCH - A. LEMAIRE, *Biblical Period Personal Seals in the Shlomo Moussaieff Collection*, Tel Aviv 2000, No. 186.

[147] L. SINGER-AVITZ, *Arad: The Iron Age Pottery Assemblages,* in *Tel Aviv* 29 (2002), p.110-214 (see p. 111, 114).

[148] This was stressed already by Y. AHARONI, *The Negeb of Judah,* in *IEJ* 8 (1958), p. 26-38 (see p. 37).

advantage that the name has apparently been preserved, although Tell al-'Ar'ara could merit the name "watch post" as well.

Secondly, there are good reasons to identify Ḫirbet al-Ġarra with *'ltwld /'Ilat-awlād/*, "Goddess of children"[149], and to understand *'-r-d-ỉ R-b-t* as "Watch post of the Lady", *Rabbat*, a well-known title of goddesses in Phoenician-Punic and Old Arabian. We may refer in particular to 'Ilat, worshipped by the Taqīf tribe in her main sanctuary of aṭ-Ṭā'if, in North Arabia, where she was called *ar-Rabbat*[150]. The full place name would have been *'Arad 'Ilat-awlād*, abridged in Hebrew lists to *'ltwld*[151], written after monophthongization *'ltld* on a "fiscal" bulla[152] from the late 7th century B.C., and reduced to *twld* in I Chron. 4, 29. *'ltwld* and *Bt(w)'l* are mentioned side by side in Josh. 15, 30; 19, 4; I Chron. 4, 29-30, just like *'-r-d-ỉ R-b-t* and *'-r-d-ỉ n b-ỉ-t Y-w-r-ḥ-m.*

Y-w-r-ḥ-m is a divine name of the same type as *Yhwh*, and *b-ỉ-t*, written in a separate oval and qualified by the hieroglyph representing a "bowl for incense with smoke rising from it", should designate the cella or the shrine of the god. The theonym is attested in Sabaic either under the full causative form *Yhrḫm*[153] or with the elision of intervocalic *h* in *Yrḫm*[154]. Egyptian *Y-w-r-ḥ-m* and Hebrew *Yrḥm-'l*[155] show the same elision of *h* and the merging *ḫ* > *ḥ*, confirmed by the absence of *ḫ*-signs in Shoshenq's notation of Negebite place names. Shoshenq's *Y-w-r-ḥ-m,* repeated in the *Y-w-r-ḥ-m* of No. 139, probably indicates a lengthened vowel *ū* after *y*. **Yūrḥim* means "Who makes happy", as suggested by Arabic *raḫama / raḫuma*, "to be enjoyable".

The worship of *'Ilat-awlād* or *Rabbat* and of *Yūrḥim-'Il* were apparently associated later in the Edomite Arad fortress of Strata X-IX. It contained a sanctuary with a cella, characterized by two raised stones: one,

149 See here below, p. 410.

150 M. HÖFNER, *Die Stammesgruppen Nord- und Zentralarabiens in vorislamischer Zeit*, in H.W. HAUSSIG (ed.), *Götter und Mythen im Vorderen Orient*, Stuttgart 1965, p. 407-481 (see p. 422).

151 Josh. 15, 30; 19, 4.

152 N. AVIGAD, *Two Hebrew 'Fiscal' Bullae,* in *IEJ* 40 (1990), p. 262-266, Pl. 28A-D (see p. 262-265, Pl. 28A-B); N. AVIGAD - B. SASS, *op. cit.* (n. 112), p. 177-178, No. 421.

153 *CIS* IV, 338, 2; 340, 1. *Yhrḫm* is the correct reading, not *Yhrhm*; cf. M. HÖFNER, *Südarabien*, in H.W. HAUSSIG (ed.), *Götter und Mythen im Vorderen Orient*, Stuttgart 1965, p. 483-552, Pls. I-IV (see p. 543); HARDING, *Arabian Names*, p. 688.

154 *RÉS* 4176, 1. Cf. LIPIŃSKI, *Semitic*, §41.11. This spelling is no "Schreibfehler", as written by M. HÖFNER, *loc. cit.* (n. 153).

155 I Sam. 27, 10; 30, 29; Jer. 36, 26; I Chron. 2, 9.26.27.42; 24, 29; 25, 33. See also here above, n. 146. The *'ry h-Yrḥm'ly* are no "cities of the Jeraḥme'elites", but either "enclosures" or a "district" with paragogic *-ī*, like in *'ry-Gl'd* (Judg. 12, 7); cf. here below, p. 323 .

painted red and somewhat larger, probably symbolized the presence of *Yūrḥim* (*'Il*), while the other one represented *Rabbat* (*'Ilat*)[156]. Two monolithic incense altars of different dimensions stood at the entrance of the cella, obviously corresponding to the two steles. One cannot expect to find a shrine of *Yūrḥim* and *Rabbat* inside the Judaean fortress of the 8th century B.C. (Stratum XI), but a cult place must have existed in its surroundings, consisting probably of a sacred open-air enclosure and of raised stones on a podium. A holy place was certainly located in the neighbourhood also at the time of Shoshenq I and in the 9th century B.C., before the Judaean occupation of the site. The mention of a *b-ỉ-t* even suggests the presence of a cella in a holy precinct, possibly with a well. The well, some 4 m in diameter, dug to a depth of 21 m and reaching the aquifer, was found in the central depression of the Bronze Age city, but seems to have been dug only in the Iron Age[157]. The inhabitants of the Iron Age settlement and of the later fortress drew water from this well[158], and one may assume that a sacred place was located in this neighbourhood. There is another possibility. The antechamber of the cella in the sanctuary of Strata X-IX had benches along the wall, probably to place offerings on them[159], and a similar disposition was found in a house exposed in Stratum XII. Now, the stone benches along the three walls of Room 933 excavated there are reminiscent of a sanctuary and one wonders whether this house of Stratum XII was no small shrine of the 9th century B.C. instead of being a dwelling of the Early Bronze Age, supposedly reused in the Iron Age[160]. Since Stratum XII was found with no conflagration layer, the pre-Judaean settlement must have been abandoned by its inhabitants, who also removed all the cultic items, transferring them to another location. This probably happened several generations after Shoshenq I's campaign.

The theonym *Yūrḥim* occurs for a second time in Shoshenq's list, apparently as first element of the compound name *Y-w-r-ḥ-m 'Iwn-nỉ-nỉ* (Nos. 139-140). This name was possibly introduced by another word - "cella", "enclosure" - in No. 138, completely destroyed. Under No. 140 one reads *'Ōnān* < **'Awnān*[161]. This is the name of a son of Judah

[156] Cf. the comparative material in U. AVNER, *Maṣṣebot Sites in the Negev and Sinai and Their Significance,* in *Biblical Archaeology Today, 1990*, Jerusalem 1993, p. 166-181.

[157] R. AMIRAN - O. ILAN, *Early Arad* II, Jerusalem 1996, p. 106-107.

[158] R. AMIRAN - R. GOETHERT - O. ILAN, *The Well of Arad,* in *Biblical Archaeology Review* 13/2 (1987), p. 40-44.

[159] Z. HERZOG, *art. cit.* (n. 106), p. 56.

[160] *Ibid.*, p. 14-15.

[161] Amorite *Aw-na-nu-um*: I.J. GELB, *Computer-aided Analysis of Amorite* (AS 21), Chicago 1980, p. 567, Nos. 988-989. Also *Am-na-nu(-um)*, *ibid.*, p. 564, Nos. 776-777,

according to biblical texts[162], but an epithet of the god 'Il according to tablets from Ugarit, where there was a "temple of 'Il the (sexually) Vigorous", *bt.'Il 'ann*[163]. The epithet is not monophtongized in Shoshenq's list, where it probably refers to *'Il* as well. The place could be another sanctuary of the Jeraḥme'elites, since one of the wives of Jeraḥme'el is supposed to be the mother of *'Ōnām*, very likely a misspelling or phonetic variant of *'Ōnān*.

A name *ỉ-d-r* (No. 116), presumably "threshing floor", follows three destroyed names (Nos. 113-115) and is immediately followed by another *ỉ-d-r* (No. 117), which might be a duplicate, derived by dittography[164]. *'I-d-r* should probably be connected with the next name (No. 118), which is unfortunately damaged, like Nos. 119-120. There is further a readable name *F-r-tỉ-m-ỉ* (No. 121), which has been related to the clan of Pelet, son of Jeraḥme'el[165]. But *F-r-tỉ-m-ỉ* can be equated also with Bēth-Peleṭ (Josh. 15, 27; Neh. 11, 26), with the gentile name *Pl*ṭ*y* in II Sam. 23, 26, and with the name Peleṭ of a Calebite clan (I Chron. 2, 47). In fact, Semitic *ṭ* is marked in Egyptian either by *t* or by *d*. The hieroglyphic spelling seems to be based on the absolute plural of the ethnic name **Pilṭiyūma*.

The next item is *Í-b-r* (No. 122), usually read *Abel*, i.e. "meadow". This reading is unlikely in the concerned area and one should interpret *Í-b-r* as the "broken" plural *Ābār* (*'b'r*) of the word *bīr*, "well". A place name "Wells" cannot be identified easily with any particular site. One may notice that the wells of Bīr 'Ar'ara provided an excellent water, and that several wells are known at Ḫirbet al-Mšāš and at Tell al-Milḥ[166], but the most famous wells were those of Bīr as-Seba'. It is possible that *Ābār* refers to them, being mentioned on the back route of the Egyptian army. The site was occupied or regularly visited in the 10th-9th centuries

with *am* used for phonemic /*aw*/; cf. E.E. KNUDSEN, *Amorite Grammar. A Comparative Statement*, in A.S. KAYE (ed.), *Semitic Studies in Honor of Wolf Leslau* I, Wiesbaden 1991, p. 866-885 (see p. 871); ID., *Amorite Names and Old Testament Onomastics*, in *Scandinavian Journal of the Old Testament* 13 (1999), p. 202-224 (see p. 213).

162 Gen. 38, 4.8-9; 46, 12; Numb. 26, 19; I Chron. 2, 3.

163 *KTU* 4.149, 17-19. See also the proper name *Bn.'Ann*: *KTU* 4. 222, 16. Under certain conditions, the diphthong *aw* was contracted at Ugarit in *ā*, like in *'ar* < *'awr*, "light". One should mistrust the usual shorthand *ô* < *aw*. The epithet *'ann* must be distinguished from the theophorous element *'ann* / *anan*(*i*) appearing in Hurrian proper names: E. LAROCHE, *Glossaire de la langue hourrite* (= *RHA* 34-35), Paris 1978-79, p. 49.

164 S. AḤITUV, *op. cit.* (n. 90), p. 51.

165 I Chron. 2, 33: Y. AHARONI, *op. cit.* (n. 95), p. 289.

166 ABEL, *Géographie* I, p. 152.

B.C., as shown by potsherds with a dark-red slip and hand burnishing, that were recovered in several excavated areas of Bīr as-Seba'[167].

The next place is again a well, *B-ỉ-r-R-wḏ3-3* (No. 123), which was interpreted as Bīr-Lawz, "Well of Almonds"[168], an unidentified site in the Negeb. It is followed by *B3-ṯ-'-n-ṯ* (No. 124), certainly a Bēth-'Anath, which ought to be looked for in the western part of the Negeb, near the coastal area. This is suggested also by *Š-r-ḥ-m* (No. 125), mentioned in Josh. 19, 6 and usually written with final *n*. The place is identified with Tell al-Far'ah South, 29 km south of Gaza[169]. The unusual spelling with three horizontal strokes, which have the phonetic value *m*(*w*), may suggest another identification, viz. with *Šilḥīm* in Josh. 15, 32[170]. However, *Šilḥīm* replaces the Sharuhen of Josh. 19, 6 and may be based on a variant pronunciation of the same place name with the alternative articulations *l/r* and *m/n* at the end of the name[171]. There is no need to assume that the scribe or the engraver of Shoshenq's list confused the hieratic ligature *n3* with hieroglyphic *mw*[172].

The toponym *'I-r-ỉm-m-ṯ-n* (No. 126) is usually read El-mattan[173]and compared to *'lmtn* in Samaria ostracon 28, 3. This reading is based on an interpretation which is grammatically impossible. One could analyze both place names as *'lm-tn*, "The Hall of the Jackal", and compare it to *Ḥăṣar Šū'āl*[174], "The Enclosure of the Fox". The toponym *'ylm* occurs as name of an Israelite encampment in the desert[175] and the same word designates a banqueting hall in Sabaic[176]. However, hieroglyphic *'I-r-ỉm-m-ṯ-n* stands rather for *'Āl-'Amtan*, "Clan of the Strongest one", an elative of *matn*, "strong". The next item is *G-r-n-ỉ* (No. 127), "Threshing floor", which appears also in *'-n-g-r-n* (No. bis 4), "The Spring of the Threshing floor", near the seacoast. Then comes the second attestation of *'I-d-m-m* (No. 128), that should probably be regarded as the generic *'ṭm* with

[167] R. GOPHNA - Y. YISRAELI, *Soundings at Beer Sheva (Bir es-Seba')*, in Y. AHARONI (ed.), *Beer-sheba* I, Tel Aviv 1973, p. 115-118, Pls. 47 and 77-79 (see p. 116, Pls. 47:3 and 78:17); N. PANITZ-COHEN, *A Salvage Excavation in the New Market in Beer-Sheba: New Light on Iron Age IIB Occupation at Beer-Sheba,* in *IEJ* 55 (2005), p. 143-155 (see p. 152).

[168] S. AḤITUV, *op. cit.* (n. 90), p. 74.

[169] S. AḤITUV, *op. cit.* (n. 90), p. 171-173.

[170] K.A. KITCHEN, *op. cit.* (n. 18), p. 441.

[171] LIPIŃSKI, *Semitic*, §17.5 and §11.7.

[172] S. AḤITUV, *op. cit.* (n. 90), p. 171, n. 499.

[173] S. AḤITUV, *op. cit.* (n. 90), p. 92.

[174] Josh. 15, 28; 19, 3; I Chron. 4, 28; Neh. 11, 27.

[175] Ex. 15, 27; 16, 1; Numb. 33, 9-10.

[176] *Sabaic Dictionary*, p. 5; M.A. GHŪL, *op. cit.* (n. 52), p. 313-314.

mimation (cf. No. 98), qualifying *G-r-n-ỉ* (No. 127): "The Threshing floor of the Redoubt / Stockade (?)" or the like.

Nos. 129-138 are all damaged, but No. 129 was restored by M. Noth as [*Š*]-*r-ḥ-ṯ*. One should rather read [*'I*]-*r-ḥ-ṯ* and interpret it as *'Āl-Ḥatt*, "Clan of Ḥatt". This is the name of a nomad group which two hundred years later surrendered to Tiglath-pileser III during his campaign in southern Palestine. Among the tribes "dwelling on the border of the countries of the setting sun", which brought camels and spices as tribute, Tiglath-pileser III lists the *āl* (URU) *Ḫa-at-te-e-a* or [*āl* (URU) *Ḫa-at*]-*ti-a-a*[177]. The cuneiform spelling of the name shows that Assyrian scribes have confused *'āl*, "clan", "tribe", with *ālu*, "town", and consequently have added to the name the ethnic ending *-iy*. The tribe in question is mentioned each time next to the Idiba'ilay, known from the Bible as *'db'l*[178] and playing a major role in Tiglath-pileser III's time, since its sheikh was appointed as warden of the area facing Egypt[179]. One can assume therefore that some of these tribes were living in the Sinai and the Negeb, while other were represented in this area by caravans coming to the emporium of Abu Ruqeish[180] or to Gaza with spices from distant places in Arabia. In an earlier period, the *'Āl-Ḥatt* may have dwelled in the Beersheba Valley, hence their mention in Sheshonq I's list and the appearance of members of the tribe in some biblical narratives. In fact, biblical texts referring to the *Ḥittīm* probably confuse these tribesmen with Neo-Hittites. The typically tribal designation of the *Bənē Ḥēt* at Hebron (Gen. 23) and Esau's marriages with "Hittite" women at Beersheba[181] strongly support this assumption, confirmed by the Semitic names and patronymics of these "Hittites"[182]. Ahimelek, the *Ḥty* from David's inner circle (I Sam. 26, 6), is in the same situation[183]. The name of the tribe *Ḥt* may be related to Arabic *ḥatt*, "fleet", "swift", attested as a Hadhramitic and Ṣafaitic proper name[184].

[177] *Tigl. III*, p. 142, Summ. 4, line 28'; p. 200, Summ. 13, line 10'. The group was also mentioned p. 168, Summ. 7, rev., line 3'. Cf. I. EPH'AL, *op. cit.* (n. 99), p. 34, 87, 89, 217.

[178] Gen. 25, 13; I Chron. 1, 28.

[179] *Tigl. III*, p. 142, Summ. 4, line 34'; p. 168, Summ. 7, rev., line 6'; p. 202, line 16; cf. p. 82, Ann. 18, line 13'. The name *'Idibi-'Ilu* appears also in Thamudic, Ṣafaitic, and Sabaic inscriptions: HARDING, *Arabian Names*, p. 31.

[180] See here below, p. 376, 378.

[181] Gen. 26, 24; 37, 46; cf. Gen. 36, 2.

[182] Even Ephron's name in Gen. 23, 8-17 (cf. 25, 9; 49, 29-30; 50, 13) is Semitic: it derives from the same root as Arabic *ya'fūr*, "gazelle", and Hebrew *'oper*, "fawn".

[183] The case of Uriah the Hittite in II Sam. 11 is different, because the actual text is based on a confusion. In reality, *'wry(h)* is the Hurrian title "Lord" and *Ḥty* is the Hurrian proper name *Ḫutiya*; cf. LIPIŃSKI, *Itineraria Phoenicia*, p. 499-500.

[184] HARDING, *Arabian Names*, p. 175.

No. 132 of Shoshenq's list was read either *'I-r-r-*[*m*], El-ra[m], or *'I-r-r-*[*ỉ-y*], El-ro'ī (Gen. 16, 13), but these are only guesses[185]. The first reading, if interpreted *'Āl-R*[*m*], can nevertheless refer to Ram, a "son" of Jeraḥme'el (I Chron. 2, 25.27) and later a well-known Ṣafaitic tribe[186]. No. 133 is probably *Y-w-r-*[*ḏ-3*], known from other sources[187] and most likely located at Ḫirbet 'Irq, 18 km south-east of Gaza, or in its vicinity, at Abu Hureira (Tel Haror)[188]. *Y-w-r-ḥ-m* (No. 139) and *'Iwn-nỉ-nỉ* (No. 140) seem to form a compound name, examined here above[189], while Nos. 141-144 are destroyed.

The restoration of No. 145 as *M-'-k*[*-ṯ*], compared with the name of Caleb's wife in I Chron. 2, 48[190], is based on a confusion of the anthroponym Maaka with an unattested place name[191]. The signs *M-'-k* were probably followed by the sole determinative of "hill country" or "foreign land". *M-'-k* can be compared to the proper name *Mā'ōk* in I Sam. 27, 2. It may have qualified a generic term in No. 144, but this oval is broken and the suggestion can only be regarded as a plausible guess. Also the *ỉ-d-r* of No. 146, "threshing floor", may have constituted the generic of a compound name, but Nos. 147-149 are completely destroyed. The final name of the section is *Y-w-r-d-n* (No. 150). It suggests an unidentified site on a route "descending" towards the Mediterranean coast.

It is reasonable to assume that Shoshenq I's campaigns aimed at bringing Canaan and the Negeb back under Egyptian control in order to benefit from the economy of the land[192]. Therefore, one can also take for granted that Shoshenq I's topographical list does not imply that all the places it mentions were destroyed. On the contrary, the list aimed at showing how widespread was pharaoh's authority. Its accuracy suggests that characteristics of particular sites were registered by professional

[185] K.A. KITCHEN, *op. cit.* (n. 18), p. 441.
[186] HARDING, *Arabian Names*, p. 286.
[187] S. AḤITUV, *op. cit.* (n. 90), p. 202-203.
[188] See here below, p. 153-154.
[189] See p. 124-125.
[190] Y. AHARONI, *op. cit.* (n. 95), p. 289.
[191] Cf. here below, p. 238-239.
[192] G.W. AHLSTRÖM, *Pharaoh Shoshenq's Campaign to Palestine*, in A. LEMAIRE - B. OTZEN (eds.), *History and Traditions of Early Israel* (VTS 50), Leiden 1993, p. 1-16. The opposite view is maintained by M. HAIMAN, *The 10th Century B.C. Settlement of the Negev Highlands of Iron Age II Israel*, in A.M. MAEIR - S. DAR - Z. SAFRAI (eds.), *The Rural Landscape of Ancient Israel* (BAR 1121), Oxford 2003, p. 71-90. According to Haiman, Shoshenq I intended to destroy the settlements which were hindering commercial relations between Egypt and Edom. This is an anachronistic view, anticipating Edom's role in the region by a whole century.

scribes and that shrines of local deities were duly noted. The repeated mentions of "stores" (*n-g-b*), "threshing floors" (*ỉ-d-r-ỉ, g-r-n-ỉ*), "enclosures" or "sheepfolds" (*h-q-r / h-g-r*), and "wells" (*í-b-r, b-ỉ-r*) reveal a continuous attention to economic aspects. Pharaoh's troops were not only supplied from the crops and folds of the Negebite population, but cattle and prisoners were very likely taken away as well. Systematic destruction was instead contra-productive, especially if Shoshenq I intended to reinstate Egyptian hegemony in the region. The settlements of the Negeb have not been "destroyed" by Shoshenq I, as one can read in some publications. Many were abandoned later, because clans have moved for other locations, fearing either a new Egyptian campaign or military interventions of Judaean kings.

A raid by people of the Negeb in Shoshenq I's period is recorded in II Chron 14, 8-14. This narrative, though theologically elaborated, is most likely based on a notice from the annals of Asa, king of Judah[193]. The suggestion that the raid in question had some connection with Osorkon I is baseless and a discussion inspired by this hypothesis is fruitless[194]. According to the chronicler, the raiding tribesmen were led by a certain Zeraḥ, obviously a Western Semite bearing an Edomite name[195]. His qualification as "Cushite" confirms the Chronicler's anachronistic misconception of history and reflects his tendency to introduce the "Cushites" in several parts of his work[196]. Instead, the mention of the border-town of Maresha (Tell Sandaḥanna), at the south-western frontier of the tiny kingdom of Judah (II Chron. 14, 8-9), and the pursuit of the enemy by the king of Judah as far as Gerar (Tell aš-Šerī'a), some 30 km further south, points clearly at the area of western Negeb, where the raiding tribesmen were active and it comes most likely from the Chronicler's source.

The last section of Shoshenq I's topographical list contained about thirty names of which only the last five are preserved. These are towns in the southern coastal region, relatively close to the eastern Delta. This at least confirms the view that the list as a whole does not follow the itinerary of a single military campaign. Two of these names are identifiable: Raphia and Lab(w)an (*R-b-w-n*). Lab(w)an is associated in Neo-Assyrian texts with the town of ^{uru}*Naḫal Muṣur*, nowadays al-'Arīš, but

[193] W. RUDOLPH, *Chronikbücher* (HAT I/21), Tübingen 1955, p. 243-244; A. ALT, *Kleine Schriften zur Geschichte des Volkes Israel* III, München 1959, p. 415-416.

[194] B.U. SCHIPPER, *op. cit.* (n. 2), p. 133-139.

[195] Cf. Gen. 36, 13.17.33; I Chron. 1, 37.44.

[196] II Chron. 12, 3; 14, 8.11-12; 16, 8; 21, 16.

its ruler is a *nasīku*[197]. This title suggests that he was the chief of a nomadic or semi-nomadic tribe, the name of which possibly reveals a link with the well at the foot of Gebel Libnī, about 45 km south of al-'Arīš[198]. This distance is acceptable, since Raphia is similarly described in Neo-Assyrian inscriptions as "close to ^{uru}*Naḫal Muṣur*", although it also lies some 45 km from al-'Arīš[199]. Other proposed locations of Lab(w)an lack any factual basis.

9th-8th centuries B.C.

The silence of Egyptian written sources concerning relations with Palestine in the 9th-8th centuries B.C. should be compensated by a more careful analysis of the pertinent archaeological material and of biblical texts.

Egypt's involvement with the Levant did certainly not cease at the death of Shoshenq I, but continued as the need was felt. Also Osorkon II (889-850 B.C.) maintained relations with Byblos where a fragment of Osorkon II's statue was found[200]. In this instance, however, no additional Phoenician inscription records the name of the king of Byblos. Material evidence of contacts with Israel at the time of Omri or Ahab is afforded at Samaria by the discovery of parts of a large alabaster vase, possibly a gift, bearing the cartouches of Osorkon II[201] and an indication of its capacity - 81 *hin* or about 40 litres. Fragments of other alabaster vases have been found as well, but without any inscription. Since alabasters were used for precious ointments and the like, the vessel with Osorkon II's cartouches does not witness only to ordinary Phoenician trade. It must be seen in the general frame of diplomatic exchanges of

[197] H. TADMOR, *The Campaigns of Sargon II of Assur: A Chronological-Historical Study*, in *JCS* 12 (1958), p. 22-40 and 77-100 (see p. 77-78); I. EPH'AL, *op. cit.* (n. 99), p. 37. Cf. here below, p. 136-140.

[198] A. ALT, *Kleine Schriften zur Geschichte des Volkes Israel* II, 2nd ed., München 1959, p. 231, n. 2.

[199] I. EPH'AL, *op. cit.* (n. 99), p. 104.

[200] P. MONTET, *Byblos et l'Égypte* II, Paris 1929, Pl. 43; ID., *La nécropole royale de Tanis* I, Paris 1947, p. 21-22; J. LECLANT, *Les relations entre l'Égypte et la Phénicie du voyage d'Ounamon à l'expédition d'Alexandre,* in W.A. WARD (ed.), *The Rôle of the Phoenicians in the Interaction of Mediterranean Civilizations*, Beirut 1968, p. 9-31 (see p. 24, n. 28, and Pl. VIIIb); B. REDFORD, *art. cit.* (n. 38), p. 15, n. 108; J. LECLANT, *Le rayonnement de l'Égypte au temps des rois tanites et libyens,* in *Tanis. L'or des pharaons*, Paris 1987, p. 77-84 (see p. 81).

[201] P. MONTET, *La nécropole*, *op. cit.* (n. 200), p. 39; I.E.S. EDWARDS, in *op. cit.* (n. 19), p. 558; K.A. KITCHEN, *op. cit.* (n. 18), p. 324-325, n. 450.

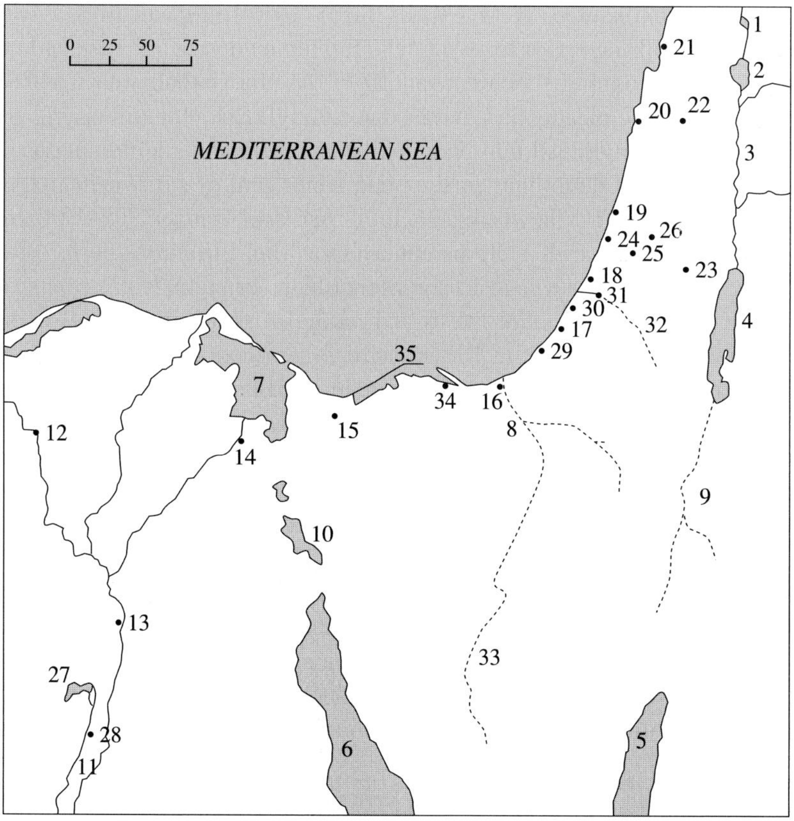

Nile delta, Sinai Peninsula, Canaan.

1 = *Ḥuleh L.*
2 = *Sea of Galilee*
3 = *Jordan R.*
4 = *Dead Sea*
5 = *G. of Aqaba*
6 = *G. of Suez*
7 = *Menzala L.*
8 = *W. al-ʿArīš*
9 = *W. Arabah*
10 = *Bitter Lakes*
11 = *Nile*
12 = Sais
13 = Memphis
14 = Tanis
15 = Migdol
16 = al-ʿArīš
17 = Raphia
18 = Gaza
19 = T. Qasile
20 = Dor
21 = Akko
22 = Megiddo
23 = Jerusalem
24 = Ashdod
25 = Ekron
26 = Gezer
27 = *Faiyūm*
28 = Heracleopolis
29 = Abu Salima
30 = Abu Ruqeish
31 = T. Ǧemmeh
32 = *W. Ġazza*
33 = *Sinai*
34 = al-Warrāda
35 = *Sirbonis L.*

luxury goods between Near Eastern kings. Royal presents from Egypt reached even Assyria, as shown by the Egyptian "tribute" represented on the Black Obelisk of Shalmaneser III[202]. As the obelisk was sculpted after 841 B.C., the exotic animals must have been sent to Assyria by Takeloth II (850-825 B.C.). This diplomatic gift is an additional reason why one should doubt that an Egyptian contingent of 1,000 men fought in 853 B.C. against the Assyrians at the battle of Qarqar[203]. Sure, there is no need whatsoever to re-invent another Muṣri in North Syria or to suppose that *Mu-uṣ-ra-a-a* in the Monolith Inscription II, 92 refers to Masuwari, i.e. Til-Barsip, like in a passage of the Sefire treaty[204]. As suggested by A. Lemaire[205], *Mu-uṣ-ra-a-a* should be regarded as a metathesis for "Ṣumuraean", a qualification of the contingent sent by the Phoenician kingdom of Ṣumur, on the Mediterranean coast. Similar mistakes in the concerned passage of the Monolith Inscription support this hypothesis[206].

Some evidence of direct contacts of Israel or Judah with Egypt is provided by the references to Tanis (Zoan) in Numb. 13, 22; Ps. 78, 12.43, and by proper names in the story of Joseph in Egypt. In fact, anthroponyms like Potiphera (*p3-dỉ-p3-r‘*, "Whom Re‘ has given"), Asenath (*nś-nỉ.t,* "Belonging to Neith"), and Zaphenath-paneah (*ḏd-p3-nṯr-ỉw.f-‘nḫ*, "God has spoken and he became alive")[207] do not become common before the Twenty-second Dynasty. Although the precise date of these biblical references remains somewhat uncertain, they belong to a period when the kings of Tanis still had a certain power.

The process of decentralization of provincial control in 8th-century Egypt was well-known in Judah, as shown by Is. 19, 11-13 and 30, 4. In particular, Is. 30, 3-4 alludes to messengers sent to Tanis and to Hanes, better known as Heracleopolis Magna, at the southern entrance of the Faiyūm. The northern Heracleopolite nome had an important Jewish community in the Ptolemaic period, as shown by a Greek archive from

[202] BM. WA. 118855: *ANEP*, No. 351 III. There is no reason to doubt that Muṣri in the accompanying inscription (*RIMA* III, text A.0.102.89, p. 150) designates Egypt. Cf. LIPIŃSKI, *Itineraria Phoenicia,* p. 208-209.

[203] *RIMA* III, text A.0.102.2, p. 23, line 92.

[204] LIPIŃSKI, *Aramaeans*, p. 204-206.

[205] A. LEMAIRE, *Joas de Samarie, Barhadad de Damas, Zakkur de Hamat: La Syrie-Palestine vers 800 av. J.-C.,* in *Avraham Malamat Volume* (ErIs 24), Jerusalem 1993, p. 148*-157* (see p. 152*).

[206] LIPIŃSKI, *Aramaeans*, p. 303.

[207] Reconstruction of the names by H. RANKE, *Die ägyptischen Personennamen* I, Glückstadt 1935, p. 123: 11; Vol. II, Glückstadt 1952, p. 334:13; cf. p. 226, n. 6 with a different explanation of the name "Asenath".

the mid-2nd century B.C.[208] and by twenty tombstones from this area (Sedment al-Gebel) with inscriptions bearing Jewish names[209]. Nothing suggests so far that there was a link between this community and the envoys sent to Hanes in the 8th century B.C. This city, called *Ḥwt-nn-nswt* in Egyptian, *Ḫi-ni-in-ši* in Neo-Assyrian, *Hnēs* in Coptic, and named Ehnasiya al-Madina nowadays, was the capital of the twenty-first nome. In the mid-8th century B.C., its high priest Peftjau-awy-Oubasti (*Pf-ṯ3w-*[*m-*]*'wỉ-B3st.t*) asserted his independence, proclaiming himself king: he adopted the pharaonic praenomen Neferkare, wrote his names in cartouches, and required documents to be dated in his regnal years[210]. He was probably visited by an envoy from Jerusalem, what is an important fact showing that the contacts of the Hebrew kingdoms in the 8th century B.C. were not limited to the nearest king of Egypt at Tanis (Zoan).

These contacts are confirmed in II Kings 17, 4, that records the sending of envoys by Hoshea, the last king of Israel (731-722 B.C.), to Sais, to the king of Egypt. The correct spelling *Sy'* of the city name can be found in Babylonian Hebrew manuscripts[211] and is confirmed by the Septuagint translation, where Σηγωρ hides *sy' 'yr* with γ marking the *'ayin* and ω corresponding to *wāw*, misread for *yōd*. In fact, some Jew-

[208] J.M.S. COWEY - K. MARESCH, *Urkunden des Politeuma der Juden von Herakleopolis (144/3-133/2 v. Chr.) (P. Polit. Iud.)* (Papyrologica Coloniensia 29), Köln 2001. A substantial Jewish community existed also at Trikomia, not far from the border with the Arsinoite nome: W. CLARYSSE, *Jews in Trikomia,* in A. BÜLOW-JACOBSEN (ed.), *Proceedings of the 20th International Congress of Papyrologists*, Copenhagen 1994, p. 193-203.

[209] A. GALAL ABD EL-FATAH - G. WAGNER, *Épitaphes grecques d'époque ptolémaïque de Sedment el-Gebel (IIe/Ier siècles): une communauté juive dans la Chôra égyptienne,* in *Comptes rendus de l'Institut de Papyrologie et d'Épigraphie de Lille* 19 (1998), p. 85-96.

[210] G. DARESSY, *Stèle du roi Pefnidubast*, in *ASAÉ* 17 (1917), p. 43-45; ID., *Fragments héracléopolitains*, in *ASAÉ* 21 (1921), p. 138-139; cf. H. GAUTHIER, *Le livre des rois d'Égypte* III, Le Caire 1914, p. 400-401; I.E.J. EDWARDS, in *op. cit.* (n. 19), p. 568.

[211] A. JEPSEN, *Liber Regum* (Biblia Hebraica Stuttgartensia 6), Stuttgart 1974, p. 96: K^Or *sy'*. The identification of *Sw'* with Osorkon IV results from the unawareness of the variant *ketīb* spelling and of the Septuagint reading, also from fanciful linguistics applied to onomastics. This identification was recently advocated by K.A. KITCHEN, *op. cit.* (n. 18), p. 372-376, 551-552, XXXIV-XXXIX; ID., *art. cit.* (n. 3), p. 126; B.U. SCHIPPER, *Wer war* "Sō', *König von Ägypten"?*, in *BN* 92 (1998), p. 71-84; ID., *op. cit.* (n. 2), p. 151-158, followed by G. VITTMANN, *Ägypten und die Fremden im ersten vorchristlichen Jahrtausend*, Mainz a/R 2003, p. 23. Without mentioning the variant *Sy'*, this reading is advocated by H. GOEDICKE, *The End of "So, King of Egypt"*, in *BASOR* 171 (1963), p. 64-66; W.F. ALBRIGHT, *The Elimination of King "So"*, in *BASOR* 171 (1963), p. 66; H.L. GINSBERG, *So*, in *Encyclopaedia Judaica*, Jerusalem 1971, Vol. 15, col. 18. Cf. also J. VON BECKERATH, *Über chronologische Berührungspunkte der altägyptischen und der israelitischen Geschichte*, in M. DIETRICH - I. KOTTSIEPER (eds.), *"Und Mose schrieb dieses Lied auf". Studien zum Alten Testament und zum Alten Orient. Festschrift für O. Loretz* (AOAT 250), Münster 1998, p. 91-99 (see p. 95-96).

ish forms of *wāw* and *yōd* are almost identical already in the early Hasmonaean period (*ca.* 175-150 B.C.)[212], when the Greek translation of the Former Prophets was most likely achieved in Alexandria. The *Vorlage* of the Septuagint thus reads: "to Sais, the city of the king of Egypt". *Sy'* matches the Neo-Assyrian spelling *Sa-a-a*, Egyptian *S3(ỉ)w*, Coptic *Sai* or *Sa*, and Greek Σαίς. It is the present-day Ṣā al-Ḥagar, on the right bank of the Rosetta branch.

The king in question must have been Tefnakht I, ruler of the West, who proclaimed himself king and extended his power in the Delta, founding the Twenty-fourth Dynasty[213]. His reign can be dated to 733-726/5 B.C. and the reign of his son and successor Bocchoris to 726/5-720 B.C.[214] As Sais was visited in 726/5 by a Samarian envoy[215], Tefnakht or Bocchoris were certainly regarded as rulers able to play a role in the Near Eastern politics. A tradition recorded by Diodorus of Sicily even shows Tefnakht (Τνεφαχθος) fighting against Arabs[216]. However, the king of Sais did apparently not attempt to aid the distant Hoshea, although Piye's stele from Napata suggests that Tefnakht's power extended over the entire eastern Delta[217]. Since it matches the information provided by II Kings 17, 4 and Diodorus, there is no need to assume that the Napata stele exaggerates the role of the ruler of Sais[218].

The last pharaoh of the Twenty-second Dynasty was Osorkon IV, called Shilkanni in Neo-Assyrian texts[219]. Since Shabako (721/20-707/6 B.C.) ascended the throne of Cush in 721 and took a first grip on Egypt in 720, it is unlikely that Re'e, "the *turtānu* of Egypt" who fought against Sargon II in 720, was a Shabako's commander, as stated by D. Kahn[220]. He was rather an officer of Osorkon IV, as generally

[212] F.M. Cross, *The Development of the Jewish Scripts*, in G.E. Wright (ed.), *The Bible and the Ancient Near East. Essays in Honor of W.F. Albright*, London 1961, p. 133-202 (see p. 138, fig. 2, line 1, and p. 168-169).

[213] I.E.J. Edwards, in *op. cit.* (n. 19), p. 574-575, with further literature.

[214] D. Kahn, *The Inscription of Sargon II at Tang-i Var and the Chronology of Dynasty 25*, in *Orientalia* 70 (2001), p. 1-18 (see p. 15-16).

[215] This date is proposed by D. Kahn, *loc cit.* (n. 214), who hesitates between Tefnakht and Bocchoris. He seems to ignore the variant spelling *Sy'*.

[216] Diodorus of Sicily, *Bibliotheca Historica* I, 45, 2.

[217] N.-C. Grimal, *La stèle triomphale de Pi('ankh)y au Musée du Caire (JE 48862 et 47086-47089)* (MIFAO 105), Le Caire 1981, see Map III on p. 245.

[218] A different opinion is advocated by D. Kessler, *Zu den Feldzügen des Tefnachte, Namlot und Pije in Mitteläygpten,* in *SAK* 9 (1981), p. 227-251 (see p. 230); B.U. Schipper, *op. cit.* (n. 2), p. 150, n. 225.

[219] Ashur Prism VA 8424, col. II, 8; cf. H. Tadmor, *art. cit.* (n. 197), p. 78.

[220] D. Kahn, *art. cit.* (n. 214), p. 8-12. Cf. A. Fuchs, *Rē'e*, in *PNA* III/1, p. 1037. The personage, bearing a name shortened from *W3ḫ-ìb-R'* or the like, has not been identified so far in Egyptian sources.

Sargon II: fragment of an Assyrian relief
(Louvre Museum).

assumed, the more so because Osorkon IV was still in power at the time of Sargon's campaign to Philistia in 716 B.C. Re'e was sent to Philistia to help Hanun of Gaza, but the expedition ended in disaster. Raphia was destroyed, Re'e fled back to Egypt, and Hanun was captured by the Assyrians. Lower Reliefs 2-13 from Room V of Sargon II's palace at Khorsabad refer to this campaign and the unnamed city of Raphia is depicted in Lower Relief 2 as an Egyptian town, without crenels. It is defended by ambidextrous Cushites, each armed with two long spears. They can positively be identified as warriors of the Twenty-fifth Cushitic Dynasty, which very likely did not affront Sargon II in 720 B.C. The reliefs sculpted a dozen years later thus offer an anachronistic view of the Egyptian enemies fought in 720 B.C.[221] Sargon II's second campaign to Philistia, in 716, brought him to uru*Naḫal Muṣur*, the "Vale of the Borderland", the present-day al-'Arīš[222], within 230 km of Tanis.

In the Neo-Assyrian period, Naḫal Muṣur was an important settlement at least from a strategic point of view. The current translation of this toponym by "Brook of Egypt" simply ignores the fact that this is the name of a town, and the suggested identification of Naḫal Muṣur with Wādī Ġazza (Naḥal Besor)[223] deepens the confusion, which goes back to the Hebrew reinterpretation of the toponym as *Naḥal Miṣrayim*. In reality, *naḫal* does not mean "river" here, "stream" or "wadi", but either "valley", like in Ṣafaitic, or "palm grove", like in Arabic[224]. This is also the meaning of Νέελ in Byzantine times, when Νεελκεράβα designated the Naḫal Qarawa, the "Vale of Qarawa", where John the Crookbacked, a disciple of St. Sabas, founded a laura[225]. As for Muṣur, it did not have the current meaning "Egypt" in this context, but designated the "Borderland"[226], usually *miṣru* in Akkadian. In particular, it was the

[221] For Hanun, see the references collected by A. FUCHS, *Ḫanūnu* 4., in *PNA* II/1, Helsinki 2000, p. 457b. Raphia was recognized on Sargon II's reliefs by M. EL-AMIN, *Die Reliefs mit Beischriften von Sargon II. in Dur-Sharrukin,* in *Sumer* 9 (1953), p. 35-59, 214-228 (see p. 35-41); cf. N. FRANKLIN, *The Room V Reliefs at Dur-Sharrukin and Sargon II's Western Campaigns,* in *Tel Aviv* 21 (1994), p. 255-275 (see p. 259-260, 264-267). Cf. here above, p. 75, and below, p. 139.

[222] References are collected by M. WEIPPERT, *Naḫalmuṣur,* in *RLA* IX, Berlin 1998-2001, p. 81-82.

[223] N. NA'AMAN, *The Brook of Egypt and Assyrian Policy on the Border of Egypt,* in *Tel Aviv* 6 (1979), p. 68-90 (see p. 74-80); ID., *The Shihor of Egypt and Shur that is before Egypt,* in *Tel Aviv* 7 (1980), p. 95-109 (see p. 105-106).

[224] J. ŁACINA, *Słownik arabsko-polski*, Poznań 1997, p. 878.

[225] CYRIL OF SCYTHOPOLIS, *Life of S. Sabas* 16.

[226] This was rightly stressed by F.-M. ABEL, *Les confins de la Palestine et de l'Égypte sous les Ptolémées* III. *La frontière asiatique du côté de l'Égypte,* in *RB* 48 (1939), p. 530-548 (see p. 534 with n. 2).

buffer area near Egypt, apparently including southern Philistia. Like Naḫal, the toponym Muṣur was borrowed from Old Arabian[227], since it occurs also in South Arabian inscriptions. If "Muṣur of the Ḥabašāt" was no Abyssinian enclave on the Yemenite coast[228], but an "Abyssinian expeditionary force" (*mṣr 'ḥbšn*)[229], at least the Minaean factories in North Arabia were called *M'n Mṣrn*[230], "Ma'in of the Borderland". They were administered by officials called *kbry Mṣrn*[231], "prefects of the Borderland".

A comparable institution is referred to by the *kāri* kur*Mu-ṣur* in Sargon II's inscriptions[232], where the phrase in question means "trading post of the Borderland". The plural seems to appear in d*Dagān* uru*Muṣurūna*[233], referring to the god Dagan worshipped by the Philistines of the Borderland, but one can read uru*Muṣ(u)run* as well, with the Arabic nunation. Since the determinative URU is used here, the city of Naḫal Muṣur must be meant.

Notwithstanding the Hebrew reinterpretation of the place name as Naḥal Miṣrayim, the Greek translator of Is. 27, 12 still knew that this was 'Ρινοκορούροι, as al-'Arīš was called in Hellenistic and Graeco-Roman times. The town of al-'Arīš is located 2 km south of the point where the Wādī al-'Arīš reaches the sea. Its palm groves give it the aspect of an oasis. This is why *Naḫal* in its name should mean "palm grove". Due to a number of geographical assets, it was Sinai's principal centre through most historic periods. Loess soil is present in patches along the bed of the wadi or hidden beneath a thin cover of sand, and water is available from wells dug in its bed, although the wadi only seasonally carries water to the sea. Land communications along the sea

227 STEPHEN OF BYZANTIUM, *Ethnica*, s.v. Αἴγυπτος, thinks instead that Egypt was called Μύσρα (corr. of Μύαρα) by the Phoenicians.

228 *Pace* A. GROHMANN, *Arabien*, München 1963, p. 25.

229 *CIS* IV, 308, 12; A. JAMME, *Sabaean Inscriptions from Maḥram Bilqiš (Mârib)* (Publications of the American Foundation for the Study of Man 3), Baltimore 1962, No. 631, 21, p. 132-133. Translation first proposed by A. JAMME, rev. in *BiOr* 14 (1957), p. 80b. See also *Sabaic Dictionary*, p. 147.

230 *RÉS* 3022, 1.4; 3535, 2. See also K. CONTI ROSSINI, *op. cit.* (n. 85), p. 79-80, No. 71. Cf. *ibid.*, p. 180, and H. WINCKLER, *Altorientalische Forschungen* I, Leipzig 1897, p. 28-30, 289-290, 337-338.

231 *RÉS* 3022, 1 = K. CONTI ROSSINI, *op. cit.* (n. 85), p. 79, No. 71, 1.

232 I. EPH'AL, *op. cit.* (n. 99), p. 101-102, n. 339.

233 *SAA* II, 2, VI, 21, with an erroneous emendation. kur*Mu-ṣu-ru-na* appears first in the latest known version of Shalmaneser III's annals for his 21st regnal year (835 B.C.). The record ends with the words: "I received the tribute of Tyrians, Sidonians, Byblians. I marched as far as Muṣuruna" (*RIMA* III, text A.0.102.16, p. 79, lines 161'-162'). The final clause was added to the earlier version of the annals (*RIMA* III, text A.0.102.14, p. 67, lines 103-104) and probably alludes to the Philistine coast, heard of in Phoenicia.

coast and the course of the wadi were easy and anchorage facilities existed on the beach near the wadi mouth. In Hellenistic and Graeco-Roman times, the city was called ‘Ρινοκόλουρα, ‘Ρινοκόρουρα, ‘Ρινοκορούροι, ‘Ρεινοκορούλοι[234], a name linked by popular etymology with the penalty of nose amputation (ῥινο-κολούω)[235]. In reality, ‘Ρι-νοκολ-ουρα may be an approximate transcription of the Egyptian toponym, possibly **R3-n-nḫr-wr*, “the Mouth of the Great Vale”, borrowing and thus preserving the name uru*Naḫal*[236].

The misinterpretation of uru*Naḫal* among biblical scholars led also to the identification of al-‘Arīš with Arṣa, conquered by Esarhadddon in 679 B.C. Now, since Naḫal Muṣur is a town according to Neo-Assyrian texts and Arṣa is located by the same texts “near (*a-na i-te-e*) Naḫal Muṣur”, both toponyms can by no means designate one and the same city. In other words, the assumption that ‘Arīš is a corrupted form of Arṣa[237] is not justified. The popular Arab explanation of ‘Arīš as “hut made of twigs” by Jacob’s sons waiting for the authorization to enter Egypt can only be regarded as folk-etymology. The origin of the toponym ‘Arīš can be explained by a popular etymology of ‘Ρινοκόλουρα, which considered it being a name of nose amputation as punishment for crime[238]. This explanation was widely known in antiquity and is reported by Diodorus of Sicily[239], Strabo[240], and Seneca[241]. A shorter Greek word, literally designating such an amputee, was ἄρις or ἄρρις, “without nose”, but it was used in the figurative sense of “smell-less” and therefore was not so offensive. One can assume that Ἄρις replaced ‘Ρινοκόλουρα to a certain extent in later Byzantine times, preparing the way for the Arabic name al-‘Arīš, that became *Laris* among the Crusaders[242] and *Larris* around 1300 A.D.[243]

[234] The frequent confusion λ/ρ in the place name reveals its Egyptian origin.

[235] F.-M. ABEL, *art. cit.* (n. 226), p. 538.

[236] Greek κ served in various occasions to transcribe a sound close to [χ], for instance in Κάρραι = *Ḫarrān*, Κάσιος = Mount Ḫazi, Κάδυτις = *Ḫa-za-ti, Ḫa-zi-ti*, “Gaza”. No certainty is possible as long as the Egyptian name of the site is not attested.

[237] F.-M. ABEL, *art. cit.* (n. 226), p. 537-539; cf. A. ALT, *op. cit.* (n. 198), p. 228.

[238] A. WIEDEMANN, *Herodot’s zweites Buch mit sachlichen Erläuterungen*, Leipzig 1890, p. 496; J. CLÉDAT, *Notes sur l’Isthme de Suez*, in *BIFAO* 18 (1921), p. 167-197 (see p. 191-193).

[239] DIODORUS OF SICILY, *Bibliotheca Historica* I, 60, 1-5; 65.

[240] STRABO, *Geography* XVI, 2, 31.

[241] SENECA, *De Ira* III, 20.

[242] WILLIAM OF TYRE, *Chronicon* XI, 31, 24; XII, 23, 23; XVII, 30, 35; XIX, 14, 8; XXI, 19, 13; 23, 18, ed. R.B.C. HUYGENS, *Guillaume de Tyr: Chronique* (CCCM 63-63a), Turnhout 1986, p. 544, 575, 804, 883, 987, 993.

[243] C. KOHLER, *Deux projets de Croisade en Terre Sainte*, in *Revue de l’Orient Latin* 10 (1905), p. 432. Cf. Ch. CLERMONT-GANNEAU, *RAO* VII, Paris 1906, p. 119.

Raphia attacked by Assyrian troops in 720 B.C.
and defended by ambidextrous Cushites
(Khorsabad, Room V, slab 2, lower register [2-L]).

Gibbethon attacked by Assyrian troops in 720 B.C.
and defended by ambidextrous Cushites
(Khorsabad, Room V, slab 5, lower register, right [5-La]).

When Sargon II reached al-'Arīš, Osorkon IV found it expedient to send a tributary gift of horses to the Assyrian king, to buy him off[244]. It is uncertain whether he acted then as an independent ruler or in quality of a vassal of Shabako, as claimed by D. Kahn[245]. In fact, the extension of Shabako's power in Egypt before *ca.* 715 is an unknown factor. At any rate, soon after 716 B.C. Osorkon IV disappeared with the Cushite occupation of the entire Egypt by Shabako.

Sargon II's campaign in 716 B.C. aimed at extending Assyrian control up to the city of Naḫal Muṣur, transferring foreign population to this area, and organizing a lucrative trade centre (*kāru*) near the border of Egypt. Sargon appointed a local chieftain, the *nasīku* of the tribe Laban[246], as his representative among the inhabitants of the region and he established his control over the commercial centre trading with Egypt: "I opened the sealed [trad]ing post of the Borderland ([*kā*]*ri Muṣur kangu aptēma*). Assyrians and Egyptians I mingled [to]gether and made them trade [with each other]"[247].

Different suggestions for the site of the *kāru* have been made. Its location at Tell Abu Salima, 30 km east of al-'Arīš and 3 km from the sea, is based on the discovery of an Assyrian fortress including living quarters, a temple, and probably offices[248]. The temple supports the identification of the site with Bitylion or Psynofir, both mentioned in the Pithom trilingual inscription of Ptolemy IV Philopator (221-204 B.C.)[249], while the fortress seems to mark a way-station on the coastal road from Raphia (Rafāḥ) to al-'Arīš. No particular findings point at the existence of a trading post at the site. Commercial activities were taking place not only at Tell Abu Ruqeish[250] and Tell

[244] H. TADMOR, *art. cit.* (n. 197), p. 78, lines 10-11.

[245] D. KAHN, *art. cit.* (n. 214), p. 9-10.

[246] H. TADMOR, *art. cit.* (n. 197), p. 78, line 7: *ša* URU *La-ba-an*, where URU stands for *'āl*, "clan", "tribe". This tribe is mentioned after Raphia (*R-p-ḥ*) in Shoshenq's topographical list: *R-b-w-n* (No. bis 2), probably the older *Labwān*, "Lion(ess)" with nunation (cf. here above, p. 129). For *lbw-*, "lion, lioness", cf. E. LIPIŃSKI, *"Lion" and "Lioness" in Northwest Semitic*, in Y. AVISHUR - R. DEUTSCH (eds.), *Michael. Historical, Epigraphical and Biblical Studies in Honor of Prof. M. Heltzer*, Tel Aviv-Jaffa 1999, p. 213-220 (see p. 214-217).

[247] H. TADMOR, *art. cit.* (n. 197), p. 34: Annals, lines 17-18; Nimrud Prism, lines 46-49.

[248] Grid ref. 0646/0708. Cf. R. REICH, *The Identification of the 'Sealed* kāru *of Egypt'*, in *IEJ* 34 (1984), p. 32-38.

[249] First published by H. GAUTHIER - H. SOTTAS, *Un décret trilingue en l'honneur de Ptolémée IV*, Le Caire 1925.

[250] Grid ref. 08610/09185: W. CULICAN, *The Graves at Tell er-Reqeish*, in *The Australian Journal of Biblical Archaeology* 2/2 (1973), p. 66-105 = W. CULICAN, *Opera Selecta*,

Gaza attacked by Assyrian troops in 720 B.C.
and defended by hooded Philistine bowmen
(Khorsabad, Room V, slabs 5 and 6, lower register [5-Lb and 6-L]).

Ǧemmeh[251]: trade involving Assyrians and Egyptians was certainly driven further west, around al-'Arīš, on the western bank of Wādī al-'Arīš[252]. Its importance and nature is revealed by the Late Egyptian loanword *ḫry*, designating a kind of myrrh[253]. The word is written *ḫl* in Demotic[254] and it appears with various spellings in Coptic texts[255]. There is little doubt that it is borrowed from Neo-Assyrian *ḫīlu*, "resin"[256]. The resin in question was probably myrrh brought by caravans from South Arabia or resin of cedar trees shipped from Phoenicia, possibly a mixture of various spices.

Göteborg 1986, p. 85-124; R. HESTRIN - M. DAYAGI-MENDELS, *Another Pottery Group from Abu Ruqeish,* in *The Israel Museum Journal* 2 (1982), p. 49-57; E. OREN - N. FLEMING - S. KORNBERG - R. FEINSTEIN - P. NAḤSHONI, *A Phoenician Emporium on the Border of Egypt,* in *Qadmoniot* 19 (1986), p. 83-91 (in Hebrew); E.D. OREN, *Ruqeish*, in *NEAEHL*, Jerusalem 1993, Vol. IV, p. 1293-1294; Y. HUSTER, *Tell er-Ruqeish,* in *ESI* 111 (2000), p. 87*-88*.

251 Grid ref. 097/088. The bibliography of G.W. VAN BEEK's excavations is collected by E. VOGEL - B. HOLTZCLAW, *Bibliography of Holy Land Sites II,* in *HUCA* 52 (1981), p. 1-98 (see p. 41: Jemmeh, Tell). Add G.W. VAN BEEK, *Jemmeh, Tell,* in *NEAEHL*, Jerusalem 1993, Vol. II, p. 667-674. One should refer in particular to the Neo-Assyrian buildings, going back to the 8th-7th centuries B.C.

252 I. EPH'AL, *op. cit.* (n. 99), p. 102-103.

253 A. ERMAN - H. GRAPOW, *Wörterbuch der ägyptischen Sprache*, Leipzig 1926-31, Vol. III, p. 323:21.

254 W. ERICHSEN, *Demotisches Glossar*, Kopenhagen 1954, p. 368.

255 W. WESTENDORF, *Koptisches Handwörterbuch*, Heidelberg 1965-77, p. 309.

256 *AHw*, p. 345-346.

Cushitic pharaohs

Yamani's revolt at Ashdod[257], followed by his flight to Egypt in 711 B.C.[258], was most likely supported by the new Cushitic dynasty, ruling in Egypt. The discovery of fragments of Egyptian faience "New Year bottles" at Ashdod, two of them bearing Egyptian inscriptions[259], implies more than ordinary relations with Egypt[260]. Since these fragments have been found in Stratum VI, represented mainly by pits witnessing an ephemeral activity after the destruction of the Stratum VIII-VII city[261], the "New Year bottles" may be related to the years of Yamani's rule. In that period, there are also signs of relations on higher level between Egypt and Transjordan. The Egyptian statuette from the time of the Twenty-fifth Dynasty, found in a Nabataean shrine at Petra[262], the presence of a "New Year bottle" in the Moabite fortress of Lahūn, on the higher Wādī Muğib[263], the fragment of an Egyptian relief chalice from Buṣeirā[264] are significant of more than ordinary trade relations, but cannot be dated in a precise way. One should also remember that a scarab of Shabako was found in Palestine at a non determinate site[265].

[257] See here above, p. 76. Yamani's revolt was the subject of a Ph. D. at the Jagellonian University, Cracow, in 1978: Z.J. KAPERA, *The Rebellion of Yamani in Ashdod. A Study in the History of Philistia between c. 713 and 709 B.C.*, Kraków 1978. A summary was published in *Folia Orientalia* 20 (1979), p. 313-314, and some parts of the work appeared in print: Z.J. KAPERA, *Was Ya-ma-ni a Cypriot*, *ibid.*, 14 (1972-73), p. 207-218; *The Ashdod Stele of Sargon II*, *ibid.*, 17 (1976), p. 87-99; *The Oldest Account of Sargon II's Campaign against Ashdod*, *ibid.*, 24 (1987), p. 29-46.

[258] A. FUCHS, *Die Annalen des Jahres 711 v. Chr. nach Prismenfragmenten aus Ninive und Assur*, Helsinki 1998, p. 124.

[259] M. DOTHAN *et al.*, *Ashdod II/III* ('Atiqot. English Series 9-10), Jerusalem 1971, p. 37 and 170-171, figs 3:15 and 96:17.

[260] This is rightly stressed by A. MALAMAT, *History of Biblical Israel*, Leiden 2001, p. 289, n. 19.

[261] I. FINKELSTEIN - L. SINGER-AVITZ, *art. cit.* (n. 7), p. 246.

[262] The statuette is housed in the Amman Museum: JAM 16193; cf. A.I. MEZA, *An Egyptian Statuette in Petra*, in *ADAJ* 37 (1993), p. 427-432, and in *JARCE* 32 (1995), p. 179-183.

[263] D. HOMÈS-FREDERICQ, *Late Bronze and Iron Age Evidence from Lehun in Moab*, in P. BIEŃKOWSKI (ed.), *Early Edom and Moab*, Sheffield 1992, p. 187-202 (see p. 197-198).

[264] A. MELLWARD, *A Fragment of an Egyptian Relief Chalice from Buseirah, Jordan*, in *Levant* 7 (1975), p. 16-18; C.-M. BENNETT, *Excavations at Buseirah (Biblical Bozrah)*, in F.A. SAWYER - D.J.A. CLONES (eds.), *Midian, Moab and Edom*, Sheffield 1983, p. 9-17 (see p. 11-13).

[265] Toronto R.O.M.A. 1718; cf. J. YOYOTTE, *Plaidoyer pour l'authenticité du scarabée historique de Shabako*, in *Biblica* 37 (1956), p. 457-476; ID., rev. in *BiOr* 14 (1957), p. 30a; ID., *Sur le scarabée historique de Shabako. Note additionnelle*, in *Biblica* 39 (1958), p. 206-210.

Hanun, his family, and dignitaries deported to Assyria
(Khorsabad, Room V, slabs 8 and 9, lower register [8-L and 9-L]).

Shebitko, nephew and successor of Shabako, tried apparently to improve his relations with Assyria and extradited Yamani to Sargon II in 707/6, in the first year of his reign (707/6-690 B.C.)[266]. However, the death of Sargon II on the battlefield in Anatolia, in 705 B.C., prompted a reversal of Shebitko's policy. This radical change is attested explicitly in Sennacherib's annals, where the unnamed "king of Cush" fighting the Assyrians in Palestine is certainly Shebitko.

The military intervention of the Cushitic pharaoh took place in 701 B.C. Its aim was to oppose Sennacherib's campaign against the Levantine kinglets, which tried to shake off the Assyrian domination after Sargon II's death. In fact, Egypt was interested in establishing a buffer-zone against the Assyrians by preserving the independence of the Syro-Phoenician and Palestinian states. Cushitic involvement is alluded to in II Kings 19, 9[267] and stated clearly in the annals of Sennacherib, who claims victory over an Egyptian expedition at Eltekeh in Philistia[268], possibly Tell aš-Šallāf[269]. The Assyrian army then turned toward Judah and conquered several towns, establishing its headquarters at Lachish,

[266] This results from Sargon II's inscription found at Tang-i War and from the Assyrian records of the events in 707/6 B.C., when Yamani arrived in Assyria: A. FUCHS, *op. cit.* (n. 258), p. 129; D. KAHN, *art. cit.* (n. 214), p. 8-9.

[267] An authorized and short assessment of the biblical accounts on Sennacherib's campaign can be found in J.A. SOGGIN, *Storia d'Israele*, Brescia 2002, p. 305-308.

[268] D.D. LUCKENBILL, *The Annals of Sennacherib* (OIP 2), Chicago 1924, p. 30-33, col. II, 78-III, 7; p. 68-69, lines 23-25; E. FRAHM, *Einleitung in die Sanherib-Inschriften* (AfO, Beih. 26), Wien 1997, p. 54 and 59, lines 43-45.

[269] Grid ref. 135/108. Cf. B. MAZAR, *The Cities of the Territory of Dan*, in *IEJ* 10 (1960), p. 65-77 (see p. 72 ff.).

but had to terminate the siege of Jerusalem abruptly, probably due to internal problems in Assyria. This event was then seen by Judaeans as a miraculous deliverance, but presented by Herodotus in a different way, from an Egyptian point of view[270].

The Cushitic pharaoh leading the Egyptian forces is called Taharqo in II Kings 19, 9[271], while Herodotus places these events during the reign of a high priest of Hephaestus, he calls Σεθῖς, possibly a confusion with Seti II (1199-1193 B.C.), the son of Merneptah. The god, viz. Ptah of Memphis, is supposed to have appeared to Sethos in a dream, like he did to Merneptah before the Libyan War[272]. This story may have prompted the idea that Sethos was a priest of Hephaestus. In reality, the pharaoh marching in 701 B.C. to meet the enemy on the eastern frontier must have been Shebitko, who had become king of Egypt in 707/6 B.C.[273] He is probably mentioned by name in Gen. 10, 7 and I Chron. 1, 9 as a son of Cush[274]. The beginning of Taharqo's reign should be placed instead in 690 B.C. The mention of this pharaoh in II Kings 19, 9 is therefore an error, easily explainable by the fact that the account was written later, under the assumption that Taharqo was already king of Egypt in 701 B.C. The Cushitic practice or law of succession may have occasioned a confusion as well, since Taharqo was a son of Piye / Piankhy[275], who

[270] HERODOTUS, *History* II, 141.

[271] The spelling *Trhqh* of his name in II Kings. 19, 9 and Is. 37, 9 is incorrect and results from a metathesis. It should have been written *Thrqh*, with *h* used as *mater lectionis* for *ō*, thus **Taharqō*. The forms Θαρακα (with variants) of the Septuagint and *Tharaca* of the Vulgate do not imply another spelling, since *h* is not transcribed; they show that final *h* was regarded as a vowel letter for *ā*. Neither the cuneiform spelling *Tar-qu-u/ú* (R. BORGER, *Die Inschriften Asarhaddons, Königs von Assyrien* [AfO, Beih. 9], Graz 1956, p. 127) nor Manethon's Τάρκος, Ταρακός, Ταράκης or *Saracus* are helpful. However, STRABO's transcriptions Τεαρκώ (*Geography* I, 3, 21) and Τεάρκονα (*Geography* XV, 1, 6) would correspond to *Thrqh*. Instead, JOSEPHUS FLAVIUS, *Jewish Antiquities* X, 1, 4, §17, calls him Θαρσίκης. Cf. J.M.A. JANSSEN, *Que sait-on actuellement du pharanon Taharqa?*, in *Biblica* 34 (1953), p. 23-43 (see p. 23-24).

[272] W.M. MÜLLER, *Egyptological Researches* I, Washington 1906, Pl. 22, lines 28-29; C. MANASSA, *The Great Karnak Inscription of Merneptah: Grand Strategy in the 13th Century BC* (Yale Egyptological Studies 5), New Haven 2003, p. 40-41, 117-119, Pl. 7, lines 28-29; K.A. KITCHEN, *Ramesside Inscriptions. Translated & Annotated. Translations* IV, Malden 2003, p. 5.

[273] Cf. p. 143, n. 266.

[274] E. LIPIŃSKI, *Les Chamites selon Gen 10, 6-10 et 1 Chr 1, 8-16*, in *ZAH* 5 (1992), p. 135-162 (see p. 146-147).

[275] The Cushitic name "Piye" was read "Piankhy" because of its Egyptian hieroglyphic spelling. For the decisive justification of its present reading, see K.H. PRIESE, *Nichtägyptische Namen und Wörter in den ägyptischen Inschriften der Könige von Kusch* I, in *Mitteilungen des Instituts für Orientforschung* 14 (1968), p. 166-191 (see p. 166-175).

Ekron attacked by Assyrian troops and defended by hooded Philistine bowmen (Khorsabad, Room V, slab 10 and 11, lower register [10-L and 11-L]).

was succeeded first by his younger brother Shabako, then by his son Shebitko, and later by Taharqo[276]. Nothing justifies D. Kahn's hypothesis that Taharqo was sent to Philistia by his brother Shebitko, although this idea was already defended by St. Gevirtz in considerations of autobiographical passages on two of the five Taharqo's steles discovered at Kawa, in Nubia[277]. In his sixth year Taharqo relates thus that as "a goodly youth, a king's brother", he came from Nubia to rejoin his brother Shebitko, who was then the reigning pharaoh[278]. In another inscription, he tells that he had left his mother as "a youth of twenty years, when he came with His Majesty to Lower Egypt". He adds that his mother came later to the north to see him[279]. Should Taharqo have led Egyptian troops in the battle of Elteqe / Altaqu in 701, when he was in his teens, he would have mentioned it, just as he recorded his voyage to Thebes, when he was "a goodly youth", and his coming to Lower Egypt, when he was twenty years old.

[276] M.F.L. MACADAM, *The Temples of Kawa* I. *The Inscriptions. Text*, Oxford 1949, p. 124-125.

[277] St. GEVIRTZ, *Patterns in the Early Poetry of Israel* (SAOC 32), Chicago 1963, p. 30-34, in particular p. 31-33, n. 17.

[278] M.F.L. MACADAM, *op. cit.* (n. 276), Stele IV, 7-8. This could have been in 705/4 B.C., when Shebitko made his solemn entry into Thebes. The latter event is dated to Shebitko's third year in Taharqo's inscription found in 1990 on the quay of Karnak; cf. J. VON BECKERATH, *Ägypten und der Feldzug Sancheribs im Jahre 701 v. Chr.*, in *UF* 24 (1992 [1993]), p. 3-8 (see p. 4, n. 11-12 with references).

[279] M.F.L. MACADAM, *op. cit.* (n. 276), Stele V, 16-17. A French translation of these passages with comments is provided by J.M.A. JANSSEN, *art. cit.* (n. 271), p. 29 and 32.

The Cushitic pharaoh, whom figurative monuments represent with Negroid features[280], was regarded at the time of Strabo as one of the great conquerors[281] and this seems to have also been the opinion of the Egyptians at the time of the Roman Empire[282]. One can hardly explain this fame by a literal interpretation of Taharqo's topographical list[283]. There was rather a conscious attempt, possibly in Persian times, at glorifying pharaohs and comparing their renown to the fame of the Achaemenid kings[284]. This phenomenon would have paralleled the "Myth of Solomon"[285], which finds its expression in biblical compositions dating precisely from the Persian period[286]. The reality was somewhat different and its visual reflex can be seen on Esarhaddon's steles, erected after the invasion of Egypt and showing Taharqo's son kneeling in front of the Assyrian king with a ring through his lip and shackled[287]. However, this was propaganda as well.

Interventions by Taharqo in Western Asia and the Levantine kinglets in particular are known from Assyrian and other sources. Traces of the passage of Egyptian envoys and of diplomatic gifts sent to Assyria can probably be recognized in Taharqo's seal used on Palmyrene tesserae in Graeco-Roman times[288], in a large Taharqo's scarab in ivory, found at

[280] H. SCHÄFER, *Eine Bronzefigur des Taharka*, in *ZÄS* 33 (1895), p. 114-116; E. BOSSE, *Zwei Kunstwerke aus der ägyptischen Sammlung der Ermitage*, in *ZÄS* 72 (1936), p. 131-133; *ANEP*, Nos. 424 and 447. Cf. here, p. 149.

[281] G. GOOSSENS, *Taharqa le Conquérant*, in *Chronique d'Égypte* 22 (1947), p. 239-244.

[282] P. MONTET, *Germanicus et le vieillard de Thèbes*, in *Mélanges 1945*. III. *Études historiques* (Publications de la Faculté des Lettres de l'Université de Strasbourg 103), Paris 1947, p. 47-79. Summary in J.M.A. JANSSEN (ed.), *Annual Egyptological Bibliography 1948*, Leiden 1949, p. 177-178.

[283] J. SIMONS, *op. cit.* (n. 77), p. 187. This list was copied from a list of Horemheb. A short and fragmentary list from Sanam only mentions Phoenicians and Libyans.

[284] J.M.A. JANSSEN, *art. cit.* (n. 271), p. 34; cf. G. POSENER, *À propos de la stèle de Bentresh*, in *BIFAO* 34 (1934), p. 75-81; J. SCHWARTZ, *Les conquérants perses et la littérature égyptienne*, in *BIFAO* 48 (1948 [1949]), p. 65-80.

[285] The formula was used by G.J. WIGHTMAN, *The Myth of Solomon*, in *BASOR* 277-278 (1990), p. 5-22.

[286] LIPIŃSKI, *Itineraria Phoenicia*, p. 217-220.

[287] B.N. PORTER, *Assyrian Propaganda for the West: Esarhaddon's Stelae for Til Barsip and Sam'al*, in G. BUNNENS (ed.), *Essays on Syria in the Iron Age* (Ancient Near Eastern Studies. Suppl. 7), Louvain 2000, p. 143-176, in particular p. 168, Fig. 15, and p. 174-175.

[288] BM. 48116; cf. B. PORTER - R.L. MOSS, *Topographical Bibliography of Ancient Egyptian Hieroglyphic Texts, Reliefs, and Paintings* VII. *Nubia, the Deserts, and Outside Egypt*, Oxford 1951, p. 39; H. INGHOLT - H. SEYRIG - J. STARCKY - A. CAQUOT, *Recueil des tessères de Palmyre* (BAH 58), Paris 1955, No. 988, p. 125, Pl. 45; R. GIVEON, *The Impact of Egypt on Canaan* (OBO 20), Freiburg-Göttingen 1978, p. 124.

Limestone stele of Shabako
(Moscow, Pushkin Museum of Fine Arts I.1.a.5646 [4118]).

Nimrud in Fort Shalmaneser[289], and in fragments of alabaster vases recovered at Ashur[290]. An inventory of the temple of Kawa in Nubia mentions gifts brought from Western Asia in the 10th year of Taharqo[291], i.e. 681 B.C., which is precisely the year of the murder of Sennacherib. One might thus assume that Taharqo took advantage of the situation in Assyria and tried to exercise his influence in Philistia and Phoenicia. Allusions to campaigns in Syro-Phoenicia, both failed and planned, may be recognized in a fragmentary inscription from Karnak, in which Taharqo addresses his prayer to the god Amon[292]. The revolt of Baal I, king of Tyre, in 671 B.C.[293], is thus explained in Esarhaddon's annals by the confidence the king of Tyre had placed in Taharqo. The Cushitic king is not mentioned in the case of Abdi-Milkūti's revolt at Sidon, in 677/6 B.C., but intrigues by Egyptians may be assumed there as well. The interventions by Egypt in the affairs of Syro-Phoenicia and Palestine prompted, from 674 to 664 B.C., repeated Assyrian invasions of Egypt. The western vassals of Assyria had to provide troops for these campaigns, directed against Taharqo, but details are not known.

The invasion of Egypt was prepared by Esarhaddon's conquest of the city of Arṣa in 679/8, followed by the deportation of its ruler, the latter's son, and all the inhabitants. The ruler bore the Old Arabian name *A-su-ḫi-li* or *A-su-ḫe-li*, which should be linked with the frequent Ṣafaitic personal name *S²ḥl*[294], not with Arabic *sahl*, "easy". Although the anthroponym *Suhayl* is attested in Arabic[295], the interpretation proposed in *PNA*[296] is questionable, because West-Semitic laryngeal *h* is rarely marked in Neo-Assyrian by signs with *ḫ*. For instance, the alleged exam-

[289] ND 7624, published by M.E.L. MALLOWAN, *Nimrud and Its Remains*, London 1966, No. 583; R. GIVEON, *op. cit.* (n. 288), p. 124 and Fig. 72a-c.

[290] İstanbul Arkeoloji Müzeleri, Inv. Nos. 9583 and 9584; cf. *AfO* 10 (1935), p. 94; B. PORTER - R.L. MOSS, *op. cit.* (n. 288), p. 397; J. MARZAHN - B. SALJE (eds.), *Wiedererstehendes Assur: 100 Jahre deutsche Ausgrabungen in Assyrien*, Mainz a/R 2003, p. 140-143..

[291] M.F.L. MACADAM, *op. cit.* (n. 276), Stele No. VI, p. 32-41, transliterated and translated also in T. EIDE - T. HÄGG - R.H. PIERCE - L. TÖRÖK (eds.), *Fontes Historiae Nubiorum* I, Bergen 1994, p. 164 ff. Cf. A.J. SPALINGER, *The Foreign Policy of Egypt Preceding the Assyrian Conquest,* in *Chronique d'Égypte* 53 (1978), p. 22-47.

[292] P. VERNUS, *Inscriptions de la Troisième Période Intermédiaire* (I), in *BIFAO* 75 (1975), p. 1-66, Pls. I-V (see p. 29-49). The inscription is transliterated and translated also in T. EIDE *et al.*, *op. cit.* (n. 291), p. 181 ff., No. 26.

[293] B.U. SCHIPPER, *op. cit.* (n. 2), p. 220, confounds the campaign against Abdi-Milkūti of Sidon with the campaign in 671 B.C.

[294] HARDING, *Arabian Names*, p. 342, s.v. *ŠḤL.*

[295] J. ŁACINA, *op. cit.* (n. 224), p. 503.

[296] K. ÅKERMAN, *Asuḫili,* in *PNA* I/1, Helsinki 1998, p. 139.

Head from a black granite statue of king Taharqo
(Cairo Museum 560).

ples with the Aramaic root *ngh*, "to shine", in proper names are uncertain, since the names in question may be formed with *ngḥ*, corresponding to Arabic *naǧaḥa*, "to succeed", "to be successful"[297]. In consequence, the interpretation of these names, as proposed in *PNA*[298], is doubtful and a negative opinion can be expressed in the case of *A-su-ḫe-li* as explained in *PNA*.

The Ṣafaitic anthroponym *S²ḥl* has been related to the Hebrew poetical name *šaḥal* of the lion[299], although Ṣafaitic *s²* normally corresponds to Hebrew *ś*. Therefore, a link with Arabic *šaḥḥala*, "to prune", has been proposed as well[300]. A derivative of *śḥl* survived with Bedouin of the Hauran

[297] J. Łacina, *op. cit.* (n. 224), p. 875.

[298] H.D. Baker - L. Pearce, *PNA* II/2, Helsinki 2001, p. 921-922.

[299] E. Littmann, *Syria. Publications of the Princeton University Archaeological Expedition to Syria in 1904-1905. Division IV. Semitic Inscriptions. Section C. Safaïtic Inscriptions*, Leiden 1943, p. 345a.

[300] Harding, *Arabian Names*, p. 342.

region as *Šaḫḫāl*[301], that belongs to the nominal pattern *qattāl* of professional names. However, a meaning like "pruner" does not suit the social and economic conditions of Ṣafaitic or Bedouin way of life. Since the basic meaning of the root *šḥl* seems to have been "to sharpen", it is probable that the connotation "to prune" of Stem II of *śḥl* has the same origin[302] and that *šḥl* and *śḥl* go back to a single Semitic root. In other words, the problem thus arisen parallels the cases of Hebrew *yš'* and Ṣabaic *ws*^{2}*'*[303], of Hebrew *šdy* and Thamudic *s*^{2}*dy*[304]. Some merging of *ś* with *š* seems to have occurred in one of the dialects concerned, probably in Hebrew. This could have happened at an early stage of the development of the language, like in Ugaritic and in Phoenician, and the resulting articulation was accepted later as the correct form of particular roots or lexemes.

Since the case of *šḥl* / *s*^{2}*ḥl* is not isolated, less likely connections can be left aside, for example with Ṣafaitic *S*^{1}*ḥly*[305], which is the Arabic noun *siḥliya*, "lizard"[306]. Its vocalization does not match *A-su-ḫe-li* and the single attestation of the uncertain *'s*^{1}*ḥl*[307] does not inspire much confidence. We assume therefore that the Ṣafaitic personal name *S*^{2}*ḥl* meant either "Lion" or "Young Lion", if we vocalize it on the pattern *fu'ēl* < *fu'ayl* (diminutive). The initial *A* in the name of the ruler of Arṣa may be a Neo-Assyrian feature, paralleled in *A-gu-su*, which corresponds to Aramaic *Gūš*[308]. However, the early use of the demonstrative and definite article *hn-* in North-Arabian may suggest a form *haś-śuḥayl*, "the young lion". The definite article seems indeed to appear in North-Arabian names, as shown by the Ṣafaitic pairs *Mlk / Hmlk*, *Msk / Hmsk*, *'wḏ / H'wḏ*, *'ḏr / H'ḏr*, etc. This usage continues in Classical and Literary Arabic, which may use the article with proper names, especially when they consist in a common noun, like *al-Ḥakam*. This is precisely the case of *s*^{2}*uḥayl*.

If the conquest of Arṣa was aimed at preparing a military basis for the invasion of Egypt, the city should be located near the border. It cannot be al-'Arīš, which was the city of the Vale of the Borderland, ^{uru}*Naḫal Muṣur*. One should thus look for a site to the west of this town, since Esarhaddon's campaign certainly aimed at extending the Assyrian control beyond al-'Arīš, already reached by Sargon II in 716 B.C.

301 E. LITTMANN, *Beduinen- und Drusen-Namen aus dem Ḥaurân-Gebiet* (Nachrichten der K. Gesellschaft der Wissenschaften zu Göttingen. Phil.-hist. Klasse 1921), Göttingen 1921, p. 12.

302 Cf. E. LIPIŃSKI, *art. cit.* (n. 246), p. 218-219, where this point has not been examined thoroughly.

303 K. CONTI ROSSINI, *op. cit.* (n. 85), p. 141.

304 E. LIPIŃSKI, *Shadday, Shadrapha, et le dieu Satrape*, in *ZAH* 8 (1995), p. 245-274 (see p. 248).

305 HARDING, *Arabian Names*, p. 312, s.v. *SḤLY*.

306 J. ŁACINA, *op. cit.* (n. 224), p. 484.

307 HARDING, *Arabian Names*, p. 41, s.v. *'SḤL*.

308 M. LUUKKO, *Agūsu*, in *PNA* I/1, Helsinki 1998, p. 56.

Esarhaddon's inscriptions situate Arṣa "near ^{uru}*Naḫal Muṣur*", but Raphia, similarly described in these inscription as "close to ^{uru}*Naḫal Muṣur*", lies about 45 km from al-'Arīš[309]. Now, the first town indicated on the map of Madaba west of 'Ῥινοκόλουρα is 'Οστρακίνη, al-Warrāda of the Arab itineraries, 36 km from al-'Arīš. This distance corresponds to a one-day journey of caravans. The nearby Cape Straki preserves the name of Ostracine, which was situated to the south of the Arab town, at the site of al-Flūsiyāt, where it was discovered in 1914[310].

According to St. Jerome, the Greek name of 'Οστρακίνη was explained by local people as a translation of *ares*, "potsherd", in Aramaic *ḥares*[311]. This popular etymology is old, since it is echoed in the Egyptian name of the site, which is mentioned in the *Pap. Demot. Cairo 31169*, dating certainly to the 4th-2nd centuries B.C.: *Mktl n-bld'*, "Tower of the Potsherds"[312]. This does not mean that "potsherd" was the original meaning of the toponym. Its true name was probably *ḥarṣa*, "the channel", an allusion to the opening of the Sirbonis Lake on the Mediterranean. The Semitic name of this opening, situated nowadays just in front of Ostracine, was translated in Greek by ἔκρηγμα. Strabo localizes it at 200 stadia (37 km) from the oriental end of the Sirbonis Lake[313] and Ptolemy assumes that Ecregma (63° 50') is only 5' east of Casius (64° 15')[314]. Instead, on the map of Madaba, Casius (*TO KACIN*) is quite close to Ostracine. The most likely solution is to locate it approximately at its present place, in front of Ostracine, and to assume that this was its location when **Ḥarṣa* got its name.

The *Arṣa* of Esarhadddon's inscriptions is thus likely to be a transcription of **Ḥarṣa*, possibly pronounced *'Arṣā* with the well-known change *ḥ* > ', attested especially in place names[315]. The 7th-century town

309 I. EPH'AL, *op. cit.* (n. 99), p. 104.

310 The Byzantine remains, discovered at the site, are described by E.D. OREN, *A Christian Settlement at Ostracine in North Sinai,* in *Qadmoniot* 11 (1978), p. 81-87 (in Hebrew); ID., *Ostrakine,* in *NEAEHL,* Jerusalem 1993, Vol. III, p. 1171-1173.

311 S. HIERONYMUS, *In Esaiam* 19, 18, ed. by M. ADRIAEN, *CCSL* 73, Turnhout 1963, p. 198:12-15. Cf. F.-M. ABEL, *Les confins de la Palestine et de l'Égypte sous les Ptolémées* V. *Stations et relais de la route gréco-romaine,* in *RB* 49 (1940), p. 63-75, 224-239, and Pls. VII-VIII (see p. 231).

312 P. CHUVIN - J. YOYOTTE, *Documents relatifs au culte pélusien de Zeus Casios,* in *Revue Archéologique* 1986-1, p. 41-63 (see p. 50).

313 STRABO, *Geography* XVI, 2, 32.

314 PTOLEMY, *Geography* IV, 5, 6 (p. 682). See now the discussion by H. VERRETH, *Lake Serbonis and Sabkhat Bardawil in the Northern Sinai,* in L. MOOREN (ed.), *Politics, Administration and Society in the Hellenistic and Roman World* (Studia Hellenistica 36), Leuven 2000, p. 471-487.

315 For a discussion of the linguistic change *ḥ* > ' in Arabic and Aramaic dialects, see G. KAMPFFMEYER, *Alte Namen im heutigen Palästina und Syrien,* in *ZDPV* 15 (1892),

could be located either at Ostracine or at al-Warrāda, the site of the harbour of Ostracine, next to the ἔκρηγμα. Instead, the identification of *Arṣa* with ^uru^*Iu-ur-za* in the Amarna letters[316] and with *Y-r-ḏ* in the Annals of Tuthmosis III[317] and the topographical lists of Tuthmosis III[318] and Shoshenq I[319] cannot be supported. Examining this question, one should also take *Tel 'Arzā* into account, where several men were killed during the Bar-Kochba revolt[320].

Several suggestions have been made for the identification of ^uru^*Iu-ur-za*, hence mistakenly also of *Arṣa*: Tell al-Fūl, Tell Ǧemmeh, Ḫirbet ʻIrq, and Abu Hureira (Tel Haror). The location of ^uru^*Iu-ur-za* at the site of Tell al-Fūl, near the junction of Wādī aṣ-Ṣarār and Wādī al-Muḫeizīn, may match the indications of the Amarna letters and of Tuthmosis III's list[321], as well as the western extent of the Bar-Kochba revolt. However, the Annals of Tuthmosis III and Row IX of Shoshenq I's topographical list indicate that *Y-r-ḏ-3* was situated in the extreme south of Palestine. B. Mazar's suggestion that 'Ιαρδά and "Ορδα reflect the late transcription of *Yurza* is most likely correct, but the proposal of identifying this place with Tell Ǧemmeh, 12 km south of Gaza, is just an unsubstantiated guess. On the Madaba map *ΟΡΔΑ* is situated between *CEANA* (Ḫirbet Siḫān)[322] and *ΦΩΤΙC* (Bīr Fṭeis)[323]. Therefore, it can by no means be identified with the site of the mosaic pavement at Kibbutz Kissufim[324], about 1 km north-west of Tell

p. 63-65 (see p. 64, n. 90); C. RABIN, *Ancient West-Arabian*, London 1951, p. 84-87; E.Y. KUTSCHER, *Studies in Galilean Aramaic*, Ramat-Gan 1976, p. 70-96, 103-104; R. ZADOK, *On West Semites in Babylonia during the Chaldean and Achaemenian Periods. An Onomastic Study*, 2nd ed., Jerusalem 1978, p. 244.

316 *EA* 314-316.

317 K. SETHE - W. HELCK, *Urkunden der 18. Dynastie*, Berlin 1906-58 (reprint, 1984), p. 846:6. Cf. S. AḤITUV, *op. cit.* (n. 90), p. 202-203; R. HANNIG, *Die Sprache der Pharaonen. Grosses Handwörterbuch Ägyptisch-Deutsch (2800-950 v. Chr.)*, 2nd ed., Mainz a/R 1997, p. 1310-1311.

318 List I, 60, in J. SIMONS, *op. cit.* (n. 77). Also in its copies: List V, 11, *ibid.*, and List Va, A39, in K.A. KITCHEN, *Ramesside Inscriptions* I, Oxford 1968-75, p. 36-37.

319 No. 133. Identification proposed by A. MAISLER (MAZAR), *Yurza. The Identification of Tell Jemmeh,* in *PEQ* 84 (1952), p. 48-51; ID., *The Campaign of Pharaoh Shishak to Palestine,* in *Volume du Congrès. Strasbourg 1956* (VTS 4), Leiden 1957, p. 57-66 (see p. 65), followed by S. AḤITUV, *op. cit.* (n. 90), p. 203, who rightly discards the proposals of N. Na'aman and A.F. Rainey (*ibid.*, n. 631).

320 Mishnah, *Yebamoth* XVI, 7. 'Αρίζα, a city of *Palaestina Prima* in the Byzantine period, is probably a different place, as suggested by the vocalization.

321 A. ALT, *Das Institut 1924*, in *Palästinajahrbuch* 21 (1925), p. 5-58 (see p. 17); ID., *Das Institut im Jahre 1932*, in *Palästinajahrbuch* 29 (1933), p. 5-29 (see p. 12-13); ABEL, *Géographie* II, p. 27.

322 Grid ref. 105/095.

323 Grid ref. 114/081.

Ǧemmeh. A similar approach to a topographical problem is founded upon a nearby complex of churches with mosaic floors, 500 m from the Kibbutz Magen[325]. According to V. Tsaferis[326], the ancient name of the site may have been Λύχνος, "Lamp", because the local tomb of Sheikh *Nūrān* could preserve the souvenir of the place name *Lychnos*, referred to by St. Jerome in his *Life of St. Hilarion*[327]. Now, *Lychnos* is located by St. Jerome near Betilium, probably Tell Abu Salima, 30 km north-east of al-'Arīš. The area in question was densely populated in the Byzantine period and the ancient name of the site should be confirmed by other means. The hill of Sheikh Nūrān was admittedly identified by W.F. Albright with Bitylion / Betilium, but A. Alt convincingly located the latter place at Sheikh Zuweid, close to Tell Abu Salima. This is most likely the location both of Bitylion and of the nearby Lychnos[328].

Another ineffective research aimed at identifying Yurza is based on ceramic and petrographic analysis of tablets *EA* 315 and 316 sent to Amarna by Pu-Ba'la, the ruler of Yurza[329]. It only provides the **possibility** of Yurza being Tell Ǧemmeh or Ḫirbet Abu Hureira (Tel Haror). Since this investigation solely considered hypotheses formulated by local scholars, nothing is said, for instance, about the suggested identification of Yurza as Tell al-Fūl. The practical results of such an analysis are thus negligible.

A. Alt has shown in a convincing way that Ὄρδα has to be located at Ḫirbet 'Irq, at the junction of Wādī aš-Šerī'a and Wādī Imleiḥ (Wādī Fṭeis), about 20 km southeast of Gaza[330]. Since the place name could be

[324] Grid ref. 0959/0893: R. COHEN, *Kissufim*, in *IEJ* 27 (1977), p. 254-256; *RB* 85 (1978), p. 104-106, and *NEAEHL*, Jerusalem 1993, Vol. III, p. 876-878 (see p. 878); S. AḤITUV, *op. cit.* (n. 90), p. 203, n. 635.

[325] Grid ref. 0948/0893: V. TSAFERIS, *Magen (1977-1978)*, in *RB* 85 (1978), p. 106-108; ID., *An Early Christian Church Complex at Magen*, in *BASOR* 258 (1985), p. 1-15; ID., *Mosaics and Inscriptions from Magen*, *ibid.*, p. 17-32; N. FEIG, *Pottery, Glass, and Coins from Magen*, *ibid.*, p. 33-40.

[326] V. TSAFERIS, *art. cit.* (n. 325), *RB* 85 (1978), p. 108, and *BASOR* 258 (1985), p. 14-15. He is following a suggestion made by A. MUSIL, *Arabia Petraea* II. *Edom* II, Wien 1908, p. 244.

[327] St. JEROME, *Life of St. Hilarion* 30, in *PL* XXIII, col. 44.

[328] W.F. ALBRIGHT, *Egypt and the Early History of the Negeb*, in *JPOS* 4 (1924), p. 131-161 (see p. 154-155); A. ALT, *Bitolion und Bethelea* and *Nachträge*, in *ZDPV* 49 (1926), p. 236-242 and 333-335. Cf. also here above, p. 140.

[329] Y. GOREN - I. FINKELSTEIN - N. NA'AMAN, *Inscribed in Clay. Provenance Study of the Amarna Letters and Other Ancient Near Eastern Texts*, Tel Aviv 2004, p. 299-301.

[330] Grid. ref. 108/086: A. ALT, *Beiträge zur historischen Geographie und Topographie des Negeb I. Das Bistum Orda*, in *JPOS* 11 (1931), p. 204-221; ID., *II. Das Land Gari*, in *JPOS* 12 (1932), p. 126-141 (see p. 126-130); ID., *Kleine Schriften zur Geschichte des Volkes Israel* III, München 1959, p. 382-400; M. AVI-YONAH, *Gazetteer of Roman Palestine* (Qedem 5), Jerusalem 1976, p. 85.

spelt also Ἄρδα[331], *d* probably represents the Aramaic spelling, while *Tel 'Arzā* in the Mishnah preserves the Hebrew spelling. As only Roman and Byzantine remains are visible at Ḫirbet 'Irq, it is possible that the older settlement, called Yurza, was situated 6 km to the east, at the site of Ḫirbet Abu Hureira, which is the largest mound in the area. Such a displacement of a settlement can be explained by a new and acute problem of water supply, caused by a natural shift of the aquifer.

Regarding the attempted identification of Arṣa with Yurza, the decisive negative argument is provided by geography and onomastics. Despite the Mishnaic spelling *'Arzā*, it is not possible to identify Ὄρδα with *Arṣa*, conquered by the Assyrians in 679 B.C., for Ὄρδα is about 75 km distant from uru*Naḫal Muṣur*, as the crow flies. Nor can we substantiate the hypothesis that Arṣa is Tell Ğemmeh, for the ostraca found at Tell Ğemmeh[332] suggest that the site was occupied in the first half of the 7th century B.C. by Philistines, not by Arabs. The town lay most likely on the territory of Gaza and could by no means be ruled by an Arab king, called *A-su-ḫi-li*. Summing up, it is clear that despite the similarity in transcription between Arṣa and Yurza (later Ιαρδα and Ορδα) these names do not refer to one and the same place. Arṣa, possibly transcribing **Ḥarṣā,* should be located in the area of Ostracine.

Going back to Esarhadddon's inscriptions, we see the king leading the Assyrian troops into Egypt. After his failure in the first campaign (673 B.C.)[333], Esarhaddon marched again in 671. The desert was crossed with the help of the Arabian sheiks and their camels. He drove the Egyptian forces before him in fifteen days all the way from the frontier to Memphis, thrice defeating them with heavy loss and wounding Taharqo himself. Memphis fell in half a day, and this was followed by deportations and plundering[334]. In autumn 669 B.C., Egypt again revolted, and while on the march to reduce it, Esarhaddon fell ill and died[335]. Ashurbanipal was immediately pressed to quash the rebellion, and succeeded in taking Memphis (667 B.C.) and Thebes (*ca.* 664 B.C.)[336]. The two statues of

331 A. ALT, *op. cit.* (n. 330), p. 385.

332 J. NAVEH, *Writing and Scripts in Seventh Century B.C.E. Philistia: The New Evidence from Tell Jemmeh,* in *IEJ* 35 (1985), p. 8-21.

333 R. BORGER, *op. cit.* (n. 271), p. 123.

334 *Ibid.*, p. 124.

335 *Ibid.*, p. 124; A.K. GRAYSON, *Assyrian and Babylonian Chronicles* (TCS 5), Locust Valley 1975, p. 86, Babylonian Chronicle 1, col. IV, 30-32; p. 127, Babylonian Chronicle 14, rev., lines 5-7.

336 M. STRECK, *Assurbanipal und die letzten assyrischen Könige bis zum Untergange Niniveh's*, Leipzig 1916, Vol. II, p. 10, col. I, 87-89; R. BORGER, *Beiträge zum Inschriftenwerk Assurbanipals*, Wiesbaden 1996, p. 20, A I 87-89; cf. p. 213.

337 W.K. SIMPSON, *The Pharaoh Taharka*, in *Sumer* 10 (1954), p. 193-194, Pls. IV-V.

Taharqo, found in the Review Palace on the mound of Nabi Yūnus at Nineveh[337], must belong to the spoils of one of these expeditions, probably in 671 B.C. Auxiliary troops of vassal states participated in these campaigns, especially Judaeans sent by king Manasseh[338]. A reference to the capture of Thebes, based on reports of eyewitnesses, is thus preserved in Nah. 3, 8-10[339]. After 664, however, the Saite Twenty-sixth Dynasty under Psammetichus I (664-610 B.C.) rejected the suzereinty of Assyria, helped by East Greek and Carian mercenaries[340], and by troops sent by Gyges of Lydia[341]. No attempt at regaining control of Egypt is recorded in Ashurbanipal's later inscriptions.

Saitic dynasty

Psammetichus I[342] was able to reunite Egypt and during a long reign marked by intimate relations with the Greeks[343] restored the prosperity of Egypt. Realizing that Assyrian power was weakening and could no longer threaten him, he attempted to preserve the existence of an Assyrian state as a buffer between Egypt and the Medo-Chaldaean axis. Probably, too, he saw the chance to regain Egypt's ancient sphere of influence in Philistia and Syro-Phoenicia. An Egyptian-Assyrian alliance came into existence, apparently *ca.* 620 B.C.[344], under the reign of Sin-šar-iškun. Egyptian forces entered in Philistia, captured the Philistine city of Ashdod[345] after a siege of twenty-nine

Cf. J. YOYOTTE, rev. in *BiOr* 14 (1957), p. 30a; E.R. RUSSMANN, *The Representation of the King in the XXVth Dynasty*, Bruxelles-Brooklyn 1974, p. 47, Nos. 7 and 8.

338 M. STRECK, *op. cit.* (n. 336), p. 138, col. I, 25; R. BORGER, *op. cit.* (n. 336), p. 18, C II 39; cf. p. 212.

339 J.R. HUDDLESTONE, *Nahum, Nineveh, and the Nile: The Description of Thebes in Nahum 3: 8-9,* in *JNES* 62 (2003), p. 97-110.

340 HERODOTUS, *History* II, 154; POLYAENUS, *Stratagems* VII, 3, both witnessing a tradition confirmed by epigraphy. Cf. O. MASSON, *Carian Inscriptions from North Saqqâra and Buchen*, London 1978; H.-J. THISSEN, *Griechen in Ägypten,* in *LÄg* II, Wiesbaden 1977, col. 898-903; G. VITTMANN, *op. cit.* (n. 211), p. 155-193, 199-209.

341 References in *PNA* III/1, p. 997, s.v. *Pišamelki.* In most Assyrian sources, Psammethicus I is referred to by his Assyrian name *Nabû-šēzibanni*; see *PNA* II/2, p. 881, s.v. 12.

342 A. SPALINGER, *Psammetichus, King of Egypt,* in *JARCE* 13 (1976), p. 133-147; 15 (1978), p. 49-57.

343 R.D. SULLIVAN, *Psammetichus I and the Foundation of Naukratis*, in W.D.E. COULSON (ed.), *Ancient Naukratis* II/1, Oxford 1996, p. 177-195.

344 This can be inferred from the data in Nabopolassar's Babylonian Chronicle; cf. A. MALAMAT, *op. cit.* (n. 260), p. 290.

345 Since Tell Esdūd was apparently not inhabited in the 7th century B.C., I. FINKELSTEIN - L. SINGER-AVITZ, *art. cit.* (n. 7), p. 231-259 (see p. 246-253), propose to locate the city of the 7th century at Mīnet-Esdūd (Ashdod-Yam), 5 km north-west of Esdūd. Sargon II's annals distinguish Ashdod and *Asdudimmu*, "Ashdod at Sea".

hours[346], and arrived in Mesopotamia at the latest in 616 B.C.[347] To ensure his control of the coastal plain, Psammetichus I established garrisons of Greek mercenaries in several places. East Greek pottery possibly reveals their presence at Meṣad Ḥashavyahu[348], 17 km south of Yavneh Yam, and at Tell Kabri[349], perhaps at other sites as well[350], but trading relations should not be excluded. A Greek inscription from the vicinity of Priene, an ancient city of Ionia, confirms the enrolment of East Greek mercenaries in Egyptian forces, as it was dedicated by a soldier who had served in the army of Psammetichus I[351].

Egyptian religious utensils and symbols, like those found in particular at Ashkelon and Ekron[352], witness an Egyptian cultural influence, but there are no proofs that the area concerned came under the direct control of the pharaohs. Instead, Egyptian suzerainty over Phoenicia[353] is implied by the inscription of an Egyptian stele[354], which commemorates

[346] The twenty-nine years of HERODOTUS' *History* II, 157, seem to result from Herodotus' misunderstanding of his Egyptian informants, apparently by taking (*h*)*ote* / (*h*)*ate* (Coptic; Demotic *ḥtỉ.t* / *htỉ.t*), "hour", for ἔτη, "years", and relating this information to the "twenty-eight years of Scythian domination in Asia", mentioned in connection with an intervention of Psammetichus I and with events at Ashkelon (I, 105-106).

[347] Tablet BM 21901, which opens with the events of 616 B.C. - after a gap of six years -, already mentions the Egyptian assistance in the fight against Nabopolassar.

[348] A. FANTALKIN, *Meẓad Ḥashavyahu: Its Material Culture and Historical Background*, in *Tel Aviv* 28 (2001), p. 3-165.

[349] W.D. NIEMEIER, *Greek Pottery: Evidence for Greek Mercenaries at Kabri*, in A. KEMPINSKI - W.D. NIEMEIER (eds.), *Excavations at Kabri: Preliminary Report of 1992-1993 Seasons 7-8*, Tel Aviv 1994, p. 31*-38*; ID., *Greek Mercenaries in Phoenicia: New Evidence from Tel Kabri*, in *AJA* 99 (1995), p. 304-305; ID., *Greek Mercenaries at Tel Kabri and Other Sites in the Levant*, in *Tel Aviv* 29 (2002), p. 328-331. However, Niemeier believes that these mercenaries were in the service of the king of Tyre, although nothing substantiates such an hypothesis. Instead, Phoenicia was depending from Psammetichus I; cf. here below with n. 354-356.

[350] A. FANTALKIN, *art. cit.* (n. 348), p. 140-141.

[351] O. MASSON - J. YOYOTTE, *Une inscription ionienne mentionnant Psammétique Ier*, in *Epigraphica Anatolica* 11 (1988), p. 171-179.

[352] They are recorded by B.U. SCHIPPER, *op. cit.* (n. 2), p. 238-239.

[353] B.U. SCHIPPER, *op. cit.* (n. 2), p. 230-231; A. MALAMAT, *op. cit.* (n. 260), p. 289-290.

[354] B. PORTER - R.L. MOSS, *Topographical Bibliography of Ancient Egyptian Hieroglyphic Texts, Reliefs, and Paintings* III/2, 2nd ed., Oxford 1978-81, p. 797 (Apis XXXVIII). There are a few differences in the readings of A. MARIETTE, *Oeuvres diverses* I, Paris 1904, p. 248-249, followed by A.J. SPALINGER, *Egypt and Babylonia: A Survey (c. 620 B.C.-550 B.C.)*, in *SAK* 5 (1977), p. 221-244 (see p. 228), and K.S. FREEDY - D.B. REDFORD, *The Dates in Ezekiel in Relation to Biblical, Babylonian and Egyptian Sources*, in *JAOS* 90 (1970), p. 462-485 (see p. 477), and of M.E. CHASSINAT, *Textes provenant du Sérapéum de Memphis*, in *Recueil de Travaux* 22 (1900), p. 163-180 (see p. 166), followed by J.H. BREASTED, *Ancient Records of Egypt* IV, New York 1906, p. 494, §966.

the burial of an Apis bull in year 52 of Psammetichus I, i.e. in 613/2 B.C., and records that its sarcophagus was made of best quality timber from Lebanon (*ḫtìw*)[355]. Lines 7-12 add that "their chiefs were subjects of the palace, with a royal courtier placed over them; and their taxes were assessed for the Residence, as though it were in the Land of Egypt"[356].

Egyptian suzerainty would be confirmed by a statue found at Arwad and allegedly bearing the name of Psammetichus I[357]. Other statues, one from black granite, found at Taanach[358], another from basalt, discovered at Tell al-Qāḍi (Tel Dan) in a level of the 7th century B.C.[359], can be dated from the same period, but their attribution remains conjectural. Instead, a basalt fragment with the cartouche of Necho II, Psammetichus I's son and successor, was found at Sidon[360]. Carchemish served as the central base of the Egyptian expeditionary corps on the Euphrates. Sir Leonard Woolley's excavations uncovered Egyptian items in "building D" of the lower city, which may have housed the offices of the Egyptian forces. A bronze seal with the cartouche of Psammetichus I was found in room 4 and several seal impressions with the cartouche of Necho II were discovered in room 5[361], which must have contained documents written on papyrus and sealed with these Egyptian bullae. The two rooms in question can thus be regarded as part of a chancellery related to the Egyptian troops garrisoned at Carchemish between 616 and 605 B.C.

In 610 B.C., the Babylonians and the Medes ejected the refugee Assyrian government from Harran, but in 609 Necho II (609-593 B.C.), who had succeeded his father, marched with a large force to Carchemish to assist Ashur-uballit II in a last attempt to retake Harran from the Babylonians[362]. Megiddo undoubtedly was a vital base or way-station for the Egyptian army in its march towards the Euphrates. At Megiddo

[355] Reading proposed by K.S. FREEDY - D.B. REDFORD, *art. cit.* (n. 354), p. 477.

[356] Translation by K.S. FREEDY - D.B. REDFORD, *ibid.*

[357] E. RENAN, *Mission de Phénicie*, Paris 1864, p. 27; W.M. MÜLLER, *Asien und Europa nach altägyptischen Denkmälern*, Leipzig 1893, p. 274, n. 2.

[358] E. SELLIN, *Tell Ta'anek*, Wien 1904, p. 66-67.

[359] A.R. SCHULMAN, *An Enigmatic Egyptian Presence at Tel Dan*, in *Festschrift Jürgen von Beckerath*, Hildesheim 1990, p. 235-244, Pls. 16-17 (see p. 239-240). It is a fragment of a statue from the period of the Twelfth Dynasty, provided with a new inscription dating from the time of the Twenty-fifth or Twenty-sixth Dynasty.

[360] F.Ll. GRIFFITH, *A Relic of Pharaoh Necho from Phoenicia*, in *PSBA* 16 (1894), p. 90-91; W.M. MÜLLER, *op. cit.* (n. 272), p. 298-299.

[361] C.L. WOOLLEY, *Carchemish* II. *The Town Defences*, London 1921, p. 125-126, Pl. 26.

[362] See J.A. BRINKMAN, *Aššūr-uballiṭ* 2., in *PNA* I/1, Helsinki 1998, p. 228a.

Stratum II, dated to 650-600 B.C.[363], a huge citadel was erected at the eastern end of the mound. The identification of its builders and the interpretation of Necho's and Josiah's encounter at the site are disputed[364]. A. Malamat suggested that the citadel was an Egyptian stronghold erected by Psammetichus I prior to 616 B.C.[365] He thinks that Josiah tried to stop Necho II and was killed in battle[366]. In fact, a battle is recorded in II Chron. 35, 20-24, followed by I Ezra 1, 23-31 and Josephus Flavius[367]. Instead, the short notice of II Kings 23, 29 mentions no battle and apparently suggests that Josiah was seized and executed, as if he were an unfaithful vassal.

A further Egyptian base on the route towards the Euphrates was Riblah, in Syria, where Necho II summoned Jehoahaz[368], Josiah's son. He deposed him, deported to Egypt, and placed his brother Eliakim on the throne as an Egyptian vassal, changing his name into Jehoiakim and laying a heavy tribute on Judah[369]. Though Necho had failed to save Assyria, the campaign of 609 consolidated the Egyptian grip on Philistia, Judah, and Syro-Phoenicia, which remained under Egyptian control until Nebuchadnezzar's campaign to the West in 605 B.C. or, at the latest, in the autumn of 604 B.C., when the king of Babylon conquered Ashkelon.

According to the Babylonian Chronicle, the decisive battle was fought at Carchemish, where the headquarters of the Egyptian army were located. Nebuchadnezzar defeated the Egyptian forces and, pursuing them southward, delivered them a second blow in the neighbourhood of Hamath[370]. The way to southern Syria and Philistia lay open. In August 605, however, the Babylonian advance was delayed by news of the death

[363] Y. Aharoni - Y. Shiloh, *Megiddo*, in *NEAEHL*, Jerusalem 1993, Vol. III, p. 1003-1024 (see p. 1023).

[364] A summary of the different opinions is given by M.A. Corral, *Ezekiel's Oracles against Tyre* (Biblica et Orientalia 46), Roma 2002, p. 25-29, but without mentioning the recent study by Z. Talshir, *The Three Deaths of Josiah and the Strata of Biblical Historiography (2 Kings xxiii 29-30; 2 Chronicles xxxv 20-5; 1 Esdras i 23-31)*, in *Vetus Testamentum* 46 (1996), p. 213-236. According to Talshir, Josiah appears in II Kings 23, 29 as a vassal summoned by his overlord, while a fictitious version of Josiah's death is presented in II Chron. 35, 20-25.

[365] A. Malamat, *op. cit.* (n. 260), p. 291.

[366] *Ibid.*, p. 293.

[367] Josephus Flavius, *Jewish Antiquities* X, 5, 1, §74.

[368] Shallum was his personal name, Jehoahaz - his throne name.

[369] II Kings 23, 31-35; II Chron 36, 1-4; I Ezra 1, 32-36; cf. Jer. 22, 10-12.

[370] Babylonian Chronicle 5, obv., lines 1-8; Jer. 46, 2. Cf. I. Eph'al, *Nebuchadnezzar the Warrior: Remarks on his Military Achievements*, in *IEJ* 53 (2003), p. 178-191 (see p. 179).

of Nabopolassar, that obliged Nebuchadnezzar to hasten to Babylon to assume the power. The Babylonian advance was resumed in 604 B.C. and Adon, king of Ekron (*p3-wr 'qrn*), requested urgent Egyptian aid against the approaching Babylonians[371]. It is doubtful whether Necho II was able to send him any help. At any rate, another Philistine town, Ashkelon, was captured in the late Autumn 604, the leading elements of its population were deported to Babylon[372], and the city was utterly destroyed[373]. Fragment B 16: 10-11 of the Lesbian poet Alcaeus juxtaposes the names of Ashkelon and Babylon, alluding to this campaign of Nebuchadnezzar II, in which Alcaeus' brother, Antimenidas, seems to have served in Babylonian ranks[374]. Greek mercenaries of the pharaoh have probably been integrated in the Babylonian army after the battle of Carchemish, in 605 B.C., and the speedy advance of Nebuchadnezzar in Syria.

Also Jer. 47, 2-7 must refer to the Babylonian campaign of 604 B.C. in Phoenicia and Philistia, since the "Foe from the North" (verse 2) is non else but Nebuchadnezzar and his army[375]. The oracle mentions Tyre and Sidon for Phoenicia, Gaza and Ashkelon for Philistia, without naming Ekron. Gaza may have been captured in 603/2, in Nebuchadnezzar's year 2. The Babylonian Chronicle for that year mentions siege towers and a large army, but the name of the town is lost in a lacuna[376]. This would date the oracle of Jer. 47, 2-7 from year 603/2 B.C. The Chronicle for Nebuchadnezzar's year 3 (602/1 B.C.) is missing almost com-

[371] *TAD* I, A1.1. The reading of the Demotic inscription, "prince of Ekron", is certain: G. VITTMANN, in B.U. SCHIPPER, *op. cit.* (n. 2), p. 240, n. 264.

[372] Babylonian Chronicle 5, obv., lines 15-20; Jer. 47, 5-7. Ashkelonian princes, seamen, craftsmen, etc., are listed among captives in Babylon some ten years later; cf. E.F. WEIDNER, *Jojachin, König von Juda, in babylonischen Keilschrifttexten,* in *Mélanges syriens offerts à M. René Dussaud,* Paris 1939, Vol. II, p. 923-935, Pls. I-V (see p. 928).

[373] L.E. STAGER, *Ashkelon and Archaeology of Destruction: Kislev 604 B.C.E.*, in *Joseph Aviram Volume* (ErIs 25), Jerusalem 1996, p. 61*-74*.

[374] See the edition by E. LOBEL - D.L. PAGE, *Poetarum Lesbiorum Fragmenta*, Oxford 1955. Cf. D. PAGE, *Sappho and Alcaeus. An Introduction to the Study of Ancien Lesbian Poetry*, Oxford 1955, p. 223-224; A. MALAMAT, *A New Record of Nebuchadnezzar's Palestinian Campaign,* in *IEJ* 6 (1956), p. 246-256 (see p. 251, n. 16); J.D. QUINN, *Alcaeus 48 (B 16) and the Fall of Ascalon (604 B.C.),* in *BASOR* 164 (1961), p. 19-20.

[375] The Babylonian invader appears as the "Foe from the North" in Jer. 1, 13.14.15; 4, 6; 6, 1.22; 10, 22; 13, 20; 15, 12; 25, 9; 46, 20.24; 47, 2. This appellation is easily understandable since the Babylonian army was approaching from the north.

[376] Babylonian Chronicle 5, obv. 21-23. The town besieged in 603/2 would have been Gaza according to A.F. RAINEY, *The Fate of Lachish during the Campaigns of Sennacherib and Nebuchadnezzar*, in Y. AHARONI (ed.), *Investigations at Lachish. The Sanctuary and the Residency* (Lachish V), *Tel Aviv* 1975, p. 47-60 (see p. 54); cf. I. EPH'AL, *art. cit.* (n. 370), p. 180, n. 4.

pletely[377], but refers to a campaign in Hatti, i.e. in Syria-Palestine. Assuming that the capture of Gaza was recorded for year 2, Ekron could then be the main target of the campaign in 602/1 B.C. If Adon's letter to the pharaoh does not date from 604/3 or 603/2 B.C., it should immediately precede the Babylonian expedition of 602/1 B.C. Ekron was captured and destroyed in one of these campaigns[378]. At any rate, the destruction level of Stratum IB at Ḫirbet al-Muqanna' (Tel Miqne) reveals a material culture from the end of the 7th century B.C.[379] In these circumstances, Jehoiakim of Judah transferred his allegiance to Nebuchadnezzar II, becoming his vassal (II Kings 24, 1)[380].

The Babylonian Chronicle for Nebuchadnezzar's year 4 (601/0 B.C.) reports a fierce battle between the king of Babylon and the king of Egypt, who was at the time Necho II:

> "In the fourth year the king of Akkad mustered his army and marched to the Hatti-land. In the Hatti-land they marched unopposed. In the month of Kislev he took the lead of his army and marched to Egypt. The king of Egypt heard (it) and mustered his army. In open battle they smote the breast (of) each other and inflicted great havoc on each other. The king of Akkad and his troops turned back and returned to Babylon"[381].

The battle must have occurred near the Egyptian border between December (Kislev) 601 B.C. and April 600 B.C., the beginning of Nebuchadnezzar's year 5. It can be judged from the entry for the following year (600/599 B.C.) that the Babylonian army suffered heavy casualties, since Nebuchadnezzar had to spend all that year in reorganizing his military forces: "In the fifth year the king of Akkad (stayed) in his own land and gathered together his chariots and horses in great numbers"[382]. No

[377] Babylonian Chronicle 5, rev., lines 2-4. W. TYBOROWSKI, *The Third Year of Nebuchadnezzar II (602 B.C.) according to the Babylonian Chronicle BM. 21946 - An Attempt at an Interpretation,* in *ZA* 86 (1996), p. 211-216, assumes that Nebuchadnezzar had to cope then with a rebellion in Babylonia.

[378] S. GITIN, *Philistia in Transition: The Tenth Century BCE and beyond,* in S. GITIN - A. MAZAR - E. STERN (eds.), *Mediterranean Peoples in Transition*, Jerusalem 1998, p. 162-183 (see p. 164b with further references). A misleading evaluation of the fragmentary passage in the Babylonian Chronicle is given by N. NA'AMAN, *Nebuchadnezzar's Campaign in Year 603 BCE,* in *BN* 62 (1992), p. 41-44.

[379] S. GITIN, *Tel Mikne-Ekron: A Type-Site for the Inner Coastal Plain in the Iron Age II Period,* in S. GITIN - W.G. DEVER (eds.), *Recent Excavations in Israel: Studies in Iron Age Archaeology* (AASOR 49), Winona Lake 1989, p. 23-58 (see p. 47-48).

[380] A. MALAMAT, *op. cit.* (n. 260), p. 312-313.

[381] Babylonian Chronicle 5, rev., lines 5-7. Translation by D.J. WISEMAN, *Chronicles of Chaldaean Kings (626-556 B.C.) in the British Museum,* London 1956, p. 71. See also *ANET*, p. 564.

[382] Babylonian Chronicle 5, rev., line 8. Translation by D.J. WISEMAN, *op. cit.* (n. 381), p. 71.

place for this clash is given in the text of the Chronicle and there are no known references in Egyptian sources with which the Babylonian record may be compared. But authors dealing with this subject seem not to have noticed that Herodotus precisely mentions this battle in his *History* II, 159: "Necho met and defeated the Syrians at Magdolos and took after the battle Kadytis, a great Syrian city".

Magdolos has generally been identified with Megiddo and the battle connected with the death of king Josiah of Judah in 609 B.C. This opinion was advocated from the mid-19th[383] to the 20th century[384], but the name recorded by Herodotus is in fact Migdol, not Megiddo[385]. As for Kadytis, conquered by Necho after the battle, this was obviously Gaza, as noticed already by F. Hitzig in 1829[386], referring to Herodotus' *History* III, 5: "From Phoenicia as far as the borders of the city of Kadytis the land belongs to the Syrians of Palestine, as they are called". Greek Καδύτις is based here on the Egyptian spelling *Q-ḏ-t* of the name of Gaza.

Assuming thus that Gaza is the Kadytis taken by Necho after "defeating the Syrians at Magdolos", it may reasonably be inferred from this succession of events that Magdolos is the Egyptian border fortress north-east of Sile, on the highway connecting Egypt with Gaza[387]. Both the battle and the capture of Gaza can safely be dated from the winter 601/600 B.C.[388]

Despite these successes, Necho II did not feel strong enough to intervene in 598/7 against the Babylonians, when Nebuchadnezzar set out for Jerusalem and captured the city[389]. However, a rebellion that flared in

[383] So, among others, F. HITZIG, *Der Prophet Jeremia* (Kurzgefasstes exegetisches Handbuch zum Alten Testament 3), Leipzig 1841, p. 364; H. WINCKLER, *Geschichte Babyloniens und Assyriens*, Leipzig 1892, p. 310.

[384] Still so H. CAZELLES, *Sophonie, Jéremie, et les Scythes en Palestine,* in *RB* 74 (1967), p. 24-44 (see p. 26); W. HELCK, *Geschichte des Alten Ägypten* (Handbuch der Orientalistik I. Abt. I/3), Leiden-Köln 1968, p. 251 with n. 3.

[385] This was stressed already by B. BEER-MORITZ, *Kadytis,* in *PW* X/2, Stuttgart 1919, col. 1478.

[386] F. HITZIG, *De Cadyti urbe Herodotea*, Leipzig 1829, p. 12 ff.; ID., *op. cit.* (n. 383), p. 364.

[387] E.D. OREN, *Migdol, A New Fortress on the Edge of the Eastern Nile Delta,* in *BASOR* 256 (1984), p. 7-44, especially p. 33-34; J. QUAEGEBEUR, *Les rois saïtes amateurs de vin,* in *Ancient Society* 21 (1990), p. 241-271 (see p. 264, n. 129).

[388] Despite his traditional dating of these events to 609 B.C. in *DEB*, Turnhout 1987, p. 518a and 829b, the writer maintains the date 601/600 B.C., proposed by him in 1972 (E. LIPIŃSKI, *The Egypto-Babylonian War of the Winter 601-600 B.C.*, in *AION* 32 [1972], p. 235-241) and accepted by several authors, among them A. MALAMAT, *op. cit.* (n. 260), p. 295, n. 33; p. 308,

[389] Babylonian Chronicle 5, rev., lines 11-13.

Babylon in 595/4, although quickly suppressed, apparently managed to raise hopes in Phoenicia, Transjordan, and Judah. In the late summer of 593 B.C., envoys from Edom, Moab, Ammon, Tyre, and Sidon met in Jerusalem to discuss plans for the revolt (Jer. 27, 3)[390]. The plot did in fact come to nothing, although Psammethicus II (595-589 B.C.) went to Palestine (*Ḫr*) in his year 4 (592 B.C.). The purpose of this campaign or journey is unknown and the event is mentioned only in a Demotic account, written in 513 B.C.[391] A priest records there that his grandfather Peṭe'isi (*P3-dỉ-3s.t*) accompanied the pharaoh on that particular occasion, which was either military or religious[392]. Under Apries (589-570 B.C.), a Lachish letter (III) sent from Jerusalem[393] informs the Lachish garrison that the commander of Judah's army went to Egypt[394], possibly with an appeal of the king to the pharaoh for aid. In fact, probably in the early summer of 588 B.C., news that Egyptian troops were advancing obliged the Babylonians to lift the siege temporarily (Jer. 37, 5) in order to confront them. However, the Egyptians were obviously driven back and the siege resumed. According to Herodotus[395], Apries led a campaign against Sidon and blockaded Tyre. This information seems to result from a misunderstanding of Herodotus' informants[396]. The pharaoh probably supported both cities against Nebuchadnezzar II, but failed to obtain tangible results.

This seems to have been the last Egyptian intervention in Syro-Phoenicia till the reign of Achoris (393-381 B.C.), when Egypt became important again on the international stage of political and military manoeuvres.

390 A. MALAMAT, *op. cit.* (n. 260), p. 312-313.

391 G. VITTMANN, *Der demotische Papyrus Rylands 9* (Ägypten und Altes Testament 38), Wiesbaden 1998, Vol. I, p. 163-165, col. XV, 17-18.

392 Cf. B.U. SCHIPPER, *op. cit.* (n. 2), p. 242-243; A. MALAMAT, *op. cit.* (n. 260), p. 317-319.

393 J.A. EMERTON, *Were the Lachish Letters Sent to or from Lachish?*, in *PEQ* 133 (2001), p. 2-15.

394 J. RENZ - W. RÖLLIG, *Handbuch der althebräischen Epigraphik*, Darrmstadt 1995, Vol. I, p. 418, lines 14-16.

395 HERODOTUS, *History* II, 161. Cf. DIODORUS OF SICILY, *Bibliotheca Historica* I, 68, 1.

396 See here below, p. 198.

CHAPTER IV

PHOENICIANS

The cities of the Phoenician coast seem to have recovered quite fast from the destructions caused by the "Sea Peoples" in the 12th century B.C. When in the first years of his reign Tiglath-pileser I (1114-1076 B.C.) reached the Mediterranean coast at Arwad, he could embark there on a ship to sail up the littoral to Ṣumur for some 20 km and kill a narwhal on high sea during this short journey. He was brought gifts by the rulers of Byblos, Sidon, and Arwad, and had massive cedars cut down on Mount Lebanon[1]. No concrete archaeological data from these sites are available so far to document possible destructions, but the excavations of Tell al-Kāzil, ancient Ṣumur, revealed several conflagrations in the 12th century B.C. and a qualitative regression of the material culture, which nevertheless preserved ancestral traditions in matters of domestic architecture and ceramics. Instead, luxurious articles do no longer appear and the palatial lifestyle has obviously come to an end[2].

The Report of Wenamon, written somewhat later, records the voyage of an Egyptian envoy to Byblos, *ca.* 1065 B.C.[3] It refers to Phoenicia, where woodwork for the holy barque of Amon-Re had to be purchased, but first mentions Dor. Dor was then the home-town of some Sicals (*Ṯ-k-r*)[4], one of the "Sea Peoples", but its ruler *b3-dỉ-r* bears a name which really is the Semitic title *badalu*, "substitute",

[1] *RIMA* II, text A.0.87.3, p. 37, lines 16-25; text A.0.87.4, p. 42, lines 24-30; p. 44, lines 67-69; text A.0.87.8, p. 49, lines 4'-6'; text A.0.87.10, p. 53, lines 28-35; text A.0.87.13, p. 60, lines 10'-13'; text A.0.87.17, p. 63, lines 2-3.

[2] E. Capet - E. Gubel, *Tell Kazel: Six Centuries of Iron Age Occupation (c. 1200-612 B.C.)*, in G. Bunnens (ed.), *Essays on Syria in the Iron Age* (Ancient Near Eastern Studies. Suppl. 7), Louvain 2000, p. 425-457.

[3] The main literature concerning the Report of Wenamon, up to 1989, has been collected by A. Scheepers, *Anthroponymes et toponymes du récit d'Ounamon*, in E. Lipiński (ed.), *Phoenicia and the Bible* (Studia Phoenicia XI; OLA 44), Leuven 1991, p. 17-83, in particular p. 17, n. 1. According to A. Egberts, *Hard Times: The Chronology of "The Report of Wenamun" Revised*, in *ZÄS* 125 (1998), p. 93-108, the events are to be dated in the early years of the Twenty-first Dynasty, *ca.* 1065 B.C. or somewhat later. For the purpose and meaning of Wenamon's mission, see G. Bunnens, *La mission d'Ounamon en Phénicie: Point de vue d'un non-égyptologue*, in *RSF* 6 (1978), p. 1-16; B.U. Schipper, *Die Erzählung des Wenamun* (OBO 209), Freiburg/Schweiz-Göttingen 2005.

[4] A. Scheepers, *art. cit.* (n. 3), p. 67-74.

"deputy"[5], and thus implies that he depended from a higher authority, possibly from the king of Tyre. The ruler of Byblos bears instead the typically Phoenician name of Sakar-Baal (*Ṯ-k-r-b-ʿ-r*)[6]. His speech to Wenamon contains an illuminating description of Phoenician shipping activity at that time. The king of Byblos says to Wenamon: "There are twenty *meneš*-ships[7] here in my harbour which are in trading association with Smendes (pharaoh *ca.* 1075 B.C.), and in Sidon, which you have passed, there must be fifty *ber*-ships[8] which are in trading association with Warkatil and are carrying (freight) to his residence", possibly on the South-Anatolian coast[9]. Maritime trade seems thus to be in full swing, even if the fleets had to be protected against piracy. From the end of the Tale of Wenamon it appears also that there were relations with Cyprus (Alashiya)[10], since from Byblos Wenamon reaches the island that belonged to the East-Mediterranean commercial circuit and had long-standing trade relations with Byblos and other Phoenician seaports.

It seems that southern Phoenicia did not suffer greatly from the invasion of the "Sea Peoples". In any case, there was no evidence for destruction at Sarepta[11], between Sidon and Tyre. Nor was there any sign of destruction in the sounding of Tyre[12]. Normal activities have been disrupted in Phoenicia for a short period and it is perhaps doubtful whether overseas commerce came there to a complete stand. The Phoenician inscription incised on a bowl from the 10th century B.C.,

[5] E. LIPIŃSKI, š u - b a l a - a k a *and* badalum, in H. HAUPTMANN - H. WAETZOLDT (eds.), *Wirtschaft und Gesellschaft von Ebla* (Heidelberger Studien zum Alten Orient 2), Heidelberg 1988, p. 257-260, especially p. 260. See also A. SCHEEPERS, *art. cit.* (n. 3), p. 38-41, and here above, p. 58.

[6] See A. SCHEEPERS, *art. cit.* (n. 3), p. 33-36.

[7] Cf. *ibid.*, p. 37-38.

[8] Cf. *ibid.*, p. 46-51.

[9] The name seems to be Hittite-Luwian, as suggested by *Wargati* in E. LAROCHE, *Les noms des Hittites*, Paris 1966, p. 204, No. 1491. It should derive from *wargant-*, "fat" (cf. J. FRIEDRICH, *Hethitisches Wörterbuch*, Heidelberg 1952-54, p. 245; E. LAROCHE, *op. cit.*, p. 335) with the suffix *-ili* or *-alli*. For other explanations of this name, see A. SCHEEPERS, *art. cit.* (n. 3), p. 46-51.

[10] Cf. *ibid.*, p. 80-83. See also P.M. BIKAI, *Cyprus and Phoenicia: Literary Evidence for the Early Iron Age*, in G.C. IOANNIDES (ed.), *Studies in Honour of Vassos Karageorghis*, Nicosia 1992, p. 241-248.

[11] The undisturbed continuation of the pottery production is significant: W.P. ANDERSON, *Sarepta* I, Beirut 1988, p. 423-425; I.A. KHALIFEH, *Sarepta* II, Beirut 1988, p. 161-162.

[12] P.M. BIKAI, *The Pottery of Tyre*, Warminster 1978, p. 8 and 73. However, it is worth stressing here that the area excavated in Tyre is tiny (150 m^2), and constitutes less than 1 per cent of the original island settlement of Tyre.

Inscription of Elibaal, king of Byblos,
on a statue of Osorkon I
(Louvre Museum, AO 9502).

found in a tomb near Cnossos[13], at least witnesses renewed trading links even between Phoenicia and Crete.

Phoenician history in Iron Age II is essentially the history of the city-states of Arwad, Byblos, Sidon, and Tyre, and of the Phoenician expansion in the Mediterranean world. Only scattered information is provided by the Assyrian annals, a small number of Phoenician inscriptions, and Hebrew and Greek literary works, that have to be used with great caution. The main source of knowledge about Iron Age Phoenicia and its trading empire are archaeological findings, although regular excavations in the core of the Phoenician territory, between the sea and the Lebanon

[13] Decipherment of the original by E. Lipiński, *Notes d'épigraphie phénicienne et punique, 1. La coupe de Tekke (Crète),* in *OLP* 14 (1983), p. 129-133 and Pl. II.

range, were rather limited in scope during the recent years, except in the ruined centre of Beirut.

Old Byblian royal inscriptions echo the situation at Byblos around the 10th century B.C., but do not contain any direct information regarding external relations[14]. However, Abibaal's dedication to the Lady of Byblos is incised on the base of a statue of Shoshenq I (*ca.* 945-924 B.C.)[15] and Elibaal's dedication to the same goddess is written on a statue of Osorkon I (*ca.* 924-889 B.C.)[16]. It is not clear why rulers of Byblos should employ pharaoh's statues for dedications to the main Byblian divinity, but this practice certainly witnesses some acknowledgement of the relationship existing between Byblos and Egypt. More attention should be paid to the sections of Tyrian annals, transmitted in a Greek version and preserved by Josephus Flavius. They offer a chronological frame for the history of Tyre and for the relations of Phoenicia with surrounding countries. Literary sources provide some information on foreign relations with Israel and Assyria. On the one hand, Tyre's wealth and importance are shown by the dynastic alliance of Israel with Tyre, whose royal princess, daughter of king Ethbaal / Ittobaal, became the wife of Ahab, Israel's heir apparent[17]. On the other hand, Arwad, Byblos, Sidon, Tyre, and other Phoenician cities paid tribute already to Ashurnasirpal II (883-859 B.C.)[18].

Tyrian king-list of the 10th-9th centuries B.C.

In his work *Against Apion*, written in *ca.* 95 A.D., Josephus Flavius preserved a passage of Menander's *Phoenician History* with extracts from Tyrian annals, providing a useful and trustworthy chronological framework for Iron Age II[19]. He thus adduces the list of Tyrian kings

[14] E. Lipiński, *Koningen van Byblos in de 10e-5e eeuw v. Chr.*, in R.J. Demarée - K.R. Veenhof (eds.), *Zij schreven geschiedenis*, Leiden-Leuven 2003, p. 253-261.

[15] *KAI* 5 = *TSSI* III, 7.

[16] *KAI* 6 = *TSSI* III, 8. See here, p. 165.

[17] H.J. Katzenstein, *The History of Tyre*, Jerusalem 1993, p. 143-147; F. Briquel-Chatonnet, *Les relations entre les cités de la côte phénicienne et les royaumes d'Israël et de Juda* (Studia Phoenicia XII; OLA 46), Leuven 1992, p. 63-70.

[18] F. Briquel-Chatonnet, *op. cit.* (n. 17), p. 74-76.

[19] Josephus Flavius, *Against Apion* I, 18, §117-126. The initial part of Menander's text is also reproduced in the *Jewish Antiquities* VIII, 5, 3, §144-146. According to A. de Gutschmid, *Kleine Schriften*, ed. Fr. Rühl, Leipzig 1889-93, Vol. IV, p. 470, 527, 529-530, Josephus drew his citations from the compilation of Alexander Polyhistor, *Περὶ Ἰουδαίων*, composed in the first part of the 1st century B.C.

who have reigned from Hiram I until the founding of Carthage in year 7 of Pygmalion. The life-span and the regnal years of each ruler are given precisely, so there is no reason to doubt the veracity of the tradition. The major chronological difficulty stems from the discrepancy between the total of 155 years and 8 months given by Josephus[20], and the figures provided for each king in the *Codex Laurentianus*, the only independent witness of the text[21], unfortunately flawed by a number of corruptions. Luckily, a Latin translation of *Contra Apionem* was made in the 6th century at the request of Cassiodorus[22]. Besides, the concerned passage was abridged by Theophilus of Antioch in his *Apology for Autolycus*[23], written about 180 A.D., and it was copied by Eusebius in his *Chronicon*. This work is lost, but its Armenian translation is preserved[24], as well as extracts with the list of Tyrian kings, inserted in the *Chronography* by George Syncellus[25] and in a 9th-century 'Εκλογὴ ἱστοριῶν[26].

The absolute chronology is provided by the date of the foundation of Carthage according to the Classical tradition and by a synchronism with the Assyrian annals of Shalmaneser III. The first information, although precise, is based on two different computations. Pompeius Trogus maintained that Carthage was founded 72 years before Rome, i.e. in 825 B.C.[27] This date was upheld by J. Liver[28], because it matches the synchronism between year 4 of Solomon, when the king began building the Temple according to I Kings 6, 1, and year 11 of Hiram, given by Josephus as the year in which Solomon started the construction of the sanctuary[29]. However, the information provided by the Tyrian annals and

[20] JOSEPHUS FLAVIUS, *Against Apion* I, 18, §126.

[21] The commonly used critical edition was prepared B. NIESE, *Flavii Josephi opera* V, Berlin 1889.

[22] C. BOYSEN (ed.), *Flavii Josephi opera ex versione latine antiqua* (CSEL 37/6), Wien 1898.

[23] THÉOPHILE D'ANTIOCHE, *Trois livres à Autolycus*, ed. G. BARDY - J. SENDER (SC 20), Paris 1948, Book III, 22, p. 246-251, with the abridged text of *Against Apion* I, 18, §117-126.

[24] A. SCHÖNE (ed.), *Eusebi Chronicorum libri duo* I, Berlin 1875 (reprint, 1967), col. 113-119, with a translation of *Against Apion* I, 17-18, §106-127.

[25] GEORGE SYNCELLUS, *Chronographia ab Adamo usque ad Diocletianum*, in L. DINDORF (ed.), *Georgius Syncellus et Nicephorius Cp.* (CSHB), Bonn 1829. English translation by W. ADLER - P. TUFFIN, *The Chronography of George Synkellos*, Oxford 2002.

[26] Edited by J.A. CRAMER, *Anecdota Graeca e codd. MSS. Bibl. Reg. Parisiensis*, Paris 1839-41, reprinted by A. SCHÖNE, *op. cit.* (n. 24), col. 114-120.

[27] JUSTINUS, *Epitome of the Philippic History of Pompeius Trogus* XVIII, 6, 9.

[28] J. LIVER, *The Chronology of Tyre at the Beginning of the First Millennium B.C.*, in *IEJ* 3 (1953), p. 113-120 (see p. 190). E. LIPIŃSKI, *Ba'li-ma'zer II and the Chronology of Tyre*, in *RSO* 45 (1970), p. 59-65, followed the same synchronism.

[29] JOSEPHUS FLAVIUS, *Jewish Antiquities* VIII, 3, 1, §62.

referred by Josephus to the Temple of Jerusalem in reality concerned building activities at Tyre[30]. In other words, this synchronism is spurious. Besides, as we shall see, it is more likely that Menander's reckoning parallels the Classical tradition based on Timaeus of Tauromenium (Taormina), not the one linked to the foundation of Rome. According to Timaeus, Carthage was founded 38 years before the first Olympiad (776 B.C.), i.e. in 814 B.C.[31] This is confirmed at first sight by Servius, who places the foundation of Carthage 60 years before that of Rome (753 B.C.), i.e. in 813 B.C.[32] However, some manuscripts give the figure 70 in both concerned passages of Servius, and this reading is consonant with Varron's chronological system followed by Servius[33]. More significant for the reliability of Timaeus' computation is the close correspondence between the story of the foundation of Carthage, as reported in a summary of Timaeus' account[34], and the brief notice of Josephus[35], deriving from Tyrian sources. Namely, the sister of a king of Tyre, called Pygmalion, i.e. Pummayon, went into exile with some followers and founded the city of Carthage in Libya. What is missing in Josephus' notice is the reason of her departure, viz. the murder of her husband by the king. Pompeius Trogus, whose narrative depends from Timaeus, adds that Pygmalion was still a child when he ascended the throne[36]. Also this circumstance corresponds to Josephus' text, from which it results that the king was then eleven years old. One may thus assume that Timaeus' account and dating are based on information stemming ultimately from Tyrian annals[37]. We can conclude therefore with a fair degree of probability that year 7 of Pygmalion, given as the date of the foundation of Carthage, corresponds to 814 B.C. of Timaeus' computation.

[30] A. DE GUTSCHMID, *op. cit.* (n. 19), Vol. II, p. 63; Vol. IV, p. 488-489.

[31] DIONYSIUS OF HALICARNASSUS, *Antiquitates Romanae* I, 74. For the "exclusive" (814/3 B.C.) or "inclusive" (813/2 B.C.) interpretation of the date, see G. BUNNENS, *L'expansion phénicienne en Méditerranée*, Bruxelles-Rome 1979, p. 132 with n. 92.

[32] SERVIUS, *Ad Aeneidem* I, 12 and 267.

[33] G. BUNNENS, *op. cit.* (n. 31), p. 252-253.

[34] *FHG* I, p. 197 (Timaeus, Frg. 23) = *FGH* IIIB, §566, F 82 = *Tractatus de mulieribus* 6, in A. WESTERMANN (ed.), *Paradoxographi Graeci*, Braunschweig 1839 (reprint, 1963), p. 215. Cf. G. BUNNENS, *op. cit.* (n. 31), p. 134-135; LIPIŃSKI, *Dieux et déesses*, p. 408-409.

[35] JOSEPHUS FLAVIUS, *Against Apion* I, 18 §125.

[36] JUSTINUS, *Epitome of the Philippic History of Pompeius Trogus* XVIII, 4, 4. Cf. G. BUNNENS, *op. cit.* (n. 31), p. 220.

[37] E. MEYER, *Geschichte des Altertums* II/2, 2nd ed., Stuttgart-Berlin 1931, p. 79, 83, 109.

As for the total of 155 years and 8 months, obtained by Josephus, it obviously includes the 53 years of Hiram's age at death instead of the 34 years of his reign[38]. A similar miscalculation occurs in Josephus' reckoning of the time-span of 143 years and 8 months between the construction of the Temple in year 12 of Hiram and the foundation of Carthage[39]. In reality, Josephus summed up all the reigns of Hiram's successors, including the forty-seven years of Pygmalion's reign[40]! Besides, he forgets here that his *Jewish Antiquities* attributed to Solomon a reign of eighty years[41], recording at the same time that the king started the construction of the Temple in his fourth regnal year, corresponding to year 11 of Hiram[42]. Solomon would thus have reigned until the time of Ethbaal I / Ittobaal I, whom Josephus nevertheless considers to be Ahab's father-in-law[43].

Another example of similar Josephus' blunders occurs in his total of "fifty-four years and three months" from the beginning of the siege of Tyre in Nebuchadnezzar's year 17 to the entry of Cyrus II to Babylon in year 14 of Hiram III[44]. In reality, the total includes the twenty years of the reign of Hiram III[45], down to 533 B.C., and its reckoning starts after the destruction of the Temple in Jerusalem in 587/6 B.C., in year 18 or 19 of Nebuchadnezzar II[46].

All this means finally that Josephus's mathematical performances must be subjected to close scrutiny and that the usually followed chronology of Tyre for the 10th-8th centuries B.C. should be lowered by at least a dozen of years, as we shall see below.

38 E. LIPIŃSKI, *art. cit.* (n. 28), p. 64.

39 JOSEPHUS FLAVIUS, *Against Apion* I, 17, §108; 18, §126. The construction of the Temple started in Hiram's year 11 according to *Jewish Antiquities* VIII, 3, 1, §62.

40 P. CINTAS, *Laurentianus, LXIX, 22, ou la torture d'un texte*, in *Mélanges A. Piganiol* III, Paris 1966, p. 1681-1692; ID., *Manuel d'archéologie punique* I, Paris 1970, p. 181-195; G. BUNNENS, *op. cit.* (n. 31), p. 218.

41 JOSEPHUS FLAVIUS, *Jewish Antiquities* VIII, 7, 8, §211, written a few years before *Against Apion*.

42 JOSEPHUS FLAVIUS, *Jewish Antiquities* VIII, 3, 1, §62.

43 JOSEPHUS FLAVIUS, *Jewish Antiquities* IX, 6, 6, §138.

44 JOSEPHUS FLAVIUS, *Against Apion* I, 21, §159. The text establishes the contemporaneity of year 14 of Hiram III and of the accession year of Cyrus II, not of his official year 1. The text says: Κῦρος ὁ Πέρσης τὸ κράτος παρέλαβεν.

45 JOSEPHUS FLAVIUS, *Against Apion* I, 21, §158.

46 JOSEPHUS FLAVIUS, *Against Apion* I, 21, §154 (cf. §160): year 18 like in Jer. 52, 29, but year 19 is given in Jer. 52, 12 and II Kings 25, 8, where the phrase with year 19 appears as a gloss. This unofficial reckoning of Nebuchadnezzar II's regnal years starts with 605 B.C., when Jer. 46, 2 already styles Nebuchadnezzar as king of Babylon and dates his victory over Necho from year 4 of Jehoiakim, king of Judah (605 B.C.).

The absolute chronology can be established further with a fair degree of probability thanks to the marble slab from Ashur published in 1951 by Fuad Safar. It gives us the annals of the first twenty campaigns of Shalmaneser III, redacted in 838 B.C. In the report on the eighteenth campaign (841 B.C.) we find a reference to a tribute paid by *Ba -'-li-ma-an-zer*, king of Tyre[47], whom J. Liver and J. M.ª Peñuela correctly identified with the king called Balezoros by Josephus Flavius[48]. His Phoenician name was no doubt *Ba'al-ma'zer*, with the *'ayin* indicated by *n*, since nasalization characterizes the pharyngeals in several Semitic languages[49], while Neo-Assyrian cuneiform script has no adequate notation of *'ayin*. The date of 841 B.C. eliminates some superfluous corrections of Josephus' text, as transmitted in the *Codex Laurentianus*, but favours a few readings preserved by the ancient extracts.

Theophilus of Antioch, George Syncellus, and the Armenian version of Eusebius' *Chronicon* attribute a reign of 17 years to Ba'al-ma'zer I, the successor of Hiram I, adding ten years to the 7 years of the *Codex Laurentianus*. The reading 7 should nevertheless be retained for two combined reasons: first, in consideration of the total of 155 years and 8 months established by Josephus Flavius in §126 for the whole period from Hiram's birth to the foundation of Carthage; second, for the necessity of following 'Εκλογὴ ἱστοριῶν, that attributes 18 years to the reign of Ba'al-ma'zer II, mentioned in Shalmaneser III's annals. Here, the *Codex Laurentianus* reads 6, Theophilus of Antioch 7, Syncellus and the Armenian version of Eusebius *Chronicon* 8. The text of 'Εκλογὴ ἱστοριῶν is trustworthy, as a rule, and the reading 18 is required by the synchronism with the Assyrian annals. However, the additional 12 years should be suppressed elsewhere, and this can happen precisely in §122,

[47] F. SAFAR, *A Further Text of Shalmaneser III from Assur,* in *Sumer* 7 (1951), p. 3-21 and Pls. I-III. A new transliteration and translation are given in *RIMA* III, text A.0.102.10, p. 54, col. IV, 10-12.

[48] J.M.ª PEÑUELA, *La inscripción asiria IM 55644 y la cronología de los reyes de Tiro,* in *Sefarad* 13 (1953), p. 217-237 and Pl. I; 14 (1954), p. 3-42, in particular 13 (1953), p. 222-223; J. LIVER, *art. cit.* (n. 28), p. 119. Twenty years later, the study by J.M.ª Peñuela prompted the critical analysis of R. VAN COMPENROLLE, *L'inscription de Salmanasar III, IM 55644, du Musée de Bagdad, la chronologie des rois de Tyr et la date de la fondation de Carthage (806/5 avant notre ère),* in *AIPHOS* 20 (1968-72 [1973]), p. 467-479. Nobody seems to have followed the idea of adding a new king to Menander's list, as proposed by W.F. ALBRIGHT, *The New Assyro-Tyrian Synchronism and the Chronology of Tyre*, in *AIPHOS* 13 (1953 = *Mélanges Isidore Lévy*, Bruxelles 1955), p. 1-9.

[49] LIPIŃSKI, *Semitic*, §17.8.

where the sentence on the usurper of the throne has been misunderstood and mistreated in the critical edition by B. Niese, who is followed by most authors. He substantially changed the text of the *Codex Laurentianus*, which inspires much confidence in this particular passage, because it does not give the name of the usurper, applying the principle of the *damnatio memoriae*, and mentions the patronymic of the lawful king: 'Υσάσταρτος ὁ Δελειαστάρτου. Instead of the inexistent and incomprehensible Μεθουσάσταρτος of the B. Niese's edition, the *Codex Laurentianus* preserves good Semitic names. The king's name *'š'štrt*, "Man of Aštart", is attested epigraphically[50], and its Greek notation with *upsilon* transcribing Phoenician-Punic *i* is consonant with a well-known scribal practice[51]. As for the patronymic, it perfectly matches the West Semitic anthroponomy of Iron Age II, providing many names with the verb *dly*, "to lift up"[52].

The text of the *Codex Laurentianus* reads: "After him Abd-Aštart, his son, who lived twenty years, reigned nine years. The four sons of his nurse conspired against him and slew him. The elder of these reigned *twelve years*. Meanwhile Iš-Aštart, son of Daliy-Aštart, who lived fifty-four years, reigned twelve years", ὧν ὁ πρεσβύτερος ἐβασίλευσεν *ἔτη δεκαδύο*, μεθ' ὃ 'Υσάσταρτος ὁ Δελειαστάρτου, ὃς βιώσας ἔτη πεντήκοντα τέσσαρα, ἐβασίλευσεν ἔτη δώδεκα. During the tenure of the anonymous usurper, a lawful king, belonging apparently to a lateral branch of the royal family, reigned somewhere on the Tyrian mainland. His twelve years of reign should not be added therefore to the twelve years of the usurper, because they were covering the same period.

However, the "twelve years" of the anonymous usurper raise a particular question, and their authenticity is doubtful. These words are missing in the Armenian version, in the 'Εκλογὴ ἱστοριῶν, and in the *Chronography* of Syncellus. This means that Eusebius did not find this information in Josephus' text or, at least, did not copy it. The usurper's distinct "twelve years" are also missing in the Latin translation of

[50] The name *'š'štrt* in *CIS* I, 846, 3 is feminine (Benz, p. 73, cf. p. 277-278) and *'š* should be regarded there as a perfect of *'wš*, "to give", but it is masculine in *CIS* I, 5129, 3-4, contrary to Lipiński, *Itineraria Phoenicia*, p. 73, n. 205, and then it parallels the royal name of the Tyrian king-list.

[51] Lipiński, *Itineraria Phoenicia*, p. 412, n. 454. This is confirmed in the list by the spelling 'Ασθάρυμος, where υμ stands for Phoenician *'im(m)*, "mother".

[52] Cf. *SAIO* I, p. 119. In proper names, the verb is often mistranslated by "safe, redeem", for example by L. Pearce, *Dalâ*, etc., in *PNA* I/2, Helsinki 1999, p. 372.

Against Apion[53]. Besides, it is striking that the *Codex Laurentianus* uses the form δεκαδύο to indicate the length of the usurper's reign, but has the older δώδεκα, when writing about Iš-Aštart. The use of δεκαδύο is attested in papyri from the 3rd century B.C. on[54], and δέκα δύο occurs in the *Codex Vaticanus* of the Septuagint, in Ex. 28, 21, a passage of the Pentateuch, which is believed to have been translated into Greek in the 3rd century B.C. However, the *Codex Alexandrinus* reads there δώδεκα, which occurs also, e.g., in III Kings 19, 19, translated probably later, perhaps in the 2nd century B.C. Δέκα δύο can thus be regarded in Ex. 28, 21 as a later scribal correction, but δέκα δύο occurs also in the *Periplus of Pseudo-Scylax* §112, considered to be a compilation of 4th century B.C. The present writer qualified this form of the numeral as "strange" in that period, and suggested that δύο was added there to an original δέκα[55]. The parallel use of δεκαδύο and δώδεκα in the very same passage of Josephus is even more "strange", and the lack of δεκαδύο in the tradition depending on Eusebius and in the Latin translation may signify that the numeral was introduced later in order to provide an antecedent to μεθ' ὅ. If the length of the usurper's reign was not indicated originally, this would mean that the months or years of his grip on power were included in the reign of Iš-Aštart. We can then suppress ἔτη δεκαδύο from the text and translate μεθ' ὅ by "thereafter", what conforms to the classical use of the preposition μετά with the accusative. Instead, if we regard these words as authentic, we should understand μεθ' ὅ in the same sense as μεθ' ἡμέρην, "during the day"[56], or more importantly μετὰ δύο ἔτη, "during two years", as written by Josephus Flavius himself[57]. Hence the translation "meanwhile" in §122. At any rate, the time-span of the usurper's reign has no influence on the chronology.

If a reign of 18 years is attributed to Ba'al-ma'zer II in *Against Apion* §124, one must keep to the 9 years of Mattan's reign despite the 29

[53] "The eldest" of the four conspirators is immediately identified with *Metuastartus*: ... *quorum senior Metuastartus filius Leastarti regnavit, qui cum vixisset annis quadraginta quattuor, regnavit annis duodecim. Post hunc frater eius Astirimus* ... ; cf. C. BOYSEN (ed.), *op. cit.* (n. 22), p. 27:11-13.

[54] H.G. LIDDELL - R. SCOTT, *A Greek-English Lexicon*, 9th ed., Oxford 1996, p. 375b.

[55] LIPIŃSKI, *Itineraria Phoenicia*, p. 463.

[56] HERODOTUS, *History* II, 150.

[57] JOSEPHUS FLAVIUS, *The Jewish War* I, 13, 1, §248; *Jewish Antiquities* XIV, 13, 3, §330. The phrase is often translated erroneously by "after two years". Comp. also μετὰ τρίτον ἔτος, "during the third year": THEOPHRASTUS, *Enquiry into Plants* IV, 2, 8.

years of the *Vorlage* of Theophilus, Syncellus, and the Armenian version. In other words, the ἔτη θ' of the *Codex Laurentianus* is no corruption of ἔτη κθ'; the latter figure is due to a deliberate change of the text: twenty years were added here to the nine years of the *Codex Laurentianus* in order to obtain the 155 years and 8 months of Josephus' total. However, Syncellus reduced the figure from 29 to 25, for he apparently noticed that there were four supernumerary years. In fact, since he attributes 8 years to Ba'al-ma'zer, he would have otherwise reached a total of 159 years and 8 months.

To summarize: The only acceptable corrections in the concerned passage of the *Codex Laurentianus* are based on the Ἐκλογὴ ἱστοριῶν. Beside the 18 years of Ba'al-ma'zer II's reign, one should notice the death of Abd-Aštart at the age of 20 instead of 29 and the death of Aštarymos at the age of 58 instead of 45. One should also follow the correct reading of the proper names Ἀβδάσταρτος, Ἀσθάρυμος, and Ἰθόβαλος. The Latin version preserves *Balbazerus* in §121, where *the Codex Laurentianus* betrays a confusion *B > E*, reading Βαλεάζερος instead of Βαλβάζερος, the β standing for a Phoenician *m*.

The *Codex Laurentianus* also provides a corrupt reading Φυσμαλιο υος, challenged by Πυγμαλίων in the text of Theophilus of Antioch and already by Timaeus. However, the ΣΜ of the *Laurentianus* probably goes back to *MM* and the *ΛΙ* of both readings is likely to be a Greek development in front of the intervocalic semi-vowel *y*, which as a rule disappears in Greek. This leads us to Φυμμαλίο(ν) υ(ἱ)ός, in Phoenician *Pummayon*, i.e. the theonym Pummay[58] extended by the suffix *-ān > -ōn* or rather by an abbreviation of *-yatōn*, "he gave". Whichever be the true form of the name, Πυγμαλίων appears as a further inner-Greek phonetic development. Geminated consonants like *mm* tend to be dissimilated in the spoken language[59], but this particular change was apparently prompted by the influence of the Greek noun πυγμή, "fist", and its derivatives, also by proper names like Πυγμᾶς, Πύγμαχος. The original Josephus' spelling seems to have been Φυμμαλίον υἱός ("son"), but we shall call this king "Pygmalion" to keep with the tradition.

Having said this, the writer proposes the following reconstruction of the Tyrian chronology, as established by Josephus' source:

[58] Lipiński, *Dieux et déesses*, p. 297-306.
[59] E. Lipiński, *Dissimilation of Gemination*, forthcoming.

Names	Age at death	Regnal years	Dates
Εἵρωμος = *Ḥīrōm* I	53	34	*ca.* 950-917
Βαλβάζερος = *Ba'al-ma'zer* I	43	7	*ca.* 916-910
'Αβδάσταρτος = *'Abd-'Aštart*	20	9	*ca.* 909-901
Anonymous usurper		(12)	*ca.* 900-889
'Υσάσταρτος = *'Iš-'Aštart*	54	12	*ca.* 900-889
'Ασθάρυμος = *'Aštar(t)-'im(m)*	58	9	*ca.* 888-880
Φέλλης = *Pillēs*	50	8 months	*ca.* 880/879
'Ιθόβαλος = *'Ittō-Ba'al* I	68	32	*ca.* 879-848
Βαλ<βά>ζερος = *Ba'al-ma'zer* II	45	18	*ca.* 847-830
Μάττηνος = *Mattān* I	32	9	*ca.* 829-821
Φυμμαλίον = *Pummayōn*	58	47	*ca.* 820-774

10th-9th centuries B.C.

If this chronology is correct, Hiram I was a contemporary of Solomon. Since the real length of David's and Solomon's reigns is unknown, we may assume that Solomon reigned for about twenty years, and Hiram could have been king already in the last days of David. It is possible therefore that the Deuteronomistic Historian found an authentic reference in his sources to relations between Tyre and Jerusalem at that time. However, we cannot pinpoint any particular passage in his work that would have an annalistic character and refer to some diplomatic contacts between the two kingdoms. Nor do we find any allusion to David or Solomon in Josephus' Tyrian sources, because his quotations from Dius and Menander, allegedly proving Hiram's involvement in the building and decoration of the Temple in Jerusalem[60], in reality concern Tyrian sanctuaries. The same must be said about Josephus' reckoning of the span of time between the construction of the Temple and the foundation of Carthage[61].

In other words, Josephus' Tyrian sources only mentioned Hiram's building and cultic activities at home, as well as his expedition against the 'Ιυκέοι, most likely the inhabitants of Akko[62]. Phoenician expansion realized by military means is thus alluded to by Menander of Ephesus who says that Hiram I "undertook a campaign against Akko, which had not paid its tribute, and when he had again made it subject to him,

[60] JOSEPHUS FLAVIUS, *Against Apion* I, 17 §113; 18, §118.

[61] JOSEPHUS FLAVIUS, *Against Apion* I, 17 §108; 18, §126; Cf. A. DE GUTSCHMID, *op. cit.* (n. 19), Vol. II, p. 63; Vol. IV, p. 488-489; E. MEYER, *op. cit.* (n. 37), p. 124, n. 1.

[62] LIPIŃSKI, *Dieux et déesses*, p. 221 with n. 21.

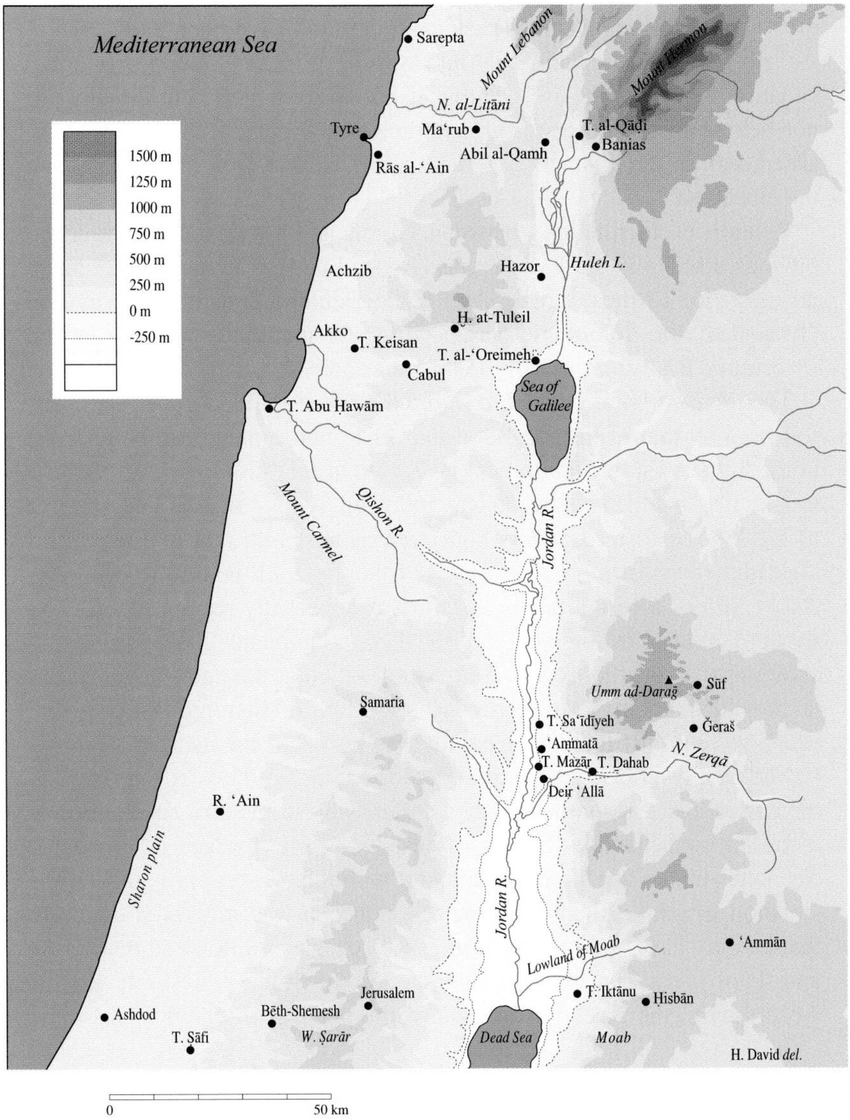

Canaan with Southern Phoenicia.

returned home"[63]. The Plain of Akko seems therefore to have belonged to Tyre in the 10th century B.C. This is the area, in any case, where some of the earliest finds of the "Phoenician culture" have been uncovered at Achzib, Tell Keisan, and Tell Abu Hawam[64]. Further south, the political situation of Dor in the 10th century is not entirely clear, but the city did not belong to the kingdom of Solomon, since one of its districts consisted only in the *nāpat Do'r*, "the marchy land of Dor", thus excluding the city itself[65].

References to relations between Hiram and David or Solomon are obvious additions due to Josephus. As said above, Tyrian annals made no reference to these kings. As for the Deuteronomistic Historian, he "furnished" the Solomonic period with later material, mainly from the 8th century B.C. and the early Persian period[66].

The reign of Hiram, which covered the space of thirty-four years, was followed by that of his son Ba'al-ma'zer I, whose name can be restored in the light of Latin *Balbazerus* and Assyrian *Ba-'-li-ma-an-zer*. He held the throne for seven years and was followed by his son Abd-Aštart. Four of the latter's foster-brothers conspired against him and murdered him after nine years of reign. The eldest of them seized the throne, while Iš-Aštart, son of a certain Daliy-Aštart, was apparently recognized as lawful king, at least in some parts of the Tyrian mainland[67]. His patronymic shows that he was no son of Abd-Aštart, killed at the age of twenty, but he may have belonged to the lineage of Hiram I. His reign lasted twelve years, which must include or parallel the period of the usurper's grip on power. His brother Aštarymos succeeded him, but he was murdered at the age of 58[68] by another brother, Pillēs, who in his turn succumbed to a conspiracy headed by the high priest of Astarte, Ittobaal I / Ethbaal I. The latter united the highest sacerdotal with the highest civil authority, a situation which was later the rule at Sidon[69]. It was suggested therefore that he may have been the high priest of Astarte at Sidon and that Sidon and Tyre were henceforth united under the rule of a single king[70]. According to the 'Ἐκλογὴ ἱστοριῶν, the reading of which seems to be

[63] JOSEPHUS FLAVIUS, *Jewish Antiquities* VIII, 5, 3, §146 = *Against Apion* I, 18 §119.
[64] J. BRIEND - J.-B. HUMBERT, *Tell Keisan (1971-1976)*, Paris 1980, p. 197-234.
[65] LIPIŃSKI, *Itineraria Phoenicia*, p. 322-328; cf. M. NOTH, *Könige* I (BKAT IX/1), Neukirchen-Vluyn 1968, p. 69-70.
[66] LIPIŃSKI, *Itineraria Phoenicia*, p. 218-220, 247, 505-507.
[67] Cf. here above, p. 171-172.
[68] Age given in the 'Ἐκλογὴ ἱστοριῶν, against 54 in the *Codex Laurentianus*.
[69] *KAI* 13 = *TSSI* III, 27, 1-2; *KAI* 14 = *TSSI* III, 28, 14-15.
[70] H.J. KATZENSTEIN, *op. cit.* (n. 17), p. 130-131.

reliable, he lived sixty-eight years, as indicated also in the *Codex Laurentianus*, and thus became king at the age of thirty-six. He had a long reign of 32 years and was obviously gifted with wide-reaching views. According to I Kings 16, 31, he gave his daughter Jezebel in marriage to Ahab, son and heir apparent of Omri, king of Israel. Also the royal epithalamium of Ps. 45 could be placed in the frame of these relations between the kingdoms of Israel and of Tyre, but nothing proves that it refers to the marriage of Ahab and Jezabel. A later occasion, perhaps at the time of Jeroboam II in the 8th century B.C., may equally be taken into account. Diplomatic marriages were aiming at strengthening military alliances and economic relations. The latter are illustrated by the excavations of Ḫirbet Rās az-Zētūn (Ḥorvat Rosh Zayit)[71].

Archaeologists propose to identify the site with biblical Cabul and this proposal is quite convincing. The main structure of the site is a fortress consisting of a central building of Phoenician-like masonry, characterized by header and stretcher construction, also called ashlar masonry. The building was surrounded by a massive wall and its cellars were predominantly used for storage of various agricultural products, mostly cereals, olive-oil, and wine. An impressive quantity of 506 storage jars have been found at the site, some containing carbonized wheat, others sealed with clay stoppers. Alongside the storage jars, a rich assemblage of Phoenician and Cypriot vessels was found, including Black-on-Red wares, Cypriot White Painted, Phoenician Bichrome and Plain wares, Red-slipped pottery. Comparing this ceramics with the pottery of other sites in North Israel, the excavators have dated the occupation of the building to the 10th-9th centuries B.C. and have concluded that this was a Phoenician stronghold, built after king Hiram of Tyre had assumed control over this region, named by him "the Land of Cabul" (I Kings 9, 10-14).

Now, the dating of the concerned pottery is controversial. According to the "short chronology" generally held in the Institute of Archaeology at Tel Aviv, the strata of the archaeological sites in North Israel, like Megiddo VA-IVB, Jokneam XV-XIV, Hazor X-IX, with comparable typical pottery should be dated to the late 10th century and the first half of the 9th century[72], thus also to the time of kings Omri and Ahab, not to

[71] Grid ref. 1718/2538: Z. GAL, *Rosh Zayit, Ḥorvat,* in *NEAEHL*, Jerusalem 1993, Vol. IV, p. 1289-1291; Z. GAL - Y. ALEXANDRE, *Ḥorbat Rosh Zayit: An Iron Age Storage Fort and Village* (IAA Reports 8), Jerusalem 2000.

[72] See, in particular, O. ZIMHONI, *The Iron Age Pottery from Tel Jezreel - An Interim Report*, in *Tel Aviv* 19 (1992), p. 57-70, especially p. 69 ; EAD., *Clues from the Enclosure-Fills : Pre-Omride Settlement at Tel Jezreel*, in *Tel Aviv* 24 (1997), p. 83-109, especially p. 89-93.

the reign of Solomon in the mid-10th century B.C., about 955-930 B.C. This is confirmed indirectly by Yardenna Alexandre, who dealt with the pottery of Ḥorvat Rosh Zayit, especially with the characteristic ovoid and short-lived type of the so-called "Hippo" storage jars[73]. Since she could not date the destruction of the Storage Fort of Ḥorvat Rosh Zayit to the 10th century B.C. because of the Black-on-Red pottery, which hardly appears in Phoenicia and in Cyprus before 875/850 B.C.[74], she assumed that the jars from Ḥorvat Rosh Zayit would represent the latest appearance of the "Hippo" jars, admitting a difference of some 30 years. This reasoning does not convince. In fact, the simultaneous presence of Red-on-Black wares, which do not occur in Phoenicia before 875 B.C., indicates that the foundation of the Storage Fort should be dated some fifty years after Solomon's death, like the strata of all the other sites with "Hippo" jars, thus providing a strong argument in favour of a lower chronology of the 10th-9th centuries B.C. Moreover, no "Hippo" jars have been found so far either at archaeological sites in Phoenicia proper or in the coastal plain of Akko, viz. at Akko, Tell Abu Hawam, or Tell Keisan. Instead, they are present at North-Israelite sites. This suggests that the Storage Fort in question has been built by Omri or Ahab at the border of their kingdom[75]. Its destruction should then be attributed to the Aramaean incursions under Hazael of Damascus, after 840 B.C. The erection of this Storage Fort at the time of Omri or Ahab appears as a sign of intense economic and commercial relations between Israel and Tyre at the time of Ethbaal I.

An act of major importance assigned to Ethbaal I in the Tyrian annals was the foundation of Botrys (Batrūn) on the Lebanese coast, north of Byblos. Still more enterprising was his initiative of creating colonies in Libya (Africa) by founding Auzia. Its exact location is unknown, but it was certainly not situated inland, in Numidia.

[73] Y. ALEXANDRE, *The 'Hippo' Jar and Other Storage Jars at Hurvat Rosh Zayit*, in *Tel Aviv* 22 (1995), p. 77-88.

[74] At Phoenician and Cypriot sites, where biblical considerations do not influence the judgment of archaeologists, the appearance of the Red-on-Black pottery is dated towards the end of Cypro-Geometric II, i.e. *ca.* 875/850 B.C. A state of art, being already fifteen years old, is provided by F. DE CRÉE, *The Black-on-Red or Cypro-Phoenician Ware*, in E. LIPIŃSKI (ed.), *Phoenicia and the Bible* (Studia Phoenicia XI; OLA 44), Leuven 1991, p. 95-102.

[75] Another border fort was built probably by Omri or Ahab at Ḫirbet at-Tuleil (Tel Harashim), about 15 km north-east of Ḥorvat Rosh Zayit; cf. D. BEN-AMI, *The Casemate Fort at Tel Harashim in Upper Galilee,* in *Tel Aviv* 31 (2004), p. 194-208, in particular p. 207-208.

Judging by the similarity of names, one might propose Marsa al-Awğia, a small harbour on the southern edge of the Greater Syrtis, but the history of this site is unknown despite its location halfway between the Altars of the Philaenoi and the *Opiros* of the Peutinger Table[76]. Another possibility would be the offshore island of Burda in the Gulf of Bomba, which could have been a typical Phoenician settlement, the more so because Herodotus mentions the nearby *Aziris*[77], the name of which seems to be based on Phoenician *ḥṣr*, corresponding to Hebrew *ḥāṣēr* < *ḥaṣir*, "enclosure". There is also the possibility of an emporium in the territory of the Adyrmachidae, at Marsa Matruḫ, ancient Paraetonium. Aegean and Cypriot pottery, found at this site[78], witnesses sea contacts with Crete, where Phoenician presence is attested from the end of the 10th or the early 9th century B.C. on[79]. However, Iron Age pottery is missing so far at Marsa Matruḫ, although this was the only place along this West-Egyptian coast convenient for a harbour[80]. At the same time, it was the terminal of an ancient caravan route from the Oasis of Siwah[81], distant about 310 km. Finally, one can suggest a more eastern site in the Gulf al-'Arab, near el-Alamein. Ramesses II had built a chain of temple-forts out to Alamein[82] and a large Hellenistic city with a harbour in a natural lagoon has been discovered in 1986 at the site of

[76] The Peutinger Table, published by K. MILLER, *Die Peutingersche Tafel*, Ravensbrug 1887 (reprint: Stuttgart 1962), bears the name of its first known proprietor: Conrad Peutinger (1465-1547), a humanist from Augsburg. On Peutinger, one can read the notice by H.-J. KIENAST - H. ZÄG, *The Revival of a Great German Library*, in *German Research* 2003-3, p. 16-19. For *Opiros*, see LIPIŃSKI, *Itineraria Phoenicia*, p. 200-202.

[77] HERODOTUS, *History* IV, 158 and 169. Cf. E. LIPIŃSKI, *The Giligamae of Herodotus IV, 169*, forthcoming.

[78] L. HULIN, *Marsa Matruh 1987. Preliminary Ceramic Report*, in *JARCE* 26 (1989), p. 115-126, in particular p. 120-121.

[79] LIPIŃSKI, *Itineraria Phoenicia*, p. 178-188. The feasibility of ancient direct navigation from Crete to Egypt is recognized by several authors since more than fifty years and the possibility of seasonal navigation in the opposite direction is now advocated by L.V. WATROUS, *Kommos* III. *The Late Bronze Age Pottery*, Princeton 1992, p. 176-178. See also J. PHILLIPS, *Aegypto-Aegean Relations up to the 2nd Millennium B.C.*, in L. KRZYŻANIAK - K. KOEPER - M. KOBUSIEWICZ (eds.), *Interregional Contacts in the Later Prehistory of Northeastern Africa*, Poznań 1996, p. 459-474, in particular p. 466.

[80] D. WHITE - A.P. WHITE, *Coastal Sites of Northeast Africa : The Case against Bronze Age Ports*, in *JARCE* 33 (1996), p. 11-30.

[81] J. LECLANT, *Per Africae sitientia*, in *BIFAO* 49 (1950), p. 193-253 (see p. 232-238).

[82] B. PORTER - R.L.B. MOSS, *Topographical Bibliography of Ancient Egyptian Hieroglyphic Texts, Reliefs, and Paintings* VII. *Nubia, the Deserts, and Outside Egypt*, Oxford 1951, p. 368-369; L. HABACHI, *Les grandes découvertes archéologiques de 1954*, in *Revue du Caire* 1955, p. 62-65.

Marina el-Alamein[83], where a large tourist centre is being built. The foundation of the ancient town goes back to the 2nd century B.C., but an older emporium may have existed in this neighbourhood, considering the presence of a natural harbour for coastal navigation between the Delta and Cyrenaica, and for overseas trade with Cyprus and Crete, as shown by the large amount of Cypriot and Cretan pottery found at the site. The place was probably called 'Αντίφραι / 'Αντίφρον in Graeco-Roman times[84].

Ethbaal I was succeeded by his son Ba'al-ma'zer II, a name given also by Hiram I to his son and successor. This may have been a conscious reference to Tyrian history and a manifestation of the dynastic principle. Of Ba'al-ma'zer II we know nothing, except that he reigned 18 years according to the 'Εκλογὴ ἱστοριῶν and paid tribute to Shalmaneser III in 841 B.C., as stated in Assyrian annals. Assyrian texts seem to imply that Ba'al-ma'zer II was king of Tyre and Sidon. While some texts report that in 841 Shalmaneser III received the tribute from the Tyrian(s) and Sidonian(s)[85], the 838 B.C. version of the annals mentions "m*Ba-'-li-ma-an-zer* the Tyrian"[86] instead of "Tyrian(s) and Sidonian(s)". Moreover, the band of the Gates of Balawat depicting "the tribute (brought) in ships from the Tyrian(s) and Sidonian(s)" shows the king of Tyre standing on the shore of an island, while tribute is being ferried from the island to the mainland in boats[87]. Insular Tyre was apparently the residence of the ruler of Tyre and Sidon.

An earlier Assyrian reference to tribute paid to Ashurnasirpal II (883-859 B.C.) by Tyre, Sidon, Byblos, and other coastal cities[88] does not give the impression that Tyre and Sidon were then governed by the same ruler. It is likely therefore that the fusion of the city-states of Tyre and Sidon happened at the time of Ethbaal I, perhaps in the very year in which he took possession of the throne of Tyre, *ca.* 875 B.C., assuming that he was previously the priest-king of Sidon[89]. Neither Tyre nor Sidon

[83] A general presentation is given by W.A. DASZEWSKI, *Marina el-Alamein - czyli odkrywanie nieznanego miasta*, in M.L. BERNHARD (ed.), *Od Nilu do Eufratu*, Warszawa 1995, p. 53-60 and Pl. I. Yearly reports appear in *Polish Archaeology in the Mediterranean*, Warsaw 1990 ff.

[84] STRABO, *Geography* XVII, 1, 14. Cf. W.A. DASZEWSKI, *art. cit.* (n. 83), p. 59-60.

[85] *RIMA* III, text A.0.102.8, p. 48, lines 25'-26'; text A.0.102.12, p. 60, line 29.

[86] *RIMA* III, text A.0.102.10, p. 54, col. IV, 10-11.

[87] *ANEP*, No. 356; *RIMA* III, text A.0.102.66, p. 141.

[88] *RIMA* II, text A.0.101.1, p. 219, lines 86-87; text A.0.101.2, p. 226, lines 29-30. See also *ANET*, p. 276b. Cf. F. BRIQUEL-CHATONNET, *op. cit.* (n. 17), p. 74-76.

[89] H.J. KATZENSTEIN, *op. cit.* (n. 17), p. 131.

are mentioned in Shalmaneser III's annals for 858 B.C., despite their listing of the members of the large anti-Assyrian alliance. It included five North-Phoenician city-states, that took part in the battle of Qarqar fought by the Syro-Phoenician coalition against Shalmaneser III, namely Ṣumur (Muṣur, Tell al-Kāzil), Arqa (Irqanata, Tell Arqa), Arwad (ar-Ruwad), Ushnu (Ušanata), and Siyan (Šian, Siano)[90]. Later in Shalmaneser III's reign, however, even Sidon and Tyre had to pay homage to the Assyrian king.

Assyrian policy towards the Phoenician cities was based on effectively exploiting the existing political structure of these mini-states and their economic potential that brought about the greatly expanded trade in the Mediterranean basin. This expansion of the Phoenician sea trade from the 9th century B.C. onwards, as far west as Spain and the Atlantic coast of Morocco, was motivated by search for new supplies of silver and gold, for cheaper and more abundant raw materials, such as elephant tusks, lead, iron, and tin. In fact, the Near Eastern market of the Phoenicians was rapidly growing not only in the Aramaean and Neo-Hittite states of Syria and south-eastern Anatolia, but now also in Assyria, where a political and military renaissance develops from the reign of Ashurnasirpal II on.

Southern Spain, called Tarshish by the Phoenicians, the Hebrews, and the Assyrians, later Tartessos by the Greeks[91], was a region rich in silver and lead, iron and tin. It was reached by Phoenician sailors and merchants not prior to the 9th century B.C.[92] and is first mentioned in a Phoenician inscription from Nora, Sardinia[93]. This text can be dated *ca.* 800 B.C. and seems to contain a reference to Cyprus, an early outpost of the Phoenician sea trade and colonization. A century of archaeological exploration has produced no evidence for any Phoenician settlement in Spain or North Africa prior to the early 8th century, but a 9th century date for the first Phoenician voyages to the western basin of the Mediter-

[90] F. Briquel-Chatonnet, *op. cit.* (n. 17), p. 77-89.

[91] M. Koch, *Tarschisch und Hispanien* (Madrider Forschungen 14), Berlin 1984; C.G. Wagner, *Tartessos en la historiografía: una revisión crítica,* in *La colonización fenicia en el sur de la Península Ibérica: 100 años de investigación*, Almería 1992, p. 81-115; Lipiński, *Itineraria Phoenicia*, p. 225-265; F. González de Canales Cerisola, *Del Occidente mítico griego a Tarsis-Tarteso. Fuentes escritas y documentación arqueológica*, Madrid 2004.

[92] J.L. López Castro, *La colonización fenicia en la Península Ibérica: 100 años de investigación,* in *La colonización fenicia en el sur de la Península Ibérica*, Almería 1992, p. 11-79; F. González de Canales Cerisola - L. Serrano Pichardo - J. Llompart Gómez, *El Emporio fenicio precolonial de Huelva* (ca. *900-770 a.C.)*, Madrid 2004.

[93] Lipiński, *Itineraria Phoenicia*, p. 234-247.

ranean can be assumed in view of the prospecting and trading activities that usually precede colonization. Besides, the Red Slip Ware, that characterizes the earliest Phoenician presence in the West, derives from a pottery type that is best represented in the East during the 9th century B.C. Instead, the hypothetical existence of a longer "pre-colonial" period, starting in the 12th century B.C., is questionable indeed. In fact, the superficial nature and the brevity of any "pre-colonial" occupation does not exclude traceable archaeological remains, especially when we consider the relatively rich material culture of the supposed early traders and sailors coming from the Levant[94].

Phoenician settlements have been founded in Malta, western Sicily, Sardinia, Ibiza, and on the coastal strips of North Africa and southern Spain[95]. The origins of the permanent colonies go back to the 8th century, that is to the time of the Neo-Assyrian empire. The Phoenician settlers were no "political" or "economic" refugees fleeing Assyrian invasions, but colonists sent overseas to provide the raw materials the mother country needed to satisfy the increasing demand for goods that resulted from the rapid expansion of the Assyrian market and the tribute imposed on the Phoenician cities. This expatriation may have helped also in solving the demographic problem raised by the increasing population of the small city-states, sometimes confined to a tiny island, like Tyre and Arwad, with a continental extension that lacked the same degree of security.

The oldest archaeologically evidenced and the most important of all the Phoenician colonies was Carthage, the New Town (*Qart ḥadašt*). The city founded at the latest in the early 8th century B.C. in a small littoral plain was characterized by a series of straight streets intersecting at right angles[96]. This example of a pre-planned town on an orthogonal grid system is paralleled in the Near East by the general layout of the network of streets in the Philistine settlement of Tell Qasile, in the 10th century B.C.[97] It certainly implies the existence of a central authority, which led finally to the creation of an independent Carthaginian state, when the

[94] M.E. Aubet, *The Phoenicians and the West: Politics, Colonies and Trade*, Cambridge 1993, p. 167-184.

[95] G. Bunnens, *op. cit.* (n. 31); O. Negbi, *Early Phoenician Presence in the Mediterranean Islands: A Reappraisal,* in *AJA* 96 (1992), p. 599-615.

[96] F. Rakob, *Karthago. Die frühe Siedlung. Neue Forschungen,* in *MDAIR* 96 (1989), p. 155-208, Pls. 34-49; Id., *Karthago* I-II, Mainz a/R 1990-97; Id., *Carthage, la ville archaïque. Nouvelles recherches,* in *CEDAC. Carthage* 16-17 (1997), p. 25-52.

[97] Z. Herzog, *The Archaeology of the City*, Tel Aviv 1997, p. 201-203.

Assyrian policy towards the cities of the Phoenician coast started to change from the reign of Tiglath-pileser III (744-727 B.C.) onward and to impose more limits to their semi-independent status[98].

Ba'al-ma'zer II was succeeded by his son Mattan I, who died at the early age of thirty-two, after a reign of only nine years (*ca.* 829-821). His succession and its aftermaths gave rise to the tale of Elissa, sister of a king of Tyre, who escaped with some followers to Libya and there founded Carthage. The tale is not preserved in its original form, but some later versions are extant. Its oldest elaborated form is narrated by Virgil[99]. A renewed inquiry into the theme of the foundation of Carthage, that has long been the subject of intense discussion, must distinguish the tale and the historiographic narrative from which the novel emerged. The tale is known mainly thanks to Virgil and Pompeius Trogus followed by Justinus, but the older narrative already associated romance to historical report, as Xenophon had done in the *Anabasis* and the *Cyropaedia*. This appears in the summary of Timaeus' account. Nevertheless there was a factual background, known to Timaeus, whose dating of the foundation of Carthage shows that he had access also to some annalistic sources of Phoenician provenance[100]. The account itself or, at least, its first part probably had a Levantine origin as well. The *Tale of the Two Brothers Ashurbanipal and Shamash-shum-ukin* from the Aramaic text in Demotic script[101] offers some striking analogies to the story of Pygmalion and of the high priest, whose wife Elissa was Pygmalion's sister. In the Aramaic text, Saritrah (Šeru'a-eṭirat), the eldest sister of both antagonists, seems to play a central role, like Elissa. At the end, Shamash-shum-ukin dies, like the high priest, while Saritrah, cursed by him (col. XX, 14-15), disappears from the scene. As for Elissa, she goes into exile.

Some dramatic events have indeed taken place at Tyre in the early years of Mattan's successor, Pygmalion. Josephus indicates that Mattan was Pygmalion's father, but the corrupt υος for υἱός was eliminated from the critical editions of *Against Apion*, creating the problem of the

[98] M. Botto, *Studi storici sulla Fenicia: l'VIII e il VII secolo a. C.* (Quaderni di orientalistica pisana 1), Pisa 1990.

[99] See the analysis of the various versions by G. Bunnens, *op. cit.* (n. 31), p. 165-172 (Virgil), 174-185 (Trogus Pompeius), 227 (Appian), 246-253 (Servius), 256-258 (John Malalas), 263-266 (Eustathius of Thessalonica).

[100] G. Bunnens, *op. cit.* (n. 31), p. 132-136 and 220.

[101] R.C. Steiner - C.F. Nims, *Ashurbanipal and Shamash-shum-ukin: A Tale of Two Brothers from the Aramaic Text in Demotic Script*, in *RB* 92 (1985), p. 60-81 and Pls. I-IV.

relationship between Mattan and Pygmalion, and opening the way to speculations, intensified because of the very name of Pygmalion, formed with a Cypriot theonym. His name certainly points at Cyprus and must witness some particular relations between Tyre and the island, where Phoenician settlement started at least in the second part of the 10th century B.C.[102] The dramatic events have another origin: Pygmalion was only eleven years old at the death of Mattan[103], and the regency was probably assumed by the high priest of Melqart, who married Elissa, the sister of Pygmalion. Fearing to be ousted by the high priest, married to Mattan's daughter, Pygmalion, when grown to manhood, murdered him and exiled his sister. This is very likely the meaning of φυγοῦσα[104] in Josephus' source: "In the seventh year of his reign, his exiled sister founded in Libya the city of Carthage". The word φυγοῦσα, interpreted in the sense of "escaped", led to the creation of the novel. The latter nevertheless contains enough elements to understand that Elissa has been sent away with a fleet and a number of people to Cyprus and from there to Libya in order to establish a Tyrian colony, situated further to the west than Auzia, created by Ethbaal I. Pygmalion's reign lasted, we are told, forty-seven years. At his death, *ca.* 774 B.C., Carthage was founded, as shown by the recent archaeological excavations, that reached levels dating to the first part of the 8th century B.C.[105]

8th century B.C.

Phoenician expansion in the Mediterranean was paralleled by an intense trade activity in the Near East, which was certainly the main cause of the diffusion of the Phoenician language, script, architecture, and cults in northern Syria, south-eastern Anatolia, and Palestine. There were also links between Phoenician and Philistine trade activities in the 8th century B.C. Thus, "the gold of Ophir" was imported from the West through the Philistine harbour of Tell Qasile[106] and Phoenician inscriptions were found in the desert station of Kuntillet 'Ağrud[107], on the road from Philistia, where some of the 'Ağrud ves-

[102] Lipiński, *Itineraria Phoenicia*, p. 42-46.

[103] This results from the life-span "58" given by the *Codex Laurentianus*.

[104] H.G. Liddell - L. Scott, *op. cit.* (n. 54), p. 1925a, III.

[105] See here above, p. 182.

[106] Lipiński, *Itineraria Phoenicia*, p. 189-221.

[107] Z. Meshel, *Kuntillet 'Ajrud. A Religious Centre from the Time of the Judaean Monarchy on the Border of Sinai*, Jerusalem 1978, inscriptions D.

sels were made[108], to the Gulf of Aqaba where perfumes and spices were coming by caravans from South Arabia[109]. Instead, the hypothesis of commercial sea links with South Arabia is problematic in consideration of the notorious difficulties of navigation in the upper reaches of the Red Sea[110].

Some northern Phoenician cities, like Ṣumur[111], were first annexed to the kingdom of Hamath and then incorporated by Tiglath-pileser III into the Assyrian provinces, but the main city-states of the seacoast, such as Arwad, Byblos, Sidon, and Tyre, remained semi-independent in the time of Assyrian hegemony[112]. Only Sidon, after an unsuccessful revolt against Esarhaddon, was turned in 676 into an Assyrian province[113]. This important period in Phoenician and Tyrian history is very partially echoed in sources preserved by Josephus Flavius.

There is a lacuna in the list of Tyrian kings, as transmitted by him, from *ca.* 773 B.C. to the reign of Elulaios, who acceded to the throne after Ethbaal II and the short reigns (*ca.* 736-727 B.C.) of Hiram II and Mattan II. Even if we assign a rather long reign to Ethbaal II and date it to *ca.* 760-737 B.C., there is still ample time in *ca.* 773-761 for at least one king who may have been "Hiram, king of the Sidonians", known from the Baal of Lebanon inscriptions, that should be dated earlier in the

[108] J. GUNNEWEG - I. PERLMAN - Z. MESHEL, *The Origin of the Pottery of Kuntillet 'Ajrud,* in *IEJ* 35 (1985), p. 270-283. The site is rightly considered to be a station on the desert road: J.M. HADLEY, *Kuntillet 'Ajrud: Religious Centre or Desert Way Station?,* in *PEQ* 125 (1993), p. 115-123.

[109] M.C.A. MACDONALD, *Trade Routes and Trade Goods at the Northern End of the "Incense Road" in the First Millennium B.C.*, in A. AVANZINI (ed.), *Profumi d'Arabia* (Saggi di storia antica 11), Firenze 1997, p. 333-350.

[110] This is confirmed by I Kings 22, 49; II Chron. 20, 37, and STRABO, *Geography* XVI, 4, 23, who notes that Aelius Gallus lost much of his large fleet on the voyage from the head of the Gulf of Suez to Leuke Kome. This is also the reason why Leuke Kome, located just below the entrance to the Gulf of Aqaba, and not Aqaba or Elath, was the head of the inland route to the Nabataean capital at Petra; cf. STRABO, *Geography* XVI, 4, 23-24; L. CASSON, *South Arabia's Maritime Trade in the First Century A.D.*, in T. FAHD (ed.), *L'Arabie préislamique et son environnement historique et culturel*, Leiden 1989, p. 187-194 (see p. 188). For Klysma, in the Gulf of Suez, see S.E. SIDEBOTHAM, *The Red Sea and the Arabia-India Trade*, in T. FAHD (ed.), *L'Arabie préislamique et son environnement historique et culturel*, Leiden 1989, p. 195-223 (see p. 201). Cf. A. LEMAIRE, *Les Phéniciens et le commerce entre la Mer Rouge et la Mer Méditerranée*, in E. LIPIŃSKI (ed.), *Phoenicia and the East Mediterranean in the First Millennium B.C.* (Studia Phoenicia V; OLA 22), Leuven 1987, p. 49-60.

[111] The identification of Ṣumur with Tell al-Kāzil seems to be well established: E. CAPET - E. GUBEL, *art. cit.* (n. 2); LIPIŃSKI, *Aramaeans*, p. 287, with former literature.

[112] See, in this connection, B. ODED, *The Phoenician Cities and the Assyrian Empire at the Time of Tiglath-Pileser III*, in *ZDPV* 90 (1974), p. 38-49.

[113] M. BOTTO, *op. cit.* (n. 98), p. 75-77; LIPIŃSKI, *Itineraria Phoenicia*, p. 17-36.

8th century B.C. than the short time-span of Hiram II (*ca.* 736-729 B.C.)[114].

The presence of Hiram's deputy on Cyprus, in the New City called like Carthage in Africa, witnesses wide-reaching economic activities, related most likely to the copper mines north of Amathus and Limassol. Remains of another economic enterprise of those years have been uncovered in the excavations of Ḫirbet Rās az-Zētūn[115], where the large complex of olive-oil presses, technically Phoenician, has been dated to the 8th century B.C.[116] After the destruction of the Israelite fort in the second part of the 9th century B.C., this site with the surrounding region has apparently been acquired by Tyre. An echo of this transaction, involving a king of Tyre and a king of Israel, probably Jeroboam II, is related in I Kings 9, 11-13, linked by the Deuteronomistic Historian or his source to the Cycle of Solomon[117].

In the coastal Sharon plain, where both Philistine and Phoenician influence was felt, between Mount Carmel in the north and the Yarkon River in the south, lies the city of Dor, which seems to have enjoyed, in the 9th-8th centuries, the status of a city-state. This is suggested at least by a seal from the second half of the 8th century B.C.[118], that belonged "to Zadoq, son of Mika(s), [son] of Krio(s), priest-king of Dor". The ruler's patronymics *Mk'* and *Kryw*, both in the genitive, are transcribed from Greek, which is not so surprising in this area and period. The seal is decorated with the winged cobra (*uraeus*), which is frequently found in Phoenico-Egyptian art and symbolizes the divine royal power. The existence of a small city-state of Dor, possibly depending from Tyre, explains why Dor later became the capital of an Assyrian province.

Nothing is known of Ethbaal II, except that he has paid a tribute to Tiglath-pileser III in 738 B.C.[119] He was followed on the throne by Hiram II, who is mentioned among Western tributaries of 738 B.C. in the Calah version of Tiglath-pileser III's annals[120]. This recension must

[114] Lipiński, *Itineraria Phoenicia*, p. 46-48.

[115] See here above, p. 177-178.

[116] Z. Gal - R. Frankel, *An Olive Oil Press Complex at Ḥurbat Rōš Zayit (Rās ez-Zētūn) in Lower Galilee*, in *ZDPV* 109 (1993), p. 128-140.

[117] E. Lipiński, *Hiram of Tyre and Solomon*, forthcoming.

[118] N. Avigad, *The Priest of Dor,* in *IEJ* 25 (1975), p. 101-105, Pl. 10C-D; N. Avigad - B. Sass, *Corpus of West Semitic Stamp Seals*, Jerusalem 1997, p. 60, No. 29; Lipiński, *Itineraria Phoenicia*, p. 326-327.

[119] *Tigl. III*, p. 106, St. IIIA, line 6.

[120] *Tigl. III*, p. 68, Ann. 13*, line [11]; p. 89, Ann. 27, line 2.

be based on a later list of tributaries, possibly from 737 B.C., when Hiram II had already succeeded Ethbaal II.

Hiram II allied in 733 or 732 B.C. with Raṣyān, king of Damascus, but was soon attacked by Tiglath-pileser III and submitted to him[121]. He has apparently been deprived of his power over Sidon where Elulaios / Luli[122] may have been appointed by the Assyrians[123]. In fact, the contents of a letter of Qurdi-Aššur-lāmur to the king implies that Hiram II had no longer power over Sidon. The letter quotes a report of Nabū-šēzib from Tyre, according to which Hiram had cut down the *ēqu* or sacred tree[124] of the temple of the gods at the entrance (SAG)[125] of Sidon and intended transporting it to Tyre, but has been prevented from doing this[126]: m⌜*Ḫi*⌝-[*r*]*u*!-*mu*[127] *ēqu ša bēt ilānišu ša rēš Ṣidūni ittikis mā ana Ṣurri lantuḫu annītu ušakli'ušu*[128] *ēqu ša ikkissuni ina šēp šadē*, "Hiram cut down the (sacred) tree of the temple of his gods, which is at the entrance to Sidon, saying: 'I shall move it to Tyre'. I made him stop this: the (sacred) tree, which he cut down, is at the foot of the mount".

Hiram II was perhaps the Tyrian king who at Ahaz request sent qualified workmen to execute works in the temple of Jerusalem, presented by the Deuteronomistic Historian as Solomon's accomplishments. However, cutting off trees on Mount Lebanon required Assyrian authoriza-

[121] *Tigl. III*, p. 186 and 188, Summ. 9, rev., lines 5-8.

[122] For this name, cf. LIPIŃSKI, *Itineraria Phoenicia*, p. 53-54.

[123] According to JOSEPHUS FLAVIUS, *Jewish Antiquities* IX, 14, 2, §284, Elulaios reigned 36 years. This is possible, if his reign, eventually in quality of *si-il-ṭa*, "potentate", has started in 733/2 B.C. For this title, see LIPIŃSKI, *Itineraria Phoenicia*, p. 54 with n. 78.

[124] Assyro-Babylonian *ēqu* is the Aramaic word *'ēq* < *'ēṣ*, "tree", which was most likely used in the Aramaic report of Nabū-šēzib from Tyre, whom Qurdi-Aššur-lāmur quotes in his Neo-Assyrian letter to the king.

[125] For the approximate meaning of SAG, "forepart", "entrance", see *ri-iš* in *RIMA* II, text A.0.89.7, p. 102, col. III, 10; p. 104, col. V, 1.

[126] Nimrud Letter XIII (ND 2686), lines 8-15, published by H.W.F. SAGGS, *The Nimrud Letters, 1952 - Part II. Relations with the West*, in *Iraq* 17 (1955), p. 126-160 (see p. 130-131 and 156, Pl. XXI).

[127] The editor of the text reads "Nergal-iddin", but [m*Ḫi*]-*ru-mu* is mentioned again with Nabū-šēzib a few lines further (rev., line 2), in a broken context, and probably at the end of the letter (rev., line 17) as well.

[128] The comments of K. FABRITIUS, *Ḫi-rūmu*, in *PNA* II/1, Helsinki 2000, p. 474, "In order to prevent this, Qurdi-Aššur-lamur gave orders and he was exiled", seem to be based on two simultaneous interpretations of *ú-sa-ak-li-ú-šú* (line 13), viz. *ušakli'ušu*, "I/he made him stop", and *ušagli'ušu*, "I/he exiled him". The context decisively favours the first interpretation, and *annītu* even excludes the second one. So there is no question of sending Hiram into exile. It is not clear whether Qurdi-Aššur-lāmur or rather Nabū-šēzib, present at Tyre, intervened in this occasion.

tion at that time and was executed under Assyrian supervision[129]. This corresponds quite well to the background of I Kings 5, 15-32, apparently elaborated by the Deuteronomistic Historian who was re-using an older text. The latter mentioned Sidonians and Byblians providing timber and participating by order of an overlord in the building of a temple or palace. The overlord in question could only be an Assyrian king, probably Tiglath-pileser III, since we know that Ahaz paid tribute to him, visited him in Damascus, and thereafter commissioned important works in the temple of Jerusalem. The account of II Kings 16, 10-11 indicates that the transformations decided by Ahaz were inspired by the architecture and decoration of the temple of Hadad at Damascus. They are not known directly[130], but we can assume that they corresponded to a pattern attested in other Syro-Phoenician sanctuaries, in particular at 'Ain Dara, in northern Syria[131]. Its architecture and final decoration, dating from the 9th-8th centuries B.C., have rightly been compared with the description of the temple of Jerusalem in I Kings 6-7[132].

The power was apparently seized at Tyre in 729 B.C. by Mattan II, whose doings were reported to Tiglath-pileser III by Qurdi-Aššur-lāmur or another Assyrian commissioner[133]. The king sent his chief eunuch to Tyre, where he received 150 or 50 talents of gold and 2,000 talents of silver from Mattan II[134]. This huge tribute was paid, probably in 728 B.C., to buy Assyrian acceptance of Mattan's usurpation of the throne[135]. However, the death of Tiglath-pileser III seems to have deprived him very soon of the sceptre, seized by Elulaios / Luli. Shalmaneser V waged then war against Elulaios and occupied the cities of the mainland, but he

[129] Nimrud Letter XII (ND 2715), published by H.W.F. Saggs, *art. cit.* (n. 126), p. 127-128. A new transliteration with a French translation is provided by G. Kestemont, *Tyr et les Assyriens,* in *Studia Phoenicia I-II* (OLA 15), Leuven 1983, p. 53-78 (see p. 74-76).

[130] The only element, so far known, is a bas-relief with a sphinx, re-examined by M. Trokay, *Le bas-relief au sphinx de Damas*, in *Religio Phoenicia* (Studia Phoenicia IV), Namur 1986, p. 99-118.

[131] 'A. Abū 'Assāf, *Der Tempel von 'Ain Dara* (Damaszener Forschungen 3), Mainz a/R 1990 ; Id., *Der Tempel von 'Ain Dara in Nordsyrien*, in *Antike Welt* 24 (1993), p. 155-171.

[132] J. H. Monson, *Solomon's Temple and the Temple at 'Ayn Dārā*, in *Qadmoniot* 29 (1996), p. 33-38 (in Hebrew).

[133] Nimrud Letter XXI (ND 2430), published by H.W.F. Saggs, *art. cit.* (n. 126), p. 141 and 160, Pl. XXXV.

[134] *Tigl. III*, p. 170, Summ. 7, rev., line 16' ("150 talents of gold"); p. 190, Summ. 9, rev., line 26 ("50 talents of gold").

[135] A. Fuchs - G. Van Buylaere, *Metenna,* in *PNA* II/2, Helsinki 2001, p. 750.

was unable to force Tyre to surrender[136]. Tyre was safe upon its island and managed to resist for five years, i.e. until the death of Shalmaneser V, followed by the Assyrian dynastic crisis in 722 B.C., when Sargon II seized the kingship.

Menander's notice, reproduced by Josephus Flavius, is perfectly clear, but its first part, recording Elulaios' expedition to Cyprus, refers to an event posterior to the campaign of Shalmaneser V. While the new Assyrian dynasty was consolidating its power basis, Elulaios restored his authority in Phoenicia and there is some ground for thinking that he transferred his residence back to Sidon, since Sennacherib shall persistently call him "king of Sidon". The policy of Sargon II seems to have been to leave Phoenicia alone and to content himself with drawing a rich tribute which the cities were quite willing to pay in return for the *pax Assyriaca*. His annals apparently do not recognize a royal dignity to Elulaios, since they name him ᵐ*Si-il-ṭa*, "the Potentate", but they seem to indicate that he received military assistance from Assyria in order to restore his authority at Citium (Cyprus). This was very likely an occasion for setting up Sargon's "Cyprus stele" in this city[137], which depended from the ruler of Sidon and Tyre, certainly instrumental in this operation. Overseas trade was the main source of the Phoenician contribution to the prosperity of the Assyrian empire, but the compound of Abu Ruqeish with its ramifications towards Egypt and Arabia played an important role as well[138]. The portrait of the king of Tyre in Ez. 28, 12-14, though written much later, may have been inspired by the figure of Elulaios, the "Splendid".

The unprecedented death of an Assyrian king on the battlefield, in early 705 B.C., led to a general revolt in the western provinces of the Empire. Elulaios was certainly one of the rulers who ceased to deliver their annual tribute to Assyria. This explains the reversal of the Assyrian policy towards him, but it was not until Sennacherib, Sargon's son and successor, had been seated for four years upon the throne that a decisive action was taken against the Phoenician king. While Sennacherib was still on his march, in 701 B.C., Elulaios took ship and removed himself to the island of Cyprus, where alone he could be safe from pursuit and capture. Sennacherib waged war against a number of Phoenician cities, but he does not claim to have taken Tyre. We may thus conclude that the

[136] JOSEPHUS FLAVIUS, *Jewish Antiquities* IX, 14, 2, §284-287.
[137] For this stele and connected questions, cf. LIPIŃSKI, *Itineraria Phoenicia*, p. 51-54, with previous literature.
[138] See here above, p. 74, 127, 140, and below, p. 376, 378.

Island City escaped him. Instead, he secured obedience of Sidon by placing over it a new king, a certain Ethbaal[139]. This practically meant a scission of the kingdom of Tyre and Sidon. The kingdom of Tyre continued nevertheless to exist on its island, and Elulaios may have ruled it further from Cyprus[140], where he died in 698 or 697 B.C.[141]

7th century B.C.

We hear nothing more of Phoenicia during the reign of Sennacherib, except that he received tribute, not only from Ethbaal, whom he had just set over Sidon, but also from Uru-milk, king of Byblos, and Abdi-le'ti, king of Arwad. The three towns probably represent the whole of Phoenicia. It is unclear who was ruling in Tyre after Elulaios. All what we know is that Baal I was there king at the time of Esarhaddon[142], who succeeded his father in 681 B.C.

It appears also that Ethbaal must have been succeeded before 681 B.C. in the government of Sidon by Abdi-Milkūti[143], but whether this change was caused by revolt at the death of Sennacherib, who had been murdered by two of his sons[144], or took place in the ordinary course, Ethbaal being succeeded by his son, is wholly uncertain. At any rate, Esarhaddon, on his accession, found Abdi-Milkūti in revolt against his authority. He had formed an alliance with Sanda-warri, king of Kundu and Sissū[145], a prince of Cilicia, and had set up as independent monarch, probably during the period when Esarhaddon had to assess his authority in Assyria and in the Sealand[146]. As soon as the Assyrian monarch found himself free to act against the two rebels, he proceeded westwards.

[139] He is called ᵐ*Tu-ba-'-lum/lu* in Sennacherib's inscriptions: D.D. LUCKENBILL, *The Annals of Sennacherib* (OIP 2), Chicago 1924, p. 30, lines 47 and 51; p. 69, line 19; p. 77, line 19; p. 86, line 14; E. FRAHM, *Einleitung in die Sanherib-Inschriften* (AfO, Beih. 26), Wien 1997, p. 53, lines 35 and 36. Cf. *ANET*, p. 287b; *TPOA*, p. 119, 122.

[140] H.J. KATZENSTEIN, *op. cit.* (n. 17), p. 251.

[141] For information on Elulaios / Luli, in Sennacherib's texts, see E. FRAHM, *Lulî,* in *PNA* II/2, Helsinki 2001, p. 668-669, also with references to very doubtful hypotheses.

[142] H.J. KATZENSTEIN, *op. cit.* (n. 17), p. 259-260, thinks that Baal I immediately succeeded Elulaios and was king for about forty years. This is not impossible, but not very likely.

[143] For Abdi-Milkūti, see K. RADNER, *Abdi-Milkūti*, in *PNA* I/1, Helsinki 1998, p. 7.

[144] For Sennacherib, see E. FRAHM, *Sīn-aḫḫē-erība*, in *PNA* III/1, Helsinki 2002, p. 1113-1127, in particular p. 1121.

[145] R. PRUZSINSZKY, *Sanda-uarri* 2., in *PNA* III/1, Helsinki 2002, p. 1088.

[146] For Esarhaddon, see B.N. PORTER - K. RADNER, *Aššūr-aḫu-iddina* 7., in *PNA* I/1, Helsinki 1998, p. 146-152.

When Abdi-Milkūti refused to submit, Esarhaddon captured and completely destroyed Sidon in early 676 B.C. The town was plundered and renamed "Quay of Esarhaddon", the treasures of the palace were carried off, and the greater portion of the population deported. All the Sidonian territory up to the present-day Al-Mina (Lebanon) was annexed[147] and Abdi-Milkūti, who had fled away by sea, was caught "like a fish out of the sea"[148], and decapitated in September/October 676 B.C. Sanda-warri was captured as well, and beheaded five months later, in February/March 675 B.C. Esarhaddon had Sidonian and Cilician magnates wear the heads of both rebels around their necks when parading in the streets of Nineveh together with singers and harpists[149].

An inscribed stele found near the citadel at Til Barsip represents Abdi-Milkūti, beheaded in 676 B.C., as a captive, standing in front of Esarhaddon and begging for clemency[150]. His name is engraved just below the figure[151]. However, the stele must date from 670/69, for the Assyrian and Babylonian heirs to the throne, appointed in 672 B.C., are represented on its lateral sides, and a second captive, kneeling in front of the king, is characterized by Nubian features. This must be Ušanahuru, crown prince of Egypt, captured by Esarhaddon in 671 B.C.[152] This means that the Assyrian campaign to Egypt in 671 forms the historical background of the stele. A similar monument, found in the eastern gate of Til Barsip, is not inscribed at all, while the text of the citadel stele breaks off abruptly, leaving ruled lines empty below it. The project of making steles for Til Barsip seems thus to have come to an abrupt end, probably because of Esarhaddon's sudden death in 669 B.C.[153] The representation of a captive Phoenician king at that date was just a wishful thinking: Assyrians probably expected capturing Baal I, king of Tyre, in the very same year, but this did not happen. The name of Abdi-Milkūti, king of Sidon, was thus engraved on the citadel stele. The parallel stele of Zincirli, likewise inscribed and dealing with Esarhaddon's campaign

[147] LIPIŃSKI, *Itineraria Phoenicia*, p. 17-36.

[148] R. BORGER, *Die Inschriften Asarhaddons, Königs von Assyrien* (AfO, Beih. 9), Graz 1956, p. 18, line 73.

[149] *Ibid.*, p. 50, lines 36-38.

[150] For both Til Barsip steles of Esarhaddon and his Zincirli stele, see B.N. PORTER, *Assyrian Propaganda for the West: Esarhaddon's Stelae for Til Barsip and Sam'al*, in G. BUNNENS (ed.), *Essays on Syria in the Iron Age* (Ancient Near Eastern Studies. Suppl. 7), Louvain 2000, p. 143-176, with former literature.

[151] R. BORGER, *op. cit.* (n. 148), p. 101, Mnm. B, line 25.

[152] *Ibid.*, p. 99, Mnm. A, line 43.

[153] B.N. PORTER, *art. cit.* (n. 150), p. 171, n. 43.

in Egypt, in 671 B.C., provides no comment to the figure of the captive Phoenician king, whose lips are pierced by rings to which run leashes coiled in Esarhaddon's left hand. Also this figure was supposed to represent Baal I, king of Tyre, but Assyrian expectations did not materialize.

In 676, after the fall of Sidon, an Assyrian governor was charged with the administration of the Sidonian territory, the southernmost part of which, with Marubbu and Sarepta, was allotted to Baal I, king of Tyre[154]. The latter appears to have been received into exceptional favour, since he is even mentioned as the first ruler in the list of Esarhaddon's tributaries who provided building material for the construction of a palace at Nineveh[155]. There are several reasons for this treatment of the king of Tyre. His fleet may have been helpful in capturing Abdi-Milkūti. In all likelihood Esarhaddon also needed its assistance in order to assess his authority on Cyprus[156] and to organize the trade along the Levantine seacoast, down to the Assyro-Phoenician emporia south-west of Gaza, especially at Abu Ruqeish. This was apparently one of the aims or the main purpose of the mutilated Esarhaddon's treaty with Baal I, which recognizes and confirms Tyrian customary rights and privileges in these matters[157]. A few years later, however, in 671 B.C., when Esarhaddon resolved again to attempt the conquest of Egypt, "Baal, king of Tyre, trusted in his friend Taharqo, king of Cush, the yoke of Ashur threw off, and made defiance"[158]. According to a summary of Esarhaddon's achievements down to 671 B.C., the king isolated Island Tyre "by cutting off the supplies of food and water"[159]. It does not appear however that these measures have then forced Baal to make his submission. In a probably later text, Esarhaddon claims to have taken away "all his cities and his belongings", but Baal was not deposed from his throne. He must have kept the control of Island Tyre, despite Esarhaddon's boast of having "conquered Tyre, which lies midst the sea"[160]. A more detailed, but badly broken account reports Baal's submission to Esarhaddon, his sending of a tribute and of daughters with dowries[161], but does not men-

[154] LIPIŃSKI, *Itineraria Phoenicia*, p. 34-36. Cf. ID., *Ba'alu,* in *PNA* I/2, Helsinki 1999, p. 242-243.

[155] R. BORGER, *op. cit.* (n. 148), p. 60, line 55.

[156] LIPIŃSKI, *Itineraria Phoenicia*, p. 62-76.

[157] *SAA* II, 5. Cf. G. PETTINATO, *I rapporti politici di Tiro con l'Assiria alla luce del "trattato tra Asarhaddon e Baal"*, in *RSF* 3 (1975), p. 145-160.

[158] R. BORGER, *op. cit.* (n. 148), p. 112, lines 12-13.

[159] *Ibid.*, p. 112, line 14.

[160] *Ibid.*, p. 86, AsBbE, lines 7-8.

[161] R. BORGER, *op. cit.* (n. 148), p. 110, Frt. A, rev., lines 2'-10'. Cf. *ANET*, p. 295b.

tion either the capture of Tyre itself or the seizing of its king as a captive[162]. The stereotyped phrase "he kissed my feet" does not even mean that Baal went personally to Nineveh to pay homage to Esarhaddon. He did it through his emissaries. The circumstances were favourable and made it imperative on the Assyrian king to overlook Baal's former treachery: Esarhaddon seriously feared internal threats and, in 670/69 B.C., took the extreme measure of murdering several of his own magnates[163]. In the same period, he apparently got a report from Egypt that his political organization of the Delta was on the verge of collapse, and he was mustering his troops to set off in 669 on a new campaign to Egypt. He fell ill on the way and died.

Baal I is mentioned again as the first ruler in a list of Ashurbanipal's vassals who joined the Assyrian king in 667 B.C. to accomplish his great enterprise - the restoration of the Assyrian dominion over the Delta and the Nile valley[164]. As the list is not identical with a similar record from Esarhaddon's time, it should reflect reality. However, this does not mean that the twenty-two vassals recorded in the list participated personally in the expedition. They had to provide troops, ships, equipment, and means, and the Tyrian navy was certainly an important operational factor in the campaign through the water meanders of the Nile delta and even in Upper Egypt. This explains why Baal I again holds the post of honour, followed by Manasseh, king of Judah, Qaws-gabri, king of Edom, Muṣuri, king of Moab, Amminadab, king of the Ammonites, three Phoenician, four Philistine, and ten Cypriot kings.

It is about four years later, in 663 or 662 B.C., that we find Baal I attacked and punished by the Assyrian monarch. The subjugation of Egypt had been in the meantime, though not without difficulty, completed by the conquest of Thebes in *ca.* 664 B.C. The Assyrian inscriptions do not make clear whether during the course of the four years' struggle, by which the re-conquest of Egypt was effected, the Tyrian ruler had given fresh offence to his suzerain, or whether it was the old perfidy, overlooked for a time but never forgotten, that was now

[162] B.N. PORTER, *art. cit.* (n. 150), p. 157, n. 31

[163] R. BORGER, *op. cit.* (n. 148), p. 124, Chron. 670/69; A.K. GRAYSON, *Assyrian and Babylonian Chronicles* (TCS 5), Locust Valley 1975, p. 86, Babylonian Chronicle 1, col. IV, 29, and p. 127, Babylonian Chronicle 14, rev., line 4.

[164] M. STRECK, *Assurbanipal und die letzten assyrischen Könige bis zum Untergange Niniveh's*, Leipzig 1916, Vol. II, p. 138-143; R. BORGER, *Beiträge zum Inschriftenwerk Assurbanipals*, Wiesbaden 1996, p. 18-20, C II 18-67, and p. 212. Cf. *ANET*, p. 294; *TPOA*, p. 131-132.

avenged by Esarhaddon's son[165]. Ashurbanipal uses a stereotyped phraseology and simply tells us that, in his third expedition, following the two campaigns to Egypt, he proceeded against Baal, king of Tyre, "who my royal will disregarded, and did not listen to the words of my lips". He says further:

> "Redoubts round him I raised, and over his people I strengthened the watch. On sea and land I seized his roads; his going out I stopped. I let scarce water and food, to preserve their lives, reach their mouths. By a strong blockade, which removed not, I besieged them. The daughter proceeding from his body and the daughters of his brothers, for concubines he brought to my presence. Yahi-milki (^{m}*Ia-ḫi-mil-ki*), his son, who had not crossed the sea, at once he sent forward, to make obeisance to me. His daughter and the daughters of his brothers with the great dowries, I received. Mercy I granted him, and the son proceeding from his body I returned to him"[166].

Thus Baal I once more escaped the fate he must have expected. Ashurbanipal was appeased by the submission made, restored Baal to his favour, and did not deprive him from the throne, but annexed the mainland territories of Tyre. Yahi-milk, who was still very young, as suggested by the words "who had not crossed the sea", had been given to Ashurbanipal as a hostage, but the Assyrian king sent him back to his father, and one can surmise that he succeeded Baal I a few years later. Neither Baal I nor his son are mentioned in later Assyrian texts, not even when Ashurbanipal suppressed a rebellion of the towns of Ushu (Palaetyros) and Akko, probably instigated by the Tyrian king. These events can be dated approximately *ca.* 644/3 B.C., in a period when Carthage was already emancipated politically and Island Tyre felt more isolated. Ashurbanipal put the leaders of the rebellion to death, the towns were plundered, and the bulk of the population carried off to Assyria[167].

The Phoenician island kings of Tyre, Arwad, and Cyprus were always more neglectful of their vassal duties than others, for it was more difficult to reach them. Assyria did not even possess a regular fleet, and could only punish a recalcitrant king of Tyre or Arwad — without mentioning the far-away kings of Cyprus — by drafting for her service the

[165] References are collected by K. Radner, *Aššur-bāni-apli*, in *PNA* I/1, Helsinki 1998, p. 159-171 (see p. 158b); E. Lipiński, *art. cit.* (n. 154).

[166] M. Streck, *op. cit.* (n. 164), p. 16-19; R. Borger, *op. cit.* (n. 148), p. 28, A II 49-62 = F I 56-69 = B II 41-61 = C III 68-90, and p. 216. Cf. *ANET*, p. 295-296; *TPOA*, p. 133.

[167] M. Streck, *op. cit.* (n. 164), p. 80-83; R. Borger, *op. cit.* (n. 148), p. 69, A IX 116-128, and p. 249.

ships and crews of some of the Phoenician coast-towns, as Sidon or Byblos. These towns were not eager of performing such a service, and probably did not maintain strong navies.

Nevertheless, Assyria exercised a control over the harbours and seems even to have obtained a concession over a quay in the port of Arwad. Such a concession, probably set forth in a treaty between the kings of Assyria and of Arwad, must have embraced a grant of partial Assyrian sovereignty over "the Assyrian harbour". We first hear of this concession in a letter of the Assyrian official Itti-Šamaš-balāṭu to king Esarhaddon[168]. The king's representative was apparently based in Ṣumur (Tell al-Kāzil)[169], which appears as an important trade centre on the Nahr al-Abraš, 3.5 km inland. The harbour of Ṣumur in Iron Age II was Ṭabbat al-Ḥammām[170], 7 km north-east of Tell al-Kāzil. Its mound is the highest point of a much larger occupied area, possibly corresponding to URU/KUR *Samsimuruna*[171] (**Šmš-'mrn*), "Sun of Amurru", the capital of a small Phoenician principality. Its kings resided previously at Ṣumur, but apparently lost the control of the city in the 8th century B.C. and shifted to a new residence near the harbour. Few of them are known by their proper name: probably Baal[172], in the second part of the 9th century B.C., perhaps Azar-Baal[173] in the 8th century B.C., then Menahem, the king of Samsimuruna who paid tribute to Sennacherib in 701 B.C.[174], finally Abi-Baal, king of Samsimuruna in the first half of the 7th century B.C.[175]

[168] *SAA* XVI, 127, 13-23.

[169] E. CAPET - E. GUBEL, *art. cit.* (n. 2); LIPIŃSKI, *Aramaeans*, p. 287, n. 219 with literature.

[170] R.J. BRAIDWOOD, *Report on Two Sondages on the Coast of Syria, South of Tartous*, in *Syria* 21 (1940), p. 183-221 and Pls. XX-XXVII.

[171] S. PARPOLA, *Neo-Assyrian Toponyms* (AOAT 6), Kevelaer-Neukirchen-Vluyn 1970, p. 303.

[172] *RIMA* III, text A.0.102.16, p. 79, lines 159'-160': m*Ba-'-il šá* ⌜KUR⌝ *Ṣ[í-mir-r]a-a-a*. The regular spelling of the toponym with ṢI is attested only from the later part of the 8th century B.C. on, i.e. a hundred years later. The earlier spelling was instead *Ṣu-mur, Ṣu-mu-ri,* etc. Baal was possibly the king who had sent a contingent of 1,000 men of Ṣumur to the battle of Qarqar, in 853 B.C.; cf. LIPIŃSKI, *Aramaeans*, p. 303 with n. 357.

[173] N. AVIGAD - B. SASS, *op. cit.* (n. 118), p. 264-265, No. 713: *l-'zm 'bd 'zrb'l.*

[174] D.D. LUCKENBILL, *op. cit.* (n. 139), p. 30, line 50; E. FRAHM, *op. cit.* (n. 139), p. 53, line 36.

[175] E. FRAHM, *op. cit.* (n. 139), p. 145; M. JURSA, *Abi-Ba'al* 1., in *PNA* I/1, Helsinki 1998, p. 8-9. His name appears very likely also on a stamp seal: P. BORDREUIL, *Inscriptions sigillaires ouest-sémitiques III*, in *Syria* 62 (1985), p. 21-29 (see p. 24-25); N. AVIGAD - B. SASS, *op. cit.* (n. 118), p. 426, No. 1122: *l-'byb'l.* The spelling with *yōd* reveals the Aramaic influence, quite comprehensible in this area.

The letter sent by Itti-Šamaš-balāṭu dates apparently from the last years of Esarhaddon, when the king had to fear some magnates at his own Court. Also his representative at Ṣumur was scared of the local merchants, who had good connections with "many in the entourage of the king"[176]. He was even afraid to act against an Aramaean agent from Ṣumur, called Il-ma'aḏi, who was travelling continuously between Assyria and Arwad, and informed Yakinlu, the king of Arwad, on every matter of interest[177]. The worse information sent by Itti-Šamaš-balāṭu to Esarhaddon concerns the measures taken by Yakinlu against the "Assyrian harbour" and the boats docking there[178]:

> "Yakinlu (m*Ik-ki-lu-ú*) does not let the boats come up to the port of the king, my lord, but has turned the whole trade for himself. He provides for anyone who comes to him, but kills anyone who docks at the Assyrian harbour, and steals his boat. He claims: 'They have written to me from the palace: Do only what is good for you!'".

Such a behaviour is unthinkable in a harbour on the mainland[179]. One should thus assume that the letter contains a report on the situation in the harbour of Arwad, where two ports can be distinguished even nowadays[180]. It does not seem that Esarhaddon did have the means and the time to react against the situation created by the successor of Mattan-Baal, who in 673/2 had contributed to Esarhaddon's rebuilding of a palace at Nineveh[181]. In 667 B.C., Yakinlu himself gave Ashurbanipal military help on the occasion of his first campaign to Egypt[182]. However, on Ashurbanipal's third campaign, in 663 or 662 B.C., after the submission of Baal I of Tyre, the Assyrian king accused Yakinlu of having been wanting in submission to his royal fathers. We may regard it as probable that his main offence was his behaviour and failure in the question of the Assyrian harbour at Arwad. Ashurbanipal let his displeasure

176 *SAA* XVI, 127, rev., lines 5-22; 128, rev., lines 1' - s. 1.

177 *SAA* XVI, 127, e. 24 - rev., line 10. Itti-Šamaš-balāṭu uses the word É in the sense "place": rev., line 8 and *SAA* XVI, 128, rev., line 4'.

178 *SAA* XVI, 127, 15-23.

179 This is why the "detaining of merchants ships in the harbour of Ṣimira", as stated by D. Schwemer, *Itti-Šamaš-balāṭu*, in *PNA* II/1, Helsinki 2000, p. 589, is out of question. Ṣumur was not immediately on the seashore and the closest harbour was situated at Ṭabbat al-Ḥammām, 7 km north-east of Tell al-Kāzil. The mouth of Nahr al-Abraš, 3.5 km to the west, was not fit for a port.

180 See the aerial photograph in G. Gerster - R.-B. Wartke, *Flugbilder aus Syrien*, Mainz a/R 2003, p. 18, Fig. 15.

181 For Mattan-Baal, see E. Frahm, *Mattan-Ba'al* 3., in *PNA* II/2, Helsinki 2001, p. 746.

182 J.S. Tenney, *Iakin-Lû*, in *PNA* II/1, Helsinki 2000, p. 488-499 (see c.).

be known at the Court of Yakinlu, and very shortly received an embassy of submission. Like Baal I of Tyre, Yakinlu sent his daughter to Nineveh to take her place in Ashurbanipal's harem, and with her he sent a large amount of valuables in the disguise of a dowry. The tokens of subjection were accepted and the Assyrian king established for Yakinlu a yearly tribute consisting of gold, purple wool, fish, and birds. When, not long afterwards, Yakinlu died, and his ten sons sought the Court of Nineveh to prefer their claims to the succession, they were received with favour. Azzi-Baal, the eldest, was appointed to the vacant kingdom, while his nine brothers were presented by Ashurbanipal with "costly clothing and rings"[183].

It is impossible to fix the year in which Phoenicia became independent of Assyria. The last trace of Assyrian military interference with destructions and deportation belongs to *ca.* 644/3, when Ashurbanipal severely punished Ushu and Akko. The latest sign of Assyrian continued domination is found in *ca.* 619 B.C., when Mannu-ki-aḫḫē, governor of Ṣumur, appears in the list of eponyms[184]. After the collapse of Assyria and an attempt by the pharaoh Necho II to re-establish Egyptian suzerainty in the Levant, Babylon became the overlord of the Phoenician coast.

6th century B.C.

However, at the beginning of the 6th century B.C. the West revolted against the Babylonians with Egypt's support. Even before the fall of Jerusalem in 587 B.C., Nebuchadnezzar II turned to the Phoenician cities and laid siege to Tyre, as the main city of the coast. This was in 588/7 B.C. One can hardly follow here the critical editions of *Against Apion*, based on the Latin version, where they read: "It was in the seventh year of his reign that Nebuchadnezzar began the siege of Tyre"[185]. This would report us to 598 B.C. Nor can we refer *regni sui* to Ethbaal III[186], not mentioned in the sentence, the subject of which is Nebuchadnezzar II. In such a hypothesis, the Latin version should at least read *regni eius*! One must obviously follow the reading of the *Codex Lauren-*

[183] References are given by J.S. TENNEY, *art. cit.* (n. 182). See also K. RADNER, *Azi-Ba'al*, in *PNA* I/1, Helsinki 1998, p. 239; LIPIŃSKI, *Itineraria Phoenicia*, p. 282.

[184] Cf. *PNA* I/1, Helsinki 1998, p. XIX.

[185] JOSEPHUS FLAVIUS, *Against Apion* I, 21, §159.

[186] H.J. KATZENSTEIN, *op. cit.* (n. 17), p. 328; cf. I. EPH'AL, *Nebuchadnezzar the Warrior: Remarks on his Military Achievements*, in *IEJ* 53 (2003), p. 178-191 (see p. 186).

tianus: ἑβδόμῳ μὲν γὰρ ἐπ' ι' τῆς Ναβουχοδονοσόρου βασιλείας, "for in the seventeenth (year) of Nebuchadnezzar's reign ...", i.e. in 588 B.C. Unfortunately, we have no cuneiform text confirming this date, because there is a large gap in Babylonian Chronicle 5, extending from 594/3 B.C. down to the third year of Neriglissar (557/6 B.C.).

A surprising notice appears in Herodotus' *History*, followed by Diodorus of Sicily. According to Herodotus, pharaoh Apries (589-568 B.C.) "marched an army to attack Sidon, and fought a naval battle with the king of Tyre"[187]. The longer notice of Diodorus of Sicily does not contain more factual data. It simply develops the topics: "He (Apries) made a campaign with strong land and sea forces against Cyprus and Phoenicia, took Sidon by storm, and so terrified the other cities of Phoenicia that he secured their submission. He also defeated the Phoenicians and Cyprians in a great sea battle, and returned to Egypt with much booty"[188].

Herodotus' report is based on a misunderstanding or a misinterpretation of an account, which very likely concerned an Egyptian attempt at relieving the siege of Tyre by Nebuchadnezzar II and helping Sidon, menaced by the Babylonians. This happened probably about 587 B.C., in the first years of Apries' reign and of the siege of Tyre.

Ez. 29, 17-20 is so far the only source stating explicitly that Nebuchadnezzar II did not capture Tyre. The reference to Egypt in v. 20 allows dating this passage from 568 B.C., when the Babylonian king was preparing himself for a confrontation with Amasis (568-526 B.C.)[189], as suggested apparently by a cuneiform text. Nothing is known about an eventual military campaign and the fragmentary tablet does not allude to any particular circumstances, but Ezekiel's text seems to be sufficiently close to the Tyrian events to provide a trustworthy information.

The siege lasted thirteen years[190]. The island city was ultimately not captured by Nebuchadnezzar II (Ez. 29, 17-20), but citizens had to be sent ashore as hostages and the presence of an exiled king of Tyre at

[187] HERODOTUS, *History* II, 161.

[188] DIODORUS OF SICILY, *Bibliotheca Historica* I, 68, 1.

[189] BM 33041, published by D.J. WISEMAN, *Chronicles of the Chaldaean Kings (626-556 B.C.) in the British Museum*, London 1956, p. 94-95, Pls. XX-XXI. Cf. *ANET*, p. 308b; E. EDEL, *Amasis und Nebukadnezar II.*, in *GM* 29 (1978), p. 13-20, in particular p. 16 and 20, n. 6; D.J. WISEMAN, *Nebuchadnezzar and Babylon*, Oxford 1985, p. 39-40; G. VITTMANN, *Ägypten und die Fremden im ersten vorchristlichen Jahrtausend*, Mainz a/R 2003, p. 41; I. EPH'AL, *art. cit.* (n. 186), p. 187-188.

[190] JOSEPHUS FLAVIUS, *Against Apion* I, 21, §156, and *Jewish Antiquities* X, 11, 1, §228.

Babylon towards the end of Nebuchadnezzar's reign shows that the city had recognized the suzerainty of its assaillant. The date of the submission was *ca.* 576/5 B.C., apparently a few months before the death of Ethbaal III.

The presence of Tyrian deportees in Mesopotamia is attested by several Babylonian tablets, which witness the existence of a settlement called *Ṣurru*, near Uruk, in the period 574-564 B.C[191]. The inhabitants of this place must have been Tyrians deported from the insular town, because the correspondence of the dates 576/5 and 574 cannot be regarded as accidental. One can surmise therefore that a certain number of Tyrian citizens have been given as hostages to Nebuchadnezzar II, then deported to Babylonia, and settled in the south of the land, near Uruk.

A further indication is provided by a register of the Court of Nebuchadnezzar, dated about 563 B.C.[192] It lists a king of Tyre as the first of a number of foreign kings exiled to Babylon[193]. He is followed by the king of Gaza, the king of Sidon, the king of Arwad, the king of Ashdod. The Tyrian king in question is very likely Baal II[194], who had remained in power during ten years[195], *ca.* 574/3-564 B.C., but had been then taken to Babylon and replaced at Tyre by "judges", who exercised their function during a few months, except for Mattan and Ger-Aštart: these seem to have shared the power for six years[196].

This institutional change, that can be dated *ca.* 563 B.C., was probably the result of a Babylonian intervention in the internal affairs of Tyre. In fact, at least five Neo-Babylonian tablets refer to troops sent then to Tyre with the king[197]. Four of them are dated between Ab the 18th of year 41 (564 B.C.) and Tishri the 15th of year 42 of Nebuchadnezzar, i.e.

[191] F. JOANNÈS, *La localisation de Ṣurru à l'époque néo-babylonienne*, in *Semitica* 32 (1982), p. 35-45; ID., *Trois textes de Ṣurru à l'époque néo-babylonienne*, in *RA* 81 (1987), p. 147-158.

[192] E. UNGER, *Babylon, die heilige Stadt*, Berlin-Leipzig 1931, p. 282-294 and Pls. 52-56; cf. *ANET*, p. 307-308. The date 570 B.C., suggested by E. Unger (*op. cit.*, p. 35), is approximate, while *ca.* 563 B.C. is based on the end of Baal II's reign at Tyre and his replacement by "judges". See here below, p. 199-200.

[193] E. UNGER, *op. cit.* (n. 192), p. 286, line 24.

[194] Not Ethbaal III, as proposed by H.J. KATZENSTEIN, *op. cit.* (n. 17), p. 326.

[195] JOSEPHUS FLAVIUS, *Against Apion* I, 21, §156.

[196] JOSEPHUS FLAVIUS, *Against Apion* I, 21, §157.

[197] R.P. DOUGHERTY, *Goucher College Cuneiform Inscriptions* I, New Haven 1923, No. 151 (date broken); ID., Vol. II, New Haven 1933, No. 135 (563 B.C.); St. ZAWADZKI, *Nebuchadnezzar and Tyre in the Light of New Texts from the Ebabbar Archives in Sippar*, in *Hayim and Miriam Tadmor Volume* (ErIs 27), Jerusalem 2003, p. 276*-281*. Cf. F. JOANNÈS, *art. cit.* (n. 191), in *Semitica* 32 (1982), p. 40; I. EPH'AL, *art. cit.* (n. 186), p. 186-187.

between 24 July 564 and 28 October 563 B.C. The date of the fifth document is damaged, but it is a receipt on the name of Ina-ṣilli-Nergal, an official active in the years 566-562 B.C.[198] There is little doubt that a military operation under the command of the king took place against Tyre in 564-563 B.C. and lasted about 15 months. This period corresponds exactly to the 15 months of the rule of the three "judges": Yakin-Baal (2 months), Kalba (10 months), and Abbar (3 months). It means that its beginning coincides with the deportation of Baal II and its end marks the beginning of the rule of Mattan and Ger-Aštart (563-558 B.C.)

During the reign of Neriglissar (560-556 B.C.), who had usurped the throne, a king Βαλάτορος has been installed by the Tyrians, probably in *ca.* 557 B.C. He reigned for one year[199]. His name most likely results from a misspelling of uncial Βαλάζορος, *Ba'al-'azōr*, "Baal helped". On his death, *ca.* 556 B.C., the Tyrians sent to Babylon for a certain Maharbaal (Μέρβαλος), who must have been a son of Baal II[200]. The situation was then changed in Babylonia, since Nabonidus had usurped the throne and become king towards the end of June 556 B.C.[201] Maharbaal was allowed to return to Tyre and, being confirmed in the sovereignty, reigned four years (*ca.* 556-553 B.C.). He was succeeded by his brother Hiram III, who remained in power twenty years (*ca.* 552-533 B.C.) and was still upon the throne when the Neo-Babylonian empire came to an end by the triumphal entry of Cyrus II to Babylon, on October the 29th, 539 B.C.[202]

We are poorly informed on the situation in Phoenicia in the 6th century B.C. and the kings of the other Phoenician city-states in the Neo-Babylonian period are so far unknown.

We can nevertheless propose the following chronological table for the rulers of Tyre in the 8th-6th centuries B.C., after Pygmalion's reign, *ca.* 820-774 B.C.

198 E. UNGER, *Nebukadnezar II. und sein Šandabakku (Oberkommissar) in Tyrus*, in *ZAW* 44 (1926), 314-317 (see p. 316). The official in question is mentioned also in a document from 576 B.C., but this was the year of the submission of Tyre.

199 JOSEPHUS FLAVIUS, *Against Apion* 1, 21, §157.

200 JOSEPHUS FLAVIUS, *Against Apion* 1, 21, §158.

201 M.A. DANDAMAYEV, *Nabonid*, in *RLA* IX, Berlin 1998-2001, p. 6-11.

202 W. HINZ, *Kyros*, in *RLA* VI, Berlin 1976-80, p. 400-403 (see p. 402a).

Chronological Table

Hiram, king of the Sidonians (?)		*ca.* 773-761
'tb'l, Tu-ba-ìl	Ethbaal II	*ca.* 760-738
Ḫi-ru-mu	Hiram II	*ca.* 737-729
Ma-te-en-ni	Mattan II	*ca.* 728-727
'Ελουλαῖος, *Lu-li-i*	Elulaios	*ca.* 732-697
----------------	------------	-------------
Ba-'-lu	Baal I	*ca.* 680-650
Ia-ḫi-mil-ki	Yahi-milk	*ca.* 650-630
----------------	------------	-------------
'Ιθωβάλος	Ethbaal III	*ca.* 600-575
Βαάλ	Baal II	*ca.* 574-564
'Εκνίβαλος	Yakin-Baal	*ca.* 564
Χέλβης	Kalba	*ca.* 564-563
Ἄββαρος	Abbar	*ca.* 563
Μύττυνος and Γεράστρατος	Mattan and Ger-Aštart	*ca.* 563-558
Βαλάτορος	Baalazor	*ca.* 557
Μέρβαλος	Maharbaal	*ca.* 556-553
Εἴρωμος	Hiram III	*ca.* 552-533

CHAPTER V

ARAMAEANS

The Aramaeans settled only in the northern regions of Canaan, but their impact on the history of the Levant was immense. Besides, it is not possible to isolate their presence in the area of Damascus, in the Beqa' Valley, and in Transjordan from their expansion in northern Syria and Upper Mesopotamia[1].

13th-10th centuries B.C.

The first explicit mentions of the Aramaeans occur in the inscriptions of Tiglath-pileser I (1114-1076 B.C.), who fought against them in the Euphrates valley from Suḫu to Carchemish and twenty-eight times crossed the river in their pursuit near Mount Bishri, west of Dēr az-Zōr, routing them from Tadmor (Palmyra) to Rapiqu on the Babylonian frontier[2]. Already Tukulti-Ninurta I (1240-1205 B.C.) regarded the Ǧebel al-Bišri as *šá-da-an Aḫ-la-mi-i*, "the mountains of the Aḫlamū"[3], who at that time were most likely Aramaeans. The name "Aḫlamū" never had a strictly ethnic significance in Akkadian, but rather denoted socio-cultural characteristics of tribesmen living and travelling over the Syrian steppe. Their name derives from a native "broken" plural *'aġlām* of *ġlm*[4], related to Arabic *ġalim*, "excited by lust", and *ġulām*, "boy, lad". In other words, they were "greedy lads".

Particular Aramaean tribes are mentioned in cuneiform sources already in the 13th century B.C., like Bēth-Zammāni in the area to the north of the Ṭūr 'Abdīn[5], the Hirana and Hasmu tribes in Upper Me-

[1] Since the present writer has recently published a synthesis on the Aramaeans (LIPIŃSKI, *Aramaeans*), this chapter may be reduced to a few general points and to some new elements resulting from fresh insights and publications.

[2] *RIMA* II, text A.0.87.1, p. 23, lines 43-63; text A.0.87.2, p. 34, lines 28-29; text A.0.87.3, p. 37-38, lines 29-35; text A.0.87.4, p. 43, lines 34-36; text A.0.87.12, p. 59-60, lines 4'-8'.

[3] *RIMA* I, text A.0.78.23, p. 273, line 70.

[4] LIPIŃSKI, *Semitic*, §31.26; cf. *AHw*, p. 21a.

[5] J.J. FINKELSTEIN, *Cuneiform Texts from Tell Billa*, in *JCS* 7 (1953) p. 111-176, especially p. 116-117, 119, 124 (No. 6), and 127 (No. 17). Cf. K. NASHEF, *Die Orts- und Gewässernamen der mittelbabylonischen und mittelassyrischen Zeit* (RGTC 5), Wiesbaden 1982, p. 74 with literature.

sopotamia[6], the Ruqahaeans, later in the mid-12th century[7], south of Ashur. Bēth-Zammāni deserves a special attention, because the present-day Diyarbakır has become its capital city, known under the name Amida[8]. The earlier name of this strategically important town seems to have been Eluḫat / Elaḫut / Eluḫut, although other identifications have been proposed. The most recent one is based on a lately published inscription of Shamshi-Adad I (1710-1679 B.C.)[9], who boasts of having taken and plundered Eluḫut, and thereafter, as it seems, received the homage of the king of Zalmaqum[10]. H. Waetzoldt thus proposes regarding Eluḫut as a city of Zalmaqum and to locate it in the area between Upper Euphrates and the western headstreams of the Ḫābūr, north of Harran[11]. However, before mentioning the capture of Eluḫut, Shamshi-Adad I's inscription refers to an earlier event of the campaign in the very damaged col. II, where one might restore URU *Ki*-[*na-bu*] (line 3). This is probably Aktepe or Tauşantepe, a city situated south-east of Diyarbakır[12], on the road from Shamshi-Adad I's capital Shubat-Enlil (Tell Leilan). Some 60 km of a slightly hilly road lead from Diyarbakır to Zalmaqum, a distance which represents a two or three days' march. About twelve lines are missing between col. III, 1-5 referring to Eluḫut and col. IV, 4 mentioning the king of Zalmaqum. There is thus ample space to record the further advance of the Assyrian army. In other words, the inscription does not endanger the identification of Diyarbakır

[6] O.R. GURNEY, *Texts from Dur-Kurigalzu*, in *Iraq* 11 (1949), p. 131-149 (see text No. 10, p. 139-140 and 148). Cf. J.-R. KUPPER, *Les nomades en Mésopotamie au temps des rois de Mari*, Paris 1957, p. 114-115; K. NASHEF, *op. cit.* (n. 5), p. 121-122 and 128; *RIMA* II, text A.0.101.1, p. 219, lines 97-98.

[7] BM 122635+122642, line 22', published by A.R. MILLARD, *Fragments of Historical Texts from Nineveh: Middle Assyrian and Later Kings*, in *Iraq* 32 (1970), p. 167-176 and Pls. XXXIII-XXXVII (see p. 172-173 and Pl. XXXIII). Cf. J.N. POSTGATE, *Taxation and Conscription in the Assyrian Empire* (Studia Pohl: Series maior 3), Rome 1974, p. 161-162; R. ZADOK, *Elements of Aramean Pre-History*, in M. COGAN - I. EPH'AL (eds.), *Ah, Assyria... Studies in Assyrian History and Ancient Near Eastern Historiography Presented to Hayim Tadmor* (Scripta Hierosolymitana 33), Jerusalem 1991, p. 104-117 (see p. 117).

[8] E. LIPIŃSKI, *Diyarbakır - An Aramaean Capital of the 9th Century B.C. and Its Territory*, in P. TARACHA (ed.), *Silva Anatolica. Anatolian Studies Presented to M. Popko*, Warsaw 2002, p. 225-239.

[9] This chronology is based on H. GASCHE - J.A. ARMSTRONG - S.W. COLE - V.G. GURZADYAN, *Dating the Fall of Babylon. A Reappraisal of Second-Milllennium Chronology*, Ghent-Chicago 1998, with the correction in *Akkadica* 108 (1998), p. 1-2.

[10] VA 15699, published by H. WAETZOLDT, *Die Eroberung Eluḫuts durch Šamši-Adad I. und der Krieg gegen Zalmaqu*, in J. MARZAHN - H. NEUMANN (eds.), *Assyriologica et Semitica. Festschrift für Joachim Oelsner* (AOAT 252), Münster 2000, p. 523-537.

[11] H. WAETZOLDT, *art. cit.* (n. 10), p. 532.

[12] LIPIŃSKI, *Aramaeans*, p. 148-149; ID., *art. cit.* (n. 8), p. 237-238.

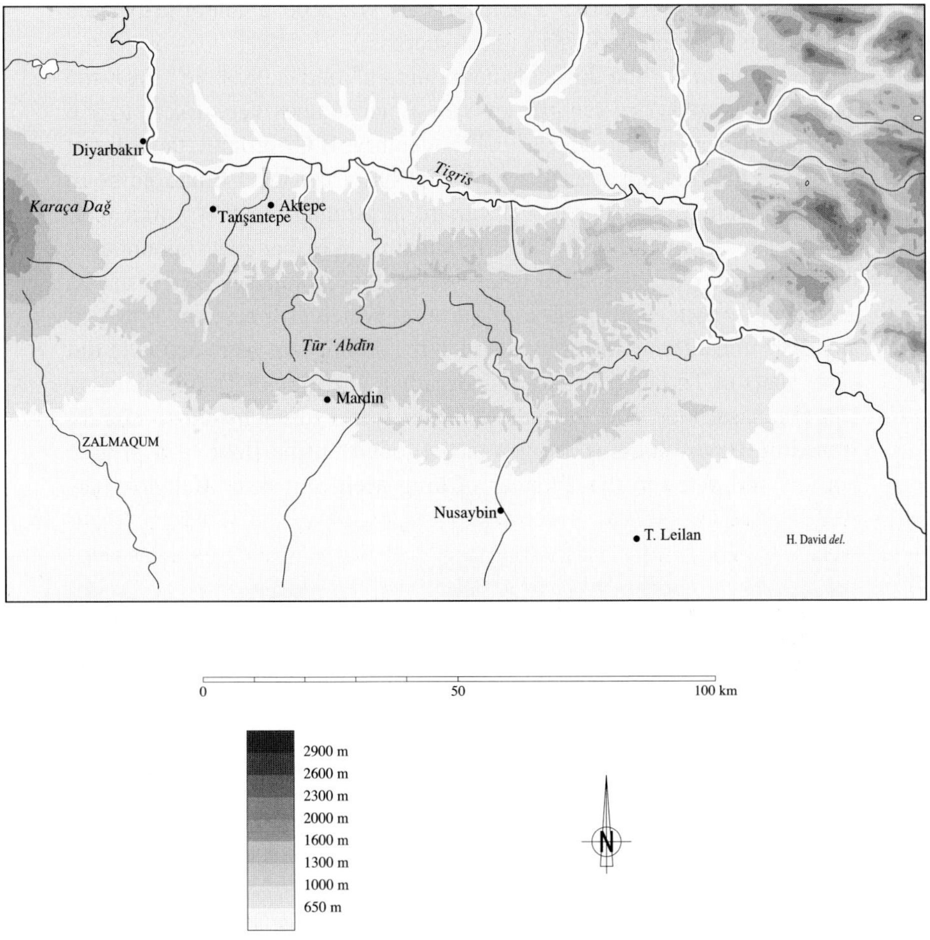

Diyarbakır and Ṭūr ʿAbdīn.

with Eluḫut. It rather confirms it, if the restitution URU *Ki-[na-bu]* is correct. In this interpretation of the campaign Shamshi-Adad apparently led his troops first north-westwards through the Ṭūr ʿAbdīn and he completed the circuit by using the large pass between the Karaça Dağ and the western slopes of the Ṭūr ʿAbdīn, and thus emerged unexpectedly at the north-eastern border of Zalmaqum. If we believe Shamshi-Adad's words, this grand sweep was a great success.

The mention of "the hosts of the mountain", the ERIM.MEŠ (kur)*Ḫar-ri*[13] and the ERIM.MEŠ *Ṭár-wi*[14], in texts of Emar alludes very likely to the Aramaeans settled in the early 12th century B.C. around the Mount Bishri[15]. *Ḫar-ri* is apparently a transcription of the local Emariote noun *harru*[16], while *ṭár-wu* must be a variant of Aramaic *ṭawr* < *ṭawru* with metathesis, both words meaning "mountain". Whether *ġūr,* "mountain", hides behind *Qūr*, the area from which the Aramaeans were native according to Am. 9,7[17], this is a question which still remains open. In any case, considering the area in which the Aramaeans were active in the early years of Tiglath-pileser I and already at the time of Tukulti-Ninurta I, we can surmise that the fall of Emar was caused by these rapidly spreading tribes. Judging from a tablet found on the floor of a private house[18] and dated to the 2nd year of king Meli-Shipak of Babylon (*ca.*

[13] D. ARNAUD, *Recherches au pays d'Aštata. Emar* VI. *Textes sumériens et akkadiens*, Paris 1985-87, No. 42 (Msk 73273), line 9; A. TSUKIMOTO, *Akkadian Tablets in the Hirayama Collection* (I), in *Acta Sumerologica* 12 (1990), p. 177-227 (see p. 190, No. 7, line 29); G. BECKMAN, *Texts from the Vicinity of Emar in the Collection of Jonathan Rosen*, Padova 1996, No. 77, line 34-35. The verb *i-la-mi-in* of the first text (line 10) was creating a problem that authors tried to resolve in different ways. The writer is finally inclined to accept the solution of S. SEMINARO, *L'accadico di Emar*, Roma 1998, p. 354. Seminaro regards the spelling with *i-* as equivalent to *u-* (cf. p. 354-355) and considers *ilammin* a D-stem.

[14] D. ARNAUD, *Textes syriens de l'âge du Bronze Récent* (Aula Orientalis. Suppl. 1), Sabadell-Barcelona 1991, Nos. 25, lines 2-3; 44, lines 2-3.

[15] E. LIPIŃSKI, *The Hosts of the Mountain*, forthcoming.

[16] Cf. *EA* 74, 20, where we find the Byblian gloss *ḫa-ar-ri*, "mountain".

[17] For the reading *Qwr* instead of *Qyr*, see LIPIŃSKI, *Itineraria Phoenicia*, p. 52, n. 66. Contrary to the writer's former opinion (*Aramaeans*, p. 40-45), the reading of the *textus receptus* is not confirmed by the mention of KUR *Ki-ri* in the Emar text Msk 73112 (D. ARNAUD, *op. cit.* [n. 13], No. 42, line 9), for the supposed KI differs from the unquestionable KI signs of the same tablet. It is not squarely identifiable with any cuneiform sign used at Emar, but is akin to an imperfectly formed ḪAR (M.R. ADAMTHWAITE, *Late Hittite Emar. The Chronology, Synchronisms, and Socio-Political Aspects of a Late Bronze Age Fortress Town* [Ancient Near-Eastern Studies. Suppl. 8], Louvain 2001, p. 263). The latter reading is supported by the parallel mention of ERIM.MEŠ *Ḫar-ri* on two other Emar tablets, referring to the same events (see here above, n. 13).

[18] D. ARNAUD, *op. cit.* (n. 13), No. 26, 9-12.

The great bend of the Euphrates.

1181-1167)[19], the fall of the city had taken place some time after 1180/79 B.C.

In the same region of the great bend of the Euphrates, a king of *Arumu* conquered Pitru and Mutkinu at the time of Ashur-rabi II of Assyria (1012-972 B.C.)[20], and the Aramaean state of Bēth-Adini certainly existed in the Middle Euphrates area by the 10th century B.C., since Adad-nirari II received a gift from its ruler in 899 B.C., after his conquest of Huzirina[21]. Further to the east, an Aramaean state was founded in the 10th century B.C. at Guzana, biblical Gozan (Tell Ḥalaf)[22], and it included the nearby city of Sikkan (Tell Fekheriye). Called Bēth-Baḫiani in Assyrian sources, it had on the east a common border with the Aramaean-held area of Nisibis, modern Nusaybin, in the foothills of Ṭūr 'Abdīn, until these territories were annexed to Assyria in 896 B.C., after a series of campaigns conducted by Adad-nirari II[23].

For northern Canaan, we dispose of the confused and late information preserved in the Bible. Ṣoba and Bēth-Reḥob most likely were one and the same Aramaean entity in the Beqa' Valley[24], while Geshur or Bēth-Maaka, ruled in the 10th century B.C. by Talmay, must have been a small Syro-Hurrian kingdom, east of the Sea of Galilee[25].

The origins of the Aramaean settlement in the Beqa' Valley are largely unknown. The most important site of the region, extensively excavated, is Kāmid el-Lōz, ancient Kumidi[26]. This city was destroyed

[19] The reign of Melishipak is dated to 1186-1172 B.C. by J.A. Brinkman, *Meli-Šipak*, *RLA* VIII, Berlin 1993-97, p. 52, but J. Boese, *Burnaburiaš II, Melišipak und die mittelbabylonische Chronologie*, in *UF* 14 (1982), p. 15-26, proposed 1181-1167 B.C., the second year being then 1180/79. These dates are followed now by H. Gasche - J.A. Armstrong - S.W. Cole - V.G. Gurzadyan, *op. cit.* (n. 9).

[20] *RIMA* III, text A.0.102.2, p. 19, lines 35-38.

[21] *RIMA* II, text A.0.99.2, p. 150, line 48.

[22] Its earliest mention in Neo-Assyrian sources dates from 894 B.C.: *RIMA* II, text A.0.99.2., p. 153, lines 100-104.

[23] *RIMA* II, text A.0.99.2, p. 149-152, lines 39-81.

[24] E. Lipiński, *Aram et Israël du Xe au VIIIe siècle av.n.è.*, in *Acta Antiqua Academiae Scientiarum Hungaricae* 27, (1979 [1981]), p. 49-102, especially p. 60-61; Id., *Aramaeans*, p. 333-334.

[25] E. Lipiński, *art. cit.* (n. 24), p. 61-63, 67, and here below, p. 238-244.

[26] Concise reports on the excavations have been provided by R. Hachmann, *Kumidi*, in *RLA* VI, Berlin-New York 1980-83, p. 330-334; Id., *Frühe Phönikern im Libanon*, Mainz a/R 1983, p. 25-37; Id., *Kamid el-Loz*, in *DCPP*, Turnhout 1992, p. 242-243. More detailed presentations of the results of the excavations can be found in the articles of Id., *Kamid el-Loz 1963-1981*, in *Berytus* 37, (1989 [1991]), p. 5-187, and H. Weippert, *Kumidi. Die Ergebnisse der Ausgrabungen auf dem Tell Kāmid el-Lōz in den Jahren 1963 bis 1981*, in *ZDPV* 114, 1998, p. 1-38. For the chronology of the site, see especially R. Hachmann, *Kāmid el-Lōz 16. 'Schatzhaus'-Studien* (Saarbrücker Beiträge zur Altertumskunde 59), Bonn 1996, p. 17-26. Iron Age settlement in the Beqa' Valley is

and burnt towards the end of the 12th century B.C. and only successive villages were built on the tell in the Iron Age, after an undetermined gap in the occupation of the site. No cultural linkage could be established between these villages and the Late Bronze city. Since the ancient name was preserved, the area had to be peopled continuously, but only remains of the period *ca.* 1100-900 B.C. have been uncovered during the excavations of the years 1963-1981. They reveal the presence of small communities living in scattered wooden houses of one or two rooms, with a relatively poor furniture. We can assume that these small settlements are Aramaean and link them with the foundation of Bēth-Reḥob, but no univocal evidence confirms this hypothesis so far. Evidence for an Aramaean cultural environment has been discovered further to the north, at Tell al-Ġasīl, 11 km north-east of Rayyaq. This is a relatively small mound where D.C. Baramki has distinguished three phases: 1100-850 (Phase I), 850-750 (Phase II), and 750-650 B.C. (Phase III)[27], but the evidence seems inadequate to provide such a precise subdivision of Iron Age II. The discovery of fifty-nine incense burners from the 9th-8th century B.C. witnesses the presence of sanctuaries in the section excavated.

The beginnings of Aramaean rule in Damascus are obscure and clouded by the repeated confusion of Aram (*'rm*) with Edom (*'dm*) in biblical manuscripts, due to the similarity of the letters *d* and *r* in Hebrew script. Nicolaus of Damascus, a Hellenistic historiographer of the 1st century B.C., writes about the wars waged by Adados, king of Damascus - obviously Hadad - against David[28]: "One of the natives, Adados by name, attained to great power and became ruler of Damascus and the rest of Syria, excepting Phoenicia. He waged war against David, king of Judaea, and, after trial in many battles, the last of which was fought beside the Euphrates, where he was defeated, he gained the reputation of being the most vigorous and courageous of kings". At first sight one would relate this account to I Kings 11, 14-22.25, dealing with

described and analyzed by L. MARFOE, *Kāmid el-Lōz* 14. *Settlement History of the Beqa' up to the Iron Age* (Saarbrücker Beiträge zur Altertumskunde 53), Bonn 1998, p. 217-236.

27 D.C. BARAMKI, *Preliminary Report on the Excavations at Tell el Ghassil*, in *BMB* 16 (1961), p. 87-97; 17 (1964), p. 47-103; 19 (1966), p. 29-49; E. GUBEL, in *Les Phéniciens et le monde méditerranéen*, Bruxelles 1986, Nos. 163-164.

28 JOSEPHUS FLAVIUS, *Jewish Antiquities* VII, 5, 2, §101. Translation by R. MARCUS, *Josephus* V, London 1934, p. 413. For Nicolaus of Damascus and his lost historical work, see B.Z. WACHOLDER, *Nicolaus of Damascus* (University of California Publications in History 75), Berkeley-Los Angeles 1962.

a prince Hadad of Aram rather than Edom[29], but the mention of the battle near the Euphrates seems to be based on a Greek version of II Sam. 8, 3, which refers to Hadadezer, described there as king of Bēth-Reḥob or Ṣoba. According to I Kings 11, 23-24, the latter's servant Rezon would have seized Damascus and become its king. However, his name simply means "prince" in Hebrew and the Greek text instead mentions Ezron[30]. The situation can be clarified only by new evidence.

However, the Deuteronomistic Historian seems to have used an early source in II Sam. 10, 15-19. His language betrays the Persian period, when *'Ēber hannāhār* designated Syria west of the Euphrates, and he connects the story with David, although the original account referred to Israel. II Sam. 10, 15 and 19b, as well as the relative sentence "which are from *'Ēber hannāhār*" and the name of David, a substitute for "the king", can be regarded as editorial, but the core of the account is probably borrowed from the annals of king Omri (I Kings 16, 27) and concerns Damascus. Even if the mention of Hadadezer in the summary of II Sam. 8 is inspired by the report of Sam. 10, 16-19a, there was very likely an original record referring to "Ben-Reḥob, king of Ṣoba", since a "Son of Ruḫubi, from the Amana (Anti-Lebanon)", is mentioned among the adversaries of Shalmaneser III in 853 B.C.

The areas settled by the Aramaeans in northern and southern Syria were separated by a large territory occupied in the early first millennium B.C. by the Neo-Hittite kingdom of Hamath. Various city-states existed in this region during the Late Bronze Age, but no direct link can be established between them and Hamath. On the contrary, there seems to be a break in the occupation of the site in Late Bronze Age II. A resettlement took place in Iron Age I, when newcomers introduced the rite of cremation burial, attested in Hamath on a large scale[31]. The importance of this practice among the "Sea Peoples" is still obscure, while cremation was a well-known Anatolian custom, best illustrated by the Hittite royal cremation, but attested also in the case of people of lower rank, especially in the Late Bronze Age[32]. This must be interpreted to mean

[29] A. LEMAIRE, *Hadad l'Édomite ou Hadad l'Araméen*, in *BN* 43 (1988), p. 14-18.

[30] LIPIŃSKI, *Aramaeans*, p. 367-371.

[31] P.J. RIIS, *Hama* III/2. *Les cimetières à crémation*, Copenhague 1948. Further research is required to appreciate the validity of J.N. TUBB's hypothesis (*An Aegean Presence in Egypto-Canaan*, in W.V. DAVIES - L. SCHOFIELD [eds.], *Egypt, the Aegean and the Levant: Interconnections in the Second Millennium BC*, London 1995), that possible Hittite refugees practised the "double-jar" burial at Tell as-Sa'īdīyeh, where this Hittite custom of Late Bronze Age Anatolia is represented by twenty-seven excavated examples.

[32] A. GOETZE, *Kleinasien*, 2nd ed., München 1957, p. 170-171; M. POPKO, *Religions of Asia Minor*, Warsaw 1995, p. 154-157.

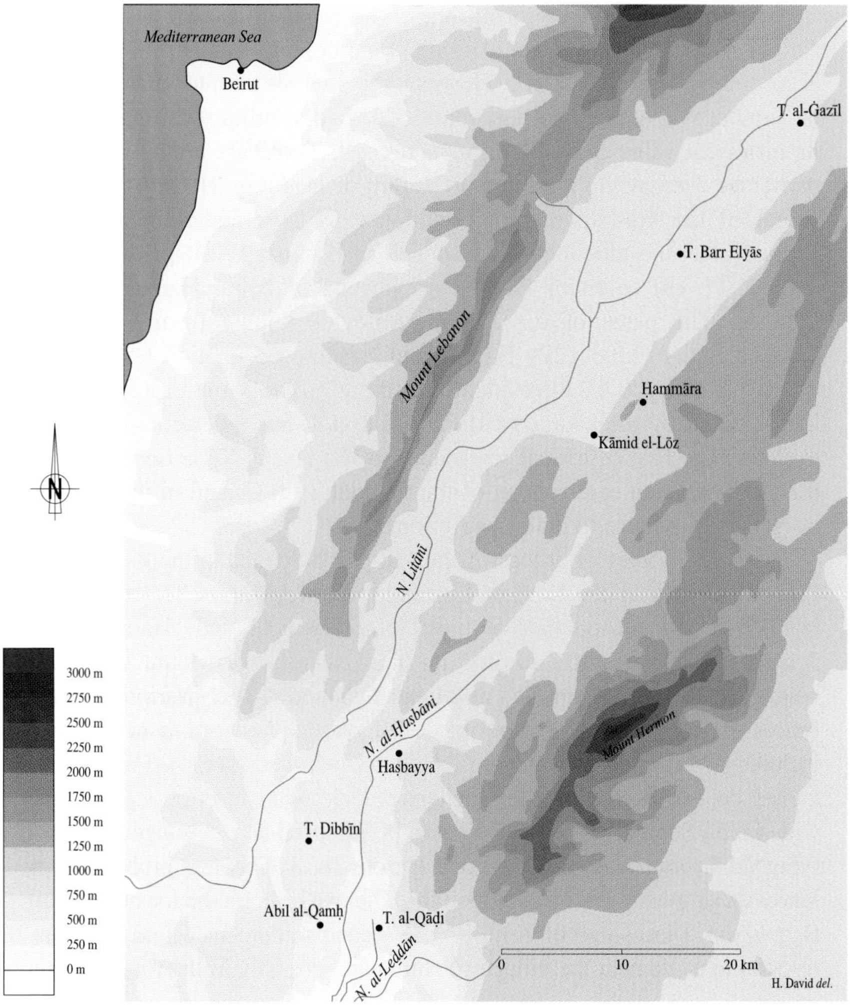

Beqaʿ Valley.

that in the second half of the 12th century Hamath saw Anatolian immigrants coming from the north and settling at the site. The reasons of this migration can only be guessed, but the raids of the Kaška people from the north and the fall of the Hittite empire with the struggles that preceded the catastrophe have certainly to be taken into account[33]. Wherever excavations have been made, they indicate that the Hittite heartland was ravaged, its cities burnt down.

[33] H. KLENGEL, *Geschichte des hethitischen Reiches*, Leiden 1999, p. 313 and 319.

A commonly held view is that the earliest named Hamathites are king To'i (*T'y*) and his son Joram (*Ywrm*), contemporaries and allies of David according to II Sam. 8, 9-10. However, this whole chapter of the Books of Samuel is a redactional summary of David's military campaigns and its historical value depends on its sources[34]. These are unknown in this particular case, while the name of Joram or Hadoram (I Chron. 18, 10) is not of the kind to inspire confidence in their authenticity, unless Hamath was the city identified as Tell al-Ḥamma West, in the Jordan Valley, 15 km south of Bēth-shan, instead of being Hamath on the Orontes. The place of the Jordan Valley is known from a stele of pharaoh Seti I (1293-1279 B.C.)[35] and Israelite occupation levels from the 10th century B.C. were identified there[36]. The same city was most likely meant by the source of II Chron. 8, 3-4, but was wrongly related to Ṣoba. The first historical references to Hamath in Syria occur then in the Neo-Assyrian inscriptions of the 9th century B.C. and in the Luwian or Neo-Hittite hieroglyphic inscriptions.

The Beqa' Valley or at least its largest part belonged to the kingdom of Hamath already at the time of Uratami, son of Urḫilina. He ruled over Hamath in the second half of the 9th century B.C. and "Hama stone" 7 records that he built a fortress in "the river-land of Mount Labrana", which can be safely identified as Mount Lebanon[37]. The inscription refers further to the people of "the land Tuhayata", *Tú-ha-ia-ta-sa* (REGIO), including "the land of Hamayara", *Ha-ma-ia+ra/i-sa* (REGIO). These place names do not occur in other hieroglyphic Luwian inscriptions, but the widespread Semitic spirantization of *b*, pronounced as *w*[38], suggests identifying *Tú-ha-ia-ta* with the *Ṭbḥt* of I Chron. 18, 8. This text probably preserves an original form of the toponym. The place should be located at Tell Barr Elyās, 7 km south of Zaḥlē[39]. The second settlement would then correspond to a site near the village of Ḥammāra, possibly Tell 'Ain al-Fawqā

[34] M. NOTH, *Überlieferungsgeschichtliche Studien*, 2nd ed., Tübingen 1957, p. 65.

[35] Text in A.K. KITCHEN, *Ramesside Inscriptions* I, Oxford 1968-75, p. 10-12. Translation by J.A. WILSON, in *ANET*, p. 253-254; cf. *ANEP*, No. 320. An additional account of this campaign is preserved on the walls of the Great Temple of Amon at Karnak. For a recent discussion, see M.G. HASEL, *Domination and Resistance: Egyptian Military Activity in the Southern Levant, ca. 1300-1185 B.C.* (Probleme der Ägyptologie 11), Leiden 1998, p. 138.

[36] Grid ref. 1973/1977: J. CAHILL - D. TARLER, *Hammah, Tell el-*, in *NEAEHL*, Jerusalem 1993, Vol. II, p. 561-562.

[37] J.D. HAWKINS, *Corpus of Hieroglyphic Luwian Inscriptions* I, Berlin 2000, p. 413-414, "Hama 7".

[38] LIPIŃSKI, *Semitic*, §11.6 and 9.

[39] E. LIPIŃSKI, *art. cit.* (n. 24), p. 66, n. 55; ID., *Aramaeans*, p. 323.

or Tell Ṣatīya al-Yamīn, both in the Wādī at-Taim, about 1 km from the village[40]. These mounds lay about 10 km south of Tell Barr Elyās.

The phonetic similitude of the names Tuhayata and *T'y*, even of Hamayara and *Ywrm*, in II Sam. 8, 9-10, may suggest the idea that both biblical anthroponyms, not attested at Hamath on the Orontes, are corruptions of place names found in the annals of a king of Israel and misinterpreted by the Deuteronomistic Historian or one of his followers redacting the sketch of II Sam. 8, 3-10, paralleled in I Chron. 18, 3-10. However, the more likely explanation is the one proposed above, viz. that the original source was referring to the city Hamath in the Jordan Valley[41].

9th-7th centuries B.C.

The Aramaean history from the 9th through the 7th centuries B.C. stands in the shadow of Assyria's expansion. Moreover, it is dominated by the Assyrian perspective, given that the chronology and the most useful information is provided by the royal annals and state archives of Assyria. The resulting picture is understandably partial and it can be corrected only by the maximal use of other sources, such as the Aramaic and Neo-Hittite inscriptions and the archaeological evidence. Yet, it must be said that the preserved inscriptions rarely refer in any detail to political developments and that archaeological evidence can only exceptionally be linked in an univocal way with historical events.

The Aramaean history of this period begins with the campaigns of Adad-nirari II (911-891 B.C.) against the Temanites of the Nisibis area, followed by a thrust to Guzana (Tell Ḥalaf) on the Upper Ḫābūr and by a march downstream through the land of Laqē, a federation of Aramaean and North Arabian tribes along the Lower Ḫābūr and the Middle Euphrates[42]. This kind of expeditions, aimed at collecting tribute and displaying Assyria's might, was imitated by Tukulti-Ninurta II (890-884 B.C.) and Ashurnasirpal II (883-859 B.C.). Tukulti-Ninurta II subjugated the Aramaean tribal state of Bēth-Zammāni on the Tigris, the capital of which was Amida, the present-day Diyarbakır, and he bound its

[40] L. MARFOE, *Kāmid el-Lōz* 13. *The Prehistoric and Early Historic Context of the Site* (Saarbrücker Beiträge zur Altertumskunde 41), Bonn 1995, p. 201, No. 066, and p. 219, No. 143.

[41] LIPIŃSKI, *Aramaeans*, p. 339-340.

[42] P.-E. DION, *Les Araméens à l'âge du fer: histoire politique et structures sociales* (Études bibliques, n.s. 34), Paris 1997, p. 56-63; LIPIŃSKI, *Aramaeans*, p. 77-117.

ruler Ammi-baal to him by an oath[43]. He also marched through the land of Laqē, collecting tribute which included gold, silver, tin, bronze vessels, also myrrh and purple wool, items that clearly indicate that international commercial transactions were flourishing in this area at the confluence of the Ḫābūr and of the Euphrates[44]. Ashurnasirpal II followed the example of his father, but clashed in the land of Laqē with the large Aramaean state of Bēth-Adini, which was established on both sides of the Middle Euphrates and was influential also in the area of Laqē[45]. This region seems to have been firmly incorporated into the Assyrian provincial system only in the early 8th century B.C. An important Neo-Assyrian town on the Ḫābūr was located at Tell aš-Šayḫ Ḥamad, ancient Dūr-Katlimmu. The publication of the Neo-Assyrian texts from this site does not confirm the identification of Dūr-Katlimmu with Magdālu: both place names occur in documents from the same period, what rather favours their distinction[46].

In the first half of the 9th century B.C., also the Neo-Hittite city-state of Masuwari (Tell Ahmar), called Til Barsip in Assyrian records and Tarbushīb in Aramaic, was dominated by Bēth-Adini. Its strong man was Hamiyatas (*ca.* 900-875 B.C.), apparently an Aramaean called 'Ammī-yaṯa', "My Ancestor has saved". He assumed the title of "ruler, king of Masuwari, servant of Tarhunza"[47], and was followed by Aḫūni (*ca.* 875-856 B.C.), probably his son, who also bore a Semitic name, viz. *'Aḫūnī*, "My little brother". He acted not only as a "Mayor of the Palace" of the Neo-Hittite dynasts, possibly still tolerated but silenced for half a century, but ruled as a full-fledged monarch[48].

[43] P.-E. DION, *op. cit.* (n. 42), p. 34-35; LIPIŃSKI, *Aramaeans*, p. 135-161. See also here above, p. 204-206.

[44] P.-E. DION, *op. cit.* (n. 42), p. 56-63; LIPIŃSKI, *Aramaeans*, p. 102-103, 517, 535-539.

[45] H.S. SADER, *Les États araméens de Syrie depuis leur fondation jusqu'à leur transformation en provinces assyriennes* (BTS 36), Beirut 1987, p. 47-98; P.-E. DION, *op. cit.* (n. 42), p. 86-98; LIPIŃSKI, *Aramaeans*, p. 163-193.

[46] *Magdālu* occurs in K. RADNER, *Die neuassyrischen Texte aus Tall Šēḫ Ḥamad* (Berichte der Ausgrabung Tall Šēḫ Ḥamad / Dūr-Katlimmu 6. Texte 2), Berlin 2002, No. 10, 3, which should be dated *ca.* 637-636 B.C. (*ibid.*, p. 35), while *Dūr-Katlimmu* is used in two documents dated after *ca.* 644 B.C.: *ibid.*, Nos. 69, 3 and 70, 5, p. 110-112. Later *Magdālu* occurs again in texts dated in 602 and 600 B.C.: *ibid.*, Nos. 39, 5 and 40, 7, p. 66-69.

[47] The title is completely preserved in the inscription Tell Ahmar 6, scheduled to be published by J.D. HAWKINS, who kindly provided the writer with his transliteration and translation of the new inscription.

[48] G. BUNNENS, *Hittites and Aramaeans at Til Barsip: A Reappraisal*, in K. VAN LERBERGHE - A. SCHOORS (eds.), *Immigration and Emigration within the Ancient Near East. Festschrift E. Lipiński* (OLA 65), Leuven 1995, p. 19-27; LIPIŃSKI, *Aramaeans*, p. 163-193.

Statue of a king of Śam'al from Zincirli, 9th century B.C.
(İstanbul Arkeoloji Müzeleri, Inv. No. 7723).

The interferences of Bēth-Adini in the land of Laqē prompted, around 870 B.C., Ashurnasirpal II's punitive campaign against Kaprabu, a stronghold of Bēth-Adini east of the Euphrates. As a result of the fall of this fortified city, Aḫūni submitted and paid tribute[49]. On his way to the west — or at least in the same period — Ashurnasirpal incorporated the

[49] H.S. Sader, *op. cit.* (n. 45), p. 94-95; P.-E. Dion, *op. cit.* (n. 42), p. 88-89; Lipiński, *Aramaeans*, p. 188-189.

Aramaean kingdom of Guzana into the Assyrian empire[50], but the appointed governor kept the royal title in his relations with the local population[51]. Following up his thrust westwards, Ashurnasirpal received tribute also from Neo-Hittite states, as well as from Gusi of Yaḫan, the eponymous ruler of Bēth-Agusi, an Aramaean state which is better known by the name of its later capital Arpad[52].

The menace threatening the Aramaean states of Syria since Ashurnasirpal II's western campaigns materialized during the reign of his son Shalmaneser III (858-825 B.C.), whose first aim was to eliminate the Aramaean tribal state of Bēth-Adini and to seize the crossing points of the great bend of the Euphrates, controlled by the Aramaeans. In four violent campaigns (858-855 B.C.), Shalmaneser III managed to conquer the territory of Bēth-Adini, to seize the control of the crossing of the Euphrates, and to dislodge Aḫūni from Til Barsip. The town was soon renamed Kar-Shalmaneser and turned into an Assyrian "royal city".

The second aim of Shalmaneser III's western policy was to extend his power to central and southern Syria[53], where two important states existed at that time: the Neo-Hittite kingdom of Hamath and the Aramaean kingdom of Damascus. Both are referred to in biblical accounts, but these can hardly be used in historical reconstructions because of their inaccurate chronological framework and the many confusions they contain.

In 853, Shalmaneser III attacked the Neo-Hittite kingdom of Hamath, but an alliance led by Hadadidri, king of Damascus, Urḫilina, king of Hamath, and Ahab, king of Israel, successfully opposed the Assyrians at Qarqar on the Orontes[54]. Shalmaneser suffered a major defeat there, since he did not attempt affronting the same coalition before 849 B.C. The campaign of 849 was followed by further expeditions in 848 and 845, which appear to have been all unsuccessful. Around 843, however, the anti-Assyrian alliance broke up. The death of Hadadidri, its main

[50] H.S. SADER, *op. cit.* (n. 45), p. 5-45; P.-E. DION, *op. cit.* (n. 42), p. 38-44; LIPIŃSKI, *Aramaeans*, p. 119-133.

[51] *SAIO* II, p. 21-24.

[52] H.S. SADER, *op. cit.* (n. 45), p. 99-152; P.-E. DION, *op. cit.* (n. 42), p. 86-98; LIPIŃSKI, *Aramaeans*, p. 195-219.

[53] J. KAH-JIN KUAN, *Neo-Assyrian Historical Inscriptions and Syria-Palestine*, Hong Kong 1995, p. 5-68.

[54] W.T. PITARD, *Ancient Damascus*, Winona Lake 1987, p. 125-132; F. BRIQUEL-CHATONNET, *Les relations entre les cités de la côte phénicienne et les royaumes d'Israël et de Juda* (Studia Phoenicia XII; OLA 46), Leuven 1992, p. 79-89; P.-E. DION, *op. cit.* (n. 42), p. 184-189; S. HAFÞÓRSSON, *A Passing Power: An Examination of the Sources for the History of Aram-Damascus in the Second Half of the Ninth Century B.C.* (Coniectanea Biblica. Old Testament Series 54), Stockholm 2006, p. 82-92, 253-255.

protagonist, and the usurpation of the throne of Damascus by Hazael[55] precipitated the events. Hamath no more appears as an ally of Damascus and the 842 edition of Shalmaneser III's annals avoids mentioning Israel among Assyria's enemies[56]. In the same year, as it seems, Hazael waged a war against Israel, which was assisted by its Judaean vassal state. Hazael won a great victory at Ramoth-Gilead, killing Jehoram, king of Israel, and Ahaziahu, his son, king of Judah[57]. As a consequence of these events, the throne of Israel was seized by Jehu, an officer of Jehoram, while Hazael began the reconquest of northern Galilee and of Gilead. He could not press his advantage further during the next following years, because Damascus had to face three Assyrian invasions in 841, 838 and 837, which were no more hindered by Hamathite resistance. Damascus, though isolated, could withstand the attacks of Shalmaneser, who in 841 ravaged the country, received the homage of Jehu, the new king of Israel, and reached the Mediterranean coast, where also Phoenician kings paid him tribute[58]. The campaigns of 838 and 837 were not fought by Shalmaneser III in person, who seems to have abandoned the struggle against Damascus at this point[59] and, in the later part of his reign, was not even in a position to intervene in North-Syrian affairs.

Probably around 830 B.C., Assyria lost control of Guzana, occupied by Kapara, apparently the ruler of the Aramaean state of the Baliḫ[60], while Hazael managed to establish Damascus as the main regional power in Syria and Palestine. Only sketchy informations are available about his military campaigns in the south, where he repeatedly invaded Israel and marched at least once to Philistia and to Judah, capturing Gath, one of the Philistine royal cities, and receiving a large tribute from king Joash of Judah[61]. Hazael's campaigns in northern Syria are known

[55] W.T. PITARD, *op. cit.* (n. 54), p. 132-138; P.-E. DION, *op. cit.* (n. 42), p. 191-194; LIPIŃSKI, *Aramaeans*, p. 376-377.

[56] E. LIPIŃSKI, *An Assyro-Israelite Alliance in 842/841 B.C.E.?*, in *Proceedings of the Sixth World Congress of Jewish Studies* I, Jerusalem 1977, p. 273-278.

[57] E. LIPIŃSKI, *art. cit.* (n. 24), p. 76-78; LIPIŃSKI, *Aramaeans*, p. 377-383; cf. H. WEIPPERT, *Ahab el campeador? Redaktionsgeschichtliche Untersuchungen zu 1 Kön 22*, in *Biblica* 69 (1988), p. 457-479. While discussing this question, S. HAFÞÓRSSON, *op. cit.* (n. 54), p. 61-63, does not notice that the Tell al-Qāḍi stele only confirms the annalistic sources of the Bible, reporting the death or fatal wounding of Jehoram at the battle of Ramoth-Gilead, as explained by E. LIPIŃSKI, *loc. cit.*, fifteen years before the discovery of the stele. But it seems, quite surprisingly, that Hafþórsson did not have access to the *Acta Antiqua* of the Hungarian Academy of Sciences.

[58] F. BRIQUEL-CHATONNET, *op. cit.* (n. 54), p. 112-115.

[59] P.-E. DION, *op. cit.* (n. 42), p. 198-199; LIPIŃSKI, *Aramaeans*, p. 384-385.

[60] *SAIO* II, p. 24-25; LIPIŃSKI, *Aramaeans*, p. 130-132.

[61] P.-E. DION, *op. cit.* (n. 42), p. 199-201; LIPIŃSKI, *Aramaeans*, p. 385-388. See also here above, p. 73.

only from a few incomplete epigraphs[62] and no information is available concerning his relations with the Aramaean kingdoms of Arpad, the "Upper-Aram", and of Śam'al or *Y'dy* (Zincirli). Both states were ruled by well established dynasties[63], founded respectively by Gush and by Gabbar. In the 9th century, Gush was followed on the throne of Arpad by Hadram, Attarsumki I, and Bar-Hadad, who dedicated, near Aleppo, a five-line Aramaic inscription to Melqart, the chief god of Tyre[64]. In Śam'al, Gabbar was succeeded by Banihu, Hayya(n), Sha'il, and Kulamuwa, who had secured Assyrian assistance against the king of Adana (Cilicia), probably in the years 839 or 834-832/1 B.C.[65]

After two decades of internal troubles in Assyria, Adad-nirari III (810-783 B.C.) was able to resume an active role in Syria[66]. Having regained the lost control of Guzana in 808 B.C., he empowered Shamshi-ilu, the new Assyrian *turtānu*, to fix the boundary between Attarsumki I of Arpad (*ca.* 830-800 B.C.) and Zakkūr, king of Hamath, on the Orontes River[67]. In fact, Zakkūr, "a man of 'Ana(h)" (Ḫana), had usurped the throne of the Neo-Hittite dynasty of Hamath in the late 9th century and he had apparently paid homage to the Assyrian king shortly after having seized the power. It is so far impossible to find a certain answer to the question whether "man of 'Ana(h)" is a generic or ethnic qualification, or rather an indication that the person in question was native from the city of 'Ana(h) on the Euphrates[68]. Even the rich Mari archives do not give a clear answer to the problem concerning the older form *Ḫanūm* of the same name[69].

[62] *SAIO* II, p. 92-93; P.-E. DION, *op. cit.* (n. 42), p. 201-203; LIPIŃSKI, *Aramaeans*, p. 388-389.

[63] H.S. SADER, *op. cit.* (n. 45), p. 99-184; P.-E. DION, *op. cit.* (n. 42), p. 99-136; LIPIŃSKI, *Aramaeans*, p. 195-219 and 233-247.

[64] É. PUECH, *La stèle de Bar-Hadad à Melqart et les rois d'Arpad*, in *RB* 99 (1992), p. 311-334, Pls. XV-XVI.

[65] P.-E. DION, *op. cit.* (n. 42), p. 108; LIPIŃSKI, *Aramaeans*, p. 242.

[66] S. PONCHIA, *L'Assiria e gli stati transeufratici nella prima metà dell'VIII sec. a.C.* (History of the Ancient Near East. Studies 4bis), Padova 1991, p. 7-20, 46-49, 88-90; J. KAH-JIN KUAN, *op. cit.* (n. 53), p. 69-106. S. HAFÞÓRSSON, *op. cit.* (n. 54), p. 112-119, 260-261, appears to be unaware of some literature referring to the subject.

[67] N. WAZANA, *Water Division in Border Agreements*, in *SAAB* 10 (1996), p. 55-66, LIPIŃSKI, *Aramaeans*, p. 214-215 and 302..

[68] LIPIŃSKI, *Aramaeans*, p. 299-301.

[69] M. ANBAR, *Ḫanûm: Nom ethnique ou générique*, in Y. SEFATI - P. ARTZI - Ch. COHEN - B.L. EICHLER - V.A. HUROWITZ (eds.), *"An Experienced Scribe who neglects Nothing" - Ancient Near Eastern Studies in Honor of J. Klein*, Bethesda 2004, p. 446-461.

Proceeding with an active policy, Adad-nirari III fought western campaigns in 805-803 against "Upper-Aram" and "Lower-Aram". The expeditions of 805 and 804 brought him "to the land of Arpad" and "to the city of Hazazu", where his main opponent was Attarsumki I[70]. Despite his defeat, Attarsumki did not lose his throne, but may have been deprived of a part of his territory. In 803, the eponymous year of Nergal-eresh, whose steles celebrate the campaign of his office term, Adad-nirari III's thrust led him as far as the city of Ba'li, in Israel or in Phoenicia, certainly beyond Damascus, where he had besieged "the Lord" of Aram (*māri'*), the aging king Hazael who died about that time and was replaced by his son Bar-Hadad II. Adad-nirari III received a considerable tribute in Damascus and, after having rescued Samaria besieged by the Aramaeans, he took a rich tribute also from Jehoash, king of Israel, and further from the city-states of Tyre and Sidon[71]. The swift success of Adad-nirari III in 803 is to be explained partly by the homage Zakkūr had paid to the Assyrian king[72]. The Calah Slab, which refers to this campaign, reports the subjugation of the Chaldaean chieftains immediately after the tribute paid by Damascus[73], thus indicating that the campaign of 802, "unto the Sea(land)", was fought in Babylonia and that 803 was the date of the last Adad-nirari III's campaign to the West, followed only in 796 B.C. by an expedition to central Syria, *ana Manṣuate*, present-day Maṣyaf.

The purpose of this campaign was to rescue Zakkūr, besieged in Hadarik/Hatarikka (Tell al-Afis) by a coalition led by Bar-Hadad II of Damascus and by the king of Arpad, who may now be securely identified with Bar-Hadad, son of Attarsumki I[74]. This city can confidently be identified with Tell al-Afis, while its location at 'Adrā / Hadra[75], about 22 km north-east of Damascus, can in the best case be regarded as "speculative"[76]. The rescue campaign manifested Assyria's loyalty towards its vassal and it ended on the territory of Hamath, at Manṣuate, without reaching the northern border of the kingdom of

[70] S. Ponchia, *op. cit.* (n. 66), p. 46-47; P.-E. Dion, *op. cit.* (n. 42), p. 127-128; Lipiński, *Aramaeans*, p. 214-215.

[71] E. Lipiński, *art. cit.* (n. 24), p. 85-87; Lipiński, *Aramaeans*, p. 390-393.

[72] J.E. Reade, *Fragments of Assyrian Monuments*, in *Iraq* 43 (1981), p. 145-156, Pls. VI-XXI (see p. 151-152, Pl. XXc); Lipiński, *Aramaeans*, p. 302 and 394.

[73] *RIMA* III, text A.0.104.8, p. 213, lines 22-23a; cf. Lipiński, *Aramaeans*, p. 392-393.

[74] E. Lipiński, *The Assyrian Campaign to Manṣuate, in 796 B.C., and the Zakir Stela*, in *AION* 31 (1971), p. 393-399; É. Puech, *art. cit.* (n. 64), p. 330-334.

[75] S. Parpola - M. Porter, *The Helsinki Atlas of the Near East in the Neo-Assyrian Period*, Helsinki 2001.

[76] Cf. A. Millard, rev. in *JSS* 50 (2005), p. 197-198.

Damascus, which was nevertheless seriously weakened by this new reverse.

Between 796 and the arrival of Tiglath-pileser III (745-727 B.C.) in Syria, only sporadic information is available about the Aramaean states[77]. The purpose of an Assyrian campaign in 775 "to the Cedar Mountain", probably the Amanus, is unknown, but in 773 the *turtānu* Shamshi-ilu brought a considerable booty from Damascus, where Hadian was then king[78]. The Assyrian campaigns of 772, 765, 755 "to Hatarikka", may have been directed against the king of Hamath or, on the contrary, be aimed at helping a loyal vassal of Assyria against enemies. Ashur-nirari V's campaign to Arpad, in 754, is certainly related to the vassalage treaty imposed by the Assyrian king upon Mati'ilu, son of Attarsumki II[79], and to the Aramaic treaties found at Sefire. They were imposed upon the same king of Arpad in favour of Bar-Ga'ya, king of *Ktk*[80]. The latter was a North-Syrian client of Assyria whose power had to be boasted in order to exercize more pressure on Arpad. In the same period, a certain gain of Israelite power at the expense of Damascus and of Hamath, probably in Gilead, in Galilee, and in the Beqa' Valley, is recorded in a few biblical passages[81], while a somewhat mutilated account of dynastic strife in Śam'al is given in an inscription of Bar-Rakkāb[82].

After re-establishing the full royal authority in Assyria and beating back an Urartian attack, Tiglath-pileser III inaugurated a new policy of violent annexation in the West[83]. He first struck at Arpad, Urartu's main Syrian ally, and captured the city in 740 B.C. after a three-year siege[84]. In 738, he defeated an alliance led by Azriyau, king of Hamath, and turned the northern regions of this kingdom into Assyrian provinces, but enthrusted a reduced Aramaean state of Hamath to Eni-ilu, an Assyrian nominee[85]. Raṣyan of Damascus took advantage of renewed Tiglath-

[77] S. PONCHIA, *op. cit.* (n. 66), p. 20-27, 49-51; J. KAH-JIN KUAN, *op. cit.* (n. 53), p. 107-134.

[78] S. PONCHIA, *op. cit.* (n. 66), p. 8-11; P.-E. DION, *op. cit.* (n. 42), p. 208-209; LIPIŃSKI, *Aramaeans*, p. 400.

[79] *SAA* II, 2.

[80] J.A. FITZMYER, *The Aramaic Inscriptions of Sefire*, 2nd ed. (Biblica et Orientalia 19/A), Roma 1995; LIPIŃSKI, *Aramaeans*, p. 230-231.

[81] P.-E. DION, *op. cit.* (n. 42), p. 207-212; LIPIŃSKI, *Aramaeans*, p. 344-345 and 401-404.

[82] *KAI* 215 = *TSSI* II, 14, 1-8.

[83] J. KAH-JIN KUAN, *op. cit.* (n. 53), p. 135-192.

[84] P.-E. DION, *op. cit.* (n. 42), p. 133-134; LIPIŃSKI, *Aramaeans*, p. 218-219.

[85] N. NA'AMAN, *Looking for KTK*, in *WO* 9 (1978), p. 220-239 (see p. 229-230, 238-239); ID., *Tiglath-pileser III's Campaigns against Tyre and Israel (734-732 B.C.E.)*, in *Tel Aviv* 22 (1995), p. 268-278 (see p. 276-277); LIPIŃSKI, *Aramaeans*, p. 315-316.

pileser III's fights against Urartu in 737-735 B.C. and concluded an anti-Assyrian alliance with Peqah of Israel, whom he apparently helped to seize the throne at Samaria[86]. But after a campaign in 734 against Philistia and the replacement of Peqah by Hoshea[87], Tiglath-pileser III attacked Damascus in 733-732[88], being assisted by some of Assyria's vassals, like Panamuwa II of Śam'al, who was killed on the battlefield[89], and probably by Shalman of Moab, who invaded the southern Gilead province of Aram-Damascus and captured the city of Bēth-Arbel (Irbid)[90]. Damascus fell in 732 and its territories were annexed to Assyria[91].

The short reign of Shalmaneser V (726-722 B.C.)[92] and the Assyrian dynastic crisis in 722 B.C. provided the opportunity for a general western revolt, that extended to newly formed Assyrian provinces. Its leader was Ilu-bi'di or Yau-bi'di, king of the still independent Hamath. After securing his position in Assyria, Sargon II (721-705 B.C.) confronted the western alliance in 720 B.C. at Qarqar. He won a decisive victory, captured Ilu-bi'di, and seized Hamath[93], where widespread destruction traces were found during the excavations. The city did not become the permanent seat of an Assyrian governor, but was subsequently incorporated into the province of Manṣuate, 38 km west of Hama. It is uncertain at what point of Sargon's policy, carried along Tiglath-pileser III's lines, the remaining Aramaean kingdoms became Assyrian provinces, namely Śam'al, whose last king was Bar-Rakkāb, son of Panamuwa II[94], and *Ktk* or Kasku (*Kṯk*), whose king Dadilu, "(Ha)dad is god", had still paid tribute to Tiglath-pileser III in 738 B.C.[95]

For most of the 7th century, the period of the *pax Assyriaca*, the conquered Aramaean territories remained firmly under Assyrian rule as provinces, usually named from the seats of the Assyrian governor. The mass deportations have certainly obliterated the Aramaean features of

[86] P.-E. DION, *op. cit.* (n. 42), p. 211-212.
[87] N. NA'AMAN, *art. cit.* (n. 85), in *Tel Aviv* 22 (1995), p. 274-275.
[88] P.-E. DION, *op. cit.* (n. 42), p. 214-215; LIPIŃSKI, *Aramaeans*, p. 406-407.
[89] *KAI* 215 = *TSSI* II, 14, 16-19.
[90] H.W. WOLFF, *Dodekapropheton 1. Hosea* (BKAT XIV/1), Neukirchen 1961, p. 243-244; W. RUDOLPH, *Hosea* (KAT XIII/1), Gütersloh 1966, p. 206-207; LIPIŃSKI, *Aramaeans*, p. 406-407. See also here below, p. 357.
[91] P.-E. DION, *op. cit.* (n. 42), p. 214-215; LIPIŃSKI, *Aramaeans*, p. 406-407.
[92] J. KAH-JIN KUAN, *op. cit.* (n. 53), p. 173-207.
[93] P.-E. DION, *op. cit.* (n. 42), p. 169; LIPIŃSKI, *Aramaeans*, p. 316-317.
[94] P.-E. DION, *op. cit.* (n. 42), p. 110-111; LIPIŃSKI, *Aramaeans*, p. 244-246.
[95] *Tigl. III*, p. 68, Ann. 13*, line 12; p. 89, Ann. 27, line 6; p. 108, Stele IIIA, line 15: *Da-di*-DINGIR ^{kur}*Kaš-ka-a-a*. Cf. LIPIŃSKI, *Aramaeans*, p. 224-225.

these areas[96], but Aramaic had become the second language of the Assyrian empire in the same period and was still widely spoken in Syria and in south-eastern Anatolia until the Islamic period, so the bulk of the population had obviously remained Aramaean, notwithstanding the arrival of new population groups.

Neo-Babylonian period

The far-reaching assimilation of the Chaldaeans to the culture and the lifestyle of the earlier Babylonians and the recorded events of their past make it difficult to distinguish properly Chaldaean traits from the general history of Babylonia in the Neo-Babylonian period. However, the case of Nabonidus constitutes an exception. The so-called "Dynastic Prophecy", which devotes a few lines to Nabonidus, states that "[he will establish] the dynasty of Harran", BALA-*e Ḫar-ra-an*^{ki} [*i-šak-kan*][97]. In the inscription of Adad-guppi, Nabonidus' mother, one reads that "he will restore Harran and make it better than it was before"[98] . Similar declarations occur in texts of Nabonidus. As they concern a ruined city at the fringes of the Empire, one must accept that Adad-guppi and Nabonidus were really native from Harran[99]. Her name is Aramaic, "Hadad is my fountain"[100], and the Moon-god worshipped by Nabonidus was the Aramaean god Śehr / Śahr[101], whose name is written *Ilte(ḫ)ri* in Neo-Babylonian texts[102]. The "Verse Account", col. V, 11, states explicitly that Nabonidus was calling him ^{d}*Il-te-ri*[103]. B. Landsberger rightly insisted on the Aramaean characteristics of Nabonidus' personality[104].

[96] The main work dealing with this subject is B. ODED, *Mass Deportation and Deportees in the Neo-Assyrian Empire*, Wiesbaden 1979.

[97] A.K. GRAYSON, *Babylonian Historical Literary Texts* (Toronto Semitic Texts and Studies 3), Toronto 1975, p. 32-33, col. II, 12.

[98] *ANET*, p. 561a, col. II, 16-17.

[99] P.-A. BEAULIEU, *The Reign of Nabonidus, King of Babylon, 556-539 B.C.* (YNER 10), New Haven 1989, p. 76-78.

[100] The predicate of her name (*gu-up-pi-'*) is a variant of *gubbu* / *kuppu*, "fountain", "well". It occurs also in the name *Gub-ba-ka-*^{d}60, "Anu is your fountain": A.T. CLAY, *Legal Documents from Erech Dated in the Seleucid Era (312-63 B.C.)* (Babylonian Records in the Library of J. Pierpont Morgan 2), New York 1913, No. 2, 3.8.11.15.

[101] LIPIŃSKI, *Aramaeans*, p. 620-623.

[102] *SAIO* II, p. 189.

[103] BM 38299, "Verse Account of Nabonidus": S. SMITH, *Babylonian Historical Texts Relating to the Capture and Downfall of Babylon*, London 1924, p. 82-91, Pls. V-X; cf. *ANET*, p. 312-315.

[104] B. LANDSBERGER, *Die Basaltstele Nabonids von Eski-Harran*, in *Halil Edhem Hatira Kitabi* I, Ankara 1947, p. 115-151, Pls. I-III (see p. 140, 146 ff.).

Nabonidus' devotion to the Moon-god manifests itself from the beginning of his reign. He dedicated his daughter as *ēntu* of the Moon-god at Ur in the second year of his reign[105] and he set out for Amman, Edom, and Arabia in the second month of his third year, when he knew that restoration works in the temple of the Moon-god at Harran were already undertaken[106].

Nabonidus stayed in Arabia for ten years (552-543 B.C.) according to his Harran inscription[107]. The "Prayer of Nabonidus" from Qumrān ascribes a length of seven years to the king's stay in Arabia and to his worshipping of false deities at Teima (*Tymn*)[108]. The number "seven" was probably inspired by the "seven years" during which Solomon's temple was built (I Kings 6, 37-38). According to the "Prayer of Nabonidus", the king started worshipping the universal god at the end of the seven-years period. This idea echoes the long prayers inserted into the middle of Nabonidus' report on his return to Babylon, recording the restoration of the ziggurat of Ur, and in his inscription where Sin "joyfully entering his temple" is portrayed as the only god recognized by the king[109]. The restoration of the Enunmaḫ, a part of the Moon-god's Ekišnugal temple at Ur, and of the ziggurat had been achieved after Nabonidus' return from Arabia[110], but one of his first deeds was certainly to go to Harran for the dedication of the Eḫulḫul. This was the second phase of his plan regarding the temple of the Moon-god at Harran, as stated in the "Verse Account": "When I have fully executed what I have planned, I shall lead him by his hand and establish him on his seat"[111]. The temple and the city lay there in ruins for fifty-four

105 P.-A. Beaulieu, *op. cit.* (n. 99), p. 127-132.

106 "Verse Account of Nabonidus", col. II, 10-17; cf. n. 103 and *ANET*, p. 313b. See also here below, p. 315.

107 *ANET*, p. 562-563 (see p. 562b and 563a). See also P.-A. Beaulieu, *op. cit.* (n. 99), p. 151, 160, 162.

108 J.T. Milik, *"Prière de Nabonide" et autres écrits d'un cycle de Daniel. Fragments araméens de Qumrân 4,* in *RB* 63 (1956), p. 407-415, Pl. I (see p. 407-411); J. Collins, *Prayer of Nabonidus*, in J. VanderKam (ed.), *Qumran Cave 4*, XVII (DJD 22), Oxford 1996, p. 83-93, Pl. VI (see p. 88).

109 P.-A. Beaulieu, *op. cit.* (n. 99), p. 60-61.

110 M.A. Dandamayev, *Nabonid*, in *RLA* IX, Berlin 1998-2001, p. 6-11 (see p. 10).

111 BM 38299, col. II, 8-9: S. Smith, *op. cit.* (n. 103) and *ANET*, p. 313b. H. Tadmor, *The Inscriptions of Nabunaid: Historical Arrangement*, in *Studies in Honor of Benno Landsberger* (AS 16), Chicago 1965, p. 351-364, failed to distinguish the starting of the restoration works at the Eḫulḫul and its solemn dedication, probably on the 17th day of Tašritu 542 or 541 B.C.: *ANET*, p. 563a, col. II, 10-14; cf. P.-A. Beaulieu, *op. cit.* (n. 99), p. 152. These two phases were already marked in col. II of the "Verse Account", as properly seen by É. Dhorme, *Recueil Édouard Dhorme*, Paris 1951, p. 345. They are paralleled in I Kings 6, 37-38, written in the same period.

years, but the Moon-god could return to his rebuilt shrine in the fatidic "seventieth year"[112] , i.e. in 542/1 or 541/0 B.C., probably on Tašrītu the 17th, when his renewed *Akītu* festival started at Harran[113]. The renewed cult activities at Harran, continued until the early Middle Ages[114], belong to the long-lived Old Aramaic tradition.

[112] *SAIO* II, p. 191 with n. 207.

[113] P.-A. Beaulieu, *op. cit.* (n. 99), p. 152.

[114] T.M. Green, *The City of the Moon God: Religious Traditions of Harran* (Religions in the Graeco-Roman World 114), Leiden 1992.

CHAPTER VI

BASHAN

Ancient Transjordan consisted of five regions, the borders of which changed sometimes, but were broadly delimitated by the physical conformation of the country itself. These regions were Bashan or Golan in the north, then southwards Gilead, further Ammon, Moab, and Edom. The degree to which the different parts of Transjordan were influenced by their neighbours depended on geography. The Bashan highland is bordered to the east by the Hauran and Syria, while Upper Jordan and the Sea of Galilee separate it from Cisjordan. The Gilead highland slopes to the east into the plateau of the Arabian Desert, while to the west it runs down into the Jordan Valley. Ammon occupies a central position at the crossroads from the Gulf of Aqaba to Syria and from Wādī Sirḥān to the Mediterranean. The tableland of Moab lies between the Dead Sea and the Arabian Desert, bordered to the north by Ammon, to the south by Edom. Edom rises eastward from the Wādī Arabah, which stretches down to the Gulf of Aqaba, but it has historical connections also with the tableland of the Negeb and the Beersheba Valley. The present chapter deals with Bashan, also in the periods preparing the Iron Age.

The land and its past

Bashan (*Baṯān*) corresponds broadly to the present-day Golan, in Arabic Ǧōlān or Ǧawlān. This is a high volcanic plateau, bordered to the south by the Yarmuk River, to the west by the Upper Jordan, the Ḥuleh Lake, and the Sea of Galilee, to the north by the slopes of Mount Hermon, and to the east by a range which rises sometimes to an altitude of more than 1,000 m. Most of its area is covered with basalt generated by lava eruptions, which occurred in the Pleistocene and later periods. In some parts, however, erosion transformed the volcanic material into fertile soil, which thanks to sufficient rainfalls was renown for its excellent pasture lands and forests, still quite large in the 19th century, but nowadays confined mainly to the area north of Banias, at the foot of Mount Hermon.

The name of the region goes back at least to the Late Bronze Age, since a city of this area, mentioned in the Amarna correspondence (*EA* 201, 4), was called ^uru^*Ṣi-ri-Ba-ša-ni*, "Spur[1] of Bashan". The same city *Ḏr-Bśn* is recorded also on a stele of a high-ranking official of Ramesses II and of Merneptah[2]. The city name seems to be shortened to *Ḏỉ3m* in an Execration Text[3] and it appears as *Ḏr* in a topographical list of Amenhotep III (1392-1354 B.C.), found at Thebes[4]. The place was identified by R. Dussaud with Izra'[5], former Zer'a and Talmudic *Zrb'y* or *Zrw'y*[6], almost 60 km east of the Sea of Galilee. The Talmudic spelling corresponds to the Syriac one and to the Greek gentile name Ζοραουηνοί[7]. These forms imply a place name **Zorawa*, which does not favour Dussaud's proposal. Instead, *Ṣyr* or *Ṣyyr* in the region of Nawā[8] may preserve the ancient toponym, which is echoed nowadays by Ṣura or Ṣurayye, 10 km to the north-east of Nawā[9].

Biblical texts praise Bashan, the "Mountain of God" (Ps. 68, 16), and make it equal with Mount Carmel (Is. 33, 9; Nah. 1, 4) and Mount Lebanon (Jer. 22, 20; Nah. 1, 4). They mention its lofty trees (Is. 2, 13; Zech. 11, 2), which Phoenicians used to build their sea-going ships (Ez. 27, 6), and its good pasture with plenty of cattle and sheep (Deut. 32, 14; Ez. 39, 18; Am. 4, 1; Ps. 22, 13). At the time of the Babylonian exile, the

[1] *Ṣi-ri* corresponds to Arabic *ẓirr*, "sharp-edged stone".

[2] A. MARIETTE, *Abydos* II, Paris 1880, Pl. 50; K.A. KITCHEN, *Ramesside Inscriptions* IV, Oxford 1982, p. 104, lines 1-15 (especially line 15); ID., *Ramesside Inscriptions. Translated & Annotated. Translations* IV, Malden 2003, p. 81-82, §68, see line 15. Cf. R. GIVEON, *Two Egyptian Documents concerning Bashan from the Time of Ramses II*, in *RSO* 40 (1965), p. 197-202 (see p. 200-202); S. AḤITUV, *Canaanite Toponyms in Ancient Egyptian Documents*, Jerusalem 1984, p. 34 and 181; R. HANNIG, *Die Sprache der Pharaonen. Grosses Handwörterbuch Ägyptisch-Deutsch (2800-950 v. Chr.)*, 2nd ed., Mainz a/R 1997, p. 1410.

[3] G. POSENER, *Princes et pays d'Asie et de Nubie*, Bruxelles 1940, *E* 19; R. HANNIG, *op. cit.* (n. 2), p. 1409.

[4] E. EDEL, *Die Ortsnamenlisten aus dem Totentempel Amenophis III.* (Bonner Biblische Beiträge 25), Bonn 1966, BN, left 6; R. HANNIG, *op. cit.* (n. 2), p. 1410.

[5] DUSSAUD, *Topographie*, p. 516; cf. ABEL, *Géographie* II, p. 10.

[6] JASTROW, p. 412a. Cf. G. REEG, *Die Ortsnamen Israels nach der rabbinischen Literatur* (BTAVO B/21), Wiesbaden 1989, p. 410-411 (*Mlḥ d-Zyzh*) and p. 544 (*Ṣyr*²).

[7] Th. NÖLDEKE, *Zur Topographie und Geschichte des Damascenischen Gebietes und der Haurângegend*, in *ZDMG* 29 (1875), p. 419-444 (see p. 434-435).

[8] Tosefta, *Shebi'it* IV, 8; Talmud Yerushalmi, *Demai* II, 2, 22d; cf. JASTROW, p. 1276b; S. AḤITUV, *op. cit.* (n. 2), p. 181; G. REEG, *op. cit.* (n. 6), p. 544.

[9] S. AḤITUV, *op. cit.* (n. 2), p. 181 with former literature. Ceramic and petrographic analysis of *EA* 201 does not provide any new information. The letter is "probably dispatched from the southern Bashan or Yarmuk Valley": Y. GOREN - I. FINKELSTEIN - N. NA'AMAN, *Inscribed in Clay. Provenance Study of the Amarna Letters and Other Ancient Near Eastern Texts*, Tel Aviv 2004, p. 216.

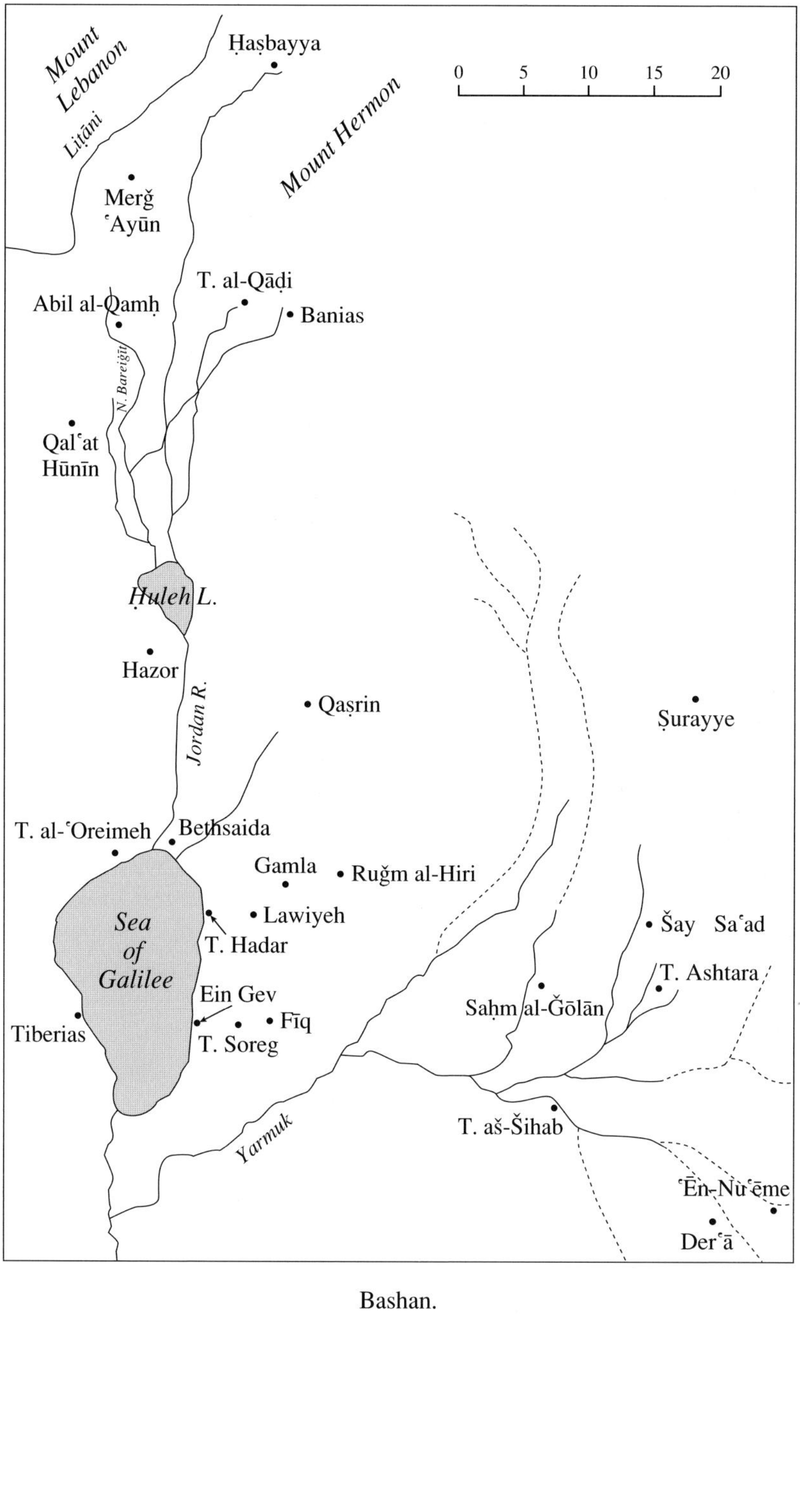
Mount
Lebanon
Liṭāni
Ḥaṣbayya
0 5 10 15 20
Mount Hermon
Merğ
ʿAyūn
T. al-Qāḍi
Abil al-Qamḥ
Banias
N. Bareiġit
Qalʿat
Hūnīn
Ḥuleh L.
Hazor
Jordan R.
Qaṣrin
Ṣurayye
T. al-ʿOreimeh
Bethsaida
Gamla
Ruğm al-Hiri
Sea
of
Galilee
Lawiyeh
T. Hadar
Šay
Saʿad
T. Ashtara
Ein Gev
Fīq
Tiberias
T. Soreg
Saḥm al-Ğōlān
T. aš-Šihab
Yarmuk
ʿĒn-Nuʿēme
Derʿā

Bashan.

return to the meadows of Bashan and Gilead was the deep aspiration of the deportees from Israel and Judah (Mich. 7, 14; cf. Ez. 39, 18).

A biblical tradition records that Moses allotted Bashan to the half-tribe of Manasseh (Numb. 32, 33-42; Josh. 17, 1.5; 22, 7), but two enclaves, Golan and Ashtarot, were attributed to the Levites of the Gershon clan (Josh. 21, 27; I Chron. 6, 56). The original aim of the so-called "Levitical cities" is not clear, but some of them were located at the fringes of the Israelite territory and seem to have had military functions rather than religious ones. At any rate, Golan, set aside also as a city of refuge (Deut. 4, 43; Josh. 20, 8), gave its name to the entire district. It was tentatively identified with Gilunu, mentioned in Amarna letter 185, 22.25[10], but this city should be located rather in the Beqa' Valley. Eusebius of Caesarea records a large village Γαυλών or Γωλάν in Batanaea[11], which G. Schumacher identified with Saḥm al-Ǧōlān[12], 8 km east of the Nahr al-'Allān, at the eastern boundary of Bashan. This identification is so far uncertain and other locations have been proposed. Toponymy might suggest identifying it with Γαλανία, mentioned on three boundary stones, dated to *ca.* 300 A.D[13]. They would indicate a location about 10 km north of the Ḥuleh Lake, but such a site does not lay in Batanaea, as understood at the time of Eusebius. There are several references to Golan in the Talmud, but some of them may allude to the entire region and not to a particular city[14].

Ashtarot is a well-known city, mentioned in Egyptian, Ugaritic, and Assyrian sources. Together with Edrei, it was believed to have been a capital of Og, king of Bashan (Deut. 1, 4; Josh. 20, 8; 21, 27). It is identified with Tell 'Ashtara, 22 km to the north-west of Der'ā (Edrei) and 34 km east of the Sea of Galilee[15]. Its mound, the largest in southern Syria, covers an area of 7 ha. This was an important town, represented even on a relief of Tiglath-pileser III's palace at Calah. The relief shows

[10] DUSSAUD, *Topographie*, p. 506, followed by some authors.

[11] EUSEBIUS OF CAESAREA, *Onomasticon*, in E. KLOSTERMANN (ed.), *Das Onomastikon der biblischen Ortsnamen*, Leipzig 1904, p. 64: 6-8.

[12] Grid ref. 238/243: G. SCHUMACHER, *Across the Jordan*, London 1886, p. 91-99.

[13] Y. AHARONI, *Three New Boundary Stones*, in *'Atiqot* (English Series) 1 (1955), p. 109-114 and Pl., see Nos. 1, 2, 17.

[14] G. REEG, *op. cit.* (n. 6), p. 169-170, only records the identification of Golan with Saḥm al-Ǧōlān.

[15] Grid ref. 2455/2460. Cf. J.G. WETZSTEIN, *Reisebericht über Hauran und die Trachonen*, Berlin 1860, p. 109-111; ABEL, *Géographie* II, p. 255; M. ASTOUR, in L.R. FISHER (ed.), *Ras Shamra Parallels* II, Rome 1975, p. 313-314; D. KELLERMANN, *'Aštārōt - 'Ašterōt Qarnayim - Qarnayim*, in *ZDPV* 97 (1981), p. 45-61; S. AḤITUV, *op. cit.* (n. 2), p. 72-73, 90-91.

Bashan seen from Umm Qais (Gadara).

a fortified city from which Assyrian soldiers are deporting the inhabitants and their cattle[16]. Remains of the double city rampart are apparently preserved at the site and Ali Abu Assaf undertook there excavations in 1966 and 1967[17]. They have been interrupted by the Six Day War and not resumed because of the proximity of the Syro-Israeli demarcation line. Tell ʻAshtara is a very promising site, as its historical past and legends suggest. Besides, its name expresses a special relation to the goddess Astarte, and the cult of Milkashtart seems to have originated in this city[18].

The tradition of Manassite settlements in Bashan, of the attribution of Ashtarot and Golan to the Levitical clan of Gershon (Josh. 21, 27; I Chron. 6, 56), and of the establishment of the city of refuge at Golan (Deut. 4, 43; Josh. 20, 8) must go back to the period when Jeroboam II

[16] BM. 118908; cf. *RLA* I, Pl. 37; *ANEP*, No. 366; *Tigl. III,* p. 210, Misc. II, 2. See here, p. 233.

[17] A. Abou Assaf, *Tell ʻAschtara in Südsyrien. Erste Kampagne 1966,* in *AAS* 18 (1968), p. 103-106; Id., *Tell ʻAschtara. Zweite Kampagne 1967,* in *AAS* 19 (1969), p. 101-102; cf. H.S. Sader, *Les États araméens de Syrie depuis leur fondation jusqu'à leur transformation en provinces assyriennes* (BTS 36), Beirut 1987, p. 268. The results of these excavations have been summarized by S. Hafþórsson, *A Passing Power: An Examination of the Sources for the History of Aram-Damascus in the Second Half of the Ninth Century B.C.* (Coniectanea Biblica. Old Testament Series 54), Stockholm 2006, p. 196-199.

[18] Lipiński, *Dieux et déesses*, p. 271-274, with former literature.

was occupying this area, as implied by I Chron. 5, 17 and Am. 6, 13. Only Qarnaim (Šayḫ Sa'd) is mentioned in Am. 6, 13, but this town lies no more than 4 km north of Ashtarot, also called Ashtarot-Qarnaim (Gen. 14, 5). Qarnaim has been chosen here by Amos for its symbolic meaning "Double-horn", suggesting power and strength. It was an important town at any rate. The basalt portal lion found at Šayḫ Sa'd, now in the Damascus Museum, must have guarded a city or palace entry. "It recalls North Syrian gate lions of the 'Syro-Hittite' type, but it is already under some Assyrian influence in the treatment of the mane; it might belong to the latter part of the ninth or the early eighth century B.C.E"[19]. This brings us to the period immediately preceding the reign of Jeroboam II. Raṣ̌yān, the last king of Damascus, has apparently re-conquered the whole region, but a few years later, in 732 B.C., it was occupied and annexed by Tiglath-pileser III[20].

No doubt, Bashan is a region, which was rich not only in woods and pasture lands, but also in myths, legends, and historical events, which is not always easy to date and classify according to their genre.

Protohistory of Bashan begins in the fourth millennium B.C., in the Chalcolithic period. This region, only sparsely inhabited in earlier times, became the centre of a highly developed culture. Surveys and the exploration of a concentration of about twenty-eight sites in the central Golan heights by Claire Epstein and a team headed by I. Ben-Efraim[21] uncovered villages with several parallel chains of abutting rectangular houses, built of large basalt stones and paved with stone slabs. In most houses, there was a bench opposite the entrance and a cultic niche with a basalt idol in the form of a human head with a depression in its upper part, probably for offerings[22]. Several idols of this type are housed in the Archaeological Museum of Qaṣrin. The largest settlements consisted of twenty to fifty houses. Economy was based on herding and agriculture with olive trees, suggesting that olive oil was first produced in Bashan during this period. Around 3300 B.C., the Chalcolithic culture was

[19] B.S. ISSERLIN, *Israelite Art during the Period of the Monarchy*, in C. ROTH (ed.), *Jewish Art*, London 1961, p. 77-118 (quotation from p. 95). Isserlin's opinion does not seem to have been known to S. HAFÞÓRSSON, *op. cit.* (n. 17), p. 199-200.

[20] LIPIŃSKI, *Aramaeans*, p. 404-407.

[21] C. EPSTEIN, *A New Aspect of Chalcolithic Culture*, in *BASOR* 229 (1978), p. 27-45, and her reports in *IEJ* from 25 (1975) to 40 (1990); I. BEN-EFRAIM, *Central Golan Heights, Survey*, in *ESI* 18 (1998), p. 5-6.

[22] C. EPSTEIN, *Basalt Pillar Figures from the Golan*, in *IEJ* 25 (1975), p. 193-200; EAD., *Basalt Pillar Figures from the Golan and the Ḥuleh Region*, in *IEJ* 38 (1988), p. 205-233. See also E. KALMACHTER, *Southern Golan Heights, Survey - 1993-1994*, in *ESI* 18 (1998), p. 7-8. See here p. 231.

Domestic idol from the Chalcolithic period in the Golan
(Excavations of Claire Epstein).

brought abruptly to an end, probably by a new population, which one is tempted to identify with Semites migrating from North Africa through Egypt and introducing the culture of the Early Bronze Age.

Surveys in Bashan have revealed enclosures constructed by the new arrivals near the junction of two deep ravines, in particular at Gamla and Lawiyeh (Mitḥam Levi'ah). These were permanent settlements[23], compactly built up and fortified. They lasted until the Early Bronze Age III, thus covering the whole span of the period *ca.* 3300-2300 B.C., at least at Lawiyeh, excavated by M. Kochavi in the years 1987-1993[24]. This

[23] Y. Olami, *The Lithic Assemblages from the Early Bronze Age Layer at Gamla,* in *Mitekufat Haeven* 22 (1989), p. 115*-128*; D. Syon - Z. Yavor, *Gamla - Old and New,* in *Qadmoniot* 34 (2001), p. 2-33 (in Hebrew), in particular p. 4-5.

[24] Grid ref. 214/250: M. Kochavi, *The Land of Geshur Project,* in *IEJ* 39 (1989), p. 1-17; 41 (1991), p. 180-184; 43 (1993), p. 185-190; 44 (1994), p. 136-141; Id., *Leviah Enclosure*, in *NEAEHL*, Jerusalem 1993, Vol. III, p. 915-916; Id., *The Land of Geshur: History of a Region in the Biblical Period,* in *J. Aviram Volume* (ErIs 25), Jerusalem 1996, p. 184-201 (in Hebrew).

city, situated 3 km east of the Sea of Galilee, had a superficies of 9 ha and its defence wall was still 5 m high in some places. Occupational remains, like pottery and cylinder-seal impressions, are similar to those found in the cities of the valleys and thus witness the same culture of the Early Bronze Age.

This culture is characterized also by megalithic burials, consisting of dolmens and tumuli, about 2,300 of which have been so far identified in Bashan[25]. The upright stones, on which a horizontal one was laid, were now and then covered by a heap of small stones, shaping tumuli, some of which have a diameter of more than 20 m. The grave proper, in which the corpse was deposited, was located under the slabs forming the pavement of the dolmen. These sepulchres belong to a homogenous model attested over 300 km from the Dead Sea to Mount Hermon[26], with examples occurring also in Syria, as far as Muslimiyeh, near Aleppo. Similar structures are found in North Africa[27], where we even encounter tumuli surrounded by several concentric circles, exactly like at Ruğm al-Hiri (Rogem Hiri), in the Golan. Also this megalithic monument dates from the Early Bronze Age[28]. The megalithic structures of Bashan are generally close to the settlements and can be regarded as an integral part of the Early Bronze Age system of cemeteries, probably reserved originally to the tribal elite, but used later also for secondary burials.

Myths and legends

The collapse of the urban civilization of the Early Bronze Age was followed about three hundred years later by the Middle Bronze Period

[25] L. VINITZKY, *The Date of the Dolmens in the Golan and the Galilee: A Reassessment,* in *Tel Aviv* 19 (1992), p. 100-112; M. ZOHAR, *Dolmens,* in *NEAEHL,* Jerusalem 1993, Vol. I, p. 352-356; I. BEN-EFRAIM, *art. cit.* (n. 21), p. 6; E. KALMACHTER, *art. cit.* (n. 22), p. 7.

[26] K. YASSINE, *The Dolmens: Construction and Dating Reconsidered,* in *BASOR* 259 (1985), p. 63-69.

[27] M. REYGASSE, *Monuments funéraires préislamiques de l'Afrique du Nord,* Paris 1950; Z. KRZAK, *Megality świata,* Warszawa 1994. The date of the North-African megaliths is somewhat uncertain, but a C-14 analysis provided the date 4095 ±210 B.P., i.e. about 3000 B.C.: B. GABRIEL, *Zur ökologischen Wandel im Neolithikum der östlichen Zentralsahara* (Berliner Geographische Abhandlungen 27), Berlin 1977, s. 1-11. Dates from the sixth and fifth millennia B.C. have been obtained as well: Z. KRZAK, *Megality śladami największych tajemnic świata,* in *Archeologia Żywa* 3/8 (1998), p. 28-31.

[28] Grid ref. 2254/2573: M. ZOHAR, *Rogem Hiri: A Megalithic Monument in the Golan,* in *IEJ* 39 (1989), p. 18-31; Y. MIZRACHI - M. ZOHAR, *Rogem Hiri,* in *NEAEHL,* Jerusalem 1993, Vol. IV, p. 1286-1287; Y. MIZRACHI - M. ZOHAR - M. KOCHAVI - V. MURPHY - S. LEV-YADUN, *The 1988-1991 Excavations at Rogem Hiri,* in *IEJ* 46 (1996), p. 167-195; S. LEV-YADUN - Y. MIZRACHI - M. KOCHAVI, *Lichenometric Studies of Cultural Formation Processes at Rogem Hiri,* in *IEJ* 46 (1996), p. 196-207.

Ashtarot: bas-relief from Tiglath-pileser III's palace at Calah
(British Museum 118908).

with its Canaanite city-states. The megalithic structures of Bashan led to the popular believe that this region was once inhabited by giants. This is probably the ultimate origin of the biblical stories about the Emim, Anakim, and Rephaim (Deut. 2, 11), whose last king was Og (Deut. 3, 1-4.10-11). He was believed to have ruled in Bashan over "sixty large walled cities with gate-bars of bronze" (I Kings 4, 13; cf. Deut. 3, 6) and to have "lived in Ashtarot and Edrei" (Josh. 12, 1; 13, 12.31). While the two cities are attested in ancient sources, Og is no real personage. Just like the Rephaim were spirits of dead ancestors, especially of royal blood, so Og bears a name, which is an ancient Semitic word meaning "corpse" or "death". It occurs in a Babylonian list of synonyms with *ú-gu* = *mu*(-*ú*)-*tum*[29], "dead", and in the Phoenician funerary inscription of Shapaṭbaal III, king of Byblos[30], cursing anybody who would dare "[to open] this sarcophagus and disturb the bones of my corpse", [... *lpt*ḥ '*]lt 'rn zn wlrgz 'ṣmy h'g*[31].

Ashtarot and Edrei, the main cities of Og, occur together in a text from Ugarit, dating back at least to the 13th century B.C. As they are

[29] *AHw*, p. 1403b.

[30] E. LIPIŃSKI, *Koningen van Byblos in de 10e-5e eeuw v. Chr.*, in R.J. DEMARÉE - K.R. VEENHOF (eds.), *Zij schreven geschiedenis*, Leiden-Leuven 2003, p. 253-261 (see p. 258-259).

[31] LIPIŃSKI, *Dieux et déesses*, p. 229 with n. 65 and former literature.

mentioned in connection with *Rapi'u*, the legend about Og, his kingdom, and the Rephaim, must be quite old. The text from Ugarit may be translated as follows[32]:

> "May [thu]s Rapi'u, the eternal king, drink,
> may the mighty and noble [god] drink,
> the god who dwells at Ashtarot,
> the god who judges at Edrei,
> who sings and plays the lire and the flute,
> with tambourine and cymbals, with castanets of ivory,
> in company of plenty of jolly mates".

Another text from Ugarit, being a ritual against snake's bites, shows that Ashtarot was the seat of the god Milk, i.e. "King", to whom an envoy should be sent to require a remedy[33]. This "King" is probably the same deity as the "eternal king" of the first text, thus one of the Rephaim, the etymological meaning of whose name is "healer".

Beside Ugaritic texts, also Egyptian monuments refer to this region. A fragmentary stele of Seti I (1293-1279 B.C.) from Tell aš-Šihab, 15 km north-west of Edrei, shows the pharaoh presenting an offering to the Egyptian god Amon-Re, who wears a crown with double plumes and holds a *was*-sceptre in his left. He is followed by the goddess Mut, his female counterpart. The particular reason why this stele was set up at Tell aš-Šihab is unknown, because its main inscription is lost[34]. The site should be identified with *Q3-m'-h3-m*, mentioned in Seti I's topographical lists and in Ramesses II's lists dependent on them. According to its place in the lists, this city should be located in Bashan, in the vicinity of Yeno'am[35], distant only 20 km, if we identify the latter with 'Ēn-Nu'ēme[36]. Another Egyptian stele, a basalt monolith more than 2 m high, stands in a Muslim sanctuary at Šayḫ Sa'd, ancient Qarnaim[37], 28 km north of Edrei. This is probably the church in which Egeria saw the famous "Stone of Job" during her pil-

[32] *KTU* 1.108, 1-5.

[33] *KTU* 1.100, 41; 1.107, 17.

[34] İstanbul Arkeoloji Müzeleri, Inv. No. 10942: W.M. MÜLLER, *The Egyptian Monument of Tell esh-Shihab*, in *PEFQ* 1904, p. 78-80; H. GRESSMANN, *Altorientalische Bilder zum Alten Testament*, 2nd ed., Berlin-Leipzig 1927, No. 90; B. PORTER - R.L.B. MOSS, *Topographical Bibliography of Ancient Egyptian Hieroglyphic Texts, Reliefs, and Paintings* VII. *Nubia, the Deserts, and Outside Egypt*, Oxford 1951, p. 383; K.A. KITCHEN, *Ramesside Inscriptions* I, Oxford 1968-75, p. 17:1-6 (the main text is lost); ID., *Ramesside Inscriptions. Translated & Annotated. Translations* I, Oxford 1993, p. 14, No. 5.

[35] S. AḤITUV, *op. cit.* (n. 2), p. 156, cf. p. 16-17, 18, 19.

[36] See here above, p. 61.

[37] Grid ref. 2473/2495. Cf. ABEL, *Géographie* II, p. 413-414; LIPIŃSKI, *Aramaeans*, p. 353, 365-366, 401-402.

Upper fragment of a basalt stele of Seti I from Tell aš-Šihab (İstanbul Arkeoloji Müzeleri, Inv. No. 10942).

grimage to the Holy Land *ca.* 400 A.D. She made the journey to the city of Job, viz. *Carneas* as Qarnaim was called in Latin, and also reports the legend of the discovery of the stele[38], which represents Ramesses II standing in front of a god[39]. This is neither Osiris nor a strange "El-qōnē-Ṣaphon"[40], but possibly "Mightiest Baal on top of

[38] *Itinerarium Egeriae* XVI, 5-7, in *Itineraria et alia geographica* (CCSL 175), Turnhout 1965, p. 57-58.

[39] G. SCHUMACHER, *Die Hiobstein, Sachrat Eijub, im Hauran*, in *ZDPV* 14 (1891), p. 142-147; Graf SCHACK-SCHACKENBURG, *Bemerkungen zu dem Hiobstein*, in *ZDPV* 15 (1892), p. 193-195; J.P. VAN KASTEREN, *Zur Geschichte von Schēch Sa'd*, in *ZDPV* 15 (1892), p. 196-211; A. ERMAN, *Das Denkmal Ramses' II. im Ostjordanland*, in *ZÄS* 31 (1893), p. 100-101; H. GRESSMANN, *op. cit.* (n. 34), No. 103; B. PORTER - R.L.B. MOSS, *op. cit.* (n. 34), p. 383; R. GIVEON, *art. cit.* (n. 2), p. 197-200.

[40] Osiris according to the information reported by K. BAEDEKER, *Palestine et Syrie*, 4th ed., Leipzig 1912, p. 156, but "El-qōnē-Ṣaphon" in the uncertain reading of K.A. KITCHEN, *Ramesside Inscriptons* II, Oxford 1969-79, p. 223, §61, and his interpretation:

the Ṣaphon", as deciphered cautiously by R. Stadelmann[41], who compares the faded hieroglyphs of the inscription with Baal's epithets in Ugaritian myths and legends.

Aqhat, the hero of another Ugaritian legend, was probably buried in a nearby region, since his tomb is located at *Knrt*[42]. The only known toponym *Knrt* is Kinneret on the north-western shore of the Sea of Gallilee, which is called *Kinnerot* in Hebrew. This city, mentioned in Josh. 19, 35, in the great topographical list of Tuthmosis III[43], and in the contemporaneous Papyrus St. Petersburg 1116A[44], was identified with Tell al-'Oreimeh, successfully excavated by A.E. Mader in 1931-1939[45], by V. Fritz in 1982-1985 and 1994-1999[46], and by the Finnish Institute in the Middle East since 2001[47]. The site was certainly well-known in

K.A. KITCHEN, *Ramesside Inscriptons. Translated & Annotated. Notes and Comments* II, Oxford 1999, p. 133-135, §61. Kitchen seems to be unaware of R. Stadelmann's study (cf. next note).

41 R. STADELMANN, *Syrisch-palästinensische Gottheiten in Ägypten* (Probleme der Ägyptologie 5), Leiden 1967, p. 44-46. Cf. W. HELCK, *Die Beziehungen Ägyptens zu Vorderasien im 3. und 2. Jahrtausend v. Chr.* (Ägyptologische Abhandlungen 5), 2nd ed., Wiesbaden 1971, p. 449, n. 28.

42 *KTU* 1.19, III, 41.

43 List I, 34, in J. SIMONS, *Handbook for the Study of Egyptian Topographical Lists relating to Western Asia*, Leiden 1937; S. AḤITUV, *op. cit.* (n. 2), p. 126.

44 Lines 69 and 186, in W. GOLÉNISCHEFF, *Les papyrus hiératiques nos 1115, 1116A et 1116B de l'Ermitage Impérial à Saint-Pétersbourg*, St. Pétersbourg 1913; cf. C. EPSTEIN, *A New Appraisal of Some Lines from a Long-known Papyrus,* in *JEA* 49 (1963), p. 49-56; D. AMIR, *Galilean Cities in the Hieratic Papyrus Leningrad 1116A*, in *Bulletin of the Israel Exploration Society* 27 (1963), p. 276-283 (in Hebrew); S. AḤITUV, *op. cit.* (n. 2), p. 126.

45 The pertinent bibliography has been collected by U. HÜBNER, *Aegyptiaca vom Tell el-'Orēme*, in *Studii Biblici Franciscani Liber Annuus* 36 (1986), p. 253-264, Pls. 5-6 (see p. 254, n. 4). In particular: A.E. MADER, *Die Ausgrabungen auf dem deutschen Besitz Tabgha am See Genesareth,* in *Biblica* 13 (1932), p. 293-297; R. KÖPPEL, *Der Tell 'Orēme und die Ebene Genesareth. Vorbereitende Untersuchungen zu einer Grabung,* in *Biblica* 13 (1932), p. 298-308; A. BEA, *Effossiones 1939 in Tel el-'Oreme factae,* in *Biblica* 29 (1939), p. 306-308, Pls. I-II.

46 V. FRITZ, *Kinneret: Ergebnisse der Ausgrabungen auf dem Tell el-'Orēme am See Gennesaret, 1982-1985* (Abhandlungen des Deutschen Palästina-Vereins 15), Wiesbaden 1990; ID., *Kinneret: Excavations at Tell el-'Oreimeh (Tel Kinrot), 1982-1985 Seasons,* in *Tel Aviv* 20 (1993), p. 187-215; V. FRITZ - D. VIEWEGER, *Vorbericht über die Ausgrabungen in Kinneret (Tell el-'Oreme) 1994 und 1995,* in *ZDPV* 112 (1996), p. 91-99; V. FRITZ, *The Decline of Chinnereth after the Campaign of Tiglath-pileser III,* in *Jahrbuch des Deutschen Evangelischen Instituts für Altertumswissenschaften des Heiligen Landes* 5 (1997), p. 59-66; V. FRITZ - S. MÜNGER, *Vorbericht über die zweite Phase der Ausgrabungen in Kinneret (Tell el-'Orēme) am See Gennesaret, 1994-1999,* in *ZDPV* 118 (2002), p. 2-32.

47 J. PAKKALA - S. MÜNGER - J. ZANGENBERG, *Kinneret Regional Project: Tel Kinrot Excavations* (Proceedings of the Finnish Institute in the Middle East 2), Helsinki 2004. An up-to-date summary of the results of the excavations is provided by S. HAFÞÓRSSON, *op. cit.* (n. 17), p. 218-222.

the Late Bronze Age, since it yielded a fragment of an Egyptian stele of Tuthmosis III or Amenhotep II[48] and a scarab of Queen Tiy[49], the consort of Amenhotep III (1392-1354 B.C.). Although the Ugaritic text reporting the burial of Aqhat contains a difficult word *mdgt* (*KTU* 1.19, III, 41), there is no doubt that the latter designates the tomb. The noun derives most likely from the same root as Arabic *duǧǧat^{un}*, "darkness". The concerned passage means therefore that Daniel "buried him in a dark place at Kinneret", where Aqhat was certainly believed to meet his ancestors.

The legend contains other elements connecting it with the region of Bashan. Daniel is regularly called "man of *Rapi'u*", the singular of "Rephaim", while "the father of the eagles", supposed to be responsible for the disappearance of Aqhat's corpse, bears the name *Hargab*, like a bird in a Babylonian lexical list[50]. Now, *kl ḥbl 'rgb* is the qualification given in Deut. 3, 4.13-14 and I Kings 4, 13 to the realm of Og[51]. *Ḥbl* designates a flock of prey birds in Ugaritic[52] and is never used with a connotation "flock" in other biblical texts. As for the Hebrew spelling *'rgb*, it parallels *hrgb* just like *'dr'y* corresponds to Ugaritic *hdr'y*[53], "Edrei", and like Hebrew *'brk* is equivalent to Phoenician *hbrk*[54], "treasurer", "steward". Therefore, *kl ḥbl 'rgb* must be a phrase borrowed from the legend of Og: it was no longer understood properly when the story of the conquest of Bashan and of the settlement of a half-tribe of Manasseh was amalgamated with the Og legend. The biblical story implies the existence of Manassite settlements in Bashan, which should probably be linked with Jeroboam II's conquests in this area[55]. In earlier times, this region belonged, at least partly, to the kings of Geshur, later to the Aramaean kingdom of Damascus.

[48] W.F. ALBRIGHT - A. ROWE, *A Royal Stele of the New Empire from Galilee*, in *JEA* 14 (1928), p. 281-287 and Pl. I; K. SETHE - W. HELCK, *Urkunden des ägyptischen Altertums* IV. *Urkunden der 18. Dynastie*, Leipzig-Berlin 1906-58 (reprint, 1984), p. 1347. A facsimile of the inscription can be found in G. FASSBECK - S. FORTNER - A. ROTTLOFF - J. ZANGENBERG (eds.), *Leben am See Gennesaret*, Mainz a/R 2003, p. 24, Fig. 38.

[49] U. HÜBNER, *art. cit.* (n. 45), p. 258 with n. 30 and Fig. 1 on p. 264.

[50] *AHw*, p. 67a, *Argabu*.

[51] The passage of I Kings 4, 13 was expanded by the Deuteronomistic Historian or his followers: the original list of governors only mentioned "Ben-Geber in Ramoth-Gilead". Cf. M. NOTH, *Überlieferungsgeschichtliche Studien*, 2nd ed., Tübingen 1957, p. 36, n. 8; ID., *Könige* I (BKAT IX/1), Neukirchen-Vluyn 1968, p. 72.

[52] *KTU* 1.18, IV, 31.

[53] *KTU* 1.108, 3.

[54] LIPIŃSKI, *Itineraria Phoenicia*, p. 124-126, 130-133.

[55] LIPIŃSKI, *Aramaeans*, p. 401-402, and here above, p. 229-230.

Bēth-Maaka

A non-Israelite realm existed in biblical times at the western boundary of Bashan, on the eastern shore of the Sea of Galilee: the kingdom of Geshur, called also Bēth-Maaka, from which the mother of Absalom was native (II Sam. 3, 3). On the east it bordered the land of Taḫaṯ, well known from Pharaonic sources[56] and mentioned in II Sam. 24, 6. This is why Taḥash appears in Gen. 22, 24 as a brother of Maaka. On the south, Bēth-Maaka reached Gilead, connected with Maaka by alleged family links (I Chron. 7, 14-16). The name of Bēth-Maaka parallels the appellations Bēth-David, Bēth-Omri, Bēth-Reḥob, used in the earlier part of the first millennium B.C., and it implies that Maaka was regarded as the founder of the dynasty and of the state.

The Bible is so far the only written source mentioning the kingdom of Geshur. Some authors dealing with the subject nevertheless continue referring to Geshur in the Amarna correspondence[57]. They are obviously not familiar with the text of Amarna letter 256, where an emendation has introduced *Gašuri* about half a century ago. In reality, Mut-Ba'li, the sender of the letter, simply informs Yanḫamu, the Canaanite commissioner of the pharaoh, that he went to rescue the ruler of Ashtarot, "when all the villages of the enemy's land were hostile", *inūma nakrū gabbi ālāni māti gārī*[58]. The foe in question was most likely the enigmatic ^{m}SILIM-^{d}MARDUK, who apparently exercised his power over a number of settlements on the way from Peḥel (Pella), Mut-Ba'li's residence, to Ashtarot, that ^{m}SILIM-^{d}MARDUK "has plundered" (*g*[*á*]*n-ba*). Despite warnings, the absence of *Gašuri* from *EA* 256 will probably take a long time to be recognized by all.

A similar problem concerns Maaka. Dwindling familiarity with literary and historical analysis, also with textual criticism, characterizes some works dealing with biblical archaeology and the narrative parts of the Bible. It happens that even an anthroponym is confounded with a country name, like in the case of Maaka[59], which the writer has already discussed in other publications[60]. One should add here that the Hebrew

[56] S. AḤITUV, *op. cit.* (n. 2), p. 185-187.

[57] Still recently G. FASSBECK *et al.* (eds.), *op. cit.* (n. 48), p. 44 and 52. Despite his cautiousness, even S. HAFÞÓRSSON, *op. cit.* (n. 17), p. 235-236, does not exclude this possibility.

[58] *EA* 256, 22-23; cf. LIPIŃSKI, *Aramaeans*, p. 336, n. 85.

[59] F. FASSBECK *et al.* (eds.), *op. cit.* (n. 48), p. 44-45.

[60] E. LIPIŃSKI, *Aram et Israël du Xe au VIIIe siècle av.n.è.*, in *Acta Antiqua Academiae Scientiarum Hungaricae* 27 (1979), p. 49-102 (see p. 61-63); LIPIŃSKI, *Aramaeans*, p. 334-337.

and Aramaic name *Mky* can by no means be regarded as a variant of *M'kh*[61]. This is an old Canaanite name, which occurs already in the Egyptian Story of Sinuhe (B 219)[62], dating from the times of the Middle Kingdom[63], in the 19th century B.C. The "forearm"-hieroglyph should not be taken there as the phonetic complement of the preceding "owl"-sign *m*, but as a consonantal *'ayin*, and the name must accordingly be read *M'kỉ*. The man in question was a prince of Qedem, a region believed to be situated east or south-east of Byblos. His name should be distinguished from the two mentions of *M-'-k-ỉ-ỉ-ỉ* in the Execration Texts[64], where the "forearm" is probably a phonetic complement of *m*, while the three "flowering reeds" must stand for the Semitic plural *-yū*, followed by the determinative of foreign countries. At any rate, these *M-'-k-ỉ-ỉ-ỉ* are no anthroponyms, as assumed by R. Zadok[65]. The hieratic spelling of the proper name *M'kỉ*, when compared with the final vowel of Hebrew, and the use of *M'kh* as a masculine name indicate that the root is *'kw/y*[66] and that *ma-* is a preformative, forming also nouns of instruments[67]. The toponym *'Akkō* seems to derive from the same root[68], which could mean "to moor" or the like. A proper name based on such a root in the area of the Sea of Galilee would be meaningful.

Three larger archaeological sites near the eastern shores of the Sea of Galilee have probably belonged in the Iron Age to the kingdom of Geshur or Bēth-Maaka, whose inhabitants were designated in the Bible by the hendiadys "Geshurites and Maakathites"[69]: Tel Hadar (Šayḫ Ḫaḍr/Ḫiḍr) in the centre[70], probably the ancient capital *Gṯr*, still mentioned under the later Aramaic form *Gtr* in Gen. 10, 23 and I Chron. 1,

[61] F. Fassbeck *et al.* (eds.), *op. cit.* (n. 48), p. 55, Fig. 87.

[62] H. Ranke, *Die ägyptischen Personennamen* I, Glückstadt 1935, p. 166:13.

[63] W.K. Simpson, *Sinuhe*, in *LÄg* V, Wiesbaden 1984, col. 950-955. See, in particular, A.M. Blackman, *Middle Egyptian Stories*, Bruxelles 1932, p. 1-41, and the translations in *ANET*, p. 18-22, and M. Lichtheim, *Ancient Egyptian Literature* I, Berkeley-Los Angeles 1973, p. 222-235.

[64] G. Posener, *op. cit.* (n. 3), *E* 37 and *E* 62; S. Aḥituv, *op. cit.* (n. 2), p. 132; R. Hannig, *op. cit.* (n. 2), p. 1343.

[65] R. Zadok, *The Pre-Hellenistic Israelite Anthroponomy and Prosopography* (OLA 28), Leuven 1988, p. 83.

[66] Contrary to the opinion of R. Zadok, *op. cit.* (n. 65), p. 83.

[67] Lipiński, *Semitic* §29.22.

[68] E. Lipiński, *Aḫat-milki, reine d'Ugarit, et la guerre du Mukiš*, in *OLP* 12 (1981), p. 79-115 (see p. 111).

[69] Deut. 3, 14; Josh. 12, 5; 13, 11.13.

[70] Grid ref. 2112/2507. Cf. W. Zwickel, *Eisenzeitliche Ortslagen im Ostjordanland* (BTAVO B/81), Wiesbaden 1990, p. 337.

17 among the sons of Aram[71], Bethsaida (et-Tell)[72], 7 km north of Tel Hadar, and Ein Gev, 7 km due south[73].

In Level IV at Tel Hadar[74], excavations uncovered several major public buildings, erected against the reused inner city wall from Late Bronze Age I. About 150 complete vessels were found in a storehouse, as well as fragments of a large Euboean open vase, which can be dated in the mid-10th century B.C. Found broken and burned, it may be older than the numerous Phoenician vessels unearthed in the same context[75]. Level IV can therefore be dated to the 10th century B.C. and its violent destruction pushed down to *ca.* 900 B.C. Since Shoshenq I's topographical list recording his campaigns in Canaan[76] does not mention any site located east of the Sea of Galilee, the destruction of Tel Hadar should be attributed to the Aramaean king Bar-Hadad I, who invaded the area around the Sea of Galilee precisely in that period (I Kings 14, 20)[77]. This would be a remarkable case of agreement between archaeological findings and the biblical narrative. We may assume in fact that Geshur depended *ca.* 900 B.C. from the Kingdom of Israel or rather formed a buffer state between Israel and Damascus, whose king took then advantage of the situation to conquer its territory.

Level VI at et-Tell (Bethsaida) reveals a fortified city, which covered an area of 8 ha[78]. Its excavated storehouse closely resembles that of Tel

[71] E. LIPIŃSKI, *Les Sémites selon Gen 10, 21-30 et 1 Chr 1, 17-23*, in *ZAH* 6 (1993), p. 193-215 (see p. 201-202). The Aramaic form *Tḥt* < *Tḫṯ* occurs similarly in II Sam. 24, 6 to designate the land of Taḫaṯ, well known from Egyptian sources (S. AḤITUV, *op. cit.* [n. 2], p. 185-187) and presented as a brother of Maaka in Gen 22, 24, where the Hebrew spelling *Tḥš* is used.

[72] Grid ref. 2083/2554.

[73] Grid ref. 2102/2435.

[74] M. KOCHAVI, *The Eleventh Century BCE Tripartite Pillar Building at Tel Hadar*, in S. GITIN - A. MAZAR - E. STERN (eds.), *Mediterranean Peoples in Transition, 13th-10th Centuries BCE*, Jerusalem 1998, p. 468-478.

[75] N. COLDSTREAM, *The First Exchange between Euboeans and Phoenicians: Who took the Initiative?*, in S. GITIN - A. MAZAR - E. STERN (eds.), *Mediterranean Peoples in Transition, 13th-10th Centuries BCE*, Jerusalem 1998, p. 353-360 (see p. 357-359); ID., *Some Aegean Reactions to the Chronological Debate in the Southern Levant*, in *Tel Aviv* 30 (2003), p. 247-258 (see p. 252-253).

[76] See here above, p. 99-130.

[77] LIPIŃSKI, *Aramaeans*, p. 372.

[78] R. ARAV - J. ROUSSEAU, *Bethsaïde, ville perdue et retrouvée*, in *RB* 100 (1993), p. 415-428; R. ARAV - R. FREUND (eds.), *Bethsaida: A City by the Northern Shore of the Sea of Galilee* I-II, Kirksville 1995-99; M. BERNETT - O. KEEL, *Mond, Stier und Kult am Stadttor. Die Stele von Betsaida (et-Tell)* (OBO 161), Fribourg-Göttingen 1998; R. ARAV, *Bethsaida*, in *Qadmoniot* 32 (1999), p. 78-91 (in Hebrew); R. ARAV - M. BERNETT, *The* bīt ḫilāni *at Bethsaida*, in *IEJ* 50 (2000), p. 47-81; F. FASSBECK *et al.* (eds.), *op. cit.* (n. 48), p. 52-76; R. ARAV, *Bethsaida*, in *IEJ* 51 (2001), p. 239-246; 55 (2005), p.

Hadar and dates from the 10th century as well. Like Tel Hadar, et-Tell was destroyed by an immense conflagration, possibly in the same circumstances. The palace discovered in Area B belongs to Level V, like the four-chambered city gate in Area A, and its construction goes back to the early 9th century B.C., as shown by the close resemblance of the earliest pottery found in the building to specimens of Hazor Level X[79]. Its erection could therefore be attributed to the reign of Bar-Hadad I. It means that it is probably posterior to the fall of the kingdom of Geshur. Nothing indicates so far that the town was called *Byt-Ṣyd(')* in the 10th-9th centuries B.C., although the proper name *Ṣayyād* is attested already in the 7th century B.C.[80] We shall see below (p. 252) that it may have been called *Lšm*, a place name of northern Canaan mentioned in Josh. 19, 47.

Ein-Gev, the third city of Bēth-Maaka, ought to be identified with the biblical Apheq (*'pq, 'pyq*). Archaeological, geographic, and phonological reasons support this identification. In fact, the Arabic name of the site was Ḫirbet al-'Ašīq. Since postvocalic *p* changes into *f* as early as the late first millennium B.C.[81], while *f* could become *ṯ* (or inversely) in some Syro-Palestinian dialects, as in *ṯum* for *fum*, "mouth"[82], *Maṣyaṯ* or *Maṣyaf*, a city name in Syria, a further change **'Aṯīq* > *'Ašīq* may be easily attributed to the semantic influence of Arabic *'ašīq*, "lover". The baseless location of a fortified city Laruba in the kingdom of Geshur, in *ca.* 838 B.C., and its identification with Ein-Gev do not need do be discussed here[83].

Now, the salvage excavation carried out in 1961 on the mound of Ein-Gev[84] and complemented by the Japanese excavations in 1990-

101-106. The results of these excavations have been summarized by S. HAFÞÓRSSON, *op. cit.* (n. 17), p. 211-218.

79 Following the "high chronology", R. ARAV - M. BERNETT, *art. cit.* (n. 78), date the construction of the palace from the 10th century B.C.

80 *PNA* III/1, Helsinki 2002, p. 1163b.

81 LIPIŃSKI, *Semitic*, §11.1 and 10

82 J. CANTINEAU, *Les parlers arabes du Ḥōrân*, Paris 1946, p. 98.

83 N. NA'AMAN, *In Search of Reality behind the Account of David's Wars with Israel's Neighbours*, in *IEJ* 52 (2002), p. 200-224 (see p. 206-207). It will suffice to notice that the place, where Shalmaneser III erected his royal image in a temple (*RIMA* III, text A.0.102.16, p. 79, lines 160'-161'), was probably called uru*Til*$_4$ *Ma-ru-ba*, with an AŠ-wedge in front of MA. *Til Ma'rūb* should be a Phoenician city, a "Mound of the Sunset", along the route of the Assyrian army on its way back to Assyria.

84 B. MAZAR - A. BIRAN - M. DOTHAN - I. DUNAYEVSKY, *'Ein Gev Excavations in 1961*, in *IEJ* 14 (1964), p. 1-49; M. DOTHAN, *Aphek on the Israel-Aram Border and Aphek on the Amorite Border*, in *Nelson Glueck Memorial Volume* (ErIs 12), Jerusalem 1975, p. 63-65 (in Hebrew); O. BAR-YOSEF - B. MAZAR - M. KOCHAVI, *'En Gev*, in *NEAEHL*, Jerusalem 1993, Vol. II, p. 409-412; M. KOCHAVI, *Land of Geshur - 1991/1992*, in *ESI* 13 (1995), p. 24-28 (see p. 27-28).

1992[85] uncovered a large fortified town, which was in existence during the 10th through the 8th centuries B.C. This town preceded Hippos / Sussita, which was built in Hellenistic times above it, overlooking the Sea of Galilee, and is commonly identified with Qal'at al-Ḥuṣn[86], while Fīq is somewhat further inland[87]. The tell of Ein-Gev is just 6 km down the slope from this place, which preserved the name of Apheq. One might thus imagine that two towns, "Lower Apheq" and "Upper Apheq", existed in the same period. However, no remains older than Late Hellenistic times have been found at Fīq[88], and the nearby Tel Soreg is too small to be identified with biblical Apheq[89]. If the Yarmuk Valley was the battlefield where Bar-Hadad II was defeated by king Jehoash[90], then the mound of Ein-Gev is more suitable for the biblical Apheq than any other site[91]. In the 10th century B.C., it belonged most likely to the kingdom of Geshur.

The kingdom of Geshur or Bēth-Maaka extended for about 40 km north of the Sea of Galilee, as far as Abel-Bēth-Maaka. This town, linked by its name to Geshur, is usually identified with the large mound of Abil al-Qamḥ, but this location is questionable from a toponymic and a historical points of view. The noun *qamḥ*, "wheat", is Aramaic and Arabic, but *'Abīl* is a very old toponym of the whole region. It occurs already in the Egyptian Execration Texts, where it is spelled *'Ibw3m*[92],

[85] M. KOCHAVI, *The Land of Geshur Project,* in *IEJ* 43 (1993), p. 185-190 (see p. 188-190); T. SUGIMOTO, *Iron Age Potteries from Tel En-Gev, Israel: Seasons 1990-1992,* in *Orient* 34 (1999), p. 1-21. Sugimoto's study of the Iron Age pottery from the Japanese excavations was apparently not accessible to S. HAFÞÓRSSON, *op. cit.* (n. 17), p. 207-211.

[86] Grid ref. 211/242: C. EPSTEIN, *Hippos (Sussita),* in *NEAEHL,* Jerusalem 1993, Vol. II, p. 634-636; A. SEGAL - J. MŁYNARCZYK - M. BURDAJEWICZ - M. SCHULER - M. EISENBERG, *Hippos-Sussita: Fifth Season of Excavations (September-October 2004) and Summary of All Five Seasons (2000-2004),* Haifa 2005; A. SEGAL - M. EISENBERG, *Hippos-Sussita of the Decapolis - First Five Years of Excavation,* in *Qadmoniot* 38 (2005), p. 15-29 (in Hebrew).

[87] Grid ref. 216/242.

[88] M. KOCHAVI, *art. cit.* (n. 84), in *NEAEHL,* Jerusalem 1993, Vol. II, p. 412. Cf. W. ZWICKEL, *op. cit.* (n. 70), p. 333.

[89] Grid ref. 2145/2424. This identification was proposed by D. BEN-AMI, *The Battle of Aphek, and Israelite Preventive War within the Borders of the Kingdom of Aram,* in *Eretz Golan* 58 (1981), p. 18-20 (in Hebrew). For the excavations of the site, cf. M. KOCHAVI, *The Land of Geshur Project,* in *IEJ* 39 (1989), p. 1-17 (see p. 6-9); 41 (1991), p. 180-184 (see p. 181); ID., *art. cit.* (n. 84), in *ESI* 13 (1995), p. 28.

[90] I Kings 20, 26-30 and II Kings 13, 17: E. LIPIŃSKI, *art. cit.* (n. 60), p. 80-85; LIPIŃSKI, *Aramaeans*, p. 397-398.

[91] Y. AHARONI, *The Land of the Bible. A Historical Geography*, London 1967, p. 304, n. 60.

[92] G. POSENER, *op. cit.* (n. 3), *E* 47.

and it is attested four times as *'Ibr* in the topographical list of Tuthmosis III[93]. The name *'Abīl* is neither related to Arabic *wābil*, "heavy downpour"[94], nor does it designate a "stream", "canal" or "water course"[95]. It means "meadow", as proposed already by W. Gesenius[96], although the latter did not know the Ethio-Semitic Gurage dialects. They preserve the old Semitic term *abəlle*, "meadow", which was borrowed by neighbouring Cushitic dialects as *abilli* or *abūlla*[97].

The name of Abel-Bēth-Maaka, attested in II Sam. 20, 14-15; I Kings 15, 20, and II Kings 15, 29, is "modernized" in II Chron. 16, 4, where the town is called Abel-mayim, "Meadow of the Waters", "Water-meadow".

Abel-mayim

The name given in II Chron. 16, 4 to Abel-Bēth-Maaka corresponds to Abel-mayin (*'bl myn*) in the Qumrān fragment 4Q213a of the Testament of Levi[98]. The Greek translation in Test. Levi 2, 7 reads 'Αβελμαούλ, 'Εβαλμαούλ or 'Αβελμαούμ. These readings result from a confusion of the letters *wāw* and *yōd*, which were almost identical in the Jewish script of the late Hasmonaean and Herodian periods[99]. The *Vorlage* was undoubtedly *'blmym* or *'blmyn*[100], where a majuscule *N* was read as *Λ*. Another passage of the Greek Test. Levi 6, 1 reveals an error

[93] List I, 15, 90, 92, 99, in J. Simons, *op. cit.* (n. 43); S. Aḥituv, *op. cit.* (n. 2), p. 45-46.

[94] This is the opinion of Abel, *Géographie* II, p. 233.

[95] W.F. Albright, *The Vocalization of the Egyptian Syllabic Orthography*, New Haven 1934, p. 39; L. Koehler - W. Baumgartner, *Lexicon in Veteris Testamenti libros*, Leiden 1958, p. 6b; D.B. Redford, *Contact between Egypt and Jordan in the New Kingdom: Some Comments on Sources*, in A. Hadidi (ed.), *Studies in the History and Archaeology of Jordan* I, Amman 1982, p. 115-119; K.A. Kitchen, *The Egyptian Evidence on Ancient Jordan*, in P. Bieńkowski (ed.), *Early Edom and Moab: The Beginning of the Iron Age in Southern Jordan*, Sheffield 1992, p. 21-34 (see p. 25).

[96] W. Gesenius - F. Buhl, *Hebräisches und aramäisches Handwörterbuch über das Alte Testament*, 17th ed., Leipzig 1915, p. 5b: "Aue". See also F. Zorell, *Lexicon Hebraicum et Aramaicum Veteris Testamenti*, Roma 1957, p. 6b: *pratum, pascuum*.

[97] W. Leslau, *Etymological Dictionary of Gurage* III, Wiesbaden 1979, p. 7-8.

[98] J.T. Milik, *Le Testament de Lévi en araméen. Fragment de la grotte IV de Qumrân*, in *RB* 62 (1955), p. 396-406, Pl. IV, in particular p. 400 and Pl. IV, col. II, 13; J. VanderKam (ed.), *Qumran Cave 4*, XVII (DJD 22), Oxford 1996, p. 30, Frg. 2, line 13.

[99] F.M. Cross, *The Development of the Jewish Scripts*, in G.E. Wright (ed.), *The Bible and the Ancient Near East. Essays in Honor of W.F. Albright*, New York-London 1961, p. 133-202, in particular p. 170, 176, 184.

[100] J.T. Milik, *art. cit.* (n. 98), p. 403.

of the translator, who read *'*byl myn* as if it were *gbl ymyn*[101], and wrote Γεβάλ ἐκ δεξιῶν. Since he calls the nearby mountain Ἄσπις, what is an approximate translation of *Śiryōn*, "breastplate" in Hebrew, the text certainly refers to Mount Hermon[102] and to Abel-mayin: "this is why this mountain is called Siryōn, near Abel-mayin".

This toponym occurred also in the Aramaic text of the Books of Enoch, but was misread by the Greek translator, who took the *mēm* for a *samek*[103]. The original uncial **ΕΒΕΛΣΑΙΝ* was further misread *ΕΒΕΛΣΑΤΑ* by a copyist. An allusion to the place name *'Abīl* still appears in I Enoch 13, 9, where the heavenly Watchers are said to have waited "weeping", in Aramaic *'ābəlīn*, for the message to be brought by Enoch. The place is clearly described in the context and the word-play *'ābəlīn* on *'Abīl-mayīn* confirms the use of the toponym in the narrative[104].

The name of *'Abīl* occurs also in the annals of Tiglath-pileser III, where the place is called *A-bi-il-mes-*⌜*qé*⌝, "Abīl of the well-watered plain". The reading *mes-*⌜*qé*⌝ seems quite clear in G. Smith's copy[105], and the previous suggestions, like ⌜*ak-ka*⌝[106], ⌜*ma-en*⌝[107] or ⌜*šiṭ-ṭi*⌝[108], should be discarded. The determination *mes-qé* transliterates Hebrew *mašqeh*, which means "well-watered plain" in Gen. 13, 10; Ez. 45, 15; Sir. 39, 23. There is no doubt that this is the same place as Abel-mayin, at the border between the kingdoms of Damascus and Bēth-Omri, i.e. Israel. Its mention parallels the biblical list of cities conquered by the Assyrian king, including Abel-Bēth-Maaka (II Kings 15, 29). The cuneiform spelling *A-bi-il* supports the reading *'by*[*l*] in Hazael's stele

[101] Cf. *ibid.*, p. 403, n. 6, and p. 404.

[102] Mount Hermon is called *Śiryōn* in Deut. 3, 9; Ps. 29, 6, possibly in I Chron. 5, 16. The same name occurs in Ugaritic (*KTU* 1.4, VI, 19.21) and in Akkadian, Hittite, and Hurrian texts from Boghazköy; cf. the references in E. LIPIŃSKI, *El's Abode: Mythological Traditions Related to Mount Hermon and the Mountains of Armenia,* in *OLP* 2 (1971), p. 13-69 (see p. 25); G.F. DEL MONTE - J. TISCHLER, *Die Orts- und Gewässernamen der hethitischen Texte* (RGTC 6), Wiesbaden 1978, p. 350-351.

[103] J.T. MILIK, *art. cit.* (n. 98), p. 404 with n. 3; ID., *The Books of Enoch: Aramaic Fragments of Qumrān Cave 4*, Oxford 1976, p. 196. For the confusion of *mēm* with *samek* in a script of the type 1QS and 1QIs[a], see also F.M. CROSS, *art. cit.* (n. 99), p. 149:5.

[104] Cf. J.T. MILIK, *op. cit.* (n. 103), p. 197.

[105] *Tigl. III*, Pls. XLIX and LI, line 6'.

[106] This was the reading of P. ROST, *Die Keilschrifttexte Tiglath-Pilesers III.*, Leipzig 1893, Vol. I, p. 78.

[107] The reading *ma* of the first sign was proposed by H. TADMOR, *The Southern Border of Aram*, in *IEJ* 12 (1962), p. 114-122 (see p. 114, n. 4), followed by LIPIŃSKI, *SAIO* II, p. 85, and *Aramaeans*, p. 289, 358, with interrogation marks.

[108] Proposed as a possible reading in *Tigl. III*, p. 139, although the situation of Abel-ha-Shittim in southern Transjordan (Numb. 33, 49) does not fit the geographical context indicated by the inscription.

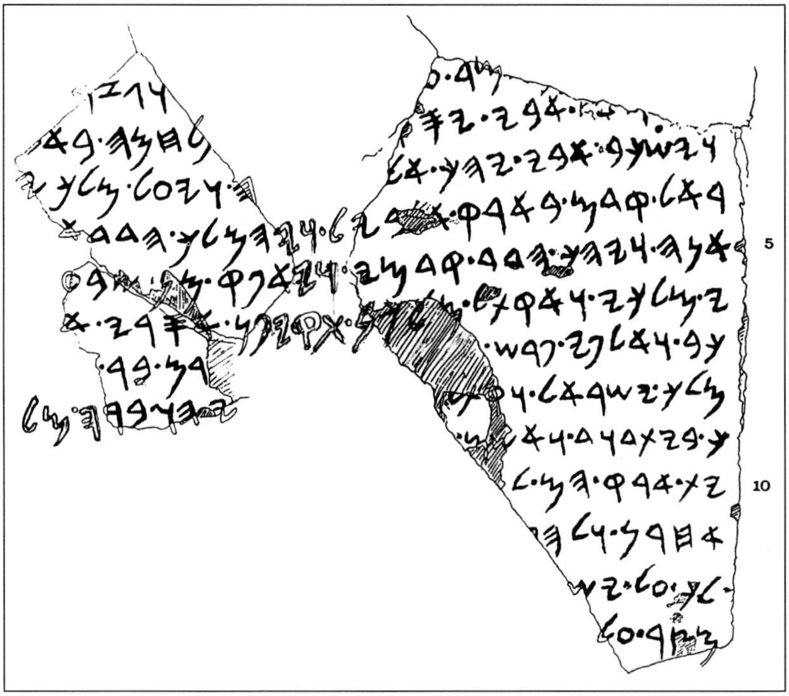

Facsimile of Hazael's inscription from Tell al-Qāḍi
(based on A. Yardeni's copy).

discovered at Tell al-Qāḍi, where *'Abīl* appears twice, without the determination *mayin*[109]. First, when the inscription recalls that Hazael's father "fought for Abīl", [*b'*]*tlḥmh.b'b*[*yl*] (line 2), and further when it records Israel's invasion of the land of Abīl: *wy'l.mlk y*[*š*]*r'l.qdm.b'rq.'by*[*l*], "and the king of Israel had already[110] entered the land of Abīl" (lines 3-4).

'Abīl most likely designates the city where the inscription was found, i.e. Tell al-Qāḍi (Tel Dan), which was identified with biblical Dan by Edward Robinson, in 1838. This mound of about 20 ha, at the foot of

[109] See Lipiński, *Aramaeans*, p. 373-374 and 378-379 with former useful literature. The recent study of the inscription by S. Hafþórsson, *op. cit.* (n. 17), p. 49-65, follows A. Biran's and J. Naveh's reconstruction of the text without noticing that the gap in the middle of the inscription implies the presence of a supplementary letter in several lines (at least in lines 4'-6'), and that there is no space at the end of line 8' for the seven letters of [*Yhwrm.ml*]. Besides, Hafþórsson assumes that both Hazael and his son Bar-Hadad II can be seen as possible authors of the Tell al-Qāḍi inscription, forgetting that Bar-Hadad II reigned almost half a century after Jehoram and Ahaziahu.

[110] The connotation "already" of *qdm* should be compared with *qdm'* in *TAD* IV, D7.8, 4.

which are the most copious sources of the Jordan, is at less than an hour's walk from Banias, at the edge of Mount Hermon, where there is another headwater of the Jordan. Excavation of Tell al-Qāḍi under the direction of A. Biran began in 1966 and is still in progress[111]. Levels of the Bronze Age are believed to confirm the identification of the site with Canaanite Laish, conquered by the Danites, and the bilingual Greek-Aramaic inscription, found in course of excavations, seems to prove that this is Dan, since it is dedicated to the "God who is in the Danite parts", *ΘΕΩΙ ΤΩΙ ΕΝ ΔΑΝΟΙΣ*.

These findings undoubtedly raise the problem of the proper identification of Tell al-Qāḍi and of Abil al-Qamḥ, since Tell al-Qāḍi is a more suitable place for "Abīl of the waters" or "Abīl of the well-watered plain" than any other site. These names hardly suit Abil al-Qamḥ, situated to the east of the Nahr Bareiġīt (Naḥal 'Ayūn). This river, which turns around Abil al-Qamḥ at the bottom of a narrow dale, is no important watercourse. In most years, it is almost dry at the end of the summer[112]. Analogous conditions must have existed in the past, even if the amount of water from the sources in the Merğ 'Ayūn reaching Abil al-Qamḥ was somewhat greater. In consequence, Nahr Bareiġīt would not justify the appellation "Meadow of the Waters", if Abel-Bēth-Maaka had to be identified with Abil al-Qamḥ.

'Αβελμαίν or Βελμαίν occurs also in Judith 4, 4, and some manuscripts have it in Judith 7, 3; 8, 3; 15, 4 as well. However, the context does not indicate its location properly and a confusion with Ibleam, called *Bil'ām* in I Chron. 6, 15, is possible, as generally assumed. The problem of the northern Abel can thus be circumscribed to a relatively small area of the Upper Jordan River and of the territory of the Danites.

Abīl is apparently called by Josephus and his contemporaries 'Αβελ(λ)ανη[113]. This is a form abridged from Abel-mayin and based on 'Αβελαν, which witnesses the well-known tendency of Galilean Aramaic to append a final *n* to undeclinable words ending in a vowel[114]. The

[111] Grid ref. 2112/2949: A. BIRAN, *Dan*, in *NEAEHL*, Jerusalem 1993, Vol. I, p. 323-332. Two volumes of the final reports are already published: A. BIRAN (ed.), *Dan* I-II, Jerusalem 1996-2002. See also the more popular presentation by A. BIRAN, *Biblical Dan*, Jerusalem 1994. The results of these excavations, as far as related to the Iron Age, have been summarized by S. HAFÞÓRSSON, *op. cit.* (n. 17), p. 222-229.

[112] ABEL, *Géographie* I, p. 169.

[113] JOSEPHUS FLAVIUS, *Jewish Antiquities* VIII, 12, 4, §305

[114] H.L. GINSBERG, *Zu den Dialekten des Talmudisch-Hebräischen*, im *MGWJ* 77 (1933), p. 413-429 (see p. 428-429); G. DALMAN, *Grammatik des jüdisch-palästinischen Aramäisch*, 2nd ed., Leipzig 1905, p. 102; E.Y. KUTSCHER, *Studies in Galilean Aramaic*, Ramat-Gan 1976, p. 61.

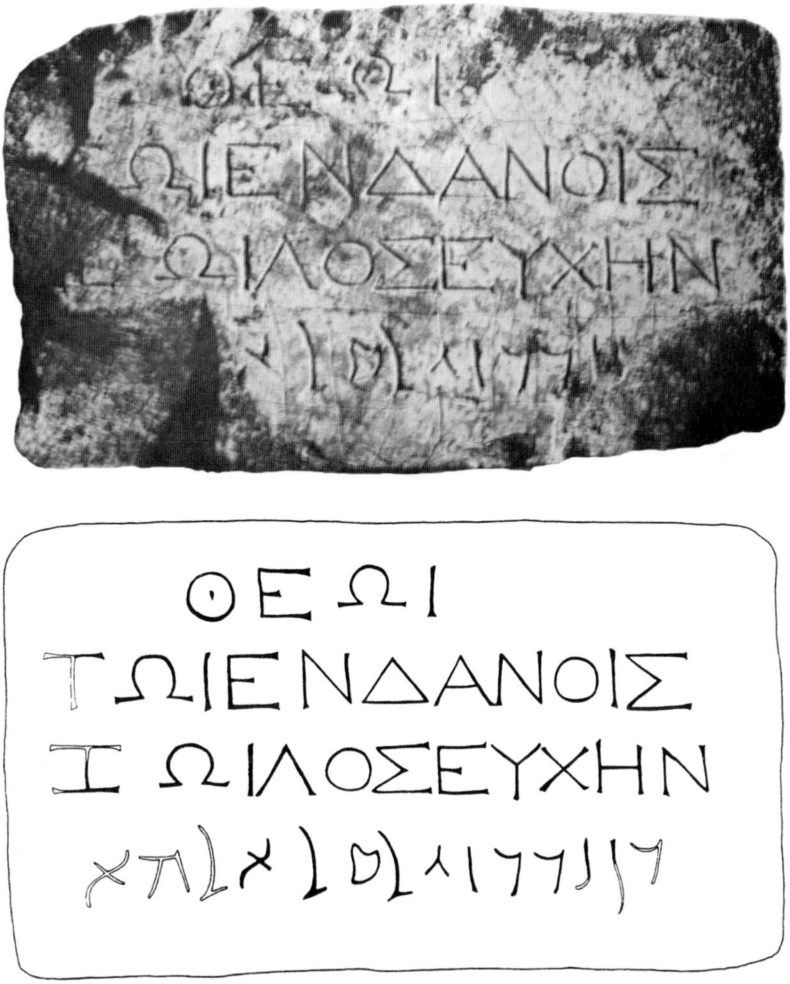

The bilingual inscription from Tell al-Qāḍi
(Excavations of Tel Dan by A. Biran).

shortened toponym was thus *'Abela*. The form with final *n* was preserved until the Middle Ages, since William, archbishop of Tyre in the 12th century, writes that *Lesen Dan*, which he locates at Banias (*Paneas*), "is called *Belinas* in the popular language", *que vulgari appellatione Belinas dicitur*[115]. This is an important record of a local tradition, which preserved the form *Abelan* with apheresis of the initial vowel *A* and the

[115] WILLIAM OF TYRE, *Chronicon* XV, 9, 1, in R.B.C. HUYGENS (ed.), *Guillaume de Tyr: Chronique* (CCCM 63-63A), Turnhout 1986, p. 685.

change of the ending *-an* into *-īn*, appearing in several Palestinian and Lebanese place names, like *'Ibillīn*, *'Ayin 'Attīn*, *Tibnīn*, *Saḫnīn*, *Ḫisfīn*, *Ḥūnīn*, etc[116]. *Bel(l)inas* occurs also in other Mediaeval sources as the name of Banias (*Paneas*)[117], for instance in a document dated *ca.* 1239[118]. Instead, *fluvius Dan*[119] is the name of the Nahr al-Leḏḏān, whose sources lay at the foot of Tell al-Qāḍi.

In another passage of the *Jewish Antiquities*[120], Abel-Bēth-Maaka is called 'Αβελωχεα. This form is not taken from the Septuagint, but implies a personal attempt by Josephus at distinguishing this particular Abel from other Abel or Abila of the region. He probably wrote 'Αβελ-ὀχέα, "Abel-the-Cave", referring to the grotto at Banias dedicated to Pan and the nymphs. The change ο > ω then represents a scribal auditory error. Also the Mishnah mentions the Cave of Paneas[121] and Josephus certainly knew it as well. It means that he was locating Abel-Bēth-Maaka on the skirts of Banias, obviously at Tell al-Qāḍi.

The ancient name of Tell al-Qāḍi does not change anything to the results of the excavation conducted by A. Biran. They have revealed an important city of the Middle Bronze Age and provided evidence of occupation in the 14th-13th centuries with a rich tomb containing Mycenaean pottery. This is a period when a topographical list of Ramesses II from Karnak mentions Abīl[122], while a trace of Egyptian passage is provided by a scarab of Ramesses II, found at Tell al-Qāḍi[123]. The excavation also uncovered remains of a later town represented by houses built of stone and mud-brick, which was deserted *ca.* 1000 B.C. The site was resettled

[116] S. WILD, *Libanesische Ortsnamen* (BTS 9), Beirut 1973, p. 71-96; E. WARDINI, *Lebanese Place-Names* (OLA 120), Leuven 2002, p. 544, reckons 57 place-names in Mount Lebanon and North Lebanon ending in *-īn*, but only 5 with the suffix *-ayn*.

[117] R. RÖHRICHT, *Studien zur mittelalterlichen Geographie und Topographie Syriens*, in *ZDPV* 10 (1887), p. 195-344 (see p. 232, 292).

[118] P. DESCHAMPS, *Étude sur un texte latin énumérant les possessions musulmanes dans le Royaume de Jérusalem vers l'année 1239,* in *Syria* 23 (1942-43), p. 86-104, in particular p. 89: 25 (Latin: *que Bellinas vulgariter appellatur*) and p. 91: 25 (Provençal: *loqual vulgarmen es appelatz Belinas*).

[119] WILLIAM OF TYRE, *Chronicon* XXI, 27, 5, in *op. cit.* (n. 115), p. 1000.

[120] JOSEPHUS FLAVIUS, *Jewish Antiquities* VII, 11, 8, §288.

[121] Mishnah, *Parah* VIII, 11. The cave is mentioned frequently in the Targum Yerushalmi and in midrashic works; cf. G. REEG, *op. cit.* (n. 6), p. 518-520.

[122] List XXIII, 1, in J. SIMONS, *op. cit.* (n. 43); S. AḤITUV, *op. cit.* (n. 2), p. 47; ABEL, *Géographie* II, p. 6. Since this list contains new place names, it is probably based on information at least partly collected during the campaign to Qadesh-on-the-Orontes in Ramesses II's fifth regnal year (1275 B.C.).

[123] A. BIRAN, *Tel Dan*, in *RB* 83 (1976), p. 278-281, Pl. XXXVII (see p. 281 and Pl. XXXVIIb).

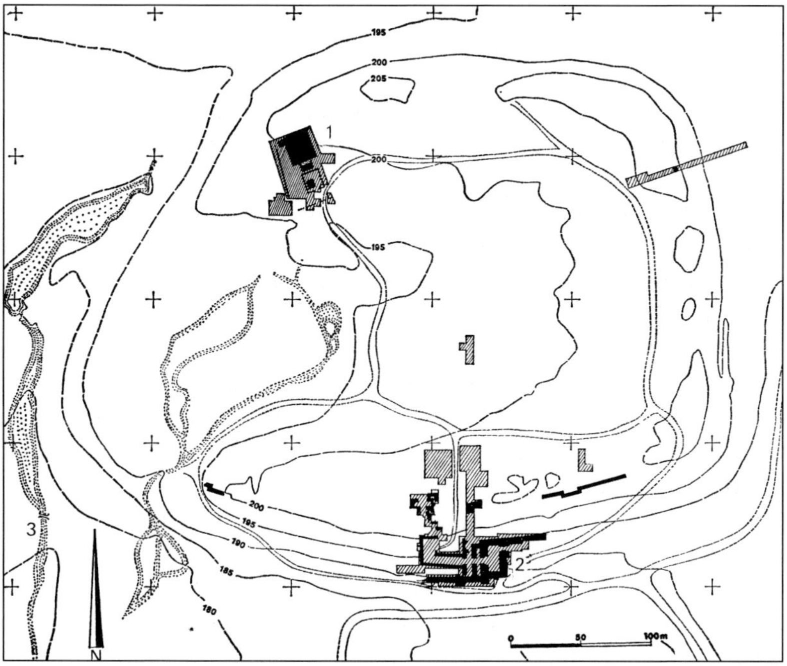

Plan of Tell al-Qāḍi according to A. Biran:
1) Site of the sanctuary; 2) City gate;
3) Nahr al-Leḏḏān.

in the 10th century B.C., which corresponds to the time of the kingdom of Bēth-Maaka. However, Tell al-Qāḍi became again a fortified town only *ca.* 900 B.C. (Stratum IVB?), when the city had become a bone of contention between the kingdoms of Damascus and Israel. After the fall of the dynasty of Omri in 842 B.C., it belonged certainly to Hazael (Stratum IVA). It appears however that the latter's inscription was broken into pieces a few years later, although no traces of an overall destruction of the city were found in the levels of that period. The limited evidence of conflagration may be connected with an Assyrian incursion, possibly in 838 or 837 B.C. In the second quarter of the 8th century B.C., Jeroboam II extended the boundaries of Israel to the north and north-east (II Kings 14, 25.28)[124]. No mention of Abīl is made, but excavations at Tell al-Qāḍi have uncovered traces of important building activities and new fortifications dating from that time.

[124] LIPIŃSKI, *Aramaeans*, p. 384-385 and 401-404.

Possible records of Israelite administration in that period have been found in the excavations of Tell al-Qāḍi and of Bethsaida. The name *Zkryw* stamped on a jar handle unearthed at Tell al-Qāḍi[125] and on another one, discovered in Area C at Bethsaida[126], is Hebrew, but palaeography points at the Aramaic script of the mid-8th century B.C. The seal impressions show no royal symbol and there is no title in the legend, but the discovery of these stamps on jar handles from both sites witnesses some link between Abīl and Bethsaida. Moreover, the presence of two impressions, made with different seals of the same type and with the same legend, indicates an official function connected with them. Potters in different towns apparently had their own stamps bearing Zakaryaw's name that they impressed on jars made for the administration and presumably intended to hold taxes in kind. These seal impressions apparently date from the period preceding the reign of Raṣyān (*ca.* 750-732 B.C.), the last king of Damascus, who probably re-conquered the whole region, but a few years later, in 732 B.C., it was occupied and annexed by Tiglath-pileser III[127]. The latter is said to have exiled the tribe of Dan to Assyria (II Kings 15, 29; cf. Judg. 18, 30), but Danite religious traditions seem to have survived down to the Roman period, especially around the pool created by the source of the Jordan River at the foot of Abel-mayim.

An additional question is raised by the Hellenistic toponyms Antioch and Daphne. Having inflicted a decisive defeat to Scopas at Banias (Paneion)[128], *ca.* 199/8 B.C., Antiochus III gave the city the name of Antioch, which did not cling to it for a long time. This new name appears in writings of Josephus Flavius and in the Talmud Yerushalmi[129]. Hence some authors have assumed that Tell al-Qāḍi, supposed to be the biblical city of Dan, was re-named in such a way[130]. However, Josephus refers twice to the 'Αντίοχου φάραγξ[131], "the Cliff of Anti-

[125] A. BIRAN, *Tel Dan: Biblical Texts and Archaeological Data*, in M.D. COOGAN - J.C. EXUM - L.E. STAGER (eds.), *Scripture and Other Artifacts*, Louisville 1994, p. 1-17 (see p. 15).

[126] R. ARAV, *art. cit.* (n. 78), in *Qadmoniot* 32 (1999), p. 88.

[127] LIPIŃSKI, *Aramaeans*, p. 404-407.

[128] POLYBIUS, *History* XVI, 18, 2; cf. JOSEPHUS FLAVIUS, *Jewish Antiquities* XII, 3, 3, §132.

[129] Talmud Yerushalmi, *Demai* II, 2, 22c:11.

[130] M. AVI-YONAH, *Gazetteer of Roman Palestine* (Qedem 5), Jerusalem 1976, p. 99. For the various opinions, see G. SCHMITT, *Siedlungen Palästinas in griechisch-römischer Zeit* (BTAVO B/93), Wiesbaden 1995, p. 55.

[131] JOSEPHUS FLAVIUS, *The Jewish War* I, 4, 8, §105; *Jewish Antiquities* XIII, 15, 3, §394.

ochus", which can designate either the rock with the grotto dedicated to the Greek god Pan or the site of Qal'at an-Namrūd[132]. Josephus also specifies once that this particular city of Antioch was close to Daphne[133], "Laurel Tree". The site of Daphne is known, because Ḫirbet Dafna, 3 km south of Tell al-Qāḍi and 6 km west of Banias[134], has preserved its ancient name, after which also the Kibbutz Dafnah was called in 1939 by its first settlers from Lithuania and Poland. The site is already mentioned under the name "Wādi ed-Dfila" by Jules de Bertou[135] and it is briefly described by Victor Guérin[136]. It cannot be identified with Tell al-Qāḍi.

Dan

Historical questions concerning Tell al-Qāḍi and Abil al-Qamḥ are related to the problem of the tribe of Dan. Following the biblical narrative, especially in Josh. 19, 40-47 and Judg. 17-18, it has long been accepted that the earlier home of the tribe of Dan was to the west of Judah. However, towns excavated in the area supposedly occupied by Dan before that tribe migrated northward, especially Timnah and Bēth-Shemesh[137], were under strong Philistine influence, judging at least from the pottery, which to a large extent also continues the traditions of the Late Bronze Age. Archaeology suggests thus that in Iron Age I this region was further inhabited by Canaanites, but belonged to the Philistine sphere of influence, despite the biblical accounts. Doubts increase when one notices that the records of the Danite migration to a new site in the far north of Canaan diverge in an essential point, for Josh. 19, 47 calls the settlement Leshem, while Judg. 18 mentions Laish. Leshem is no early form of Laish, with mimation, as it has been accepted since P. de Lagarde[138], since the Middle-Bronze toponym is known to have

[132] A. SCHLATTER, *Zur Topographie und Geschichte Palästinas*, Stuttgart 1893, p. 314-320, rightly concluded that Antioch must be near Banias.

[133] JOSEPHUS FLAVIUS, *Jewish Antiquities* XVII, 2, 1, §24. Cf. *Dapnē* in the Targum Yerushalmi I to Numb. 34, 11.

[134] Grid ref. 209/292: G. SCHMITT, *op. cit.* (n. 130), p. 131.

[135] J. DE BERTOU, *Voyage depuis les sources du Jourdain jusqu'à la Mer Rouge,* in *Bulletin de la Société de Géographie* 1838, p. 31 of the offprint.

[136] V. GUÉRIN, *Description géographique, historique et archéologique de la Palestine* III/2. *Galilée*, Paris 1880, p. 342-344.

[137] See here above, p. 56.

[138] P. DE LAGARDE, *Übersicht über die im Aramäischen, Arabischen und Hebräischen übliche Bildung der Nomina*, Göttingen 1889, p. 20, 190; G. KAMPFFMEYER, *Südarabisches*, in *ZDMG* 54 (1900), p. 621-660 (see p. 631).

been *Lawišum*[139]. Neither is there any evidence that Leshem is a scribal error, a corrupt spelling of Laish, as A. Malamat assumed[140]. The insertion of Judg. 17-18 in the Deuteronomistic History did simply non affect the name of Leshem in Josh. 19, 47. Manuscripts of the Septuagint only witness a variant spelling Λασεν or Λεσεν.

Both places are supposed to have been named Dan after the conquest. As the wording of the concerned clauses is identical in both passages (Josh. 19, 47b; Judg. 18, 28b), they can be attributed to the post-Deuteronomistic redactor, although the two place names are different, and one should not attempt at identifying them at any cost.

The name *Lšm* appears now on a potsherd from the 8th century B.C., found at Bethsaida. It is followed by the Egyptian sign *'anḫ*[141], which is often represented in the hand of a deity[142]. It has obviously a religious significance, the more so because the potsherd comes from a cultic environment. The inscription can hardly be understood as "for the name of ...": it must refer to a holy place at Leshem. This kind of inscription, so far unique, can be compared with the Judaean seal impressions on jar handles, which consist of a place name and a symbol, viz. a winged sun disc. The question is whether *Lšm* can be the ancient name of Bethsaida and the *'anḫ* sign an indication of one of its civic cultic sites, to which the vessel was given or simply belonged. There are so far no contra-indications.

The tradition reported in Josh. 19, 47 may have attributed the destruction of Level VI at et-Tell to the Danites, whether they were really responsible for it or not. In any case, the change of the city name in Dan is a redactional feature. The spelling *Lšm* may hide an ancient **Lṯm*, in which case the toponym could match the Egyptian place name *Rṯnw*, certainly in Canaan or in the Beqa' Valley[143]. In fact, the *ṯ* of the toponym in the Story of Sinuhe, which goes back to the 19th century B.C., must still indicate the sound *č*, close to Semitic *ṯ*, not *s* like in Neo-Egyptian texts. As for the use of *n* in stead of *m*, this can be one of the numerous cases of the *n/m* interchange in the Egyptian spelling, espe-

[139] See here below, p. 256-257.

[140] A. MALAMAT, *History of Biblical Israel*, Leiden 2001, p. 184.

[141] See lately R. ARAV, *Et-Tell / Betsaida*, in G. FASSBECK *et al.* (eds.), *op. cit.* (n. 48), p. 52-69, in particular p. 68-69 with Fig. 115.

[142] An example is provided by the Melqart stele from Northern Syria; cf. *ANEP*, No. 499.

[143] R. HANNIG, *op. cit.* (n. 2), p. 1361. The place name is missing in S. AḤITUV, *op. cit.* (n. 2).

cially in proper names and other Semitic words[144]. The place name might also occur as *Rwṯn* or *Rtn* in the topographical lists of Tuthmosis III (No. 64). Egyptian texts distinguish "Upper" or "Southern" *Rṯnw* and "Lower" or "Northern" *Rṯnw*. The exact meaning of this distinction cannot be established so far from a geographic point of view.

The case of Laish is different, because the city is located precisely "in the valley leading to Bēth-Reḥob", i.e. to the Beqaʿ Valley[145]. The text obviously refers to the southern gateway of the Beqaʿ Valley, on the international highway, which runs northward from Hazor to the important mound of Abil al-Qamḥ, to ʿIyyōn and the Lebanese Beqaʿ. Amenhotep II followed it up to the Orontes River and Ramesses II took the same route on his campaign against Qadesh. This was also a convenient entry for invading Canaan or Israel from the north. Bar-Hadad I, king of Damascus, proceeding westward from his capital through Rashayya, followed this route when he conquered ʿIyyōn, Dan, Abel-Bēth-Maaka (I Kings 15, 20). The biblical text describing this invasion from the north and listing Dan after ʿIyyōn and before Abel-Bēth-Maaka seems to place Dan precisely at the site of Abil al-Qamḥ. Dan occurs also in the itinerary of Joab's men conducting the Davidic census. They went to Gilead, Bashan, and thereafter followed the route of Dan and Yaʿan[146], in the direction of Sidon: "they came to Gilead and to the land of Taḫṯim[147], to Ḥadashay[148], and they came to Dan, Yaʿan[149], and so round towards Sidon" (II Sam. 24, 6)[150]. Dan is no longer mentioned in II Kings 15, 29,

[144] For a discussion of the *m/n* interchange in Egyptian, see K. SETHE, *Das ägyptische Verbum in Altägyptischen, Neuägyptischen und Koptischen* I, Leipzig 1899, p. 127, §220; A. ERMAN, *Ägyptische Grammatik*, Berlin 1928, §123; G. FECHT, *Wortakzent und Silbenstruktur. Untersuchungen zur Geschichte der ägyptischen Sprache*, Glückstadt 1960, p. 175, §360; V.I. DAVIS, *Syntax of the Negative Particles* bw *and* bn *in Late Egyptian*, Munich 1973, Pl. 5; J. OSING, *Die Nominalbildung des Ägyptischen* II, Mainz a/R 1976, p. 689; R.J. DEMARÉE, *A Letter of Reproach*, in E. TEETER - J. LARSON (eds.), *Gold of Praise. Studies on Ancient Egypt in Honor of Edward F. Wente*, Chicago 1999, p. 75-82 (see p. 79, n. *s*).

[145] E. LIPIŃSKI, *art. cit.* (n. 60), p. 60-68; ID., *Aramaeans*, p. 319-345.

[146] Perhaps Meğdel Yūn, east of Sidon: DUSSAUD, *Topographie*, Map III, A, 3.

[147] *Tḥš* in Gen. 22, 24; *Táḫ-ši* in *EA* 189, rev., line 12; *Tḫšy* in Egyptian (S. AḤITUV, *op. cit.* [n. 2], p. 185-187).

[148] Greek Αδασαι. One can compare this place name with Dayr al-ʿAdas, north of Ṣanamein: DUSSAUD, *Topographie*, Map II, A, 1.

[149] *Yʿn* is usually corrected in *ʿyn*, following E. KLOSTERMANN, *Die Bücher Samuelis und der Könige* (Kurzgefasster Kommentar zu den Heiligen Schriften), Nördlingen 1887, but *Yʿn* occurs also in *Papyrus Anastasi* I, 22, 1 (S. AḤITUV, *op. cit.* [n. 2], p. 196). This does not mean that the papyrus refers to the same place.

[150] Most translations of this passage disregard the Hebrew text, which does not seem to be corrupt.

where Tiglath-pileser III is said to have taken 'Iyyōn, Abel-Bēth-Maaka, and Hazor.

Deuteronomistic History obviously collected various traditions, which referred to different places, like Leshem and Laish, and perhaps to distinct cult sites, like those of the bull worship, the introduction of which later tradition ascribed to Jeroboam I (I Kings 12, 28-30), and of Micha's graven image, which the Danites set up as symbol of their cult (Judg. 18, 30-31). However, Micha's silver idol must have been a bull statuette in the mind of the redactor who connected Micha's story with the legend of the Danite settlement[151]. Further association of the local cult with a priesthood tracing its descent from Moses (Judg. 18, 30-31) reminds us of an exegesis of Ex. 32, which assumes that the original account — a *hagios logos* of a bull shrine — made Moses himself, not Aaron, the originator of the cult[152], and explained that this was the divinely communicated form under which Yahwe wished to be worshipped.

The criticism of the Danite cult, obvious in the actual account of Judg. 17-18, was dated recently from exilic[153] or postexilic times, about 500-300 B.C.[154] It does not need to be directed only against practices from the past, since the bull cult seems to have continued among Danites down to Hellenistic and Roman times. The Book of Jubilees, whose original is dated now from the 2nd century B.C., gives to Dan's wife the name of Egla (Jub. 34, 20), "Heifer", and a bull statuette from the late Hellenistic or early Roman periods was found in 1975 at Tell al-Qāḍi, in Area T, where stood the sanctuary built next to the main Jordan's spring[155]. The bilingual dedication to the unnamed deity, worshipped "in

[151] For the redactional connection of two independent themes, see H.-D. NEEF, *Michas Kult und Jahwes Gebot: Jdc 17, 1-18, 31*, in *ZAW* 116 (2004), p. 206-222.

[152] H. VALENTIN, *Aaron* (OBO 18), Freiburg/Schweiz-Göttingen 1978, p. 299-302. The suspended *n* in the masoretic text of Judg. 18, 30 aims likewise at replacing Moses' name by Manasseh: E. MARTÍN CONTRERAS, *Continuity of the Tradition: Masorah with Midrashic Explanations*, in *JSS* 50 (2005), p. 329-339 (see p. 333-334).

[153] H.-D. NEEF, *art. cit.* (n. 151), especially p. 220-221.

[154] U.F.W. BAUER, *"Warum nur übertretet ihr SEIN Geheiss!" Eine synchrone Exegese der Anti-Erzählung von Richter 17-18* (Beiträge zur Erforschung des Alten Testaments 45), Frankfurt a/M-Bern 1998, in particular p. 436-443. Idiosyncrasy burdens this dating when one assumes that Judg. 17-18 was inspired by the Phocaean story of the founding of Marseille, reported by STRABO, *Geography* IV, 1, 4. This idea, put forward by N. NA'AMAN, *The Danite Campaign Northward (Judges xvii-xviii) and the Migration of the Phocaeans to Massilia (Strabo iv 1, 4)*, in *Vetus Testamentum* 55 (2005), p. 47-60, betrays a poor acquaintance with literary genres, in particular the widespread genre of Foundation Stories of cities and sanctuaries.

[155] A. BIRAN, *Tel Dan*, in *RB* 83 (1976), p. 278-281 (see p. 281). The criticism of the Danite cult is also manifest in Am. 8, 14, which cannot be dated easily: H.M. BARSTAD, *The Religious Polemics of Amos* (VTS 34), Leiden 1984, p. 185-191, with former literature.

the Danite parts", was found in 1976 in the same area, and Josephus Flavius still refers to the "bull sanctuary" at the headwaters of the Jordan[156]. The cult continued at this site until the 4th century A.D. I Kings 12, 28-30 certainly referred to the same holy place, the location of which only increases the problem of the identification of *'Abīl* and of Dan, which Talmudic and mediaeval texts even locate at Banias / Paneas. It is doubtful whether the worship of Pan at Banias played a role here. Pan was usually represented as more or less bestial in shape, generally having horns, legs, and ears of a goat. Did his aspect suggest a relation to the Danite bull-cult? The sanctuary of Pan at Banias has not been erected before the 3rd century B.C., but it was used until the 5th century A.D.[157], like the temple at the headwater of the Jordan River at Tell al-Qāḍi. At any rate, one should be aware that the accounts of Judg. 17-18 and the notice of I Kings 12, 28-30 do not belong to the earliest references to Dan.

The earliest Hebrew texts bringing some information about the tribe of Dan are the Blessing of Moses (Deut. 33, 22) and the Song of Deborah (Judg. 5, 17)[158]. Both are remarkable poetic compositions, which preserve old records over Dan's origins and area of settlement. The Blessing of Moses reveals that the Danites came from Bashan, which is mentioned in the verse:

> "Dan is a lion's whelp,
> that leaps forth from Bashan".

The poet has the origin of the Danites in his mind and alludes at their incursions and final settlement to the west of the mountain ranges and oak forests of Bashan. This is confirmed by the Song of Deborah, whose sarcastic question refers to the dwellings of the Danites. They were living in the marches of the Ḥuleh Lake and earned their livelihood on boats, while fishing and hunting the water fauna:

> "And Dan, why does he live on ships?"

We may assume that their original settlement in the area of the lake and its swamps consisted of bog or lakeshore dwellings, perhaps similar

[156] JOSEPHUS FLAVIUS, *The Jewish War* IV, 1, 1, §3.

[157] A.M. BERLIN, *The Archaeology of Ritual: The Sanctuary of Pan at Banias / Caesarea Philippi,* in *BASOR* 315 (1999), p. 27-45.

[158] The original form of the Song is rightly dated in the 11th century B.C. by H.-D. NEEF, *Deboraerzählung und Deboralied. Studien zu Jdc 5, 1-5, 31,* presented by W. THIEL in *OLZ* 99 (2004), col. 617-619. The erroneous tracks followed by M. WALTISBERG, *Zum Alter der Sprache des Deboraliedes 5*,* in *ZAH* 12 (1999), p. 218-232, lead him to the conclusion that the Song was composed between the 5th and the 3rd centuries B.C.!

in some cases to the structures described by Herodotus, who tells us in the 5th century B.C. that dwelling platforms were erected at Lake Prasias, in Thracia[159]. Permanent and seasonal water bodies covered considerable parts of the Ḥuleh Valley even in the Roman and Byzantine periods, leaving only its circumference for human habitation. Seasonal inundations and water-logged grounds affected the land cultivation in a large area, permitting regular farming on a fraction of the valley's total expanse[160], especially in the north, around the impressive mound of Abil al-Qamḥ, "the Meadow of the Wheat"[161].

Abil al-Qamḥ

The general physiognomy of the Abil al-Qamḥ shows a powerfully walled Bronze Age city, which covers a superficies of about 18 ha. The mound is well over 800 m long from the south to the north and 200-250 m broad. Its steep slopes rise more than 15 m above the surrounding terrain and its small acropolis, about 1.5 ha in extent, stands another 10 m above the lower city. Pottery found on the surface of the tell dates from the Early Bronze Age and later periods[162]. This site is surrounded by excellent farming lands and gets up to 820 mm of annual rainfall. It is located at the crossroads of two international highways, the north-south road from the Beqa' Valley to Hazor and the east-west road from Damascus to Tyre.

There is a striking parallelism between the results of W.G. Dever's survey of the mound in 1973[163] and the information provided by inscriptions and literary sources. In the Middle Bronze Age, major city defences and pottery reveal an important city, which is mentioned in the Execration Texts, the Mari tablets, and the topographical list of Tuthmosis III, always assuming that this is Laish. The spellings *3wśỉ* in the Execration Texts and *Rwś* in the topographical list[164] suggest reading *La-wi-*

[159] HERODOTUS, *History* V, 16.

[160] Y. KARMON, *The Huleh Valley,* in *IEJ* 3 (1953), p. 4-25; ID., *The Northern Hula Valley: Its Natural and Cultural Landscape*, Jerusalem 1957 (in Hebrew).

[161] Grid ref. 2045/2960.

[162] The site was surveyed in 1973 by W.G. DEVER, *'Abel-Beth-Ma'acah: "Northern Gateway of Ancient Israel"*, in L.T. GERATY - L.G. HERR (eds.*), The Archaeology of Jordan and Other Studies Presented to S.H. Horn*, Berrien Springs 1986, p. 207-222. For older literature see M. AVI-YONAH, *Abel-Beth-Maacah,* in *Encyclopædia Judaica* 2, Jerusalem 1971, col. 60-61.

[163] W.G. DEVER, *art. cit.* (n. 162), p. 220-221.

[164] S. AḤITUV, *op. cit.* (n. 2), p. 130.

Boat of the 1st century B.C. or A.D.
excavated near the Kibbutz Ginosar on the Sea of Galilee.

*ši-im*ki (genitive) at least on one of the Mari tablets, where this toponym appears between Muzunnum and Hazor[165]. Hazor is well known and

[165] G. Dossin, *La route de l'étain en Mésopotamie au temps de Zimri-Lim*, in *RA* 64 (1970), p. 97-106 (see p. 98, line 21). The text was published again in *ARMT* XXIII, Paris 1984, No. 556. The same volume contains the publication of another tablet, which mentions a city bearing the same name (*ARMT* XXIII, 535, IV, 27), but situated between

Muzunnum is currently identified with Mušunipa, about 30 km south-west of Aleppo[166]. However, the Semitic name Sumu-Eraḫ of the ruler of Muzunnum and the perfect correspondence of the possible reading *Mu-ṣú-un-ni-im* (genitive) with *M-ḏ-n* in the topographical list of Tuthmosis III[167] and *M-ḏ3-w-n* in Amenhotep III's list found at Thebes[168] suggest distinguishing the two places and situating Muṣunnum in southern Syria or in the Beqa' Valley[169]. The mention of Muṣunnum on another Mari tablet seems to favour such a location, as the proper names appearing there are Semitic as well[170]. Instead, the *Mu-šu-ni* or *Mu-šu-un-ni-e* of the Alalakh tablets[171] may be identified with Mušunipa.

There is a probable gap in the occupation of Abil al-Qamḥ after the campaigns of Tuthmosis III, and the revival during the Amarna age does not seem to have given the city a semi-independent status with a local ruler. It was a relatively unimportant settlement in Iron Age I, what would explain its seizure by the tribe of Dan according to one of the sources of Judg. 17-18. The city apparently developed in the late 10th century B.C., justifying its mention in II Sam. 24, 6 and in the notice of I Kings 15, 20 and II Chron. 16, 4, listing cities conquered by Bar-Hadad I *ca.* 900 B.C. This list seems to follow a route: 'Iyyōn, Dan, Abel-Bēth-Maaka / Abel-mayim. 'Iyyōn has been located at Tell Dibbīn, between the Nahr al-Liṭāni and the Nahr al-Ḥaṣbāni. Abil al-Qamḥ, situated 9 km south of Tell Dibbīn, should be the site of Dan, ancient Laish, which was a fortified city according to II Sam. 20, 14. Abel-Bēth-Maaka / Abel-mayim, mentioned next, must then correspond to Tell al-

Aleppo and Ugarit. A. MALAMAT, *Mari and the Early Israelite Experience*, Oxford 1989, p. 58, distinguishes the two cities, because one of them is connected with Hazor. One should add that these toponyms mean "Lion" and can thus appear in various regions. A third city with such a name occurs probably in *ARMT* VII, 180, II, 35: *La-úš* (*Lawuš*), but the signs are somewhat uncertain.

[166] LIPIŃSKI, *Aramaeans*, p. 249-250, 297-298, with former literature. Add: J.A. BELMONTE MARÍN, *Die Orts- und Gewässernamen der Texte aus Syrien im 2. Jt. v. Chr.* (RGTC 12/2), Wiesbaden 2001, p. 202.

[167] List I, 20, in J. SIMONS, *op. cit.* (n. 43).

[168] E. EDEL, *op. cit.* (n. 4), BN, left 5, p. 16-17; cf. S. AḤITUV, *op. cit.* (n. 2), p. 145.

[169] A. MALAMAT, *Syro-Palestinian Destinations in a Mari Tin Inventory*, in *IEJ* 21 (1971), p. 31-38 (see p. 34-35). A location in this area was already assumed by G. DOSSIN, *art. cit.* (n. 165), p. 102, while Y. AHARONI, *op. cit.* (n. 91), p. 146, located *M-ḏ-n* (No. 20) in the Damascus region.

[170] H. LIMET, *Textes administratifs relatifs aux métaux* (ARMT XXV), No. 134, rev., line 4.

[171] D.J. WISEMAN, *The Alalakh Tablets*, London 1953, Nos. 139, 1 and 343, 5. Cf. M. DIETRICH - O. LORETZ, *Die soziale Struktur von Alalaḫ und Ugarit* (II), in *Die Welt des Orients* 5 (1969-70), p. 57-93 (see p. 66-67, No. 11); J.A. BELMONTE MARÍN, *op. cit.* (n. 166), p. 201.

Qāḍi, 8 km east of Abil al-Qamḥ, as the crow flies. The same route was followed by Tiglath-pileser III, but the text of II Kings 15, 29 does not mention Dan.

A severe conflagration in the mid-9th century B.C. is revealed by the partly restorable store-jar of unusual type, recovered at the site from a tick layer of ash and debris, visible in the cut for the modern road. The date is provided by a perfect parallelism between the jar and vessels from Hazor Stratum IX[172]. The destruction might be linked with an Assyrian incursion, as in 838 or 837 B.C.[173] This event marked a new decline of the town, but surface surveys indicate that the site has considerable 8th-century pottery, especially in the upper city, which seems to be a citadel, possibly built by Jeroboam II[174]. Instead, few potsherds from the Roman period were found at the site, probably a hamlet, which should correspond to the Talmudic *Kpr Dn* and to the village of Dan, originally recorded by Eusebius at a distance of 14 miles west of Paneas, as we shall see below. There are virtually no potsherds from the Byzantine period, while considerable fine painted and glazed ware appears in Arabic times, when a larger settlement was obviously established on the mound, eventually called *Cafardani*.

When Josephus refers to the city of Dan in the context of Judg. 17-18, he localizes it "not far from Mount Lebanon and from the sources of Lesser Jordan, in front of a great valley, at one day journey from Sidon"[175]. He obviously thinks of the high plateau bordered on the west by the steep slopes of Mount Lebanon and on the east by the headwaters of the Jordan River, looking northward to the Beqa' Valley. This site corresponds to the mound of Abil al-Qamḥ. In another passage, Josephus says that Dan "is close to the sources of the Lesser Jordan"[176], but he apparently identifies the place with the Bull Shrine. Elsewhere, he simply mentions Dan between 'Iyyōn and Abelane[177], as he calls the biblical Abel-Bēth-Maaka (I Kings 15, 20).

The first passage of the *Jewish Antiquities* seems to distinguish the city of Dan from the mighty Jordan's source called "Dan" and helps understanding the account of *Genesis Apocryphon* XXII, 4-10 about Abram chasing the kings who have captured Lot and set out for their country:

[172] W.G. DEVER, *art. cit.* (n. 162), p. 215.
[173] LIPIŃSKI, *Aramaeans*, p. 384-385, and here above, p. 249.
[174] W.G. DEVER, *art. cit.* (n. 162), p. 214-215, 220-221.
[175] JOSEPHUS FLAVIUS, *Jewish Antiquities* V, 3, 1, §178.
[176] *Ibid.*, VIII, 8, 4, §226.
[177] *Ibid.*, VIII, 12, 4, §305.

"The kings had taken the way of the Great Valley (Jordan Valley) towards their country, making slaves, plundering, destroying, killing, and heading for the country of Damascus. And Abram wept for Lot, his brother's son. Then Abram summoned all his courage, rose up, and chose among his servants three hundred and eighteen men drilled in the fight, and Arnam, Eshcol, and Mamre set out with him. He went in pursuit of them until he reached Dan and found them encamped in the Valley of Dan (*Bq't Dn*). He fell upon them by night from all four sides, slaughtered some of them during the night, and pursued them, as all of them went fleeing before him as far as Helbon, which is situated to the north of Damascus (25 km)".

The Beqa' of Dan leading to Helbon is the southern part of the Beqa' Valley, the entrance to which is watched by Abil al-Qamḥ. It appears therefore that this was the location of Dan in the 1st century B.C., when 1QApGen was written.

After the *Genesis Apocryphon* and the *Jewish Antiquities* we must wait until Eusebius of Caesarea to get a concrete information about a village called Dan or Kfar Dan. Procopius of Gaza has preserved extracts from Eusebius' lost work 'Εβραϊκαὶ ἑρμενεῖαι and he also had knowledge of a description of Palestine by Eusebius, who regarded these compositions as a preparation of his *Onomasticon*, completed before 324 A.D. Procopius' commentary to the *Octateuch* in the *Codex Monacensis gr. 358* provides a quotation from Eusebius' text, which refers to "the village called Dan, at 14 miles from Paneas on the road to Tyre"[178]. This can be a reference to *Kpr Dn*, mentioned in the treatise *Demai* II, 2, 22c of the Talmud Yerushalmi[179]. Dealing with the question of produce not certainly tithed, R. Yose of Kfar Dan inquires about the practice followed at Bēth-shan, apparently quite distant from his residence. As the same section of the tractate *Demai* also mentions Paneas, we are probably in northern Palestine. If R. Yose is Yose the Galilean, the reference to Kfar Dan could date from the beginning of the 2nd century A.D. The 14 Roman miles of Eusebius' text correspond in fact to the distance from Banias to Abil al-Qamḥ by the ancient road and the Ǧisr al-Ġaǧar: the time of walking a horse about 3½ hours[180]. It is probable therefore that *Kpr Dn* was the name of Abil al-Qamḥ in Talmudic times.

[178] J.P. MIGNE, *Patrologia Graeca* 87, col. 333A, quoted by E. KLOSTERMANN, *op. cit.* (n. 11), p. 76.

[179] G. REEG, *op. cit.* (n. 6), p. 338-339, records the identifications of *Kpr Dn* with Dan and Banias. They are deprived of any concrete basis and contradict Eusebius' text, preserved by Procopius of Gaza.

[180] K. BAEDEKER, *op. cit.* (n. 40), p. 259-260.

The village is apparently attested at the time of the Crusades as *Cafardani*. This place was identified with Kfar Dūnīn, on the road to Tyre, 27 km west of Banias as the crow flies[181]. But Kfar Dūnīn hardly derives from Kfar Dan, and S. Wild rightly proposes two different explanations of the toponym[182]: *Dūnīn* may go back to **Adūnīn* < 'Αδωνεῖον, with the frequent loss of the initial vowel, or it witnesses an assimilation *l* > *n* in the word *dawlīn*, "buckets" or "noria" in Jewish Aramaic[183]. Mediaeval *Cafardani*, located in the hinterland of Tyre, might thus be built at the site of the village recorded by Eusebius *ca.* 300 A.D. It was controlled in the Crusader period by the nearby *Castrum Novum* or *Chastiau Neuf / Castel Nau*, destroyed by Nūr ad-Dīn in 1167, but rebuilt in 1178. It is identified with Qal'at Ḥūnīn (Margaliot Fortress, alt. 900 m)[184].

Eusebius changed his original notice in the *Onomasticon*, no longer referring to *Kpr Dn*, but taking the Dan source of the Jordan River into account. He was probably influenced by the Talmudic interpretation of "Jordan" as a combination of the names of the river's two sources: *Yə'ōr*, "stream", actually an Egyptian loanword, and *Dan*, the name of the second source. For this purpose, Eusebius simply changed the "14 miles" into "4 miles" (p. 76:7), i.e. 6 km. In reality, there are only 2.5 Roman miles by the ancient road from Banias to the source of Nahr al-Leḏḏān, at the foot of Tell al-Qāḍi (Tel Dan). Except for this small change, Eusebius kept the original wording of the notice, which mentions a village. This does not match the archaeological findings of Tell al-Qāḍi: they include a Roman fountain house and a sanctuary in use until the mid-4th century A.D., later even a Byzantine church[185].

St. Jerome, who never visited this region, did not correct the notice in his translation of the *Onomasticon*, written between 387 and 390 A.D. On the contrary, he used *uiculus*, "small village" in his translation[186] and

[181] Grid ref. 117/145 of the map 1: 20,000 published by the Direction des Affaires Géographiques, Beyrouth 1970. R. RÖHRICHT, *art. cit.* (n. 117), does not provide any argument in favour of his identification of *Cafardani* and similar toponyms with Kfar Dūnīn; cf. p. 265, n. 6; p. 286, n. 7; p. 294, n. 11.

[182] S. WILD, *op. cit.* (n. 116), p. 88.

[183] J. LEVY, *Neuhebräisches und chaldäisches Wörterbuch über die Talmudim und Midraschim* I, Leipzig 1876, p. 383; JASTROW, p. 283-284.

[184] Grid ref. 20110/29175. Cf. I. SHAKED, *Margaliot Fortress,* in *ESI* 16 (1997), p. 17-18. For its strategic importance see, for instance, P. DESCHAMPS, *art. cit.* (n. 118), p. 101.

[185] Architectonic elements of the church have been found during the excavation of Tell al-Qāḍi: A. BIRAN, *Tel Dan*, in *RB* 82 (1975), p. 562-566 (see p. 562). A photograph of the Roman fountain house is given in *RB* 82 (1975), Pl. XLVa.

[186] St. Jerome often translates κώμη by *uiculus* with no obvious reason. Cf. J. WILKINSON, *L'apport de Saint Jérôme à la topographie,* in *RB* 81 (1974), p. 245-257 (see p. 248, n. 56).

added an explanation of *Yə'ōr*[187]. He clarifies his interpretation of the name "Jordan" in his Questions on the Hebrew of the Book Genesis[188], but locates Dan at Paneas (Banias) in his Commentaries to the Gospel of Matthew 16, 13[189] and to the Book of Amos 8, 11-12[190]. Instead, he seems to follow Eusebius in his Commentary to the Book of Ezekiel 27, 9 and 48, 21-22[191]. The identification of Dan with Banias (*Pmy's*) occurs also in Rabbinic writings[192], which do not distinguish the two sites, distant less than an hour's walk from one another. The Talmudic interpretation of the name of Jordan, followed by St. Jerome, was generally accepted in the Byzantine period and in the Middle Ages, while the third headstream of the river, the Nahr al-Ḥaṣbāni, was regarded then as Jordan's tributary. The site of Tell al-Qāḍi was abandoned in the later Arab period, but a *weli* was built on top of the mound under a big oak[193].

The Christian village of Abil al-Qamḥ existed already in the 19th century, but was deserted in 1948 and destroyed some time thereafter. Its name means "Abil of the Wheat" and implies a contrast with "Abīl of the Waters", *'Abil-mayin*. The name chosen for the Christian village, which was built on the mound, apparently supposes a short-distance migration, possibly caused by floods affecting the crops and the livelihood of the migrants in their original settlement. In other words, the toponym seems to record and to explain a change of habitat. The seasonal rise of the waters in the headstreams of the Jordan River regularly overflowed the plain, but the migration - if caused by repeated floods - was probably occasioned by exceptional situations. Only excavations on the mound of Abil al-Qamḥ, inspired by the desire of discovering not only the remote past of the site, but also its more recent history, may shed a light on the origins and date of this village.

[187] S. HIERONYMUS, *Liber locorum*, in E. KLOSTERMANN (ed.), *op. cit.* (n. 11), p. 77.

[188] S. HIERONYMUS, *Hebraicae quaestiones in libro Geneseos* 14, 14, in P. DE LAGARDE (ed.), *CCSL* 72, Turnhout 1959, p. 19: 3-8.

[189] S. HIERONYMUS, *Commentarii in Matthaeum*, in D. HURST - M. ADRIAEN (eds.), *CCSL* 77, Turnhout 1969, p. 139: 9-11.

[190] S. HIERONYMUS, *Commentarii in Prophetas Minores*, in M. ADRIAEN (ed.), *CCSL* 76, Turnhout 1969, p. 333: 261.

[191] S. HIERONYMUS, *Commentarii in Hiezechielem*, in Fr. GLORIE (ed.), *CCSL* 75, Turnhout 1964, p. 374: 1204-1208 and p. 739: 1862. Cf. J. WILKINSON, *art. cit.* (n. 186), p. 255-256.

[192] G. REEG, *op. cit.* (n. 6), p. 518-520.

[193] K BAEDEKER, *op. cit.* (n. 40), p. 260. The oak was believed to mark the grave of a *qāḍi*, "judge", what some regard as a translation of Dan, at least according to the popular etymology of Gen. 30, 6.

"Waters of Dan"

The place called Abel-mayin is located in I Enoch 13, 9 between Mount Lebanon and Mount Hermon, and Enoch's dream takes place "at the waters of Dan, in the territory of Dan, to the south-west of Hermon" (I Enoch 13, 7). There is little doubt that the "Waters of Dan" designate the mighty fountain which issues from the western base of Tell al-Qāḍi and is the largest of the sources of the Jordan River. "Abel of the Waters" must then refer to the mound itself . Also Levi purifies himself in the flowing waters of the stream, consults his father Jacob at Abel-mayin, and goes then "sitting at [the waters of Dan]", *wytbt 'nh* '[*l my Dn*][194].

Dan appears in this context as the name of the pool formed by the constant flow of water from the source at the western base of the mound. The Nahr al-Leḏḏān rises from this pool[195], called by metonymy *dan*(*nu*), literally "vat". This interpretation is supported by the meaning of *dan*, container, large cask or vat[196] in Ugaritic[197], Aramaic[198], Neo-Assyrian and Neo-Babylonian[199], in Arabic (*dann*), and the word is borrowed in Greek as δάν(ν)α[200]. It is etymologically linked to Arabic *wadana*, "to soak", "to inundate", attested also by the Sabaic verb *wdn*, "to prepare for flood-irrigation"[201]. According to al-Layṯ b. al-Muẓaffar, the editor of al-Ḫalīl b. Aḥmad's *Kitāb al-'ayn* (8th century A.D.), *dīn* meant "rain that falls continuously on a place and soaks it with

[194] 4Q213a, Frg. 2, line 14: J.T. Milik, *art. cit.* (n. 98), p. 400 and Pl. IV; J. VanderKam (ed.), *op. cit.* (n. 98), p. 30. Cf. J.T. Milik, *art. cit.* (n. 98), p. 400-403. The phrase *'l my Dn* occurs also on the fragment 5Q9, 5, 3: M. Baillet - J.T. Milik - R. de Vaux, *Les 'Petites Grottes' de Qumrân* (DJD 3), Oxford 1962, p. 180 and Pl. XXXVIII.

[195] Abel, *Géographie* I, p. 162 and Pl. XIV, 1.

[196] The entry *DNN* in D. Cohen, *Dictionnaire des racines sémitiques*, La Haye-Leuven 1970 ff., p. 283-284, contains words, which probably do not belong to a single Afro-Asiatic root, while some derivatives are not included.

[197] *KTU* 1.3, I, 12; 1.16, III, 14 (*lḥm.*[*b*]*.dnhm*); 2.38, 18. Cf. G. del Olmo Lete - J. Sanmartín, *Diccionario de la lengua ugaritica* I, Sabadell 1996, p. 134b (*dn* II) and 135a (*dnt* II).

[198] S.A. Kaufman, *The Akkadian Influences on Aramaic* (AS 19), Chicago 1974, p. 46. M. Sokoloff, *A Dictionary of Jewish Babylonian Aramaic of the Talmudic and Geonic Periods*, Ramat-Gan 2002, p. 343-344, regards *dannā* as a loanword borrowed from Akkadian *dannu*. It seems instead that this is a West Semitic word, borrowed by Neo-Assyrian and Neo-Babylonian from Aramaic. At least one of the Aramaic pronunciations must have been *dān*, as suggested by the Mandaic spelling *d'n'* and Rabbinic Hebrew *dwn*, i.e. *dōn* < *dān*.

[199] *AHw*, p. 161b; *CAD*, D, p. 98-99.

[200] J.T. Milik, *Dédicaces faites par des dieux*, Paris 1972, p. 200-201.

[201] *Sabaic Dictionary*, p. 156.

water"[202]. The primary root must be *dan*, as confirmed by Egyptian *dn*, "to fill with water", "to overflow"[203]. The root was eventually extended by a prefix *wa-*[204]. In this hypothesis, the Talmudic and later tradition regarding Dan as the name of one of the sources of the Jordan River appears as correct and it preserves an old micro-toponym.

Place names based on such a root will of course be common, and there are a number of toponyms in the region formed apparently with the element *dan*. Eusebius mentions a village called Βηρ Δαν south or south-east of Gaza[205]. The place should correspond to the *Bə'ēr mayim ḥayyīm* of Gen. 20, 20 and its name may be echoed by the Ḫirbet Umm Ğirār, "the site of the jars", 3 km north of Tell Ğemmeh. Dannāh in the Judaean highland (Josh. 15, 49) and *Dn-hbh* (Gen. 36, 32; I Chron. 1, 43) can also be related to the same root, but no concrete information is available about these sites. The same must be said about Ḫirbet ad-Danna[206], near Balu'a in Transjordan, and about ad-Dānā in central Syria[207]. Kfar Dān in the northern Beqa' Valley bears the same name as Dan, but the present site does not seem to have been occupied before the Ottoman period[208]. Besides, William of Tyre mentions *Caphardan* in northern Syria[209]. One could refer further to ad-Dānā, west of Aleppo, Danabu and Dennaba in the area of Damascus, and Maḥaneh-Dan in the Shephelah (Judg. 13, 25; 18, 12), between Zorah and Eshtaol. This place name served as a key element in developing the story of the earlier Danite settlement in the area of Bēth-Shemesh and of the tribe's migration to the north. In reality, Maḥaneh-Dan signifies "Camp of the Vat" or "Pool". The site has not been identified so far, but there are several springs in the area, the most important one being 'Ain Faṭīr, east of Beit al-Ğemāl[210].

[202] Quotation by M.A. GHŪL, *Early Southern Arabian Languages and Classical Arabic Sources,* Irbid 1993, p. 108.

[203] A. ERMAN - H. GRAPOW, *Wörterbuch der ägyptischen Sprache* V, Leipzig 1931, p. 464:3; R. HANNIG, *op. cit.* (n. 2), p. 981.

[204] LIPIŃSKI, *Semitic*, §43. 6-8.

[205] EUSEBIUS OF CAESAREA, *Onomasticon*, in E. KLOSTERMANN (ed.), *op. cit.* (n. 11), p. 166:23.

[206] ABEL, *Géographie* II, p. 303.

[207] LIPIŃSKI, *Aramaeans*, p. 259, n. 46.

[208] L. MARFOE, *Kāmid el-Lōz 13. The Prehistoric and Early Historic Context of the Site* (Saarbrücker Beiträge zur Altertumskunde 41), Bonn 1995, p. 297, No. 452. Cf. DUSSAUD, *Topographie*, Map III, C, 1; S. WILD, *op. cit.* (n. 116), p. 225 (grid ref. 179/229).

[209] WILLIAM OF TYRE, *Chronicon* XI, 25, 16; XIII, 16, 26-27; XIII, 21, 35, in *op. cit.* (n. 115), p. 533, 605, 614.

[210] ABEL, *Géographie* II, p. 317.

The incubation and the visionary dreams of Enoch and of Levi show that the site at the "Waters of Dan" was a sacred place. This is confirmed by the bilingual Greek-Aramaic inscription from the late 3rd or 2nd century B.C., found at the site and dedicated to an unnamed deity. This is also implied by the architectural remains of the place dating from the early first millennium B.C. to the 4th century A.D.[211] This unnamed deity is mentioned already in Am. 8, 14a and "Spring of living water" is used as a divine epithet in Jer. 2, 13 and 17, 13. It is quite normal therefore that the "Waters of Dan" became a holy place[212]. Josephus Flavius only refers to the "Lesser Jordan below the sanctuary of the Golden Calf"[213], certainly alluding to the site at the Jordan's source "called Dan"[214].

In conclusion, since Tell al-Qāḍi must have been *'Abīl*[215], eventually *'Abīl mayim/n* or *'Abīl-mašqeh*, Abil al-Qamḥ was Laish, called later Dan and Kfar Dan. The "Waters of Dan" and the Bull Shrine were located at the western base of Tell al-Qāḍi, at the pool called "Dan". In I Enoch 13, 7, the "Waters of Dan" are said to be "in the land of Dan", the bilingual inscription from Tell al-Qāḍi is dedicated to the god "who is in the Danite parts"[216], and the biblical phrase "from Dan to Beersheba" must refer to the "land of Dan" around the headwaters of the Jordan. The tribe was probably named after the territory, which in turn had gotten its name from the powerful spring and its pool, called *Dan*. Tribesmen must have given this name also to a town, probably at the site of the later Kfar Dan and Abil al-Qamḥ.

211 A. BIRAN, *"To the God who is in Dan"*, in A. BIRAN (ed.), *Temples and High Places in Biblical Times*, Jerusalem 1981, p. 142-151.

212 For the religious symbolism of the flow of water in Hellenistic times, see J.H. CHARLESWORTH, *Les Odes de Salomon et les manuscrits de la Mer Morte,* in *RB* 77 (1970), p. 522-549 (see p. 534-538).

213 JOSEPHUS FLAVIUS, *The Jewish War*, IV, 1, 1, §3.

214 JOSEPHUS FLAVIUS, *Jewish Antiquities* I, 10, 1, §177.

215 Mentioned also in II Sam. 20, 18 without any qualification.

216 The Aramaic text must be read: [*d*]*n ndr Zyls l'*[*lh'*], "[Th]is vowed Zoilos to the G[od]". Dan is not mentioned in the Aramaic inscription.

CHAPTER VII

GILEAD

Gilead seems to have originally designated the mountainous area of Ağlūn, north of the Jabboq or Nahr az-Zerqā, as well as the region south of the river with the present-day Ğebel Ğal'ad, Ḫirbet Ğal'ad and Ḫirbet Ğal'ud, 300 m north of the preceding ruin; both preserve the ancient name. Ḫirbet Ğal'ad is the site of a Byzantine settlement[1], which was probably called Γαλαάδ[2], since Eusebius erroneously located there Ramoth-Gilead, "which still exists about 15 miles west of Philadelphia"[3], present-day Amman. Gilead is sometimes used in a wider and more general sense to denote the region extending from the river Arnon to the base of Mount Hermon. It is a country of high forest ridges lying between the Jordan and the desert plateau. Whilst the gentle declivities towards the desert were bare of trees, the western slopes, still in the 19th century, were well clothed with oak, terebinth, and pine. Gilead appeared in the main as a fertile and beautiful land.

Early history

The early history of Gilead is similar to that of Bashan, and the Jabboq River, although dividing the region in northern and southern Gilead[4], did not constitute a real border. North Gilead extends north-south for some 50 km between the Yarmuk and the Jabboq Rivers. It represents the richest part of the lands of Transjordan with a rainfall of 700-800 mm a year. This explains the existence of several perennial streams descending from the fertile highlands westward to the Jordan, as well as the presence of early civilization in the Jordan Valley and in the foothills. The eastern side of the valley was always a densely settled region. Tell aš-Šuna, located about 4 km south-east of the confluence of

[1] Grid ref. 2235/1695: R. de Vaux, *Exploration de la région de Salṭ*, in *RB* 47 (1938), p. 398-425, Pls. XVII-XXIII (see p. 416-417, Nos. 43-44).

[2] R. de Vaux, *Notes d'histoire et de topographie transjordaniennes*, in *Vivre et Penser* 1 (1941), p. 16-47 (see p. 28, n. 5).

[3] Eusebius of Caesarea, *Onomasticon*, in E. Klostermann (ed.), *Eusebius: Das Onomastikon der biblischen Ortsnamen*, Leipzig 1904, p. 144:4-6 and 146:3-4.

[4] Deut. 3, 12; Josh. 12, 2.5; 13, 31.

the Jordan and Yarmuk Rivers, Ṭabaqat Faḥl, better known as Pella, both mounds of Tell al-Ḫandaqūq, Tell as-Sa'īdīyeh, Tell al-Qaws were flourishing cities already in the Early Bronze Age. The same must be said about Irbid and Tell al-Ḥuṣn in north Gilead. The Middle and Late Bronze periods witness the same development, which continues until the Iron Age.

Like Bashan, Gilead is a land of dolmens. The largest dolmen field in this area is situated 5 km east of Tell ad-Dāmiya, which dominates the confluence of the Nahr az-Zerqā and the Jordan. It covers a superficies of about 4 km^2 and consists of remnants of at least 200 megalithic monuments. They date from the same period as the dolmens on the Golan Heights[5]. The huge Tell Umm Ḥamād Šarqī, about 5 km north-east of ad-Dāmiya, dates also from those times, but apparently continued to be occupied in Early Bronze Age II[6]. It yielded great masses of potsherds belonging to the last centuries of the fourth millennium B.C. Next to it rises Tell Umm Ḥamād Ġarbī with extensive pottery remains from Early Bronze IV and Middle Bronze I.

The unique walled town of Jawa (Ǧāwā) North, located on the Wādī Rağil in the basalt wilderness north-east of Mafraq, dates also from the Proto-Urban period. It covers an area of 10 ha and was occupied eventually by 2,500 inhabitants. In spite of its massive fortifications on two levels, of an elaborate water conservation system with dams across the wadis and reservoirs, and of enclosures for the safekeeping of domestic animals, this town was abandoned after about three generations[7]. Such an establishment is incomparably more advanced than the contemporary settlements farther west and implies the arrival of a new population of cattle pastoralists.

Gilead is described in the Bible as a pasture land[8], an allusion to its mainly semi-nomadic or semi-sedentary population of pastoralists. Their clans were regarded as forming Gilead, mentioned in the Song of Deborah among the Transjordanian tribes, which did not participate in the war

[5] R.W. DAJANI, *Excavations in Dolmens*, in *ADAJ* 12-13 (1967-68), p. 56-64; D. GILEAD, *Burial Customs and the Dolmen Problem*, in *PEQ* 100 (1968), p. 16-26; J. UNDELAND, *A Cultic Slab at Damiya*, in *ADAJ* 18 (1973), p. 55-59. See also here above, p. 232.

[6] Grid ref. 2055/1730: A.V.G. BETTS, *Excavations at Tell Um Hammad 1982-1984: The Early Assemblages (EB I-II)*, Edinburgh 1992. Cf. G. PHILIP, *Jawa and Tell Um Hammad - Two Early Bronze Age Sites in Jordan. Review Article*, in *PEQ* 127 (1995), p. 161-170.

[7] S.W. HELMS, *Jawa, Lost City of the Black Desert*, London 1981; E.V.G. BETTS, *Excavations at Jawa 1972-1986*, Edinburgh 1991. See here, p. 270 and 271.

[8] Numb. 32, 1; Jer. 50, 19; Mich. 7, 14.

Tell aš-Šuna: circular mud-brick building
from the later part of the Early Bronze Age I.

against Sisera (Judg. 5, 15). The dozens of small Iron Age I sites in Gilead should be related to these clans, dating roughly to the 11th century B.C. The Bible seems to have preserved some records from those times, although they are presently embedded in later traditions.

A number of settlements — allegedly sixty (Deut. 3, 4; I Kings 4, 13), thirty (Judg. 10, 4) or twenty-three (I Chron. 2, 22) — were forming the Hawwoth-Jair, consistently located in Gilead, "as far as the border of the Geshurite and Maakathite" (Deut. 3, 14), i.e. in the region south of the Yarmuk River. The word *ḥwt* is always written in this way and vocalized as a plural[9]. It occurs frequently in Ugaritic[10], also in the syllabic

[9] Numb. 32, 41; Deut. 3, 14; Josh. 13, 30; Judg. 10, 4; I Kings. 4, 13; I Chron. 2, 23.

[10] G. del Olmo Lete - J. Sanmartín, *Diccionario de la lengua ugaritica* I, Sabadell 1996, p. 185.

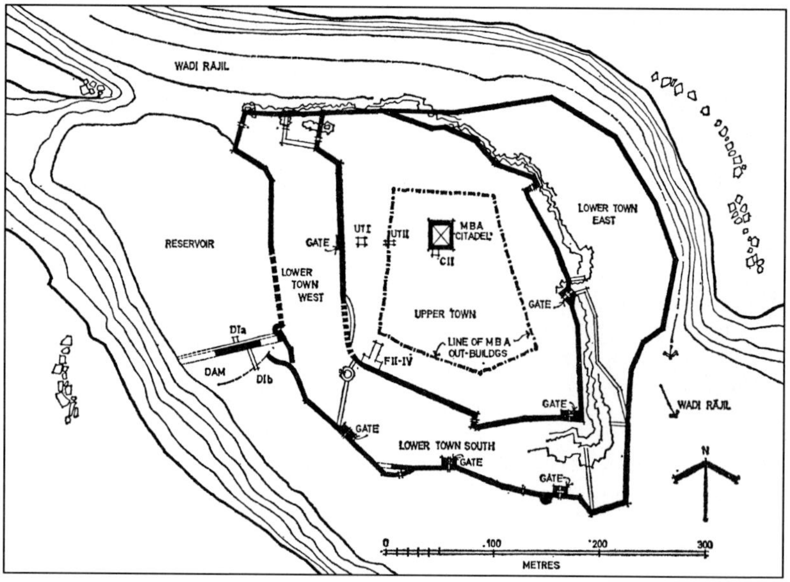

Plan of the site of Jawa (Ǧāwā) North according to S.W. Helms.

spelling *ḫu-wa-tum*[11], and it means "country", as shown by the contexts and by its equivalence with Sumerian KALAM[12]. The Hivites mentioned in the stereotyped list of the pre-Israelite populations of Canaan[13] are designated by the same word: they are just "country-men" or "natives"[14]. The feminine ending *-t* is replaced in these cases by the gentile suffix *-ī*, in agreement with the rules of the Hebrew grammar[15]. The noun *ḥwt* is related etymologically and semantically to Egyptian *ḥw.t*, which means "settlement", "house"[16], and often occurs in place names[17].

Ḥawwoth-Jair is thus a "Country of Jair", who has been linked with Makīr in a rather complicated way (I Chron. 2, 21-23), but was regarded

[11] J. NOUGAYROL, in *Ugaritica* V, Paris 1968, p. 243, No. 137, II, 10'.

[12] *Ibid.*, p. 242-243, No. 137, II, 10'.

[13] Gen. 10, 17; Ex. 3, 8.17; 13, 5; 23, 23; 33, 2; 34, 11; Deut. 7, 1; 20, 17; Josh. 3, 10; 9, 1; 11, 3; 12, 8; 24, 11; Judg. 3, 5; I Kings. 9, 2; I Chron. 1, 15; II Chron. 8, 7.

[14] E. LIPIŃSKI, *Les Chamites selon Gen 10, 6-10 et 1 Chr 1, 8-16,* in *ZAH* 5 (1992), p. 135-162 (see p. 157).

[15] The gentile form of *Yəhūdāh* is *Yəhūdī*, that of *Timnāh* is *Timnī*. However, the gentile derivative of *Bēt-Ma'akāh* is *Ma'ᵃkātī*.

[16] A. ERMAN - H. GRAPOW, *Wörterbuch der ägyptischen Sprache*, Leipzig 1926-31, Vol. III, p. 1; R. HANNIG, *Die Sprache der Pharaonen. Grosses Handwörterbuch Ägyptisch-Deutsch (2800-950 v.Chr.)*, 2nd ed., Mainz a/R 1997, p. 515-516.

[17] R. HANNIG, *op. cit.* (n. 16), p. 1363-1369.

Photograph of the site of Jawa (Ǧāwā) North
with the water reservoir and the dam on the left.

more often as a son of Manasseh[18]. These connections certainly reveal attempts at integrating the Country of Jair in a common Israelite framework. Since its mentions in Judg. 10, 4 and I Kings 4, 13 must be regarded as later additions to ancient lists of respectively the "minor judges" of Israel[19] and the royal districts[20], the aggregation of the Country of Jair to the "family" of Manasseh may be ascribed to the reign of

[18] Numb. 32, 41; Deut. 3, 14; I Kings. 4, 13; cf. Josh. 13, 30.

[19] Judg. 4, 4-5 + 10, 1-5 + 12, 7-15 + I Sam. 7, 15-17a. The basic study remains that of M. Noth, *Das Amt des "Richters Israels"*, in *Festschrift A. Bertholet*, Tübingen 1950, p. 404-417. See also H. Niehr, *šāpaṭ*, in *ThWAT* VIII, Stuttgart 1985, col. 408-428, especially col. 423-424, and E. Lipiński, *Juge*, in *DEB*, Turnhout 1987, p. 703-704, both with literature.

[20] The classical essay by A. Alt, *Kleine Schriften zur Geschichte des Volkes Israel* II, 2nd ed., München 1959, p. 76-89, does not yet consider the probably correct explanation of the lack of Judah in the list by its composition at the time of Omri or Ahab.

Jeroboam II, just like the Manassite settlements in Bashan (Josh. 13, 30)[21].

The actual shape of the story of Jephthah (Judg. 10, 6-12, 7) betrays the hand of later redactors, but the protagonist of the original account is likely to have been a **qaṣ́yān* (*qṣyn*) or "war-lord" (Judg. 11, 6.11), chosen by the tribal chiefs of Gilead, called *śārē Gilə'ād* (Judg. 10, 18). They were gathering at the central shrine of the tribe, at *Miṣpeh Gilə'ād* (Judg. 10, 18; 11, 11.29.34), which should be located in the tribal heartland. The place is mentioned also in Gen. 31, 47-49[22], where Jacob's dealings with Laban are finished off. The general context suggests a site north of the Jabboq. Around 400 A.D., Egeria went on a pilgrimage to the memorial of Jephthah at Tishbe[23]. This shows that Miṣpeh-Gilead, the "Watch-post of Gilead", was looked for in the mountainous area to the south of Wādī al-Yābis. There is a Tell al-Maṣfa north of Sūf, but it is no conspicuous place[24]. Qal'at Rabaḍ (alt. 997 m) would have been a convenient site, but we do not know whether there was an ancient settlement or a shrine at this place before the erection of the fortified castle in 1184. Several other heights could be considered. It seems, at any rate, that Ağlūn was the heartland of the Gilead clans. This is confirmed by the role played by the city of Jabesh in the early period[25]. Eusebius locates it six Roman miles south-east of Pella, on the road to Ğerash[26]. Its accepted identification is with Tell al-Maqlūb[27], despite a different opinion of Nelson Glueck.

The area of Gilead was included in the survey of the western half of Transjordan, conducted by N. Glueck between 1933 and 1947. His sur-

[21] See here above, p. 229-230.

[22] R. DE VAUX, *art. cit.* (n. 2), p. 27-28.

[23] *Itinerarium Egeriae* XVI, 1, in *Itineraria et alia geographica* (CCSL 175), Turnhout 1965, p. 56-57. Egeria calls the place: *Memoria sancti Gethae.*

[24] ABEL, *Géographie* II, p. 390.

[25] Judg. 2, 8-14; I Sam. 11, 1-11; 31, 11-13; II Sam. 2, 4-6; I Chron. 10, 11-12. See also the fragment of 4QSam[a] published by F.M. CROSS, *The Ammonite Oppression of the Tribes of Gad and Reuben: Missing Verses from 1 Samuel 11 found in 4QSamuel[a]*, in E. TOV (ed.), *The Hebrew and Greek Texts of Samuel*, Jerusalem 1980, p. 105-119 = H. TADMOR - M. WEINFELD (eds.), *History, Historiography and Interpretation*, Jerusalem 1983, p. 148-158. The official edition of the text: F.M. CROSS - D.W. PARRY - R.J. SALEY - E. ULRICH, *Qumrân Cave 4*, XII*: The Samuel Scrolls from Cave 4* (DJD 17), Oxford 2005, p. 66-67, Pl. X. Cf. A. ROFÉ, *The Acts of Nahash according to 4QSam[a]*, in *IEJ* 32 (1987), p. 129-133.

[26] EUSEBIUS OF CAESAREA, *Onomasticon*, in E. KLOSTERMANN (ed.), *op. cit.* (n. 3), p. 110:11-13.

[27] Grid ref. 2144/2011: M. NOTH, *Jabes-Gilead. Ein Beitrag zur Methode alttestamentlicher Topographie*, in *ZDPV* 69 (1953), p. 28-41. Cf. W. ZWICKEL, *Eisenzeitliche Ortslagen im Ostjordanland* (BTAVO B/81), Wiesbaden 1990, p. 294.

Qalʿat Rabaḍ (Aǧlūn).

vey was site-oriented and still presents the best global picture of settlement, as shown by a recent reassessment of the results of his research[28]. For the dating of his finds, Glueck relied heavily on excavations and surveys conducted in Cisjordan. Recent changes in the chronology of the end of Late Bronze II and of Iron Age I must of course lead to a re-evaluation of his conclusions. Besides, written documentation can be linked to archaeological information only after its critical analysis. This concerns biblical texts in particular, for they generally echo historical events, rarely describing them directly.

In such a way, a new historical phase of events in Gilead seems to be reflected in the Bible when Makīr is presented as the father of Gilead[29] in spite of the Song of Deborah, which distinguishes between Makīr and the Gilead tribe. The latter resides in Transjordan and does not participate in the war against Sisera (Judg. 5, 15), contrary to Makīr, mentioned along with Ephraim and Benjamin (Judg. 5, 14), obviously in Cisjordan, while Manasseh is yet missing. It is reasonable to suppose therefore that the Makīr tribe dwelled first west of the Jordan River. Later, around the 10th century B.C., some clans crossed to the eastern side (cf. Josh. 13, 31), thus Makīr becoming the "father" of Gilead. According to Numb. 12, 39-42, the Makīr clans settled between the Yarmuk and the Jabboq, thus facing the area of Bēth-shan. One can thus assume that the original home of the Makīr tribe was the Bēth-shan Valley. As eponym and ancestor of an important tribe, viewed later as part of Manasseh, Makīr must have been a venerated figure, which one is inclined to link to *M'-k3-r3*, represented on the Bēth-shan stele from the time of the Eighteenth Egyptian Dynasty, *ca.* the 14th century B.C.[30] The enthroned elderly god may be the divinized ancestor and eponym of the tribe, but the latter may also have borne a name based on the theonym. It is unlikely that *Makīr* is a passive participle of *mkr* and means "bought"[31]. One should probably regard it as a denominative participle,

[28] A short presentation is provided by E.J. VAN DER STEEN, *Nelson Glueck's Surveys in Eastern Palestine: A Reassessment*, in *Albright News* 9 (2004), p. 11. Some particular reassessments of N. Glueck's work are given by EAD., *Tribes and Territories in Transition. The Central East Jordan Valley in the Late Bronze Age and Early Iron Ages: A Study of Sources* (OLA 130), Leuven 2004, p. 80-81, 92-94, 213-231, 235-248.

[29] Numb. 26, 29; Josh. 17, 1; I Chron. 2, 21; 7, 14.

[30] E. LIPIŃSKI, *Resheph Amyklos*, in E. LIPIŃSKI (ed.), *Phoenicia and the East Mediterranean in the First Millennium B.C.* (Studia Phoenicia V; OLA 22), Leuven 1987, p. 87-99 (see p. 87-91, with further literature). Good photographs of the stele can be found in H.O. THOMPSON, *Mekal, the God of Beth-shan*, Leiden 1970, Pl. V, and in *CAH. Plates to Vol. I & II. New Ed.*, Cambridge 1977, Pl. 101.

[31] M. NOTH, *Die israelitischen Personennamen im Rahmen der gemeinsemitischen Namengebung*, Stuttgart 1928, p. 232.

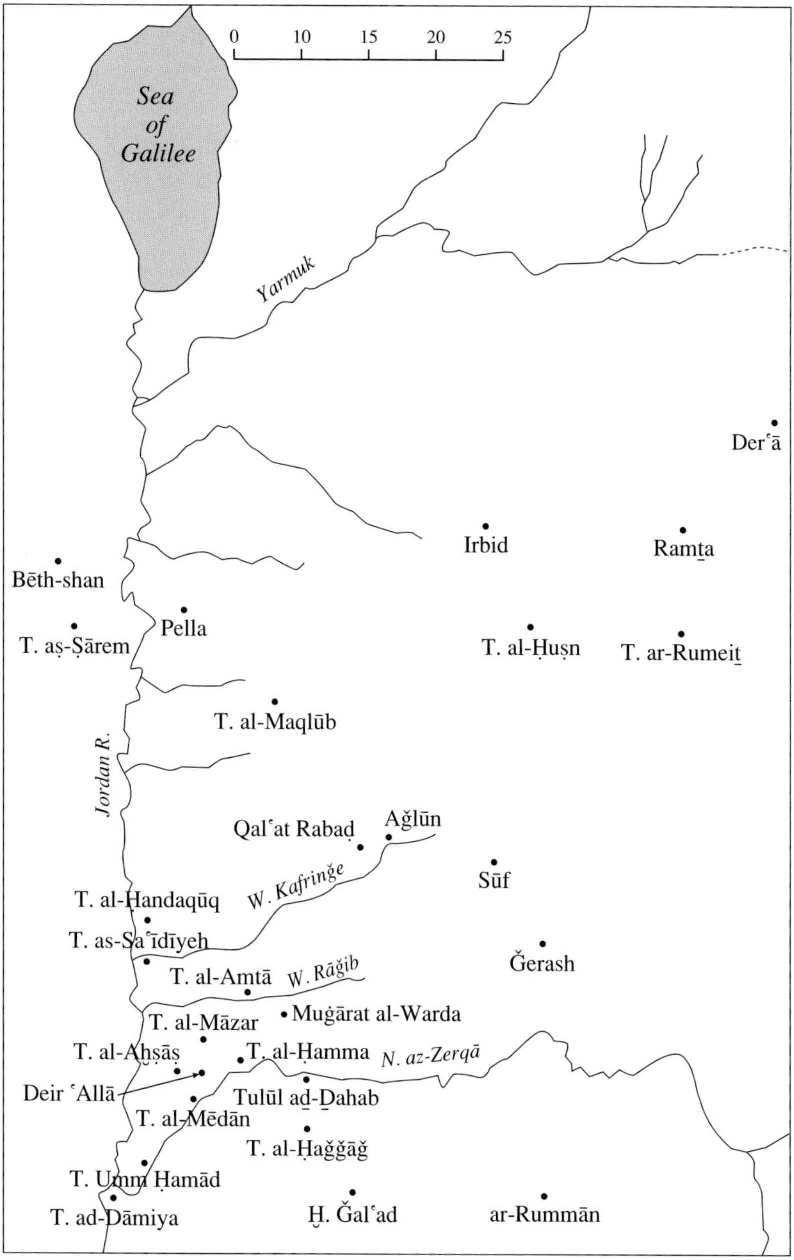
0 10 15 20 25
Sea of Galilee
Yarmuk
Der'ā
Irbid
Ramta
Bēth-shan
Pella
T. aṣ-Ṣārem
T. al-Ḥuṣn
T. ar-Rumeiṯ
T. al-Maqlūb
Jordan R.
Qal'at Rabaḍ
Ağlūn
Sūf
W. Kafrinğe
T. al-Ḫandaqūq
T. as-Sa'īdīyeh
Ğerash
T. al-Amtā
W. Rāğib
T. al-Māzar
Muġārat al-Warda
T. al-Aḫṣāṣ
T. al-Ḥamma
N. az-Zerqā
Deir 'Allā
Tulūl aḏ-Ḏahab
T. al-Mēdān
T. al-Ḥağğāğ
T. Umm Ḥamād
T. ad-Dāmiya
Ḫ. Ğal'ad
ar-Rummān

Gilead.

derived from *kūr / kīr* and meaning "smelter". In fact, the *yōd* is never missing in the spelling of the name and hieroglyphic *k3* in *M'-k3-r3* can stand for *ky*, later *kei*[32]. Such a name, borne by a deity, recalls Hephaestus and Koṯar-wa-Ḫasis.

Makīr's mother is said to have been an Aramaean (I Chron. 7, 14), and he married Maaka according to I Chron. 7, 16. These references suggest that the Makīr clans settled in an area bordering Bēth-Maaka, along the Yarmuk and the Wādī aš-Šellāle, and that they were mixed with the Aramaean population of the Bashan and the Hauran, progressing further southwards[33]. This seems to reflect a situation of the 10th and 9th centuries B.C., when this region formed two districts of the Kingdom of Israel: Ramoth-Gilead and Maḥanaim (I Kings 4, 13a.15). Both towns were also "Levitical cities" (Josh. 21, 38) and Ramoth-Gilead was a "city of refuge" as well (Deut. 4, 43; Josh. 21, 38).

The appearance of the Manassites east of the Jordan River hints at conditions created in the early 8th century B.C., when Jeroboam II extended the territory of the Kingdom of Israel to the north and north-east. Jair, dubbed son of Manasseh[34], was settled of old in north Gilead, between the Jabboq and the Yarmuk[35], while Nobah, allegedly another son of Manasseh, is located in the eastern part of the region (Numb. 32, 42; cf. Judg. 8, 11). Further tribal connections of the Nobah clans are unknown.

Ramoth-Gilead

An important centre of northern Gilead in the Iron Age was Ramoth-Gilead, chief-town of a district, "Levitical city", and "city of refuge". It is often identified with Tell ar-Rumeiṯ, also called Tell Ramith, 7 km south of ar-Ramṯa and 17 km east of Irbid.

This identification was first proposed by N. Glueck[36]. Soundings were carried out on the mound by P.W. Lapp in 1962, and an excavation under his direction followed in 1967[37]. The Iron Age occupation consists

[32] A. GARDINER, *Egyptian Grammar*, 3rd ed., Oxford 1957, p. 430.

[33] LIPIŃSKI, *Aramaeans*, p. 353-363.

[34] See here above, p. 271-272.

[35] Numb. 32, 41; cf. Deut. 3, 14; Judg. 10, 4; I Kings. 4, 13.

[36] Grid ref. 2455/2116: N. GLUECK, *Ramoth-Gilead*, in *BASOR* 92 (1943), p. 10-16; ID., *Exploration in Eastern Palestine* IV (AASOR 25-28), New Haven 1951, p. 98-100; ID., *The River Jordan*, New York 1968, p. 139.

[37] P.W. LAPP, *Tell er-Rumeith*, in *RB* 70 (1963), p. 406-411; ID., *Tell er-Rumeith*, in *RB* 75 (1968), p. 98-105; N.L. LAPP, *The Tale of the Tell. Archaeological Studies by Paul*

of four strata (VIII-V) covering at most 200 years and apparently ending with a destruction by Tiglath-pileser III in 732 B.C. Ar-Rumeiṯ was a small rectangular fortress, measuring *ca.* 37 m by 32 m with a total superficies of about 0.12 ha. The earliest pottery found in Stratum VIII was dated by P.W. Lapp to the later part of the 10th century B.C., but it may belong rather to the early 9th century. In this case, the fortress would have been erected by Omri. Parts of the east gateway complex were uncovered. Stratum VII provided evidence of a massive destruction in mid-9th century. It could be connected with the battle of Ramoth-Gilead in 842 B.C. The destruction level is followed by a careful town planning in Stratum VI, dating probably from the reign of Hazael, king of Damascus. This stratum was destroyed by fire about half a century later, perhaps at the time of Jeroboam II. The occupied area of Strata VI and V extended beyond the fort to the north and the east. Following the destruction of Stratum V, there was a brief period of occupation, but the site was soon abandoned.

The small size of Tell ar-Rumeiṯ does not favour its identification with an administrative centre of Gilead, as specified in I Kings 4, 13. At any rate, the name of the mound is a Semitic *quṭayl*-diminutive of *Ramṯ-*, which indicates that it is a relatively recent toponym. Since Stratum II showed occupation lasting until mid-7th century A.D. and Stratum I consisted of several post-Byzantine sepultures, the toponym might go back to those times and designate the site as the "small Ramṯa". Ramṯa derives unquestionably from Aramaic *Rāmātā'*, "the heights", which is a perfect translation of Hebrew *hā-Rāmōt*[38], transliterated 'Αραμωθα by Josephus Flavius[39]. The spirantization of postvocalic *t* gave *ṯ*, which remained after the elision of the second *a* and brought about the proper name *Ramṯa*. It is quite possible that ar-Ramṯa (alt. 607 m) is built above

W. Lapp, Pittsburgh 1975, in particular p. 111-119; EAD., *Rumeith, Tell er,* in *NEAEHL*, Jerusalem 1993, Vol. IV, p. 1291-1293. The results of these excavations have been summarized by S. HAFÞÓRSSON, *A Passing Power: An Examination of the Sources for the History of Aram-Damascus in the Second Half of the Ninth Century B.C.* (Coniectanea Biblica. Old Testament Series 54), Stockholm 2006, p. 202-204. Cf. W. ZWICKEL, *op. cit.* (n. 27), p. 315.

38 M. NOTH, *Könige* I (BKAT IX/1), Neukirchen-Vluyn 1968, p. 57, induces from the Septuagint and Peshitta transcriptions, as well as from *Rmh* in II Kings 8, 29, that the original toponym was *Rāmat*, a singular. However, the lack of a *mater lectionis* explains the Greek and Syriac transcriptions, while II Kings 8, 29 is a redactional addition to the annalistic record: LIPIŃSKI, *Aramaeans*, p. 380. The Deuteronomistic redactor regarded *Rmt Gl'd* as a construct state followed by a qualification, but this was not the case, as shown by the frequent spelling *R'mt* with *aleph*, excluding the reading *Rəmat,* and by *Rāmōt bag-Gilə'ād* in Deut. 4, 43; Josh. 20, 8; 21, 36; I Chron. 6, 65. *Rmt* was a plural.

39 JOSEPHUS FLAVIUS, *Jewish Antiquities* IX, 6, 1, §105; 6, 2, §112.

the ruins of the biblical Ramoth-Gilead[40], but accumulated layers of remains from the last centuries discourage any serious research. Surface surveys on the large mound nevertheless yielded a great quantity of potsherds from Iron Age I and II, while the originally plural form of the toponym seems to hint at the administrative centre of the Heights of Gilead without suggesting that it is built on "heights". Its situation on the ancient Roman road connecting the Hauran with the Mediterranean and the remarkable coincidence of the names support this identification, although only deep soundings or excavations could give a definitive proof.

Josephus' 'Αραμωθα with initial *'A* is paralleled by 'Ασωφων, 'Αραβαθα[41], and such a prefixing of *'A* is not particular to him. Αρημωθ occurs in the Septuagint (Josh. 20, 8), just as Αρμαθαιμ or Αριμαθαια is used for Ramathaim[42]. This *A* reflects the addition of a determinate article in front of place names, a feature which occurs also in Punic and Arabic, especially when the toponym is a common noun[43]. Where the Hebrew text has no *mater lectionis* indicating *ō* Josephus transliterates 'Αραμαθη or 'Ραμθη[44], but once he writes 'Αρίμανον[45], possibly referring to ar-Rummān, south of Ğerash. Eusebius mistakenly identifies Ramoth-Gilead with a village near the Jabboq River or the present-day as-Salṭ[46], in the Ğebel Ğal'ād, allegedly 15 Roman miles west of Amman (Philadelphia)[47]. St. Jerome follows Eusebius without correcting this erroneous information.

Another site, still identified by some authors with Ramoth-Gilead[48], is Tell al-Ḥuṣn / Ḥiṣn, 8.5 km south-east of Irbid. This is one of the

[40] Grid ref. 2450/2186: R. SMEND, *Beiträge zur Geschichte und Topographie des Ostjordanlandes,* in *ZAW* 22 (1902), p. 129-158 (see p. 158); G. HÖLSCHER, *Bemerkungen zur Topographie Palästinas,* in *ZDPV* 29 (1906), p. 133-151 (see p. 137). Cf. W. ZWICKEL, *op. cit.* (n. 27), p. 315; E.A. KNAUF, *The Mists of Ramthalon, or: How Ramoth-Gilead Disappeared from the Archaeological Record,* in *BN* 110 (2001), p. 33-36.

[41] JOSEPHUS FLAVIUS, *Jewish Antiquities* XIII, 12, 5, §338; XIV, 1, 4, §18.

[42] ABEL, *Géographie* II, p. 428.

[43] LIPIŃSKI, *Semitic*, §67.11-13.

[44] JOSEPHUS FLAVIUS, *Jewish Antiquities* VIII, 15, 3, §399; 15, 5, §411; 15, 6, §417.

[45] JOSEPHUS FLAVIUS, *Jewish Antiquities* IV, 7, 4, §173.

[46] P.M. SÉJOURNÉ, *Chronique de Jérusalem,* in *RB* 2 (1893), p. 228-244 (see p. 230-231); É. NODET, *Flavius Josèphe: Les Antiquités Juives* II, Paris 1995, p. 42, n. 7. Cf. here above, p. 267.

[47] EUSEBIUS, *Onomasticon*, in *op. cit.* (n. 3), p. 144:4-6 and p. 146:3-4.

[48] M. WEIPPERT, *Israélites, Araméens et Assyriens dans la Transjordanie septentrionale,* in *ZDPV* 113 (1997), p. 19-38 (see p. 32-33). For a discussion of the different opinions see also J. BRIEND, *Ramot-Galaad,* in *DBS* IX, Paris 1977, col. 1101-1104, 1113.

largest ancient mounds of Gilead (*ca.* 5 ha). Its top is well over 200 m long and nearly as broad. It raises more than 13 m above the surrounding terrain, and surface surveys, made already by N. Glueck[49], revealed pottery representing all the periods from the Early Bronze Age to Iron Age II. Fragments of Hellenistic, Roman, and Mediaeval Arabic ceramics were found as well, beside ruins on top of the mound, possibly going back to Roman times. Buildings of the nearby village have stone blocks, some of them inscribed, incorporated in their walls. The ancient name of the site is unknown and its identification with Ramoth-Gilead is generally abandoned nowadays in favour of Tell ar-Rumeiṯ, which is a questionable location of the biblical city at any rate.

A dwelling and a burial cave have been discovered fortuitously 1 km south of Tell al-Ḥuṣn and subsequently excavated by G.L. Harding[50]. The cave was obviously reused and Harding interpreted the older pottery as Early Bronze II and the more recent one as Early Bronze IV / Middle Bronze I. Instead, B.S.J. Isserlin argued for Early Bronze I and early Middle Bronze I. This cave does not help identifying the Iron Age mound.

Irbid, less than 30 km south-east of the Sea of Galilee, covers the ancient city of Arbela or Bēth-Arbel (Hos. 10, 14), whose name it preserved with the slight change *l* > *d*[51]. The mound covered a superficies of about 350 m by 400 m, and sections of the city wall with its massive stones were still visible until 1937. W.F. Albright visited the site in 1929 and identified potsherds from the Early Bronze Age through Iron Age II. Four tombs from Late Bronze II and the Iron Age were excavated in 1958-1959[52], and some of the objects found are housed in the small Archaeological Museum of Irbid. The importance of the town in Iron Age II is stressed by the mention of its conquest by the king of Moab in Hos. 10, 14.

[49] Grid ref. 2330/2102: N. GLUECK, *op. cit.* (n. 36), *River Jordan*, p. 163, and *Exploration...* IV, p. 96-97, 113, 161-165. See also A. LEONARD, *The Jerash-Tell el-Ḥuṣn Highway Survey,* in *ADAJ* 31 (1987), p. 359-368. Cf. W. ZWICKEL, *op. cit.* (n. 27), p. 313.

[50] G.L. HARDING, *Four Tomb Groups from Jordan (*Palestine Exploration Fund. Annual 6), London 1953, with contributions by G.R. DRIVER, B.S.J. ISSERLIN, and O. TUFNELL.

[51] Grid ref. 2298/2184: C.J. LENZEN - E.A. KNAUF, *Irbid (Jordanie),* in *RB* 85 (1988), p. 239-247. Cf. W. ZWICKEL, *op. cit.* (n. 27), p. 311-312; LIPIŃSKI, *Aramaeans*, p. 354-355, with former literature.

[52] R.W. DAJANI, *Iron Age Tombs from Irbed,* in *ADAJ* 8-9 (1964), p. 99-101; ID., *Four Iron Age Tombs from Irbid,* in *ADAJ* 11 (1966), p. 88-101.

Maḥanaim

Maḥanaim is the second royal administrative centre of Gilead, mentioned in I Kings 4, 14. Saul's crippled son took refuge at Maḥanaim according to II Sam. 2, 8-9, and later on David retired there from his son Absalom (II Sam. 17, 24.27). The historical value of these reports cannot be checked, but such accounts show at least that Maḥanaim was regarded as a place suitable for taking refuge in case of danger. The earliest identification of Maḥanaim with Ḫirbet al-Maḫna, 3.5 km north of Ağlūn, proposed by Estori ha-Parḥi (14th century)[53], has been discarded by most modern scholars, because the site does not seem to have the characteristics required by the biblical contexts[54]. Gustav Dalman was the first to point at the twin site of Tulūl aḏ-Ḏahab on the Jabboq (Nahr az-Zerqā)[55]. However, the toponymic ending *-ayim* represents no dual[56] and therefore does not favour this place in a particular way. R. de Vaux and M. Noth suggested Tell al-Ḥağğāğ, uphill and to the south of the Jabboq[57]. None of these sites has ever been excavated and the mention of Maḥanaim in the list of Shoshenq I (No. 22)[58] is not very helpful: the toponym is placed between the unknown *Š3-w3-d* and Gibeon, and as such does not suggest any concrete location. The choice depends thus from an accurate survey of the site and of its surroundings, and from the characteristics required by the biblical accounts. The western mound of Tulūl aḏ-Ḏahab seems to meet all the criteria for identifying it as Maḥanaim[59].

[53] ESTORI HA-PARḤI, *Sefer Kaftor wa-Feraḥ*, Venice 1549. Critical edition: *Kaftor wa-Feraḥ*, ed. A.M. LUNCZ, Jerusalem 1897.

[54] The identification of Maḥanaim with Ḫirbet al-Maḫna, along the Roman road from Pella to Ğerash, is nevertheless accepted by ABEL, *Géographie* II, p. 373-374, and N. GLUECK, *op. cit.* (n. 36), *Exploration...* IV, p. 234.

[55] G. DALMAN, *Mahanaim*, in *Palästinajahrbuch* 9 (1913), p. 68-73, Pl. 5; ID., *Am Jabbok und in Mahanaim*, in *Palästinajahrbuch* 11 (1915), p. 156-160. N. GLUECK, *Exploration in Eastern Palestine* III (AASOR 18-19), New Haven 1939, p. 232-235, would look there for Penuel. See here below, p. 292.

[56] LIPIŃSKI, *Semitic*, §29.54.

[57] Grid ref. 2154/1732: the site, 150 x 50 m large, yielded mainly early Iron Age pottery. Cf. R. DE VAUX, *art. cit.* (n. 2), p. 30-31; M. NOTH, *Beiträge zur Geschichte des Ostjordanlandes*, in *Palästinajahrbuch* 37 (1941), p. 50-101 (see p. 82-86), followed by K.-G. SCHUNCK, *Erwägungen zur Geschichte und Bedeutung von Mahanaim*, in *ZDMG* 113 (1963), p. 34-40. Cf. R.L. GORDON - L.E. VILLIERS, *Tulūl edh-Dhahab and Its Environs. Surveys of 1980 and 1981. A Preliminary Report*, in *ADAJ* 27 (1983), p. 275-289; E.J. VAN DER STEEN, *op. cit.* (n. 28), p. 231, 250.

[58] S. AḤITUV, *Canaanite Toponyms in Ancient Egyptian Documents*, Jerusalem 1984, p. 134; R. HANNIG, *op. cit.* (n. 16), p. 1348.

[59] R.A. COUGHENOUR, *A Search for Maḥanaim*, in *BASOR* 273 (1989), p. 57-66.

In its middle course, the Nahr az-Zerqā flows in a deep narrow ravine which cleaves the mountains of Gilead. The site of Tulūl aḏ-Ḏahab can thus appear as a hiding place and a place of refuge. The western mound is surrounded on its three sides by a curve of the river and was thus easily defensible[60]. It was fortified by casemate walls, which enclosed an area of 220 m by 170 m, commanded an excellent view of the plain leading to the Jordan Valley, and thus possessed the characteristics of a strategic position. An accurate survey of the site yielded Iron Age potsherds[61], contemporary of the biblical accounts, which date from Iron Age II. R.A. Coughenour's exploration in 1978 also found a track leading directly northwards from Tell aḏ-Ḏahab al-Ġarbī to the Muġārat al-Warda iron mine *via* the village of Lakšeba[62]. Its map distance amounts only to 3.2 km. This is an important information, which reveals a new aspect of the role of Maḥanaim in the Iron Age.

The southern Ağlūn district was a centre of ancient iron metallurgy, as shown by the abundance of iron slag in the area. The main source of iron ore is in this mountainous region, which is called "Iron Mountain" by Josephus Flavius[63], Talmudic sources[64], and even Venerable Bede (672/3-735) and Peter the Deacon (13th century), who mention the *Mons Ferreus*[65]. The largest mining facilities and remains of smelting operations, including a 30 ton slab of slag, are found at Muġārat al-Warda[66]. Evidence for an early iron metallurgy in this area is provided by the proper name Barzillay, "Iron smith", attested precisely in the Jordan Valley (II Sam. 21, 8) and in Gilead[67]. Local mines could have supplied

[60] A description of the site is provided by R. DE VAUX, *art. cit.* (n. 1), p. 412-413. He refers to potsherds from the late Iron Age period, without specifying.

[61] R.L. GORDON, *An Interim Report on the Site Survey of Tell edh-Dhahab el-Gharbī*, in *Newsletter of ASOR* 8 (1981), p. 4-5; R.L. GORDON - L.E. VILLIERS, *art. cit.* (n. 57), p. 275-285, 287; R.L. GORDON, *Telul edh-Dhahab Survey (Jordan) 1980 and 1982*, in *MDOG* 116 (1984), p. 131-137; E.J. VAN DER STEEN, *op. cit.* (n. 28), p. 230-231, 249.

[62] R.A. COUGHENOUR, *art. cit.* (n. 59), p. 63 with Fig. 2 on p. 61.

[63] JOSEPHUS FLAVIUS, *The Jewish War* IV, 8, 2, §454.

[64] Mishnah, *Sukka* III, 1; Talmud Yerushalmi, *Shebi'it* IX, 2; *Sukka* III, 1, 53c; Babylonian Talmud, *Erubin* 19a; *Sukka* 32b. Cf. G. REEG, *Die Ortsnamen Israels nach der rabbinischen Literatur* (BTAVO B/21), Wiesbaden 1989, p. 224.

[65] BEDA VENERABILIS, *De locis sanctis* IX, 4, and PETRUS DIACONUS, *De locis sanctis* IX, 4, in *Itineraria et alia geographica* (CCSL 175), Turnhout 1965, p. 268-269.

[66] R.A. COUGHENOUR, *art. cit.* (n. 59), p. 62-63; M. GOODWAY, *News of Archaeometallurgy. Newsletter* 6/3 (1983), p. 1-3, reporting on the work of R.A. Coughenour; J.D. MUHLY, *Metalle. B. Archäologisch,* in *RLA* VIII, Berlin 1993-97, p. 119-136 (see p. 122). All the pottery can safely be dated to the Iron Age according to E.J. VAN DER STEEN, *op. cit.* (n. 28), p. 230, 248 (Fig. 9-40).

[67] II Sam. 17, 27; 19, 32-40; I Kings 2, 7; Ezra 2, 61; Neh. 7, 63.

the iron ore used in making the iron and steel artefacts from Iron Age I found in the Baq'a Valley (Jordan) and Pella burial caves[68], as well as the iron objects from Phase IX (9th century B.C.) at Deir 'Alla[69].

The storyteller of II Sam. 17, 27-29 probably had Tulūl aḏ-Ḏahab in his mind, close to the iron mines of Muġārat al-Warda. His short account follows the well-known scheme of three friends or visitors, used in the episode of the "three men" visiting Abraham (Gen. 18, 2) , in the story of the three friends of Job (Job 2, 11), even in the tradition about the magi offering three gifts to Jesus at Bethlehem (Matth. 2, 11) and named Melkon or Melchior, Balthasar, and Gaspard in an Armenian apocryphal work of the 6th century A.D.[70] Story telling and writing is characterized by a spontaneous tendency at providing concrete data and names. Living in a period in which the area of Maḥanaim belonged to the Ammonites or at least was close to their territory, the storyteller of II Sam. 17, 27-29 first mentions Shobi, son of Nahash, from the Ammonite capital. The proper names of the two remaining figures are suggested by nouns designating metallurgical professions: *Makīr*, the "smelter"[71], and *Barzillay*, the "iron smith", whom J. Gray characterizes as "head of a smith-caste"[72]. The proximity of Muġārat al-Warda seems to have inspired the storyteller.

N. Glueck noted the abundance of iron slag also in other parts of the Aǧlūn area, possibly near Ḫirbet al-Maḫna, but this site lacks the features of a refuge place. Besides, the account of Jacob's encounter with the messengers of Elohim at Maḥanaim, in Gen. 32, 2-3, is related to Gen. 32, 23-33, where the struggle with Elohim[73] is placed near the ford of the Jabboq River[74] and not far from Succoth, mentioned in Gen. 33,

[68] P.E. McGovern - V. Pigott - M. Notìs, *The Earliest Steel from Transjordan,* in *University of Pennsylvania Museum of Applied Science. Center for Archaeology Journal* 2 (1983), p. 35-39; P.E. McGovern, *The Innovation of Steel in Transjordan,* in *Journal of Metals* 40/10 (1988), p. 50-52.

[69] G. van der Kooij - M.M. Ibrahim, *Picking up the Threads... A Continuing Review of Excavations at Deir Alla, Jordan*, Leiden 1989, p. 56, cf. p. 99, Nos. 73-78.

[70] St. Ephraem (*ca.* 306-373 A.D.) seems to be the first writer to give them names, but different from the traditional ones. Cf. J.C. Marsh-Edwards, *The Magi in Tradition and Art,* in *Irish Ecclesiastical Record* 85 (1956), p. 1-9 (see p. 6-7). The adoration of *three* magi is represented also on small artefacts from the 6th century A.D.: L.Y. Rahmani, *The Adoration of the Magi on Two Sixth-Century C.E. Eulogia Tokens,* in *IEJ* 29 (1979), p. 34-36 and Pl. 8, B-C-D.

[71] Cf. here above, p. 274, 276.

[72] J. Gray, *I & II Kings*, London 1964, p. 100.

[73] Gen. 32, 29. 31; cf. Hos. 12, 4b-5a.

[74] Gen. 32, 2-3 is not related to Gen. 28, 11-19, as proposed by E. Blum, *Die Komposition der Vätergeschichte*, Neukirchen-Vluyn 1984, p. 141, because the latter account refers to a completely different region. It belongs to the Yahwistic tradition (cf. Gen. 28, 13.16).

17b. The ford was probably located east of Deir 'Alla, in the triangular valley in which the river bends to the south-west. The distance from Deir 'Alla to Tulūl aḏ-Ḏahab amounts to 7 km, and Tell al-Aḫṣāṣ, a probable site of Succoth, lies only 1.5 km further to the west[75]. Tell aḏ-Ḏahab al-Ġarbī is thus the most likely location of Maḥanaim. The smaller eastern mound[76] was instead a fort measuring 130 m by 50 m and dating from the same period as the city proper. It should not be regarded as a distinct town. However, some authors distinguish two settlements there, since the site consists in two ruined mounds: one north of the Jabboq, the other on its south side. Because of the huge curve of the river, the two ruins are beside each other on an east-west axis. The eastern site, Tell aḏ-Ḏahab aš-Šarqī, lies on the south bank. The western site, Tell aḏ-Ḏahab al-Ġarbī, is on the northern bank. Now, the widely held identification of Tell aḏ-Ḏahab aš-Šarqī with Penuel contradicts the biblical account of Gen. 32, 22-24, the author of which certainly knew the region. In fact, Jacob's people, coming from the north, crossed the river at a ford, while Jacob remained alone on its northern bank. Josephus understood it perfectly, since he wrote that Jacob "remained on the other side"[77]. As a matter of fact, Gen. 32, 22-24 does not agree with Gen. 33, whose author assumes that Jacob's family is on the same side of the river as Jacob himself, when they meet Esau coming from the south. It is obvious, however, that there are several sources at the basis of the actual account and there is no point at trying to conciliate the various episodes.

The main Iron Age sites, recently excavated and being further studied, lay in the Jordan Valley: Pella, Tell as-Sa'īdīyeh, Tell al-Mazār, Deir 'Alla.

Pella and Tell as-Sa'īdīyeh

Pella, present-day Ṭabaqat Faḥl, is situated on the lower slopes of the Gilead tableland, 22 km south of the Sea of Galilee and 4 km east of the Jordan River, across the Jordan Valley from Bēth-shan[78]. The mound is some 400 m long by 240 m wide and it rises about 30 m high, with a copious spring flowing from its southern base. The city is mentioned in

[75] See here below, p. 292-293.
[76] Grid ref. 2153/1772; cf. W. Zwickel, *op. cit.* (n. 27), p. 249-250.
[77] Josephus Flavius, *Jewish Antiquities* I, 20, 2, §331.
[78] Grid ref. 2078/2064; cf. W. Zwickel, *op. cit.* (n. 27), p. 292-293.

an Execration Text (*E* 8), in later Egyptian records of the Eighteenth and Nineteenth Dynasties[79], and in Amarna letters 255 and 256. Excavations produced evidence of Iron Age occupation, especially in Iron Age I, which shows no break of continuity with the Late Bronze Age. The city apparently had a reduced population in the Iron II period, at least until the 8th-7th centuries, when its population expanded again. However, Pella appears to have been unoccupied from the early 6th until at least the end of the 4th century B.C. and it plays no role in the biblical tradition[80].

The situation is somewhat different on the impressive mound of Tell as-Sa'īdīyeh, located only 1.8 km from the Jordan River[81], immediately east of a ford. It rises on the south bank of Wādī Kafrinğe, approximately midway between the Sea of Galilee and the Dead Sea. The site consists of two mounds, the western one (al-Ġarbī), lower in elevation, and the eastern (aš-Šarqī), which is the main tell. The upper tell was excavated by J.B. Pritchard in 1964-1967, the lower one in 1964-1965, when the cemetery dating to the end of the Late Bronze and to Iron Age I was uncovered. New excavations, directed by J.N. Tubb, were conducted on both tells from 1985 to 1996[82].

The important city of Early Bronze II, attested also on the lower tell, was destroyed *ca.* 2700 B.C. and remained uninhabited throughout the Early Bronze III period, but graves of Early Bronze IV and Middle Bronze II type did appear in the excavation. A new fortified city was erected in the Late Bronze Age, and the cemetery excavated on the lower mound revealed an Egyptian outpost from the 13th-12th centuries B.C. with graves containing Mycenaean, Cypriot, and Egyptian wares. Bronze stands, a cauldron, axes, spearheads witness a flourishing bronze industry and a prosperous city. Stratum XII on the upper tell, dated by

[79] S. AḤITUV, *op. cit.* (n. 58), p. 153-154.

[80] A synthesis of the research is presented by R.H. SMITH, *Excavations at Pella of the Decapolis, 1979-1985*, in *National Geographic Research* 1 (1985), p. 470-489, and ID., *Pella*, in *NEAEHL*, Jerusalem 1993, Vol. III, p. 1174-1180, with former literature. One should add: A.B. KNAPP, *Society and Polity at Bronze Age Pella: An Annales Perspective*, Scheffield 1993. Several recent articles concern the Christian period.

[81] Grid ref. 2045/1861. Cf. W. ZWICKEL, *op. cit.* (n. 27), p. 264.

[82] J.N. TUBB, *Sa'idiyeh, Tell*, in *NEAEHL*, Jerusalem 1993, Vol. III, p. 1295-1300, with former literature; ID., *Tell es-Sa'idiyeh...*, in *ADAJ* 30 (1986), p. 115-129; 32 (1988), p. 41-58; *Levant* 20 (1988), p. 23-88; 22 (1990), p. 21-42; J.N. TUBB - P.G. DORRELL, *Tell es-Sa'idiyeh...*, in *Levant* 23 (1991), p. 67-86; *PEQ* 125 (1993), p. 50-74; 126 (1994), p. 52-67; J.N. TUBB - P.G. DORRELL - F.J. COBBING, *Tell es-Sa'idiyeh...*, in *PEQ* 128 (1996), p. 16-40, 54-77; S. LEACH - E. REGA, *Interim Report on the Human Skeletal Material Recovered from the 1995 Tell es-Sa'idiyeh Excavations, Areas BB and DD*, in *PEQ* 128 (1996), p. 131-138. See also E.J. VAN DER STEEN, *op. cit.* (n. 28), p. 64-68.

the excavators to the 12th century B.C., seems to have yielded some pottery belonging to the later part of the 9th century B.C.[83] However, Stratum XII lies immediately below Stratum VII, dated now to *ca.* 825-790 B.C., and the potsherds in question obviously slid from the higher to the lower level. One must also keep in mind that a clear differentiation should be made between ceramic assemblages and architectural contexts, which can belong to an earlier period and be reused after clearing of buildings. At any rate, the 9th century town was walled, well built, and the stepped water system, found in the excavation, parallels similar structures in Cisjordan. This level was destroyed by heavy fire, perhaps during the Assyrian invasion of the region by Adad-nirari III, in 803 B.C.[84] The sequence of later occupation levels down to the late 8th century B.C. shows an industrial quarter, but the city had also a well-planned residential area, which was destroyed, probably by the Assyrians in 732 B.C. Remains from Persian and Hellenistic times were encountered as well, especially an official building on the acropolis. Its earlier phases go back to the late 7th century B.C., while its final use dates from the Persian period. Also a cemetery from Persian times was uncovered.

N. Glueck's identification of Tell as-Saīdīyeh as biblical Ṣarethan[85] depends finally on the analysis of literary sources. Ṣarethan occurs in three biblical texts and in a Talmudic quotation. Its location is uncertain, mainly because pertinent biblical passages are usually emended or read superficially, while the Talmudic tradition is regarded as unreliable. The text of Josh. 3, 16, in which *mṣd* is generally mistranslated by "near, next to", simply states that Adam, the present-day Tell ad-Dāmiya, lies on the eastern bank of the Jordan River like Ṣarethan. It says that Jordan "pilled up like a bank for a long way back, as far as Adam, **which is a town on the side** (*miṣṣad*)[86] **of Ṣarethan**". I Kings 7, 46 concerns the casting of Hiram's huge bronze artefacts: "In the plain of the Jordan he cast them in the thickness of the soil, **between Succoth and Ṣarethan**". The last words specify the location, which is already indicated at the beginning of the sentence. However, the phrase "in the thickness of the soil" was emended in 1895 by G.F. Moore in his commentary on Judges,

[83] A. Mazar, *Archaeology of the Land of the Bible, 10,000-586 B.C.E.*, New York 1990, p. 401, n. 21.

[84] Lipiński, *Aramaeans*, p. 395-396.

[85] N. Glueck, *op. cit.* (n. 36), *River Jordan*, p. 126-130, and *Exploration*... IV, p. 334-347; Id., *Transjordan*, in D.W. Thomas (ed.), *Archaeology and Old Testament Study*, Oxford 1967, p. 426-453 and Pl. XIX (see p. 431-432).

[86] Cf. Ex. 25, 22; 37, 18; I Sam. 23, 26; II Sam. 13, 34; Ez. 4, 8.

where he proposed to read *bəma'ᵃberet 'ᵃdāmā*, "at the ford of Adamah"[87], thus connecting both places with ad-Dāmiya. This proposal was widely held for almost half a century[88] and it led to various hypothetical locations of Ṣarethan. The third text, I Kings 4, 12, describes the fifth district of the Kingdom of Israel. Authors generally do not pay any attention to the postposition *-h* of *Ṣrtn-h*, which expresses motion towards the place[89], and they transpose the mistranslated phrase "which is by Ṣarethan" at the end of the sentence. In reality, the passage should be translated as follows: "... and the entire Bēth-shan (region), **which extends nearly to Ṣarethan** (*Ṣrtn-h*), from the Lowland of Jezreel and from Bēth-shan as far as Abel-Meholah, as far as the ford of Jokmeam".

By emending other place names in the Hebrew Bible, some authors try to find supplementary attestations of Ṣarethan. The present writer does not intend to discuss the results of such research. Instead, he wants to stress that the actual mentions of Ṣarethan seem to be limited to glosses, which should help locating other places; they are indicated above in thick-faced letters. These glosses can be attributed to a Deuteronomistic Historian's follower, who was referring to a town well-known in his own days, probably around the 5th century B.C. The place name does not occur in other sources. Moreover, neither the Greek translators of the Bible nor Eusebius understood the passage in I Kings 4, 12; the Septuagint read Σιρα in I Kings 7, 46 and has a different text in Josh. 3, 16. The toponym was obviously unknown in the 3rd or early 2nd century B.C. among the translators of the Bible working at Alexandria.

The texts do not suggest that Ṣarethan was in the immediate neighbourhood of ad-Dāmiya[90], but Josh 3, 16 indicates that the town lay in Transjordan. This excludes the Cisjordanian locations, viz. on the lower course of the Wādī Far'a, as proposed by H. Guthe[91], on Qarn Sarṭaba, as argued by F.-M. Abel[92], or at Ḫirbet al-Qārūr, opposite the outlet of the Wādī ar-Rāğib, as proposed by A. Alt[93]. The topographic indications

[87] G.F. MOORE, *Judges* (ICC), Edinburgh 1898, p. 212-213.

[88] The return to the text was prompted by the article of N. GLUECK, *Three Israelite Towns in the Jordan Valley: Zarethan, Sukkoth, Zaphon*, in *BASOR* 90 (1943), p. 2-23 (see p. 13-14).

[89] LIPIŃSKI, *Semitic*, §32.20.

[90] Grid ref. 2018/1679. Ṣarethan was even localized at ad-Dāmiya by N. GLUECK, *art. cit.* (n. 88), who later proposed Tell as-Sa'īdīyeh; see above, n. 85.

[91] H. GUTHE, *Zarethan und die Erzgiesserei Salomos*, in K. BUDDE (ed.), *Vom Alten Testament. Marti-Festschrift* (BZAW 41), Giessen 1925, p. 96-108, in particular p. 105-106.

[92] ABEL, *Géographie* II, p. 450.

[93] A. ALT, *Das Institut im Jahre 1927*, in *Palästinajahrbuch* 24 (1928), p. 5-74 (see p. 44).

of I Kings 4, 12 show that Ṣarethan must be located south of Bēth-shan, even below Abel-Meholah, as far as the ford at Joqmeam. If the latter place is identified with a well-known ford close to the outlet of the Wādī Kafrinğe[94], the site of Tell as-Sa'īdīyeh, 1.8 km to the east, would agree with the location of Ṣarethan 12 Roman miles from ad-Dāmiya, as stated by Rabbi Johanan (3rd century A.D.): "Rabbi Johanan said: 'Adam is a town and Ṣarethan is a town; they are 12 miles from one another'"[95]. Instead, Tell Suleiḫāt, 8 km north of Tell as-Sa'īdīyeh, suggested by W.F. Albright[96], seems to lay too far away, since the 12 miles, if taken seriously, must represent the distance by ancient roads, not as the crow flies. As for the identification of Ṣarethan with Tell Umm Ḥamād, proposed by B. Mazar[97], one should notice that this is a large (90 x 50 m) Early Bronze I-II mound (Tell Umm Ḥamād Šarqī), situated about 5 km north-east of ad-Dāmiya[98]. Next to it, Tell Umm Ḥamād Ġarbī[99] shows extensive pottery fragments belonging mainly to Middle Bronze I. This twin mound can hardly be taken into consideration for Iron Age I.

If the post-Deuteronomistic glosses referring to Ṣarethan belong to the period around the 5th century B.C., the identification of Tell as-Sa'īdīyeh as Ṣarethan matches the archaeological findings, in particular the discovery of an official building on the acropolis and of a cemetery, both dating from the Persian period.

Also W.F. Albright's identification of Tell as-Sa'īdīyeh with *Ṣpn* is based on literary sources[100]. According to Judg. 12, 1, the Ephraimites forded the Jordan at *Ṣpn*, just like the army of Ptolemy Lathyrus did it at 'Ασωφων in the 1st century B.C.[101] However, the shortest way from the

[94] Abel, *Géographie* II, p. 448.

[95] Talmud Yerushalmi, *Sōṭāh* VII, 5, 21d. Cf. G. Reeg, *op. cit.* (n. 64), p. 552-553. For vague and unspecified reasons this information is discarded by Y. Aharoni, *The Land of the Bible. A Historical Geography,* London 1967, p. 115.

[96] W.F. Albright, *The Jordan Valley in the Bronze Age*, in *AASOR* 6 (1926), p. 13-74 (see p. 47). For this site, cf. also F.-M. Abel, *Exploration de la vallée du Jourdain,* in *RB* 19 (1910), p. 532-556; 20 (1911), p. 408-436; 21 (1912), p. 402-423; 22 (1913), p. 218-243, see 20 (1911), p. 416; Abel, *Géographie* II, p. 34, 273.

[97] B. Maisler (Mazar), *Canaan on the Threshold of the Age of the Patriarchs*, in *To the Memory of M.D.U. Cassuto* (ErIs 3), Jerusalem 1954, p. 18-32 (in Hebrew), in particular p. 26.

[98] See here above, p. 268, n. 6. For Iron Age I-II potsherds, see E.J. van der Steen, *op. cit.* (n. 28), p. 227-228, 246 (Figs. 9-32, 33, 34).

[99] Grid ref. 2053/1724.

[100] Numb. 26, 15; Josh. 13, 27; Judg. 12, 1. The Greek transliterations show that no *wāw* was indicated in *Ṣpn* in the manuscripts used as *Vorlage* by the translators of the 3rd or 2nd century B.C. and that they did not know the correct form of the toponym.

[101] Josephus Flavius, *Jewish Antiquities* XIII, 12, 5, §338.

area of Shechem to Gilead would lead through the Wādī al-Buqei'a to the ford south of the outlet of the Wādī ar-Rāğib. Now, Talmud Yerushalmi identifies *Ṣpwn* with 'Amtan / 'Amtu[102], the present-day Tell al-'Am(ma)tā on the north bank of Wādī ar-Rāğib, about 5 km north-east of the ford. Basing his position on the Talmudic equation, N. Glueck thus identified *Ṣpn* with Tell al-Qaws, a prominent and strategically strong position above Tell al-'Am(ma)tā. Pottery on the surface of this double mound dates from the Iron Age, while its northern part mainly yielded potsherds from the Early Bronze Age[103]. Its date seems to indicate that this was the earliest site of 'Am(ma)tā, where most of the pottery can be dated to later Iron Age II, and to the Roman, Byzantine, and Arabic periods[104]. At a certain point, this site apparently took over the role of *Ṣpn* in that neighbourhood[105]. Its identification with *Ṣpn* may be justified in Talmudic times, but an independent site, closer to the river, seems to be required for *Ṣpn* by the literary sources. The right solution probably consists in identifying *Ṣpn* with Tell al-Mazār, which in fact is closer to the Jordan River.

Tell al-Mazār and Deir 'Alla

Tell al-Mazār is located in the middle Jordan Valley, 2 km south-west of Tell al-'Am(ma)tā[106]. The site was excavated in 1977-1981 by K. Yassine. Occupation levels with architectural remains, roughly dated from the 8th through the 4th century B.C., have been uncovered on the mound[107] and a large public building from the early 9th century has been found on the small Mound A (1,200 m^2), about 400 m north-west of the main tell[108]. The building in question was destroyed *ca.* 800 B.C. by a heavy conflagration, probably at the same time as Phase IX at the nearby

[102] *Shebi'it* IX, 2, 38d; cf. G. Reeg, *op. cit.* (n. 64), p. 494-495 and 548.

[103] Grid ref. 2087/1834; cf. W. Zwickel, *op. cit.* (n. 27), p. 264; E.J. van der Steen, *op. cit.* (n. 28), p. 216-217, 236-237 (Figs. 9-5, 6, 7).

[104] Grid ref. 2085/1829; cf. W. Zwickel, *op. cit.* (n. 27), p. 263. For the pottery, see E.J. van der Steen, *op. cit.* (n. 28), p. 217-218, 237-238 (Figs. 9-8, 9, 10).

[105] Y. Aharoni, *op. cit.* (n. 95), p. 115.

[106] Grid ref. 1959/1718. Cf. A. de Groot, *Mazar, Tell,* in *NEAEHL*, Jerusalem 1993, Vol. III, p. 989-991.

[107] K. Yassine, *Tell el Mazar, Field I Preliminary Report of Area G, H, L, and M: The Summit,* in *ADAJ* 27 (1983), p. 495-513.

[108] K. Yassine, *The Open Court Sanctuary of the Iron Age I Tell Mazar Mound A,* in *ZDPV* 100 (1984), p. 108-118, and in K. Yassine, *The Archaeology of Jordan: Essays and Reports*, Amman 1988, p. 115-135. The excavator's dating of the building to Iron Age I is too high.

Deir 'Alla[109]. The area was abandoned until the 5th century B.C., when it was used as a cemetery[110]. The floor plan of the building on Mound A can be recovered only in part, but it included casemate rooms along one side of a large courtyard. This disposition recalls the compound around Palace 6000 at Megiddo[111], which should be dated to the early 9th century B.C. There is no reason to accept the identification of this building as an "open court sanctuary", as suggested by the excavator. It may have been a large farmhouse or an offiсlal building, possibly related either to Omri's conquests in Transjordan, recorded in the Mesha inscription[112], or to the metallurgy which is well attested in this area. Slag deposits are found at various sites in the vicinity. A large scale iron smelting installation from the early 8th century B.C. has been identified at Tell al-Ḥamma East, 2.5 km east of Deir 'Alla, where an Iron Age I foundry for casting bronze was apparently discovered[113]. Besides, metal works, that seemingly date to the same period, have been uncovered at Tell al-Mazār, but the finds are still under study[114].

If Tell al-Mazār does not yield architectural remains after the 4th century B.C., this can mean that the settlement was relocated in the neighbourhood, perhaps at Tell al-Ġazāla, 1.5 km to the north-east, where Roman and Byzantine ceramics was found besides potsherds from the second half of the Late Bronze Age and the Iron Age[115]. The name of the Iron Age settlement, vocalized *Ṣāpōn*, was apparently no longer understood. However, Josephus Flavius, who records the actual pronunciation of the place name 'Ασωφων[116], preserves its original form *ha-Ṣōp̄ōn*. This shows that the toponym, attested also as the name of a clan of Gad (Numb. 26, 15), does not mean "North", but is a derivative either of *ṣpn*, which has the connotation "to shelter" in poetic texts (Ps. 27, 5; 31, 21;

[109] G. VAN DER KOOIJ - M.M. IBRAHIM, *op. cit.* (n. 69), p. 88.

[110] K. YASSINE, *Tell el Mazar I: Cemetery A*, Amman 1984. Cf. ID., *Burial Customs and Practices in Ancient Ammon*, in B. MACDONALD - R.W. YOUNKER (eds.), *Ancient Ammon*, Leiden 1999, p. 137-151. See also A.M. DISI *et al.*, *Tell el Mazar: Study of the Human Skeletal Remains*, in *ADAJ* 27 (1983), p. 515-548.

[111] A. MAZAR, *op. cit.* (n. 83), p. 389-390.

[112] See here below, p. 336.

[113] For Tell al-Ḥamma East (Grid ref. 2112/1778), see E.J. VAN DER STEEN, *op. cit.* (n. 28), p. 195-196; cf. W. ZWICKEL, *op. cit.* (n. 27), p. 250. For Deir 'Alla, see G. VAN DER KOOIJ - M.M. IBRAHIM, *op. cit.* (n. 69), p. 87, but doubts have been expressed E.J. VAN DER STEEN, *op. cit.* (n. 28), p. 63.

[114] R.A. COUGHENOUR, *art. cit.* (n. 59), p. 62.

[115] Grid ref. 2076/1812; cf. W. ZWICKEL, *op. cit.* (n. 27), p. 263; E.J. VAN DER STEEN, *op. cit.* (n. 28), p. 219-220, 239-240 (Figs. 9-12, 13).

[116] JOSEPHUS FLAVIUS, *Jewish Antiquities* XIII, 12, 5 §338.

83, 4) and in proper names[117], or of *śyp*, "to stay as guest". It should thus mean "shelter", and it might be a noun of the **ṣawpan* type. Unfortunately, such a place name does not suggest any particular location.

The impressive mound of Deir 'Alla is located west of the bend of Nahr az-Zerqā, 3 km south of Tell al-Mazār. The excavation directed by H.J. Franken have yielded important results, but the Talmudic identification of *Tr'lh* with Succoth[118] raises as many questions as ever. At any rate, *Tr'lh* does obviously not designate the mound in the sense of the Hebrew word *tr'lh*, "staggering", which occurs in Is. 51, 17.22 and in Ps. 60, 5. It is based on Aramaic *tr''lh*, "Gate of God", used in parallelism with "Gate of Heaven" in Gen. 28, 17: it alludes to the account in Gen. 32, 25-31, and interprets Penuel, "Face of God". In the current pronunciation, the glottal stop of the divine name was assimilated to the voiced pharyngeal *'ayin*, as happens regularly in proper names[119]. The Aramaic place name, which must be quite old, was thus pronounced **Tera'lah*, still echoed in Deir 'Alla. Aramaic is the language of a prophecy by Balaam, discovered at Deir 'Alla[120], and the area was densely occupied in the Persian period, when both excavated sites of Tell al-Mazār and Deir 'Alla provide proofs of Aramaic literacy. Both places yielded ostraca, which can be dated to the 6th-4th centuries B.C.[121], as well as seals datable to the same period[122]. An Aramaic place name "Gate of God", translating "Penuel", fits in perfectly with this situation. It is uncertain whether the redactors of the Talmud Yerushalmi still understood the meaning of the toponym, but their identification was based on a tradition preceding the late Roman or early Byzantine times. No traces of these periods have been found on the mound, but there were some farms in the neighbourhood, and a Byzantine graveyard was discovered in 1960-1961 about 1 km east of the tell[123]. Toponymic tradition could thus live forth and locate Succoth in an approximate way, close to Penuel (Judg. 8, 8.16-17).

[117] M. NOTH, *op. cit.* (n. 31), p. 178.

[118] Talmud Yerushalmi, *Shebi'it* IX, 2, 38d.

[119] E. LITTMANN, *Semitische Parallelen zur assimilatorischen Wirkung des 'Ajin*, in *ZÄS* 47 (1910), p. 62-64; *SAIO* I, p. 106, 122, 125.

[120] *SAIO* II, p. 103-170, with former literature.

[121] K. YASSINE - J. TEIXIDOR, *Ammonite and Aramaic Inscriptions from Tell el-Mazār in Jordan*, in *BASOR* 264 (1986), p. 45-50; G. VAN DER KOOIJ - M.M. IBRAHIM, *op. cit.* (n. 69), p. 69-70 and 107, No. 151.

[122] K. YASSINE, *Ammonite Seals from Tell el-Mazar*, in A. HADIDI (ed.), *Studies in the History and Archaeology of Jordan* I, Amman 1982, p. 189-194; G. VAN DER KOOIJ - M.M. IBRAHIM, *op. cit.* (n. 69), p. 70 and 106, No. 140.

[123] G. VAN DER KOOIJ - M.M. IBRAHIM, *op. cit.* (n. 69), p. 90.

Excavations at Deir 'Alla.

Deir 'Alla was a fairly large sanctuary already in the Late Bronze Age and its name Penuel should go back to that time. Its destruction in an earthquake is dated in the early 12th century B.C. by an Egyptian faience vase with the cartouche of Queen Tewosret. The inhabitants of the following period were in part metal workers, and they practiced animal husbandry and farming. The most spectacular find of the Iron Age was a ruined building of the 9th century B.C. with a plastered wall, inscribed in Aramaic[124] with the text of the prophecy by Balaam, son of Beor, also known from Numb. 22-24. The site is probably referred to in Numb. 22, 5, which locates Balaam's residence "on the river, in the country of the

[124] For the excavations, see H.J. FRANKEN - J. KALSBEEK, *Excavations at Deir 'Alla. A Stratigraphical and Analytical Study of the Early Iron Age Pottery*, Leiden 1969; G. VAN DER KOOIJ - M.M. IBRAHIM, *op. cit.* (n. 69); H.J. FRANKEN, *Excavations at Deir 'Alla. The Late Bronze Age Sanctuary*, Leuven 1992; G. VAN DER KOOIJ, *Deir 'Alla*, in *NEAEHL*, Jerusalem 1993, Vol. I, p. 338-342. For the pottery, see also E.J. VAN DER STEEN, *op. cit.* (n. 28), p. 170-193.

sons of Ammon"[125]. There is no unequivocal evidence that the Iron Age settlement was walled, but in Phase K, dating from the end of the 11th century B.C., there was a round tower made of mud-bricks with a diameter of *ca.* 7 m[126]. If the identification of Deir 'Alla as Penuel is correct, this is likely to be the tower destroyed by Gideon, who had slain the men of the city according to Judg. 8, 17. The settlement is possibly mentioned as *Pr-nw-3r* in the list of Shoshenq I (No. 53)[127].

If Deir 'Alla is ancient Penuel, the twin mound of Tulūl aḏ-Ḏahab, identified with Penuel by S. Merrill in 1881, must be Maḥanaim, as seen above[128]. One element is certain: Penuel is the holy place, where Jacob saw "God face to face" (Gen. 32, 31). It can indeed be called "Gate of God", *Tr'(')lh*. In this case, Succoth must correspond not to Deir 'Alla, but to another mound in its neighbourhood, while Maḥanaim should be regarded as the name of Tulūl aḏ-Ḏahab.

Succoth was identified by some authors with Tell al-Aḫṣāṣ or al-Ḫiṣāṣ[129], which should be distinguished from the small Tell ar-Rabī'[130], situated beside Tell al-Aḫṣāṣ. The latter is a large mound. It yielded potsherds from the early Iron Age, but also from Iron Age II, down to the 6th century B.C.[131] It is situated 2.5 km south-west of Deir 'Alla and this location suits the biblical account. The mound was identified with Succoth also because *'aḫṣāṣ* is an exact translation of *sukkōt*, "boots". However, to be translated into Arabic, "Succoth" should have been used down to the Islamic-Arabic period. Now, this is unlikely, because Eusebius was unable to localize Succoth, while St. Jerome only refers vaguely to a Transjordanian place in the region of Bēth-shan: *est autem usque hodie civitas trans Iordanem hoc vocabulo inter partes Scythopoleos*[132]. The name of Tell al-Aḫṣāṣ can thus be quite recent and have alluded originally to boots for cattle, erected on the mound by semi-nomad tribes, which were living in this part of the valley in the recent centuries. Cattle like to stay on the mound during the hotter months of

125 *SAIO* II, p. 111-113.

126 G. van der Kooij - M.M. Ibrahim, *op. cit.* (n. 69), p. 81.

127 S. Aḥituv, *op. cit.* (n. 58), p. 154; K.A. Kitchen, *The Third Intermediate Period in Egypt (1100-650 B.C.)*, 3rd ed., Warminster 1995, p. 438.

128 See here above, p. 280-283.

129 Abel, *Géographie* II, p. 470.

130 Grid ref. 2063/1777; cf. E.J. van der Steen, *op. cit.* (n. 28), p. 222-223 and 229.

131 The date *ca.* 900, given by W. Zwickel, *op. cit.* (n. 27), p. 247, is too early, as the pottery in question goes down to the late 7th or 6th century. Cf. E.J. van der Steen, *op. cit.* (n. 28), p. 222-223, 241-242 (Figs. 9-18, 19).

132 S. Hieronymus, *Hebraicae quaestiones in libro Geneseos* 33, 17.

the year, as there is always breeze[133]. Besides, there was another mound 2.5 km south of Deir ʻAlla, viz. Tell al-Mēdān, also called Tell Šuʻba, which still rose some fifty years ago close to the Jabboq River. It yielded Iron Age pottery as well[134]. In the opinion of the biblical storyteller, Penuel and Succoth were sites close to one another. If Deir ʻAlla is identified as Penuel, both al-Aḫṣāṣ and al-Mēdān can correspond to Succoth. To establish the probable historical relations between these sites archaeological excavations or deep soundings should be conducted at Tell al-Aḫṣāṣ and Tell at al-Mēdān. However, the latter practically disappeared before the East Jordan Valley Survey of 1975-1976 could visit the site, which is situated in the middle of arable land, much in demand in the second half of the 20th century[135].

[133] G. van der Kooij - M.M. Ibrahim, *op. cit.* (n. 69), p. 12-13, cf. p. 90.

[134] Grid ref. 2086/1758. Cf. W. Zwickel, *op. cit.* (n. 27), p. 246; E.J. van der Steen, *op. cit.* (n. 28), p. 224-225, 243 (Fig. 9-23).

[135] E.J. van der Steen, *op. cit.* (n. 28), p. 224.

CHAPTER VIII

AMMON

The Ammonites, known from biblical, epigraphic, and archaeological sources, derive their name from a presumed ancestor and eponym *'Ammān*. This is an Amorite name, attested since the early second millennium B.C., especially in the Mari archives[1]. Its base is formed by the noun *'amm*, "forefather" in ancient Semitic[2], with the affix *-ān*. The form *'Ammōn*, witnessing the change *ā* > *ō*, is Hebrew, while Akkadian and Greek notations, based on the spoken language, show that the Ammonites were calling themselves *Banī 'Ammān*[3], their land was *Bēt 'Ammān*[4], and their capital was called *Rabbat 'Ammān*[5], present-day Amman. Despite the antiquity of the name, no literary sources from the Bronze Age, not even the Egyptian topographical lists, mention the region occupied by the Ammonites in the Iron Age. It means that it fell outside the Pharaonic sphere of influence, although archaeological findings reveal a cultural and economic impact of Egypt.

Territory

The eastern border of the Ammonite territory was the desert, i.e. the limit of any permanent settlement or the 200 mm annual rainfall line. The central Jabboq, flowing east to west, constituted their northern border (Deut. 3, 16; Josh. 12, 2). The western one extended from the con-

[1] M. BIROT, in *ARM* XVI/1, Paris 1979, p. 98-99, s.v. *Ḫamman(um)*. Cf. J.J. STAMM, *Zur Ursprung des Namens der Ammoniter,* in *Archiv Orientální* 17 (1948), p. 179-182 = J.J. STAMM, *Beiträge zur hebräischen und altorientalischen Namenkunde* (OBO 30), Freiburg/Schweiz-Göttingen 1980, p. 5-8.

[2] The semantic shift from "first agnate" to "paternal uncle" seems to imply a tribal power structure in which the "father" of the clan was succeeded after his demise by a brother, thus an "uncle".

[3] Cf. the singular *Ba-an Am-ma-na-a-a* in H.W.F. SAGGS, *The Nimrud Letters, 1952. - Part II: Relations with the West,* in *Iraq* 17 (1955), p. 126-160 (see No. XVI, 36, p. 134-135).

[4] *Bēt-Am-man-a-a*, for instance in *SAA* VII, 58, I, 6' and 10'; *SAA* XI, 33, 2.

[5] 'Ραββατάμμανα in a Zenon Papyrus from 259 B.C., published by C.C. EDGAR, *Zenon Papyri* I (CGC), Le Caire 1925, Pap. 59003, in POLYBIUS, *History* V, 71, 4, and STEPHEN OF BYZANTIUM, *Ethnica*, s.v.

fluence of the Jabboq River and of Wādī ar-Rumaymīn southward, along the ridge of mountains dividing the upper Jabboq tributaries from the upper beds of Wādī aš-Šu'ayb, Wādī al-'Azrāq, Wādī aṣ-Ṣīr, Wādī an-Nuṣariyāt, and Wādī Ḥisbān. Important settlements along the western boundary were Jogbehah (al-Ǧubeiḥa) and Ya'zer (Ḫirbet Ġazzir). On the south, at Nā'ūr, the border turned eastward, passing north of the Moabite territory.

According to Numb. 32, 35, Ya'zer and Jogbehah belonged to the tribe of Gad, which also tried to occupy the territory situated further to the south and described in Numb. 32, 34-36[6]. However, the Mesha stele already indicates that the Gadites have been repulsed from this region after the fall of the Omrides[7], i.e. after *ca.* 840 B.C., and also in the east they have certainly lost ground. Dibon, Ataroth, and Aroer belonged to the Moabites *ca.* 825 B.C., while Ya'zer and Jogbehah were in Ammonite hands at the latest in the 7th century B.C. The large rectangular structure of Qaṣr al-Ḫilda al-Aǧbeiḥāt / Ǧubeiḥa (34 x 45 m) must be close to the ancient settlement of Jogbehah, as the name suggests. It yielded potsherds not older than the 7th century B.C.[8] An initial Iron II occupation was confirmed by the excavation of two tombs near the fort[9], which presents the characteristics of the Ammonite Iron II round towers and rectangular or square buildings. In the vicinity, there are two other structures of this type, viz. a rectangular one and a "tower" or *ruǧm*[10]. These constructions witness the Ammonite occupation of the area, abandoned by the Gadites. The situation is apparently similar at Ḫirbet Ġazzir, 4 km south of as-Salṭ. This is a strategic site, which most likely corresponds to Ya'zer[11]. A rectangular *qaṣr*, measuring about 10 m by 15 m, is built on bedrock on a spur of the hill. The stones are laid in

[6] One of the cities mentioned in this passage, viz. Atrot-Shaphan, has not been identified so far.

[7] Mesha inscription, lines 10 ff. See here below, p. 336.

[8] Grid ref. 2003/1559: K. YASSINE, *The Archaeology of Jordan: Essays and Reports*, Amman 1988, p. 17; R.G. KHOURI, *Amman. A Brief Guide of Antiquities*, Amman 1988, p. 23.

[9] Grid ref. 2303/1565: K. YASSINE, *op. cit.* (n. 8), p. 11-31.

[10] Grid ref. 2315/1576 and 2316/1590. The latter structure has a diameter of 15 m: N. GLUECK, *Exploration of Eastern Palestine* III (AASOR 18-19), New Haven 1939, p. 172, No. 234.

[11] Grid ref. 218/158: R. DE VAUX, *Notes d'histoire et de topographie transjordaniennes*, in *Vivre et Penser* 1 (1941), p. 16-47 (see p. 25-27). A summary presentation of the various opinions is provided by B. MACDONALD, *Ammonite Territory and Sites*, in B. MACDONALD - R.W. YOUNKER (eds.), *Ancient Ammon*, Leiden 1999, p. 30-56 (see p. 34-35).

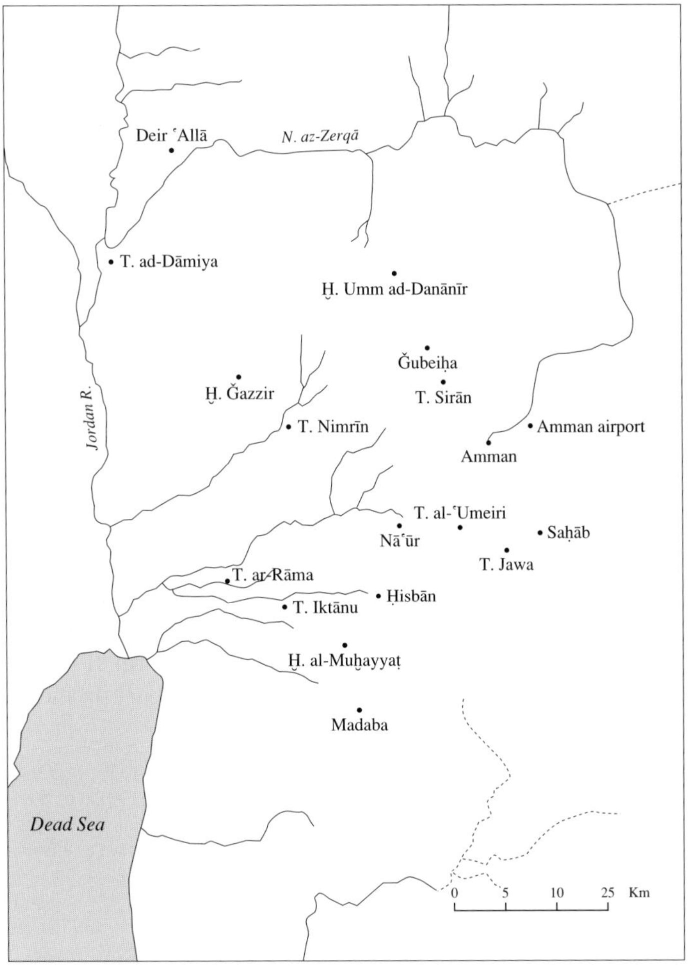

Ammon.

courses, using a headers and stretchers technique in the corners. The pottery from the surface is said to be Iron Age I-II without any later potsherds[12]. This seems to be an Ammonite *qaṣr*, dating from the 8th-7th centuries B.C. like other buildings of this type[13]. The presence of older pottery could indicate that the site was previously occupied by Gadites.

[12] R. DE VAUX, *Exploration de la région de Salṭ*, in *RB* 47 (1938), p. 398-425, Pls. XVII-XXIII (see p. 405, No. 8; Pls. XVII, 1, and XVIII, 1).

[13] R. KLETTER, *The Rujm El-Malfuf Buildings and the Assyrian Vassal State of Ammon*, in *BASOR* 284 (1991), p. 33-50.

Bēth-Nimra and Bēth-Haram, reckoned in Numb. 32, 36 among Gadite cities, are located further west. Bēth-Nimra is identified with Tell Nimrīn, west of Amman, at the entrance of the Jordan Valley. Excavations conducted at the site from 1989 uncovered levels from Early Bronze IV to Hellenistic times. At least five phases of the Iron Age, from the 10th to the 6th century B.C. have been distinguished[14]. Bēth-Haram can be identified as Tell ar-Rāma, further south, 4 km west of al-Hammam[15]. This was a significant population centre in the Iron Age. In the 8th century B.C., one of these sites or the nearby Tell Iktānu[16] was probably the residence of the prince of Bēth-Ṭāb'il, a small princedom, whose head has been candidate to the throne of Judah according to Is. 7, 6[17]. A Nimrud letter sent by Qurdi-Aššur-lāmur[18] to Tiglath-pileser III informs the king about the coming of a messenger from mDINGIR-*a-a-nu-ri*[19] kur*Ṭa-ab-i-la-a-a*[20], "Ilāya-nūr of Ṭāb'il", adding that the man is called m*E-za-zu*[21], i.e. *'Āzāz,* a personal name attested also in I Chron. 5, 8. The messenger brought news concerning the nearby country of Moab, attacked by Qedarites[22].

Also the Land of Ṭōb, where Jephthah the Gileadite settled according to Judg. 11, 3.5, and the men of Ṭōb, who allegedly fought on the side of the Ammonites (II Sam. 10, 6.8)[23], can most likely be linked with Bēth-Ṭāb'il. *Ṭōb* is only a shortened and Hebraized form of Ṭāb'il, used also with the suffix *-ī* as the patronymic *Ṭwby* of Tobit[24]. In the writer's

[14] Grid ref. 2096/1450. Preliminary reports by J.W. FLANAGAN, D.W. MCCREERY and K. YASSINE, *Tell Nimrin...*, in *ADAJ* 34 (1990), p. 131-152; 36 (1992), p. 89-112; 38 (1994), p. 205-244; 40 (1996), p. 271-292.

[15] Grid ref. 2111/1371: ABEL, *Géographie* II, p. 273; W. ZWICKEL, *Eisenzeitliche Ortslagen im Ostjordanland* (BTAVO B/81), Wiesbaden 1990, p. 162.

[16] Cf. LIPIŃSKI, *Aramaeans*, p. 371.

[17] W.F. ALBRIGHT, *The Son of Tabeel (Isaiah 7:6),* in *BASOR* 140 (1955), p. 34-35.

[18] His name is shortened in the letter to Qurdi-Aššur; cf. G. VAN BUYLAERE, *Qurdi-Aššūr-lāmur,* in *PNA* III/1, Helsinki 2002, p. 1021-1022.

[19] It is obvious that this name does not mean "Ea is my light", as stated by F.M. FALES, *Aia-nūrī,* in *PNA* I/1, Helsinki 1998, p. 92. The name is *'Ilāya-nūr*, "My god is a light", with the suffixed Arabic theophorous element *'Ilā(h)*. The *y* of *'Ilāy* is sometimes marked in Ammonite seal legends, like in *'ly-dn*, "My god is strong"; cf. N. AVIGAD - B. SASS, *Corpus of West Semitic Stamp Seals*, Jerusalem 1997, p. 335-336, No. 698, and p. 336-337, No. 702. A different name ⸢*A-a*⸣?*-nu-ḫu /Yanūḫ/* should be read in V. DONBAZ - S. PARPOLA, *Neo-Assyrian Legal Texts in Istanbul* (Studien zu den Assur-Texten 2), Saarbrücken 2001, No. 188, left edge 1 (cf. note on p. 134), and one should cancel *Aia-nūri* in *PNA* I/1, p. 92.

[20] It is impossible to interpret kur*Da-ab-i-la-a-a* as Dibonite, as done by G.W. VERA CHAMAZA, *Die Rolle Moabs in der neuassyrischen Expansionspolitik* (AOAT 321), Münster 2005, p. 78 and 137, and Ilāya-nūr is no Assyrian official (*ibid.*, p. 78).

[21] Nimrud letter XIV, 4-6, published by H.W.F. SAGGS, *art. cit.* (n. 3), p. 131-133.

[22] See here below, p. 357-358.

[23] For the question of Maaka, chieftain of Ṭōb, see LIPIŃSKI, *Aramaeans*, p. 333-337.

[24] J.T. MILIK, *La Patrie de Tobie,* in *RB* 73 (1966), p. 522-530, connects the Book of

opinion, the basic text of the topographical indications of Tobit 1, 2 in the long version of the *Codex Sinaiticus*, which appears to be also the version of the Qumrān fragments, consisted only of the words ἐκ Θίσβης ... ἐξ ἀριστερῶν Φογωρ, "from Thisbe, ... north of Peor". Tishbe is Tishbe in Gilead (I Kings 17, 1) and Peor is Bēth-Pe'ōr, possibly Tell Iktānu[25]. The other topographical indications, introduced by ἥ ἐστιν, are a gloss connecting Tobit with the tribe of Naphtali, what is done also in verses 4-5 of chapter 1[26]. The story was thus connected initially with the region of Bēth-Ṭāb'il.

Nothing indicates so far that this western area of Transjordan belonged to the Ammonites in the Iron Age. It was close to Moab and Aramaic influence was strong in the entire region. Instead, Ammonite expansion westward did not begin before the end of the 7th century B.C. It is occasionally recorded in the Bible. A gloss in Numb. 21, 24, better preserved in the Septuagint, explains that "Ya'zer is the border of the Ammonites". They were still occupying the new site of the town at Ḫirbet as-Sūq, when Judah Maccabee conquered the place (I Macc. 5, 8). The area around Deir 'Alla is placed in Ammonite territory by Numb. 22, 5[27], and Jer. 49, 1-5 clearly states that the Ammonites took possession of the territory of Gad. Finally, Judg. 11, 13 says that the Ammonites extended "from the Arnon to the Jabboq and to the Jordan", approximately describing the situation in the 6th century B.C. or somewhat later in the Persian period, at the time of the post-Deuteronomistic redactions.

Early history

The ancient history of the Ammonite country, known mainly from archaeological surveys and excavations, is clearly divided into periods of urban life and prosperity, separated by centuries during which the area seems to have been inhabited by nomad tribes with an Amorite background. Such a period of prosperity occurred during the Middle Bronze Age, but came to an end *ca.* 1500 B.C., after which the country returned to its nomadic or semi-nomadic status for more than 200 years. New people then came and rebuilt the cities. As for the Ammonites,

Tobit with the dynasty of the Tobiads, whose main centre was 'Irāq al-Amīr, west of Amman, at least from the beginning of the 2nd century B.C.

[25] LIPIŃSKI, *Aramaeans*, p. 360-361.

[26] The writer does not agree here with J.T. MILIK, *art. cit.* (n. 24), who considers all the topographical indications to be authentic.

[27] *SAIO* II, p. 111.

whose initial tribal area was very likely the Baq'a Valley[28], 25 km northwest of Amman, they pushed first to the south and assumed the control of the caravan routes between Egypt, Mesopotamia, and Arabia. This undoubtedly brought wealth to the country.

Nelson Glueck's synthesis[29], the later developments in the research, and recently published states of art[30] are well-known and do not need to be summarized here again.

Saḥāb and Tell al-'Umeiri, respectively south-east and south-west of Amman, already reveal an urbanization process indicating that the land of the Ammonites was the most developed area of Transjordan in Iron Age I[31]. The casemate wall and the dry moat of Tell al-'Umeiri, the pillared houses of Saḥāb, "collared-rim" pithoi and "jar coffins" evidence a material culture comparable with that of urban centres in Cisjordan. Saḥāb, that was already inhabited in the Middle and Late Bronze periods, is one of the largest Iron I sites of Jordan, covering about 25 ha and thus having a population of about five or six thousand people, if we use the population coefficient of 200-250 persons per built up hectare.

About 4 km north-east of Amman, a square stone structure on a side of 15 m was discovered in 1955 during works at the Amman airport[32]. It contained fragments of Egyptian stone vessels, masses of Cypriot and Mycenaean IIIB pottery, weapons, and dispersed bone remains of some cremated human bodies. The local pottery would suggest that the building continued in use until the mid-12th century or *ca.* 1100, rather than *ca.* 1200 B.C. Its interpretation as temple of human sacrifice or the like

[28] P.E. McGovern, *Baq'a Valley,* in *NEAEHL*, Jerusalem 1993, Vol. I, p. 144-147.

[29] N. Glueck, *Explorations in Eastern Palestine* I (AASOR 14), Philadelphia 1934, p. 81-83; Id., *Explorations in the Land of Ammon,* in *BASOR* 68 (1937), p. 13-21; Id., *Explorations in Eastern Palestine* III (AASOR 18-19), New Haven 1939.

[30] B. Oded, *'Ammōn,* in *Enṣiqlopēdiya Miqrā'īt* VI, Jerusalem 1971, col. 254-271 with bibliography; U. Hübner, *Die Ammoniter: Untersuchungen zur Geschichte, Kultur und Religion einer Transjordanischen Volkes im 1. Jahrtausend v. Chr.* (Abhandlungen des Deutschen Palästina-Vereins 16), Wiesbaden 1992; B. MacDonald - R.W. Younker (eds.), *Ancient Ammon*, Leiden 1999.

[31] Grid ref. 2452/1425 and 2341/1420. Cf. M.M. Ibrahim, *Archaeological Excavations at Sahab, 1972*, in *ADAJ* 17 (1972), p. 23-36; Id., *Second Season of Excavations at Sahab, 1973*, in *ADAJ* 19 (1974), p. 55-61; Id., *Third Season of Excavatios at Sahab, 1975*, in *ADAJ* 20 (1975), p. 69-82; B. de Vries, *Archaeology in Jordan,* in *AJA* 95, (1991), p. 253-280, especially p. 266-268; L.G. Herr, *The Bronze and Iron Ages at Tell el-'Umeiri, Jordan*, in *Qadmoniot* 28 (1995), p. 83-89 (in Hebrew). Cf. W. Zwickel, *op. cit.* (n. 15), p. 203-204 and 212.

[32] Grid ref. 2430/1535. The literature has been collected by R. Hachmann, *Kāmid el Lōz* 16. *'Schatzhaus'-Studien* (Saarbrücker Beiträge zur Altertumskunde 59), Bonn 1996, p. 242-248: "Der spätbronzezeitliche Quadratbau von Amman".

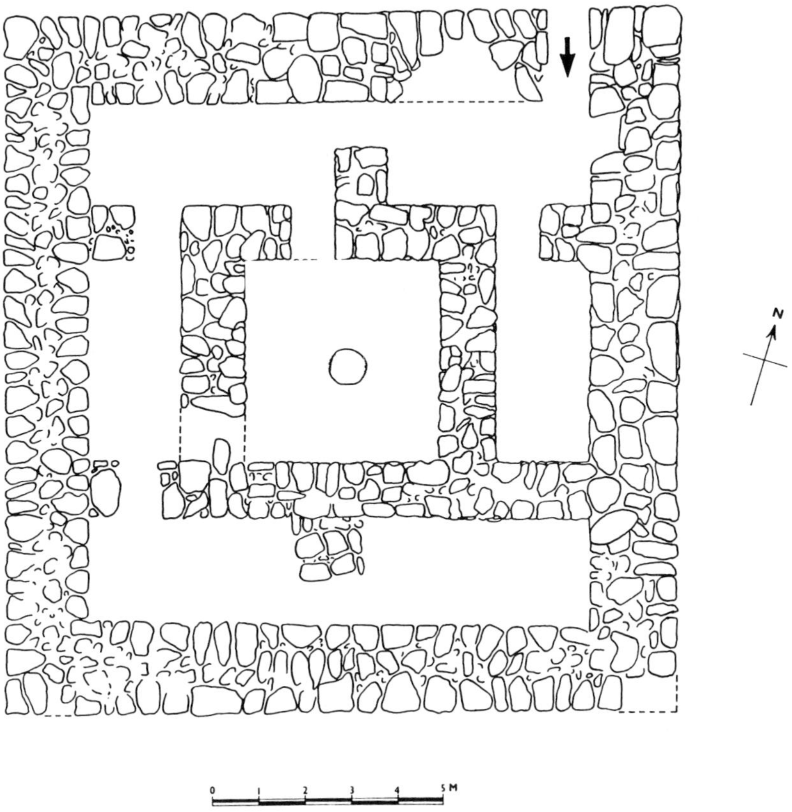

Plan of the fortified residence at the Amman airport.

is not convincing and the opinion considering it as a tower-like residence[33], a *migdal*, is more appealing, the more so that comparable structures were discovered at El-Mabrak[34], 4 km to the south-east, at Ḫirbet Umm ad-Danānīr, and at Ruǧm al-Ḥinw East[35], both in the Baq'a Val-

[33] V. Fritz, *Erwägungen zu dem spätbronzezeitlichen Quadratbau bei Amman*, in *ZDPV* 87 (1971), p. 140-152. See also E.J. van der Steen, *Tribes and Territories in Transition. The Central East Jordan Valley in the Late Bronze Age and Early Iron Ages: A Study of the Sources* (OLA 130), Leuven 2004, p. 55-58, 161.

[34] K. Yassine, *El Mabrak: An Architectural Analogue of the Amman Airport Building?*, in *ADAJ* 27 (1983), p. 491-494 = K. Yassine, *op. cit.* (n. 8), p. 61-64. Subsequent investigation by M. Waheeb, *A Fortified Agricultural Complex East of Amman (Late Bronze Age-Iron Age): Preliminary Report*, in *ADAJ* 36 (1992), p. 399-408 (in Arabic), revealed associated installations, regarded by the author as belonging to an agricultural complex.

[35] Ḫirbet Umm ad-Danānīr (grid ref. 2273/1659) was excavated by P.E. McGovern, *The Late Bronze and Early Iron Ages of Central Transjordan. The Baq'ah Valley Project*

ley. A similar structure, square with sides about 10 m, was discovered further west, close to Ḫirbet al-Muḫayyaṭ[36]. The weapons and the burnt remains of exsanguine human bodies, discovered in the edifice of the Amman airport[37], suggest an attack putting an end to the occupation of the site by some wealthy people, possibly living in the middle of an agricultural complex. The attackers may have been the Ammonites, who have then started to settle and to occupy the country. Discussing the alternative hypothesis that the new settlers in the area could have been Reubenites, would not lead to any result[38].

Ammonite expansion northward, from the Baq'a Valley across the Nahr az-Zerqā, does not seem to have been successful, despite the biblical references to Ammonite incursions into Gilead[39] and the additional story in 4QSam[a], which reports the alleged oppression of the Gadites and Reubenites by Nahash, king of Ammon[40]. While this account, inserted between I Sam. 10, 27a and 10, 27b, is most likely a midrashic development added to an earlier version of the text[41], the account of David's first Ammonite war[42] contains unlikely elements, like the unforgivable insult to David's ambassadors (II Sam. 10, 1-5; I Chron. 19, 1-5) and the intervention of Hadadezer, supposed to be king of Ṣoba in the

1977-1981, Philadelphia 1986, who still speaks of "cultic installations" (p. 63), despite the fact that the pottery was domestic in character; cf. E.J. van der Steen, *op. cit.* (n. 33), p. 59-60. See further P.E. McGovern, *The Baq'ah Valley Project: Khirbet Umm ad-Dananir and al-Qeṣir*, in *ADAJ* 32 (1989), p. 123-126. - Ruǧm al-Ḥinw East (grid ref. 2284/1655), to the east of Ḫirbet Umm ad-Danānīr, was excavated likewise by P.E. McGovern, *Test Soundings of Archaeological and Resistivity Survey Results at Rujm al-Ḥenu*, in *ADAJ* 27 (1983), p. 105-141; Id., *op. cit.* (n. 35), p. 5, 11-13.

[36] F. Benedettucci - R. Sabelli, *The Edifice at Rujm al-Mukhayyat*, in M. Piccirillo - E. Alliata (eds.), *Mount Nebo: New Archaeological Excavations 1967-1997*, Jerusalem 1998, p. 128-131.

[37] An interesting comparison is made by W. Zwickel, *I Sam 31, 12f. und der Quadratbau auf dem Flughafengelände bei Amman*, in *ZAW* 105 (1993), p. 165-174.

[38] See here below, p. 326. For this Reubenite hypothesis, see L.G. Herr, *Tall al-'Umayri and the Reubenite Hypothesis*, in *F.M. Cross Volume* (ErIs 26), Jerusalem 1999, p. 64*-77*, referring to F.M. Cross, *Reuben, First-Born of Jacob*, in *ZAW* 100 (1988), *Supplement*, p. 46-65. For similar reasons, it is not necessary to discuss here the article by M. Cogan, *The Men of Nebo - Repatriated Reubenites*, in *IEJ* 29 (1979), p. 37-39.

[39] Judg. 10, 7-11, 33; I Sam. 11, 1-11; Am. 2, 13-15.

[40] F.M. Cross, *The Ammonite Oppression of the Tribes of Gad and Reuben: Missing Verses from 1 Samuel 11 found in 4QSamuel[a]*, in E. Tov (ed.), *The Hebrew and Greek Texts of Samuel*, Jerusalem 1980, p. 105-119 = H. Tadmor - M. Weinfeld (eds.), *History, Historiography and Interpretation*, Jerusalem 1983, p. 148-158. The official edition of the text: F.M. Cross - D.W. Parry - R.J. Saley - E. Ulrich, *Qumrân Cave 4, XII: The Samuel Scrolls from Cave 4* (DJD 17), Oxford 2005, p. 66-67, Pl. X.

[41] A. Rofé, *The Acts of Nahash According to 4QSam[a]*, in *IEJ* 32 (1987), p. 129-133.

[42] II Sam. 10; I Chron. 19.

Lebanese Beqa'. It cannot be taken at its face value, but possibly uses historical records, especially from the 9th century B.C., as suggested by the name of the Aramaean king, who must be Hadadezer of Damascus, ruling *ca.* 880-843 B.C. The names of the Ammonite kings Nahash[43] and Hanūn[44] may be historical as well, and the account of Davidic attempts at conquering Madaba[45] and the Ammonite capital[46] appear as reflexes of real endeavours to control commercial routes, especially the "King's Highway"[47].

Omri's conquests north of the Arnon River (Wādī al-Muğib), recorded in the Mesha inscription, would fit in a clearer pattern, if they were related to an attempt at dominating the Ammonite territory and thus controlling the "King's Highway". An allegedly earlier event of this kind is reported in II Sam. 12, 26-31, an episode of David's second Ammonite war, which seems to belong to an early version of the story of "David's Succession". The storyteller indulged a folkloristic feature by mentioning the crown "which weighed a talent of gold and was set with precious stones" (II Sam. 12, 30), but he must have heard of the Ammonite *atef*-crown, represented in the 8th-7th centuries B.C. on limestone sculptures showing a male head[48]. He was aware also of "the water city" (II Sam. 12, 27), which most likely corresponded to a walled compound at Rās al-'Ain, at the source of Nahr az-Zerqā, south-west of the Ğebel al-Qal'ah. The upper city of Rabbat-Amman and the royal palace were in fact supplied with water from Rās al-'Ain and the seizure of this site was an obvious prelude to the capture of the city proper.

The story and the ancient poem on Sihon, king of Heshbon, in Numb. 21, 21-32, allude to wars between Ammonites and Moabites, perhaps in the 9th century B.C. These wars are referred to also by a fragmentary Moabite inscription, in which a king of Moab from the early 8th century B.C. boasts of buildings he erected by setting Ammonite prisoners to work[49].

43 I Sam. 11, 1-2; 12, 2; II Sam. 10, 2; I Chron. 19, 1-2.

44 II Sam. 10, 1-4; II Chron. 19, 2-6.

45 I Chron. 19, 7; cf. II Sam. 10, 6-14; I Chron. 19, 7-15.

46 II Sam. 11, 1; 12, 26-31; I Chron. 20, 1-3.

47 Y. AHARONI, *The Land of the Bible. A Historical Geography*, London 1967, p. 49-52.

48 See here below, p. 310, 313.

49 S. AḤITUV, *A New Moabite Inscription,* in *Israel Museum Archaeological Studies* 2 (2003), p. 3-10; ID., *A New Royal Inscription from Moab*, in *Qadmoniot* 37 (2004), p. 88-92 (in Hebrew). Cf. here below, p. 329, 342, 344.

Early royal names

Sihon's name is Ammonite and should be interpreted as **Ṯīḥān*, with Hebrew *s* marking an Ammonite /ṯ/, like in the case of *B'lys* (Jer. 40, 14)[50]. It occurs still in Ṣafaitic (*Ṯḥn*)[51] and Nabataean (*Šyḥn*)[52]. The name is a derivative in *-ān* of the same root as Akkadian *šīḫu*, "lofty", "tall". The name of king *Nāḥāš*, "Serpent", which appears also on a Hebrew bulla[53], should be regarded as Ammonite or as an Hebrew adaptation of Ammonite **Lāḥāš*, which occurs on two seals[54] and on an ostracon from Ḥisbān, dated to the 6th century B.C.[55] The name can hardly mean "Whisper" and it should not be related to *hal-Lōḥēš* in Neh. 3, 12 and 10, 25. The presence of the article shows that this is no real proper name, but a nickname. Since names of animals, especially those of totems like the serpent[56], are often used as personal names, *Lḥš* should very likely be regarded as a dialectal variant of *Nḥš*. In fact, the widespread alternation *l/n*, especially at the beginning of words[57], suggests such an interpretation.

Also Hanūn, a son of Nahash, bears a name attested on an Ammonite seal[58] and in line 10 of the Nimrud ostracon[59]. The name of Shobi, another son of Nahash according to II Sam. 17, 27, is frequently attested in Ṣafaitic and Thamūdic[60], in Nabataean[61], and in Palmyrene[62]. Greek

[50] See here below, p. 340 with n. 125.

[51] HARDING, *Arabian Names*, p. 143.

[52] A. NEGEV, *Personal Names in the Nabatean Realm* (Qedem 32), Jerusalem 1991, p. 63, No. 1122.

[53] R. DEUTSCH, *Biblical Period Hebrew Bullae: The Josef Chaim Kaufman Collection*, Tel Aviv 2003, No. 103 and p. 414.

[54] N. AVIGAD - B. SASS, *op. cit.* (n. 19), p. 434, No. 1146 (*l-Lḥš*), and perhaps p. 339, No. 909 (*l-'lrm L*[*ḥ*]*š*).

[55] F.M. CROSS, *An Unpublished Ammonite Ostracon from Ḥesbān*, in L.T. GERATY - L.G. HERR (eds.), *The Archaeology of Jordan and Other Studies Presented to S.H. Horn*, Berrien Springs 1986, p. 475-489, line 1: *lḥ˻š˼˻b˼n* […]. For the excavations of Ḥisbān, see L.T. GERATY, *Heshbon*, in *NEAEHL*, Jerusalem 1993, Vol. II, p. 626-630, with former literature.

[56] Cf. Numb. 21, 8-9.

[57] LIPIŃSKI, *Semitic*, §17.3-4.

[58] N. AVIGAD - B. SASS, *op. cit.* (n. 19), p. 346, No. 932.

[59] F. ISRAEL, *Die Sprache des Ostrakons aus Nimrud*, in *UF* 21 (1989), p. 233-235; ID., *Ammonite Inscriptions*, in *OEANE*, New York 1997, Vol. I, p. 105-106.

[60] HARDING, *Arabian Names*, p. 310, sub *SBY*, with a questionable interpretation.

[61] A. NEGEV, *op. cit.* (n. 52), p. 61, No. 1093.

[62] J.K. STARK, *Personal Names in Palmyrene Inscriptions*, Oxford 1971, p. 50, with an erroneous explanation on p. 113.

Statue of an Ammonite king, late 8th century B.C.
(Amman, Archaeological Museum, J. 1657).

Σαβεῖς[63] is likely to provide the correct vocalization *Šābey*, the active participle of *šby*, "to capture", thus "captor, raider", by no means "captive", Arabic *sabīy*. The masoretic vocalization of the name is not supported by any tradition, as shown by the Septuagint and by Josephus Flavius. *Šby* is not attested so far in Ammonite epigraphy, but the presence of this name in Ṣafaitic and Nabataean inscriptions shows that it belongs to the traditional anthroponomy of this Transjordanian area. The name of the first Ammonite king mentioned in Neo-Assyrian texts is in the same situation[64].

[63] *CIS* II, 4124, 1.

[64] Ba'šā, mentioned in the annals of Shalmaneser III, is no Ammonite king, but the ruler of Bēth-Reḥob in the Beqa' Valley, contrary to the opinion of R. DEUTSCH, *A Royal*

The well-known Ammonite statuette from the Amman Archaeological Museum (Inv. J. 1656) bears a name written *Šnb* according to F. Zayadine[65], who rightly equated the personage in question with the Ammonite king whose name is written *Sa-ni-bu* or *Sa-ni-pu* in the annals of Tiglath-pileser III[66]. The last cuneiform sign of the name can be read indifferently *bu* or *pu* [67], but the examination of the inscription leaves no doubt that the name should be read *Šnpy*:

[*s*]*ml Yrḥ'zr*	"Statue of Yariḥ'ezer,
[*b*]⸢*r*⸣ *Zkr br Šnpy*	son of Zakkūr, son of Śanīpu".

Šnpy is written with a *p*[68] and a final angular *yōd*, similar to the slightly damaged z-shaped *zayin*. Instead, the *yōd* of line 1 still has a curved head, familiar in early scripts. Both forms may alternate in the same inscription. The last letter of line 2 is by no means an *aleph* or a scratch. It reveals the maintenance of case endings in a "classical" form of the spoken Ammonite language in the 8th century B.C. The *yōd* of the genitive is exceptionally indicated in this case, because the inscription is written in Aramaic, as shown by the use of *br*. Case endings were also indicated in the contemporaneous Aramaic inscriptions in the Śam'alian dialect.

The name *Śanīpu* is well attested in Nabataean and Ṣafaitic onomastics, with two attestations of *Šnypw* in Nabataean[69] and twenty-one published attestations of *S²nf* in Ṣafaitic[70]. The name might also occur in early cuneiform texts where the same person, living in Sippar at the time of Hammurabi, is called *Sa-ni-bu/pu-um* or *Za-ni-bu/pu-um*[71].

Ammonite Seal Impression, in Y. AVISHUR - R. DEUTSCH (eds.), *Michael. Historical, Epigraphical and Biblical Studies in Honor of Prof. M. Heltzer*, Tel Aviv-Jaffa 1999, p. 121-125 (see p. 124). Cf. E. LIPIŃSKI, *Ba'sa*, in *PNA* I/2, Helsinki 1999, p. 275; ID., *Aramaeans*, p. 343.

[65] F. ZAYADINE, *Note sur l'inscription de la statue d'Amman J. 1656*, in *Syria* 51 (1974), p. 129-136 and Pls. III-IV. An excellent colour photograph of the statuette was published in *La voie royale. 9000 ans d'art au Royaume de Jordanie*, Paris 1986, p. 97 and frontispiece; cf. p. 105-106, No. 129. See also the next page.

[66] *Tigl. III*, p. 170, Summ. 7, rev., line 10'.

[67] This is by no means a "vocalic interchange", as stated by W.E. AUFRECHT, *Corpus of Ammonite Inscriptions*, Lewistone-Queenston-Lampeter 1989, p. 109.

[68] The letter has been recognized by É. PUECH, *L'inscription de la statue d'Amman et la paléographie ammonite*, in *RB* 92 (1985), p. 5-24 (see p. 8), but this reading is recused by F. ZAYADINE, in *La voie royale*, *op. cit.* (n. 65), p. 106.

[69] A. NEGEV, *op. cit.* (n. 52), p. 65, No. 1166.

[70] HARDING, *Arabian Names*, p. 359; F.V. WINNETT - G.L. HARDING, *Inscriptions from Fifty Safaitic Cairns*, Toronto 1978, p. 587.

[71] I.J. GELB, *Computer-aided Analysis of Amorite* (AS 21), Chicago 1980, p. 128.

Limestone statue of Yariḥʿezer, early 7th century B.C.
(Amman, Archaeological Museum, J. 1656).

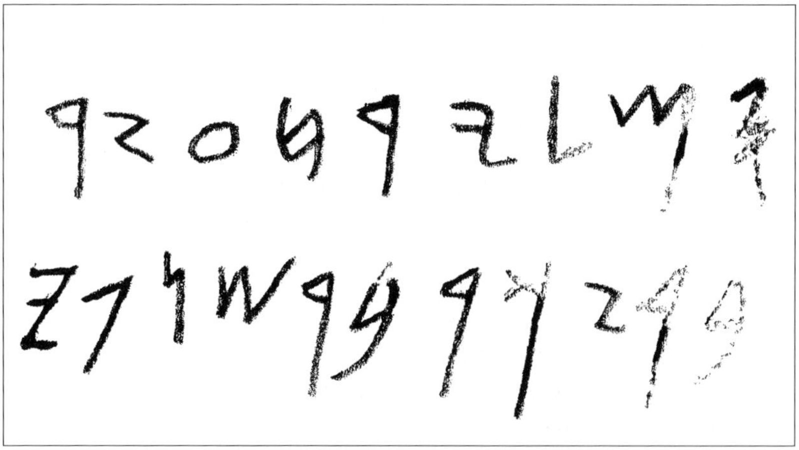

Inscription of Yariḥʿezer's statue.

The *Śanīpu* appears as a good Semitic name of the *qatīl*-type. Its meaning is less evident. Sabaic s^2nf means "side"[72] and post-biblical Hebrew *sānīp* designates a "side-piece"[73], already in the Mishnah[74]. In Ethio-Semitic, the same root has the connotation "inactive, indolent", derived from the notion of side-stepping. *Śanīpu* could thus mean "indolent", even "lazy", but the nuance of a term is related to its context, and the semantic range of a word in one language is not necessarily the same as that in another. We shall not know the Ammonite connotation of the root as long as the word does not appear in a context.

History of the 9th-6th centuries B.C.

The land of the Ammonites, with a superficies estimated at *ca.* 1500 km^2, had no direct access to the Mediterranean and to the Red Sea, but it occupied a key place on the lucrative trade routes from Arabia to the Mediterranean and to Syria[75]. The main Ammonite settlement was Rabbat-Amman, present-day Amman whose location made it an ideal site for the capital of the country and a royal city. It is situated next to the

[72] *Sabaic Dictionary*, p. 133.

[73] JASTROW, p. 1007b.

[74] Mishnah, *Kelayim* XXI, 3.

[75] M.C.A. MACDONALD, *Trade Routes and Trade Goods at the Northern End of the 'Incense Road' in the First Millennium B.C.*, in A. AVANZINI (ed.), *Profumi d'Arabia* (Saggi di storia antica 11), Firenze 1997, p. 333-350.

abundant source of the Jabboq (Nahr az-Zerqā) and could draw its wealth from fertile agriculture land and international trade conducted along the north-south "King's Highway" and along the Wādī Sirḥān, that connected Dumat al-Ǧandal (al-Ǧōf) with Kaf, near the present Saudi-Jordanian border. It was surrounded by other important cities as Tell Jawa (Ǧāwā) South[76] and Tell al-'Umeiri[77], 13 km south of Amman, and its territory was protected in the Assyrian period (730-620 B.C.) by massive round, rectangular, or square structures, which were situated within sight of each other and obviously had also guarding and warning functions. However, the location of many "towers" on hillsides, rather than hilltops, overlooking arable wadis, seems to indicate that they were usually associated with agricultural or agro-pastoral activities, and served as shelters, storage places, and watchtowers, especially before and during the harvest period.

The Ammonite history in Iron Age II is poorly documented[78], but the carefully written Amman Citadel[79] inscription from the late 9th century or the beginning of the 8th century B.C.[80] strongly suggests that this is a fragment of a royal inscription. Its right side is lost with the first words of line 1, but there is little doubt that the text records temple instructions of Milkom, the chief god of the Ammonites. The person addressed in the first place is probably the king, who received the command through the medium of a spokesman or spokeswomen of the deity, and promulgates the divine ordinance. The language of the inscription is a Canaanite dialect, similar to Moabite and Hebrew, but the script is closely related to the Aramaic one. We do not know the name either of this king or of the Ammonite king whose subjects were captured by the Moabites in the

[76] Grid ref. 2392/1401: Preliminary reports by P.-M.M. DAVIAU,... *Tell Jawa...*, in *ADAJ* 36 (1992), p. 145-162; 37 (1993), p. 325-340; 38 (1994), p. 173-194; 40 (1996), p. 83-100; R.W. YOUNKER - P.-M.M. DAVIAU, *Is Mafa'at to be found at Tell Jawa (South)?*, in *IEJ* 43 (1993), p. 23-28.

[77] Grid ref. 2342/1420: W. ZWICKEL, *op. cit.* (n. 15), p. 203-204, with literature. See further: R.W. YOUNKER *et al.*, ... *Madaba Plains Project...*, in *AUSS* 28/1 (1990), p. 5-52; 31/3 (1993), p. 205-238; 34/1 (1996), p. 65-92; 35/2 (1997), p. 227-240; L. GERATY *et al.*, *Madaba Plains Project...*, in *ADAJ* 33 (1989), p. 145-176; L.G. HERR, *The Settlement and Fortification of Tell al-Umayri in Jordan during the LB/Iron I Transition*, in L.E. STAGER - J.A. GREENE - M.D. COOGAN (eds.), *The Archaeology of Jordan and Beyond. Essays in Honour of J.A. Sauer*, Winona Lake 2000, p. 167-179.

[78] However, see U. HÜBNER, *op. cit.* (n. 30), and B. MACDONALD - R.W. YOUNKER (eds.), *op. cit.* (n. 30).

[79] Grid ref. 2386/1516.

[80] Published by S. HORN, *The Ammān Citadel Inscription*, in *ADAJ* 12-13 (1967-68), p. 81-83, Pl. LIV, and in *BASOR* 193 (1969), p. 2-13. Cf. U. HÜBNER, *op. cit.* (n. 30), p. 17-21, with literature.

Limestone head of an Ammonite king, 7th century B.C.
(Amman, Archaeological Museum, J. 4767).

early 8th century and set to work at royal building projects[81]. The first king mentioned in Assyrian records is Śanīpu, who appears among the tributaries of Tiglath-pileser III, probably in 734 B.C.[82] Like in the other states of the region, subjection to Assyria took the form of periodic gifts

[81] See here above, p. 303, n. 49, and below, p. 329, 342, 344.

[82] *Tigl. III*, p. 170, Summ. 7, rev., line 10'. Cf. H.D. BAKER - R. ZADOK, *Sanīpu*, in *PNA* III/1, Helsinki 2002, p. 1090.

Bronze bottle from Tell Sirān, lines 1-4 are visible
(Amman, Archaeological Museum, J. 12943).

or "tributes", as well as of corvée and military aid to the Assyrian king. An Assyrian letter from Nimrud (Calah), addressed to Sargon II (721-705 B.C.), mentions an Ammonite delegation which visited Calah with other western missions bringing presents to the Assyrian king[83].

As mentioned above, Śanīpu is named in the Ammonite inscription engraved on the statuette of his grandson Yariḥ'ezer[84], who does not seem to have become king. He lacks the royal title, does not wear the *atef*-crown, and grasps a drooping lotus blossom, which characterizes the funerary iconography[85]. At least from 701 through 673 B.C., the king of the Ammonites was Padō-Il[86], known from the inscriptions of Sennacherib[87] and of Esarhaddon[88], as well as from the seal of one of his ministers[89]. He did not join the Judaean rebellion against Sennacherib in

[83] *SAA* I, 110, rev., line 7.

[84] See here above, p. 306, n. 65.

[85] R. Dussaud, *L'art phénicien du IIe millénaire*, Paris 1949, p. 90: "La fleur est dressée si le personnage est vivant, inclinée si le personnage est décédé".

[86] P.C. Ambos, *Padû-il*, in *PNA* III/1, Helsinki 2002, p. 978-979.

[87] D.D. Luckenbill, *The Annals of Sennacherib* (OIP 2), Chicago 1924, p. 30, line 55; E. Frahm, *Einleitung in die Sanherib-Inchriften* (AfO, Beih. 26), Wien 1997, p. 53, line 37.

[88] R. Borger, *Die Inschriften Asarhaddons, Königs von Assyrien* (AfO, Beih. 9), Graz 1956, p. 60, line 62.

[89] U. Hübner, *op. cit.* (n. 30), p. 75-76, No. 65, with literature; N. Avigad - B. Sass, *op. cit.* (n. 19), p. 321, No. 857.

701, but declared his allegiance to the Assyrian monarch by paying him tribute. An administrative document from Nineveh records his visit at the royal court of Assyria and the present of two gold rings that was offered to him on this occasion, while the members of his suite received each a silver ring[90].

Sennacherib probably marched through the Ammonite territory in 691, after his campaign against Qedarite Arabs, whom he pursued all along the Wādī Sirḥān from al-Ǧōf (*Adummatu*) to Kaf (*Kapanu*)[91], southeast of Amman. In 673, Padō-Il is mentioned among the western vassals of Assyria who had to supply building material for the construction of Esarhaddon's palace in Nineveh[92]. He was succeeded by Amminadab I, known from the legend of his ministers' seals[93], from the inscriptions of Ashurbanipal[94], and from the inscription on the Tell Sirān[95] bronze bottle[96]. He had to put his army at Ashurbanipal's disposal for the campaign against Egypt in 667 B.C. and pay him a heavy tribute. An Assyrian document registering 2 minas of gold, i.e. about 1 kg, paid by the Ammonite king probably dates from this period. The comparison of this tax with the 1 mina of gold given by the ruler of Moab according to the same text and the equivalent 10 minas of silver paid by the king of Judah[97] shows that the land of the Ammonites was economically much stronger. This is confirmed not only by the allusion of the Song of Songs 6, 12 to the splendour of "Amminadab's chariots", but also by the partly excavated royal residence in Amman, dating to the 8th-7th century B.C.[98], and by the outstanding quality of objects found in the 7th-6th century levels of Milkom's temple in the Amman Citadel[99].

[90] *SAA* VII, 58, I, 4'-10'.

[91] E. Frahm, *op. cit.* (n. 87), p. 131, lines 53'-9''; cf. p. 135.

[92] R. Borger, *op. cit.* (n. 88), p. 60-61, col. V, 73b-VI, 1.

[93] U. Hübner, *op. cit.* (n. 30), p. 53-54, Nos. 14-15, with literature; N. Avigad - B. Sass, *op. cit.* (n. 19), p. 321-322, Nos. 858-859.

[94] R. Borger, *Beiträge zum Inschriftenwerk Assurbanipals*, Wiesbaden 1996, p. 19 and 212, C II 48; cf. P. Villard, *Ammi-nadbi*, in *PNA* I/1, Helsinki 1998, p. 105.

[95] Grid ref. 2342/1581.

[96] Published by F. Zayadine - H.O. Thompson, *The Ammonite Inscription from Tell Siran*, in *Berytus* 22 (1973), p. 115-140. Cf. U. Hübner, *op. cit.* (n. 30), p. 26-30, with literature; D. Kinet, *Die Bronze Flasche aus Tell Siran*, in F. Ninow (ed.), *Wort und Stein. Studien zur Theologie und Archäologie. Festschrift für U. Worschech*, Frankfurt a/M 2003, p. 133-144. See here p. 311.

[97] *SAA* XI, 33.

[98] J.-B. Humbert - F. Zayadine, *Trois campagnes de fouilles à Ammân (1988-1991): troisième terrasse de la Citadelle (Mission franco-jordanienne)*, in *RB* 99 (1992), p. 214-260, Pls. IV-XIV (see p. 249-258).

[99] Grid ref. 2386/1516: M. Najjar, *Amman Citadel Temple of Hercules Excavations. Preliminary Report*, in *Syria* 70 (1993), p. 220-225 (see p. 222-223).

Limestone head of an Ammonite king, 7th century B.C.
(Former collection of Moshe Dayan).

The Ammonite limestone sculptures showing standing figures or life-size human heads[100] recall Iron Age Cypriot sculpture and Phoenician art: they date from the same period, like the Ammonite tombs with rich groups of pottery[101]. In that period, the city of Amman as such (URU *Am-ma-a-*[*na*]) is mentioned for the first time in an Assyrian text[102]. Ammonite position within the Assyrian imperial framework was beneficial to the economic growth and to the prosperity of the land. There is no evidence that the weakening of the Assyrian power and the transition to Babylonian rule at the end of the 7th century brought about an immediate change.

Amminadab I was followed on the throne by Hissil-Il and by Amminadab II[103], whose reigns should be placed in the 7th century B.C. The fragmentary Amman Theater[104] inscription, dated around 600 B.C., might then mention a king Abinad[ab][105], bearing the same name as the donor of a votive seal dedicated to Astarte of Sidon in the late 7th century B.C.[106] The Ammonite king Barak-Il, whose royal seal impression has been published recently, seems to have reigned also towards the end of the 7th century B.C.[107], but the king who sent a delegation to Jerusalem in 594 B.C. (Jer. 27, 2) was probably Baalis, known from Jer. 40, 14 and from the seal of one of his ministers[108]. The purpose of the Jerusalem meeting was to organize a general rebellion against Babylonia, but there is no evidence about its outcome and Ammon's actual role. A few years later, however, some events seem to suggest that the

[100] A. ABOU-ASSAF, *Untersuchungen zur ammonitischen Rundbildkunst*, in *UF* 12 (1980), p. 7-102; A. MAZAR, *Archaeology of the Land of the Bible: 10,000-586 B.C.E.*, New York 1990, p. 543; T. ORNAN, *A Man and His Land: Highlights from the Moshe Dayan Collection*, Jerusalem 1986, p. 38-39, No. 13; A.-J. 'AMR, *Four Ammonite Sculptures from Jordan*, in *ZDPV* 106 (1990), p. 114-118, Pls. 7-8.

[101] K. YASSINE, *Burial Customs and Practices in Ancient Ammon*, in B. MACDONALD - R.W. YOUNKER (eds.), *Ancient Ammon*, Leiden 1999, p. 137-151, with former literature.

[102] *SAA* XI, 1, II, 12.

[103] According to the inscription of the Tell Sirān bottle; cf. U. HÜBNER, *op. cit.* (n. 30), p. 26-30.

[104] Grid ref. 2389/1512.

[105] Published by R.W. DAJANI, *The Amman Theatre Fragment*, in *ADAJ* 12-13 (1967-68), p. 65-67. Cf. U. HÜBNER, *op. cit.* (n. 30), p. 21-23.

[106] U. HÜBNER, *op. cit.* (n. 30), p. 51-52, No. 12; N. AVIGAD - B. SASS, *op. cit.* (n. 19), p. 328-329, No. 876.

[107] This date is suggested by palaeography, but the editor of the clay bulla, R. DEUTSCH, *art. cit.* (n. 64), p. 121-125, dates it about 675 B.C. Besides, there is a seal probably belonging to one of the king's ministers: N. AVIGAD - B. SASS, *op. cit.* (n. 19), p. 324, No. 863..

[108] U. HÜBNER, *op. cit.* (n. 30), p. 86-87, No. 88; B. BECKING, *Baalis, the King of the Ammonites. An Epigraphical Note on Jeremiah 40:14,* in *JSS* 38 (1993), p. 15-24; N. AVIGAD - B. SASS, *op. cit.* (n. 19), p. 322, No. 860.

Ammonites have adopted a neutral or even hostile policy towards Babylonia[109]. Especially, the involvement of Baalis in the plot to murder Gedaliah, the Babylonian deputy in Judah (Jer. 40-41), appears as a hostile act. While nothing proves that Ammon was subjugated by the Babylonians in 604 B.C.[110], Nebuchadnezzar II conducted a campaign against the Ammonites and the Moabites in 582/1, putting an end to their independence or semi-independence[111]. However, most of the widespread destructions, noticeable in the north-western region of the country, do probably not date from this Babylonian invasion, but from events that took place a quarter of a century later. A revolt broke out in the area of Amman in the early reign of Nabonidus, who suppressed it in 553 "decapitating the people who lived in Amman"[112]. This destruction of the city by the Babylonians corresponds to the end of Stratum VI of the Third Terrace in the Lower City of the Amman Citadel[113].

From Amman, Nabonidus went first to Edom, where traces of his passage are visible[114], and then continued to Teima without returning to Babylon[115]. The "Verse Account of Nabonidus" records that he set out for Teima after having initiated the restoration of the Eḫulḫul at Harran, "when the 3rd year came"[116]. He stayed in Arabia for ten years (552-543 B.C.) according to his Harran inscription[117]. During his sojourn at

[109] U. Hübner, *op. cit.* (n. 30), p. 198-205.

[110] This unsubstantiated thesis is defended by O. Lipshits, *Ammon in Transition from Vassal Kingdom to Babylonian Province,* in *BASOR* 335 (2004), p. 17-52.

[111] Flavius Josephus, *Jewish Antiquities* X, 9, 7, §181-182.

[112] "Royal Chronicle", col. IV, 50-64, published by W.G. Lambert, *A New Source for the Reign of Nabonidus,* in *AfO* 22 (1968-69), p. 1-8. The relevant passage is used by P.-A. Beaulieu, *The Reign of Nabonidus, King of Babylon, 556-539 B.C.* (YNER 10), New Haven 1989, p. 166-167, who identifies uru*Am-ma-na-nu* with Anti-Lebanon (p. 168 with n. 13). This does not correspond to the context and the use of the determinative URU excludes this explanation, although kur*Am-ma-na-nu* occurs in the "Nabonidus Chronicle"; cf. A.K. Grayson, *Assyrian and Babylonian Chronicles* (TCS 5), Locust Valley 1975, p. 104-111, Chronicle 7, col. I, 11; it refers to the mountainous area north of Amman (cf. Abel, *Géographie* I, p. 68). The ending *-ānu* is the nunation, which is extensively used in proper names, in Classical Arabic as well as in North Arabian (*tanwīn*), for example *Tym'* and *Tymn*, *Rḥbt* and *Rḥbtn*, *Ḥgr* and *Ḥgrn*.

[113] Grid ref. 2386/1516: J.-B. Humbert - F. Zayadine, *op. cit.* (n. 98), p. 247-249.

[114] See here below, p. 418, 420.

[115] Cf. P.-A. Beaulieu, *op. cit.* (n. 112), p. 150.

[116] BM 38299, col. II, 17: S. Smith, *Babylonian Historical Texts relating to the Capture and Downfall of Babylon*, London 1924, p. 82-91, Pls. V-X; cf. *ANET*, p. 312-315 (see p. 313b). The chronology of Nabonidus' life and reign was the subject of much sterile discussion.

[117] *ANET*, p. 562-563 (see p. 562b and 563a). See also P.-A. Beaulieu, *op. cit.* (n. 112), p. 151, 160, 162.

Amman Citadel Inscription
(Amman, Archaeological Museum, J. 9000).

Teima, where he is mentioned in local inscriptions[118], Nabonidus seized some other cities between Teima and Yathrib (Medina), inflicting defeat on the Arabs, but texts do not contain any further reference to Amman and the Ammonites.

Religion

The main Ammonite deity was Milkom[119], whose name consists simply of the word "king" with suffixed mimation. Since El or Il appears as theophorous element in many Ammonite personal names, it has been suggested that Milkom is just an Il's epithet[120]. So far there is no evidence supporting this opinion. On the contrary, Milkom's typical characteristics must have presented some analogy with those of Hellenistic Heracles, who took Milkom's place in Graeco-Roman times[121]. The limestone sculptures showing a male head wearing an *atef*-crown are sometimes believed to be representations of Milkom, but these crowned heads rather portray Ammonite kings[122], as indicated by their attitude which is identical with that of Yariḥ'ezer's statuette. They may eventually portray kings deified after their death. Unfortunately, the figure from the Amman Citadel grasping a drooping lotus blossom is headless[123], but the bent-arm position of full-body statues with *atef*-crowns suggests that also these figures grasped an object. As for the double-faced female heads from Amman Citadel, they are probably decorative elements of some official building[124] and no divine images. The Citadel

[118] W.W. Müller - S.F. Al-Said, *Der babylonische König Nabonid in taymanischen Inschriften*, in *BN* 107-108 (2001), p. 109-119; Y. Grundfest - M. Heltzer, *Nabonid, King of Babylon (556-539 B.C.E.), in Arabia in Light of New Evidence*, in *BN* 110 (2001), p. 25-30.

[119] H. Niehr, *Religionen in Israels Umwelt. Einführung in die nordwestsemitischen Religionen Syrien-Palästinas* (Die neue Echter-Bibel. Ergänzungsband 5 zum Alten Testament), Würzburg 1998, p. 211-212; É. Puech, *Milcom*, in *DDD*, 2nd ed., Leiden-Grand Rapids 1999, p. 575-576.

[120] J.H. Tigay, *'You shall have no Other Gods'* (HSM 31), Atlanta 1986, p. 19-20.

[121] The Amman Citadel temple of Heracles most likely occupies the site of the temple of Milkom, the main Ammonite deity. Its excavations started in 1990: M. Najjar, *art. cit.* (n. 99).

[122] S.H. Horn, *The Crown of the King of the Ammonites*, in *AUSS* 11 (1973), p. 170-180; H. Weippert, *Palästina in vorhellenistischer Zeit* (Handbuch der Archäologie. Vorderasien II/1), München 1988, p. 669-670; U. Hübner, *op. cit.* (n. 30), p. 267-268; *Jordanie sur les pas des archéologues*, Paris 1997, p. 83, 86-87.

[123] A. Abou-Assaf, *art. cit.* (n. 100), p. 27-28, Pl. 7.

[124] K. Prag, *Decorative Architecture in Ammon, Moab and Judah*, in *Levant* 19 (1987), p. 121-127 (see p. 123-126); *Jordanie, op. cit.* (n. 122), p. 85. See here p. 4.

inscription is an important religious document from the period *ca*. 800 B.C., but it is incomplete. No ritual or mythological texts are available and we lack any information about Ammonite literature.

CHAPTER IX

MOAB

The most extensive literary source for the history of Moab is the Old Testament, in which this area appears as a distinct political entity at the time of the Exodus and of the conquest. This anachronistic view of the legendary and mythical past, as well as the passages about Moab in the time of David and Solomon, reflect a 9th- or 8th-century Judaean perspective. An independent approach and further archaeological research are needed here. One should also remind that the earlier appearance of Moab in Egyptian texts shows knowledge of a geographical name, written with a determinative sign for a foreign land or hill country, not of a state or kingdom. As for the place names *T-b-n* and *B-t-r-t* in Ramesses II's inscriptions, they are still a cause for debate[1]. It will suffice to stress here that the risky identification of the second toponym with the *Raba Batora* of the *Peutinger Table* cannot by-pass al-Laǧǧūn, the *Betthoro* of the *Notitia Dignitatum Or.* XXXVII, 22, compiled *ca.* 393-405 A.D. Even more hazardous is the recent equation of *B-t-r-t* with the Ǧebel Baṭrā, where no town existed in the 13th century B.C. These place names will be examined below.

The land and its early history

The formation of the Moabite state cannot be dated long before 900 B.C. As said above, older Egyptian mentions of Moab do not refer to a state, but to an ancient geographic area of southern Jordan, which later gave its name to the newly created territorial state of the first millennium

[1] S. TIMM, *Moab zwischen den Mächten* (Ägypten und Altes Testament 17), Wiesbaden 1989, p. 5-60; M. WEIPPERT, *Moab*, in *RLA* VIII, Berlin 1993-97, p. 318-325 (see p. 318-319); M.G. HASEL, *Domination and Resistance: Egyptian Military Activity in the Southern Levant, ca. 1300-1185 B.C.* (Probleme der Ägyptologie 11), Leiden 1998, p. 159-166; E.J. VAN DER STEEN, *Tribes and Territories in Transition. The Central East Jordan Valley in the Late Bronze Age and the Early Iron Ages: A Study of Sources* (OLA 130), Leuven 2004, p. 23; B. ROUTLEDGE, *Moab in the Iron Age: Hegemony, Polity, Archaeology*, Philadelphia 2004, p. 58-60. For a general approach from the biblical perspective, see for instance: M. MILLER, *Ancient Moab: Still largely Unknown*, in *BA* 60 (1997), p. 194-204. The bibliography concerning Moab has been collected by E. NINOW, *Index Librorum de Rebus Moabiticis Conscriptorum*, Frankfurt a/M 2002.

B.C. A difficult question is that of identifying the origin of the Moabite population, which increased significantly during the Iron Age. Considering the short distance between this region and the Arabian Peninsula, we might deal here with the same population which spread through the desert areas. The qualification of Moabites in Numb. 24, 16 as "sons of Sheth", i.e. Sutaeans, does not solve the problem, because the name of the "Sutaeans" was used as an antonomasia for "nomads" already in the Amarna period[2]. A characteristic element is the worship of the Moabite god Chemosh[3], but he does not appear in Old Arabian inscriptions or names, while the cult of *Kamiš* at Ebla, *ca.* 2300 B.C., is chronologically too distant to allow some concrete conclusions. Besides, Chemosh is not attested in Amorite anthroponomy and we cannot yet establish whether Nergal's by-name *Kammuš* and the Ugaritic theonym *Ṭṯ-w-Kmṯ* (with variant spellings) refer to the same deity as the Moabite god Chemosh.

Some biblical texts clearly connect Moab with the Midianites (Numb. 22, 4.7; 25; 31, 1-11), and one could thus assume that the population settled in Moab around the 10th century B.C. originated from Midian. The "oasis urbanism", emerged in the 13th century B.C. at Qurayya[4], 80 km northwest of Tabuk, came to an end in the late 11th century. The profits of metallurgical activity at Timna, further north, had then ceased with the collapse of Egyptian power, while the use of camels as pack animals had gained prominence, causing a return to a nomadic life-style[5], with

[2] However, M. HELTZER, *The Suteans*, Naples 1981, p. 81-83, considers them as an ethnic entity. The connection of the *bny št* of Numb. 24, 16 with the *šwtw* of the Egyptian Execration Texts is certainly anachronistic, despite K.A. KITCHEN, *The Egyptian Evidence on Ancient Jordan*, in P. BIEŃKOWSKI (ed.), *Early Edom and Moab*, Sheffield 1992, p. 21-34 (see p. 21).

[3] For this deity, see H. NIEHR, *Religionen in Israels Umwelt. Einführung in die nordwestsemitischen Religionen Syrien-Palästinas* (Die neue Echter-Bibel. Ergänzungsband 5 zum Alten Testament), Würzburg 1998, p. 213-216; H.-P. MÜLLER, *Chemosh*, in *DDD*, 2nd ed., Leiden-Grand Rapids 1999, p. 186-189.

[4] P.J. PARR, *Aspects of the Archaeology of North-West Arabia in the First Millennium BC*, in T. FAHD (ed.), *L'Arabie préislamique et son environnement historique et culturel*, Leiden 1989, p. 39-66 (see p. 40-43); ID., *Edom and the Hedjaz*, in P. BIEŃKOWSKI (ed.), *Early Edom and Moab*, Sheffield 1992, p. 41-46.

[5] P.J. PARR, *art. cit.* (n. 4), in T. FAHD (ed.), p. 43. For this process, see I. FINKELSTEIN - A. PEREVOLOTSKY, *Processes of Sedentarization and Nomadization in the History of Sinai and the Negev*, in *BASOR* 279 (1990), p. 67-88. It appears however that the renomadization was not complete in the central regions of North Arabia: G. BAWDEN - C. EDENS, *Tayma Painted Ware and the Hejazi Iron Age Ceramic Tradition to Appear*, in *Levant* 20 (1988), p. 197-213; C. EDENS - G. BAWDEN, *History of Tayma' and Hijazi Trade during the First Millennium B.C.*, in *JESHO* 32 (1989), p. 48-103; G. BAWDEN, *Continuity and Disruption in the Ancient Hejaz: An Assessment of Current Archaeological Strategies*, in *Arabian Archaeology and Epigraphy* 3 (1992), p. 1-22.

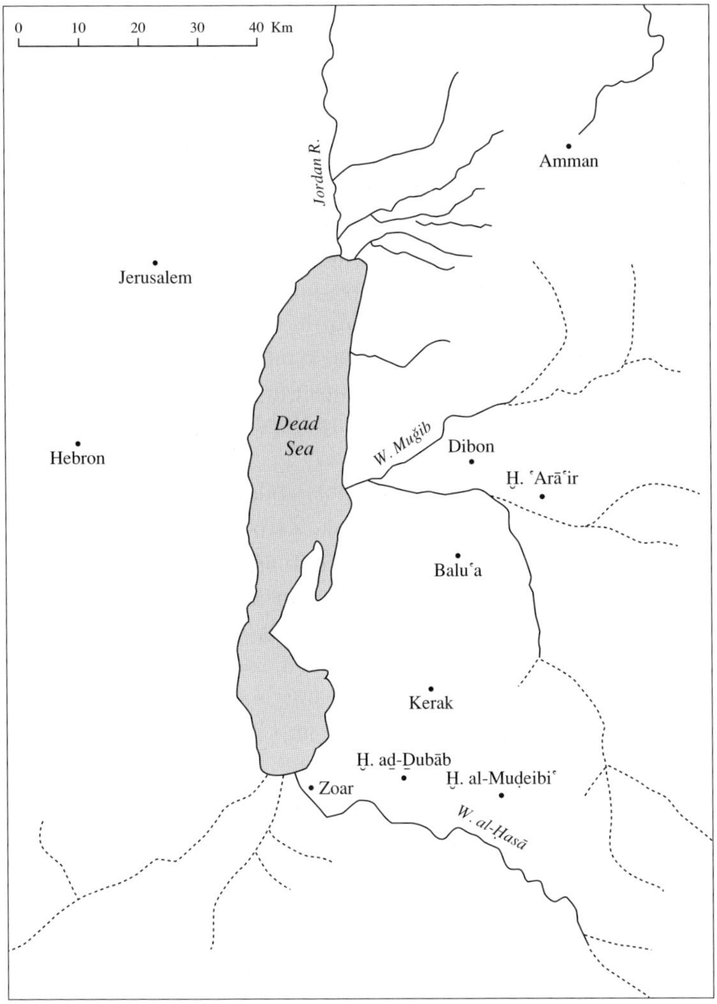

Moab.

the important difference that now the tamed dromedary was utilized for travelling and raiding. However, a new settlement process took place after a short time in Moab: this area best fitted a combination of agriculture and sheep/goat husbandry, and it lay on the main trade route through Transjordan, the "King's Highway". The presence of the camel in north-western Arabia is proved by its representation on a painted potsherd from Qurayya[6], while the multi-coloured Moabite potsherds from

[6] M.L. INGRAHAM *et al.*, *Preliminary Report on a Reconnaissance Survey of the Northwestern Province*, in *Atlal* 5 (1981), p. 59-84.

the Kerak plateau's Iron II repertoire[7] may appear as later derivatives of the Qurayya painted ware. In other words, there seems to be a link between the two cultures[8], although the cult of Chemosh is not attested so far in Midian. The lack of such an important element is disturbing in a culture-historical approach, but we have no written records from the Midianite area that would date back to Late Bronze II or Iron Age I. Since Ebla texts attest the worship of *Kamiš*, supposedly the same god as Chemosh, we can just surmise that this is a very old Semitic deity. The meaning of the name is unknown, unless we take the Neo-Assyrian equation GUD, "bull" = *Ka-mu-uš* = ^{d}*Ka-mu-uš* GUD at its face value[9], but the bull figure was a widespread divine symbol in the Ancient Near East. The compound name of Ashtar-Chemosh in the Mesha inscription (line 17) connects the Moabite deity with the North-Arabian stellar upper-god Ashtar.

The Kerak plateau or Moabite tableland, between Wādī al-Muğib (Arnon) in the north and Wādī al-Ḥasā (Zered) in the south, constitutes the original territory of Moab[10]. Its obvious centre is Kerak[11], the ancient capital, where the fragmentary inscription of Mesha or of his father Chemoshyatt was discovered in a foundation trench cut for a new building[12]. Another important centre was called **Rabbat Mō'āb*. Its name is so far attested only in Greek transcriptions: 'Αραβαθα in Josephus Flavius[13], 'Ραββαθμω(α)βα in Ptolemy, in Greek papyri belonging to archives found in the Judaean Desert[14], and on coins struck under Septimius Severus (193-211)[15]. Eusebius of Caesarea calls it 'Ραββαθ Μωαβ

[7] R.M. BROWN, *Ceramics from the Kerak Plateau*, in J.M. MILLER (ed.), *Archaeological Survey of the Kerak Plateau*, Atlanta 1991, p. 169-279 (see p. 198, 202-203); cf. R.H. DORNEMANN, *The Archaeology of Transjordan in the Bronze and Iron Ages*, Milwaukee 1983, p. 65.

[8] The possibility of a Midianite involvement in Moab's emergence has been considered by P.J. PARR, *Contacts Between NW Arabia and Jordan in the Late Bronze and Iron Ages*, in A. HADIDI (ed.), *Studies in the History and Archaeology of Jordan* I, Amman 1982, p. 127-134.

[9] A. DEIMEL, *Šumerisches Lexikon* II/2, Roma 1930, p. 515, No. 13e.

[10] G.L. MATTINGLY, *A New Agenda for Research on Ancient Moab*, in *BA* 60 (1997), p. 214-221.

[11] Grid ref. 2170/0660; cf. W. ZWICKEL, *Eisenzeitliche Ortslagen im Ostjordanland* (BTAVO B/81), Wiesbaden 1990, p. 103-104.

[12] *TSSI* I, 17, p. 83-84; S. TIMM, *op. cit.* (n. 1), p. 269-277.

[13] JOSEPHUS FLAVIUS, *Jewish Antiquities* XIV, 1, 4, §18.

[14] PTOLEMY, *Geography* V, 16, 4; N. LEWIS, *The Documents from the Bar-Kokhba Period in the Cave of Letters. Greek Papyri*, Jerusalem 1989, Nos. 16, 11; 25, 22.56.

[15] F. DE SAULCY, *Numismatique de la Terre Sainte*, Paris 1874, p. 354 ff.; G.F. HILL, *A Catalogue of the Greek Coins in the British Museum. Arabia*, London 1922, p. XLII-XLIII; H. SEYRIG, *Les dieux armés et les Arabes en Syrie*, in *Syria* 47 (1970), p. 77-112,

or 'Αρεοπολις[16]. The *Codex Vaticanus graecus 1456* of Eusebius' work has the reading 'Αρσοπολις, which corresponds to the legend 'Αρσαπολις of the city coins from the reign of Elagabalus (218-222)[17]. This name means "City of Ares", the Greek war-god, which was identified with the Moabite god Chemosh. The city is situated at ar-Rabba[18], 22 km south of the Wādī al-Muğib (Arnon). The toponym Marma al-'Eyr, near Rabba[19], still preserves the old name of the Moabite tableland, called *'ār* in the Bible. This word does not mean "city", like Hebrew *'īr*, despite some ancient interpretations[20]. It designated the region of central Moab.

Mesha's father, Chemoshyatt, who was king for thirty years (*ca.* 890-860 B.C.), probably extended the Moabite territory to the north and annexed the area between the Wādī al-Muğib and Wādī al-Wāla with the town of Dibon. This town became the residence of Mesha, who called himself "the Dibonite". In the northeast, Moab's influence reached at least the Wādī aṯ-Ṯamad, where a characteristic Moabite inscription (*sydn*) and Moabite pottery was found at the site of Ḫirbet al-Mudayyina[21]. Mesha endeavoured to expand his kingdom further to the north by

Pl. IX (see p. 96 and 112); A. SPIJKERMAN, *The Coins of the Decapolis and the Provincia Arabia*, Jerusalem 1978, p. 264 ff.

[16] EUSEBIUS OF CAESAREA, *Onomasticon*, in E. KLOSTERMANN (ed.), *Eusebius: Das Onomastikon der biblischen Ortsnamen*, Leipzig 1904, p. 124:13-17..

[17] G.W. BOWERSOCK, *The Arabian Ares*, in E. GABBA (ed.), *Tria Corda. Scritti in onore di Arnaldo Momigliano* (Bibliotheca di Athenaeum 1), Como 1983, p. 43-47; ID., *An Arabian Trinity*, in *Christians among Jews and Gentiles. Essays in Honor of Krister Stendahl*, Philadelphia 1986, p. 17-21. See also A. SPIJKERMAN, *Unknown Coins of Rabbath Moba - Areopolis*, in *Studii Biblici Franciscani Liber Annuus* 34 (1984), p. 347-352; E.A. KNAUF, *Arsapolis. Eine epigraphische Bemerkung*, in *Studii Biblici Franciscani Liber Annuus* 34 (1984), p. 353-356. There is no confusion here between *E* and *Σ*, since Ares, mentioned on some coins, and the Arabic god Arṣu were identified in Palmyra: *PAT* 0197, A, line 20; B, line 12.

[18] Grid ref. 2203/0755; cf. W. ZWICKEL, *op. cit.* (n. 11), p. 121.

[19] A. MUSIL, *Arabia Petraea* I. *Moab*, Wien 1907, p. 369.

[20] The spelling *'yr* for *'r* occurs in the Samaritan Pentateuch, Numb. 21, 15, and in 1QIs[a] 15, 1, where Peshitta translates '(*y*)*r* by *q[e]rītā*, "city". Targum Onqelos to Numb. 21, 15.28; Deut. 2, 9.18.29, and Targum Jonathan to Is. 15, 1 replace *'ār* by the city name *Lḥyt*; cf. here below, p. 354. For the meaning of '*r*, see ABEL, *Géographie* II, p. 248; M. WEIPPERT, *Ar und Kir in Jesaja 15, 1. Mit Erwägungen zur historischen Geographie Moabs*, in *ZAW* 110 (1998), p. 547-555. The same Transjordanian word occurs in *'ry Gl'd* (Judg. 12, 7), where the *yōd* marks the paragogic vowel *-i*. Contrary to the opinion of ABEL, *Géographie* II, p. 351, the word *'yr* in Numb. 22, 36; Deut. 2, 36; Josh. 13, 9.16; II Sam. 24, 5 does not mean "city", but "gorge", "canyon". It is related to Arabic *ġawr, ġār, ġōr*, "depression", "cave", and designates "the canyon which is in the middle of the Arnon valley". The geographical indication "south of the canyon" in II Sam. 24, 5 is erroneous; it should be "north of the canyon".

[21] Grid ref. 2363/1109. Cf. P.-M.M. DAVIAU, *Moab's Northern Border: Khirbat al-Mudyna on the Wadi ath-Thamad*, in *BA* 60 (1997), p. 222-228.

annexing the land of Madaba, the land of Ataroth, Nebo, and Jahaz, which Mesha claims to have conquered all from the Israelites.

To understand this situation one must turn to events in Israel. An important development in Israel's history was Omri's accession to the throne. He founded Samaria, which became Israel's capital from then on[22], and introduced the cult of Yahwe of Samaria therein[23], while Omri's daughter Athaliahu[24] and his grandsons Ahaziahu and Jehoram received Yahwistic names. Omri recovered northern Galilee from the Aramaeans[25] and extended Israel's territory in Transjordan as far as the land of Moab[26], east of the Dead Sea. Israel's wealth in this period is shown by the carved ivories found in the royal palace in Samaria[27] and by the dynastic alliance with Tyre, whose royal princess, daughter of king Ethbaal, became the wife of Ahab, Israel's heir apparent[28]. On the other hand, Omri's daughter Athaliahu was married to Jehoshaphat, king of Judah[29], in order to strengthen Judah's ties with Israel and to prepare an Omride's bid for the throne of the House of David. A significant indicator of the importance of Omri's dynasty as political factor is that Assyrian records refer to Israel as the "House of Omri"[30] and that Ahab

[22] I Kings. 16, 24; cf. A. Mazar, *Archaeology of the Land of the Bible: 10,000-586 B.C.E.*, New York 1990, p. 406-410.

[23] This divine name is attested by one of the inscriptions from Kuntillet 'Ağrud; cf. Z. Meshel, *Kuntillet 'Ajrud. A Religious Centre from the Time of the Judaean Monarchy on the Border of Sinai*, Jerusalem 1978, Fig. 12; J. Naveh, *Graffiti and Dedications*, in *BASOR* 235 (1979), p. 27-30 (see p. 28); P. Beck, *The Drawings from Ḥorvat Teiman (Kuntillet 'Ajrûd)*, in *Tel Aviv* 9 (1982), p. 3-68, Pls. 1-16 (see p. 45-47).

[24] II Kings 8, 26; II Chron. 22, 2.

[25] Hazor was in Israelite hands in the period immediately preceding *ca.* 850/840 B.C. and corresponding to Stratum IXA, clearly distinguished from Stratum VIII, which probably represents the Aramaean reoccupation of the area under Hazael, in the third quarter of the 9th century B.C. Comp. I. Finkelstein, *Hazor and the North in the Iron Age: A Low Chronology Perspective*, in *BASOR* 314 (1999), p. 55-70; Id., *Hazor XII-XI with an Addendum on Ben-Tor's Dating of Hazor X-VII*, in *Tel Aviv* 27 (2000), p. 231-247 (see p. 240-244). These strata are dated about fifty years earlier by A. Ben-Tor - D. Ben-Ami, *Hazor and the Archaeology of the Tenth Century B.C.E.*, in *IEJ* 48 (1998), p. 1-37; A. Ben-Tor, *Responding to Finkelstein's Addendum*, in *Tel Aviv* 28 (2001), p. 301-304.

[26] This results from the Mesha inscription: *TSSI* I, p. 74-76.

[27] J.W. & G.M. Crowfoot, *Samaria-Sebastia II. Early Ivories from Samaria*, London 1938.

[28] H.J. Katzenstein, *The History of Tyre*, Jerusalem 1973, p. 143-147; F. Briquel-Chatonnet, *Les relations entre les cités de la côte phénicienne et les royaumes d'Israël et de Juda* (Studia Phoenicia XII; OLA 46), Leuven 1992, p. 63-70.

[29] The Chronicler still had access to a source dealing with the events of the 9th century and independent from the Books of Kings. He knew that Jehoshaphat's wife belonged to Omri's family (II Chron. 18, 1), but he tried to accord this information with his main source.

[30] S. Parpola, *Neo-Assyrian Toponyms* (AOAT 6), Kevelaer-Neukirchen-Vluyn 1970, p. 82-83.

was able to supply great contingents of troops to oppose Shalmaneser III at Qarqar in 853 B.C.[31]

Biblical chronology applied to older Hebrew sources referring to this period is extremely problematic, but a plausible reconstruction of events is possible thanks to Assyrian, Aramaic, and Moabite inscriptions, all dating from the 9th century B.C. It suggests the following sequence of events.

In consequence of Ahab's quiet death in *ca.* 852 B.C., his son Ahaziahu became king of Israel, but his unexpected death in 851 brought his brother Jehoram to power in Samaria. After Jehoshaphat's death, the latter also became king of the vassal state of Judah, but in 842 he entrusted its rule to his son Ahaziahu[32]. While Ahab's relations with Damascus were placed on a peaceful footing, Hadadidri's apparently violent death and Hazael's successful bid for the Aramaean throne *ca.* 843 B.C.[33] radically changed the political situation. Hazael's attempt to conquer Gilead and northern Galilee led to a great battle at Ramoth-Gilead, probably in 842 B.C. Hazael boasts of his victory in the Tell al-Qāḍi inscription: "[I killed Jeho]ram, son of [Ahab], king of Israel, and I killed [Ahaz]iahu, [his] son, [ki]ng of the House of David"[34]. Following this battle, Omri's dynasty was continued by one of Jehoram's generals, Jehu, called "son of Omri" in Assyrian texts. He allegedly wiped out the family of Omri (II Kings 9-10), founding a dynasty that ruled Israel for the next hundred years. Jehu paid homage to Shalmaneser III in 841[35], when the Assyrian army marched from the Hauran to the Mediterranean, but the next forty years of Israel's history were marked by the loss of all the Transjordanian possessions to Damascus in the north and to Moab in the south,

The land of Madaba has been in the hands of the Omrides for forty years (*ca.* 880-840 B.C.) and the land of Ataroth was settled by the tribe of Gad from time immemorial. This information, provided by the Mesha inscription (line 10), raises the intricate question of the Israelite tribe of

[31] F. Briquel-Chatonnet, *op. cit.* (n. 28), p. 79-81.

[32] Chronicler's independent source reported obviously that "all Jehoshaphat's sons" have been murdered by Jehoram, his successor to the throne (II Chron. 21, 2-4), but the Chronicler tried once again to accord this information with his main source, namely the Books of Kings.

[33] P.-E. Dion, *Les Araméens à l'âge du fer: histoire politique et structures sociales* (Études bibliques, n.s. 34), Paris 1997, p. 191-194; Lipiński, *Aramaeans*, p. 376-377.

[34] A. Biran - J. Naveh, *The Tel Dan Inscription: A New Fragment,* in *IEJ* 45 (1995), p. 1-18. There is no space at the end of line 8 to restore the name of *Yhwrm*. Comparison with other lines only allows the reading *br*[*h.ml*]*k*, with three missing letters and a dot; cf. Lipiński, *Aramaeans*, p. 378-379.

[35] F. Briquel-Chatonnet, *op. cit.* (n. 28), p. 112-115.

Reuben, supposed to have occupied the territories located north of the Arnon River (Wādī al-Muǧib) according to Numb. 32, 1-38 and Josh. 13, 15-28.32. This area is nevertheless called "Moab" in the topographical list of Ramesses II at Luxor, thus in the 13th century B.C.[36]

Reuben

The tribe of Reuben is probably mentioned among the Shasu clans in an Egyptian topographical list of the 14th century B.C.[37] and it reappears in the Song of Deborah (Judg. 5, 15b-16), almost three hundred years later. Its members were pastoralists with great "men of sound mind", but they preferred listening to "narrow-minded men". This opposition is expressed by **ḥăqīqē-lēb* and **ḥăqīrē-lēb*, corresponding to Arabic *ḥaqīq*, "competent", and *ḥaqīr*, "vulgar":

> "By the water-channels of Reuben
> there are great men of sound mind.
> Why do you sit (then) between the folds
> to listen to the bleating of the flocks?
> Near the water-channels of Reuben
> there are great, narrow-minded men".

The Blessing of Moses, composed in a somewhat later period, only contains a short prayer for Reuben's survival (Deut. 33, 6), and at least two Reubenite clans, viz. Carmi and Hezron, are later integrated in the tribe of Judah[38]. It is probably no accident that no "judges" came in the 11th century from the tribe of Reuben. Besides, the tribe is not mentioned either in the list of the districts of the Kingdom of Israel (I Kings 4, 8-19) or in the Mesha inscription, though Gad is, also in I Kings 4, 19 according to the Septuagint. It appears therefore that one cannot expect to find recognizable traces of Reuben in the northern part of the Moabite territory, which was allotted to this tribe according to Numb. 32 and Josh. 13.

The four "Levitical cities" situated in Reuben's alleged realm, north of the Arnon River, viz. Bezer, Jahaz, Qedemot, and Mepha'at (I Chron.

[36] K.A. KITCHEN, *art. cit.* (n. 2), p. 27-28. The pertinent biblical passages have been analyzed by M. WÜST, *Untersuchungen zu den siedlungsgeographischen Texten des Alten Testaments I. Ostjordanland* (BTAVO B/9), Wiesbaden 1975, especially p. 59-185.

[37] See here below, p. 363-364.

[38] Carmi: Josh. 7, 1.18; I Chron. 4, 1; Hezron: Numb. 26, 21; I Chron. 4, 1. These clans are regarded as Reubenite in Gen. 46, 9; Ex. 6, 14; Numb. 26, 6; I Chron. 5, 3.

6, 63-64), seem to have bordered the desert. They may represent some outposts of the kingdom of Omri and Ahab before this entire area was conquered by the Moabites in the last years of the Omride dynasty and in the aftermath of its fall, *ca.* 840 B.C. If their location on the edge of the desert is confirmed, the "Levitical cities" on the "Reubenite" territory would appear as military stations defending the border of the Omride kingdom from incursions of the desert people, and this would possibly disclose an original function of such cities[39]. I Chron. 6, 63-64 seems to list them in a topographical sequence from the north to the south.

Bezer (*Bṣr, Bṣrh*), first mentioned, is an ancient **Bṯ̣rt*, "fenced place", a toponym related to Arabic *bẓr*, "to be inaccessible". **Buṯ̣artu* is still echoed by the spelling *B-w-t-ỉ-r-t-ỉ* (*B-t-r-t*) of a topographical list of Ramesses II, while the later form of the name appears also in Rabbinic sources[40]. The place is usually identified with Umm al-ʻAmad[41], 14 km north-east of Madaba. This is a large site, about 400 m in diameter, which is in part covered by the buildings of a modern village. It yielded potsherds from Iron Age I and II, as well as pottery fragments from the Persian period. Bezer is mentioned in the Mesha inscription (line 27), where the king says that he "rebuilt it, for it was in ruins", and he adds immediately that "all Dibon was a bodyguard" (line 28). It seems therefore that Bezer should be located not too far from Dibon. Instead of being identified with Umm al-ʻAmad, it should probably be situated at Ǧalūl[42], 5 km east of Madaba and 26 km north-east of Dibon. This is a large mound, measuring 240 m by 300 m and showing traces of occupation since the Bronze Age. Excavations undertaken in 1992, 1994, and 1996 have recovered remains from the 10th to the 4th centuries B.C. The finds of the Late Iron Age II and of the Persian period suggest that the town was at least from the later part of the 7th century in the Ammonite sphere of influence[43]. More recent periods are attested as well and would explain the mention of Bezer in Talmudic texts.

[39] A particular attention to these cities was already paid by J.A. DEARMAN, *The Levitical Cities of Reuben and Moabite Toponymy*, in *BASOR* 276 (1989), p. 55-66.

[40] A reliable copy of the hieroglyphic inscription is provided by K.A. KITCHEN, *Ramesside Inscriptions* II, Oxford 1969-79, p. 180:2. The Rabbinic texts are referred to by G. REEG, *Die Ortsnamen Israels nach der rabbinischen Literatur* (BTAVO B/51), Wiesbaden 1989, p. 134-135.

[41] Grid ref. 2355/1328: ABEL, *Géographie* II, p. 264; cf. W. ZWICKEL, *op. cit.* (n. 11), p. 176.

[42] Grid ref. 2312/1254: W. ZWICKEL, *op. cit.* (n. 11), p. 159; J.A. DEARMAN, *art. cit.* (n. 39), p. 61.

[43] The earliest indication is provided by an Ammonite stamp seal from the late 7th century B.C.: R.W. YOUNKER, *An Ammonite Seal from Tall Jalul, Jordan: The Seal of*

The second city is Jahaz (*Yhṣ, Yhṣh*), which A. Musil proposed to locate at Umm al-Walīd[44], but only a few potsherds from Iron Age II were found at this site[45]. Jahaz was a relatively important city, which was captured by Mesha (lines 19-20). F.-M. Abel proposed to identify it with Ǧalūl[46], but Ǧalūl is situated 5 km east of Madaba, while Eusebius clearly states that Jahaz lays between Madaba and Dibon, thus further south[47]. Following the letter of Eusebius' text R. de Vaux thus identified Jahaz with Ḫirbet Libb[48], 12 km north of Dibon. Potsherds from Iron Age I and II are well represented on the mound[49], but the latter does not have the strategic importance of Ḫirbet al-Mudayyina, on the southern bank of Wādī aṯ-Ṯamad[50]. This is a relatively small tell (*ca.* 1 ha), with a walled area of about 160 m by 40 m. It yielded much pottery from Iron Age I and II, dating down at least to *ca.* 600 B.C.[51] The mound is located 20 km south-east of Madaba and about 16 km north-east of Dibon, thus fitting the identification of Eusebius. The site is being excavated since 1995 by P.-M. Michèle Daviau[52]. The discovery of a Phoenician inscription, datable to *ca.* 600 B.C., should be mentioned in particular[53]. Ḫirbet

'Aynadab Son of Zedek'il, in *F.M. Cross Volume* (ErIs 26), Jerusalem 1999, p. 221*-224*. In general, see R.W. Younker *et al.*, ... *Madaba Plains Project...*, in *AUSS* 31/3 (1993), p. 205-238; 34/1 (1996), p. 65-92; 35/2 (1997), p. 227-240.

44 Grid ref. 2350/1175: A. Musil, *op. cit.* (n. 19), p. 107, 122.

45 W. Zwickel, *op. cit.* (n. 11), p. 154.

46 Grid ref. 2312/1254: Abel, *Géographie* II, p. 354. The opinions regarding the location of Jahaz are summarized by S. Loewenstamm, *Yahaṣ, Yahaṣāh*, in *Enṣiqlopēdiya Miqrā'īt* III, Jerusalem 1958, col. 571-572 (in Hebrew).

47 Eusebius of Caesarea, *Onomasticon*, in E. Klostermann (ed.), *op. cit.* (n. 16), p. 104:11-12.

48 Grid ref. 2223/1128; cf. R. de Vaux, *Notes d'histoire et de topographie transjordaniennes*, in *Vivre et Penser* 1 (1941), p. 16-47 (see p. 20); Id., rev. in *RB* 69 (1962), p. 472. Cf. W. Zwickel, *op. cit.* (n. 11), p. 152.

49 This is not the case of Ḫirbet Iskander, on the Wādī al-Wāla, identified with Jahaz by K.-H. Bernhardt, *Beobachtungen zur Identifizierung moabitischer Ortslagen*, in *ZDPV* 76 (1960), p. 136-158 (see p. 151-158).

50 Grid ref. 2363/1109: J.A. Dearman, *The Location of Jahaz*, in *ZDPV* 100 (1984), p. 122-126; Id., *art. cit.* (n. 39), p. 61-63; cf. W. Zwickel, *op. cit.* (n. 11), p. 153.

51 B. Routledge, *A Comment on A.F. Rainey's 'The New Inscription from Khirbet el-Mudeiyineh'*, in *IEJ* 53 (2003), p. 192-195.

52 P.-M.M. Daviau, *Moab's Northern Border: Khirbat al-Mudayna on the Wadi ath-Thamad*, in *BA* 60 (1997), p. 222-228; R. Chadwick - P.-M.M. Daviau - M. Steiner, *Four Seasons of Excavations at Khirbat al-Mudayna on the Wadi ath-Thamad, 1996-1999*, in *ADAJ* 44 (2000), p. 257-270; P.-M.M. Daviau - M. Steiner, *A Moabite Sanctuary at Khirbet al-Mudayna*, in *BASOR* 320 (2000), p. 1-21; P.-M.M. Daviau - P.E. Dion, *Moab comes to Life*, in *Biblical Archaeology Review* 28/1 (2002), p. 38-49; P.-M.M. Daviau - P.E. Dion, *Economy-Related Finds from Khirbat al-Mudayna*, in *BASOR* 328 (2002), p. 31-48.

53 P.E. Dion - P.-M.M. Daviau, *An Inscribed Incense Altar of Iron Age II at Ḫirbet el-Mudēyine (Jordan)*, in *ZDPV* 116 (2000), p. 1-13. The interpretation of the inscription

al-Mudayyina appears to have been rebuilt and heavily fortified at the beginning of the 8th or the end of the 9th century B.C. The town was protected by a casemate wall system. An exceptionally well-preserved six-chambered gate, measuring 15.80 m by 16.35 m, has been exposed and dated by radiocarbon C-14 to the first half of the 8th century B.C.[54] Small towers were flanking its front bastions. A similar, but four-chambered gate has been discovered at Ḫirbet al-Muḍaybi'[55], about 20 km south-east of Kerak. This is a large rectangular fort (*ca.* 0.75 ha), measuring 83.5 m by 88.75 m and dated likewise by radiocarbon C-14 to the early 8th century B.C. It has corner towers, mid-wall buttresses, and its monumental gate was flanked by two solid towers. Both fortifications appear to be posterior by *ca.* half a century to the building activities of Mesha. They must date from the time of his successor, whose name does not appear on the fragment of the recently published Moabite inscription[56], in which the king explicitly records the building of a large gateway with a moat: "With Ammonite captives [I dug] the moat of a powerful gate", *b'sry.bny'mn* [*krty.'t.*] *mkrt.š'r.'dr* (lines 3'-4'). Halfway between these two fortresses there is another Ḫirbet al-Mudayyina, surnamed al-'Aliya[57]. It is situated about 27 km south-east of Dibon and was occupied only in the Iron I period[58]. It should, of course, be distinguished from the Ḫirbet al-Mudayyina on the Wādī aṯ-Ṯamad[59].

The third "Levitical city" is Qedemot (*Qdmwt*, *Qdmt*), which F.-M. Abel placed at Qaṣr az-Za'farān[60], 17 km north-east of Dibon, or at Ḫirbet ar-Rumēl[61], 12 km north-east of Dibon. This toponym may

was improved by A.F. Rainey, *The New Inscription from Khirbet el-Mudeiyineh,* in *IEJ* 52 (2002), p. 81-86. For further comments, see Lipiński, *Itineraria Phoenicia*, p. 139-140, and for the dating, B. Routledge, *art. cit.* (n. 51).

54 R. Chadwick *et al.*, *art. cit.* (n. 58), p. 258-267; cf. B. Routledge, *op. cit.* (n. 1), p. 175-176.

55 Grid ref. 2306/0502: G. Mattingly, *A New Agenda for Research on Ancient Moab*, in *BA* 60 (1997), p. 214-221; Id. *et al.*, *Al-Karak Resources Project 1997: Excavations at Khirbat al-Muḍaybi*, in *ADAJ* 43 (1999), p. 127-144.

56 S. Aḥituv, *A New Moabite Inscription*, in *Israel Museum Archaeological Studies* 2 (2003), p. 3-10; Id., *A New Royal Inscription from Moab*, in *Qadmoniot* 37 (2004), p. 88-92 (in Hebrew).

57 Grid ref. 2328/0767 or 2330/0768; cf. W. Zwickel, *op. cit.* (n. 11), p. 128-129.

58 B. Routledge, *Seeing through Walls: Interpreting Iron Age I Architecture at Khirbat al-Mudayna al-'Aliya*, in *BASOR* 318 (2000), p. 37-70.

59 See J.M. Miller, *Six Khirbet el-Medeinehs in the Region East of the Dead Sea*, in *BASOR* 276 (1989), p. 25-28.

60 Grid ref. 2328/1140 and 2336/1146: Abel, *Géographie* II, p. 217 and 415; cf. W. Zwickel, *op. cit.* (n. 11), p. 153.

61 Grid ref. 2331/1097; cf. W. Zwickel, *op. cit.* (n. 11), p. 150.

designate an "Eastern" desert, like in Deut 2, 26, but it does not suit a town. *Qdmt*, as the toponym is spelled in Josh. 13, 18, should probably be regarded as an old scribal mistake for *Qrywt*, an important Moabite city, mentioned in the Mesha inscription (lines 12-13), in Jer. 48, 24.41; Am. 2, 2, and in the Genesis Apocryphon 21, 29. The confusion *d/r* is very common and *yw* happen to be read as *m*[62]. If this "Levitical city" was indeed *Qrywt*, it could be identified with Ḫirbet Qurayyāt 'Alēyān[63], 12 km north-east of Dibon. This high hill, covered with potsherds from Iron Age I-II, certainly corresponds to an ancient site and it perfectly suits a holy place of the Moabite upper-god Chemosh, referred to in Mesha's inscription (line 13).

The fourth "Levitical city" is Mepha'at (*Myp't, Mwp't*), the name of which designates a "beautiful place". The Hebrew noun *yp'h* means "beauty", speaking especially of a town (Ez. 28, 7.17), and *Myp't* is a derivative with prefixed *ma-*, used in particular with nouns of place[64]. Such a name can be given to several settlements and it appears also in South Arabian as the name of the major town of *Myf't* or Μαίφα. Its identification with Ḫirbet Nēfa'a, near Amman, or with a site close to the latter place, which yielded no Iron Age potsherds, should thus be based on additional arguments. The change of the preformative *m* into *n* constitutes no problem, since this shift is widely attested in Semitic languages when the root morpheme contains a labial, especially as first radical consonant[65]. The problem is historical, since Jer. 48, 21 considers Mepha'at a Moabite city, while Tell Jawa (Ǧāwā) South[66] — associated since Ch. Clermont-Ganneau[67] with biblical Mepha'at, because it is close to Ḫirbet Nēfa'a — lies clearly on Ammonite territory, 10 km south of the Amman Citadel[68].

[62] F. DELITZSCH, *Die Lese- und Schreibfehler im Alten Testament*, Berlin-Leipzig 1920, p. 120-121, §132e-f.

[63] Grid ref. 2338/1045: K.-H. BERNHARDT, *art. cit.* (n. 49), p. 136-151; W. ZWICKEL, *op. cit.* (n. 11), p. 149. R. BOLING, *Levitical Cities: Archaeology and Texts*, in A. KORT - S. MORSCHAUSER (eds.*), Biblical and Related Studies Presented to S. Iwry*, Winona Lake 1985, p. 23-32 (see p. 25), proposed locating Qedemot at as-Sālīya (grid ref. 2375/0959); cf. also J.A. DEARMAN, *art. cit.* (n. 39), p. 63. This location disrupts the topographical sequence north-south, although the vestiges match the requirements of an Iron II site: W. ZWICKEL, *op. cit.* (n. 11), p. 145.

[64] LIPIŃSKI, *Semitic*, §29.21.

[65] LIPIŃSKI, *Semitic*, §29.26.

[66] Grid ref. 2392/1401; cf. W. ZWICKEL, *op. cit.* (n. 11), p. 200.

[67] Ch. CLERMONT-GANNEAU, *RAO* IV, Paris 1901, p. 56-60.

[68] R.W. YOUNKER - P.M.M. DAVIAU, *Is Mefa'at to be found at Tell Jawa (South)?*, in *IEJ* 43 (1993), p. 23-28; R.W. YOUNKER, *Identity of Tell Jawa (South): Mephaath or Abel Keramim?*, in D. MERLING (ed.), *To Understand the Scriptures. Essays in Honor of W.H. Shea*, Berrien Springs 1997, p. 257-263.

The site of Mepha'at has been found at Ḫirbet Umm ar-Raṣāṣ, as proposed by the excavators M. Piccirillo and T. Attiyat[69]. Among the exceptional finds from the Byzantine and Early Arab periods, uncovered at the site, one should mention the Greek dedication of a mosaic by "the administrator of Mephaon (ἄρχοντι Μεφαον) and all the Christ-loving people of Kastron Nephaon (Κάστρου Νφαων)"[70]. There is little doubt that Μεφαον / Νφαων[71] is the same place as the biblical Mepha'at and that it should be identified with the site of Ḫirbet Umm ar-Raṣāṣ. The unfounded objections formulated against this identification[72] can be easily discarded, the more so because the site yielded Iron Age pottery. Deeper soundings made in 1989 and 1990 in the area of the St. Stephen church provided potsherds from the 7th century B.C.[73] and unspecified Iron Age pottery was found on the mound located to the north-east of the castle[74].

Umm er-Raṣāṣ is situated 13 km east of Dibon, 5 km south-east of Ḫirbet Qurayyāt 'Alēyān, presumably the biblical *Qrywt*, and 4 km north-east of Ḫirbet al-Ǧumayyil[75], which has been identified as *Bēt-Gāmūl* in the Plain of Moab[76]. The identification of Umm ar-Raṣāṣ as Mepha'at perfectly suits Eusebius' notice: "where a military guard encamps at the edge of the desert"[77]. The place is recorded also among the cities of Arabia in the *Notitia Dignitatum* (*ca.* 393-405 A.D.)[78].

[69] M. Piccirillo - T. Attiyat, *The Complex of St. Stephen at Um er-Rasas - Kastron Mefaa. First Campaign Aug. 1986*, in *ADAJ* 30 (1986), p. 341-351; M. Piccirillo, *Mosaics of 785 A.D. at Um er-Rasas (K. Mefaa)*, in *Holy Land* 7/2 (1987), p. 59-75; Id., *Le iscrizioni di Um er-Rasas - Kastron Mefaa in Giordania, I (1986-1987)*, in *Studii Biblici Franciscani Liber Annuus* 37 (1987), p. 177-239, Pls. 1-30; Id., *L'identificazione storica delle rovine di Umm er-Raṣāṣ - Kastron Mefaa in Giordania*, in *Biblica* 71 (1990), p. 527-541 and 4 Pls.; Id., *Umm er-Rasas*, in *NEAEHL*, Jerusalem 1993, Vol. IV, p. 1490-1493. Other reports of the excavations at Umm ar-Raṣāṣ do not concern the identification of the site.

[70] A good photograph was published by M. Piccirillo, *art. cit.* (n. 69), in *Studii Biblici Franciscani Liber Annuus* 37 (1987), p. 184.

[71] Written phonetically without ε because a vowel precedes *N* < *M*, changed in a position contiguous to φ.

[72] Y. Elitzur, *The Identification of Mefa'at in View of the Discoveries from Kh. Umm er-Raṣāṣ*, in *IEJ* 39 (1989), p. 267-277; Z. Kallai, *A Note on 'Is Mefa'at to be found at Tell Jawa (South)?' by R.W. Younker and P.M.M. Daviau*, in *IEJ* 43 (1993), p. 249-251.

[73] M. Piccirillo, *art. cit.* (n. 69), in *Biblica* 71 (1990), p. 540-541.

[74] W. Zwickel, *op. cit.* (n. 11), p. 149.

[75] Grid ref. 2348/1002: W. Zwickel, *op. cit.* (n. 11), p. 149.

[76] Jer. 48, 23: M. Avi-Yonah, *Bēt-Gāmūl*, in *Enṣiqlopēdiya Miqrā'īt* II, Jerusalem 1954, p. 70 (in Hebrew).

[77] Eusebius of Caesarea, *Onomasticon*, in E. Klostermann (ed.), *op. cit.* (n. 16), p. 128:21.

[78] *Notitia Dignitatum Or.* XXXVII, 8, 19, in O. Seeck (ed.), *Notitia Dignitatum utriusque Imperii*, Berlin 1876, p. 80-81.

The name of the city appears surprisingly on a carnelian scaraboid of uncertain provenance, acquired in London and published by N. Avigad[79]. It is decorated with a four-winged figure holding a papyrus flower in each hand and wearing a debased Egyptian crown. This motive occurs on several West Semitic seals, in particular on three Moabite scaraboids, which are inscribed *l-Kmšṣdq*[80], *B'lntn*[81], and *l-Kmš'r*[82]. The inscription reads *Myp'h* without the customary preposition *l-*. This omission is known from many seals, but it raises a serious question in this particular case, because the owner's name is identical with the name of a city. The latter is written with a final *t* in the Bible, but the spelling with *-h* probably reflects a later pronunciation. N. Avigad dates the seal from the 7th century B.C. and points at the close resemblance between the *m* of the seal and the Hebrew letter. However, this is certainly no Hebrew *m* from the 7th century B.C. Both palaeography and iconography rather suggest dating the scaraboid to the mid-8th century B.C., while the city name engraved in the exergue seems to indicate that this is no private stamp-seal, but a city seal, used possibly by a successor of one of those "captains of centuries", whom Mesha let rule over the cities of his land (lines 28-29)[83].

The four "Levitical cities" in the "Reubenite" area, listed from the north to the south, appear as a chain of fortified places along the eastern side of the Plain of Madaba. They aimed, as it seems, at protecting Madaba, Dibon, and the "King's Highway" from raiders coming from the east. The presence of this list in Josh. 21, 36-37 and I Chron. 6, 63-64 (cf. Josh. 13, 18) can best be explained by dating its origin from the time of the Omrides, no doubt occupying also Dibon[84] and Madaba[85], where

[79] N. AVIGAD, *The Seal of Mepha'ah*, in *IEJ* 40 (1990), p. 42-43 and Pl. 6A; N. AVIGAD - B. SASS, *Corpus of West Semitic Stamp Seals*, Jerusalem 1997, p. 434-435, No. 1147, cf. p. 505.

[80] VA 2826: K. GALLING, *Beschriftete Bildsiegel des ersten Jahrtausends v. Chr., vornehmlich aus Syrien und Palästina*, in *ZDPV* 64 (1941), p. 121-202 (see No. 92); N. AVIGAD - B. SASS, *op. cit.* (n. 79), p. 382, No. 1036; L. JAKOB-ROST, *Die Stempelsiegel im Vorderasiatischen Museum*, 2nd ed., Berlin 1997, p. 62-63, No. 176.

[81] P. BORDREUIL, *Catalogue des sceaux ouest-sémitiques inscrits*, Paris 1986, p. 57-58, No. 61; N. AVIGAD - B. SASS, *op. cit.* (n. 79), p. 377, No. 1020.

[82] R. DEUTSCH - M. HELTZER, *Windows to the Past*, Tel Aviv-Jaffa 1997, p. 59-61, No. 109 (32). This seal provides a variant design: the figure raises the arms and holds no papyrus flowers.

[83] See here below, p. 337.

[84] Grid ref. 2240/1010; cf. W. ZWICKEL, *op. cit.* (n. 11), p. 148; G. REEG, *op. cit.* (n. 40), p. 206.

[85] Grid ref. 2256/1253; cf. W. ZWICKEL, *op. cit.* (n. 11), p. 157; G. REEG, *op. cit.* (n. 40), p. 407-408.

Iron Age material was found in multiple burial caves[86]. Excavations on the mound itself (*ca.* 16 ha) were started in 1995. The earliest levels reached so far belong to Iron Age II and can thus date to the Omride period[87]. As for Dibon, some pottery prior to the time of Mesha or the mid-9th century B.C. has been found[88], but there is no evidence for a royal city before that period[89]. The Moabite conquest of the "Reubenite" territories north of the Arnon River is reported in the Mesha inscription.

Mesha inscription

The Mesha stele was discovered in 1868 by a German missionary at Ḏībān (< Ḏaybān, cf. p. 107), the biblical Dibon, most likely at its original place, which the engraved inscription seems to call *qrḥh*[90].

The word *qrḥh,* occurring in lines 3, 21, 24, 25, has often been considered a place name. *Qrḥh* was thus regarded either as a quarter of

[86] G.L. Harding - B.S.J. Isserlin, *An Early Iron Age Tomb from Madaba*, in *Palestine Exploration Fund. Annual* 6 (1953), p. 27-47; M. Piccirillo, *Una tomba del Ferro I a Madaba (Madaba B, Moab)*, in *Studii Biblici Franciscani Liber Annuus* 25 (1975), p. 199-224; Id., *Chiese e mosaici di Madaba*, Jerusalem 1989, p. 316-317; H.O. Thompson, *An Iron Age Tomb at Madaba*, in L.T. Geraty - L.H. Herr (eds.), *The Archaeology of Jordan and Other Studies Presented to S. Horn,* Berrien Springs 1986, p. 331-363; E.J. van der Steen, *op. cit.* (n. 1), p. 51, 135-136, 157 (Fig. 6-6).

[87] T.P. Harrison, *Investigations of Urban Life in Madaba, Jordan,* in *BA* 60 (1997), p. 53-54; Id., *Tell Madaba*, in V. Egan - P. Bikai - K. Zamora (eds.), *Archaeology in Jordan,* in *AJA* 104 (2000), p. 561-588 (see p. 579-581); Id. *et al.*, *Urban Life in the Highlands of Central Jordan: A Preliminary Report of the 1996 Tall Madaba Excavations,* in *ADAJ* 44 (2000), p. 211-230.

[88] E.J. van der Steen, *op. cit.* (n. 1), p. 134-135, 157 (Fig. 6-5).

[89] B. MacDonald, *East of the Jordan. Territories and Sites of the Hebrew Scriptures* (ASOR Books 6), Boston 2000, p. 76, sees Dibon as the capital of Moab and identifies it with biblical ʻAr-Moab. However, ʻAr Moab in Numb. 21, 28 is no city name, but "the precinct of Moab", the Moabite tableland, and there is no city name ʻAr-Moab in Is. 15, 1. The two words *ʻĀr* and *Mō'āb* should be separated and the passage interpreted as follows: "On the night when Ar is sacked, Moab meets her doom; on the night when Qir is sacked, Moab meets her doom". Both words, *ʻār* and *qīr*, "city", are Moabite and refer to the territory and to the capital city.

[90] For the text, see for instance: *KAI* 181; *TSSI* I, 16. The language of the inscription was studied by A.H. van Zyl, *The Moabites*, Leiden 1960, p. 161-189; S. Segert, *Die Sprache der moabitischen Königsinschrift,* in *Archiv Orientální* 29 (1961), p. 197-267; F.I. Andersen, *Moabite Syntax,* in *Orientalia* 35 (1966), p. 81-120; K.P. Jackson, *The Language of the Mesha Inscription*, in A. Dearman (ed.), *Studies in the Mesha Inscription and Moab*, Atlanta 1989, p. 96-130; A. Niccacci, *The Stele of Mesha and the Bible: Verbal System and Narrativity,* in *Orientalia* 63 (1994), p. 226-248; A.F. Rainey, *Meshaʻ and Syntax*, in J.A. Dearman - M.P. Graham (eds.), *The Land that I Will Show You: Essays on the History and Archaeology of the Ancient Near East in Honour of J.M. Miller*, Sheffield 2001, p. 287-307.

Dibon[91], where the stele was found, apparently *in situ*, or it was identified with Kerak, the ancient Moabite capital[92]. The phrase *kl r'š qrḥh*, "every bald head", in Is. 15, 2 and Jer. 48, 37, was also interpreted as a word play on the name of *Qrḥh*[93], while M.-J. Lagrange translated *Kmš b-Qrḥh* in line 3 of the inscription by "Chemosh (dwelling) in *Qrḥh*"[94]. In reality, *qrḥ* is an ancient North-West Semitic noun, which means "citadel" or the like[95]. It appears in the Assyro-Babylonian *malku* = *šarru* list of synonyms, where the equation *qé-er-ḫu* = *du-u-ru* (I, 236) implies a meaning "fort" or "fortified place"[96]. The sense "acropolis" or "citadel" is corroborated by the use of *Qé-er-ḫa-am*ᵏⁱ and *qé-er-ḫi* at Mari and at Chagar Bazar[97]. The final *-h* of *qrḥh* in the Mesha inscription seems to be a pronominal suffix referring either to Chemosh (line 3) or to Dibon (lines 3 [cf. *Dybny* in line 2] and 21), and to *qr*, "town" (lines 24 and 25). Unfortunately, the excavations conducted in 1950-1955 and 1965 by F.V. Winnett, W.L. Reed, A.D. Tushingham, and W.H. Morton on the mound of Dibon[98] did not manage to elucidate this point of the topography of the ancient town, despite the discovery of a city gate and of a large building from the 9th century B.C.[99] A pilot season conducted in 2004 by B.W. Porter, B.E. Routledge, and D. Steen may prelude to renewed excavations of the site.

[91] F.V. WINNETT, *Excavations at Dibon in Moab 1950-51*, in *BASOR* 125 (1952), p. 7-19 (see p. 6-7); W. RÖLLIG, in *KAI* II, p. 172; *TSSI* I, p. 78.

[92] ABEL, *Géographie* II, p. 418; R. DE VAUX, rev. in *RB* 69 (1962), p. 472.

[93] E. EASTERLEY, *Is Mesha's* qrḥh *mentioned in Isaiah XV 27?*, in *Vetus Testamentum* 41 (1991), p. 215-220, following ABEL, *Géographie* II, p. 418.

[94] M.-J. LAGRANGE, *L'inscription de Mésa*, in *RB* 10 (1901), p. 522-545 (see p. 527-528), still followed by K. GALLING, *Textbuch zur Geschichte Israels*, Tübingen 1950, p. 48.

[95] E. LIPIŃSKI, *North-West Semitic Inscriptions*, in *OLP* 8 (1977), p. 81-117 (see p. 95-96).

[96] A. DRAFFKORN KILMER, *The First Tablet of* malku = šarru *together with Its Explicit Version*, in *JAOS* 83 (1963), p. 421-446 (see p. 428).

[97] J.-M. DURAND, *Villes fantômes de Syrie et autres lieux*, in *MARI* 5 (1987), p. 199-234 (see p. 225); Ph. TALON, *Old Babylonian Texts from Chagar Bazar* (Akkadica. Supplementum 10), Brussels 1997, No. 77, 19'. See also the Additional note on p. 359-360.

[98] Grid ref. 2240/1010; cf. W. ZWICKEL, *op. cit.* (n. 11), p. 148.

[99] *The Excavations at Dibon (Dhībân) in Moab* I: *The First Campaign, 1950-1951*, by F.V. WINNETT; II: *The Second Campaign, 1952*, by W.L. REED (AASOR 36-37), New Haven 1964; A.D. TUSHINGHAM, *The Excavations at Dibon (Dhībân) in Moab. The Third Campaign, 1952-1953* (AASOR 40), Cambridge, Mass. 1972; W.H. MORTON, *The 1954, 55, and 65 Excavations at Dhiban in Jordan*, in A. DEARMAN (ed.), *Studies in the Mesha Inscription and Moab*, Atlanta 1989, p. 239-246; A.D. TUSHINGHAM, *Dibon*, in *NEAEHL*, Jerusalem 1993, Vol. I, p. 350-352. See also B. ROUTLEDGE, *op. cit.* (n. 1), p. 161-175.

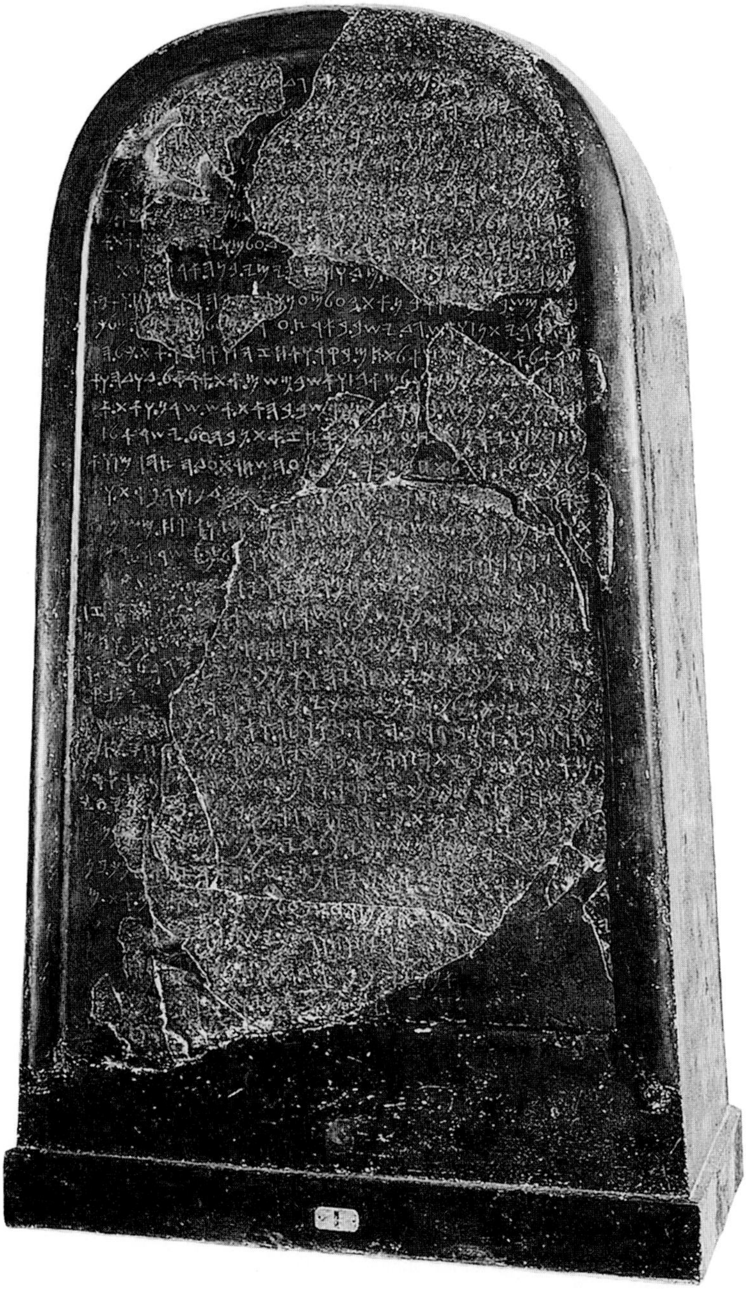

Inscription of Mesha, king of Moab
(Louvre Museum, AO 5066 + AO 2142).

Translation

“[1]I am Mesha, son of Chemosh[yatt][100], king of Moab, the [2]man of Dibon. My father had reigned over Moab for thirty years, and I became king [3]after my father. I made this high place for Chemosh in his/its citadel. [I] built it being [4]victorious[101], because he saved me from all the kings and let me triumph over all my adversaries. Omri [5]was king of Israel and he had oppressed Moab many days, for Chemosh was angry with his land. [6]And his son (Ahab) succeeded him and he also said: ‘I will oppress Moab’. In my days C[hemosh][102] spoke [7]and I triumphed over him and over his house, and Israel perished utterly for ever, although Omri had occupied the land [8]of Madaba, and had dwelt there in his days and half the days of his son, forty years. But [9]Chemosh dwelt there in my days.

And I built Baal-Meon, and I made a reservoir in it, and I built [10]Qiryatēn. Now, the men of Gad had dwelt in the land of Ataroth from of old, and the king of [11]Israel had built Ataroth for him, but I fought against the town and took it, and I slew all the people of [12]the town in due homage to Chemosh and to Moab. And I brought from there Uriel, its warden[103], and [13]I dragged him before Chemosh at Qerioth, and I settled there men of Sharon and men of [14]Maḥaroth. And Chemosh said to me: ‘Go, take Nebo from Israel!’ So I [15]went by night and fought against it from the break of dawn until noon, and I took [16]it and slew it all, seven thousand men and boys, women and girls, [17]and pregnant females, for I devoted it to Ashtar-Chemosh. And I took from there the[18][r]ams of Yahwe and dragged them before Chemosh. Now, the king of Israel had built [19]Jahaz, and he had dwelt there while he was fighting against me, but Chemosh drove him out before me, [when] [20]I took from Moab two hundred men, all its host[104], and I set it against Jahaz, and I took it [21]in order to attach it to Dibon.

It was I who built its citadel, the wall of the garden and the wall [22]of the acropolis. I also built its gates and I built its towers and [23]I built the king’s house, and I made both reservo[irs for wa]ter inside [24]the town. And there was no cistern inside the town, in its citadel, so I said to all the people: ‘Let each of you make for [25]yourselves a cistern in his house!’ And I dug the ditches[105] for

[100] The second part of the name is restored from the fragmentary inscription found at Kerak: *TSSI* I, 17, line 1.

[101] The new sentence following the stroke engraved after *bqrḥh* should be restored *bn*[*t*]⸤*h*⸥[.*n*⸥*š*‘, “I built it being victorious”. The participle niphal of *yš*‘ is used here as an adverbial accusative with the connotation “victorious”, which occurs also in Hebrew, at least in Deut. 33, 29 and Zech. 9, 9.

[102] At the end of line 6 there are traces of two letters, which were probably followed by a third one. The traces suggest restoring ⸢*k*⸣⸤*m*][*š*], as proposed already by M. SCHLOTTMANN, *Die Siegessaüle Mesa’s*, Halle 1870, whose view was shared by Ch. CLERMONT-GANNEAU, *La Stèle de Dhiban ou Stèle de Mesa, roi de Moab*, Paris 1870, p. 54.

[103] Cf. here below, p. 339-340.

[104] The singular suffixed noun *ršh* should be related to the root *ršš*, the causative of which is attested in Sabaic (*hrs*[1]) with the meaning “perform military service”: *Sabaic Dictionary*, p. 118. The noun *rš* must then mean “army”, “host”, or the like.

[105] The feminine plural *mkrtt* derives from the same root *kry*, “to dig”, as the perfect *krty*. This is not a form of the verb *krt*, “to hew”, “to fell”, as often assumed. The noun

its citadel with Israelite captives. [26]I built Aroer and I made the highway in the Arnon. [27]And I built Bēth-Bamoth, for it had been destroyed. I built Bezer, for it lay in ruins.

[28]And [the m]en of Dibon were in battle array[106], for all Dibon was a bodyguard[107]. And I let [29][the captains] of centuries rule in the towns which I had added to the land. And I built [30][Bēth-Mad]aba and Bēth-Diblatēn and Bēth-Baal-Meon, and I set there [31]my shepherds [in order to tend] the sheep of the land. As for Hawronēn, there had dwelt the Hou[se of Da]vid[108] [...[32]...], but Chemosh said to me: 'Go down, fight against Hawronēn!' And I went down and [33][I fought against the town and I took it], and Chemosh [dwelt] there in my days, and the moth? [re]moved injustice? from there[109]... [34][... of sh]ame tore apart?. And I ... [35][...]."

Mesha first records the rebuilding of Baal-Meon and of Qiryatēn (lines 10-11). The first town, also called Bēth-Baal-Meon (line 30)[110], Bēth-Meon (Jer. 48, 23), Beon or Βαιάν[111], was a "Reubenite" city[112]. Eusebius identifies it with Βεελμαούς, 9 miles from 'Εσβοῦς (Ḥisbān)[113]. This is certainly the present-day Mā'īn[114], 15 km south-west of Ḥisbān and 8 km south-west of Madaba. An important mosaic pavement of a Byzantine church was discovered there. It is characterized by a topographical frame representing churches of the Holy Land and naming the respective towns. The church of Baal-Meon is pictured in front of a lateral gate of the nave with the inscription *BEΛEMOYNIM*,

mkrt can thus mean "ditch, fosse, moat". In the present context, the ditches seem to belong to the system of water supply.

[106] Cf. Hebrew *ḥ^a^mušīm* in Ex. 13, 18; Josh. 1, 14; 4, 12; Judg. 7, 11. This interpretation was already considered by Ch. CLERMONT-GANNEAU, *op. cit.* (n. 102), p. 40.

[107] Cf. Hebrew *mišma'at* in I Sam. 22, 14; II Sam. 23, 23; I Chron. 11, 25. Cf. M. WEIPPERT, *Meša und der Status von "ganz Dibon"*, in F. NINOW (ed.), *Wort und Stein. Studien zur Theologie und Archäologie. Festschrift für U. Worschech*, Frankfurt a/M 2003, p. 323-328.

[108] Cf. A. LEMAIRE, *'House of David' Restored in Moabite Inscription*, in *Biblical Archaeology Review* 20/3 (1994), p. 30-37; ID., *La dynastie davidique* (byt dwd) *dans deux inscriptions sémitiques du IXe s. av. J.-C.*, in *Studi epigrafici e linguistici* 11 (1994), p. 17-19.

[109] There seems to be a stroke after *'š*, thus indicating the end of the sentence. The image of the clause *w'l.[n]dh.mšm.'š*, if properly understood, is paralleled in Is. 50, 9; 59, 8; Hos. 5, 12, and one can refer also to Ps. 39, 12 and Job 13, 28. The word *ss*, "moth", is used in a similar context in the Aramaic inscription of Sefire I, A, 31, and *sāsu* appears in the Epic of Gilgamesh XII, 93-94. Other interpretations of the sentence are possible, because *'š* can stand for various roots, e.g. Old Arabian *'ws^1*, "plague", or *ġwṯ*, "help", while *'l* can also mean "yoke".

[110] Cf. Josh. 13, 17, and Talmudic texts: G. REEG, *op. cit.* (n. 40), p. 93-95.

[111] Numb. 32, 3; Jub. 29, 10; E. KLOSTERMANN (ed.), *op. cit.* (n. 16), p. 44:14.

[112] Numb. 32, 38; Josh. 13, 18; I Chron. 5, 8; Ez. 25, 9.

[113] E. KLOSTERMANN (ed.), *op. cit.* (n. 16), p. 44:21-46:2

[114] Grid ref. 219/121.

which certainly refers to the very town of Baal-Meon[115]. Mesha does not say that he conquered the city, but he makes a boast of having rebuilt it and made a reservoir there for storing water (line 9). The meaning of *'šwḥ*, "water reservoir", is certain[116]. The word occurs also in line 23 and possibly on the small fragment from Dibon ('*]šwḥ*[)[117]. It corresponds to Hebrew *'šyḥ*, which is used in Sir. 50, 3 and four times in the Copper Scroll from Qumrān (3Q15): 5, 6; 7, 4; 10, 5; 11, 12[118]. The Septuagint translates *'šyḥ* in Sir. 50, 3 by λάκκος (ὡσει θαλάσσης = *kym*), which designated great rectangular pools, built in free-stones. Mesha further records that he settled his shepherds there to tend the sheep (lines 30-31), which were an important economic resource of the country. II Kings 3, 4 even reports that "Mesha, king of Moab, was a sheep-breeder: he used to supply the king of Israel regularly with the wool of a hundred thousand lambs and a hundred thousand rams".

Mesha further boasts of having rebuilt Qiryatēn (lines 9-10), which is the same city as the biblical Qiryataim, also a "Reubenite" town, often mentioned in the Scripture: Numb. 32, 37; Josh. 13, 19; Jer. 48, 1.23; Ez. 25, 9. Eusebius identifies it with the village of Καραιάθα, 10 miles west of Madaba[119]. The place should not be identified with Ḫirbet Qurayyāt 'Alēyān[120], but with Ḫirbet al-Qurayya[121], 10 km west of Madaba as the crow flies. This is a well protected, steep mound, measuring 120 m by 80 m and yielding large quantities of Iron Age potsherds.

Mesha further mentions his conquest of the Gadite town of Ataroth (lines 10-14). This is the biblical city of *'Aṭārōt* (Numb. 32, 3.34), the name of which means "crown", thus confirming its identification with the crown-shaped Ḫirbet 'Aṭārūz[122]. This mound is situated 13 km north-west of Dibon and 4 km north-east of the Hasmonaean fortress of Machaerus, the present-day Ḫirbet al-Mukāwir[123]. Ḫirbet 'Aṭārūz is pro-

[115] R. DE VAUX, *Une mosaïque byzantine à Ma'in*, in *RB* 47 (1938), p. 227-258, Pls. X-XVI (see p. 250 and Pl. XVI, 1).

[116] Despite the doubt expressed in *DNWSI*, p. 122, where the Hebrew parallels are not mentioned.

[117] W.F. ALBRIGHT - R.E. MURPHY, *A Fragment of an Early Moabite Inscription from Dibon*, in *BASOR* 125 (1952), p. 20-23.

[118] J.T. MILIK, *Le rouleau de cuivre de Qumrân (3Q15). Traduction et commentaire topographique*, in *RB* 66 (1959), p. 321-357 (see p. 338 with n. 2); ID., *Le rouleau de cuivre provenant de la grotte 3Q (3Q15)*, in M. BAILLET - J.T. MILIK - R. DE VAUX, *Les 'Petites Grottes' de Qumrân* (DJD 3), Oxford 1962, p. 199-302 (see p. 244, §70).

[119] E. KLOSTERMANN (ed.), *op. cit.* (n. 16), p. 112:14-17

[120] Grid ref. 2338/1045: ABEL, *Géographie* II, p. 419.

[121] Grid ref. 2159/1242: W. ZWICKEL, *op. cit.* (n. 11), p. 156.

[122] Grid ref. 2132/1094: W. ZWICKEL, *op. cit.* (n. 11), p. 147.

[123] Grid ref. 210/108: G. REEG, *op. cit.* (n. 40), p. 236-238.

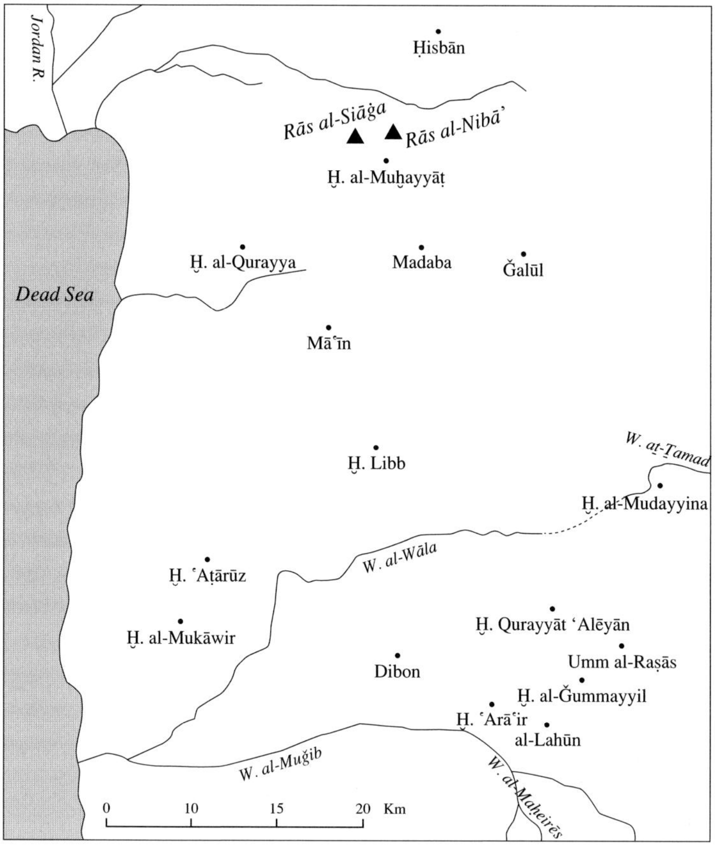

Territory conquered by Mesha in the North.

tected by a wall and a moat; it yielded a large amount of potsherds going back to Iron Age I and II. Mesha boasts of having slain all its inhabitants, apparently as accomplishment of a vow made to the god Chemosh and to the people of Moab. In fact, the term *ryt* has rightly been linked to Sabaic *rwt / ryt* with a derivative used of outstanding or deferred obligations[124]. Mesha dragged the Gadite chief Uriel from there to Qerioth, where he obviously sacrificed him to Chemosh. It is remarkable that the "warden" (*dwd*) of Ataroth bears the same name *'r'l* as the last son of Gad according to Gen. 46, 16 and Numb. 26, 17. If it is the same

[124] *Sabaic Dictionary*, p. 119; cf. S. SEGERT, *art. cit.* (n. 90), p. 244. The reading *ryt* is certain: A. SCHADE, *New Photographs Supporting the Reading* ryt *in Line 12 of the Mesha Inscription,* in *IEJ* 55 (2005), p. 205-208.

person, this may indicate that the tribe of Gad ceased to exist as an independent tribal entity after the conquest of Ataroth by Mesha. His name is vocalized *'Ar'ēlī* in the Hebrew Bible, i.e. "My God has shined", but the *Vorlage* of the Septuagint and of the Vulgate in Numb. 26, 17 reads *'ry'l*, which may be consonant with the Moabite spelling *'r'l* and suggests the name *'Urī-'El*, "El is my light". The title *dwd* given to the man in the Mesha inscription is related to Arabic *ḏāwid* (> *ḏā'id*), "defender, protector". Just like the shibboleth incident in Judg. 12, 6 and the name *B'lyš' / B'lys* show that the Gileadites and Ammonites have retained /ṯ/[125], so does *dwd* indicate that the Gadites also kept pronouncing /ḏ/, which was realized or noted as /d/ by the Moabites. The name of David probably witnesses a similar situation in the Ephrathite dialect[126].

Mesha settled at Ataroth people from Sharon and Maḥaroth. Sharon, mentioned also in I Chron. 5, 16, is a plain, and its Moabite name is very likely a synonym of the Hebrew *Mīšōr*, which mainly designates the region between the Arnon River and Wādī al-Wāla[127]. As for *Mḥrt*, it must be the region of the Wādī al-Maḥeirēs, which is the name of the upper course of the Wādī al-Muğib, having its source at al-Lağğūn (alt. 690 m)[128].

Thereafter Mesha reports his conquest of Nebo, a supposed "Reubenite" town (Numb. 32, 38). He slew all the Israelite population and dragged all the lambs of Yahwe before Chemosh, certainly to be sacrificed to the upper-god of the Moabites (lines 14-18). The number of seven thousand people (line 16) slain at Nebo cannot be taken at its face value. It is a literary figure occurring in other texts: a remnant of seven thousand out of the whole population of Israel will be spared according to I Kings 19, 18 and only seven thousand men managed to fly from the Ammonites, as reported in 4QSam[a], lines 8-9[129]. "Seven thousand" appears therefore as a stereotyped figure, used in contexts of disaster and war. As for "the [r]ams of Yahwe", [']*ly Yhwh* (lines 17-18), this restitution is based on the use of the verb *sḥb*, employed especially with

[125] G.A. RENDSBURG, *The Ammonite Phoneme /Ṯ/*, in *BASOR* 269 (1988), p. 73-79; ID., *More on Hebrew šibbōlet*, in *JSS* 33 (1988), p. 255-261.

[126] The case of the Ephrathites is described accurately by M. KOCHAVI, *Ephrath*, in *Encyclopaedia Judaica* 6, Jerusalem 1971, col. 815: "... the Ephrathites, who possibly were of different origin, also penetrated into the Bethlehem district... Jesse, David's father, was called 'Ephrathite'...". *Dybn* /Ḏaybān/ offers another example.

[127] ABEL, *Géographie* I, p. 430.

[128] Grid ref. 2326/0719.

[129] F.M. CROSS - D.W. PARRY - R.J. SALEY - E. ULRICH , *Qumrân Cave 4*, XII. *The Samuel Scrolls from Cave 4* (DJD 17), Oxford 2005, p. 66-67, Pl. X.

Rās Siyāġa (Mount Nebo).

sheep (Jer. 49, 25; 50, 45), but also with a corpse or a captive dragged to be put to death (II Sam. 17, 13; Jer. 22, 19), like in lines 12-13. Cattle belonging to a sanctuary is oftentimes said to be the property of the deity. For instance, "sheep of Adad", *immeri Adad*, are mentioned in the Old Babylonian period[130], and "bulls and sheep of Nabū" are referred to in a letter to a Neo-Assyrian king[131]. It seems that the frequently encoun-

[130] G. Dossin, *Prières aux "dieux de la nuit" (AO 6769)*, in *RA* 32 (1935), p. 179-186 (see p. 181, line 10).
[131] *SAA* X, 353, rev., line 4.

tered restitution and translation "vessels of Yahwe" (lines 17-18) can be safely discarded.

Nebo was certainly the site of an important Yahwistic sanctuary and it is identified with Ǧebel Šayhān, opposite Jericho. This high mountain has two peaks: Rās al-Nibā' (alt. 835 m) and Rās Siyāġa (alt. 710 m). In the Bible, the peak of Mount Nebo is called Pisgah and was regarded as the place where Moses stood and beheld the Promised Land before dying. Although the higher Rās al-Nibā' retains the ancient name, scholars consider the second peak[132] the more likely site of Mount Nebo, close to the "Reubenite" town (Numb. 32, 38) conquered by Mesha. Ḫirbet al-Muḫayyaṭ[133], 12 km south of Ḥisbān, seems to correspond to Eusebius' location of the "Reubenite" Ναβώθ, 8 miles south of 'Εσβοῦς[134]. Although N. Glueck found many potsherds from Iron Age I and II inside the fortified area[135], the excavations of a tomb and of a cave recovered no evidence of an occupation anterior to Iron Age II, i.e. the 10th-9th centuries B.C.[136] Another site taken into consideration is Ḫirbet 'Uyūn Mūsā[137], situated north-east of Rās Siyāġa. It yielded potsherds from Iron Age I-II and from the Persian Period, and still shows some architectural remains, like a large tower and traces of a wall closing an area of about 200 m by 80 m.

Mesha further reports his capture of the fortified city of Jahaz (lines 18-21)[138] and describes his urbanistic activity at Dibon, the present-day Ḏibān (lines 21-26)[139]. His use of Israelite prisoners as manpower is paralleled in the recently published Moabite inscription from the early 8th century B.C., where the king insists upon his setting of Ammonite captives to work at his building projects[140]. He says in lines 3'-5': "With Ammonite captives [I dug] the moat of a powerful gate and [I folded

[132] Grid ref. 219/131; cf. G. REEG, *op. cit.* (n. 40), p. 232.

[133] Grid ref. 2206/1286; W. ZWICKEL, *op. cit.* (n. 11), p. 157.

[134] E. KLOSTERMANN (ed.), *op. cit.* (n. 16), p. 136:9-13.

[135] N. GLUECK, *Exploration in Eastern Palestine* II (AASOR 15), New Haven 1935, p. 110-111, No. 239.

[136] E. ALLIATA, *La ceramica dello scavo della capella del prete Giovanni a Kh. el Mukhayyat,* in *Studii Biblici Franciscani Liber Annuus* 38 (1988), p. 317-360 (see p. 321-323, 335, 342, 344, 346, 348-349, 353); M. PICCIRILLO, *Campagna archeologica al Monte Nebo,* in *Studii Biblici Franciscani Liber Annuus* 38 (1988), p. 457-458; F. BENEDETTUCCI, *The Iron Age*, in M. PICCIRILLO - E. ALLIATA (eds.), *Mount Nebo: New Archaeological Excavations 1967-1997*, Jerusalem 1998, p. 110-127 (see p. 111-125).

[137] Grid ref. 2202/1318: cf. W. ZWICKEL, *op. cit.* (n. 11), p. 164.

[138] See here above, p. 328-329.

[139] See here above, p. 336-337.

[140] S. AḤITUV, *art. cit.* (n. 56).

Ḫirbet al-Mu ayyaṭ (Nebo town).

th]ere the flock and the cattle. And the Ammonite saw that he was weak in every [...]", *b'sry.bny'mn* [*krty.'t.*] *mkrt.š'r.'dr.wmqnh.whbqr* [*hrbṣty.š*]⌊*m*⌋*.wyr'.bny'mn.ky.ḥlh.bkl.*[...].

Mesha also linked the northern part of the kingdom with the Kerak plateau by building a road in Arnon's massive canyon[141] and by restoring the fortress Aroer, which overlooks the highway. A section of a road, probably dating to Iron Age II, eventually to Mesha's time, has been now identified in Moab[142]. It seems to confirm Mesha's words. Aroer, often mentioned in the Bible[143], was identified with Ḫirbet 'Arā'ir[144]. It is a large site of *ca.* 100 m by 200 m, where the excavations of 1964-1966 have identified six levels, dating from the Late Bronze Age to the 7th century B.C., but no structures have been found which could be dated before the time of Mesha[145].

Mesha further records the rebuilding of some ruined cities. He thus mentions Bēth-Bāmōt and Bezer (line 27), one of the "Levitical cities" in the "Reubenite" territory[146]. Bēth-Bāmōt should be identified with *Bmwt* (Numb. 21, 19-20) and *Bmwt B'l*[147], which Eusebius locates in the Arnon area, ἐν τῷ 'Αρνωνᾷ[148]. This is confirmed by the context of the Mesha inscription and suggests identifying this place with al-Lahūn[149], excavated since 1977[150]. The enclosed settlement of this site, measuring

[141] The canyon of Wādī al-Mužib explains the use of *mslt* in line 26; cf. J.A. DEARMAN, *Settlement Patterns and the Beginning of the Iron Age in Moab*, in P. BIEŃKOWSKI (ed.), *Early Edom and Moab*, Sheffield 1992, p. 65-75 (see p. 70). There is no "aural error" or "poor carving" in the inscription, contrary to the opinion of N.L. TIDWELL, *Mesha's* hmslt b'rnm: *what and where?*, in *Vetus Testamentum* 46 (1996), p. 490-497.

[142] A. KLONER - C. BEN-DAVID, Mesillot *on the Arnon: An Iron Age (Pre-Roman) Road in Moab*, in *BASOR* 330 (2003), p. 65-81.

[143] ABEL, *Géographie* II, p. 250.

[144] Grid ref. 2281/0981; cf. W. ZWICKEL, *op. cit.* (n. 11), p. 144.

[145] E. OLÁVARRI, *Sondages à 'Arô'er sur l'Arnon*, in *RB* 72 (1965), p. 77-94, Pls. I-IV; ID., *Fouilles à 'Arô'er sur l'Arnon. Les niveaux du Bronze Intermédiaire*, in *RB* 76 (1969), p. 230-259, Pls. I-V; ID., *Aroer*, in *NEAEHL*, Jerusalem 1993, Vol. I, p. 89-92.

[146] See here above, p. 327.

[147] Numb. 22, 41; Josh. 13, 7, and Talmudic texts quoted by G. REEG, *op. cit.* (n. 40), p. 129-130.

[148] E. KLOSTERMANN (ed.), *op. cit.* (n. 16), p. 44:7-8.

[149] Grid ref. 2309/0957; cf. W. ZWICKEL, *op. cit.* (n. 11), p. 145.

[150] A general presentation of the site and the results of the excavations are provided by D. HOMÈS-FREDERICQ, *Ontdek Lehun en de Koningsweg... De belgische opgravingen in het antieke Jordanië*, in *Phoenix* 47 (2001), p. 117-147. See also D. HOMÈS-FREDERICQ, *Late Bronze and Iron Age Evidence from Lehun in Moab*, in P. BIEŃKOWSKI (ed.), *Early Edom and Moab*, Sheffield 1992, p. 187-202; EAD. (ed.), *Lehun et la Voie Royale / en de Koningsweg*, Bruxelles/Brussel 1997; EAD. - M. DE DAPPER - B.-M. DE VLIEGHER, *Lehun: A Geo-Archaeological Approach of the Belgian Excavations in Jordan*, in K. VAN LERBERGHE - G. VOET (eds.), *Languages and Cultures in Contact* (OLA 96), Leuven 1999, p. 177-199.

Tell Ḥisbān (Heshbon).

ca. 2 ha, lays 7 km east of Dibon and 3 km east of Aroer. The site has been almost continuously inhabited since Palaeolithic times and the Iron Age II settlement with casemate walls can date from the reign of Mesha.

Lahūn is situated on a steep promontory, a place suitable for a Bēth-Bāmōt, "House of High Places". Referring to some biblical passages[151], F. Aspesi has argued that *Bt-Bmt* was a temple[152]. The name of Bāmōth-Baal implies the existence of a sanctuary, so far not identified in the excavation. Since "Baal" is linked to the name of the settlement, the sanctuary should go back to the times of its foundation in the 12th or 11th century B.C. and the plural *bāmōt* could reflect a local tradition about seven altars, echoed in Numb. 23, 1-4. The general context of the Mesha inscription nevertheless suggests the rebuilding of a town. The site was clearly occupied in the Iron IIC period (*ca.* 700-550 B.C.), as witnessed by the discovery of an Egyptian Twenty-sixth Dynasty "New Year's" bottle[153] and of a cosmetic palette from the same period[154]. At least one published vessel from the enclosed settlement[155] belongs typologically in Iron IIB (*ca.* 850-700 B.C.). The occupation of the settlement in this period explains its mention on the Mesha stele and in Numb. 21, 19-20; 22, 41; Josh. 13, 17. The place must have been widely known, since Numb. 22, 41-23, 13 locates there an episode involving Balaam and Balaq, king of Moab. Since a Rabbinic tradition inflated the importance of Balaam, it is understandable that Bāmōth-Baal occurs several times in Talmudic literature. Josephus Flavius records the episode[156], but does not name the place.

After having mentioned the military organization of the Dibon region (lines 28-29), Mesha records his building activity at Madaba[157] and Bēth-Diblatēn, a town mentioned also in Jer. 48, 22. It is often identified with Ḫirbet Dulēlat aš-Šarqīya[158], but this site only yielded a few sherds

[151] I Kings 12, 31; 13, 32; II Kings 17, 29.32; 23, 19.

[152] F. Aspesi, *A proposito di un "toponimo" moabita*, in *Atti del Sodalizio Glottologico Milanese* 25 (1984 [1985]), p. 70-77.

[153] D. Homès-Fredericq, *Un goulot de bouteillle de Nouvel An, trouvé à Lehun (en Jordanie)*, in J. Quaegebeur (ed.), *Studia Paulo Naster oblata* II. *Orientalia antiqua* (OLA 13), Leuven 1982, p. 79-92.

[154] D. Homès-Fredericq, *A Cosmetic Palette from Lehun, Jordan*, in St. Bourke - J.-P. Descoeudres (eds.), *Trade, Contact, and the Movement of Peoples in the Eastern Mediterranean. Essays in Honor of J.B. Hennessy*, Sydney 1995, p. 265-270.

[155] D. Homès-Fredericq, *art. cit.* (n. 150), in P. Bieńkowski (ed.), Fig. 16:8c.

[156] Josephus Flavius, *Jewish Antiquities* IV, 6, 2-6, §102 ff.

[157] Grid ref. 2256/1253: W. Zwickel, *op. cit.* (n. 11), p. 157. Cf. here above, p. 325, 332-333.

[158] Grid ref. 2285/1163. Cf., for instance, Abel, *Géographie* II, p. 269.

from the Iron Age[159]. It is more likely that the hill with the ruins of Ḫirbet Libb[160] is the ancient Diblatēn/Diblataim. In fact, it yielded large quantities of potsherds from Iron Age I and II. The shortened form *Dibla-* of the toponym, attested as *T-ỉ-b-w-ỉ-n-ỉ-w* (*T-b-n*) in a topographical list of Ramesses II[161], was apparently changed in *Libba*, perhaps in early Nabataean times and possibly as a result of the alternation *d/l*, which explains the passage Arbel > Irbid. Josephus Flavius does not record the ancient name of the place after Λίββα, as often assumed because of an emendation of the text, but he mentions the "Spring of Lot", Ναβαλώθ[162], i.e. *Naba' Lōṭ*. This site is called *ΤΟ ΤΟΥ ΑΓΙΟΥ Λ[ΩΤ]* on the Madaba map, which locates the Byzantine church of St. Lot at the foot of the highland, east of Zoar. The remains of the building have been identified above the northern bank of Wādī al-Ḥasā, half an hour walk from Ḫirbet aš-Šēḫ 'Īsā[163].

Mesha had thus rebuilt several towns in the north and lines 30-31 refer again to Bēth-Baal-Meon, first named in line 9. His achievements in the south were possibly recorded on the Kerak stele[164]. In fact, one should keep in mind that the Moabite territory reached the Wādī al-Ḥasā, and that the large fortress of Ḫirbet al-Mudayyina[165] was very likely a Moabite stronghold[166], possibly built by Mesha.

The partial presentation of the events of Mesha's reign on the Dibon stele can perhaps be explained by the aim of the royal inscriptions. They were not intended to exist as abstract records of the past, but were exhibited in an open-court complex and associated with the activities of state and city officials, able to read and to comment alphabetic inscriptions. It was important to record at Dibon the events of the northern part of the kingdom, in which Dibonites have personally taken part as fighters or

[159] W. ZWICKEL, *op. cit.* (n. 11), p. 152.

[160] Grid ref. 2223/1128: W. ZWICKEL, *op. cit.* (n. 11), p. 152.

[161] A reliable copy of the hieroglyphic inscription is provided by K.A. KITCHEN, *op. cit.* (n. 40), p. 180. The spelling of the name implies the presence of a vowel after *b*. For the alternation *l/n*, see LIPIŃSKI, *Semitic* §17.3-4. Besides, one should keep in mind the constant Egyptian spelling *K-b-n* or *K-p-n* of the name of Byblos, *Gbl* in Semitic.

[162] JOSEPHUS FLAVIUS, *Jewish Antiquities* XIV, 1, 4, §18. Only Libba - Λέμβα by dissimilation - is mentioned in another passage of the *Jewish Antiquities* XIII, 15, 4, §397.

[163] Grid ref. 1950/0481: H. DONNER - E.A. KNAUF, *Ghor eṣ-Ṣāfī et Wadi el-Kerak (1983)*, in *RB* 92 (1985) p. 429-430 and Pl. XVIIb (see p. 430). Cf. H. DONNER - H. CÜPPERS, *Die Mosaikkarte von Madaba* I, Wiesbaden 1977, Pls. 21 and 110.

[164] *TSSI* I, 17, p. 83-84; S. TIMM, *op. cit.* (n. 1), p. 269-277.

[165] Grid ref. 2239/0421: W. ZWICKEL, *op. cit.* (n. 11), p. 78.

[166] B. MACDONALD, *A Moabite Fortress on Wadi al-Hasa? A Reassessment of Khirbet al-Medeinah*, in L.E. STAGER - J.A. GREENE - M.D. COOGAN (eds.), *The Archaeology of Jordan and Beyond. Essays in Honor of J.A. Sauer*, Winona Lake 2000, p. 317-327.

officials. Similar circumstances possibly explain the contents of the fragmentary inscription of Hazael at Tell al-Qāḍi, where Abīl seems to be mentioned twice and were wars against Israel are the most significant events recorded on the stele[167]. Dibon was no exclusive capital of Moab and monuments similar to the Mesha stele could have existed at Kerak, especially when it became the "New town" (*Qīr ḥadaš*[*t*]) of the kingdom.

An important event at the southern border of Moab is nevertheless mentioned in the last lines of the inscription from Dibon. It is the conquest of Hawronēn, which apparently was then in Judaean hands[168], but the capture of which was perhaps accomplished with the help of Dibonite fighters. This city — no doubt the same as biblical Horonaim[169] — was situated on the road that went up from Zoar (aṣ-Ṣāfī)[170] to Qīr-ḥadaš(t) (Kerak)[171] and has been located by A. Musil at the village of al-'Irāq[172]. Other localizations have been proposed as well, but the discovery of a Roman road climbing directly from the area aṣ-Ṣāfī to the Moabite tableland finally gives concrete chances of solving the question, for one can assume that this road followed an older track[173]. Most of the Roman thoroughfares were constructed along routes set out in earlier times and the mentions of "the ascent of Luhith" in Is. 15, 5 and of "the descent of Horonaim" in Jer. 48, 5 point precisely at the road climbing east of Zoar up to the Transjordanian tableland.

Is. 15, 5-6 seems to indicate an itinerary Zoar - Luhith - Horonaim - Wādī Nemeira. The "ascent of Luhith" and the "road to Horonaim" are two parallel and synonymous appellations of the ancient road in Is. 15, 5, while an additional information is provided in the following verse by the mention of the "waters of Nimrim", the Wādī Nemeira, whose sources are near al-'Irāq. Luhith was a well-known place in Nabataean and Roman times. It is mentioned in the Nabataean inscription *CIS* II, 196, 4 and in its duplicate *RÉS* 674[174]. Although both inscriptions were

[167] See here above, p. 245-246.

[168] The restoration of "House of David" in Mesha 31 was proposed quite convincingly by A. LEMAIRE, *art. cit.* (n. 108). See here above, p. 337.

[169] Is. 15, 5; Jer. 48, 5. Cf. Y. AHARONI, *The Land of the Bible. A Historical Geography*, London 1967, p. 57.

[170] Grid ref. 1944/0492: cf. W. ZWICKEL, *op. cit.* (n. 11), p. 71.

[171] Grid ref. 2170/0660: cf. W. ZWICKEL, *op. cit.* (n. 11), p. 103-104.

[172] A. MUSIL, *op. cit.* (n. 19), p. 72-73.

[173] C. BEN-DAVID, *The 'Ascent of Luhith' and the 'Road to Horonaim': New Evidence for Their Identification*, in *PEQ* 133 (2001), p. 136-144, where also the various opinions are summarized.

[174] J. STARCKY, *Inscription de Madaba*, in *La Voie Royale. 9000 ans d'art au Royaume de Jordanie*, Paris 1986, p. 189-190, No. 243.

found at Madaba, they should not allude to another place called Luhith[175]. Luhith has replaced 'Ar in Targum Onqelos to Numb. 21, 15.28; Deut. 2, 9.18.29[176], in Targum Jonathan to Is. 15, 1[177], and in Targum Yerushalmi to Numb. 21, 15[178]. It is written there without the internal *mater lectionis* for *ū*, like in Nabataean, and has consequently been vocalized in a different way in the preserved manuscripts.

Since Papyrus Yadin 44, line 5, refers to Luhith as to a locality of Mahoz Eglatain[179], in the Zoar area[180], Luhith should be situated near the start of the ascent to the Moabite tableland. This is confirmed by Josephus Flavius who mentions Eglatain instead of Luhith: 'Ορωναΐμ, 'Αγελεθων, Ζόαρα[181], and 'Αγαλλαθων, Ζώαρα, 'Ωρωναΐμ[182]. Luhith could possibly be located at Qaṣr aṭ-Ṭūba or Ḫirbet al-Fās[183], about 4 km east of aṣ-Ṣāfī. As for Horonaim / Hawronēn, the Mesha stele suggests that it was a relatively important place, at least from the strategic point of view. At first sight, the settlement situated along the recently discovered Roman road and corresponding best to the available information seems to be Ḫirbet aḏ-Ḏubāb[184], 17 km south-west of Kerak and 15 km east of aṣ-Ṣāfī as the crow flies. It was already identified as Horonaim by A.H. van Zyl[185] and is apparently preferred by C. Ben-David[186]. In fact, it lies at ancient crossroads, was a walled settlement, and measured 130 m by 32 m, being thus somewhat smaller than the enclosure of Ḫirbet al-Mudayyina (160 x 40 m), but almost four times larger than the fort of Tell ar-Rumeiṯ (37 x 32 m).

It should be stressed, however, that P. Bieńkowski's soundings at Ḫirbet aḏ-Ḏubāb revealed no pottery earlier than Iron Age II and no architectural remains preceding the Nabataean period[187]. This means that the

175 R. SAVIGNAC - J. STARCKY, *Une inscription nabatéenne provenant du Djôf*, in *RB* 64 (1957), p. 196-217, Pl. V (see p. 200-202).

176 A. SPERBER, *The Bible in Aramaic* I, Leiden 1959, p. 259, 260, 292, 293.

177 A. SPERBER, *The Bible in Aramaic* III, Leiden 1962, p. 32.

178 A. DÍEZ MACHO, *Neophyti I. Targum Palestinense* IV. *Numeros*, Madrid 1974, p. 197.

179 Y. YADIN - J.C. GREENFIELD - A. YARDENI - B. LEVINE, *The Documents from the Bar-Kokhba Period in the Cave of Letters. Hebrew, Aramaic and Nabatean-Aramaic Papyri*, Jerusalem 2002, p. 44.

180 *Ibid.*, p. 8-9.

181 JOSEPHUS FLAVIUS, *Jewish Antiquities* XIII, 15, 4, §397.

182 JOSEPHUS FLAVIUS, *Jewish Antiquities* XIV, 1, 4, §18.

183 A. MUSIL, *op. cit.* (n. 19), p. 72 and 75, n. 7 (Ḫ. al-Fās), cf. p. 180-188 (Q. aṭ-Ṭūba).

184 Grid ref. 2095/0495.

185 A.H. VAN ZYL, *op. cit.* (n. 90), p. 64-65.

186 C. BEN-DAVID, *art. cit.* (n. 173).

187 P. BIEŃKOWSKI, *Observations on Late Bronze-Iron Age Sites in the Wadi Hasa, Jordan*, in *Levant* 27 (1995), p. 29-37; P. BIEŃKOWSKI *et al.*, *Soundings at Ash-Shorabat and Khirbet Dubab in the Wadi Hasa, Jordan: The Stratigraphy*, in *Levant* 29 (1997),

wall preserved at the site does not date back to Mesha's time, but that the place was occupied around the 9th century B.C. and possibly earlier, since the uncertain date of the pottery attributed by the Central Moab Survey to the Late Bronze and Iron I periods does not exclude its partly earlier date. Ḫirbet aḏ-Ḏubāb belongs in any case to a cluster of five sites, measuring about 6 km in diameter, where a greater concentration of pottery implies rainfall and soils more favourable for settlement and agriculture[188]. An alternative location of Horonaim / Hawronēn is Ḫirbet Madīnat ar-Rās[189], 3 km north-west of Ḫirbet aḏ-Ḏubāb. N. Glueck had dated this fort from the Iron Age[190]. The road from these sites to Kerak leads northwards through al-'Irāq and 'Aiy.

Mesha's victory at Horonaim can very likely be linked with Jehoram's campaign against Moab, mentioned in the account of II Kings 3[191], when the attackers chose "the way of Edom", that goes around the Dead Sea on the south. The invading forces obviously finished by being defeated by Mesha, as conceded implicitly in II Kings 3, 27b. The storyteller of II Kings 3, 4-27 provides a Judaean version of the events, in which king Jehoshaphat of Judah and an unnamed king of Edom play a role. The ultimate source was certainly North Israelite and it was based on a historical record of Mesha's rebellion against the Omrides: "When Ahab was dead, the king of Moab rebelled against the king of Israel. And king Jehoram went forth at that time from Samaria and mustered all Israel" (II Kings 3, 5-6). The exact date of the Moabite expedition is unknown, but comparison with the Mesha inscription seems to indicate that the biblical account does not refer to the beginning of the Moabite rebellion, which dates back to Ahab's reign (lines 6-7), but rather to its later stages, when Mesha had already fortified the northern border of his kingdom. The expedition was apparently aimed at by-passing the forts built by Mesha and attacking the old Moabite capital Kerak from the

p. 41-70; P. Bieńkowski - R. Adams, *Soundings at Ash-Shorabat and Khirbet Dubab in the Wadi Hasa, Jordan: The Pottery*, in *Levant* 31 (1999), p. 149-172, in particular p. 168-170.

188 B. Routledge, *op. cit.* (n. 1), p. 79-81.

189 Grid ref. 2059/0511; cf. W. Zwickel, *op. cit.* (n. 11), p. 81.

190 N. Glueck, *Explorations in Eastern Palestine* III (AASOR 18-19), New Haven 1939, p. 86-89, No. 94.

191 A too "theological" evaluation of II Kings 3 undermines the article by Ph. Stern, *Of Kings and Moabites: History and Theology in 2 Kings 3 and the Mesha Inscription*, in *HUCA* 64 (1993), p. 11-14. A midrashic development of the account can be found in II Chron. 20. Beside biblical commentaries, one can see A.F. Rainey, *Mesha's Attempt to invade Judah (2 Chron 20)*, in G. Galil - M. Weinfeld (eds.), *Studies in Historical Geography and Biblical Historiography* (VTS 81), Leiden 2000, p. 174-176.

southern end of the Dead Sea, by "the road of Horonaim" (Is. 15, 5) or "the descent of Horonaim" (Jer. 48, 5)[192].

Jehoram's Edomite war, recorded in II Kings 8, 20-22, is very likely the same war as the Moabite expedition of Jehoram, son of Ahab. In fact, Jehoram of Judah and Jehoram of Israel are one and the same person[193], and the expedition "through the wilderness of Edom" (II Kings 3, 9) follows the same route as Jehoram's retreat "to Zoar[194] with all his chariots" (II Kings 8, 21). The ultimate source of the latter account may have been Judaean, while the first one was apparently Israelite.

The borders of Moab do not seem to have changed in a noticeable way after the reign of Mesha (*ca.* 860-825 B.C.). However, the "Lowlands of Moab" (*'Arbōt Mō'āb*)[195], on the eastern bank of the Jordan River, opposite Jericho, may have been annexed in a later period, since they are not mentioned in the Mesha inscription.

Sculptures

The reign of Mesha or of his father Chemoshyatt may have been the period, in which the Balu'a stele and the Šīḥān stele have been sculpted. The Balu'a stele, found in 1930[196], consists of a basalt block with two panels[197]. The top one bears an inscription, so worn that only the baselines of the text are still visible. The lower and larger part of the stele depicts a local ruler standing between a god handing him a sceptre and a goddess assisting to this investiture scene. The style of the relief is Egyptianizing, but there are several atypical features. The headdress of the ruler is similar to the headscarves worn by the Shasu in Egyptian reliefs, the lunar symbol and the sun-disk in a crescent, flanking the cen-

[192] Y. AHARONI, *op. cit.* (n. 169), p. 309.

[193] See LIPIŃSKI, *Aramaeans*, p. 378-379, n. 176, and here above, p. 217.

[194] The *mater lectionis* for *ō* was badly inserted, as shown by the Σιωρ of the Septuagint, and the *w* was later read as *y*, thus *Ṣ'yr* instead of *Ṣw'r*.

[195] Numb. 22, 1; 25; 31, 12; 33, 48; 36, 13. Cf. F.-M. ABEL, *Exploration du sud-est de la vallée du Jourdain*, in *RB* 40 (1931), p. 214-226, 375-400, pl. VI-IX, XI-XII; 41 (1932), p. 77-88, 237-257, pl. I-VI, in particular 40 (1931), p. 223 ff.; 41 (1932), p. 78 ff.

[196] G. HORSFIELD - L.-H. VINCENT, *Une stèle égypto-moabite au Balou'a*, in *RB* 41 (1932), p. 417-444, Pls. IX-XV.

[197] The pertinent bibliography - without the first publication (!) - was recently collected by I. CORNELIUS, *The Many Faces of the Goddess. The Iconography of the Syro-Palestinian Goddesses Anat, Astarte, Qedeshet, and Asherah c. 1500-1000 BCE* (OBO 204), Fribourg-Göttingen 2004, p. 112-113, with a photograph on Pl. 3.3. One can add: B. ROUTLEDGE, *op. cit.* (n. 1), p. 82-85 and 231 (notes); E.J. VAN DER STEEN, *op. cit.* (n. 1), p. 24.

tral figure, belong to the Levantine iconography, and some characteristics in the dress, like the *atef*-crown of the goddess, and the proportions of the figures are non-Egyptian. The inscription, as seen by G. Horsfield and L.-H. Vincent in 1930[198], then by W.A. Ward and M.F. Martin in 1964[199], was probably engraved in cursive hieratic or pseudo-hieratic Egyptian script. The use of such a script on a stele does not match Egyptian tradition, and the current state of the stele, viewed a few years ago by the writer in the Amman Archaeological Museum, excludes any improved reading in the future. The stele obviously deteriorated since its discovery in 1930.

The stature of the local ruler, standing between deities and dressed in a "gala" robe, implies that Egypt had lost every influence in this area at the time of the carving of the relief with the royal investiture scene. Now, the Timna copper mine was operational at least until the time of Ramesses V (1145-1141 B.C.)[200] and scarabs with the name of Ramesses X (1108-1098 B.C.) have been found at Tell al-Far'ah South[201] and at Ḫirbet al-Mšāš (Tel Masos)[202], 120 km from the southern border of Moab. No Moabite ruler would have imagined and dared to commission such a relief before the 11th century B.C. The scene of investiture also implies the existence of an organized society with a ruler at its head[203]. It does not seem that this condition was realized long before the reigns of Chemoshyatt and of Mesha. Therefore, the dating of the stele to the 9th century B.C., as proposed by H. Weippert[204], seems to be the most adequate proposal.

Considering our actual knowledge of the Moabite history, the discovery of the stele at Balu'a, in an area which has not been occupied by the Omrides, and the probable use of a kind of hieratic script for its inscription suggest that the ruler depicted on the stele was Chemoshyatt, the father of Mesha, or a somewhat earlier ruler, possibly Balaq, "king of Moab" according to Numb. 22, 10; 23, 7; Josh. 24, 9; Judg. 11, 25; Mich. 6, 5, assuming that he is a historical figure. The occupation of the

198 See here above, p. 351, n. 196.

199 W.A. WARD - M.F. MARTIN, *The Balu'a Stele: A New Transcription with Palaeographic and Historical Notes*, in *ADAJ* 8-9 (1964), p. 5-29.

200 B. ROTHENBERG, *The Egyptian Mining Temple at Timna*, London 1988, p. 277.

201 W.M.F. PETRIE, *Beth Pelet* I, London 1930, p. 7, Pl. XXII, 202.

202 B. BRANDL, *The Tel Masos Scarab: A Suggestion for a New Method for the Interpretation of Royal Scarabs*, in *Scripta Hierosolymitana* 28 (1982), p. 371-405.

203 K.A. KITCHEN, *The Egyptian Evidence on Ancient Jordan*, in P. BIEŃKOWSKI (ed.), *Early Edom and Moab*, Sheffield 1992, p. 21-34 (see p. 29).

204 H. WEIPPERT, *Palästina in vorhellenistischer Zeit* (Handbuch der Ärcheologie: Vorderasien II/1), München 1988, p. 666-667.

Stele of Baluʿa
(Amman, Archaeological Museum).

site of Balu'a in the transitional Late Bronze-Early Iron Age, not yet ascertained on the basis of the pottery[205], cannot prove a significantly higher date of the stele. Its discovery at Balu'a can instead lead to the assumption that Balu'a was a royal centre in the 9th century B.C. U. Worschech suggested that the ancient name of the city was 'Ar-Moab[206]. Such a toponym can mean "Precinct of Moab"[207], but "precinct" may have a larger connotation and designate a "district" or a "region", as shown by M. Weippert in this particular case[208].

One should rather regard *Bālū'* as the ancient name of the town, preserved in the Midrashic account of Gen. 14, 2.8 and in Genesis Apocryphon 21, 25.31. The place was later equated with Zoar in two glosses of Gen. 14, 2.8, just like the Targums have identified the Moabite *'Ār* with Luhith[209]. When Gen. 14 was written, probably in the 5th-4th century B.C., the site of Balu'a was still occupied, as shown by the uncovered pottery from the Persian period[210]. There must have been a local tradition among the "sons of Lot" (Deut. 2, 9.19; Ps. 83, 9), which regarded *Bālū'* as a royal city. This was later forgotten and *Bl'* was thus identified with the better known Zoar, just like *'Ār* was equated with Luhith, a place close to Zoar and still attested in Roman and Byzantine times as Λουειθά[211].

The dating of the heavy, likewise basalt stele from Šīḥān is more difficult. This stele was discovered in 1851 by F. de Saulcy at Ruğm al-'Abd, near Ḫirbet Šīḥān[212], which occupies a hill about 15 km southwest of Dibon[213]. The archaeological context is unknown and the monument

[205] E.J. VAN DER STEEN, *op. cit.* (n. 1), p. 48 and 133-134, 156 (Fig. 6-2).

[206] U. WORSCHECH, *Ar Moab,* in *ZAW* 109 (1997), p. 246-253, in particular p. 250-253.

[207] LIPIŃSKI, *Itineraria Phoenicia*, p. 412.

[208] M. WEIPPERT, *Ar und Kir in Jesaia 15, 1. Mit Erwägungen zur historischen Geographie Moabs,* in *ZAW* 110 (1998), p. 547-555. The use of *'ār* in Deut. 2, 9 and the parallelism *Śē'īr // 'Ār* in Deut. 2, 29 confirm this interpretation. Instead, the etymological link between Moabite *'r* and Ugaritic *ġr*, "mountain", suggested by M. Weippert (*ibid.*, p. 552-553), should assume that the word was pronounced /γūr/, but there is no evidence so far that this was the case.

[209] See here above, p. 349.

[210] U. WORSCHECH, *art. cit.* (n. 206), p. 246.

[211] EUSEBIUS OF CAESAREA, *Onomasticon*, in E. KLOSTERMANN (ed.), *op. cit.* (n. 16), p. 122: 28-29. See also here above, p. 348-349.

[212] Grid ref. 2201/0877; cf. W. ZWICKEL, *op. cit.* (n. 11), p. 137. Ancient remains are visible on top of the Ğebel Šiḥān (alt. 1065 m).

[213] L.F. DE SAULCY, *Narrative of a Journey round the Dead Sea and in the Bible Lands, 1850 and 1851*, London 1854, p. 324 and 333, Pl. 17. The stele was acquired in 1884 by H. D'ALBERT, DUC DE LUYNES, *Voyage d'exploration à la Mer Morte, à Pétra et sur la rive gauche du Jourdain*, Paris 1874, p. 170-182. Cf. A. CAUBET, in *F. de Saulcy (1807-1880) et la Terre Sainte*, Paris 1982, p. 187-189, No. 242.

Basalt stele from Šīḥān
(Louvre Museum, AO 5055).

only represents the central part of the original stele with the relief. It may have been brought from another place, as suggested by P. Amiet[214], and F. Zayadine thinks that it may come from the same site as the Balu'a stele[215]. There are about 4 km from Balu'a to Ḫirbet Šīḥān, but the latter place was a fortified site as well and may have been the original place of the monument. The suggested dates range from the third millennium down to the 9th-8th centuries B.C. The latter is probably the correct date, argued on basis of stylistic details and circumstantial evidence[216]. The warrior depicted on the stele, dressed in a short kilt and holding a spear, probably represents a war god, whom the Mesha inscription would suggest identifying with Chemosh. A fragment of a similar basalt statue, showing the knees to mid-hip of an armed figure, is on display in the Kerak Archaeological Museum. Its provenance is unknown and it is unpublished[217], but its stylistic resemblance to the warrior of the Ruǧm al-'Abd stele suggests attributing both sculptures to the same royal workshop, which could be dated to the 9th century B.C.

The presence of experienced relief sculptors in Moab is confirmed by a basalt orthostat found at Kerak[218]. The hind-quarters of a lion, skilfully carved in relief, are a part of a larger slab, which possibly belonged to a series or a pair of orthostats lining a courtyard or a gateway. The Proto-Aeolic capital reused in a modern wall at 'Ain Sāra, down the slope of Kerak[219], also witnesses the presence of a royal building. Both underline the importance of Kerak as the ancient Moabite capital and royal residence.

History of the 8th-6th centuries B.C.

The mention of Zoar with Luhith and Horonaim in Is. 15, 5 may imply that Zoar belonged to Moab in the 8th century B.C. In the north,

[214] P. Amiet, *Stèle moabite de Shihân*, in *La Voie Royale. 9000 ans d'art au Royaume de Jordanie*, Paris 1987, p. 84-85, No. 110.

[215] F. Zayadine, *Sculpture in Ancient Jordan*, in P. Bieńkowski (ed.), *The Art of Jordan*, Phoenix Mill 1991, p. 31-61 (see p. 37).

[216] E. Warmenbol, *La stèle de Ruǧm el-'Abd (Louvre AO 5055): Une image de divinité moabite du IXème-VIIIème siècle av.n.è.*, in *Levant* 15 (1983), p. 63-75. See also G.L. Mattingly, *The Culture-Historical Approach and Moabite Origins*, in P. Bieńkowski, *Early Edom and Moab*, Sheffield 1992, p. 55-64, in particular p. 60, where the author suggests the Early Iron Age.

[217] It is nevertheless mentioned and described by B. Routledge, *op. cit.* (n. 1), p. 178 and 180.

[218] G. Horsfield - L.-H. Vincent, *art. cit.* (n. 196), p. 438 and Pl. XV, 4; R. Canova, *Iscrizioni e monumenti protocristiani del paese di Moab*, Roma 1954, p. 8-9 with Fig. 4.

[219] H. Donner - E.A. Knauf, *art. cit.* (n. 163), p. 430 and Pl. XVIIb.

Copy of the inscription of Shiqquṣ-Chemosh.

relations between Moab and the Jordan Valley are possibly attested in the 9th century B.C. by the inscription *l-Šqṣ-Kmš* incised after firing on a "Hippo" jar from Tell aṣ-Ṣārem (Tel Reḥov), dated by the excavator to the second half of the 9th century B.C.[220], but the "Lowland of Moab" (*'Arbōt Mō'āb*)[221], on the eastern bank of the Jordan River, must have been occupied by the Moabites only in the 8th century B.C. The following step was the Gilead expedition of king Shalman of Moab, who razed Bēth-Arbel according to Hos. 10, 14. Since this city is believed to be Irbid in Gilead[222], Shalman's attack may have coincided with Tiglath-pileser III's campaign and capture of Damascus in 733-732 B.C. It is quite possible, in fact, that the king of Moab had become a vassal of Assyria already in 734 B.C.[223] and that he intervened in the war against Aram-Damascus like king Panamuwa II of Śam'al, who perished then while fighting for Tiglath-pileser III[224]. It is interesting to see that Ilāya-

[220] Published by A. MAZAR, *Three 10th-9th Century B.C.E. Inscriptions from Tēl Reḥōv*, in C.G. DEN HERTOG *et al.* (eds.), *Saxa loquentur. Festschrift für V. Fritz* (AOAT 302), Münster 2003, p. 171-184 (see p. 178-181). A completely lying *ṣade* is so far un-attested elsewhere, but the down-stroke bends back to the left on Aramaic clay tablets from Ashur (mid-7th century B.C.), which also provide the best parallels of the *kāf*. The date assigned to the inscription incised after firing on the "Hippo" jar may be too high. "Shiqquṣ-Chemosh" must mean "Tabu of Chemosh", i.e. an exclusive property of the Moabite god. See also the abridged name *Šqṣ* in R. DEUTSCH - M. HELTZER, *New Epigraphic Evidence from the Biblical Period*, Tel Aviv-Jaffa 1995, p. 88-92, No. (78)3, line 5.

[221] LIPIŃSKI, *Aramaeans*, p. 359, n. 69.

[222] ABEL, *Géographie* II, p. 249, 267-268. Cf. F.-M. ABEL, *Topographie des campagnes machabéennes*, in *RB* 32 (1923), p. 495-521; 33 (1924), p. 201-217, 371-387; 34 (1925), p. 194-216; 35 (1926), p. 206-222, 510-533, in particular 33 (1924), p. 380 ff.; ID., *Le circuit de Transjordanie*, in *RB* 37 (1928), p. 425-433, 590-60, especially p. 427. See also here above, p. 347.

[223] *Tigl. III*, p. 170, Summ. 7, rev., line 10'. The denial of the identity of the Assyrian vassal with the Shalman of Hos. 10, 14 by S. TIMM, *op. cit.* (n. 1), p. 319-320, lacks any concrete basis.

[224] *KAI* 215 = *TSSI* II, 14, 16-19.

nūr, prince of Ṭāb'il, sends a messenger to Qurdi-Aššur-lāmur[225] in order to inform Tiglath-pileser III that tribesmen of Qedar had invaded Moab and "caused a bloodshed in the City of Moab", probably Qir-Moab (Kerak). This event is recorded in a Nimrud letter, which interestingly enough uses the phonetic spelling ^{kur}*Gi-di-ra-a-a* for "Qedarite"[226], thus witnessing the voiced pronunciation of *qāf* like later in Hijazi.

Moab is mentioned several times in the Assyrian correspondence and administrative records at the time of Tiglath-pileser III and of Sargon II[227], and it may have played a role in the rebellion of Yamani of Ashdod against Sargon II. Yamani sought support from his neighbours in Philistia, Judah, Edom, and also Moab, but the surviving records do not reveal whether Moab actually sided with Yamani[228]. In any case, there appears to be no doubt that Moab's rulers thereafter realized the wisdom of faithfulness to their Assyrian overlord. When Sennacherib entered Palestine in 701 B.C. to quell the revolt led by Hezekiah of Judah, king Chemosh-nadbi of Moab bowed before him with the kings of Ammon, Edom, and many other rulers[229]. King Muṣuri was equally submissive to Esarhaddon about 673 B.C.[230] and to Ashurbanipal in 667/6[231]. So far as the sources show, it was only under Ashurbanipal, around 650 B.C., that Assyrian troops actually entered Moab in the war against North Arabs who belonged to the tribal confederacy of Qedar. According to the earlier Ashurbanipal's Prisms B and C, dating from *ca.* 649-647 B.C.,

225 G. Van Buylaere, *Qurdi-Aššūr-lāmur*, in *PNA* III/1, Helsinki 2002, p. 1021-1022.

226 Nimrud letter XIV, 8-15: H.W.F. Saggs, *The Nimrud Letters, 1952 - Part II: Relations with the West*, in *Iraq* 17 (1955), p. 126-160 (see p. 131-133). Cf. also here above, p. 298.

227 Nimrud letter L, 13: H.W.F. Saggs, *The Nimrud Letters, 1952 - Part V*, in *Iraq* 21 (1959), p. 158-179 (see p. 159); S. Dalley - J.N. Postgate, *The Tablets from Fort Shalmaneser* (CTN 3), London 1984, No. 143, II, 12'; *SAA* I, 110, rev., line 7; *SAA* VII, 57, III, 4'; *SAA* XI, 33, 4. The discussion of Neo-Assyrian texts by S. Timm, *op. cit.* (n. 1), p. 303-399, is partly outdated, while G.W. Vera Chamaza, *Die Rolle Moabs in der neuassyrischen Expansionspolitik* (AOAT 321), Münster 2005, is unfortunately not aware of the recent literature on the subject. Besides, some parts of this work do not deal really with Moab.

228 H. Winckler, *Die Keilschrifttexte Sargons*, Leipzig 1889, p. 188, line 30. See also here above, p. 76, 142.

229 D.D. Luckenbill, *The Annals of Sennacherib* (OIP 2), Chicago 1924, p. 30, line 56; E. Frahm, *Einleitung in die Sanherib-Inchriften* (AfO, Beih. 26), Wien 1997, p. 53, line 37. Cf. A. Berlejung, *Kammūsu-nadbi*, in *PNA* II/1, Helsinki 2000, p. 600.

230 R. Borger, *Die Inschriften Asarhaddons, Königs von Assyrien* (AfO, Beih. 9), Graz 1956, p. 60, line 56. Cf. M. Jursa, *Muṣuri*, in *PNA* II/2, Helsinki 2001, p. 772. The seal of *Mṣry* may have belonged to the king of Moab; cf. P. Bordreuil, *op. cit.* (n. 81), p. 60-61, No. 65; N. Avigad - B. Sass, *op. cit.* (n. 79), p. 413, No. 1093.

231 R. Borger, *Beiträge zum Inschriftenwerk Assurbanipals*, Wiesbaden 1996, p. 19 and 212, C II 41.

Chemosh-'aśa, king of Moab, managed then to capture 'Ammu-laddin, king of Qedar[232].

Assyria has never put Moab under direct rule, probably because it preferred leaving to its kings the difficult task of coping with the tribal structure of Moabite society[233] and of exercising a control over the trade routes through the desert. In 605/4 B.C., Moab most likely evaded the Babylonian threat, unlike other countries of the area, but Jer. 27, 3 suggests that its king played a part around 594/3 in an anti-Babylonian coalition, soon disbanded due to a quick intervention of Nebuchadnezzar II. Lachish ostracon 8 still mentions a king of Moab about 587 B.C.[234], but Flavius Josephus dates the conquest of the land by Nebuchadnezzar II to 582/1, apparently in connection with a Palestinian uprising[235].

Additional note

The word *qrḫ* in question is generally transcribed *kerḫu(m)/kirḫu(m)* by Assyriologists[236]. However, the initial signs KI and KIR can always be read *qí/qé* and *qir/qer*, while the initial spelling with GI favours the reading *qì/qè*, thus *qerḫu(m)/qirḫu(m)*. J.-Cl. Margueron is probably right to regard *adaššum* and *qerḫum* in the Mari archives as terms designating the "lower city" and the "upper city"[237]. Both words are Semitic and there is no reason why one should consider them to be Hurrian loanwords in Akkadian, as proposed by V. Haas and I. Wegner[238]. *Adaššum* is no doubt the North-west Semitic noun *ḥadaṯtum* > *hadaṯtum*, "new (town)", referring to the new city quarters built around the original core of the settlement. *Qerḫum* is etymologically related to or identical with North-west Semitic *qerḫum*, "bald head". Initially, it

232 *Ibid.*, p. 115 and 244, B VIII 39-50 = C X 48-62. Cf. P. VILLARD, *Ammi-ladin*, in *PNA* I/1, Helsinki 1998, p. 104-105; A. BERLEJUNG, *Kamās-ḫaltâ*, in *PNA* II/1, Helsinki 2000, p. 600.

233 R.W. YOUNKER, *Moabite Social Structure*, in *BA* 60 (1997), p. 237-248.

234 A. LEMAIRE, *Inscriptions hébraïques* I. *Les ostraca* (LAPO 9), Paris 1977, p. 124-126.

235 JOSEPHUS FLAVIUS, *Jewish Antiquities* X, 9, 7, §181-182.

236 *AHw*, p. 467-468; *CAD*, K, Chicago 1971, p. 404-405.

237 J.-Cl. MARGUERON, *Mari, métropole de l'Euphrate au IIIe et au début du IIe millénaire av. J.C.*, Paris 2004, p. 446.

238 V. HAAS - I. WEGNER, *Stadtverfluchungen in den Texten aus Boğazköy, sowie die hurritischen Termini für "Oberstadt", "Unterstadt" und "Herd"*, in U. FINKBEINER - R. DITTMANN - H. HAUPTMANN (eds.), *Beiträge zur Kulturgeschichte Vorderasiens. Festschrift für R.M. Boehmer*, Mainz a/R 1995, p. 187-194 (see p. 191-192).

must have designated the "hill without vegetation", where the original walled city was built. The latter was surrounded by gardens and fields, where the new town, *adaššum*, developed in the course of time.

CHAPTER X

EDOM

The geographical notion of Edom goes back to the Late Bronze Age, when the syllabically written name *'I-d-m*, followed by the determinative of foreign lands or mountains, appears in Egyptian hieroglyphic inscriptions. The land of Edom had, however, other names and appellations, both prosaic and poetic. "Seir" is the most common equivalent of "Edom" and it occurs already as KUR.ḪA *Še-e-ri*^{ki}, "Mount Seir", in a letter of the ruler of Jerusalem to the pharaoh, in the 14th century B.C.[1] This toponym designated the highland which extends from the Dead Sea and Wādī al-Ḥasā to the Gulf of Aqaba and from the desert to the Negebite highland. The population of this large area was often called *Š3św* in Neo-Egyptian texts. This is a derivative of *š3ś*, "to travel", "to transit", and it qualified the inhabitants of the region as nomads or semi-nomads.

Shasu

In fact, the meagre remains of the small Iron I-IIA settlements in Edom do not confirm the biblical traditions concerning this area in the time of the Exodus, of the Judges, and of David's and Solomon's United Monarchy. They rather suggest the presence of semi-nomadic seasonal settlements, unlike the towns or villages called *dmỉ* in Ramesses II's topographical list at Luxor referring to his Moab campaign, probably after 1271 B.C.[2] The population of the settlements in Edom could be linked with the Shasu (*Š3św*) tribesmen, often mentioned in Egyptian texts[3]. Their name, which derives from *š3ś*, "to wander", designates

[1] *EA* 288, 26.

[2] P. HAIDER, *Zum Moab-Feldzug Ramses' II.*, in *SAK* 14 (1987), p. 107-123. See below, n. 23.

[3] The comprehensive work on the subject is that by R. GIVEON, *Les bédouins Shosou des documents égyptiens* (DMOA 18), Leiden 1971. For the questionable relocation of the Shasu in Lebanon and coastal Syria, see M.C. ASTOUR, *Yahweh in Egyptian Topographical Lists*, in M. GÖRG - E. PUSCH (eds.), *Festschrift Elmar Edel* (Ägypten und Altes Testament 1), Bamberg 1979, p. 17-34. Recent overviews are provided by M.G. HASEL, *Domination and Resistance: Egyptian Military Activity in the Southern Levant, ca. 1300-1185 B.C.* (Probleme der Ägyptologie 11), Leiden 1998, p. 217-239; E.J. VAN DER STEEN, *Tribes and Territories in Transition. The Central East Jordan Valley in the Late Bronze Age and Early Iron Ages: A Study of the Sources* (OLA 130), Leuven 2004, p. 19-22.

nomads living mainly on the Sinai Peninsula, in the Negeb, and southern Transjordan. The *'-y-n Š3-św*, mentioned in Amenhotep III's (1392-1354 B.C.) topographical list from Qōm al-Ḥēṭān, at Thebes[4], has been identified with ^{uru}*E-ni-ša-si*$_{20}$ or ^{uru}*E-ša-sí* /*'Ēššāsi*/ in the Amarna correspondence[5], which suggests locating this town in the northern Beqa' Valley. However, the geographical context leaves no doubt that we are dealing here with an Egyptian interpretation or adaptation of a West Semitic toponym, probably meaning "Spring of the Plunderer" (*'n šs). In other words, *'-y-n Š3-św* is no correct phonetic notation of the place name, which would have required the use of *ṯ* instead of *ś*. This occurrence of *Š3-św* cannot be regarded therefore as a genuine attestation of Shasu nomads in the Beqa' Valley[6].

T3-Š3-św, "Land of the Shasu", is sometimes qualified in Egyptian sources by a geographical name as Seir (*T3-Š3św Ś'r* / *Ś'rr*)[7] or Yahwe (*T3-Š3św Yhw3*)[8], referring to Mount Seir[9] or to Mount Yahwe[10]. One of the Shasu-lands was probably the territory of Reuben, whose original name was **Rababan*: *T3-Š3-św R-b-b3-b3-n-3*[11]. By dissimilation, the

[4] E. Edel, *Die Ortsnamen aus dem Totentempel Amenophis III.*, Bonn 1966, p. 25, Cn, left 11.

[5] Respectively *EA* 187, 12 and 363, 4 (with the assimilation *-nš-* > *-šš-*). Cf. M. Weippert, *Die Nomadenquelle*, in A. Kuschke - E. Kutsch (eds.), *Archäologie und Altes Testament. Festschrift für K. Galling*, Tübingen 1970, p. 259-273; Id., *Semitische Nomaden des zweiten Jahrtausends*, in *Biblica* 55 (1974), p. 265-280 (see p. 273); A.F. Rainey, *El Amarna Tablets 359-379* (AOAT 8), Kevelaer-Neukirchen-Vluyn 1970, p. 91; Id., *Toponymic Problems: 'Ain-Shasu*, in *Tel Aviv* 2 (1975), p. 13-16.

[6] Pace M.C. Astour, *art. cit.* (n. 3), p. 29.

[7] Amara West, N 93, in H.W. Fairman, *Preliminary Report on the Excavations at 'Amārah West, Anglo-Egyptian Sudan, 1938-9*, in *JEA* 25 (1939), p. 139-144, Pls. XIII-XVI (see Pl. XIV, 4); cf. R. Giveon, *op. cit.* (n. 3), p. 75, also for the spelling *Ś-'-r-r*; K.A. Kitchen, *The Egyptian Evidence on Ancient Jordan*, in P. Bieńkowski (ed.), *Early Edom and Moab: The Beginning of the Iron Age in Southern Jordan* (Sheffield Archaeological Monographs 7), Sheffield 1992, p. 21-34, especially p. 26-27; R. Hannig, *Die Sprache der Pharaonen. Grosses Handwörterbuch Ägyptisch-Deutsch (2800-950 v. Chr.)*, 2nd ed., Mainz a/R 1997, p. 1379.

[8] Amara West, N 97, in H.W. Fairman, *art. cit.* (n. 7), Pl. XIV, 4 (last right); cf. R. Giveon, *op. cit.* (n. 3), No. 6a, p. 26-28 (Soleb), and No. 16a, p. 74-77 (Amara West); cf. M. Weippert, *Jahwe*, in *RLA* V, Berlin-New York 1976-80, p. 246-253, especially p. 250.

[9] Gen. 36, 8.9; Deut. 1, 2; 2, 1.5; Josh. 15, 10; 24, 4; Ez. 35, 2.3.7.15; I Chron. 20, 22.23.

[10] Numb. 10, 33. Gen. 22, 14 is doubtful and Is. 2,3; 30, 29; Mich. 4, 2; Zech. 8, 3; Ps. 24, 3 refer to the Temple Mount. Elsewhere *Yhwh* is replaced by *(h)'lhym*: Ex. 3, 1; 4, 27; 18, 5; 24, 13; I Kings 19, 8.

[11] Amara West, N 94, in H.W. Fairman, *art. cit.* (n. 7), Pl. XIV, 4; cf. R. Giveon, *op. cit.* (n. 3), p. 75; R. Hannig, *op. cit.* (n. 7), p. 1359.

first *b* later became *w* (**Rwbn*), like in *kwkb* < *kbkb*, "star". Since *wāw* was no *mater lectionis*, an *aleph* was added in the script (*R'wbn*) to prevent the reading Ρουβην. As this Shasu-land is mentioned in the Amara list next to *T3-Š3św Ś'rr*, it was very likely located in southern Palestine or in Transjordan. This list appears to have been copied from Amenhotep III's temple at Soleb, in Sudan[12], and therefore witnesses the existence of the tribe of Reuben in the 14th century B.C.[13] The spelling and the geographical context preclude the identification of the toponym with *R-b-n* in Tuthmosis III's list (No. 10)[14], in the northern Beqa' Valley. The following *T3-Š3-św Pys-pyś*[15], a plural by reduplication[16], is closely related to the Sabaic tribal name *Fys²n*[17]. Next comes *T3-Š3-św Ś3-m3'-mỉ-t-ỉ*[18], identified with the Edomite tribe *Šammāh* in Gen. 36, 13.17[19].

Some Shasu tribesmen were migrating seasonally to Egypt in search of suitable pasture grounds, but Papyrus Harris I contains a summary of the wars of Ramesses III (1182-1151 B.C.) against the Shasu of Seir[20]:

> "I destroyed the people of Seir among the Shasu tribes. I razed their tents: their people, their property, and their cattle as well, without number, pinioned and carried away in captivity as the tribute of Egypt. I gave them to the Ennead of the gods as slaves for their houses".

In ancient Hebrew literature, the hill country of Seir is located both east and west of Wādī Arabah. It is identified with Edom (Gen. 36, 8-9.21), and the land of Edom is repeatedly referred to as the land of Seir[21]. The geographic term "Edom" appears for the first time in Egyptian records during the reign of Merneptah (1212-1202 B.C.). It occurs in

[12] H.W. FAIRMAN, rev. in *JEA* 26 (1940), p. 165.

[13] The problem of the Reuben tribe, examined by U. SCHORN, *Ruben und das System der zwölf Stämme Israels. Redaktionsgeschichtliche Untersuchungen zur Bedeutung des Erstgeborenen Jakobs* (BZAW 248), Berlin 1997, should be submitted to a fresh analysis in the light of this information from the 14th century B.C. The tribe of Joseph is attested earlier, in the Execration Texts *e* 21 (*'Iysỉpỉ*) and *E* 12 (*'Isỉpỉ*).

[14] *Pace* M.C. ASTOUR, *art. cit.* (n. 3), p. 20, 23.

[15] Amara West, N 95, in H.W. FAIRMAN, *art. cit.* (n. 7), Pl. XIV, 4; cf. R. GIVEON, *op. cit.* (n. 3), p. 75; R. HANNIG, *op. cit.* (n. 7), p. 1335.

[16] LIPIŃSKI, *Semitic* §31.21.

[17] HARDING, *Arabian Names*, p. 474.

[18] Amara West, N 96, in H.W. FAIRMAN, *art. cit.* (n. 7), Pl. XIV, 4; cf. R. GIVEON, *op. cit.* (n. 3), p. 75; R. HANNIG, *op. cit.* (n. 7), p. 1381.

[19] M. WEIPPERT, *art. cit.* (n. 5), in *Biblica* 55 (1974), p. 271.

[20] Papyrus Harris I, 76, 9-11. Text in W. ERICHSEN, *Papyrus Harris I. Hieroglyphische Transkription* (Bibliotheca Aegyptiaca 5), Bruxelles 1933, p. 93; P. GRANDET, *Le Papyrus Harris I* (Bibliothèque d'étude 109-110), Le Caire 1994, p. 337. English translation by J.A. WILSON, in *ANET*, p. 262. Cf. K.A. KITCHEN, *art. cit.* (n. 7), p. 27.

[21] Gen. 32, 3; Numb. 24, 18; Josh. 24, 4.

Papyrus Anastasi VI, in a passage in which an official on the eastern frontier of Egypt reports the passage of "the Shasu tribes of Edom" into the better pasture lands of the eastern Nile delta[22]. The name of the upland of Moab, east of the Dead Sea, occurs first in inscriptions of Ramesses II (1279-1212 B.C.)[23] and it must refer to the tribal territory of some Shasu clans as well.

Names of Shasu clans with the theophorous element *Q3wś* or *Q3wṯ* occur in hieroglyphic inscriptions of Ramesses II and Ramesses III[24], and Qaws appears as the main deity of the Edomites in the first millennium B.C. Hebrew literature refers however to a cult of Seir, condemned in Lev. 17, 7; II Kings 23, 8; II Chron. 11, 15, but still attested in Roman times by the Ṣafaitic proper name S^2*ʻr'l*, "Seir is god"[25]. This worship probably originated from the cult of Mount Seir deified, which obviously implies that Seir originally designated a particular holy spot. It is tempting to identify it with Ǧebel aš-Šera', south-east of Petra, since the Nabataean god Dusares (*Dwšr'*) is obviously "He-of-the -Šara'(-mountain)". Although a merging *ʻr > r* in *šaʻrā*, "scrub land", is phonetically possible, the different vocalization still creates a difficulty, so far not resolved. At any rate, the existence of a divine name Seir is not contradicted by the fact that "goats" are called *śeʻīrīm* in Hebrew. Goats may have been, for instance, totem-animals, but *śʻyr* may have other meanings as well, as indicated e.g. by Arabic *šaʻīra*, "cultic practice", and its plural *šaʻā'ir*, "places of worship". Too little is known about the religious beliefs of the Proto-Edomites to speculate further.

One can assume in the same way that the Shasu of *Yhw3* were worshippers of Yahwe, called — as often among Semites — by the same

[22] Text in A.H. GARDINER, *Late Egyptian Miscellanies* (Bibliotheca Aegyptiaca 7), Bruxelles 1937, p. 76-77. English translation by J.A.WILSON, in *ANET*, p. 259. Cf. K.A. KITCHEN, *art. cit.* (n. 7), p. 27.

[23] S. SIMONS, *Handbook for the Study of Egyptian Topographical Lists Relating to Western Asia*, Leiden 1937, List XXd, 10. See also K.A. KITCHEN, *Ramesside Inscriptions* II, Oxford 1969-79, p. 185 (Cw 14); cf. ID., *Some New Light on the Asiatic Wars of Ramesses II*, in *JEA* 50 (1964), p. 47-70, especially p. 49; S. TIMM, *Moab zwischen den Mächten*, Wiesbaden 1989, p. 6 and 15; K.A. KITCHEN, *art. cit.* (n. 7), p. 27-29, which reflect a misunderstanding of the archaeological evidence and of the culture of (semi-)nomadic pastoralists. A recent discussion can be found in M.G. HASEL, *op. cit.* (n. 3), p. 159-166.

[24] J. SIMONS, *op. cit.* (n. 23), p. 158, List XXIII (Ramesses II), 7.8.11.13.21; p. 168-169, List XXVII (Ramesses III), 85.89.100.101.103, apparently copied on List XXIII; cf. B. ODED, *Egyptian References to the Edomite Deity Qaus*, in *AUSS* 9 (1971), p. 47-50; E.A. KNAUF, *Qaus in Ägypten*, in *GM* 73 (1984), p. 33-36, with questionable interpretations of some names.

[25] HARDING, *Arabian Names*, p. 351.

name as God's mountain[26]. The deity was even identified with the mountain[27], which was considered therefore as sacred, and this belief is expressed vividly by the biblical phrase *hr h-hr*[28], the original meaning of which was "the mountain of the Mountain". One can surmise that *hhr* hides *Yhw* in these cases. We can assume that some of the *Yhw* worshippers had emigrated to Egypt or were taken there as captives, and that a number of them managed later to return to their home-land, especially when Egyptian control in southern Canaan had faded in the late 12th and the 11th centuries B.C. Such a migration could have happened less likely in the 13th century, at the time of Ramesses II, despite S.I. Groll's endeavour to deduce this date from the Ramesside letter preserved by Papyrus Anastasi VIII[29]: "the place, time, drought, troubled conditions and Semitic presence are authentic historical motifs which relate Papyrus Anastasi VIII to the story of the Exodus and the story of the Exodus to the middle years of Ramesses II"[30].

Material traces of those people can hardly be discovered, all the more so as the general picture of the Iron I period arising from the excavations and surveys in the large area of the Judaean Desert, the Negeb, southern Transjordan, and the Sinai Peninsula is one of relatively few permanent settlements. The only larger site is Ḫirbet al-Mšāš (Tel Masos), the material culture of which is close to that of coastal Palestine and completely unlike that of the Israelite settlements in the central hill country[31]. The question of the ethnic identification of its population cannot be answered in a positive way. Yet, it is in these southern areas that we

[26] E.A. KNAUF, *Midian*, Wiesbaden 1988, p. 43-63.

[27] Similar cases are collected by W.G. LAMBERT, *The God Aššur*, in *Iraq* 45 (1983), p. 82-86.

[28] Numb. 20, 22.23.25.27; 21, 4; 33, 37.38.39.41; 34, 7.8; Deut. 32, 50.

[29] A transcription of the papyrus is provided by 'A. EL-MOHSEN BAKIR, *Egyptian Epistolography from the Eighteenth to the Twenty-First Dynasty* (Bibliothèque d'étude 48), Le Caire 1970, Pls. 28-32. The letter was translated with a philological commentary by S.I. GROLL, *Unconventional Use of the System of Shifters as a Means of Signaling the Use of Different Sources: Papyrus Anastasi VIII in the Light of the "Standard Theory"*, in *Lingua Aegypta* 5 (1997), 43-56.

[30] Conclusions reached by S.I. GROLL, *The Historical Background to the Exodus: Papyrus Anastasi VIII*, in M. SIGRIST (ed.), *Études égyptologiques et bibliques à la mémoire du Père B. Couroyer* (Cahiers de la Revue Biblique 36), Paris 1997, p. 109-114, quotation from p. 114. The text lacks any concrete and direct evidence related to the Exodus. Similar views are expressed by D.B. REDFORD in the last chapter of his *Egypt and Canaan in the New Kingdom* (Beer-Sheva IV), Beersheba 1990, and elsewhere. The Shasu are confused there with the hill country groups of central Palestine and with proto-Israel.

[31] I. FINKELSTEIN, *The Archaeology of the Israelite Settlement*, Jerusalem 1988, p. 41-46.

must look for the nuclear group which initiated Yahwism and was responsible for the traditions concerning slavery in Egypt, the Exodus, Mount Sinai, and the role of Moses[32].

The precise situation of Mount Yahwe is unknown, although Numb. 10, 33 explicitly locates it in Midian. This corresponds to the area close to the Gulf of Aqaba or Elath, where the copper mines of Timna attest the Egyptian presence at least to the reign of Ramesses V (1145-1141 B.C.)[33]. The handmade pottery in elaborate black and red hand-painted designs, found there and conventionally called "Midianite", originated in the north-western part of the Arabian Peninsula ("Qurayya painted ware"), with a second group produced in Edom[34]. It sporadically occurs also in southern Canaan until the 11th or even 10th century B.C. The ethnic identification of the potters cannot be established, but their vessels are similar in shape to the so-called "Negebite ware", found together with wheel-made pottery in the enclosures and small settlements of the central Negeb highlands, the oasis of 'Ain al-Qudeirat (Qadesh-Barnea), and in Edom[35]. The Negeb settlements can be dated about the 11th/10th century B.C. It is unlikely that they reflect a royal policy aimed at securing the routes crossing the Negeb and exercising a control on the southern border of Judah (Josh. 15, 2-3). They were simple enclosed settlements established in regions that best fitted the combination of sheep/goat pastoralism and desert agriculture[36].

32 The Egyptian origin of the name of Moses is explained by J.G. GRIFFITHS, *The Egyptian Derivation of the Name Moses*, in *JNES* 12 (1953), p. 225-231.

33 B. ROTHENBERG, *The Egyptian Mining Temple at Timna*, London 1988, p. 277.

34 B. ROTHENBERG - J. GLASS, *The Midianite Pottery*, in J.F.W. SAWYER - D.J.A. CLINES (eds.), *Midian, Moab, Edom*, Sheffield 1983, p. 65-124; B. ROTHENBERG, *op. cit.* (n. 33), p. 100-101 (group originating in Edom); E.A. KNAUF, *op. cit.* (n. 26), p. 15-25; J. GUNNEWEG - Th. BEIER - U. DIEHL - D. LAMBRECHT - H. MOMMSEN, *'Edomite', 'Negbite' and 'Midianite' Pottery from the Negev Desert and Jordan: Instrumental Neutron Activation Analysis Results*, in *Archaeometry* 33 (1991), p. 239-253.

35 However, the typology of the "Negebite ware" has not been established to date: G.D. PRATICO, *Nelson Glueck's 1938-1940 Excavations at Tell el-Kheleifeh: A Reappraisal*, in *BASOR* 259 (1985), p. 1-32, especially p. 23-24, with references; N. LAPP, *"Who is This that comes from Edom?"*, in M.D. COOGAN - J.C. EXUM - L.E. STAGER (eds.), *Scripture and Other Artifacts. Essays on the Bible and Archaeology in Honor of Philip J. King*, Louisville 1994, p. 216-229, especially p. 223-224 with references. - It should be stressed that no archaeological or textual data support the view that Tell al-Qudeirat is Qadesh-Barnea. Since Israeli authors systematically use this misnomer, it is mentioned eventually in parenthesis. Tell al-Qudeirat might correspond to the *Ḥăṣar 'Addār* of Numb. 34, 4, a text from the late 4th century B.C.

36 This is the opinion of I. FINKELSTEIN - A. PEREVOLOTSKY, *Processes of Sedentarization and Nomadization in the History of Sinai and the Negev*, in *BASOR* 279 (1990), p. 67-88, but see also S.A. ROSEN, *Nomads in Archaeology: A Response to Finkelstein and Perevolotsky*, in *BASOR* 287 (1992), p. 75-85.

Judah

Judah, which seems to have become a tribal entity only in David's times[37], originated from tribes and clans living close to these sparsely populated regions: a few Reubenite and Simeonite clans and, above all, Kenizzite, Kenite, Calebite, Jeraḥme'elite, and Ephrathite tribes living in and around "the land full of ravines" (*'ereṣ yəhūdā*), which gave its name to the tribe of Judah[38]. When the latter came into existence, it was given an eponym, Judah, who was subsequently integrated in the pan-Israelite framework of the patriarchal traditions. This could not have happened before the mid-10th century B.C. The components of the tribe were in part of Edomite stock, like *Qənaz* (Gen. 36, 11.15; I Chron. 1, 36), whose name may be related to Liḥyanite *'nzh*[39]: one can assume in fact that initial *q* was here marking /γ/, like in Old Aramaic, and that this phoneme weakened dialectally into /ʕ/. The Calebite clans were regarded as belonging to the same group and they occupied Hebron according to Josh. 14, 12-15 and 15, 13.

David was proclaimed king in Hebron by the elders of the clans living in the Judaean hills, probably because he was a renowned war-lord native from the local clan of Ephrath and related by marriage to the southern clans of Jezreel and of Carmel. According to II Samuel 5, 5, he ruled in Hebron for seven and a half years, and then was elected king of Israel by the elders of the league, threatened by the Philistines who have killed Saul and his sons at the battle of Gilboa, *ca.* 975 B.C. Hebron was no city in the 10th century B.C. and the few potsherds of "collared-rim" jars and hand-burnished vessels discovered on the Tell ar-Rumēda[40] just indicate a small-scale occupation before the 8th century B.C., thus revealing a minor settlement, like Jerusalem itself. This situation matches the notice of II Sam. 2, 1-3, which records the occupation of the site by David and his family.

David connected the Judaean hill country with the central Cisjordanian highland after having ousted the last ruler of Hurrian descent from

[37] E. Lipiński, *Juda et 'tout Israël': analogies et contrastes*, in Id. (ed.), *The Land of Israel: Cross-Roads of Civilizations* (OLA 19), Leuven 1985, p. 93-112, especially p. 99-102. For an archaeological description of the area, see A. Ofer, *The Judean Hills in the Biblical Period*, in *Qadmoniot* 31 (1998), p. 40-52 (in Hebrew).

[38] E. Lipiński, *L'étymologie de "Juda"*, in *Vetus Testamentum* 23 (1973), p. 380-381.

[39] Harding, *Arabian Names*, p. 444.

[40] Grid ref. 1598/1030. Cf. A. Ofer, *Tell Rumeideh (Hebron)*, in *ESI* 5 (1987), p. 92-93; 6 (1988), p. 92-93; E. Eisenberg - A. Nagorski, *Tel Ḥevron (Er-Rumeidi)*, in *ESI* 114 (2002), p. 91-92.

Jerusalem[41] and having made it his residence. Jerusalem was then a small settlement, the size of which amounted to *ca.* 4 ha with a population of a few hundred inhabitants. From this tiny basis of his power, David managed to protect the hill country of Judah and of central Palestine against the Philistines, but nothing indicates that he ever conquered and kept an effective control on a part of the coastal plain. He may have been more successful in the Beersheba Valley[42], where Stratum IX at Tell as-Seba', ancient Beersheba, and an early phase of Stratum III at Ḫirbet al-Mšāš[43] might coincide with an occupation of this area by David[44]. David's possible success in this region and the military backing for his continuing authority probably stemmed from the backward Judaean highland and the adjacent Ephrathite area. As for the enclosed settlements of the Negeb highlands, they are more likely enclosures of the local Shasu population, often abandoned toward the end of the 10th century B.C. or somewhat later.

The Hebrew noun *'ămālēq(ī)*, which designates the population of the Negeb and the adjoining deserts, does not refer to a mythical tribe, unknown in historical sources: it was probably meaning "enclosure". Possibly it could also designate lowland enclosed by mountains. This apparently Hurro-Urartian loanword is attested in cuneiform script under the form *ḫa-mi-luḫ-ḫi* on the "Broken Obelisk" of Ashur-bēl-kala (1073-1056 B.C.). The king says there: "I rebuilt from top to bottom the storehouses of my lordly palace, which are at the fore part (*šá ri-iš*) of the enclosure (*ḫa-mi-luḫ-ḫi*)"[45]. Since syllabic Hurrian *ḫ* often corresponds to *ġ* in Ugaritic, this sound may be expressed approximately in Hebrew by *'ayin* or a voiced *qōf*. If this is correct, we may assume that the word was used also in Canaan to designate the enclosures of semi-nomadic populations and people who inhabit an enclosure, an enclosed space. The final *-i* of *'ămālēqī* belongs to the Hurro-Urartian derivational suffix *-ḫi / -ġi*, but was probably regarded as the Hebrew ethnic ending *-ī*, thus "enclosure-man". However, this is not the case in Judg. 12, 15:

[41] LIPIŃSKI, *Itineraria Phoenicia*, p. 498-500.

[42] Cf. Z. HERZOG, *The Beer-sheba Valley*, in I. FINKELSTEIN - N. NA'AMAN (eds.), *From Nomadism to Monarchy*, Jerusalem 1994, p. 122-149.

[43] Grid ref. respectively 1348/0726 and 146/069.

[44] For a higher dating of these strata, see Z. HERZOG - L. SINGER-AVITZ, *Redefining the Centre: The Emergence of State in Judah*, in *Tel Aviv* 31 (2004), p. 209-244.

[45] *RIMA* II, text A.0.89.7, p. 104, col. V, 1-2; cf. *AHw*, p. 338: "eingezäuntes Grundstück". One should perhaps refer also to *ḫamarḫi* (*AHw*, p. 315b), assuming a change *l/r*, for grain had to be brought *ana ḫamarḫi*, "to the enclosure (?)".

Ceramic cult stand, *ca.* 1000-800 B.C., allegedly found in the Judaean Highland (Reuven and Edith Hecht Museum, University of Haifa).

"... in the Land of Ephraim on the Hill of the Enclosure (*ha-'ămālēqī*)". This must be a reference to the tribal and cultic centre of Ephraim.

The original meaning of *'ămālēq(ī)* can explain some difficult passages in ancient texts, like the Song of Deborah, which must date from the same period as the "Broken Obelisk". The text says of Ephraim: *šoršām ba-'ămālēq* (Judg. 5, 14), "their root is in the Enclosure", probably the sacred one, mentioned in Judg. 12, 15. Some Septuagint manuscripts and the Latin Vulgate version are likely to preserve the original text of Judg. 1, 16, where their *Vorlage* should have been translated: "and he settled by the enclosure" (αμαληκ). It is clear, however, that the word was no longer understood in a later period and was then used as if it was the name of a hostile people. David's fight against the "Amalekites" (I Sam. 30) would have been directed in reality against the enclosure settlements of the northern Negeb.

David's possible interest in the Negeb and its trade roads might have paralleled his attempts to control both the "King's Highway" (Numb. 20, 17; 21, 22), running through Transjordan from Arabia to Damascus, and the northern section of the "Way of the Sea" (Is. 9, 1), leading from Egypt to Damascus or to northern Syria. These attempts — if attested historically — could have led to wars with the settling Ammonites and with the Aramaeans, which had gotten control over Damascus and the Beqa' Valley in the 11th or 10th century B.C. They would precede, at any rate, the emergence of an Edomite kingdom.

Edomite State

The formation of the Edomite State cannot be dated before the late 9th century B.C.[46] Earlier mentions of Edom either refer to the geographic region east and west of the Arabah, or imply a confusion of *'rm* (Aram) with *'dm* (Edom), due to the similarity of the Hebrew letters *d* and *r*, or belong to biblical accounts projecting realities of the 8th-6th centuries into a remote past. Settlements of Iron Age I and early Iron Age II in Edom were supposed to occur in the mining district of Wādī Feinan[47],

[46] I Kings 22, 48a; II Kings 8, 20-22. Cf., in general, J.R. Bartlett, *Edom and the Edomites*, Sheffield 1989; Id., *Edom*, in D.N. Freedman (ed.), *Anchor Bible Dictionary*, Garden City 1992, p. 287-295; D.V. Edelman (ed.), *'You shall not abhor an Edomite for he is your brother'. Edom and Seir in History and Tradition* (Archaeology and Biblical Series 3), Atlanta 1995.

[47] Grid ref. 1972/0041; cf. W. Zwickel, *Eisenzeitliche Ortslagen im Ostjordanland* (BTAVO B/81), Wiesbaden 1990, p. 44.

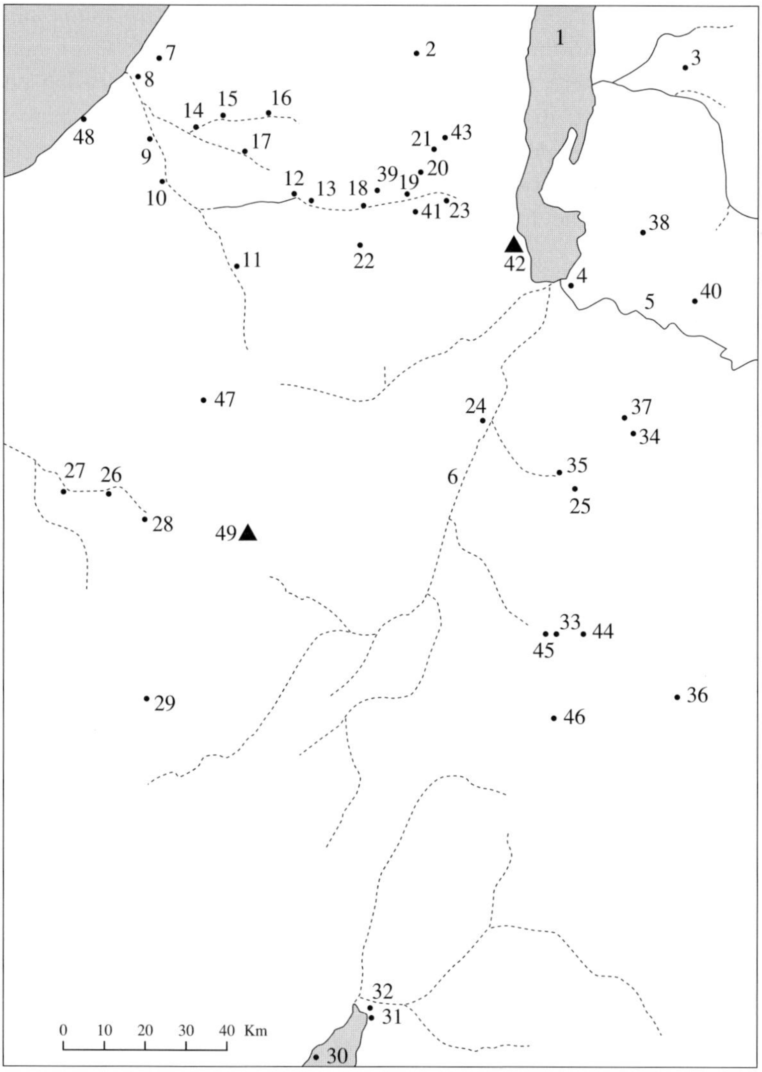

Edom and the Negeb.

1 = *Dead Sea*
2 = Hebron
3 = Dibon
4 = Zoar
5 = *W. al-Ḥasā*
6 = *W. Arabah*
7 = Gaza
8 = T. Aǧǧūl
9 = T. Ǧemmeh
10 = T. al-Farʿah
11 = Ḫalaṣa
12 = Bīr as-Sebaʿ
13 = T. as-Sebaʿ
14 = Ḫ. ʿIrq
15 = Abu Hureira
16 = T. aš-Šerīʿa
17 = Bīr Fṭeis
18 = Ḫ. al-Mšāš
19 = T. al-Milḥ
20 = Ḫ. al-Quṣeifa
21 = T. ʿArad
22 = Bīr ʿArʿara
23 = Ḫ. al-Ġazza
24 = ʿAin al-Ḥuṣb
25 = Feinan
26 = ʿAin al-Qudeirat
27 = ʿAin al-Quṣeima
28 = ʿAin Qedeis
29 = Ḳuntillet ʿAǧrud
30 = *Ǧ. al-Farʿūn*
31 = Aqaba
32 = T. al-Kheleifeh
33 = Petra
34 = Buṣeirā
35 = Ḫ an-Naḥās
36 = Maʿān
37 = Selaʿ
38 = Kerak
39 = Ḫ. al-Ġarra
40 = Ḫ. al-Muḍeibiʿ
41 = Ḫ. Qiṭmīt
42 = *Ǧ. Usdum*
43 = Ḫ. Ṭāyeb
44 = Ṭawilān
45 = Umm al-Biyāra
46 = Ġrāra
47 = ʿAbda
48 = Abu Ruqeish
49 = *Naqb al-ʿArūd*

where charcoal samples from houses, especially at Ḫirbet an-Naḥās, have been dated to the 12th-9th centuries B.C. on ground of C-14 data[48], and associated there with the "Qurayya painted ware", revealing contacts with Midian, in north-western Saudi Arabia. However, analyses based on charcoals, not on short-lived samples, risk to result in too high dates. Therefore, a more cautious approach would situate this industrial activity between the 11th and 8th centuries B.C., thus also in the period when the Edomite statehood was emerging[49]. A fort was then erected at Ḫirbet an-Naḥās, while copper production shifted to other sites in the area. Its steady continuation can safely be assumed, even if some recent surveys and excavations in Wādī Feinan have provided only scattered fragments of Iron Age pottery from the 7th-6th centuries B.C., while most of the evidence dates from much earlier or later periods[50].

Feinan was known to biblical authors. It appears as the name of an Edomite chieftain[51] and as toponym[52], but no particular information is provided. Except Ḫirbet an-Naḥās, there is a conspicuous lack of settlement traces between the Early Bronze and Iron Age II in the entire neighbouring area of Wādī al-Ḥasā[53]. Nor do researches in other Edomite sites reveal any unequivocal settlement before the end of the 9th or early 8th century B.C., while the majority of sites in Edom can be dated only from the 7th century B.C.[54] This situation undoubtedly under-

[48] T.E. LEVY - R.B. ADAMS - M. NAJJAR - A. HAUPTMANN - J.D. ANDERSON - B. BRANDL - M.A. ROBINSON - T. HIGHAM, *Reassessing the Chronology of Biblical Edom: New Excavations and ¹⁴C Dates from Khirbet en-Nahas (Jordan),* in *Antiquity* 78 (2004), p. 865-879.

[49] These dates weaken the position of I. FINKELSTEIN, *Khirbet en-Nahas. Edom and Biblical History,* in *Tel Aviv* 32 (2005), p. 119-125, who tries to show that the results of the Ḫirbet an-Naḥās excavations have no bearing on the early history of Edom. He also confuses Assyrian domination and diplomatic contacts, shown by presents exchanged between monarchs, but labelled "tribute" by Assyrian scribes.

[50] G.W. BARKER *et al.*, *The Wadi Faynan Project. Southern Jordan,* in *Levant* 29 (1997), p. 19-40; ID., *Environment and Land Use in the Wadi Faynan, Southern Jordan: The Second Season of Geoarchaeology and Landscape Archaeology (1997),* in *Levant* 30 (1998), p. 5-25, in particular p. 20-21. For an earlier view, see E.A. KNAUF - C. LENZEN, *Edomite Copper Industry*, in A. HADIDI (ed.), *Studies in the History and Archaeology of Jordan* III, Amman 1987, p. 83-88.

[51] Gen. 36, 41; I Chron. 1, 52.

[52] Numb. 33, 42-43, where one should read *Pynn* with the Septuagint, instead of *Pwnn*.

[53] P. BIEŃKOWSKI *et al.*, *Soundings at Ash-Shorabat and Khirbat Dubab in the Wadi Hasa, Jordan: The Stratigraphy,* in *Levant* 29 (1997), p. 41-70.

[54] See, in general, the various contributions in P. BIEŃKOWSKI (ed.), *Early Edom and Moab*, Sheffield 1992. Cf. also B. MACDONALD, *The Southern Ghors and Northeast 'Arabah Archaeological Survey*, Sheffield 1999.

mines the historical value of the biblical traditions regarding the relations between Israel-Judah and Edom[55], as well as the hypothesis regarding Shoshenq I's campaign in the Negeb as an attempt at destroying settlements which hindered commercial relations between Egypt and Edom[56].

Even during the peak of Iron Age occupation between the late 8th and the 6th century B.C., Buṣeirā is the only Edomite settlement east of the Arabah that deserves to be classified as city[57], while the other sites rather represent villages or hamlets. The population of Buṣeirā was smaller than suggested by the surface of the site, because about 40% of its superficies was occupied by temples or palaces of the acropolis (*ca.* 0.32 ha). Edom's economic growth and expansion westward were then prompted by the newly emerging trade routes from the Arabian Peninsula, probably focused on aromatics[58], and by the export of raw materials from the copper mines in the Wādī Feinan, apparently operational around the 7th century B.C. These trade routes were directed northwards, to Moab, Ammon, and Syria, but increasingly westwards, through the Negeb to the Mediterranean.

The Negeb trade route

Kuntillet 'Ağrud[59], a single period site on the Negeb trade route, belongs to an early phase of this period, viz. to the second part of the 8th century B.C. The site was usually dated between 830 and 750 B.C. on basis of ceramic typology[60] and fifteen carbon C-14 results[61], but the long-lived samples of wooden beams used for the analysis may give too

[55] A study of these traditions is provided by N. NA'AMAN, *Israel, Edom and Egypt in the 10th Century B.C.E.*, in *Tel Aviv* 19 (1992), p. 71-93.

[56] M. HAIMAN, *The 10th Century B.C. Settlement of the Negev Highlands of Iron Age II Israel*, in A.M. MAEIR - S. DAR - Z. SAFRAI (eds.), *The Rural Landscape of Ancient Israel* (BAR 1121), Oxford 2003, p. 71-90.

[57] Grid ref. 2077/0170; cf. W. ZWICKEL, *op. cit.* (n. 47), p. 48.

[58] C. EDENS - G. BAWDEN, *History of Taymā' and Hejazi Trade during the First Millennium B.C.*, in *JESHO* 32 (1989), p. 48-103; L. SINGER-AVITZ, *Beersheba: A Gateway Community in Southern Arabian Long-Distance Trade in the Eighth Century B.C.E.*, in *Tel Aviv* 26 (1999), p. 3-75. The bulk of the Tell as-Seba' documentation dates in reality from the 7th century B.C.

[59] Grid ref. 0940/9560.

[60] E. AYALON, *The Iron Age II Pottery Assemblage from Horvat Teiman (Kuntillet 'Ajrud)*, in *Tel Aviv* 22 (1995), p. 141-205.

[61] D. SEGAL, *^{14}C Dates from Horvat Teiman (Kuntillet 'Ajrud) and Their Archaeological Correlation*, in *Tel Aviv* 22 (1995), p. 208-212.

high dates[62], while a new examination of the pottery shows that it cannot be dated before the mid-8th century B.C.[63] Also palaeography supports a lower date, viz. between *ca.* 750 and 675 B.C. A particular attention was paid by A. Lemaire to a characteristic cursive hook at the extremity of the foot of *yōd*, exactly like in Arad ostracon 72[64], which Y. Aharoni connected with Stratum X on palaeographic grounds[65], while A. Lemaire related it to Stratum IX[66]. These levels can be dated only by reference to Stratum XI, which apparently ended at about the same time as Level IV at Lachish[67]. Now, Kathleen Kenyon noticed already that the end of Lachish Level IV can represent Sennacherib's attack in 701 B.C.: "It could be that the destruction recorded by Ussishkin as ending Level IV but without evidence of burning is really that of the Assyrian attack"[68]. Further finds, especially the recovery of complete pottery vessels in domestic structures[69] and the absence of a layer of collapse between floors of dwellings[70] indicate immediate repair of the destruction caused at the end of Level IV and continued occupation of the site. All this perfectly matches the written and iconographic records of Sennacherib's attack. On the famous Lachish relief from Sennacherib's palace, diachronic scenes, like the storming of the city and the driving out of its inhabitants, are dramatically combined by the artist in a single perspective, while the town is neither burned nor its walls being demolished[71]. In fact, the city-walls were only slightly damaged, as "the Assyrians forced their way into the city by climbing above the nearly

[62] I. FINKELSTEIN, *Bible Archaeology or Archaeology of Palestine in the Iron Age? A Rejoinder*, in *Levant* 30 (1998), p. 167-174 (see p. 171). Short-lived organic material, e.g. the fruit of the date-palm or reed-matting, is highly desirable for absolute dating. Wood samples are instead long-lived and could be quite old by the time they found their way into a particular building.

[63] L. SINGER-AVITZ, *Arad: The Iron Age Pottery Assemblages,* in *Tel Aviv* 29 (2002), p. 110-214 (see p. 163).

[64] A. LEMAIRE, *Date et origine des inscriptions hébraïques et phéniciennes de Kuntillet 'Ajrud,* in *Studi epigrafici e linguistici* 1 (1984), p. 131-143, in particular p. 134-136, where the author proposes a higher date, viz. between *ca.* 800 and 725.

[65] Y. AHARONI, *Arad Inscriptions*, Jerusalem 1975, p. 97.

[66] A. LEMAIRE, *Inscriptions hébraïques I. Ostraca* (LAPO 9), Paris 1977, p. 219.

[67] L. SINGER-AVITZ, *art. cit.* (n. 63), p. 114, 162.

[68] K.M. KENYON, *Archaeology in the Holy Land*, 4th ed., London 1979, p. 297.

[69] D. USSISHKIN (ed.), *The Renewed Archaeological Excavations at Lachish (1973-1994)*, Tel Aviv 2004, Vol. I, p. 83.

[70] O. ZIMHONI, *The Pottery of Levels V and IV and Its Archaeological and Chronological Implications*, in D. USSISHKIN (ed.), *op. cit.* (n. 69), Vol. IV, p. 1643-1788 (see p. 1706).

[71] *ANET*, Nos. 372-373.

intact walls"[72]. This was less a matter of chance than a deliberate strategy, as Lachish had to become the headquarters of Sennacherib and of his army[73]. If Arad Stratum XI ends therefore in the late 8th B.C., Stratum X must begin shortly after this date and the occupation of Kuntillet 'Ağrud can hardly precede the last quarter of the 8th century B.C.

Its foundation on the road leading in Antiquity from the Mediterranean, through Tell al-Qudeirat (Qadesh-Barnea), to the Gulf of Aqaba is a product of this commercial activity. The choice of the site in the middle of the desert was dictated by its location at the junction of several natural routes and by the presence of wells in its immediate neighbourhood. It was a kind of "caravansary" or way-station, which apparently had a religious significance for the travellers[74]. Its residents did not belong to the desert population, since no Negebite handmade pottery was found at the site. Typological study as well as petrographic and neutron activation analyses of ceramics indicate its origin mainly from Judah, Philistia, and Samaria[75], while Phoenician connections are revealed by some inscriptions[76]. A drawing painted on one of the Judaean pithoi ridicules a royal couple, recognizable by the crowns[77]. These figures were abusively called "deities" by authors eager for sensation. We do not know which king and queen were supposed to be represented in such a way. Would it be Hezekiah with his consort? The Hebrew ink-inscription written later on the undecorated surface of the

[72] D. USSISHKIN, *Excavations and Restoration Work at Tel Lachish 1985-1994: Third Preliminary Report*, in *Tel Aviv* 23 (1996), p. 3-60 (see p. 18).

[73] II Kings 18, 14; 19, 8; Is. 36, 2; 37, 8; II Chron. 32, 9. In the "Azekah fragment" (E. FRAHM, *Einleitung in die Sanherib-Inschriften* [AfO, Beih. 26], Wien 1997, p. 229-232), line 5', Sennacherib most likely calls Lachish his army unit's place, when he describes Azekah as a city located "between my [ar]my unit ([*ki-i*]*ṣ-ri-ia*) and the land of Judah". Azekah, identified as Tell Zakariya, lies in fact about half-way between Tell ad-Duweir (Lachish) and Jerusalem. This means that Sennacherib's "Letter to the God" was written from the perspective of his stay at Lachish.

[74] Z. MESHEL, *Kuntillet 'Ajrud. A Religious Centre from the Time of the Judaean Monarchy on the Border of Sinai*, Jerusalem 1978; ID., *Teman, Horvat*, in *NEAEHL*, Jerusalem 1993, Vol. IV, p. 1458-1464.

[75] Y. GOREN, *Petrographic Analyses of Ḥorvat Teiman (Kuntillet 'Ajrud) Pottery*, in *Tel Aviv* 22 (1995), p. 206-207; J. GUNNEWEG - I. PERLMAN - Z. MESHEL, *The Origin of the Pottery of Kuntillet 'Ajrud*, in *IEJ* 35 (1985), p. 270-283.

[76] Z. MESHEL, *op. cit.* and *art. cit.* (n. 74).

[77] Cf. Jer. 13, 18. This drawing appears in many publications showing a penis or tale on both figures; for example: Z. MESHEL, *op. cit.* (n. 74), Fig. 12. Originally the right figure did not have it and should be identified as female: U. AVNER, *Maẓẓebot Sites in the Negev and Sinai and Their Significance*, in *Biblical Archaeology Today, 1990*, Jerusalem 1993, p. 166-181 (see p. 172, Fig. 24, and p. 179-180, n. 37). See here p. 377.

pithos, but encroaching upon the king's crown, has no relation to the drawing[78].

The wording of the fragmentary Phoenician inscriptions, painted on a wall plaster and apparently expressing some blessings, is not particularly important, but their presence seems to establish a link between Kuntillet 'Ağrud and the large Assyro-Phoenician emporium, erected precisely in the second half of the 8th century B.C. at the site of Abu Ruqeish or Tell ar-Reqeish (Tel Qatif), 15 km south-west of Gaza[79]. Its rectangular area, bordering the coast, comprises between 8 and 10 ha. It was surrounded by a massive brick wall, being in places 6.2 m tick and 5 m high, and reinforced by rectangular towers. The site was discovered in 1940 among the coastal dunes and partially excavated in 1940, 1973, and 2000. The area inside the wall was hardly examined, but a nearby cemetery revealed rich finds with distinct Phoenician and Assyrian features[80]. Considering the date of the foundation of this site, one is entitled to assume that it should have a relation to Tiglath-pileser III's endeavour to control the lucrative desert trade from Arabia to the Mediterranean[81], as soon as he occupied the area in 734 B.C., forcing vassalage on Hanun, king of Gaza. One can further argue that the "caravansary" of Kuntillet 'Ağrud was built in the same period, probably under Assyrian pressure, and that this short-lived site was operational between *ca.* 725 and 705 B.C., when a general rebellion broke out on the sudden death of Sargon II. No Edomite pottery, except some possible specimens[82], was discovered at the site, what can mean that it did not depend from Edom. Petro-

[78] The inscription was first deciphered by J. NAVEH, *Graffiti and Dedications*, in *BASOR* 235 (1979), p. 27-30 (see p. 28). It was added after the drawing was made: P. BECK, *The Drawing from Ḥorvat Teiman (Kuntillet 'Ajrud)*, in *Tel Aviv* 9 (1982), p. 3-68, Pls. 1-16 (see p. 46).

[79] Grid ref. 08610/09185.

[80] W. CULICAN, *The Graves at Tell er-Reqeish*, in *The Australian Journal of Biblical Archaeology* 2/2 (1973), p. 66-105 = W. CULICAN, *Opera Selecta*, Göteborg 1986, p. 85-124; A. BIRAN, *Tell er-Ruqeish to Tell er-Ridan*, in *IEJ* 24 (1974), p. 141-142, Pls. 24-25; R. HESTRIN - M. DAYAGI-MENDELS, *Another Pottery Group from Abu Ruqeish*, in *The Israel Museum Journal* 2 (1982), p. 49-57; E. OREN - N. FLEMING - S. KORNBERG - R. FEINSTEIN - P. NAḤSHONI, *A Phoenician Emporium on the Border of Egypt*, in *Qadmoniot* 19 (1986), p. 83-91 (in Hebrew); E.D. OREN, *Ruqeish*, in *NEAEHL*, Jerusalem 1993, Vol. IV, p. 1293-1294; Y. HUSTER, *Tell er-Ruqeish*, in *ESI* 111 (2000), p. 87*-88*.

[81] C.S. EHRLICH, *The Philistines in Transition. A History from ca. 1000-730 B.C.E.*, Leiden 1996, p. 86-104.

[82] E. AYALON, *art. cit.* (n. 60), p. 151. For a description of Edomite pottery, also called "Buṣeirā pottery" by reference to the main Iron Age site in Edom, see M.F. OAKESHOTT, *The Edomite Pottery*, in J.F.A. SAWYER - D.J.A. CLINES (eds.), *Midian, Moab and Edom*, Sheffield 1983, p. 53-63; E. MAZAR, *Edomite Pottery at the End of the Iron Age*, in *IEJ* 35 (1985), p. 253-269.

King and Queen painted on a pithos from the Jerusalem area,
found at Kuntillet ʿAğrud, late 8th century B.C.
(after Z. Meshel's and P. Beck's drawings).

Inscriptions from Tell al-Qudeirat:
[ʾ]*dmy*, left, and *lʾdnṣ*[*dq*], right.

graphic and neutron activation analyses show a preponderance of ware coming from Philistia, except for the large whole-mouth pithoi. These storage jars, not used for the transport of goods, have been produced in the Jerusalem area. The Hebrew ink inscriptions and the paintings occur at least on four of them. It would seem that these pithoi represent an urgent supply imposed by the Assyrians on the king of Judah. Instead, actual administration of the "caravansary" was probably in the hands of some Phoenician attendants from Abu Ruqeish, who were staying at Kuntillet ʿAǧrud and had painted the short Phoenician inscriptions on a wall. Following the events of 705 B.C., the site had to be abandoned at the end of the 8th century B.C.

The discussion on the origin and aim of Kuntillet ʿAǧrud is frequently linked to the question of Tell al-Qudeirat, although the first site has never been a fortress. ʿAin al-Qudeirat is a rich spring which waters a fertile oasis at the junction of desert routes from the Gulf of Aqaba to the Mediterranean and to Egypt. The nearby mound of Tell al-Qudeirat[83], believed by some to be the biblical Qadesh-Barnea, is the site of a rectangular Iron Age II fortress, which already raised the interest of C.L.

[83] Grid ref. 0955/0062. In the Wādī al-ʿAin, to the north-east of the mound and at a walking distance of thirty minutes, A. MUSIL, *Arabia Petraea* II. *Edom* II, Wien 1908, p. 156-157, had seen "Nabataean and Liḥyanite inscriptions", which have been recorded in 1937 and published by R. DE VAUX - R. SAVIGNAC, *Nouvelles recherches dans la région de Cadès,* in *RB* 47 (1938), p. 89-100 and Pls. VIII-IX (see p. 91-92 and 97-100). The older graffiti are Nabataean, the somewhat later ones, Thamudic. They show that the wadi was used as a caravan route in Roman times.

Wooley and T.E. Lawrence in 1914[84]. Soundings were carried out at the site in 1956 by M. Dothan[85] and large-scale excavations conducted in 1976-1982 by R. Cohen[86]. The fortress was built in the 8th or early 7th century B.C. at the place of an earlier enclosed settlement, which had an oval layout. Contrary to Kuntillet 'Ağrud, it could be regarded as an Edomite way-station, since Tell al-Qudeirat's handmade and wheel-made pottery is said to be most closely paralleled by that of Tell al-Kheleifeh[87]. The analysis of stratigraphic data led D. Ussishkin to the convincing conclusion that a single rectangular fortress was built above the oval enclosure[88]. Its interior may have had four occupational phases in the 8th-7th centuries B.C., but there are no clear indications for the destruction of the fortress before the end of the 7th century B.C.

The development of the caravan trade from Arabia to the Mediterranean, noticeable from the 8th century B.C. and echoed by Am. 1, 6-7, who refers to the slave trade between Gaza and Edom, explains the erection of the fortress at this particular site. The script of two inscribed fragments, discovered in the ruins, resembles the 8th/7th century Hebrew scripts, but the names do not suggest Judaean connections. The broken basis of a lamp still bears five signs, incised before firing. They can be read *l-'dn*⌜*ṣ*⌝[*dq*], "Belonging to Adoniṣedeq". The theophorous element "Ṣedeq" is reminiscent of "Malkiṣedeq", a name occurring on a stamp seal[89], the script of which appears to be Edomite: the baseline of *bēt* is strongly dipping and the *daleth* has no leg or a very short one. The second fragment preserves three letters, likewise incised before firing. They probably constitute the end of the ethnic name "Edomite": [...']*dmy*. "Edomite" (*'dmy*) occurs instead of a proper name in line 4 of an ostracon, the script of which is similar to that of the Arad ostraca from Stra-

[84] C.L. Woolley - T.E. Lawrence, *The Wilderness of Zin (Archaeological Report)*, in *Palestine Exploration Found. Annual* 3 (1914-15), p. 64-67.

[85] M. Dothan, *The Fortress of Kadesh-Barnea*, in *IEJ* 15 (1965), p. 134-151.

[86] R. Cohen, *Kadesh-Barnea*, in *IEJ* 26 (1976), p. 201-202; 28 (1978), p. 197; 30 (1980), p. 235-236; 32 (1982), p. 70-71, 266-267; Id., *Excavations at Kadesh-Barnea 1976-1978*, in *BA* 44 (1981), p. 93-107; Id., *Did I Excavate Kadesh Barnea?*, in *Biblical Archaeology Review* 7/3 (1981), p. 20-33; Id., *Kadesh-Barnea: A Fortress from the Time of the Judaean Kingdom*, Jerusalem 1983; Id., *Excavations at Kadesh-Barnea 1976-1982*, in *Qadmoniot* 16 (1983), p. 2-14 (in Hebrew); I. Gilead - R. Cohen, *Kadesh-Barnea*, in *NEAEHL*, Jerusalem 1993, Vol. III, p. 841-847.

[87] See already G.D. Pratico, *art. cit.* (n. 35), p. 22.

[88] D. Ussishkin, *The Rectangular Fortress at Kadesh-Barnea*, in *IEJ* 45 (1995), p. 118-127.

[89] R. Deutsch - M. Heltzer, *West Semitic Epigraphic News of the 1st Millennium BCE*, Tel Aviv 1999, p. 32-35, No. 130 (32). See also *l-Ṣdq*, probably Edomite, in Y. Aharoni, *op. cit.* (n. 65), p. 108-109, No. 93.

"Negebite" ware from Tell al-Qudeirat
(Excavations of R. Cohen).

tum VI (early 6th century B.C.)[90]. Among the other finds of Tell al-Qudeirat there are five ostraca with West-Semitic letters, likewise similar to the Hebrew scripts of the late 8th or 7th century B.C., and a large ostracon with numbers and measurements in hieratic script[91]. These are school exercises, obviously aimed at preparing scribes who would intervene in trade transactions. They do not prove that the fortress was in Judaean hands. Nor does the pottery, not yet fully analyzed, offer a decisive answer to this question, although a relatively large amount of painted Edomite vessels suggests an Edomite presence. This ware is reminiscent of potsherds found at Tell as-Seba' (Tel Beersheba) and Ḫirbet al-Ġarra (Tel 'Ira) in levels dated in a conventional chronology to the last third of the 8th century B.C.[92], but belonging rather to the 7th cen-

[90] M. Heide, *Wheat and Wine. A New Ostracon from Shlomo Moussaieff Collection*, in *BN* 114-115 (2002), p. 40-46.

[91] A. Lemaire - P. Vernus, *Les ostraca paléo-hébreux de Qadesh-Barnéa*, in *Orientalia* 49 (1980), p. 341-345, Pls. LXXI-LXXIII; Id., *L'ostracon paléo-hébreu n° 6 de Tell Qudeirat (Qadesh-Barnéa)*, in M. Görg (ed.), *Fontes atque Pontes. Festgabe für H. Brunner*, Wiesbaden 1983, p. 302-326.

[92] L. Singer-Avitz, *'Busayra Painted Ware' at Tel Beersheba*, in *Tel Aviv* 31 (2004), p. 80-89.

tury B.C.[93] like the bulk of the pottery and like similar ware from Buṣeirā: two comparable decorated bowls have been discovered there in Stratum IV, dated by E. Mazar from the first half of the 7th century B.C.[94] All this can mean that the fortress of Tell al-Qudeirat, situated on the trade route between Tell ar-Reqeish and the Gulf of Aqaba, was built at the end of the 8th or in the early 7th centuries B.C. in order to foster the traffic, supported both by the Assyrians and the Edomites. The Edomite economy and even the State itself seem to be derivatives of this "international" trade, while the internal exchange of goods appears to have been minimal in Edom, as shown by the great variety of pottery assemblages[95]. The turbulent times following the death of Sargon II do not seem to have disturbed the unfolding of commercial activities along the Negeb routes. Trade even increased in the following century, answering the demand for aromatics and raw materials. The fortress was destroyed in a great conflagration, possibly at the time of the first Nebuchadnezzar II's attack against Egypt, in 601 B.C.[96]

Elath

Ancient Elath certainly corresponds to Tell al-Kheleifeh (Tell al-Ḫulayfi)[97], a mound situated on the trade route, some 500 m from the northern shore of the Gulf of Aqaba. Following F. Frank[98], N. Glueck had identified this site with Ezion-Geber, the supposed port of call of Solomon's trade with Ophir[99]. Linking the results of his excavations to biblical texts, he interpreted the earliest architectural remains of the site as a casemate enclosure from the time of Solomon, followed by a larger fortress (*ca.* 60 x 60 m), built in the first half of the 9th century B.C. by Jehoshaphat and rebuilt in the following century by Uzziah, king of Judah (II Kings 14, 22). The stronghold would have been occupied later

[93] See here below, p. 410.

[94] It is not clear why E. MAZAR, *art. cit.* (n. 82), p. 261, wants to link these bowls to Stratum II, which she dates from the last quarter of the 7th century: *ibid.*, p. 263.

[95] P. BIEŃKOWSKI - E.J. VAN DER STEEN, *Tribes, Trade, and Towns: A New Framework for the Late Iron Age in Southern Jordan and the Negev,* in *BASOR* 323 (2001), p. 21-47 (see p. 26-28).

[96] Cf. here above, p. 160-161.

[97] Grid ref. 1476/8845; cf. W. ZWICKEL, *op. cit.* (n. 47), p. 11; G.D. PRATICO, *Kheleifeh, Tell el-*, in *NEAEHL*, Jerusalem 1993, Vol. III, p. 867-870.

[98] F. FRANK, *Aus der 'Arabah I. Tell el-Chlēfi,* in *ZDPV* 57 (1934), p. 243-245.

[99] N. GLUECK's publications referring to Tell al-Kheleifeh have been collected by G.D. PRATICO, *art. cit.* (n. 35), p. 30.

by the Edomites (II Kings 16, 6) and replaced by a new settlement, associated with Edomite wheel-made pottery of the 8th-6th centuries B.C. However, Tell al-Kheleifeh can certainly be identified with Elath, for the site of the Nabataean, Roman, Byzantine, and early Islamic city of Aila(t) is situated at Aqaba[100]. A confusion occurs in later biblical texts between Elath and Ezion-Geber, which possibly corresponds to the island of Ǧazīrat al-Far'ūn in the Gulf of Aqaba. One should certainly recuse the identification of *Š-b-p3-r-ṯ n G-b-r-ỉ* in Shoshenq I's topographical list[101] with Ezion-Geber[102]. This toponym and the following one, *Š-b-p3-r-ṯ w-r-k-y-t*[103], contain the noun *šplt*, "lowland", "Shephelah". Considering their place in the list, both should refer to the Beersheba Valley[104]. They have no relation to Ezion-Geber or Elath. As for the biblical accounts of Solomon's and Jehoshaphat's maritime endeavours[105], they date from the early Persian period[106], when Phoenician presence is attested at Tell al-Kheleifeh by two Phoenician ostraca and two Phoenician names occurring on an Aramaic ostracon[107].

II Kings 16, 6 recognizes that Elath was an Edomite town in the last third of the 8th century B.C. This date corresponds to the period when the fortress of Tell al-Kheleifeh was built. Instead, puzzling is the reference to the earlier Judaean occupation of the site and the mention of the building of Elath by king Uzziah / Azariah of Judah some fifty years earlier. This record of II Kings 14, 22 seems to be linked in the mind of the Deuteronomistic Historian to the short report of the war of Amaziah

[100] Grid ref. 149/883. Cf. D. Whitcomb, *Aqaba 1989-90*, in *Syria* 70 (1993), p. 239-244; Id., *The Fourth Gate of Ayla: A Report on the 1992 Excavations at Aqaba,* in *ADAJ* 37 (1993), p. 533-548; S.Th. Parker, *Preliminary Report on the 1994 Season of the Roman Aqaba Project,* in *BASOR* 305 (1997), p. 19-44; A. Retzleff, *A Nabataean and Roman Domestic Area at the Red Sea Port of Aila,* in *BASOR* 331 (2003), p. 45-65. Aila has been completely destroyed in the 1068 A.D. earthquake, as recorded in written sources.

[101] Nos. 73-74. The list should be used according to the readings of its definitive publication in *Reliefs and Inscriptions at Karnak* III. *The Bubastite Portal* (OIP 74), Chicago 1954, Pls. 2-9.

[102] Y. Aharoni, *The Land of the Bible. A Historical Geography*, London 1967, p. 288. This identification was already discarded by K.A. Kitchen, *The Third Intermediate Period in Egypt (1110-650 B.C.)*, 3rd ed., Warminster 1995, p. 439.

[103] Nos. 75-76. See here above, p. 111-112 and 116.

[104] See here above, p. 116.

[105] I Kings 9, 26-28; 10, 11-12.22; 22, 49-50.

[106] Lipiński, *Itineraria Phoenicia*, p. 217-223, 247.

[107] A. Lemaire, *Les Phéniciens et le commerce entre la Mer Rouge et la Mer Méditerranée*, in E. Lipiński (ed.), *Phoenicia and the East Mediterranean in the First Millennium B.C.* (Studia Phoenicia V; OLA 22), Leuven 1987, p. 49-60 (see p. 56); Id., *Kheleifeh, Tell el,* in *DCPP*, Turnhout 1992, p. 247.

against the Edomites in II Kings 14, 7: "He smote Edom in the Valley of Salt, ten thousand, and seized the Rock by war, and called its name Joqtheel until this day". If the Valley of Salt (*Gy'-hmlḥ*) is not simply the Wādī Arabah, it might be Bīr Mulēḥ[108], 12 km south-east of aṣ-Ṣāfī, and the Rock (*Sl'*) would then be as-Sil'[109], 18 km to the south, not Petra, as assumed by the Septuagint. In the original source, the Elath of II Kings 14, 22, spelled Αἰλώθ or 'Ελώθ in the Septuagint, was not Tell al-Kheleifeh, but a place within a single day's journey south of Jerusalem. It is mentioned in the Mishnah[110], means "Terebinth(s)", and is located at Ramath al-Ḫalīl, 3 km north of Hebron[111].

It is hard to believe that the Deuteronomistic Historian has just invented the story. He probably found a notice concerning a building activity at this holy place in the annals of the kings of Judah and linked this information with the record on wars against the Edomites. His source seems instead to have connected the "building of *'Ēlat* / *'Ēlōt*" with the burial of king Amaziah, who was murdered, like his father Joash, after a campaign against the Edomites and a disastrous war against Israel. These regicides have probably been prompted not by the foreign policy of the kings, but by the suspicion of some people at the Court that Joash, proclaimed king on the overthrow of Athaliahu[112], did not really belong to David's lineage, but was a son of the high priest Yehoyada. It did not matter that Joash prevented an attack on Jerusalem by Hazael, king of Damascus, by paying him a heavy tribute: he was killed a few years later in a conspiracy. His son Amaziah managed to succeed him to the throne, but was murdered in his turn. The double name of Azariah / Uzziah in the Bible seems to represent an additional

[108] Grid ref. 2033/0388; cf. W. ZWICKEL, *op. cit.* (n. 47), p. 60.

[109] Grid ref. 2049/0214; cf. W. ZWICKEL, *op. cit.* (n. 47), p. 53; S. HART, *Sela': The Rock of Edom?*, in *PEQ* 118 (1986), p. 91-95.

[110] Mishnah, *Maaṣer Sheni* V, 2.

[111] Grid ref. 160/107; cf. ABEL, *Géographie* II, p. 375-376; M. AVI-YONAH, *Gazetteer of Roman Palestine* (Qedem 5), Jerusalem 1976, p. 99-100. Fifteen pottery fragments, dated by W.F. Albright to the 9th-8th centuries B.C. and to the 7th-6th centuries by L.-H. Vincent, have been found in the excavation of the site: L.-H. VINCENT, *L'année archéologique 1927-8 en Palestine*, in *RB* 38 (1929), p. 92-114, Pl. III (see p. 108-109); R. DE VAUX, rev. in *RB* 65 (1958), p. 595. The 8th century would correspond to the reign of Uzziah / Azariah. Unfortunately, these sherds are not published in the report of E. MADER, *Die Ergebnisse der Ausgrabungen im heiligen Bezirk Râmet el-Ḫalîl in Süd-palästina 1926-1928*, Freiburg im Br. 1957.

[112] The seven years of Athaliahu's reign might coincide with the reigns of Jehoram and of his son Ahaziahu in Judah. The report on her killing all the royal seed of Judah may refer to the same event as the killing of all Jehoshaphat's sons by Jehoram.

symptom of the continuing dynastic crisis; it may even hide the replacement of Amaziah's son by a descendant of a lateral Davidic lineage. At that time, Tell al-Kheleifeh did certainly not constitute a major concern at the Court of Jerusalem.

Technical analysis of the material from N. Glueck's excavations at Tell al-Kheleifeh was made by G.D. Pratico[113]. It showed that the site was initially occupied by an enclosed settlement, similar to a caravansary and characterized by "Negebite" handmade pottery (Period I). Thereafter two phases should be distinguished in the fortress with a solid "offsets / insets" wall, built in the second half of the 8th century B.C. (Periods II and III). However, the rich finds of Edomite wheel-made ware cannot be tied to any particular phase[114]. The fortress appears thus as an Edomite stronghold of the late 8th and the 7th centuries B.C., as shown by the pottery, the Edomite ostraca published by N. Glueck[115], and the stamp impression appearing on many handles of Edomite cooking pots and other vessels. It bears the inscription: *l-Qws'nl 'bd hmlk*, "Belonging to Qaws'anal, servant of the king"[116]. The personal name is obviously Edomite and the script is datable to the 7th century B.C., confirming the control exercised then by the kings of Edom over this strategic site and over the desert routes to Egypt and to the Mediterranean. It seems therefore that Tell al-Kheleifeh has never been in Judaean hands, although finds of Judaean pottery witness the existence of some contacts between this site and the northern highland. Decisively more important was the discovery of a great jar with incised South Arabian monograms

[113] G.D. Pratico, *art. cit.* (n. 35); Id., *Nelson Glueck's 1938-1940 Excavations at Tell el-Kheleifeh. Reappraisal*, Atlanta 1993; Id., *art. cit.* (n. 97).

[114] G.D. Pratico, *op. cit.* (n. 113), p. 71.

[115] N. Glueck, *Ostraca from Elath*, in *BASOR* 80 (1940), p. 3-10, and 82 (1941), p. 3-11; Id., *Tell el-Kheleifeh Inscriptions*, in H. Goedicke (ed.), *Near Eastern Studies in Honor of W.F. Albright*, Baltimore 1971, p. 225-242. The latter group contains Phoenician and Aramaic ostraca, also from the early Hellenistic period, as shown by the Aramaic transcriptions of the Greek words καρπολόγος, "fruit-harvester", and τοπεῖον, "rope", in Ostracon 2069:

qrplgs ṭpy'n 1	"fruit-harvester, rope 1
ḥmr ṭpy'n 2	ass-driver, rope 2
ḥmr 5	ass-driver 5".

The *aleph* in *ṭpy'n* indicates that *yōd* is no *mater lectionis* for *ī*.

[116] N. Glueck, *The First Campaign at Tell el Kheleifeh (Ezion-Geber)*, in *BASOR* 71 (1938), p. 3-18 (see p. 16-18); Id., *The Topography and History of Ezion Geber and Elath*, in *BASOR*, 72 (1938), p. 2-13 (see p. 12); G.D. Pratico, *art. cit.* (n. 35), p. 21, Fig. 17, and p. 24; R.A. DiVito, *The Tell el-Kheleifeh Inscriptions*, in G.D. Pratico, *op. cit.* (n. 113), p. 53-55; N. Avigad - B. Sass, *Corpus of West Semitic Stamp Seals*, Jerusalem 1997, p. 389-390, No. 1051.

South Arabian monograms from Tell al-Kheleifeh
(Archival photograph of N. Glueck's excavations).

in the Edomite fortress of Period III (8th/7th century B.C.)[117]. It clearly manifests the role of Tell al-Kheleifeh in the international trade of the 8th-7th centuries B.C. between South Arabia, the Levant, and the Mediterranean world. The two monograms consist of the combined letters *l* + s^1 and *ḥ* + ʿ, perhaps followed by another monogram on the lost part of the jar. Their meaning is so far unclear, but they may refer to the proprietor of the jar and its contents.

ʿAin al-Ḥuṣb

A strategic site on the north-western border of Edom was ʿAin al-Ḥuṣb (ʿEn Ḥaẓeva)[118], situated about 35 km south of Zoar, at the cross-roads of the north-south and east-west routes, from Moab to the Gulf of Aqaba and to Egypt. The site must be identified with Tamar in the Desert (I Kings 9, 18), as shown convincingly by Y. Aharoni[119]. Ez. 47, 19 and 48, 28 seems to locate Tamar at the south-eastern corner of the future Holy Land and the gloss *b'rṣ*, originated in I Kings 9, 18 from a misread *b'dm*, correctly located Tamar in Edom[120].

The large fortress of Stratum V, excavated in 1992-1994[121], has been built by the Edomites. It is dated to the 8th century B.C. by the pottery found in one of casemate rooms, and its four-chambered gate closely resembles that of Ḫirbet al-Muḍeibiʿ[122], which was founded perhaps in the first half of the 8th century B.C. It measured *ca.* 50 x 50 m in its first phase (Stratum VB) and was later enlarged to *ca.* 100 x 100 m (Stratum VA). If all this area was built up, the number of residents can be estimated at 200-250 persons. The date of Stratum VB suggests connecting

[117] G. Ryckmans, *Un fragment de jarre avec caractères minéens à Tell el-Kheleyfeh*, in *RB* 48 (1939), p. 247-249, Pl. VI; *RÉS* 4918 bis. Cf. N. Glueck, *The Other Side of the Jordan*, New Haven 1940, p. 105-108; Id., *Iron II Pottery from Tell el-Kheleifeh*, in *Yediot* 31 (1966-67), p. 124-127 (see p. 125); Id., *Some Ezion-Geber: Elath Iron Age Pottery*, in *W.F. Albright Volume* (ErIs 9), Jerusalem 1969, p. 51*-59* (see p. 53* and Pl. VI, 4). See here p. 385.

[118] Grid ref. 1734/0242.

[119] Y. Aharoni, *Tamar and the Roads to Elath*, in *IEJ* 13 (1963), p. 30-42.

[120] The frequent confusion *d/r* does not need to be discussed, while the misreading of *m* as *ṣ* can be explained by the similarity of the zigzag-head of *mēm* with a top of *ṣade* resembling the old *zayin*.

[121] R. Cohen, *Ḥaẓeva, Meẓad*, in *NEAEHL*, Jerusalem 1993, Vol. II, p. 593-594; R. Cohen - Y. Israel, *The Iron Age Fortress at ʿEn Ḥaṣeva*, in *BA* 58 (1995), p. 223-235; Id., *The Excavations at ʿEin Ḥaẓeva / Israelite and Roman Tamar*, in *Qadmoniot* 29 (1996), p. 78-92 (in Hebrew) and Pls. I-III; Id., *ʿEn Ḥazeva - 1990-1994*, in *ESI* 15 (1996), p. 110-116; P. Beck, *Horvat Qitmit Revisited via ʿEn Ḥazeva*, in *Tel Aviv* 23 (1996), p. 102-114.

[122] See here above p. 329.

Ceramic cult vessel representing a worshipper
from the Edomite shrine of 'Ain al-Ḥuṣb, ancient Tamar
(Excavations of R. Cohen and Y. Israel).

its construction with the invasion of Edom by king Amaziah of Judah (804-776 B.C.). It is also possible that the earliest fort (Stratum VI), the remains of which have been exposed under the gate of Stratum VB[123], existed already at the time of Amaziah and played a role in the battle of the Valley of Salt (II Kings 14, 7), possibly the Wādī Arabah. Since the earliest fortress of 'Ain al-Ḥuṣb was not built before the end of the 9th or the 8th century B.C., it is useless to discuss its attribution to Solomon in I Kings 9, 18.

[123] R. COHEN - Y. YISRAEL, *art. cit.* (n. 121), in *ESI* 15 (1996), p. 114.

The fortress of Stratum IV is badly preserved. The architectural remains are scanty, but there is some characteristic pottery of the 7th century B.C. and the finds in this stratum include a stone seal carved with a horned altar flanked by two facing figures and the Edomite inscription *l-Mškt bn Wḥzn*, "Belonging to *Mškt*, son of *Wḥzn*"[124], two North Arabian names meaning "Steadfast" and "Violent"[125]. Moreover, a unique assemblage of sixty-three complete cult vessels and seven stone altars have been found in a *favissa* close to the wall. The pottery items are similar to the figures found in the Edomite temple at Ḫirbet Qiṭmīt[126], and they witness the existence of an Edomite shrine in the 7th and the first half of the 6th century B.C. The building of these fortresses certainly implies the intervention of a royal administration. One can also assume that a "servant of the king" commanded them, like Qaws'anal at Elath.

There were small Edomite forts also on the western shore of the Dead Sea, like at Meṣad Gozal[127], just north of the Ǧebel Usdum. This square fort measured about 20 m by 20 m. A smaller one has been discovered southward, 3.5 km west of 'Ain 'Arūs.

Edomite kings

Our knowledge of the Edomite kings is very limited. The so-called Edomite king-list in Gen. 36, 31-39 and I Chron. 1, 43-50 is compiled from two different sources[128], one of which has to do with Edomite rulers: Jobab, son of Zeraḥ, Husham, Shalmah[129], Shaul, and Baal-hanan, son of Akbar. They may have ruled in Buṣeirā (Boṣrah) from the

[124] R. COHEN - Y. YISRAEL, *art. cit.* (n. 121), in *Qadmoniot* 29 (1996), p. 83, and in *ESI* 15 (1996), p. 112, Fig. 116; J. NAVEH, *A Sixth Century Edomite Seal from 'En Hazeva*, in *'Atiqot* 42 (2001), p. 197-198.

[125] HARDING, *Arabian Names*, p. 545 (*MSKT*), and the Arabic adjectives *waḫḫāz* and *wāḫiz* with mimation.

[126] See here below, p. 394, n. 169, and p. 400.

[127] Grid ref. 186/060: Y. AHARONI, *Meṣad Gozal*, in *RB* 72 (1965), p. 562-563.

[128] This has been demonstrated by J.R. BARTLETT, *The Edomite King List of Genesis XXXVI. 31-39 and I Chron. I. 43-50*, in *Journal of Theological Studies*, n.s. 16 (1965), p. 301-314. A similar conclusion was reached by M. WEIPPERT, *Remarks on the History of Settlement in Southern Jordan during the Early Iron Age*, in A. HADIDI (ed.), *Studies in the History and Archaeology of Jordan* I, Amman 1982, p. 153-162, especially p. 155, where the author rightly doubts that the second source mentions Moabite kings, as proposed by Bartlett. The names suggest that these kings were Aramaeans: LIPIŃSKI, *Aramaeans*, p. 358-363.

[129] The reading *Śmlh* of the Hebrew manuscripts should be corrected with the *Codex Alexandrinus* into *Šlmh*, changed by metathesis. This name may be an abridged form of *S¹lmtqs¹*, "Bounty of Qaws"; cf. HARDING, *Arabian Names*, p. 326.

end of the 9th to the late 8th century B.C.[130] The first ruler bears the same name as king Jobab of Midian in Josh. 11, 1[131] and he was a member of the *Ḏrḥ*-tribe (Zeraḥ). A tribe bearing such a name is well known from Sabaic texts[132], but a chieftain Zeraḥ appears also in the account of II Chron. 14, 8-14, referring to nomads or semi-nomads in the western Negeb[133]. The name and patronymic of Jobab seem to reveal trade relations with the Arabian Peninsula in a period in which Midian has lost its former importance[134]. The last ruler in the source bears, instead, a Phoenician name[135], which may reflect contacts with Levantine merchants using the Negeb route through Kuntillet ʻAǧrud, where their presence is attested by Phoenician inscriptions[136] dating to *ca.* 725-705 B.C.[137] There are thus good reasons to assume that the pertinent source of the king-list preserves genuine historical material from the 8th century B.C.[138], although no king of the list bears a name with the theophorous element "Qaws". The reigns of the five Edomite rulers of the king-list may cover a span of about one century, thus bringing us to the late 9th century B.C. This is also the period when Edom is first mentioned in known Assyrian inscriptions. The so-called Calah Slab lists it between Israel and Philistia among western countries that paid tribute to Adad-nirari III[139] after the surrender of Damascus, most likely in 803, when

[130] C.-M. BENNETT, *Excavations at Buṣeirā (Biblical Bozrah)*, in J.F.A. SAWYER - D.J.A. CLINES (eds.), *Midian, Moab and Edom*, Sheffield 1983, p. 9-17, in particular p. 11, considered the very end of the 9th century B.C. as a possible date for the town wall of Buṣeirā. Further study of early Edomite pottery should elucidate this question. In LIPIŃSKI, *Itineraria Phoenicia*, p. 196, line 9, one should read: "Edom, which did not exist as *State* before the 8th century B.C.".

[131] The unknown place name *Mdwn* (cf. Josh. 12, 19) of the manuscripts should be corrected into *Mdyn*, considering the easy confusion of *y* and *w* in the Jewish script of the Hasmonaean and Herodian periods. The old form of the toponym apparently gave rise to the name of Ḫirbet Madīn, a site southwest of Tiberias, which local tradition connects with Jethro, the priest of Midian, whose grave is venerated nearby.

[132] HARDING, *Arabian Names*, p. 252.

[133] Cf. here above, p. 129.

[134] For the importance of Midian in the late second millennium B.C., cf. E.A. KNAUF, *Midian*, Wiesbaden 1988.

[135] E. LIPIŃSKI (ed.), *Dictionnaire de la civilisation phénicienne et punique*, Turnhout 1992, p. 58.

[136] Z. MESHEL, *op. cit.* and *art. cit.* (n. 74).

[137] See here above, p. 373-378.

[138] E.A. KNAUF, *Alter und Herkunft der edomitischen Königsliste Gen 36, 31-39,* in *ZAW* 97 (1985), p. 245-253, dates the king-list to the early Persian period. The compilation of the two sources may have taken place in that period, but the pertinent Edomite source does not post-date the 8th century B.C., since it does not even mention Qaws-malaka.

[139] *RIMA* III, text A.0.104.8, p. 213, line 12.

the Assyrians reached ^{uru}*Ba'li*[140], somewhere in Israel or on the South-Phoenician coast. This confirms the existence of the Edomite state in the late 9th century B.C.

The first king of Edom known from Assyrian sources is Qaws-malaka, who is mentioned in a list of tributary kings from the reign of Tiglath-pileser III (744-727 B.C.)[141]. The list is not dated, but is likely to record the tribute paid between 734 and 732 B.C. Qaws-malaka is the first example of a personal name honouring the national deity of Edom after a long gap extending from the time of Ramesses II and Ramesses III, whose topographical lists at Karnak and at Medinet Habu contain five names with the theophorous element Qaws followed by a predicate[142].

After the list of Tiglath-pileser III's tributaries, a Nimrud letter from the earlier part of Sargon II's reign reports the arrival of envoys from the west, bringing tribute. Edom is mentioned there together with Gaza, Ashdod, and Ekron[143]. To the same period may belong a list of wine allocations from Nimrud, recording in sequence men of Ashdod, Edom, and Gaza[144]. Edom was also one of the neighbours whose support was required by Yamani of Ashdod on the eve of his rebellion against Sargon II[145]. Besides, Edom is mentioned in an Assyrian list of place names, apparently after Philistia and Ashkelon[146]. These texts are relevant inasmuch as they seem to imply particular links of Edom with the Philistine cities. This can best be explained by Edom's role in the 8th century trade between the Gulf of Aqaba or the Arabah and Philistia through the Negeb. The initial, probably peaceful and transitory use of sites such as 'Ain al-Ḥuṣb ('En Ḥaẓeva)[147], Ḫirbet al-Ġazza (Ḥorvat 'Uza)[148], Ḫirbet Qiṭmīt (Ḥorvat Qitmit)[149], Ḫirbet 'Ar'ara (Tel

[140] A.R. MILLARD, *The Eponyms of the Assyrian Empire: 910-612 BC* (SAA Studies 2), Helsinki 1994, p. 34 and 110. Cf. LIPIŃSKI, *Itineraria Phoenicia*, p. 13-15.

[141] *Tigl. III*, p. 170, Summ. 7, rev., line 11'. Cf. J. LLOP, *Qauš-malaka*, in *PNA* III/1, Helsinki 2002, p. 1011. The same name appears in Liḥyanite: HARDING, *Arabian Names*, p. 491.

[142] See here above, p. 364, n. 24.

[143] *SAA* I, 110, rev., lines 10-13.

[144] S. DALLEY - J.N. POSTGATE, *The Tablets from Fort Shalmaneser* (CTN 3), London 1984, No. 135, 6-8.

[145] H. WINCKLER, *Die Keilschrifttexte Sargons*, Leipzig 1889, p. 188, line 29.

[146] *SAA* XI, 1, II, 9-11.

[147] Grid ref. 1734/0242. Cf. here above, p. 386-388.

[148] Grid ref. 1657/0687. See here below, p. 404-409.

[149] Grid ref. 1564/0665. See here below, p. 400.

'Aro'er)[150], and Tell al-Milḥ (Tel Malḥata)[151] by Edomites trafficking with the Philistine cities on the Mediterranean might thus go back to the second half of the 8th century B.C., while their settlement marked by new constructions and sanctuaries would date there from the 7th century. A more precise dating of Edomite pottery can be helpful in these matters.

Edom's rulers seem to have generally remained faithful to their Assyrian suzerain[152]. Thus, in 701 B.C., when Sennacherib marched against Jerusalem, king Ilāya-rām of Edom paid tribute to him together with other rulers of the region[153]. King Qaws-gabri was equally submissive to Esarhaddon about 673[154] and to Ashurbanipal about 667[155]. A clay impression of his royal seal, restored convincingly as *Qwsg*[*br*] *mlk* '[*dm*], was found at Umm al-Biyāra[156], the highest mountain overlooking Petra from the west[157]. The seal impression of Qaws-gabri is still the only example of a king's seal from Edom, but two seals of king's min-

150 See here below, p. 409.

151 Grid ref. 152/069. See here below, p. 398-400.

152 For Edom's relations with Assyria, see especially C.-M. BENNETT, *Neo-Assyrian Influence in Transjordan*, in A. HADIDI (ed.), *Studies in the History and Archaeology of Jordan* I, Amman 1982, p. 181-187; A.R. MILLARD, *Assyrian Involvement in Edom*, in P. BIEŃKOWSKI (ed.), *Early Edom and Moab*, Sheffield 1992, p. 35-39.

153 D.D. LUCKENBILL *The Annals of Sennacherib* (OIP 2), Chicago 1924, p. 30, line 57, where the correct reading should be mDINGIR-*a-a-ram-mu* (cf. *ibid.*, p. 169), also in E. FRAHM, *op. cit.* (n. 73), p. 53, line 37. It is evident that mDINGIR-*a-a-ram-mu* is *'Ilāya-rām*, "My god is exalted", with the Arabic theophorous element *'ilā*(*h*). By no means can the name be interpreted "Ea is exalted", as done by K. RADNER, *Aia-rāmu* 2, in *PNA* 1/1, Helsinki 1998, p. 92. The name of the king probably appears as *'lrm* on the seal of one of his ministers: N. AVIGAD - B. SASS, *op. cit.* (n. 116), p. 324, No. 864. The seal should then be considered Edomite, as suggested by the form of the *mēm*, instead of being Ammonite.

154 R. BORGER, *Die Inschriften Asarhaddons, Königs von Assyrien* (AfO, Beih. 9), Graz 1956, p. 60, line 56. Cf. J. LLOP, *Qauš-gabri*, in *PNA* III/1, Helsinki 2002, p. 1011.

155 R. BORGER, *Beiträge zum Inschriftenwerk Assurbanipals*, Wiesbaden 1996, p. 18 and 212, C II 40. Cf. M. COGAN, *A Plaidoyer on Behalf of the Royal Scribes*, in M. COGAN - I. EPH'AL (eds.), *Ah, Assyria... Studies in Assyrian History and Ancient Near Eastern Historiography Presented to Hayim Tadmor*, Jerusalem 1991, p. 121-128 (see p. 122-123), and A.R. MILLARD, *art. cit.* (n. 152), p. 36.

156 C.-M. BENNETT, *Fouilles d'Umm el-Biyara: Rapport préliminaire,* in *RB* 73 (1966), p. 372-403, Pls. XIV-XXV (see p. 399-401 and Pl. XXIIb). A better reproduction can be found in P. BIEŃKOWSKI (ed.), *Early Edom and Moab*, Sheffield 1992, p. 101, Fig. 11:2, and N. AVIGAD - B. SASS, *op. cit.* (n. 116), p. 388, No. 1049. Besides, there is a scaraboid, found in Babylon, probably with the name of the same king: *l-Qwsgbr* / [*mlk* *'d*]*m* ? or [*bn 'lr*]*m* ?; cf. L. JAKOB-ROST - I. GERLACH, *Die Stempelsiegel im Vorderasiatischen Museum*, 2nd ed., Mainz a/R 1997, No. 186; N. AVIGAD - B. SASS, *op. cit.* (n. 116), p. 387-388, No. 1048.

157 Grid ref. 1919/9717. Cf. W. ZWICKEL, *op. cit.* (n. 47), p. 34.

isters, "royal servants", have been found in excavations. They are a clear evidence of a royal administration in Edom in the 7th century B.C. One seal from the first half of the 7th century was found at Buṣeirā[158], a site excavated from 1971 through 1974 and in 1980[159].

Buṣeirā, biblical Boṣrah, is well known from prophetic references in the Bible[160] and it is attested archaeologically at least from the 8th century onwards[161]. It must be distinguished from Boṣrah, south of the Hauran mountains, where Iron Age pottery has been found as well. Buṣeirā is built on a promontory *ca.* 22 km south of Ṭafīla and 4 km west of the "King's Highway". It was a substantial administrative centre dominated by palatial and temple buildings, and fortified by a casemate town wall. A battered enclosure separated the "acropolis" from the lower town which consisted of ordinary domestic buildings and is hidden to the south under the present-day village.

A tentative chronological list of Edomite kings, known from epigraphic and literary sources, may be proposed by way of a conclusion of this section:

Jobab, son of Zeraḥ	*ca.* 835-815
Husham	*ca.* 815-795
Shalmah	*ca.* 795-775
Shaul	*ca.* 775-755
Baal-hanan, son of Akbar	*ca.* 755-735
Qaws-malaka	*ca.* 735-710
Ilāya-rām	*ca.* 710-685
Qaws-gabri	*ca.* 685-665

Edom and the Beersheba Valley

The Edomite fortresses of Tell al-Kheleifeh and 'Ain al-Ḥuṣb do not witness an expansion on former Judaean territory, but the situation is somewhat different in the Beersheba Valley, and later in the Shephelah

[158] Grid ref. 2077/0170. Cf. W. ZWICKEL, *op. cit.* (n. 47), p. 48.

[159] C.-M. BENNETT, *Excavations at Buseirah, Southern Jordan, 1973: Third Preliminary Report,* in *Levant* 7 (1975), p. 1-19, in particular p. 4, Fig. 3, and p. 18-19 (A. LEMAIRE); É. PUECH, *Documents épigraphiques de Buseirah,* in *Levant* 9 (1977), p. 11-20 (see p. 12-13); N. AVIGAD - B. SASS, *op. cit.* (n. 116), p. 388, No. 1049.

[160] Is. 34, 6; 63, 1; Jer. 49, 13.22; Am. 1, 12.

[161] P. BIEŃKOWSKI, *Umm el-Biyara, Tawilan and Buseirah in Retrospect,* in *Levant* 22 (1990), p. 91-109; ID. (ed.), *op. cit.* (n. 156), p. 101-104.

and in the highland around Hebron. The westward thrust of the Edomites is echoed in the oracles of the Judaean prophets of the 6th-5th centuries against Edom, inspired mainly by Edom's expansion to the detriment of Judah[162]. This process began in the mid-8th century B.C. and continued unabated until the Persian period. The settlement of Edomite population west of Wādī Arabah followed the same route and started at least in the early 7th century B.C.[163] The distinction made recently between Edomite mercantile activity and the political influence of Edom west of Wādī Arabah[164] overlooks the nature of the Edomite state brought into existence by the needs of the international trade in this particular area of the Levant[165]. Edomite expansion westward was favoured by the development of international trade in the Assyrian empire. The Beersheba Valley played here a significant role as a transit zone between the Arabian Peninsula, the shores of the Mediterranean, and Egypt. Archaeological findings illustrate the importance of this trade, facilitated by the use of camels. Its beginnings can be dated to the second half of the 8th century B.C. and its traces are being discovered all along the route crossing the Beersheba Valley, where several mounds have been excavated in the last decennia.

Edomite pottery has been identified in various sites of the northern Negeb in strata dated from the end of the 8th century to the early 6th century B.C. It occurs also further to the west at Tell as-Seba' (Tel Beersheba), on the southern edge of the Judaean highland at Tell 'Arad, also near the coastal area at Tell aš-Šerī'a (Tel Sera') and Tell al-Ğemmeh (Tel Gamma). One should note that this Edomite pottery was found to have been manufactured locally, whenever it was subjected to neutron activation analysis or petrographic study. In other words, as L. Singer-Avitz rightly stresses, it was no Edomite import, with the exception of

[162] Convenient summaries are given by J.M. MYERS, *Edom and Judah in the Sixth-Fifth Centuries B.C.*, in H. GOEDICKE (ed.), *Near Eastern Studies in Honor of W.F. Albright,* Baltimore 1971, p. 377-392; C.R. MATHEWS, *Defending Zion. Edom's Desolation and Jacob's Restoration (Isaiah 34-35) in Context* (BZAW 236), Berlin 1995; J. LINDSAY, *Edomite Westward Expansion: The Biblical Evidence,* in *Ancient Near Eastern Studies* 36 (1999), p. 48-89.

[163] Contrary to the opinion of N. GLUECK, *The Boundaries of Edom,* in *HUCA* 11 (1936), p. 141-157, who dated this expansion to the late postexilic period (see p. 157).

[164] J.R. BARTLETT, *Edomites and Idumaeans,* in *PEQ* 131 (1999), p. 102-114.

[165] E.A. KNAUF, *The Cultural Impact of Secondary State Formation: The Cases of the Edomites and the Moabites*, in P. BIEŃKOWSKI, *Early Edom and Moab*, Sheffield 1992, p. 47-54; E.A. KNAUF-BELLERI, *Edom: The Social and Economic History*, in D. EDELMAN (ed.), *"You shall not abhor an Edomite, for he is your brother". Edom and Seir in History and Tradition*, Atlanta 1995, p. 93-117 (see p. 108-111).

cooking pots[166]. The relevant question, that she does not address, is the peculiar case of this kind of vessels. Particular attention was given to their preparation, as they had to withstand heat. Specially mixed clay was thus used in order to reduce the porosity of the vessel and to prevent its cracking under heat. Edomites seem to have privileged raw materials from their homeland.

I. Beit-Arieh noticed in 1995 at Tell al-Milḥ, in Area H, that all the cooking pots of the 8th century were of Judaean type, while those of the later stratum were of Edomite type[167]. This seems to imply a substantial change in the population of the site, but the continuing presence of other Edomite ware apparently signifies that qualified Edomite potters had established workshops in the Beersheba Valley and the northern Negeb since the early 7th century B.C., depending on the sites. In the same way, the discovery of Edomite ostraca witnesses the presence of Edomite scribes. The earliest inscription seems to come from Strata X-IX at Arad. Moreover, the discovery of a large number of Edomite cult vessels not only at 'Ain al-Ḥuṣb[168], but also at Ḫirbet Qiṭmīt[169] and Tell al-Milḥ[170], witnesses the existence of Edomite sanctuaries in this area.

Arad

The Iron Age II settlement was confined at Arad to a citadel on the highest part of the Early Bronze Age city. It was about 50 x 50 m in size, with *ca.* 50 occupants. After Amaziah's campaign against Edom (II Kings 14, 7), *ca.* 780 B.C., a violent conflagration destroyed the Arad casemate fortress of Stratum XI and a solid-walled stronghold replaced it in the early 7th century B.C.[171] Its Strata X-IX must date from the first half of the 7th

[166] L. SINGER-AVITZ, *art. cit.* (n. 92), p. 84-85 with further literature. See, in particular, J. GUNNEWEG - Th. BEIER - U. DIEHL - D. LAMBRECHT - H. MOMMSEN, *art. cit.* (n. 34).

[167] I. BEIT-ARIEH, *Tel Malḥata - 1995*, in *ESI* 18 (1998), p. 106-107.

[168] See here above, p. 386, n. 121.

[169] For the Edomite shrine discovered at the site, see I. BEIT-ARIEH, *An Edomite Shrine at Horvat Qitmit*, in *Y. Yadin Volume* (ErIs 20), Jerusalem 1989, p. 135-146 (in Hebrew); ID., *The Edomite Shrine of Ḥorvat Qitmit in the Judean Desert,* in *Tel Aviv* 18 (1991), p. 93-116; ID., *Qitmit, Ḥorvat,* in *NEAEHL*, Jerusalem 1993, Vol. IV, p. 1230-1233; ID. (ed.), *Ḥorvat Qitmit. An Edomite Shrine in the Biblical Negev,* Tel Aviv 1995; J. GUNNEWEG - H. MOMMSEN, *Instrumental Neutron Activation Analysis and the Origin of Some Cult Objects and Edomite Vessels from the Horvat Qitmit Shrine,* in *Archaeometry* 32 (1990), p. 7-18; P. BECK, *Transjordanian and Levantine Elements in the Iconography of Qitmit,* in *Biblical Archaeology Today, 1990*, Jerusalem 1993, p. 231-236; EAD., *Ḥorvat Qitmit Revisited via 'En Ḥazeva,* in *Tel Aviv* 23 (1996), p. 102-114.

[170] I. BEIT-ARIEH (ed.), *op. cit.* (n. 169), p. 315, Fig. 9:4.

[171] Since the pottery of Arad Stratum XI is very similar to that of Lachish Stratum IV, that ended with Sennacherib's attack in 701 B.C. (cf. here above, p. 374-375), this is the

century B.C.[172] The considerable difference in the fortifications and vessel types between Stratum XI and Strata X-IX[173] does not indicate a gap in the occupation of the site, but another centre of power planning and erecting the new fortress. As Edomite pottery and Assyrian finds, like a bronze weight in the shape of a crouching lion[174], first appear in Strata X-IX, they were very likely built by the Edomite central authority to watch the trade route through the Beersheba Valley. This is also suggested by significant findings belonging to that period. The two inscribed offering dishes, found near the altars of the 7th century shrine at Arad[175], bear each a roughly scratched North Arabian inscription *yḥ*[176]. There can be little doubt that this is an abbreviation of *yd ḥrm*, "possession of the sanctuary", according to an old connotation of *yd*, "hand", preserved in Islamic law. The slightly different shape of *ḥ* in these inscriptions represents the two varieties of the Teimanite *ḥ*. This is an interesting feature, since Teimanites and Sabaeans were associated in the huge caravan attacked by Ninurta-kudurrī-uṣur, the ruler of Sūḫu[177]. It is unlikely that this association was an exceptional case. The fragmentary vessel found in Arad Stratum IX with the name of the fortress written several times, also from left to right[178] like some North Arabian inscriptions, exhibits an Edomite legless *daleth*.

The presence of two steles in the cella[179], paralleled by two asymmetric incense altars, is certainly a feature alien to the Yahwistic tradition[180].

approximate date of the destruction of Arad Stratum XI. This means that the erection of the new stronghold cannot be dated to the mid-8th century B.C., as proposed by Z. HERZOG, *The Fortress Mound at Tel Arad: An Interim Report*, in *Tel Aviv* 29 (2002), p. 3-109 (see p. 26).

172 They are dated from the 8th century B.C. by Z. HERZOG, *art. cit.* (n. 171), in particular p. 14 and 98.

173 L. SINGER-AVITZ, *art. cit.* (n. 63), p. 162.

174 Inscribed lion weights appear in Assyria in the last quarter of the 8th and the early 7th centuries B.C.: F.M. FALES, *Assyro-Aramaica: The Assyrian Lion-Weights*, in K. VAN LERBERGHE - A. SCHOORS (eds.), *Immigration and Emigration within the Ancient Near East. Festschrift E. Lipiński* (OLA 65), Leuven 1995, p. 33-55.

175 Y. AHARONI, *op. cit.* (n. 65), p. 117-119, Nos. 102-103.

176 These are neither 7th-century Phoenician inscriptions, as argued by F.M. CROSS, *Two Offering Dishes with Phoenician Inscriptions from the Sanctuary of 'Arad*, in *BASOR* 235 (1979), p. 75-78, nor Proto-Hebrew (?) inscriptions. The alleged *kāf* of A.F. RAINEY, in Z. HERZOG (ed.), *Beer-sheba* II. *The Early Iron Age Settlements*, Tel Aviv 1984, p. 32, quoted recently by Z. HERZOG, *art. cit.* (n. 171), p. 56, 58, should be dated back to the 11th century B.C.! See here p. 396-397.

177 *RIMB* II, text S.0.1002.2, p. 300, col. IV, 26'-38'.

178 Y. AHARONI, *op. cit.* (n. 65), p. 114-115, No. 99.

179 Z. HERZOG, *art. cit.* (n. 171), p. 63, tries to present the smaller stele as a "roughly worked slab of flint", but on p. 57 he squarely mentions the "stone stele found embedded into the back wall of the later Stratum IX *debir*".

180 The two tablets housed in the Ark of the Covenant may have been stone relics from pre-Yahwistic times, but they never appear in the biblical tradition as divine symbols.

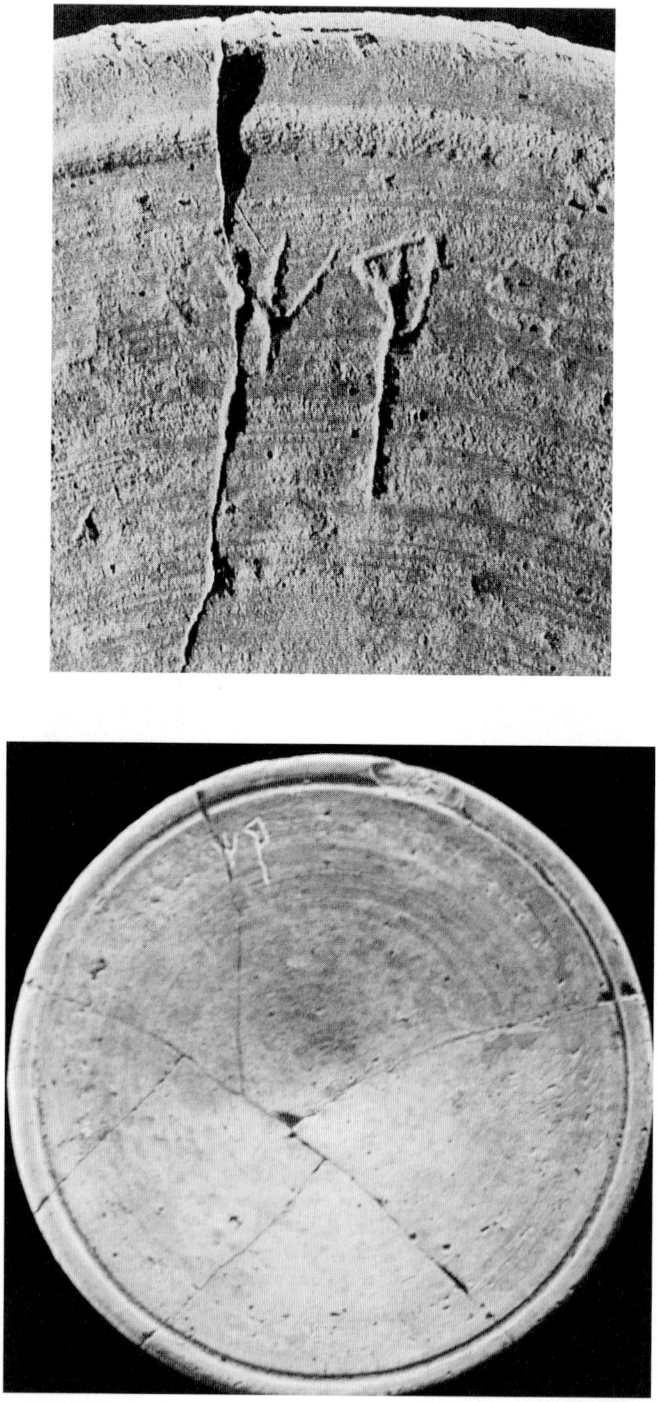

Inscription on an offering dish from the Tell ʿArad sanctuary
(Y. Aharoni, *Arad Inscriptions*, No. 102).

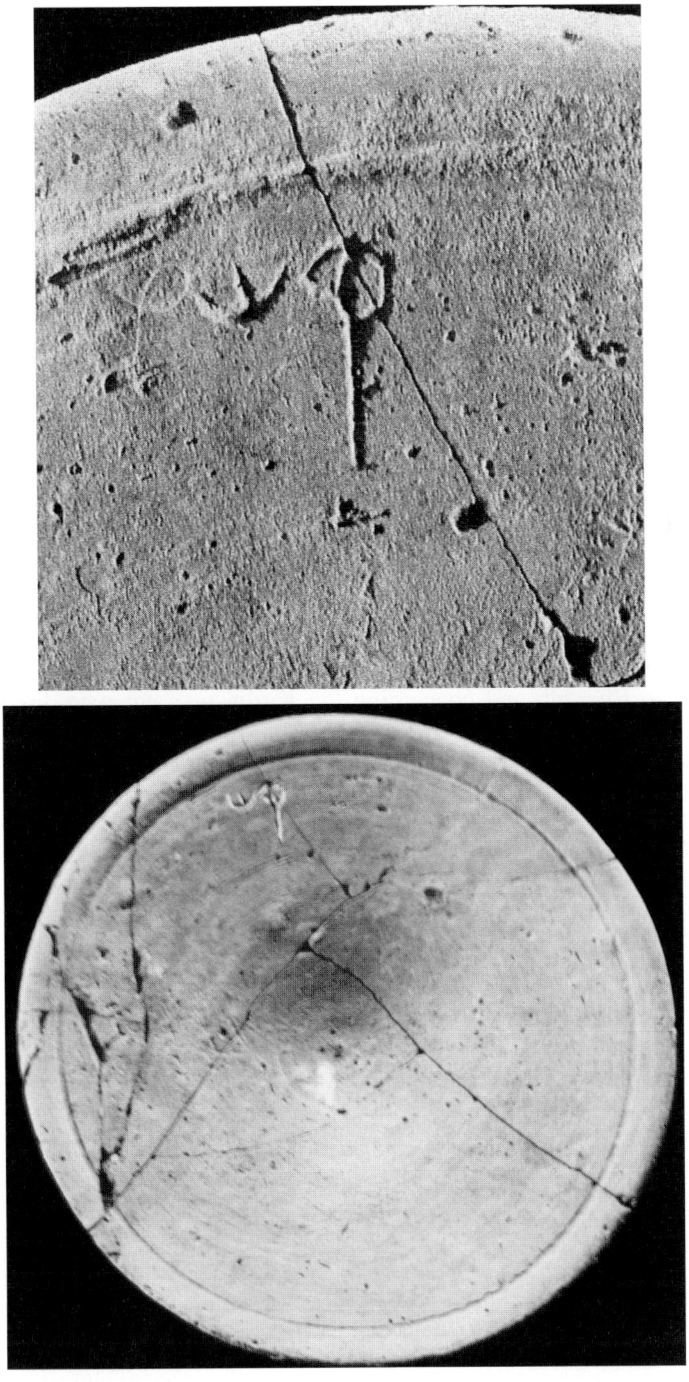

Inscription on an offering dish from the Tell ʿArad sanctuary (Y. Aharoni, *Arad Inscriptions*, No. 103).

The steles symbolize a couple of divinities, possibly ’Il and ’Ilat, as suggested by the North Arabian inscriptions on the two offering dishes. As for the presence of a few Hebrew ostraca (Nos. 59-72) and of "Judaean" pottery in Strata X-IX, it does not have any political significance in the concerned area, on the skirts of the hill-country of Judah.

The fortress has been later occupied by the king of Judah, probably in the second half of the 7th century B.C., perhaps as late as the collapse of the Assyrian power *ca.* 620 B.C. The stronghold of Arad was thus rebuilt in Stratum VIII, *ca.* 620 B.C. There were significant changes in the internal layout of the fortress. In particular, the shrine of foreign gods was suppressed, two buildings were expanded, and the gate structure was modified. The destruction undoubtedly parallels that of Lachish Level III in 598/7 B.C., while Strata VII-VI correspond to Lachish Level II and represent the early 6th century B.C. with a caesura in 587/6 and an epilogue lasting approximately until the flight of Judaeans to Egypt (Jer. 41, 11 - 43, 7) and the third deportation from Judah in the 23rd year of Nebuchadnezzar II's reign (Jer. 52, 30), in 582/1 B.C. The Kittim of the Arad letters from Stratum VI and the *Ynm* of the jar No. 19 from the same room 637 are probably Greek mercenaries of the Babylonian army, garrisoned or operating in southern Judah after 587/6 B.C. The orders given to Elyashib and concerning the Kittim may emanate directly or indirectly from Gedaliah, appointed by the Babylonians as governor of Judah after the capture of Jerusalem.

Malḥata

Tell al-Milḥ (alt. 639 m)[181], better known as Tel Malḥata, is a mound with a superficies of *ca.* 1.5 ha, 14 m high, situated on lowland, 12 km south-west of Tell ‘Arad. The occupation started there in the 8th century B.C., at the site of a former Middle Bronze city. Contrary to Arad, which was only a fortress, this was a town. One can estimate its population at 300-400 inhabitants, women and children included. Renewed excavations brought to light a large amount of pottery datable to the 7th century B.C., including a great percentage of Edomite vessels[182]. Besides, an

[181] Grid ref. 152/069: M. KOCHAVI, *Tel Malḥata,* in *RB* 79 (1972), p. 593-596; ID., *Malhata, Tel,* in *NEAEHL*, Jerusalem 1993, Vol. III, p. 934-936; I. BEIT-ARIEH, *The Excavations at Tel Malḥata - An Interim Report,* in *Qadmoniot* 31 (1998), p. 30-39 (in Hebrew).

[182] Its dating to the 8th century B.C. is based, of course, on its similarity with the pottery of Lachish Stratum III, wrongly dated from the 8th century B.C.: L. SINGER-AVITZ, *art. cit.* (n. 58), p. 56-57, with reference to I. Beit-Arieh and E. Brand. Cf. I. BEIT-ARIEH, *Tel Malḥata - 1998*, in *ESI* 112 (2000), p. 115*. See here below, p. 416.

Edomite ostracon with a list of names was found in the excavation[183]. As mentioned above, in the earlier ceramic assemblage all the cooking pots were of Judaean type, while they were all of Edomite type in the destruction stratum dated by the excavator to the early 6th century B.C.[184]

The problems attending the identification of many sites with ancient names are well known. Tell al-Milḥ is generally regarded as the Μαλιάτθα of Ptolemy and the Μαλαθα of Josephus Flavius[185], who considers it an Idumaean city. Eusebius calls it Μαλααθα and localizes it at 4 miles from Arad and 20 miles from Hebron[186], not far from Jattir[187]. The reference to Jattir can be explained by the relative importance of the place in Roman-Byzantine times, but the distance indicated by Eusebius from Arad to Μαλααθα would exclude the latter's identification with Tell al-Milḥ. Eusebius also records Μωλαδά, but he does not identify it[188]. The reason is his confusion of *Mōlādāh*[189] with Malḥata, that also the *Notitia Dignitatum Or.* XXXIV mentions as *Moleatha* with the camp of a Roman cohort[190], still clearly recognizable before the excavation of Tell al-Milḥ. The 4 miles reported by Eusebius bring us to Ḫirbet al-Quṣeifa (Ḥorvat Kasif), about half-way between Tell 'Arad and Tell al-Milḥ. It is unlikely that a civil settlement, distant 6 km from the fortress, would bear the same name in Eusebius' own opinion[191]. There is rather a confusion between two sites, the second one being certainly more important in Byzantine times, since remains of three Byzantine churches have been found at Ḫirbet al-Quṣeifa[192]. The logical conclusion is that Moladah should be identified with Ḫirbet al-Quṣeifa, 12 km south-east of Jattir[193].

183 M. Kochavi, *art. cit.* (n. 181), in *RB* 79 (1972), p. 595-596.

184 See here above, p. 394, n. 167.

185 Ptolemy, *Geography* V, 16, 4 (p. 996); Josephus Flavius, *Jewish Antiquities* XVIII, 6, 2, §147.

186 Eusebius of Caesarea, *Onomasticon*, in E. Klostermann (ed.), *Eusebius: Das Onomastikon der biblischen Ortsnamen*, Leipzig 1904, p. 14:1-3.

187 *Ibid.*, p. 88:4. This is Ḫirbet 'Attīr, 26 km north-east of Beersheba.

188 *Ibid.*, p. 130:6.

189 Josh. 15, 26; 19, 2; Neh. 11, 26; I Chron. 4, 28.

190 O. Seeck (ed.), *Notitia Dignitatum utriusque Imperii*, Berlin 1876, p. 74:45. The work can be dated to *ca.* 393-405 A.D.

191 A. Alt, *Limes Palaestinae*, in *Palästinajahrbuch* 26 (1930), p. 43-82 (see p. 49-50); Id., *Kleine Schriften zur Geschichte des Volkes Israel* III, München 1959, p. 395-396; M. Avi-Yonah, *op. cit.* (n. 111), p. 78.

192 E. Mader, *Altchristliche Basiliken und Lokaltraditionen in Südjudäa*, Paderborn 1918, p. 225 ff.

193 A site close to Jattir has been proposed for Moladah by Y. Govrin, *The Naḥal Yattir Site Moladah in the Inheritance of the Tribe of Simeon*, in *'Atiqot* 20 (1991), p. 13-23 (in Hebrew with English summary)

Moladah and Malḥata must be distinguished at any rate. In fact, an ostracon from the nearby Ḫirbet al-Ġazza (Ḥorvat 'Uza), dating to the 7th century, mentions a certain "'Amadyahu, son of Zakkūr, from Moladah", *'mdyhw.bn.Zkr.m-Mldh*[194], while *Mlḥt* occurs on an Idumaean ostracon from Maqqedah, dating to the second half of the 4th century B.C.[195] The identification of Tell al-Milḥ with Moladah goes back to E. Robinson[196], whose proposals should always be considered with circumspection. Other identifications have been proposed, but they do not present conclusive evidence. They are either based on incomplete documentation or amount to guesses.

Qaws

The Edomite shrine of Ḫirbet Qiṭmīt, a single period site of the 7th century B.C.[197], is situated only 5 km south-east of Tell al-Milḥ. The relatively high percentage of Edomite pottery points to a direct connection with Edom, while the preponderance of cultic vessels indicates that the site was not domestic in nature. No evidence of destruction by human hand was found, which means that the site has been abandoned, possibly when the collapse of the Assyrian power in the region signified a stagnation and the end of the lucrative trade through the Beersheba Valley in the last quarter of the 7th century B.C. At any case, there is a complete absence of Neo-Babylonian and Persian pottery.

This open-air shrine consisted of a double complex of structures and enclosures (1300 m^2) with stone altars, a plastered basin, and dressed stones. The excavations of 1984-1986 brought there to light remains of about 800 figurines and cult objects, mostly of local origin, as suggested by the neutron activation analysis of twenty-three samples. Six short Edomite inscriptions are incised on potsherds, some with the name of the main Edomite and Idumaean god Qaws (Nos. 2, 3, 4), and a stamp seal bears the legend *l-Šwbn-Qws*, "Belonging to Shuban-Qaws" (No. 7). There is no doubt that Qaws was the main deity of the

[194] I. Beit-Arieh, *The Ostracon of Aḥiqam from Ḥorvat 'Uza*, in *Tel Aviv* 13-14 (1986-87), p. 32-38, Pl. 2:2, line 2.

[195] I. Eph'al - J. Naveh, *Aramaic Ostraca of the Fourth Century BC from Idumaea*, Jerusalem 1996, No. 108, 3. The *ḥ* is somewhat blurred, but the reading seems to be correct.

[196] E. Robinson - E. Smith, *Biblical Researches in Palestine, Mount Sinai and Arabia Petraea* II, Boston 1841, p. 619-622.

[197] Grid ref. 1564/0665. Cf. here above, p. 394, n. 169.

Edomites[198] and that this name implies a community of worshippers that is quite different from the "people of Chemosh " settled in Moab. Their proper names reveal their North Arabian origin[199], while names with the theophorous element Qaws establish a link with the Shasu of Late Bronze II and with the Liḥyanites of Dedan in the Neo-Babylonian and Persian periods[200]. The origin and nature of this deity is important also in order to understand the provenance and the cultural connections of the Edomites.

The divine name Qaws cannot mean "bow", as still assumed sometimes[201] on basis of a superficial comparison of *Qws* with the modern pronunciation of classical and literary Arabic *qaws*, which is a derivative of *qš*. Instead, the theonym is always spelled *qws* in West Semitic script and qws^1 in Liḥyanite, which does not use s^3 [202]. As early as 1887, Theodor Nöldeke explicitly rejected the derivation of the divine name from *qaus*, "bow"[203], but evidence sometimes needs many years to be recognized by all. The ancient pronunciation was nevertheless *Qaws*, as shown by the usual spelling *Qws* of the name in Semitic texts, indicating that *wāw* was a semi-vowel initially, not a *mater lectionis*.

[198] E. A. KNAUF, *Qôs*, in *DDD*, 2nd ed., Leiden-Grand Rapids 1999, p. 674-677, with a very incomplete bibliography. One should mention in particular: J.T. MILIK, *Nouvelles inscriptions nabatéennes,* in *Syria* 35 (1958), p. 227-251, Pls. XVIII-XXI; ID., *Notes d'épigraphie orientale 2. À propos du dieu édomite Qôs,* in *Syria* 37 (1960), p. 95-96; Th. VRIEZEN, *The Edomite Deity Qaus*, in *Oudtestamentische Studiën* 14 (1965), p. 330-353; J. STARCKY, *Le temple nabatéen de Khirbet Tannur,* in *RB* 75 (1966), p. 206-235, Pls. XV-XX (see p. 208-221); J. NAVEH, *The Scripts of Two Ostraca from Elath,* in *BASOR* 183 (1966), p. 27-30 (see p. 28-30); M. DU BUIT, *Qôs*, in *DBS* IX, Paris 1979, col. 674-678; H. NIEHR, *Religionen in Israels Umwelt. Einführung in die nordwestsemitischen Religionen Syrien-Palästinas* (Die neue Echter-Bibel. Ergänzungsband 5 zum Alten Testament), Würzburg 1998, p. 217.

[199] One should refer in particular to the two names *Mškt*, "Tenacious", and *Wḥzm*, "Violent", engraved on the seal from 'Ain al-Ḥuṣb ('En Ḥaẓeva); cf. here above, p. 388.

[200] HARDING, *Arabian Names*, p. 164 ($Gltqs^1$, "Splendor of Qaws"), 400 ($'bdqs^1$, "Servant of Qaws"), 491 (Qws^1br, "Qaws is loyal", and Qws^1mlk, "Qaws is king", perhaps Qws^1t). Two names appear also in Minaic inscriptions, but most likely designate Liḥyanites; cf. HARDING, *Arabian Names*, p. 102 ($Brqs^1$, "Qaws is loyal"), 326 (S^1lmtqs^1, "Bounty of Qaws"). The spelling with s^1 results from the merging of s^1 and s^3 in Liḥyanite, that only uses the signs s^1 and s^2, like other North Arabian dialects. Cf. LIPIŃSKI, *Semitic,* § 14.3. The monophthongization of *aw* takes place when the theonym is the second element of the name.

[201] J.R. BARTLETT, *op. cit.* (n. 46), p. 200-204; E. A. KNAUF, *art. cit.* (n. 198), p. 676-677.

[202] See here above, n. 200.

[203] Th. NÖLDEKE, rev. of J. WELLHAUSEN'S *Reste arabischen Heidentums* (Berlin 1887), in *ZDMG* 41 (1887), p. 707-726 (see p. 714).

Another explanation of the theonym has been proposed recently by L. Zalcman[204], who relates *qws* to Hebrew *qwṣ*, "to feel a sickening dread". The interchange of *ṣ* and *s* is attested in some Arabic dialects, when the word contains an emphatic consonant. The phonological tendency at work consists then either in turning all consonants, especially *s*, into emphatic ones or making the whole word non-emphatic[205]. The name *Qws* contains an emphatic sound, but the theonym *Qws* is never written *Qwṣ*. The Idumaean one-word names *Qwṣ*, *Qwṣy*, *Qṣ'*, *Qṣy* are based on the noun *qwṣ*, "thorn", that also forms biblical proper names. As for the examples of the interchange of *ṣ* and *s* quoted by Zalcman, they are not adequate. The difference between *śḥq* and *ṣḥq* < *ṣ́ḥq*, "to laugh", goes back to allophones of the lateral phoneme *ś/ṣ́*, while the variant forms *mṣyqyn* and *msyqyn*, "tax collectors", *qpṣ* (Hebrew) and *qps* (Syriac), "to shrink", *'qṣ* and *'qs*, "to bend", occur in texts of the Byzantine period, when the phonetic distinction *s/ṣ* was weakened and the spellings sometimes blundered. In good method, one cannot transfer such data of Talmudic Hebrew and Syriac to the Edomite of the mid-first millennium B.C.

If Qaws was a Weather-god, as some authors have argued on textual or iconographic ground[206], his name could be related to a variant of the root attested in Arabic as *ġayṯ*, "(abundant) rain". Qaws would then be the god responsible for bringing rain. This view is defensible in theory. In fact, like Ammonite and Gileadite, Edomite has probably preserved the phoneme /θ/, which was marked by *samek* in Hebrew and in the Aramaic inscription of Tell Fekheriye. Likewise, Edomite must have preserved /γ/. This approximate sound was marked in old Aramaic by *qōf*, and one can assume that this practice was borrowed by Edomite scribes together with the Aramaic script[207]. All this would mean that the spelling

[204] L. ZALCMAN, *Shield of Abraham, Fear of Isaac, Dread of Esau*, in *ZAW* 117 (2005), p. 405-410.

[205] J. CANTINEAU, *Le dialecte arabe de Palmyre*, Beyrouth 1934, p. 39-40; ID., *Les parlers arabes du Ḥōrān*, Paris 1946, p. 103; C. RABIN, *Ancient West-Arabian*, London 1951, p. 195-196.

[206] J.A. DEARMAN, *Edomite Religion, A Survey and Examination of Some Recent Contributions*, in D.V. EDELMAN (ed.), *'You shall not abhor an Edomite for he is your brother'. Edom and Seir in History and Tradition* (Archaeology and Biblical Series 3), Atlanta 1995, p. 119-136; P. BECK, in I. BEIT-ARIEH (ed.), *Ḥorvat Qitmit. An Edomite Shrine in the Biblical Negev*, Tel Aviv 1995, p. 187-189; EAD., *art. cit.* (n. 121), p. 107-111.

[207] There is no evidence that Hebrew script was first adopted by the Edomites, but was modified in the 8th century B.C. under the influence of Aramaic script. This was the opinion of J. NAVEH, *art. cit.* (n. 198), p. 27-30; ID., *Early History of the Alphabet. An Introduction to West-Semitic Epigraphy and Palaeography*, Jerusalem 1982, p. 102-105.

of the name in the Persian period, attested by many proper names of the Aramaic ostraca from Idumaea[208], follows an old scribal tradition. However, what is disturbing in this hypothesis is the absence of any variant despite the approximate spelling of the theonym. This interpretation should therefore be abandoned and one ought to pay a closer attention to the composite Aramaic-Idumaean theonym in Greek dress *ΠΑΚΕΙΔΟΚΩΣΟΣ*[209]. Here, Qaws is identified with a divine "Overseer", *Paqīdā*, attested by two inscriptions found at Ğerash[210]. If the equivalence is correct, Qaws might be a name derived from the same root *gws* as Arabic *ğāsa*, "to look around", but in Edomite a voiced *qāf*[211] would of old have replaced the North Arabian *gāf*, adding a pharyngeal emphasis. Whether Qaws was then imagined as a tribal "overseer" or as a heavenly and lunar "overseer" of flocks, this is a matter for further speculation.

Chronology helps also distinguishing the Edomite theonym *Qws* from *qyś*, which designates a holy grove in Nabataean inscriptions, especially in the phrase *Mnwtw w-qyšh*[212], "Manawat and her grove", comparable to *Dwšr' w-mwtbh*, "Dushara and his throne", and to *Yhwh w-'šrth*, "Yahwe and his shrine". The Aramaic word *qyś* > *qys*, "grove, wood",

Instead, the formal script shows some analogies with Moabite: L.G. HERR, *The Scripts of Ancient Northwest Semitic Seals*, Missoula 1978, p. 161; ID., *Formal Scripts of Iron Age Transjordan*, in *BASOR* 238 (1980), p. 21-34 (see p. 29-31).

208 A provisional list is provided by A. LEMAIRE, *Nouvelles inscriptions araméennes d'Idumée* II, Paris 2002, p. 279-280.

209 A. PLASSART, *Les sanctuaires et les cultes du Mont Cynthe* (Exploration archéologique de Délos 11), Paris 1928, p. 266; P. ROUSSEL - M. LAUNEY, *Inscriptions de Délos (nos 2220-2879)*, Paris 1937, No. 2311. Cf. L.-H. VINCENT, *Le dieu saint Paqeidas à Gérasa*, in *RB* 49 (1940), p. 98-129, Pls. I-VI (see p. 102-105).

210 C.B. WELLES, in C.H. KRAELING, *Gerasa, City of Decapolis*, New Haven 1938, p. 575-616, see Nos. 17 and 18, Pls. CVIa and XCVIIIc; cf. L.-H. VINCENT, *art. cit.* (n. 209), p. 99-101, Fig. 1 and Pl. I.

211 It appears in some cuneiform spellings, like *gi-ra-a* for *qīrā*, "the city", or *Gi-id-ra-a-a* for "Qedarite" (see LIPIŃSKI, *Aramaeans*, p. 41, n. 100, and here above, p. 358). - *Qāf* replaces *gāf* also in Hijazi *qaṣṣa* or *qiṣṣa* and South Arabian *qṣ* for common Arabic *ğaṣṣ* and Syriac *geṣṣā*, "plaster" (cf. C. RABIN, *op. cit.* [n. 205], p. 125), but emphatic *ṣ* can play a role here. This is not the case of *ngd* and *nqd*, apparently going back to the same root that means "to set out"; cf. E. LIPIŃSKI, *"Leadership". The Roots* DBR *and* NGD *in Aramaic*, in M. DIETRICH - I. KOTTSIEPER (eds.), *"Und Mose schrieb dieses Lied auf". Studien zum Alten Testament und zum Alten Orient. Festschrift für O. Loretz* (AOAT 250), Münster 1998, p. 501-514 (see p. 509-514). Derivatives with *qāf* are attested in Ṣafaitic and Nabataean proper names, thus in the former Edomite area.

212 See the discussion in J.F. HEALEY, *The Nabataean Tomb Inscriptions at Mada'in Salih* (JSS, Suppl. 1), Oxford 1993, p. 119-120.

attested also in Akkadian (*qīšu*), appears later as theophorous element in Arabic proper names, like ʻAbd-al-Qais, Imru'-al-Qais[213].

Ramath-Negeb and ʻArʻarah

About 5 km north-east of Ḫirbet Qiṭmīt, the site of Ḫirbet al-Ġazza (Ḥorvat ʻUza), excavated in 1982-1986, has yielded a complete Edomite ostracon. The site consisted in a new, rectangular fort, measuring 51 m by 42 m and surrounded by a wall 1.50 m thick[214]. Its superficies of 0.21 ha could be occupied by 40-50 persons, women and children included, but an unwalled settlement developed outside the fort, increasing the total inhabited area to 0.9 ha with a population that can be estimated at 150-200 persons. This fort has been built in the 7th century B.C., about 10 km south of the fortress of Tell ʻArad, as a Judaean outpost at the Edomite border. The ancient name of the site, which is situated on the Wādī al-Qeini, was believed to be *Qynh*, as indicated by the name of the wadi[215]. This methodologically correct approach is nevertheless challenged by the summary of an aetiological account in Judg. 1, 16. The storyteller explains the origin of a Kenite settlement in the Judaean Desert, near Arad, by the immigration of a Kenite clan from Tamar, the present-day ʻAin al-Ḥuṣb. The name of the place is not given, but it had to be related to *Qyny*, "Kenite", thus *Qynh*. The summary is based on an ancient account, for it still uses the terms *ngb* and *ʻmlqy* in their original sense of "store" and "enclosure"[216]. Some explanatory notes have been added, but they do not disturb the initial notice: "The sons of the Kenite ... went up from the city of Tamar ... to the Desert of Judah, which is beside the Store of Arad, and (the Kenite) went and dwelled next to the enclosure". The enclosure is obviously the one of Arad and the nearby Kenite settlement was probably *Qynh*, identified by Y. Aharoni with Ḫirbet Ṭāyeb (Ḥorvat Ṭob)[217], about 4 km north-east of Arad. The set-

[213] Cf. M. Höfner, in H.W. Haussig (ed.), *Götter und Mythen im Vorderen Orient*, Stuttgart 1965, p. 460-461.

[214] Grid ref. 1657/0687: I. Beit-Arieh - B. Cresson, *Ḥorvat ʻUza: A Fortified Outpost on the Eastern Negev Border*, in *BA* 54 (1991), p. 126-135; I. Beit-Arieh, *ʻUza, Ḥorvat*, in *NEAEHL*, Jerusalem 1993, Vol. IV, p. 1495-1497.

[215] This identification, proposed by A. Musil, *Arabia Petraea* II, *Edom* II, Wien 1908, p. 19-20, was followed by Abel, *Géographie* I, p. 273; II, p. 88, 149, 417-418; A. Lemaire, *op. cit.* (n. 66), p. 191, and by the excavators of Ḫirbet al-Ġazza.

[216] See here above, p. 109-110 and p. 368, 370.

[217] Y. Aharoni, *Three Hebrew Ostraca from Arad,* in *BASOR* 197 (1970), p. 16-42 (see p. 22-24); Id., *op. cit.* (n. 65), p. 146-148 (in Hebrew). Aharoni has thus abandoned his previous identification of *Qynh* with Ḫirbet al-Ġazza.

tlement is mentioned in Josh. 15, 22 among the localities of the tribe of Judah and it appears with Arad in Arad ostracon 24, line 12. A Kenite settlement at Ḫirbet Ṭāyeb fits these occurrences of *Qynh* and concretizes the role played by the Kenites in stories related to David (I Sam. 27, 10; 30, 29).

Y. Aharoni identified Ḫirbet al-Ġazza with Ramath-Negeb[218], where *ngb* is used in its original meaning of "store" or "supplies", not in the topographic sense of "southern region". In other words, Ramath-Negeb means "Hill of the Store". The site is located at the eastern end of the Beersheba Valley, thus fitting its mention in Josh. 19, 8, where Ramath-Negeb seems to be situated at the border of the territory allotted to the tribe of Simeon. It guards the access to the valley by the road coming from the Wādī Arabah and from Edom, and is therefore exposed to Edomite attacks. It is listed in I Sam. 30, 24.27 among the beneficiaries of the booty taken by David from the "Amalekites". It is more important to pay attention to Arad ostracon 24, where Ramath-Negeb is mentioned twice. It results from the context that the town was threatened by the Edomites and that military help had to be sent urgently from other forts[219], namely from Arad and Qinah. The ostracon can be dated palaeographically to the late 7th or early 6th centuries B.C., but it was found in a stratigraphically undetermined area on the western side of the mound, not with the ostraca forming the so-called "Elyashib archive". It was written before the events of 598/7, perhaps about 609 B.C., when Egyptian troops had penetrated in Judah, creating conditions that could favour an Edomite attack. Despite its fortifications with solid walls and a six-chambered gate, Ramath-Negeb was taken and destroyed, most likely by the Edomites, deprived of their lucrative trade after the fall of the Assyrian empire. The date of 586 B.C., proposed by several authors, is not based on archaeological data, while literary sources, like the Bible, do not appear to have been available to them. The oracle of Jer. 13, 18-19, addressed to Jehoiachin and the queen mother (cf. II Kings 24, 8.12), clearly was uttered just prior to Jerusalem's surrender in 597 B.C.

[218] See the references in n. 217. A. LEMAIRE's identification of Ramath-Negeb with Ḫirbet al-Ġarra (*op. cit.* [n. 66], p. 191-192) is contradicted by Arad ostracon 24, since troops from *Qynh*, supposedly Ḫirbet al-Ġazza, the first major Judaean stronghold on the road from Edom, should be sent westwards to protect Ḫirbet al-Ġarra. As for ABEL's opinion, *Géographie* II, p. 344, one should stress that there is hardly any phonetic correspondence between Ḥaṣar Gadda (Josh. 15, 27) and Ḫirbet al-Ġazza.

[219] Y. AHARONI, *op. cit.* (n. 65), p. 48-51; A. LEMAIRE, *L'ostracon 'Ramat-Négeb' et la topographie historique du Négeb,* in *Semitica* 23 (1973), p. 11-26; ID., *op. cit.* (n. 66), p. 188-195. However, Lemaire's identification of Ramath-Negeb with Ḫirbet al-Ġarra cannot be accepted (see here above, n. 218).

"Say to the king and the queen mother:
'Humble yourself, sit down,
for from your heads has fallen
your proud crown.
The storage cities[220] are bolted
and none can open.
All Judah has been deported:
it has been deported completely'".

Edom's active participation in Babylonian hostilities against Jehoiakim of Judah (608-598 B.C.) and his son Jehoiachin (598-597 B.C.), even prior to the events of 598-597 B.C., can be assumed on the basis of the Syriac text of II Kings 24, 2, which reads "Edom" instead of "Aram". A similar change should then be adopted in Jer. 35, 11, and these events be associated, at least in a general way, with Arad ostracon 24 ordering the dispatching of Judaean troops to Ramath-Negeb in order to prevent its capture by the Edomites. The role played by Edomites at least from 598/7 on is echoed also in Is. 34, 1-17; Jer. 49, 7-22, and in the booklet of Obadiah. It does not concern Jerusalem directly, but the Judaean cities in the Beersheba Valley, the northern Negeb, and even the Judaean highland.

The discovery of 22 Hebrew ostraca and inscriptions in the gatehouse of the Ḫirbet al-Ġazza fortress and only of one Edomite ostracon gives the impression that the fort was in Judaean hands. The presence of an ostracon with a Hebrew literary text[221] even suggests that a professional Hebrew scribe had been working there for some time. Moreover, a small fort (21 x 25 m) was discovered at Ḥorvat Radum, some 2 km south of Ḫirbet al-Ġazza, and it yielded five Hebrew ostraca as well[222]. The linkage of Baalath-Beer to Ramath-Negeb in Josh. 19, 8, where Simeon's eastern border is fixed, suggests that Baalath-Beer, "The Mistress of the Well", is the ancient name of Ḥorvat Radum.

The Edomite letter addressed to Lamalek or (E)limelek with a blessing by Qaws and practical dispositions[223] seems to imply that the fort of

[220] For the meaning of *ngb*, see here above, p. 109-110. The same phrase has a completely different meaning in Jer. 32, 44; 33, 13; Obadiah 20. "Storage cities" are towns with royal storehouses, large pillared buildings like the so-called "stables of Solomon" at Megiddo.

[221] I. Beit-Arieh, *A Literary Ostracon from Ḥorvat 'Uza*, in *Tel Aviv* 20 (1993), p. 55-63.

[222] Grid ref. 1659/0665: I. Beit-Arieh, *Radum*, in *NEAEHL*, Jerusalem 1993, Vol. IV, p. 1254-1255.

[223] I. Beit-Arieh - B. Cresson, *An Edomite Ostracon from Horvat 'Uza*, in *Tel Aviv* 12 (1985), p. 96-101 and Pl. 12:2. Cf. also W. Zwickel, *Das 'edomitische' Ostrakon aus*

Ḫirbet al-Ġazza was under Edomite control and that the addressee was its commander. It is possible that the fortress changed hands without any fight leaving permanent traces or that the small Judaean garrison simply abandoned the site, which was immediately occupied by the Edomites. This could have happened at the time of one of the Babylonian invasions of Judah, in 597 or 587 B.C., but possibly earlier, in the troublesome years when the Egyptian forces of Necho entered Palestine, about 609 B.C. In fact, the palaeography of the two published Hebrew ostraca suggests an earlier date than that of the ostraca from Stratum VI at Arad. Since the *yōd* of both ostraca still has its foot-stroke, a date *ca.* 610-590 B.C. would be appropriate. The Ahiqam ostracon from Ḫirbet al-Ġazza might be a message announcing to the Judaean commander of the fort that three supplementary men will be sent to reinforce the small garrison[224]. The patronymic and the origin of the second man suggest however that he or his father were native from Edom, despite his own Yahwistic name:

1) *⌜š⌝lm.l’ḥqm.bn.Mšlm*	“Greetings! To Ahiqam, son of Meshullam.
2) *‘mdyhw.bn.Zkr.m-Mldh*	‘Amadyahu, son of Zakkūr, from Moladah.
3) *Hš‘yhw.bn.Nwy.m-Rptn*	Hosha‘yahu, son of Nawiy, from Raptān.
4) *Mky.bn.Hṣlyhw.m-Mqdh*	Maki, son of Hiṣṣilyahu, from Maqqedah.”

The name *Nwy* still occurs in Ṣafaitic inscriptions and means “Neighbour” or “Friend”[225]. The toponym *Rftn* is attested in a Minaean inscription[226]. This is certainly a different place, but derivatives of the common noun *rpt*, “stall”, with the widespread suffix *-ān* can occur in various regions. The patronymic and the toponym seem to be related to Arabic and should therefore be regarded as Edomite. The name *Hš‘yhw* is instead Hebrew and would thus attest a case of an Edomite settled in a Judaean community. Settlements with a mixed population would of course accept easier Edomite rule.

The analysis of the four proper names in the Edomite ostracon is also informative, as none of them is Yahwistic. They imply a non-Judaean population:

1) *’mr.Lmlk.’mr.l-Blbl*	“Lamalek speaks: Say to Bulbul:
2) *hšlm.’t.whbrktk*	Are you well? I recommend you

Ḫirbet Ġazza (Ḥorvat ‘Uza), in *BN* 41 (1988), p. 36-40; H. Misgav, *Two Notes on the Ostraca from Ḥorvat ‘Uza*, in *IEJ* 40 (1990), p. 215-217.

224 I. Beit-Arieh, *The Ostracon of Aḥiqam from Horvat ‘Uza*, in *Tel Aviv* 13-14 (1986-87), p. 32-38, Pl. 2.

225 Harding, *Arabian Names*, p. 604.

226 *RÉS* 2754, 2 = Halévy 169; cf. Harding, *Arabian Names*, p. 252.

3) *l-Qws.w't.tn.'t.h'kl*	to Qaws. And now: Give the grain,
4) *'šr.'md.'ḥ'mh.yšlḥ*?	which is with Aḥimmahu; he should send? (it).
5) *whrm.'z'l.'l mz[r'.tn*?]	And set 'Azzi'il over the sow[ing. Give?]
6) [*'t*?].*ḥmr.h'kl*	[a] donkey-load of the grain".

If the name of the sender consists of the preposition *l* and of the noun *mlk*, "king", it would be a typical name of Court officials: "Belonging to the king"[227]. The addressee bears a one-word name which can be compared with Arabic *bulbul*, "nightingale", and with the Old Babylonian proper name *Ba-al-ba-lum* /*Balbal-um*/[228], with the mimation characteristic of that period.

The keeper of the grain bears a name which is attested also on two apparently Hebrew seal impressions, but neither patronymic is Yahwistic: *'ḥ'mh Dml'* and *l-'ḥ'mh Krmy*[229].

The name occurs quite often in Neo-Assyrian and Neo-Babylonian texts, and has a parallel in Sabaic. The Neo-Assyrian spellings are PAP-*im-me-e*, PAP-*im-me*, PAP-*me-e*[230], while Neo-Babylonian texts provide the form ŠEŠ-*im-me-e*/*'*[231]. Both logograms PAP and ŠEŠ stand for *aḫu*, "brother". From the comparison of these names it is evident that they mean "The brother of his mother", *'Aḫ-'immeh*, i.e. "his uncle". This interpretation is confirmed by the Babylonian name *A-ḫi-um-mi-šu*[232], which has the same meaning. The noun "mother" is usually vocalized *'imm*, but one also encounters ŠEŠ-*um-me-e*[233], with a secondary form *'umm* resulting from the labialization of the vowel *i* under the influence of the nasal labial *m*. The *aleph* can be dropped in the middle of the name, which was then pronounced *'Aḫimmeh* or *'Aḫummeh*, and could be written PAP-*me-e* in cuneiform and *'ḫmh* in West Semitic script[234]. These names are paralleled in Sabaic by *'ḫt-'mhw*[235], "The sister of his mother", and they mean that a newborn child takes the place of the deceased maternal uncle or aunt in the family. This

[227] One may compare the contemporaneous West Semitic feminine name *Le-be-el*, "Belonging to the husband / Baal / lord"; cf. C. AMBOS, *Le-Bēl*, in *PNA* II/2, Helsinki 2001, p. 659. In North Arabian, one finds *L-'l*, "Belonging to God", *L-S*[1]*ms*[2], "Belonging to the Sun-god", *L-'m*, "Belonging to the Ancestor", *L-Qs*[2] or *L-Qys*[2], "Belonging to Qayš": HARDING, *Arabian Names*, p. 508, 515, 517, 519, 520.

[228] I.J. GELB, *Computer-aided Analysis of Amorite* (AS 21), Chicago 1980, p. 116.

[229] R. DEUTSCH, *Biblical Period Hebrew Bullae. The Josef Chaim Kaufman Collection*, Tel Aviv 2003, Nos. 70 and 71, p. 407.

[230] A. BERLEJUNG - K. RADNER, *Aḫ-immê*, in *PNA* I/1, Helsinki 1998, p. 65-66.

[231] K.L. TALLQVIST, *Neubabylonisches Namenbuch*, Helsingfors 1905, p. 4a.

[232] J.J. STAMM, *Die akkadische Namengebung*, Leipzig 1939, p. 302.

[233] A. BERLEJUNG - K. RADNER, *art. cit.* (n. 230), p. 66, No. 5.

[234] P. BORDREUIL - A. LEMAIRE, *Nouveaux sceaux hébreux, araméens et ammonites*, in *Semitica* 26 (1976), p. 45-63 (see p. 48); N. AVIGAD - B. SASS, *op. cit.* (n. 116), p. 418, No. 1104.

[235] HARDING, *Arabian Names*, p. 29.

reveals a strong feeling of the continuation of the family and of the permanence of the “Name”.

The fourth person mentioned in the letter is *‘z’l*, “God is strong”. The name is attested also at Ḫirbet al-Ġarra, where *l-‘z*⌜’⌝[*l*] is incised on the shoulder of a pithos from Stratum VII[236], and it occurs likewise in Liḥyanite[237]. It should be vocalized *‘Azzi-’Il*, despite the absence of gemination in its cuneiform notations[238].

About 8 km south-west of Ḫirbet Qiṭmīt and 7 km south of Tell al-Milḥ, the prominent Ḫirbet ‘Ar‘ara (Aroer) overlooks an important well. A Herodian fort was built there above an Iron Age fortress from the late 8th-7th centuries B.C., which enclosed an area of about 1 ha, doubled by quarters built outside the wall with offsets[239]. The rich ceramic material from this period includes Edomite pottery, which may attest to the cultural closeness of Edom. According to I Sam. 30, 24.28, Aroer is one of the cities in the Negeb to which David distributed the booty taken from the “Amalekites”, and it is believed to be included in the southern district of Judah, in Josh. 15, 22, where *‘r‘rh* should be read instead of *‘d‘dh*. The discovery of jar handles with the Hebrew *lmlk* and *zyp* inscriptions[240], on the one hand, and of a jasper seal with the Edomite inscription *l-Qws’*[241] and an incomplete Edomite ostracon[242], on the other, leads to raising the same question as in the case of Ḫirbet al-Ġazza, viz.: Did this settlement with some 400-500 inhabitants pass at a certain moment in Edomite hands?

236 I. Beit-Arieh, *Tel ‘Ira: A Stronghold in the Biblical Negev*, Tel Aviv 1999, p. 410-411.

237 Harding, *Arabian Names*, p. 417.

238 J.A. Brinkman, *Azi-il*, in *PNA* I/1, Helsinki 1998, p. 239. Cf. I.J. Gelb, *op. cit.* (n. 228), p. 15 and 268, sub ‘AZZ.

239 Grid ref. 1479/0623: A. Biran - R. Cohen, *Aroer*, in *IEJ* 26 (1976), p. 138-140; 27 (1977), p. 250-251, Pl. 38; 28 (1978), p. 197-199, Pl. 32C-D; 31 (1981), p. 131-132, Pl. 24A-D; 32 (1982), p. 161-163, Pl. 23; Id., *Aroër*, in *RB* 83 (1976), p. 256-257, Pls. XXVI-XXVII; 84 (1977), p. 273-275, Pl. IXd; 85 (1978), p. 425-427, Pl. XXVIII; 86 (1979), p. 465-466; 89 (1982), p. 240-245, Pl. VIII; Id., *Aroer in the Negev*, in *Y. Aharoni Volume* (ErIs 15), Jerusalem 1981, p. 250-273 (in Hebrew); A. Biran, *Aroer (in Judea)*, in *NEAEHL*, Jerusalem 1993, Vol. I, p. 89-92.

240 A. Biran - R. Cohen, *art. cit.* (n. 239), in *RB* 83 (1976), p. 257.

241 A. Biran - R. Cohen, *art. cit.* (n. 239), in *IEJ* 26 (1976), p. 139 and Pl. 28B, and in *RB* 84 (1977), p. 274 and Pl. IXd; N. Avigad - B. Sass, *op. cit.* (n. 116), p. 392-393, No. 1055.

242 A. Biran - R. Cohen, *art. cit.* (n. 239), in *RB* 85 (1978), p. 427 and Pl. XXVIIIe; J. Naveh, *Published and Unpublished Aramaic Ostraca*, in *‘Atiqot. English Series* 17 (1985), p. 114-121, Pls. XIX-XX (see p. 120-121, Pl. XX, 13).

Eltolad and Ḥormah

An important settlement has been excavated at Ḫirbet al-Ġarra (Tel 'Ira)[243], about 4 km northwest of Tell al-Milḥ. Stratum VII of Ḫirbet al-Ġarra goes back to the first half of the 7th century B.C.[244] and one may assume that the city of this phase occupied the entire mound, which extends over some 2.5 ha, with a population estimated at *ca.* 500-600 inhabitants. This was therefore the largest town in the region and it was variously identified in the past[245]. An important new element is provided by a "fiscal" bulla of Eltolad, published in 1990 by N. Avigad[246]. It dates very likely from the 26th year of Josiah's reign over Judah, i.e. from 613 B.C.: *b-26 šnh 'ltld lmlk*, "in year 26. Eltolad for the king". The ancient place name *'Arad 'Ilat-awlād*[247] is attested here with the reduction of the diphthong *aw* > *ō*, which is quite normal in Hebrew. The use of a "fiscal" bulla seems to indicate that the town was relatively important. This is why we suggest identifying it with Ḫirbet al-Ġarra.

Ḫirbet al-Mšāš (Tel Masos)[248], 2.5 km south-west of Ḫirbet al-Ġarra, was reoccupied towards the end of Iron Age I (Stratum III), after a gap of several centuries[249]. From the exceptional size of the settlement, covering an area of about 6 ha, one may infer that it was an agricultural centre and a trading point for the entire region, at least in the period 950-875 B.C. The abundant water supply and the fertility of the soil explain the existence of this large, unfortified village, which does not show major destruction layers for more than a century. It was completely abandoned in the 9th century, probably for a more strategic and easier defensible position. In the 7th century, however, a new settlement, also unwalled, was established near the wells, about 500 m from the Middle Bronze earth rampart of Ḫirbet al-Mšāš. Its area may be estimated at 0.5 ha,

[243] Grid ref. 1487/0713. Cf. I. Beit-Arieh, *op. cit.* (n. 236); Id., *'Ira, Tel*, in *NEAEHL*, Jerusalem 1993, Vol. II, p. 642-646.

[244] Comparison with the pottery of Lachish Stratum III, dated to the 8th instead of the 7th century B.C., leads L. Singer-Avitz, *art. cit.* (n. 92), p. 84-86, to the unlikely dating of Stratum VII at Ḫirbet al-Ġarra from the second half of the 8th century B.C.

[245] A. Lemaire, *op. cit.* (n. 66), p. 191-192, who proposes Ramath-Negeb, hardly acceptable (see here above, p. 405, n. 218).

[246] N. Avigad, *Two Hebrew 'Fiscal' Bullae*, in *IEJ* 40 (1990), p. 262-266, Pl. 28A-D (see p. 262-265, Pl. 28A-B); N. Avigad - B. Sass, *op. cit.* (n. 116), p. 177-178, No. 421.

[247] See here above, p. 123.

[248] Grid ref. 146/069.

[249] V. Fritz - A. Kempinski (eds.), *Ergebnisse der Ausgrabungen auf der Ḫirbet el-Mšāš (Tel Māśōś) 1972-1975*, Wiesbaden 1983; A. Kempinski, *Masos, Tel*, in *NEAEHL*, Jerusalem 1993, Vol. III, p. 986-989. The chronology of Z. Herzog - L. Singer-Avitz, *art. cit.* (n. 44), p. 222-223, still seems to be too high.

what implies a population of 100-125 inhabitants. The whole site was identified with the biblical Ḥormah in the territory of Simeon[250]. The rampart and the remains of the early Iron Age settlement were certainly recognizable in Iron Age II. An aetiological story thus explained the visible ruins by telling its destruction (*ḥērem*) by the Israelites entering Canaan (Numb. 21, 3; Judg. 1, 17) and taking revenge of a battle lost there in a first attempt at reaching the Judaean highland (Numb. 14, 45; Deut. 1, 44). The name Ḥormah, "wholly destruction", attested also in other passages of the Bible[251], is no real place name. The toponym obviously refers to conspicuous ruins and implies the existence of the aetiological legend. According to Judg. 1, 17, Ḥormah would have replaced the ancient name Zephath. The Middle Bronze toponym was of course long forgotten and an actual settlement could hardly be called Ḥormah. Zephath may instead have been the name of the early Iron Age locality, prior to the appearance of the aetiological legend. The presence of Edomite pottery on the 7th-century small tell[252], as well as of two ostraca, confirms the general picture of the situation in the region.

Tell as-Seba‘

At Tell as-Seba‘ (Tel Beersheba)[253], painted Edomite ware appears already in the earlier phase of Strata III-II, destroyed in a huge conflagration *ca.* 600 B.C.[254] The city is still mentioned in Arad ostracon 3,

[250] Y. AHARONI, *The Negeb*, in D.W. THOMAS (ed.), *Archaeology and the Old Testament Study*, Oxford 1967, p. 384-403 (see p. 400-401); R. DE VAUX, *Histoire ancienne d'Israël* (I), Paris 1971, p. 490-491, 500; A. LEMAIRE, *op. cit.* (n. 66), p. 193; etc. But see the objections formulated already by F. CRÜSEMANN, *Überlegungen zur Identifikation der Ḫirbet el-Mšāš (Tēl Māśōś)*, in *ZDPV* 89 (1973), p. 211-224, in particular p. 214-218, although his identification of Ḫirbet al-Mšāš with Ziqlag is questionable as well.

[251] Josh. 12, 14; 15, 30; 19, 4; I Sam. 30, 30; I Chron. 4, 30. V. FRITZ, *Israel in der Wüste*, Marburg 1970, p. 89-93, regards the biblical account of Numb. 21, 1-3 and Judg. 1, 17 as an aetiology of the place name. However, "Ḥormah" has been **created** by the aetiology, just like the story of the battles between the Israelites and the king of Arad, who appears with the king of Ḥormah, side by side, in Josh. 12, 14. The aetiological legends have been conceived by the storyteller to explain the conspicuous ruins of the Early Bronze site at Arad and of the early settlement at Ḫirbet al-Mšāš.

[252] O. ZIMHONI, *The Pottery*, in V. FRITZ - A. KEMPINSKI (eds.), *Ergebnisse der Ausgrabungen auf der Ḫirbet el-Mšāš (Tel Māśōś) 1972-1975*, Wiesbaden 1983, p. 127-130 (see p. 129 and Pl. 164:7-10).

[253] Grid ref. 1348/0726: Z. HERZOG, *Beersheba*, in *NEAEHL*, Jerusalem 1993, Vol. I, p. 161-173.

[254] Cf. K.M. KENYON, *The Date of the Destruction of Iron Age Beer-Sheba*, in *PEQ* 108 (1976), p. 63-64. K.M. Kenyon observed that pottery assemblages in Stratum II of Tell as-Seba‘ precede the ceramics of Lachish Level III and thus suggested to date them

lines 3-4, that might refer to the impoverished town of Stratum I, as suggested by the order to bring wine and wheat to Beersheba. The life conditions were quite different in an earlier period. The city, distant 75 km from Jerusalem as the crow flies, enjoyed an unprecedented prosperity in the 7th century B.C., which was precisely the period of the *pax Assyriaca*. Large amounts of Edomite pottery can then be found in settlements laying along the road from Edom to the Mediterranean, e.g. at Ḫirbet al-Ġarra[255] and Tell as-Seba'[256]. Also cuboid limestone altars appear at that time in Stratum II of Tell as-Seba'[257]. These small altars have four short, square legs, and a cavity containing traces of soot is hollowed on top of the cube. These are obviously incense altars, well attested in South Arabia and already described in 1922 by A. Grohmann[258]. The number of published items increased considerably since that time[259]. In particular, several altars of this type have been found in Hadhramaut, at al-Ḥureidha in the Wādī 'Amd[260], in Qataban, at Hağar bin Ḥumeid, some 13 km south of Timna[261], but also in central Arabia, at Qaryat al-Faw[262]. The complex of al-Ḥureidha can be dated to the 7th-5th centuries B.C. by objects reflecting foreign influence. This date roughly corresponds to the period when similar altars appear in Southern Palestine[263], especially at

from the mid-7th century B.C. The earlier phase of Strata III-II may therefore go back to the first half of the 7th century B.C. Present-day Israeli archaeologists generally date the destruction of Lachish Stratum III and Tell as-Seba' Stratum II to 701 B.C., a "mythopeic" reference to Sennacherib's campaign in Judah. See here below, p. 415-416.

[255] Tel 'Ira, Stratum VII: L. FREUD, *Iron Age*, in I. BEIT-ARIEH (ed.), *op. cit.* (n. 236), p. 189-289.

[256] Tel Beersheba, Strata III and II: L. SINGER-AVITZ, *art. cit.* (n. 58 and 92).

[257] E. STERN, *Limestone Inscense Altars*, in Y. AHARONI (ed.), *Beer-sheba* I, Tel Aviv 1973, p. 52-53 and Pls. 29 and 52; L. SINGER-AVITZ, *art. cit.* (n. 58), p. 41-44.

[258] A. GROHMANN, *Südarabien als Wirtschaftsgebiet* I, Wien 1922, p. 115-119.

[259] The list established by W. ZWICKEL, *Räucherkult une Räuchergeräte. Exegetische und archäologische Studien zum Räucheropfer im Alten Testament* (OBO 97), Freiburg/Schweiz-Göttingen 1990, p. 70-74 ("Die Räucherkästschen von der arabischen Halbinsel"), can be enlarged, as shown by W.W. MÜLLER in his review of the book: *BiOr* 49 (1992), col. 265-266.

[260] G. CATON THOMPSON, *The Tombs and Moon Temple of Hureidha (Hadhramaut)* (Reports of the Research Committee of the Society of Antiquaries of London 13), London 1944, p. 49-50, Pls. XVI-XVII.

[261] G.W. VAN BEEK (ed.), *Hajar bin Ḥumeid. Investigations at a Pre-Islamic Site in South Arabia*, Baltimore 1969, p. 272-273.

[262] A.R. AL-ANSARY, *Qaryat al-Fau. A Portrait of Pre-Islamic Civilization in Saudi Arabia*, Riyadh 1982, p. 73, Figs. 7-8.

[263] W. ZWICKEL, *op. cit.* (n. 259), p. 91-109, offers a catalogue of 65 pre-Hellenistic specimens found in Palestine, with drawings and respective publication places, as well as a map of the concerned sites (p. 75). See besides: I. BEIT-ARIEH, *op. cit.* (n. 236), p. 275-276; ID., *art. cit.* (n. 181), p. 37; R. COHEN - Y. YISRAEL, *art. cit.* (n. 121), in *Qadmoniot* 29 (1996), Figs. on top of p. 84, where the photographs show at least one altar of this type; L. SINGER-AVITZ, *art. cit.* (n. 58), p. 41-44, and *art. cit.* (n. 63), p. 161-162.

Tell as-Seba‘ (Beersheba), on the trade route from Arabia to the Mediterranean, and at sites closer to the seacoast, like Tell Ǧemmeh[264] and Tell al-Far‘ah South[265]. The specimens attributed to the Persian period and found at Gezer[266], Lachish[267] or Samaria[268] can be related, if properly dated[269], to the Arabian units of the Achaemenian army, stationed in Palestine and worshipping ‘Ashtarum[270]. Several specimens of these incense altars, found in Saba, Hadhramaut, Qataban, and Ma‘in, are provided with short South Arabian inscriptions[271].

The South Arabian origin of these altars, found mainly in funerary and domestic contexts, has already been noticed by W.F. Albright[272], but

[264] W.M.Fl. PETRIE, *Gerar*, London 1928, Pls. XL-XLI and XLII, 5-6.

[265] E. MACDONALD - J.L. STARKEY - L. HARDING, *Beth Pelet* II, London 1932, Pls. LXXXVIII, 14 and XCIII, 662.

[266] R.A.S. MACALISTER, *The Excavation of Gezer* II, London 1912, p. 443-445, Figs. 524-526.

[267] O. TUFNELL *et al.*, *Lachish* III, London 1953, Pls. 68-71.

[268] G.A. REISNER - C.S. FISHER - D.G. LYON, *Harvard Excavations at Samaria 1908-1910*, Cambridge Mass. 1924, Pl. 80a-c.

[269] Such limestone cubes could easily be reused. Their dating to the Persian period is therefore questionable. In particular, the decoration of the Samaria altar shows surprising resemblance to the engravings of one of the Tell as-Seba‘ specimens and should probably be dated to the 7th century as well. In this case, it is a new witness of trade links with South Arabia, to be mentioned next to the Beitīn stamp.

[270] E. LIPIŃSKI, *The Cult of Ashtarum in Achaemenian Palestine*, in L. CAGNI (ed.), *Biblica et Semitica. Studi in memoria di Francesco Vattioni*, Napoli 1999, p. 315-323. The spelling *‘štrm* with mimation occurs in several inscriptions from the Sharon plain: R. DEUTSCH - M. HELTZER, *Forty New Ancient West Semitic Inscriptions*, Tel Aviv-Jaffa 1994, p. 69-89. It apparently matches the Hadhramitic orthography of the divine name *‘s³trm* (*RÉS* 4065; A.G. LUNDIN, *Die Inschriften des antiken Raybūn*, in *Mare Erythraeum* 1 [1997], p. 19-25), but the inscriptions are written in West Semitic script, in Phoenician or Aramaic, and South Arabia was not under Achaemenid rule. The worshippers of *‘štrm* must thus be North-Arabians, perhaps from Teima or Dedan. The theonym *‘štrm* is written with mimation like the names of *Mlkm*, the Ammonite national god, and of *Wdm*, the moon-god Wadd worshipped in Ma‘in, but originated from North Arabia.

[271] At least 31 inscribed examples are actually published. The oldest ones may easily date from the 5th century B.C.: A. JAMME, *Deux autels à encens de l'Université de Harvard*, in *BiOr* 10 (1953), p. 94-95, Pl. XIV; *ANEP*, Nos. 579 and 581; *Corpus des inscriptions et antiquités sud-arabes* I/2, Louvain 1977, p. I.275-I.292; S. ANTONINI, *Nuovi incensieri iscritti yemeniti*, in *Oriens Antiquus* 27 (1988), p. 133-141, Pls. IV-VI; W.W. MÜLLER, rev. in *BiOr* 49 (1992), col. 265-266.

[272] W.F. ALBRIGHT, *Some Recent Publications*, in *BASOR* 98 (1945), p. 27-31 (see p. 28), and 132 (1953), p. 46-47; ID., *L'archéologie de la Palestine*, Paris 1955, p. 156-158. See further: M. FORTE, *Sull'origine di alcuni tipi di altarini sud-arabici*, in *AION* 29 (1967), p. 97-120, in particular p. 104-108, 115-118, and 120. M. O'DWYER SHEA, *The Small Cuboid Incense-Burner of the Ancient Near East*, in *Levant* 15 (1983), p. 76-109, rightly observes that there are good reasons for thinking that the obsolete dating of the Arabian specimens to the 5th-1st centuries B.C. is too low. In the writer's opinion, the oldest, not inscribed examples, must go back at least to the 8th century B.C., since they are present in the Beersheba Valley in the 7th century B.C.

One of the incense altars from Tell as-Seba', 7th century B.C.
It is decorated with a camel and a snake, framed by a row of triangles.
(Photo: Excavations of Y. Aharoni).

poor acquaintance with the pertinent material led some authors astray. No disquisition is needed to see that these altars can by no means be related to a Phoenician workmanship of the Persian period, as stated surprisingly by E. Stern[273]. Nor can they be linked to the small chests of clay from the third and mid-second millennium B.C. found at sites along the great bend of the Euphrates, in northern Syria[274]. As for the similar Babylonian altars made of clay[275], the oldest of which date to the 7th-6th

[273] E. STERN, *Limestone Incense Altars*, in Y. AHARONI (ed.), *Beer-sheba* I, Tel Aviv 1973, p. 52-53, Pls. 29 and 52; ID., *Material Culture of the Land of the Bible in the Persian Period*, Warminster 1982, p. 182-195.

[274] L. SINGER-AVITZ, *art. cit.* (n. 58), p. 44.

[275] L. ZIEGLER, *Tonkastschen aus Uruk, Babylon und Assur,* in *ZA* 47 (1942), p. 224-240. A single specimen was found in Ashur.

centuries B.C., they derive very likely from South Arabian prototypes as well, and should be related to the presence of Old Arabian tribes in Babylonia[276] and to the inscriptions in "South Arabian" script found at several Babylonian sites[277].

Some cuboid altars are decorated with incised figures of animals, humans, and plants, framed by a row of triangles reminiscent of the oldest Nabataean tombs at Petra and Hegra. These are characterized by a façade ornamented by a single or double row of crenelations above the entrance[278]. It is reasonable to assume that the same patterns have inspired the decoration of the limestone incense altars and of the oldest Nabataean tombs.

Stratum II at Tell as-Seba‘, to which seven cuboid limestone altars belong, should be dated to the 7th century B.C.[279], the period of the *pax Assyriaca*. These altars are thus roughly contemporaneous with the South Arabian monograms of Tell al-Kheleifeh and pinpoint the route of the caravans toward the Mediterranean. Their discovery at Tell as-Seba‘ may even indicate that South Arabian merchants were settled in the town or at least disposed there of some facilities. The Old Arabian inscription *khn,* incised on a small limestone object, and the dromedary bones found in Stratum II of Tell as-Seba‘ confirm such a general socio-economic context, as well as small alabaster or limestone stoppers of South Arabian origin[280]. Also the altars from Tell Ǧemmeh and the large amount of dromedary bones excavated at this site[281] can very likely be dated from the 8th-7th centuries B.C. on.

The role of Tell as-Seba‘ in the trade with Arabia is witnessed also by the Edomite ware. Since the pottery assemblages of Strata III-II at Tell as-Seba‘ are similar to those of Level III at Lachish, these layers are

276 LIPIŃSKI, *Aramaeans*, p. 409-489.

277 One can find references in I. EPH‘AL, *"Arabs" in Babylonia in the 8th century B.C.*, in *JAOS* 94 (1974), p. 108-115 (see p. 109-110, n. 12). The list is not complete; it does not refer to the three fragments found in 1926-27 at Ur and published in *RÉS* 3934-3936.

278 A. NEGEV, *The Nabateans and the Provincia Arabia,* in *ANRW* II/8, Berlin 1977, p. 520-686, Pls. I-XLVIII (see p. 574-575, Pls. VIII-IX); *Inoubliable Petra,* Bruxelles 1980, p. 36, Fig. 17.

279 Since Stratum II at Tell as-Seba‘ should be dated from the 7th century B.C. (see K.M. KENYON, *art. cit.* [n. 254]), the dates proposed by L. SINGER-AVITZ, *art. cit.* (n. 58), p. 41, 52, must be lowered; cf. also EAD., *'Busayra Painted Ware' at Tel Beersheba,* in *Tel Aviv* 31 (2004), p. 80-89.

280 L. SINGER-AVITZ, *art. cit.* (n. 58), p. 50-52, and *art. cit.* (n. 63), p. 162.

281 P. WAPNISH, *Camel Caravans and Camel Pastoralists at Tell Jemmeh,* in *JANES* 13 (1981), p. 101-121.

wrongly dated from the second half of the 8th century B.C.[282] and their destruction attributed to Sennacherib's campaign in 701 B.C.[283] In the original view of the first excavator of Lachish, J.L. Starkey[284], followed by number of distinguished archaeologists[285], Level III at Lachish was destroyed in the first Babylonian invasion of Judah in 598/7 B.C. This opinion is supported not only by the palaeography and the orthography of the legends in the seal impressions on jar handles from Lachish Level III[286]. It is confirmed also by the perfect correspondence between the destruction traces of Level IV, which did not end by fire, and the records of the Assyrian campaign against Judah and Lachish in 701 B.C.[287] The presence of Sennacherib's headquarters at Lachish indicate that the city was not razed and burnt during the campaign of 701 B.C. Strata III-II at Tell as-Seba', parallel to Lachish Level III, must thus date from the 7th century B.C.

Biblical texts, especially Am. 1, 11-12 dating from the second half of the 8th century B.C., refer nevertheless to destructions and massacres caused in that period by Edomites, possibly responsible also for the end of Strata V-IV at Tell as-Seba':

> "For three crimes of Edom
> and for four, I will not revoke it:
> Because he pursued his brother with the sword,
> and destroyed his womenfolk,
> I will send fire upon Teiman,
> and it shall devour the buildings of Buṣeirā".

[282] L. Singer-Avitz, *art. cit.* (n. 92), p. 81-82.

[283] I. Finkelstein - N. Na'aman, *The Judahite Shephelah in Late 8th and Early 7th Centuries BCE,* in *Tel Aviv* 31 (2004), p. 60-79 (see p. 64-66 and 69-75).

[284] J.L. Starkey, *Lachish as Illustrating Bible History,* in *PEQ* 69 (1937), p. 171-179 (see p. 175); Id., *Excavations at Tell ed-Duweir,* in *PEQ* 69 (1937), p. 228-241 (see p. 236).

[285] W.F. Albright, *Some Recent Publications,* in *BASOR* 132 (1953), p. 46-47; Id., *Recent Progress in Palestinian Archaeology: Samaria-Sebaste III and Hazor I,* in *BASOR* 150 (1958), p. 21-25 (see p. 24); G.E. Wright, rev. of O. Tufnell *et al.*, *Lachish* III*: The Iron Age* (Oxford 1953), in *Vetus Testamentum* 5 (1955), p. 97-105 (see p. 100-104), and in *JNES* 14 (1955), p. 133-135; B.W. Buchanan, rev. in *AJA* 58 (1954), p. 335-339; K.M. Kenyon, in J.W. & G.M. Crowfoot - K.M. Kenyon, *Samaria-Sebaste* III. *The Objects from Samaria*, London 1957, p. 204-208; Ead., *op. cit.* (n. 68), p. 295-302; R. de Vaux, rev. in *RB* 66 (1959), p. 298.

[286] See already L.G. Herr, *The Scripts of Ancient Northwest Semitic Seals*, Missoula 1978, p. 86-94. For the spelling *-yh* of the theophorous element in proper names, see R. Zadok, *The Pre-Hellenistic Israelite Anthroponomy and Prosopography* (OLA 28), Leuven 1988, p. 185. See also here above, p. 80.

[287] See here above, p. 374-375.

Such a text may have been inspired by similar events in other places as well, like Arad where the Judaean fortress of Stratum XI has been destroyed towards the end of the 8th century B.C.

Am. 1, 6 and 9 curses Gaza and Tyre for selling an "entire population" to Edom. While "Edom" might be a scribal error for "Aram" in verse 9 concerning Tyre, the role of Edomites as middlemen in the trade of slaves dragged from Gaza to Arabia fits the general picture of such a long-distance commerce[288]. Although the booklet of Obadiah was written after the fall of Jerusalem in 587 B.C., as verses 10-14 suggest, it alludes also to earlier events and looks for the day when Judah would regain her land, occupied by the Edomites. The same perspective explains the oracles of Is. 34, 1-17 and Jer. 49, 7-22.

Moreover, Arad ostracon 40, found in Stratum VIII and thus dating to the late 7th century B.C., is a letter sent from a Judaean outpost, perhaps Ḫirbet al-Ġazza, to Malkiyahu, apparently the commander of the fortress of Arad[289]. The senders of the letter, Gemaryahu and Nehemyahu, mean that "the king of Judah should know [that we are un]able to send the [reinforcement because of the out]burst of the evil that Edom [has caused]", *yd‘.mlk.Yhwd[h.ky.’y]nnw.yklm.lšlḫ.’t h[‘zr$^{?}$.bṣ]’t hr‘h.’š[r.]’d[m.hby’$^{?}$]* (lines 13-15). The destruction of several sites should probably be linked to attacks by Edomites towards the end of the 7th or in the early 6th centuries B.C., in the aftermaths of Nebuchadnezzar II's campaigns against Philistia and Judah. At Tell as-Seba‘, an attempt was made at the beginning of the 6th century to rebuild the town destroyed by the Babylonians. The traces of this reconstruction, referred to as Stratum I, were probably a local initiative that was soon abandoned[290]. Instead, after the destruction of Stratum VIII at Tell ‘Arad, probably in similar circumstances, the fortress has been rebuilt (Strata VII-VI)[291].

Although the existence of unwalled settlements in the Beersheba Valley reveals a certain sense of security in the period of the *pax Assyriaca*,

288 H.W. Wolff, *Dodekapropheton 2. Joel und Amos* (BKAT XIV/2), Neukirchen-Vluyn 1969, p. 191-192; W. Rudolph, *Joel-Amos-Obadja-Jona* (KAT XIII/2), Gütersloh 1971, p. 133; Sh.M. Paul, *Amos*, Minneapolis 1991, p. 57.

289 Y. Aharoni, *op. cit.* (n. 65), p. 72-76; A. Lemaire, *op. cit.* (n. 66), p. 207-209. All the *yōd* of the ostracon still have their foot-stroke, missing in the ostraca of Stratum VI. Stratigraphy, ceramic evidence, and palaeography thus contradict the attribution of the ostracon to Stratum VI, as argued by N. Na’aman, *Ostracon 40 from Arad Reconsidered*, in C.G. den Hertog *et al.* (eds.), *Saxa loquentur. Festschrift für V. Fritz* (AOAT 302), Münster 2003, p. 201-204.

290 Y. Aharoni (ed.), *Beer-sheba* I, Tel Aviv 1973, p. 11-12.

291 See here above, p. 398.

the events at the end of the 8th century prepared a progressive Edomite penetration in this area, followed by a worsening situation of the Judaean towns and villages in the 6th century. Edomite settlement extended progressively to the Judaean highland and the eastern Shephelah. Instead, the mention of Edom in connection with Dedan and Teiman in Is 21, 13; Jer. 49, 8; Ez. 25, 3, offers no sufficient basis for assuming the existence of Edomite colonies at Dedan and Teima, the North Arabian caravan cities.

Babylonian period

Assyria had never put Edom under direct rule, most likely because its economic interests were favoured in that way by the trade connections between Edom and the coast through the Negeb[292], and because Edom's rulers had realized the wisdom of a policy which was loyal towards their overlord. They may have followed a similar policy when the Babylonians took it over from the Assyrians, though their diplomatic posture at the beginning of the Neo-Babylonian period is in doubt. Jer. 27 might suggest that Edom took part *ca.* 593 B.C. in an anti-Babylonian alliance, although the text does not reveal whether Edom actually sided with Zedekiah of Judah. Jer. 27, 3 implies at least that there was an Edomite king in the first decade of the 6th century B.C. The denunciations against Edom in Obadiah 10-14 indirectly witness Edom's submission to Babylon and this is the most likely explanation for its freedom to expand in southern Judah[293], which was later called Idumaea.

The situation changed in the mid-6th century. A palatial building of Buṣeirā shows evidence of destruction by fire, probably during an attack by the Neo-Babylonians[294]. Since Josephus does not mention Edom when recording a campaign of Nebuchadnezzar II in southern Transjordan[295], this destruction of the site must date from the reign of Nabonidus (556-539 B.C.), who ravaged Edom in 553 B.C.[296] and is probably rep-

[292] A. MAZAR, *Archaeology of the Land of the Bible: 10,000-586 B.C.E.*, New York 1990, p. 442-444; I. FINKELSTEIN, *Ḥorvat Qiṭmīt and the Southern Trade in the Late Iron Age II*, in *ZDPV* 108 (1992), p. 156-170; L. SINGER-AVITZ, *art. cit.* (n. 58).

[293] P.K. MCCARTER, *Obadiah 7 and the Fall of Edom*, in *BASOR* 220-221 (1975-76), p. 87-91.

[294] C.-M. BENNETT, *op. cit.* (n. 130), p. 15.

[295] JOSEPHUS FLAVIUS, *Jewish Antiquities* X, 9, 7, §181-182.

[296] Chronicle of Nabonidus, No. 7, col. I, 17 ([kur/uru*Ú*]-*du-um-mu ittadû*, "they threw Edom down", in A.K. GRAYSON, *Assyrian and Babylonian Chronicles* (TCS 5), Locust

Umm al-Biyāra seen from Petra.

resented on the rock relief of Sela', near Buṣeirā[297]. The same period is marked by evident traces of destruction at other Edomite sites, such as Umm al-Biyāra[298], Ṭawilān[299], the fort of Ġrāra[300], and Tell al-Kheleifeh[301]. According to the fragmentary Babylonian chronicles, Nabonidus also captured Petra, called *Ruq-qú*[!]*-ni* (*Ruqqumu*) in the text[302], and ended his campaign at Dedan[303], in northern Arabia. It is uncertain as yet whether the "war against Dedan" (*ḏr Ddn*), mentioned in four North Arabian inscriptions from Ǧebel Ġunaym[304], 14 km south of Teima, refers to this final stage of Nabonidus' campaign. More information is needed.

An unknown factor is the situation in the Negeb and the Beersheba Valley, where Edomite influence and presence were conspicuous until

Valley 1975, p. 105 and 282. Cf. W.G. LAMBERT, *Nabonidus in Arabia,* in *Proceedings of the Fifth Seminar for Arabian Studies*, London 1972, p. 53-64; J. LINDSAY, *The Babylonian Kings and Edom, 605-550 B.C.,* in *PEQ* 108 (1976), p. 23-39; J.R. BARTLETT, *From Edomites to Nabataeans,* in *PEQ* 111 (1979), p. 53-66; P.-A. BEAULIEU, *The Reign of Nabonidus, King of Babylon, 556-539 B.C.* (YNER 10), New Haven 1989, p. 166, with no comments.

297 S. DALLEY - A. GOGUEL, *The Sela' Sculpture: A Neo-Babylonian Rock Relief in Southern Jordan,* in *ADAJ* 41 (1997), p. 169-176; F. ZAYADINE, *Le relief néobabylonien à Sela' près de Tafileh: interprétation historique,* in *Syria* 76 (1999), p. 83-90.

298 Grid ref. 1919/9717; cf. W. ZWICKEL, *op. cit.* (n. 47), p. 34. The sequence all over the site shows collapse, abandonment, and further collapse; cf. P. BIEŃKOWSKI (ed.), *Early Edom and Moab*, Sheffield 1992, p. 93-95; ID., *Umm el-Biyara*, in *NEAEHL*, Jerusalem 1993, Vol. IV, p. 1488-1490.

299 Grid ref. 1975/9704; cf. W. ZWICKEL, *op. cit.* (n. 47), p. 34. Stratum V provides evidence of fire or destruction in the three main excavated areas: P. BIEŃKOWSKI, *Tawilan*, in *NEAEHL*, Jerusalem 1993, Vol. IV, p. 1446-1447; C.-M. BENNETT - P. BIEŃKOWSKI, *Excavations at Tawilan in Southern Jordan* (British Academy Monographs in Archaeology 8), London 1996.

300 Grid ref. 1908/9515; cf. W. ZWICKEL, *op. cit.* (n. 47), p. 28. See, in particular, S. HART, *Excavations at Ghrareh, 1986: Preliminary Report,* in *Levant* 20 (1988), p. 89-99.

301 Grid ref. 1476/8845. Clear traces of destruction by fire have been noted; see G.D. PRATICO, *art. cit.* (n. 35), p. 2; ID., *op. cit.* (n. 113), passim.

302 A.K. GRAYSON, *op. cit.* (n. 296), p.106, Chronicle 7, col. I, 19, used by P.-A. BEAULIEU, *op. cit.* (n. 296), p. 166. The unknown [uru]*Ruq-di-ni* should be corrected into [uru]*Ruq-qú*[!]*-ni*, considering that the signs DI and KU are very similar in Neo-Babylonian script. The form *Ruqquni* corresponds to the older Greek transcription Ῥοκόμ of *Rqm*, the Semitic name of Petra, often personified in the Bible: I Chron. 2, 43-44; 7, 16; Numb. 31, 8; Josh. 13, 21. The change *m*/*n* is quite common, especially at the end of a word.

303 The king of Dedan is mentioned in the "Royal Chronicle" published by W.G. LAMBERT, *A New Source for the Reign of Nabonidus,* in *AfO* 22 (1968-69), p. 1-8, in particular p. 6, col. V, 20: LUGAL *šá Da-da-na*. For Dedan and Nabonidus' Arabian campaign generally, see P.-A. BEAULIEU, *op. cit.* (n. 296), p. 168-185, and here above, p. 317, n. 118.

304 F.V. WINNETT - W.L. REED, *Ancient Records from North Arabia* (Near and Middle Eastern Series 6), Toronto 1970, p. 102-103, 223, 226, Nos. 20-23; cf. p. 91-92.

the end of the 7th or the beginning of the 6th century B.C. In the 4th century B.C., the Aramaic ostraca from Tell as-Seba'[305] provide proper names with the Arabic *-u* ending, like *Zbdw* (No. 4, 2), *Nḥrw* (No. 15)[306], *Ntynw* (Nos. 33, 2; 34, 5; 35, 3), *Zbydw* (Nos. 33, 5; 34, 4; 35, 2), *Ḥdlw* (No. 37, 2), *Mlkw* (No. 38, 5), *Whbw* (No. 39, 4), *'mw* (Nos. 40, 4; 42, 2), *'wtw* (No. 42, 4), *Ḥlpw* (No. 44, 1). Other names contain the Edomite theophorous element *Qws*[307], attested also at Tell al-Far'ah[308] and Tell 'Arad[309]. Names with the Arabic *-u* ending occur likewise at Ḫirbet al-Ġarra (Tel 'Ira)[310] and Tell 'Arad[311]. These anthroponyms either signify a continuation of the previous situation in the area or more likely result from the massive Edomite move westwards during the Persian period, as witnessed in particular by the Aramaic ostraca from Maqqedah.

[305] J. NAVEH, *The Aramaic Ostraca*, in Y. AHARONI (ed.), *Beer-sheba* I, Tel Aviv 1973, p. 79-82 and Pls. 35-38; ID., *The Aramaic Ostraca from Tel Beer-sheba (Seasons 1971-1976)*, in *Tel Aviv* 6 (1979), p. 182-198 and Pls. 24-31.

[306] The name is attested in Ṣafaitic: HARDING, *Arabian Names*, p. 583. It probably means "skilled".

[307] Nos. 8, 2; 14, 1.4; 28, 2; 33, 3.4; 34, 1.6; 36, 1.6; 37, 1.4; 41, 4.6; 42, 3.

[308] J. NAVEH, *Published and Unpublished Aramaic Ostraca*, in *'Atiqot. English Series* 17 (1985), p. 114-121 and Pls. XIX-XX (see No. 3).

[309] J. NAVEH, in Y. AHARONI, *Arad Inscriptions*, Jerusalem 1975, p. 167-204 (see Nos. 1, 1; 10, 1; 20, 1; 21, 1; 33, 1; 43, 1).

[310] J. NAVEH, *art. cit.* (n. 308), No. 8.

[311] J. NAVEH, in *op. cit.* (n. 309), No. 27, 1; 39, 3.5; 40, 2.

INDICES

1. Index of personal names

A

B

C

D

E

G

H

I

J

P

Q

R

S

Yariḥ'ezer, son of Zakkūr 306-308, 311
Yaṣi-Dagan 29
Yasod 88
Yau-bi'di, king of Hamath 221
Yaukin 86
Yehoyada, high-priest 383
Yose, rabbi 260

Z

Zadoq 186
Zaphenath-paneah 132
Zakaryaw 250
Zakkūr, king of Hamath 218f.
Zedekiah, king of Judah 418
Zeraḥ 129, 388f., 392
Zu-Ashtarti, ruler of Emar 29

Proper names in Semitic alphabetic script

'dn 68
'dnš 68
'ḥ'mh 408f.
'ḥzyh 80
'ḥqm 407
'ẖt'mhw 408f.
'kys, 'kyš 66
'klyn 69
'lydn 116
'lyqm 66
'nš 68
's^{1}*ḥl* 150
(')*rẖlk* 67
'š'štrt 171
Blbl 407f.
B'l' 69
B'lys 314f.
B'lntn 332
B'lšm' 68
Brṣyh 70
Brqs^{1} 401
Glyt 70
Gltqs^{1} 401
Dgprt 67f.
Dml' 408
Drymš 66
Hmlk 150
Hmsk 150
Hrš 68
H'wḏ 150
H'ḏr 150
Hṣlyhw 407
Hš'yhw 407
Whbw 421
Wḥzn 388
Wnnt 68
Zbdw 421
Zbydw 421
Zyls 247, 265
Zkr 407
Zkryw 250
Ḥdlw 421
Ḥlpw 421
Ḥmš 69
Ḥty 127
Ṭb 69
Ṭwby 298
Ywkn 86
Yrḥm'l 123
Yrḥ'zr 306-308, 311
Klyṭbš 69
Kmš'r 332
Kmšdn 116
Kmšṣdq 332
Krmy 408
Kryw 186
Kš 68
Lḥš 304
Lmlk 406f.
Mk' 186
Mky 239, 407
Mlk 150
Mlkw 421
Msk 150
M'k 66, 128
M'kh 239
Mšlm 407
Mškt 388
Nwy 407
Nḥš 304
Nḥrw 421
Ntn 69
Ntynw 421
Qws^{1}*br* 401

Proper names in cuneiform script

Proper names in Greek alphabetic script

Proper names in Lycian epichori script

2. Geographical and ethnical index

General geographic notions, like Canaan, Israel (except in particular cases), Levant, Mediterranean Sea, Middle East, Mesopotamia, Palestine, Syria, Syro-Phoenicia, Trans-jordan, Western Asia, are not included in the index. Numbers in italics denote map.

A

Abar-Nahara 65, 210
'Abda, see Oboda
Abelan(e) 246f., 259
Abel-Bēth-Maaka 12, 242, 244, 246, 253f., 258
Abel-mayim/n 12, 243-251, 258, 262f.
Abel-Meholah 286f.
A-bi-il-mes-qé 244, 265
Abīl 242-246, 249f., 255, 265, 348
Abil al-Qamḥ *175, 211,* 242, 246, 251, 253, 256-262, 265
Abu Hureira *71, 113,* 128, 152-154, *371*
Abu Ruqeish 47, *71,* 74, 77, *113,* 127, *131,* 140, 189, 192, *371,* 376, 378, 381
Abu Ṣalābīḫ *25*
Abu Salima *131,* see Tell Abu Salima
Achaeans 36f., 51
Achzib 96, *175,* 176
Adam, see Tell ad-Dāmiya
Adana (Cilicia) 42, 218
'Adrā 219
Adyrmachidae 179
Aegean 34-36, 49f., 52, 58, 67, 93, 95
Ağlasun, see Sagalassos, Shagalasha
Ağlūn 267, 272f., *275,* 281f.
Ahhiyawa, see Achaeans
Aḫlamū 30, 203
al-Aḥwat 54
Aila(t), see Elath
'Ain 'Arūs 388
'Ain Dara 188
'Ain Faṭīr 264
'Ain al-Ḥuṣb *371,* 386-388, 390, 392, 394, 401
'Ain Qadeis *113,* 119f., *374*
'Ain al-Qudeirat *113,* 119f., 366, *371,* 375, 378-381
'Ain al-Quṣeima *113,* 119f., *371*
'Ain Sāra 356
'Aiy 350
Akkad 160
Akko 54, *131,* 174, *175,* 176, 178, 194, 197, 239
Aktepe 204, *205*
Alalakh 258
el-Alamein 179
Alashiya, see Cyprus
'Āl-Gad 117
'Āl-'Amtan 126
Aleppo *207,* 218, 232, 258
Alexandria 134, 226
'Āl-Ḥatt 127
'Āl-Hilāl 114
Al-Mina (Lebanon) 191
'Āl-Ram 128
Altaqu, see Elteqe
Altars of the Philaenoi 179
"Amalekites" 368, 370, 405, 409
Amanus 220
Amara West 363
Amathus 186
Amida 204, 213
Amman *32, 175,* 223, 267, 278, 295, *297,* 298, 300, 308f., 314-317, 330
Amman airport *297,* 300-302
'Ammatā *175,* see 'Amtan
Ammon, Ammonites 11f., 162, 193, 225, 282, 292, 295f., *297,* 298-318, 342, 344, 370, 373
'Amtan, 'Amtu *175,* 288
Amurru 32, 43-45, 47, 299
'Ana(h) 218
Anatolia 23, 26, 28, 34, 37, 48, 52, 67, 69, 78, 92, 94, 164, 181, 210
Anṣariyah range 33
Antioch 250f.
Antiphrai, Antiphron 180
Apasa, see Ephesus

B

C

D

E

F

G

H

I

M

Q

R

S

T

Y

Z

Geographical and ethnical names in Egyptian texts (simplified transcription)

3. Index of divine names

4. Subject index

5. Index of biblical texts

6. Index of rabbinic texts

7. Index of Semitic inscriptions and papyri

8. Index of cuneiform texts

9. Index of Egyptian documents

10. Index of Greek and Latin authors

11. Index of Greek and Latin inscriptions and papyri

12. Index of modern authors

A

Abel, F.-M. 15, 62, 108, 110, 112, 114f., 117, 121, 125, 136, 138, 151f., 226, 228, 234, 243, 246, 248, 264, 272, 278, 280, 286f., 292, 298, 327-329, 334, 338, 340, 344, 346, 351, 357, 383, 404f.
Abū ʻAssāf, ʻA. 188, 229, 314, 317
Adams, R. 350, 372
Adamthwaite, M.R. 30, 206
Adler, W. 167
Adriaen, M. 151, 262
Aharoni, Y. 61f., 114, 116, 119f., 122, 125, 128, 158, 228, 242, 258, 287f., 303, 348, 351, 374, 379, 382, 386, 388, 395-397, 405f., 411, 417
Aḥituv, S. 61, 112, 114-117, 125f., 128, 152f., 226, 228, 234, 236, 238-241, 243, 248, 252f., 256f., 280, 284, 292, 303, 329, 342
Ahlström, G.W. 128
Åkerman, K. 148
Albright, W.F. 40, 86, 133, 153, 170, 237, 243, 287, 298, 338, 413, 416
Alexandre, Y. 177f.
Alliata, E. 242
Al-Said, S.F. 317
Alt, A. 43, 54, 59, 66, 83, 112, 129f., 138, 152-154, 271, 286, 399
Altenmüller, H. 24
Ambos, P.C. 311, 408
Amiet, P. 356
Amir, D. 236
Amiran, R. 124
ʻAmr, A.-J. 314
Anbar, M. 218
Andersen, F.I. 333
Anderson, J.D. 372
Anderson, W.P. 164
al-Ansary, A.R. 412
Antonini, S. 412
Arav, R. 240f., 250, 252
Armstrong, J.A. 28, 204, 208
Arnaud, D. 28-30, 206
Artzy, M. 36
Aspesi, F. 246
Astour, M.C. 30, 228, 361-363
Attiyat, T. 331
Aubet, M.ª E. 182
Aufrecht, W.E. 306
Avigad, N. 86, 92, 116, 122f., 186, 195, 298, 304, 311f., 314, 332, 358, 384, 391f., 408-410
Avi-Yonah, M. 153, 250, 256, 331, 383, 399
Avner, U. 124, 375
Ayalon, E. 373, 376

B

Badre, L. 34, 43
Baedeker, K. 61, 235, 260, 262
Baillet, M. 263
Baillie, M.G.L. 35
Baker, H.D. 66, 149, 310
Barajo, T.J. 49
Baramki, D.C. 209
Bardy, G. 167
Barkay, G. 80
Barker, G.W. 372
Barnett, R.D. 40, 42, 44
Barstadt, H.M. 254
Bartlett, J.R. 370, 388, 393, 401, 420
Bar-Yosef, O. 241
Bauer, U.F.W. 254
Baumgartner, W. 243
Bawdens, G. 320, 373
Bea, A. 236
Beaulieu, P.-A. 222-224, 315, 420
Bechtel, F. 67
Beck, P. 324, 376, 386, 394, 402
Beckerath, J. von 133, 145
Becking, B. 314
Beckman, G. 29, 206
Beer-Moritz, B. 161
Beeston, A.F.L. 21
Beier, Th. 366, 394
Beit-Arieh, I. 394, 398, 400, 404, 406, 409f., 412
Belmonte Marín, J.A. 258
Ben-Ami, D. 178, 242, 324
Ben-David, Ch. 344, 348

L

Ł

M

LIST OF MAPS, TEXT FIGURES, AND ILLUSTRATIONS

ORIENTALIA LOVANIENSIA ANALECTA

1. E. Lipiński, Studies in Aramaic Inscriptions and Onomastics I.
2. J. Quaegebeur, Le dieu égyptien Shaï dans la religion et l'onomastique.
3. P.H.L. Eggermont, Alexander's Campaigns in Sind and Baluchistan and the Siege of the Brahmin Town of Harmatelia.
4. W.M. Callewaert, The Sarvāṅgī of the Dādūpanthī Rajab.
5. E. Lipiński (ed.), State and Temple Economy in the Ancient Near East I.
6. E. Lipiński (ed.), State and Temple Economy in the Ancient Near East II.
7. M.-C. De Graeve, The Ships of the Ancient Near East (c. 2000-500 B.C.).
8. W.M. Callewaert (ed.), Early Hindī Devotional Literature in Current Research.
9. F.L. Damen, Crisis and Religious Renewal in the Brahmo Samaj Movement (1860-1884).
10. R.Y. Ebied - A. Van Roey - L.R. Wickham, Peter of Callinicum, Anti-Tritheist Dossier.
11. A. Rammant-Peeters, Les pyramidions égyptiens du Nouvel Empire.
12. S. Scheers (ed.), Studia Paulo Naster Oblata I. Numismatica Antiqua.
13. J. Quaegebeur (ed.), Studia Paulo Naster Oblata II. Orientalia Antiqua.
14. E. Platti, Yaḥyā ibn ʿAdī, théologien chrétien et philosophe arabe.
15. E. Gubel - E. Lipiński - B. Servais-Soyez (eds.), Studia Phoenicia I-II.
16. W. Skalmowski - A. Van Tongerloo (ed.), Middle Iranian Studies.
17. M. van Mol, Handboek Modern Arabisch.
18. C. Laga - J.A. Munitiz - L. Van Rompay (eds.), After Chalcedon. Studies in Theology and Church History.
19. E. Lipiński (ed.), The Land of Israel: Cross-Roads of Civilizations.
20. S. Wachsmann, Aegeans in the Theban Tombs.
21. K. Van Lerberghe, Old Babylonian Legal and Administrative Texts from Philadelphia.
22. E. Lipiński (ed.), Phoenicia and the East Mediterranean in the First Millennium B.C.
23. M. Heltzer - E. Lipiński (eds.), Society and Economy in the Eastern Mediterranean (1500-1000 B.C.).
24. M. Van de Mieroop, Crafts in the Early Isin Period.
25. G. Pollet (ed.), India and the Ancient World.
26. E. Lipiński (ed.), Carthago.
27. E. Verreet, Modi Ugaritici.
28. R. Zadok, The Pre-Hellenistic Israelite Anthroponomy and Prosopography.
29. W. Callewaert - M. Lath, The Hindī Songs of Nāmdev.
30. A. Shisha-Halevy, Coptic Grammatical Chrestomathy.
31. N. Baum, Arbres et arbustes de l'Égypte ancienne.
32. J.-M. Kruchten, Les Annales des prêtres de Karnak.
33. H. Devijver - E. Lipiński (eds.), Punic Wars.
34. E. Vassilika, Ptolemaic Philae.
35. A. Ghaith, La Pensée Religieuse chez Ǧubrân Ḫalil Ǧubrân et Mi â'îl Nuʿayma.
36. N. Beaux, Le Cabinet de curiosités de Thoutmosis III.
37. G. Pollet - P. Eggermont - G. Van Damme, Archaeological Sites of Ancient India.
38. S.-A. Naguib, Le Clergé féminin d'Amon thébain à la 21e dynastie.
39. U. Verhoeven - E. Graefe (eds.), Religion und Philosophie im Alten Ägypten.
40. A.R. George, Babylonian Topographical Texts.
41. A. Schoors, The Preacher Sought to Find Pleasing Words. Part I.
42. G. Reinink - H.E.J. Van Stiphout (eds.), Dispute Poems and Dialogues in the Ancient and Mediaeval Near East.

43. C. TRAUNECKER, Coptos. Hommes et dieux sur le parvis de Geb.
44. E. LIPIŃSKI (ed.), Phoenicia and the Bible.
45. L. ISEBAERT (ed.), Studia Etymologica Indoeuropaea Memoriae A.J. Van Windekens dicata.
46. F. BRIQUEL-CHATONNET, Les relations entre les cités de la côte phénicienne et les royaumes d'Israël et de Juda.
47. W.J. VAN BEKKUM, A Hebrew Alexander Romance according to MS London, Jews' College no. 145.
48. W. SKALMOWSKI - A. VAN TONGERLOO (eds.), Medioiranica.
49. L. LAUWERS, Igor'-Severjanin, His Life and Work — The Formal Aspects of His Poetry.
50. R.L. VOS, The Apis Embalming Ritual. P. Vindob. 3873.
51. Fr. LABRIQUE, Stylistique et Théologie à Edfou. Le rituel de l'offrande de la campagne: étude de la composition.
52. F. DE JONG (ed.), Miscellanea Arabica et Islamica.
53. G. BREYER, Etruskisches Sprachgut im Lateinischen unter Ausschluß des spezifisch onomastischen Bereiches.
54. P.H.L. EGGERMONT, Alexander's Campaign in Southern Punjab.
55. J. QUAEGEBEUR (ed.), Ritual and Sacrifice in the Ancient Near East.
56. A. VAN ROEY - P. ALLEN, Monophysite Texts of the Sixth Century.
57. E. LIPIŃSKI, Studies in Aramaic Inscriptions and Onomastics II.
58. F.R. HERBIN, Le livre de parcourir l'éternité.
59. K. GEUS, Prosopographie der literarisch bezeugten Karthager.
60. A. SCHOORS - P. VAN DEUN (eds.), Philohistor. Miscellanea in honorem Caroli Laga septuagenarii.
61. M. KRAUSE - S. GIVERSEN - P. NAGEL (eds.), Coptology. Past, Present and Future. Studies in Honour of R. Kasser.
62. C. LEITZ, Altägyptische Sternuhren.
63. J.J. CLÈRE, Les Chauves d'Hathor.
64. E. LIPIŃSKI, Dieux et déesses de l'univers phénicien et punique.
65. K. VAN LERBERGHE - A. SCHOORS (eds.), Immigration and Emigration within the Ancient Near East. Festschrift E. Lipiński.
66. G. POLLET (ed.), Indian Epic Values. *Rāmāyaṇa* and its impact.
67. D. DE SMET, La quiétude de l'Intellect. Néoplatonisme et gnose ismaélienne dans l'œuvre de Ḥamîd ad-Dîn al-Kirmânî (Xe-XIe s.).
68. M.L. FOLMER, The Aramaic Language in the Achaemenid Period. A Study in Linguistic Variation.
69. S. IKRAM, Choice Cuts: Meat Production in Ancient Egypt.
70. H. WILLEMS, The Coffin of Heqata (Cairo JdE 36418). A Case Study of Egyptian Funerary Culture of the Early Middle Kingdom.
71. C. EDER, Die Ägyptischen Motive in der Glyptik des Östlichen Mittelmeerraumes zu Anfang des 2. Jts. v. Chr.
72. J. THIRY, Le Sahara libyen dans l'Afrique du Nord médiévale.
73. U. VERMEULEN - D. DE SMET (eds.), Egypt and Syria in the Fatimid, Ayyubid and Mamluk Eras. Proceedings of the 1st, 2nd and 3rd International Colloquium organized at the Katholieke Universiteit Leuven in May 1992, 1993 and 1994.
74. P. ARÈNES, La déesse Sgrol-Ma (Tara). Recherches sur la nature et le statut d'une divinité du bouddhisme tibétain.
75. K. CIGGAAR - A. DAVIDS - H. TEULE (eds.), East and West in the Crusader States. Context - Contacts - Confrontations. Acta of the Congress Held at Hernen Castle in May 1993.
76. M. BROZE, Mythe et Roman en Egypte ancienne. Les Aventures d'Horus et Seth dans le papyrus Chester Beatty I.
77. L. DEPUYDT, Civil Calendar and Lunar Calendar in Ancient Egypt.
78. P. WILSON, A Ptolemaic Lexikon. A Lexicographical Study of the Texts in the Temple of Edfu.
79. A. HASNAWI - A. ELAMRANI - M. JAMAL - M. AOUAD (eds.), Perspectives arabes et médiévales sur le tradition scientifique et philosophique grecque.

80. E. LIPIŃSKI, Semitic Languages: Outline of a Comparative Grammar.
81. S. CAUVILLE, Dendara I. Traduction.
82. C. EYRE (ed.), Proceedings of the Seventh International Congress of Egyptologists.
83. U. VERMEULEN - D. DE SMET (eds.), Egypt and Syria in the Fatimid, Ayyubid and Mamluk Eras II.
84-85. W. CLARYSSE - A. SCHOORS - H. WILLEMS (eds.), Egyptian Religion. The Last Thousand Years.
86. U. VERMEULEN - J.M. VAN REETH (eds.), Law, Christianity and Modernism in Islamic Society.
87. D. DE SMET - U. VERMEULEN (eds.), Philosophy and Acts in the Islamic World Proceedings of the Eighteenth Congress of the Union européenne des Arabisants et Islamisants held at the Katholieke Universiteit Leuven.
88. S. CAUVILLE, Dendara II. Traduction.
89. G.J. REININK - A.C. KLUGKIST (eds.), After Bardaisan. Studies on Continuity and Change in Syriac Christianity in Honour of Professor Han J.W. Drijvers.
90. C.R. KRAHMALKOV, Phoenician-Punic Dictionary.
91. M. TAHTAH, Entre pragmatisme, réformisme et modernisme. Le rôle politico-religieux des Khattabi dans le Rif (Maroc) jusqu'à 1926.
92. K. CIGGAAR - H. TEULE (eds.), East and West in the Crusader States. Context — Contact — Confrontations II. Acta of the Congress held at Hernen Castle, the Netherlands, in May 1997.
93. A.C.J. VERHEIJ, Bits, Bytes, and Binyanim. A Quantitative Study of Verbal Lexeme Formations in the Hebrew Bible.
94. W.M. CALLEWAERT - D. TAILLIEU - F. LALEMAN, A Descriptive Bibliography of Allama Muhammad Iqbal (1877-1938).
95. S. CAUVILLE, Dendara III. Traduction.
96. K. VAN LERBERGHE - G. VOET (eds.), Languages and Cultures in Contact: At the Crossroads of Civilizations in the Syro-Mesopotamian Realm.
97. A. CABROL, Les voies processionnelles de Thèbes.
98. J. PATRICH, The Sabaite Heritage in the Orthodox Church from the Fifth Century to the Present. Monastic Life, Liturgy, Theology, Literature, Art, Archaeology.
99. U. VERHOEVEN, Untersuchungen zur Späthieratischen Buchschrift.
100. E. LIPIŃSKI, The Aramaeans: Their Ancient History, Culture, Religion.
101. S. CAUVILLE, Dendara IV. Traduction.
102. U. VERMEULEN - J. VAN STEENBERGEN (eds.), Egypt and Syria in the Fatimid, Ayyubid and Mamluk Eras.
103. H. WILLEMS (ed.), Social Aspects of Funerary Culture in the Egyptian Old and Middle Kingdoms.
104. K. GEUS - K. ZIMMERMANN (eds.), Punica — Libyca — Ptolemaica. Festschrift für Werner Huß, zum 65. Geburtstag dargebracht von Schülern, Freunden und Kollegen.
105. S. CAUVILLE, Dendara. Les fêtes d'Hathor.
106. R. PREYS, Les complexes de la demeure du sistre et du trône de Rê. Théologie et décoration dans le temple d'Hathor à Dendera.
107. A. BLASIUS - B.U. SCHIPPER (eds.), Apokalyptik und Ägypten. Eine kritische Analyse der relevanten Texte aus dem griechisch-römischen Ägypten.
108. S. LEDER (ed.), Studies in Arabic and Islam.
109. A. GODDEERIS, Economy and Society in Northern Babylonia in the Early Old Babylonian Period (ca. 2000-1800 BC).
110. C. LEITZ (Ed.), Lexikon der ägyptischen Götter und Götterbezeichnungen, Band I.
111. C. LEITZ (Ed.), Lexikon der ägyptischen Götter und Götterbezeichnungen, Band II.
112. C. LEITZ (Ed.), Lexikon der ägyptischen Götter und Götterbezeichnungen, Band III.

113. C. LEITZ (Ed.), Lexikon der ägyptischen Götter und Götterbezeichnungen, Band IV.
114. C. LEITZ (Ed.), Lexikon der ägyptischen Götter und Götterbezeichnungen, Band V.
115. C. LEITZ (Ed.), Lexikon der ägyptischen Götter und Götterbezeichnungen, Band VI.
116. C. LEITZ (Ed.), Lexikon der ägyptischen Götter und Götterbezeichnungen, Band VII.
117. M. VAN MOL, Variation in Modern Standard Arabic in Radio News Broadcasts.
118. M.F.J. BAASTEN - W.Th VAN PEURSEN (Eds.), Hamlet on a Hill. Semitic and Greek Studies Presented to Professor T. Muraoka on the Occasion of his Sixty-Fifth Birthday.
119. O.E. KAPER, The Egyptian God Tutu. A Study of the Sphinx-God and Master of Demons with a Corpus of Monuments.
120. E. WARDINI, Lebanese Place-Names (Mount Lebanon and North Lebanon).
121. J. VAN DER VLIET, Catalogue of the Coptic Inscriptions in the Sudan National Museum at Khartoum (I. Khartoum Copt).
122. A. ŁAJTAR, Catalogue of the Greek Inscriptions in the Sudan National Museum at Khartoum (I. Khartoum Greek).
123. H. NIEHR, Ba'alšamem. Studien zu Herkunft, Geschichte und Rezeptionsgeschichte eines phönizischen Gottes.
124. H. WILLEMS - F. COPPENS - M. DE MEYER - P. DILS (Eds.), The Temple of Shanûr. Volume I : The Sanctuary, The *Wabet*, and the Gates of the Central Hall and the Great Vestibule (1-98).
125. K. CIGGAAR - H.G.B. TEULE (Eds.), East and West in the Crusader States. Context – Contacts – Confrontations III.
126. T. SOLDATJENKOVA - E. WAEGEMANS (Eds.), For East is East. Liber Amicorum Wojciech Skalmowski.
127. E. LIPIŃSKI, Itineraria Phoenicia. Studia Phoenicia 18.
128. D. BUDDE, S. SANDRI, U. VERHOEVEN (eds.), Kindgötter im Ägypten der griechisch-römischen Zeit. Zeugnisse aus Stadt und Tempel als Spiegel des Interkulturellen Kontakts.
129. C. LEITZ (ed.), Lexikon der ägyptischen Götter und Götterbezeichnungen Band VIII.
130. E.J. VAN DER STEEN, Tribes and Territories in Transition.
131. S. CAUVILLE, Dendara V-VI. Traduction. Les cryptes du temple d'Hathor.
132. S. CAUVILLE, Dendara V-VI. Index phraséologique. Les cryptes du temple d'Hathor.
133. M. IMMERZEEL, J. VAN DER VLIET, M. KERSTEN, C. VAN ZOEST (eds.), Coptic Studies on the Threshold of a New Millennium. Proceedings of the Seventh International Congress of Coptic Studies. Leiden, August 27 - September 2, 2000.
134. J.J. VAN GINKEL, H. MURRE-VAN DEN BERG (H.L.), T.M. VAN LINT (eds.), Redefining Christian Identity. Cultural Interaction in the Middle East since the Rise of Islam.
135. J. MONTGOMERY (ed.), 'Abbasid Studies. Occasional Papers of the School of 'Abbasid Studies, Cambridge, 6-10 July 2002.
136. T. BOIY, Late Achaemenid and Hellenistic Babylon.
137. B. JANSSENS, B. ROOSEN, P. VAN DEUN (eds.), Philomathestatos. Studies in Greek Patristic and Byzantine Texts Presented to Jacques Noret for his Sixty-Fifth Birthday.
138. S. HENDRICKX, R.F. FRIEDMAN, K.M. CIAŁOWICZ, M. CHŁODNICKI (eds.), Egypt at its Origins. Studies in Memory of Barbara Adams.
139. R. ARNZEN, J. THIELMANN (eds.), Words, Texts and Concepts Cruising the Mediterranean Sea. Studies on the Sources, Contents and Influences of Islamic Civilization and Arabic Philosophy and Science.

140. U. VERMEULEN, J. VAN STEENBERGEN (eds.), Egypt and Syria in the Fatimid, Ayyubid and Mamluk Eras IV.
141. H.T. DAVIES, Yūsuf al-Shirbīnī's Kitāb Hazz al-Qūḥuf bi-Sharḥ Qaṣīd Abī Shādūf.
142. P. VAN NUFFELEN, Un héritage de paix et de piété. Étude sur les histoires ecclésiastiques de Socrate et de Sozomène.
143. A. SCHOORS, The Preacher Sought to Find Pleasing Words II. A Study of the Language of Qoheleth. Part II: Vocabulary.
144. M.E. STONE, Apocrypha, Pseudepigrapha and Armenian Studies. Collected Papers: Volume 1.
145. M.E. STONE, Apocrypha, Pseudepigrapha and Armenian Studies. Collected Papers: Volume 2.
146. M. CACOUROS, M.-H. CONGOURDEAU, Philosophie et sciences à Byzance de 1204 à 1453. Les textes, les doctrines et leur transmission.
147. K. CIGGAAR, M. METCALF (eds.), East and West in the Medieval Eastern Mediterranean I.
148. B. MICHALAK-PIKULSKA, A. PIKULSKI (eds.), Authority, Privacy and Public Order in Islam.

PRINTED ON PERMANENT PAPER • IMPRIME SUR PAPIER PERMANENT • GEDRUKT OP DUURZAAM PAPIER - ISO 9706

N.V. PEETERS S.A., WAROTSTRAAT 50, B-3020 HERENT